The Renaissance in Europe: A Reader

The Renaissance in Europe
A Reader

Edited by Keith Whitlock

Yale University Press
New Haven and London
in association with The Open University

First published 2000

Copyright © 2000 selection and editorial matter. The Open University; individual items, the contributors

The publishers have made every effort to trace the relevant copyright holders to clear permissions. If any have been inadvertently omitted this is deeply regretted and will be corrected in any future printing.

Set in Adobe Garamond and Helvetica Condensed by Best-set Typesetter Ltd, Hong Kong Printed in Great Britain by Biddles Ltd, Guildford and Kings Lynn

ISBN 0-300-082185 (hbk.)
      0-300-082231 (pbk.)

Library of Congress Cataloging-in-Publication Data

The Renaissance in Europe : a reader / edited by Keith Whitlock.
      p.   cm.
    Includes index.
    ISBN 0-300-08218-5 (cloth : alk. paper.) – ISBN 0-300-08223-1
(pbk. : alk. paper)
    1. Renaissance.   2. Europe – Civilization.   3. Humanism.
I. Whitlock, Keith.
CB361.R386   2000
940.2′1 – dc21   99-41078
                                                              CIP

A catalogue record for this book is available from the British Library

10 9 8 7 6 5 4 3 2 1

Summary

Contents

Illustrations

Introduction

This volume of readings is an integral part of the Open University course AA305, *The Renaissance in Europe: A Cultural Enquiry*, a third-level honours programme which, in the best traditions of the Open University, is multidisciplinary, shaped in its teaching and choice of texts by scholars from the fields of Music, History, Literature, History of Science, History of Art and Architecture, Philosophy and Classics. We offer no apology for a selection that may startle for its breadth, its juxtapositioning and numerous departures from convention. We hope it will attract the professional scholar, the undergraduate and the curious general reader.

These readings have been chosen to explain, to supplement and to problematise the set texts and teachings of *The Renaissance in Europe*. A word about both is therefore due by way of clarification. In its multidisciplinary period studies, the Open University has always treated a wide range of cultural phenomena and artefacts as texts for the purposes of exploration and analysis. Since the university's distance teaching is multimedia, the cultural phenomena subjected to scrutiny and discussion may range from a humanist dialogue to an Elizabethan poem or play, from patronage in Italian court architecture, art and music to the staging of demonology for the Jacobean court in England, from anatomy to dance, and from printing and religious reform to astronomy. Further, as the course is European in scope, the cultural phenomena may occur as widely as Naples, Cracow, Scotland or El Escorial over a period roughly from 1350 to 1630.

The course teaching of *The Renaissance in Europe* is organised into three books published by Yale, each offering a distinctive focus, bearing the titles respectively of *The Impact of Humanism*, *Courts, Patrons and Poets* and *Challenges to Authority*; a volume of primary sources called *The Renaissance in Europe: An Anthology*, also published by Yale; and audio and video materials produced by the BBC for students' home use. Additionally our students must acquire *The Penguin Book of Renaissance Verse* (ed. Norbrook and Woodhuysen, 1993), Montaigne's *The Complete Works* (ed. Screech, Penguin 1991), Alison Cole's *Art of the Italian Renaissance Court* (Everyman 1997), Dekker and Rowley's *The Witch of Edmonton* (ed. Corbin and Sedge, Manchester University Press 1999), Shakespeare's *The Merchant of Venice* (ed. Halio, Oxford University Press, 1993), Machiavelli's *The Prince* (trans. Bull, Penguin, 1999) and a bilingual facing text of the proto-picaresque *Lazarillo de Tormes*, of 1554 and David Rowland's English translation of 1586, (ed. Whitlock, Aris and Philips, 2000), a crucial reading in the evolution of Western prose fiction, and not previously available in this form.

A part of the appeal of a course such as *The Renaissance in Europe* is that a familiarisation with, and understanding of, the past helps us to grapple with some of the problems facing Europe at the beginning of the twenty-first century where so many of us live or visit. The first of our teaching books, *The Impact of Humanism*, sets up a debate with Burckhardt's seminal book *The Civilization of the Renaissance in Italy* (trans. Middlemore, Penguin Classics, 1990) and his broad thesis that the period 1350–1500 in Italy saw the origins of modern individualism, the modern state and secular society. Burckhardt's thesis may be regarded as the starting-point for serious study of the Renaissance and a defining moment in historical scholarship. Historians may love or hate Burckhardt, but they cannot ignore him. Teaching and texts qualify and debate with his assumptions, arguments and choice of evidence. There are detailed case studies of Valla's *On the True and False Good*, Machiavelli's *The Prince*, and other examples drawn from humanism, the recovery of classical learning, the fine arts and political history.

Courts, Patrons and Poets, the second teaching book, looks at the role of respective courts and patronage in Renaissance Europe with particular attention to Budapest, Milan, Urbino, Mantua, Florence, and London, in terms of music, architecture, painting, poetry and drama, including Shakespeare's *The Merchant of Venice*.

Challenges to Authority, the third teaching book, continues the exploration of the Renaissance and humanism in the context of religion and religious reform, science, medicine, anatomy, Galileo's use of astronomy at the Medicean court, and demonology. There are studies of the two German cities of Zwickau and Augsburg, the proto-picaresque *Lazarillo de Tormes* in its 1586 English translation by David Rowland, Pico della Mirandola's *The Witch*, Dekker and Rowley's *The Witch of Edmonton* and Montaigne's *Essays*.

The selected readings of this volume do not carry the heavy scholarly annotation of their originals but have been prepared to speed the undergraduate for whom time may be of the essence. Those who wish to go more deeply should engage with the full Open University programme, or at least consult the source texts from which our readings have been drawn.

Finally I would like to acknowledge the active assistance of the AA305 course team in the preparation of the Reader.

Section One

The Impact of Humanism

1   Richard Danson Brown 'From Burckhardt to Greenblatt: New Historicisms and Old'

Source: written for this reader.

At the beginning of *The Civilization of the Renaissance in Italy*, Burckhardt admits that 'To each eye, perhaps, the outlines of a given civilization present a different picture' (p. 19). We have different images – different pictures – of the Renaissance and the individuals who lived at that time. But not only do we have different pictures of the past, the pictures we share are themselves subject to revision and reinterpretation as time goes on. Burckhardt's Renaissance, though highly influential and arguably still relevant, is not the Renaissance we see today. The outlines of the picture have changed.

This essay examines the images provided by New Historicism, a movement of the late twentieth century which has had a significant impact on the interpretation of the Renaissance. Though New Historicists are, typically, literature specialists with a central interest in sixteenth-century English literature, this movement has had a widespread influence across the Humanities through its interdisciplinary approach. For example, Richard Helgerson's *Forms of Nationhood* (1992) considers the construction of English nationhood not only in conventional literary forms like poetry and drama, but also in law, theology, map making and travel narratives. At its best, New Historicist scholarship studies the cultures of the past in all their various forms, without privileging one discourse above another. As we shall see, New Historicism also significantly revises Burckhardt's model of the Renaissance.

(1)   NEW VS. OLD HISTORICISM

So what is New Historicism? The adjective 'New' suggests that such Historicism must logically be understood in relation to an 'Old' Historicism – the question would then be 'What is Old Historicism?' Unsurprisingly, there is no movement which defines itself as Old Historicism. Like any label, New Historicism attempts to seduce its audience by laying claim to a novelty it may or may not actually possess. In this context, I am reminded of the repackaging during the 1990s of the British Labour Party as 'New Labour' in opposition to and revolt from 'Old Labour'. People only became conscious of Old Labour as a political grouping with the advent of New Labour. According to its adherents, the novelty of New Labour lies in its move away from the centralising, state-control model of democratic socialism of Old Labour; similarly, New Historicism attempts to modify older historicism by refiguring and reconceiving the ways in which historical evidence may be used to illuminate cultures of the past.

For example, in his essay 'Invisible Bullets' (1981), Stephen Greenblatt reads Shakespeare's History plays through his retelling Thomas Harriot's 1588 account of his visit to Virginia. According to Greenblatt, Harriot's account of the colonisation of America is punctuated by an ambiguous dynamic: by reporting how English colonisers deceived Algonquin Indians, Harriot invites 'a skeptical critique of the function of Christian morality in the New World' which is then immediately closed off (p. 39). By juxtaposing Harriot with Shakespeare, Greenblatt argues that Shakespeare exhibits a similar dynamic: his plays open up potential critiques of power – say in the character of Prince Hal – which are then contained. In this way, Shakespeare's Histories, and indeed the whole production of the drama in late sixteenth-century England, become embroiled in that other infinitely more treacherous Elizabethan project of colonisation.

What does an 'Old Historicist' make of similar texts? E. M. W. Tillyard's *Shakespeare's History Plays* (1944) reads the Histories through the examination of sixteenth-century historiography – the Tudors' dynastic interpretation of fourteenth- and fifteenth-century English history. In this reading, Shakespeare's plays enact orthodox Tudor history: God punishes usurpers and eventually saves England by delivering it into the hands of the Tudors. Greenblatt and Tillyard contextualize Shakespeare's Histories very differently. Tillyard takes the narrative sources of Shakespeare's plays and argues that the plays replicate the political and moral values contained in the sources; Greenblatt juxtaposes Shakespeare with a text which has no explicit connection with the Histories to illuminate what he sees as a common dynamic within Elizabethan culture.

Indeed, when we read Tillyard and Greenblatt, we are comparing scholars writing at vastly different times and in the context of different institutional influences and pressures. So Hugh Grady argues that Tillyard's over-riding concern with the theme of order is a product both of English anxiety about disorder during the Second World War and Tillyard's own position as a Cambridge professor trying to reconcile conflicting intellectual traditions. In this reading, Tillyard was 'a consummate English moderate who had remarkable success in what was a nearly impossible balancing act' (Grady, p. 170). Tillyard was caught between a positivist commitment (dating back to the nineteenth-century) to the idea that the study of literature is morally improving, and a modernist aesthetic which is more sceptical about the moral value of literature. By contrast Greenblatt writes as an American academic based in California attempting to study Renaissance literature through the adoption of a range of theoretical positions. Greenblatt's concern with the uses and abuses of power can be traced to his engagement with the ideas of the French historian Michel Foucault, whose primary concern was with the ways in which power informs and constructs human identity. We could also note that Greenblatt and his fellow American New Historicists were attuned to how power was used in Renaissance England at precisely the historical moment when the right-wing Republican administration of Ronald Reagan governed twentieth-century America. Analysing past cultures' tensions and incongruities is often a way of exploring the related dynamics which underlie your own society. My point is that historcisms of all kinds are themselves shaped by the historical and ideological pressures which inform the mental worlds of their proponents.

How then do these different methodologies influence the interpretation of literary texts? The interpretative differences between Tillyard and Greenblatt can be seen through their readings of Shakespeare's Prince Hal in *Henry IV*, who notoriously spends his time 'With unrestrained loose companions' (*Richard II*

V.iii.7) like Sir John Falstaff. For Tillyard, Hal is a hero figure – 'a man of large powers, Olympian loftiness' (p. 269); for Greenblatt, Hal is 'a conniving hypocrite' (p. 41). Where Tillyard's Hal glamorously embodies Tudor ideas of kingship, Greenblatt's is a compromised representative of the morally ambivalent cultural practices he anathematises in Elizabethan colonialism. Tillyard celebrates Hal while Greenblatt rubbishes him. But paradoxically, both critics view the Histories as texts which support ruling class ideology. The key difference is in the way they arrive at these conclusions: Hal is Shakespeare's 'studied picture of the kingly type' (Tillyard, p. 269), or Hal's 'ideal image' requires 'the constant production of its own radical subversion and the powerful containment of that subversion' (Greenblatt, p. 41).

The issue here is not which interpretation is the most convincing, but rather the distance between Old and New Historicist examinations of the same text. Perhaps one of the more immediately striking differences between Greenblatt and Tillyard is in terms of the complexity of their written style – curiously, the more recent writer is the more complex of the two. In the sentence just quoted, you must work out what is meant by 'the constant production of its own radical subversion' by reading on: Greenblatt means that the 'ideal image' of Hal is subverted by the play's presentation of him as a hypocrite; this subversion is in turn 'contained' by the audience's '"ironical acceptance"' of Hal's authority. I am not sure that either interpretation convinces me. Neither critic considers the possibility that Shakespeare's Histories could modify Tudor political orthodoxy while avoiding the risks of wholesale subversion. For example, the extent to which *Henry V* (c. 1599–1600) is a straightforward glorification of English militarism has been increasingly questioned during the course of the twentieth century. Though at one level the play can lend itself to propagandist readings and productions, in comparison with its major dramatic source, *The Famous Victories of Henry V* (printed 1598), Shakespeare's play is sceptical about the necessity and cost of war. This interpretative shift can be gauged by comparing Laurence Olivier's 1944 film, which aims to glorify Henry and the English war effort while Britain was again at war in Europe, with Kenneth Branagh's 1989 film, which offers a more realistic sense of war. The idea that Shakespeare's Histories could embody a sceptical (rather than a subversive) critique of Tudor ideology is paradoxically one which neither Tillyard nor Greenblatt explores, though for very different reasons. More recent historicists like Peter Erickson have however tried to advance 'a model of Elizabethan culture that recognises the room for artistic maneuver [sic] between the two extremes of total affirmation of royal mythology and all-out, open subversion' (Highley, p. 4).

(2)   BURCKHARDT, NEW HISTORICISM AND THE UNFREE SUBJECT

A more detailed overview of New Historicism in relation to Burckhardt's picture of the Renaissance may be derived from John Martin's article, 'Inventing Sincerity, Refashioning Prudence: the Discovery of the Individual in Renaissance Europe' (1997) (Text 2). According to Martin, the central innovation of New Historicism is the sense that the self is not 'an autonomous entity' but is 'a site on which broader institutional and political forces are inscribed' (p. 1313). Helgerson provides an alternative formulation: 'people themselves, whether individually or in groups, are made and imagined. Their identity – *our* identity – is a structure, a cultural construct' (p. 13). The human subject, which for centuries had been assumed to be autonomous and independent, is revealed as being unfree – put bluntly, we are the products of cultural forces as much as buildings or books. Martin then makes the point that Burckhardt's *Civilization* 'now serves as a canonical marker of a paradigm surpassed' (p. 1317). Exactly reversing Burckhardt's idea that the modern individual develops in the Renaissance, New Historicist scholars seek to reveal the process whereby the idea of the self is constructed in response to the pressures of competing power systems. In Greenblatt's famous formulation, the self is something *fashioned* in the Renaissance rather than something which, according to Burckhardt, *develops* in the Renaissance. Martin also points out (pp. 1314–20) the influence of New Historicism on other Humanities disciplines like the History of Science (Biagioli on Galileo) and Art History (Koerner on Dürer). As a concept for the interpretation of the Renaissance, self-fashioning has been powerfully influential.

   These are complex arguments which it is often difficult to grasp. As Martin notes (p. 1316), Greenblatt himself registers some resistance to the idea of the unfree subject by telling a personal anecdote in the Epilogue to *Renaissance Self-Fashioning* which signals his desire 'to sustain the illusion that I am the principal maker of my own identity' (Greenblatt, *Renaissance Self-Fashioning*, p. 257). But note that word 'illusion': Greenblatt *feels* that he is an independent self – as do the sixteenth-century writers he discusses – but he actually *thinks* otherwise. The differences between Burckhardt and Greenblatt can be seen from Burckhardt's section 'The Development of the Individual' and from Greenblatt's comparison of More and Tyndale in *Renaissance Self-Fashioning*:

> . . . at the close of the thirteenth century Italy began to swarm with individuality; the ban laid upon human personality was dissolved; and a thousand figures meet us each in its own special shape and dress . . . among these many-sided men, some who may truly be called all-sided tower above the rest. Before analysing the general phases of the life and culture of this period, consider . . . the figure of one of these giants – Leon Battista Alberti (b. 1404?, d. 1472) . . . He learned music without a master . . . he acquired every sort of accomplishment and dexterity, cross-examining artists, scholars . . . To all this must be added his literary works, first those on art, which are landmarks and authorities of the first order for the Renaissance of form . . . then his Latin prose writings . . . his elegies [and] eclogues . . . But the deepest spring of his nature has yet to be spoken of – the sympathetic intensity with which he entered into the whole life around him. At the sight of noble trees and waving cornfields he shed tears; handsome and dignified old men he honoured as 'a delight of nature' . . . It need not be added that an iron will pervaded and sustained his whole personality; like all the great men of the Renaissance, he said, 'Men can do all things if they will'. (Burckhardt, *The Civilization of the Renaissance in Italy*, pp. 98, 102–03)

For More the self is poised between an ironic, self-conscious performance, grounded upon hidden reserves of private judgment and silent faith, and an

absorption into a corporate unity that has no need for pockets of privacy . . .
For Tyndale, the self is likewise poised, but between poles quite different
from those glimpsed in More . . . Tyndale's own sense of his identity is marked
precisely by his refusal to make a part for himself in the midst of the ongoing
performance. As a tutor in Gloucestershire he did not keep silent, cloaking
his judgments behind a cover of affability, but quarreled openly and violently
with those whose views of the Church he could not accept, until he was forced
to depart for London . . . If there is none of More's calculated role-playing,
there is equally none of his absorption into a visible corporate body . . . Identity then is not defined by participation in a body – hence in visible, communal rituals – but by a place in a schema of communication, legal relationships
and obedience. The book – for Tyndale, the printed book in the vernacular –
displaces the communal body. (Greenblatt, *Renaissance Self-Fashioning*, pp.
157–59)

So which writer makes the stronger argument? Burckhardt is not really arguing
at all. Rather, he fleshes out his picture – that 'many-sided men' or modern individuals emerged in Italy between the thirteenth and fifteenth centuries – through
anecdotes and snapshots, like the lengthy description of Leon Battista Alberti's
accomplishments. We might say that Burckhardt's case for the emergence of the
individual rests on such evidence as Alberti shedding tears 'At the sight of noble
trees and waving cornfields'. Paradoxically, like Burckhardt, Greenblatt also uses
anecdotes; indeed, later in the same chapter he cites Burckhardt with qualified
approval: 'Despite its age and its well-documented limitations, one of the best
introductions to Renaissance self-fashioning remains Burckhardt's *Civilization of
the Renaissance in Italy* . . . But his . . . assertion that . . . men emerged at last as
free individuals must be sharply qualified' (*Renaissance Self-Fashioning*, pp.
161–62). Greenblatt's anecdotes firmly locate his sixteenth-century subjects in
relation to power systems: for him their identities are fashioned by these interactions. He does not recount Tyndale's career to illustrate his personality – as
Burckhardt would have done – but to elucidate the dynamic within Tyndale's life
between his rejection of the Catholic Church and his corresponding submission
to the Bible.

  The real issue is not which writer is the more skilful at putting his case, but
which model of the Renaissance is the more persuasive. Martin concludes his
summary of the New Historicist contribution to the question of identity in the
Renaissance by asking 'Are we simply to accept the view that the self . . . is a mere
cultural artifact . . . ?' (p. 1320). This is the issue which divides Burckhardt and
Greenblatt. Again, there is no simple answer to these questions. The New Historicist construction of the self has been immensely influential in literary studies
– much of the most significant new work in Renaissance literature since the 1980s
has either come from a New Historicist perspective, or has had to engage with
that perspective. But I find Greenblatt's discussions of Spenser and Shakespeare
often comically reductive, as when he makes assertions like 'Spenser loves power
and attempts to link his own art ever more closely with its symbolic and literal
embodiment' (p. 174). My problem here is not so much with Greenblatt's reading

of Spenser's poetry (which is often subtle and sensitive), but with the fact that for Greenblatt apparently all Renaissance writers 'love power' – this particular obsession would seem to be characteristic of More, Tyndale, Wyatt, Marlowe, Shakespeare and Spenser. We might suggest again that Greenblatt's preoccupation with power is as symptomatic of the period in which he was writing as was Tillyard's concern with order or indeed Burckhardt's interest in the individual. In short, Greenblatt's Renaissance is not a 'better' Renaissance than Burckhardt's but a different one, as fuelled by late twentieth-century American concerns as Burckhardt's was by late nineteenth-century European concerns.

Martin offers a related critique of the New Historicist view of the Renaissance. His article focuses on the refashioning of the traditional virtue of prudence and the invention of sincerity during the fifteenth and sixteenth centuries. So he contends that there was a genuine growth in the consciousness of individual subjectivity during the Renaissance. He summarises:

> The language of prudence and sincerity points to a sense of interiority . . . relatively immune to the sort of ideological forces . . . of the church or the monarchy that Greenblatt and other New Historicists have seen as determining . . . the formation of Renaissance identities.

(pp. 1339–40)

In other words, not every element in Renaissance culture is reducible to the discourses of power New Historicists are particularly attuned to. While power remains an important consideration in any cultural transaction, Martin usefully reminds us that it is not the only narrative that we should be attending to. As I remarked in relation to Greenblatt's 'Invisible Bullets' essay, Shakespeare's History plays could operate somewhere in between the poles of enacting Tudor ideology and outright subversion: I would suggest that Shakespeare was capable of making *artistic* decisions with *political* implications which were independent of the controlling influence of state power.

Martin concludes his essay by asserting 'the enduring significance of Burckhardt's questions' (p.1341). Indeed, much work following on from the first wave of New Historicism revisits Greenblatt's notion of the unfree subject, and by implication Burckhardt's model of the Renaissance discovery of the individual. As you may have spotted, Greenblatt pays little attention to the formation of female identity during the Renaissance: like Burckhardt, he focuses on the 'many-sided *men*' of Renaissance culture. He is absorbed by power and the play between discourses of power and the literary texts which he believes were shaped by those discourses. Because the majority of women were excluded from such power, books like *Renaissance Self-Fashioning* and Helgerson's *Forms of Nationhood* have little to say about the construction of female roles at this time. As an example of feminist New Historicism, Frances Dolan's *Dangerous Familiars* (1994) (Text 34), suggests through its examination of representations of domestic crime in sixteenth- and seventeenth-century England that there was the possibility of what she calls contingent and circumscribed 'human agency in historical process' (p. 5). By trying to explain the behaviour of wives who murdered their husbands, the writers of these pamphlets paradoxically confer a subjectivity on their subjects. Dolan's book is also interesting because while revising some New Historicist assumptions, it nonetheless participates in the central manoeuvres of the movement: the pamphlets she discusses alongside texts like *Othello* and *The Winter's Tale* are given the same level of attention – no attempt is made to differentiate between the literary quality of her chosen texts.

Another criticism that has been levelled at New Historicism relates directly to this open-ended attitude towards cultural artefacts. For New Historicists, notions of artistic value are themselves culturally formed. The way Burckhardt (like many others) privileges Shakespeare and Leonardo as pre-eminent artists possessed of special gifts is from this perspective a dubious practice: by elevating Shakespeare and Leonardo, you exclude hundreds of other voices. The process of 'canon formation' (the construction of a select list of masterpieces like *Hamlet* and the 'Mona Lisa') becomes not just an issue of artistic taste but of the deliberate exclusion of divergent voices. New Historicists demonstrate their resistance to these traditional critical manoeuvres by extending the parameters of what should be discussed. A good example of this work is the growing attention paid to women writers of the Renaissance – a group which the traditional male-centred canon had excluded. But New Historicists can be accused of simply transferring value from traditional artists like Shakespeare and Leonardo either to neglected artists, or indeed to modern historians. The same need to privilege is constant, though the object of the critic's admiration has shifted.

Before closing, we must offset these criticisms with some sense of the value of the New Historicist approach. As Martin points out, the attention that has been paid to self-fashioning has helped to refocus attention on Burckhardt's questions and the whole issue of the formation of the modern individual. By resisting Burckhardt's picture, New Historicists have, in Heather Dubrow's phrase, 'sparked interest in tensions' within Renaissance culture (p. 42). Rather than being the progressive new age envisaged by Burckhardt, the Renaissance emerges as a cross-European cultural moment during which questions of identity were re-negotiated in response to rapidly changing social pressures. I would not be surprised if you find the whole idea of the unfree subject both a bit outrageous and mildly repellent – as Greenblatt's anecdote at the close of *Renaissance Self-Fashioning* is intended to show, we are very attached to the idea of our autonomy within larger social structures. Personally, I remain to be convinced whether my identity is a socially produced sample – an agglomeration of clichés and partly remembered texts – or whether it remains my own uniquely self-authored individuality. But I am sure that the New Historicist inspection of the construction of the self has changed both how I look at the past and how I look at myself. Identity – for so long something we took for granted – has become something we have to prove.

In summary:

- New Historicism reacts against 'old' historicism by reconceiving how historical context should be used to illuminate the study of cultural artefacts;
- Characteristically, that reconception focuses on issues of power and identity:

power shapes or fashions identity and so shapes the artefacts produced by past cultures;

• New Historicism therefore sees Burckhardt's model as fundamentally outdated by stressing the restrictions on individual autonomy in any given culture;

• New Historicism is vulnerable to criticism in its obsession with issues of power; its initial insensitivity to the formation of female identities; while the whole notion of the unfree subject remains contentious.

FURTHER READING

Dolan, Frances E., *Dangerous Familiars: Representations of Domestic Crime in England 1550–1700* (Ithaca and London: Cornell University Press, 1994)

Dubrow, Heather, 'Twentieth Century Shakespeare Criticism' in *The Riverside Shakespeare: Second Edition* (ed. G. Blackmore Evans and J. J. M. Tobin. Boston and New York: Houghton Mifflin Co., 1997)

Greenblatt, Stephen, 'Invisible Bullets' in *Shakespearean Negotiations: The Circulation of Social Energy in Renaissance England* (Oxford: The Clarendon Press, 1988)

Renaissance Self-Fashioning: From More to Shakespeare (Chicago and London: Chicago University Press, 1980)

Helgerson, Richard, *Forms of Nationhood: the Elizabethan Writing of England* (Chicago and London: Chicago University Press, 1992)

Highley, Christopher, *Shakespeare, Spenser, and the Crisis in Ireland* (Cambridge: Cambridge University Press, 1997)

Martin, John, 'Inventing sincerity, refashioning prudence: the discovery of the individual in Renaissance Europe', *American Historical Review* 102 (1997)

Tillyard, E. M. W., *Shakespeare's History Plays* (London: Chatto and Windus, 1944)

2 John Martin 'Inventing Sincerity, Refashioning Prudence: The Discovery of the Individual in Renaissance Europe'

Source: from *American Historical Review*, 102 (5) December 1997 pp. 1309–17, 1320–42.

In the Middle Ages both sides of human consciousness – that which was turned within as that which was turned without – lay dreaming or half awake beneath a common veil. The veil was woven of faith, illusion and childish pre-possession, through which the world and history were seen clad in strange hues. Man was conscious of himself only as member of a race, people, party, family, or corporation – only through some general category. In Italy this veil first melted into air; an *objective* treatment and consideration of the state and of all things of this world became possible. The *subjective* side at the same time asserted itself with corresponding emphasis; man became a spiritual *individual*, and recognized himself as such. In the same way the Greek had once distinguished himself from the barbarian, and the Arab had felt himself an individual at a time when other Asiatics knew themselves only as members of a race.

It will not be difficult to show that this result was due above all to the political circumstances of Italy.

Jacob Burckhardt, *The Civilization of the Renaissance in Italy* (1860)

More than one hundred and thirty years after its publication, Burckhardt's masterpiece *The Civilization of the Renaissance in Italy* continues to stimulate much of the most creative scholarship in late medieval and early modern European history. This book, to be sure, has never generated a scholarly consensus on the nature of the Renaissance. It has, however, accomplished something far more valuable. Ever since its publication, *The Civilization of the Renaissance in Italy* has consistently invited corrections, modifications, and refutations; it has become a classic, compelling each new generation of readers to come to terms with its arguments. Period subspecialists define themselves and examine their presuppositions in relation to this text. Intellectual and cultural historians who focus on the Middle Ages, for instance, have mustered considerable evidence that many of the humanistic and even individualistic ideals Burckhardt viewed as originating in Italy in the Renaissance had in fact emerged much earlier. [. . .] But for the majority of social historians, Burckhardt served primarily as a marker of what they were not. Where Burckhardt had focused on the writings of a few exceptionally talented figures, they would privilege the experience of ordinary people (merchants, artisans, peasants, vagabonds); where he had viewed the state abstractly, in nearly Nietzschean terms, as a 'work of art,' they had begun to decipher the social and institutional forces that shaped it; and, finally, where he had appeared to 'celebrate' individualism, they would demonstrate the vitality of corporate and collective experience.

This essay, by contrast, is an effort to underscore the importance of what I believe should still be called 'the discovery of the individual' for our understanding not only of high culture – art, music, literature, and intellectual history – but also for our grasp of social and political history as well. This does not mean that we must approach the Renaissance in traditional Burckhardtian terms. To the contrary, recent philosophical, anthropological, and literary models of the individual have so transformed our understanding of the human person that it is no longer possible to base our analysis of the origins of individualism on the traditional humanistic assumptions that Burckhardt took as a given. We are, in other words, no longer in the comfortable position of believing, as Burckhardt and many of his nineteenth-century contemporaries did, that the individual existed prior to history; that, if the individual was not a central concern of the Middle Ages, this was due to a veil 'of faith, illusion and childish prepossession'; that, finally, what emerged in the Renaissance was man *as he really is*. For in recent years, many analysts, inspired by post-structuralist and postmodern arguments and insights, have begun to argue that individualism itself is a construction, that, indeed, the human self is in many ways nothing more than a fiction, and that it is above all what might be called the Renaissance representations of the self as an individual, expressive subject that require explanation.

In the first part of this essay, therefore, I examine in some detail what I believe to be the most significant recent challenge to Burckhardt's understanding of individualism – namely, the work of the Renaissance literary historian Stephen Greenblatt and the New Historicists he has inspired. As I shall try to make clear, there is much in the New Historicist scholarship that should interest historians, whether social or intellectual, and that needs to be taken seriously. Indeed, at their best, these scholars offer tantalizing insights into the play of social forces and ideological currents on Renaissance texts and Renaissance selves. Yet, as I shall argue, their accounts are, paradoxically, profoundly ahistorical. On the one hand, their analytical strategies tend to view the formation of the Renaissance self from within a synchronic framework, one frozen in time, with little sense of the operation of more slowly developing historical – or diachronic – forces on the process of what has come to be called 'Renaissance self-fashioning.'[1] On the other hand, their analyses also tend to be based on a totalizing view of politics and power in the Renaissance world – a view that leaves little room for oppositional or dissenting voices. Accordingly, in the second part of this essay, I try to correct this by offering an alternative approach to a salient aspect of the history of the formation of Renaissance selves. In particular, I examine the effort on both theoretical and practical levels during the Renaissance period to redefine certain moral categories relating to sincerity and prudence and the relation of these redefinitions to the formation of an increased sense of subjectivity and individualism. My claim is not that these shifts alone were responsible for the generation of individualism in the Renaissance. As Michael Mascuch has recently cautioned in his study of the self in seventeenth-century England, 'individualism is a multidimensional phenomenon, an amalgam of practices and values with no discernible center. A variety of forces – social, economic, political, intellectual – contributed to its making, each one of which was paramount at some time or another, either separately or jointly with others. Thus a single account of individualism cannot possibly represent its development, its contours, its functions.'[2] Nonetheless, the evidence I have gathered does suggest that this shift in moral vocabulary played a significant role in the construction of new notions of individualism in the Renaissance world.

Over the past few decades, scholars have approached the problem of the emergence of the modern self from a variety of perspectives. [. . .] But, as I indicated above, the most influential and innovative treatment of the Renaissance self is found in the work of Stephen Greenblatt and, most notably, in his now classic study *Renaissance Self-Fashioning: From More to Shakespeare*. This book, which was first published in 1980, has proven enormously influential. This is especially true in Greenblatt's own field of literature, where his ideas have been fundamental for the development of New Historicism, a critical movement that, in its reaction against the formalist or idealist readings of the New Critics, has sought to read literary texts as cultural artifacts or practices, dialectically related to the specific cultural, social, and political contexts in which they were written. In addition – and what is decisive here – the New Historicists also view the self, like a text, not as an autonomous entity but rather as a site on which broader institutional and political forces are inscribed. [. . .] Self-fashioning has become a central theme in the exploration of Renaissance and early modern culture generally. It is deployed in a variety of fields: in social history, art history, intellectual history, the history of science, and it even has important implications for the study of the self in other times and places.

On many levels, this development is not surprising. As a descriptive category, self-fashioning seems to capture much of what is popularly believed about Renaissance life. As Greenblatt notes, 'the simplest observation we can make is that in the sixteenth century there appears to be an increased self-consciousness about the fashioning of human identity as a manipulable, artful process.' Above all, self-fashioning appears to make sense of a world in which the court was central to literary life – for this was a world in which prudent accommodation and even deception were often seen as virtues. And indeed, the Renaissance world was a theatrical age – an age of masks, of masquerades, of role playing, of the studied nonchalance of *sprezzatura* [ease of manner in style or performance], even of 'honest dissimulation.' Clearly, at least among the privileged orders, men and women were often conscious of fashioning particular selves in order to survive or advance in the high-stakes world of court society.

But self-fashioning is not only powerful descriptively, it is also heuristically powerful. At a point when social history appears to have reached an impasse in its ability to offer convincing explanations of cultural developments, self-fashioning holds out the promise of offering scholars new ways of thinking about the interplay of social and cultural life. As Greenblatt himself notes, 'self-fashioning derives its interest precisely from the fact that it functions without regard for a sharp distinction between literature and social life.' In short, it seems to offer a way around both idealist accounts of culture such as those found in traditional histories of literature and ideas and those Marxist accounts that privilege the infrastructure to such a degree that cultural life is viewed passively, as a mere reflection of social relations. In theoretical terms, we might say, self-fashioning avoids both the abstract aestheticism of formal analyses and the reflectionist assumptions of much Marxist theory. Throughout his work, Greenblatt deftly merges a consideration of ideas and social life; he argues against theories that deny 'any relation between the play and social life' and those that affirm 'that the latter is "the thing itself," free from interpretation.' In his view, 'Social actions are themselves always embedded in systems of public signification, always grasped, even by their makers, in acts of interpretation, while the words that constitute the works of literature that we discuss here are by their very nature the manifest assurance of a similar embeddedness.' Other scholars have fastened onto this dimension of his ideas. As the historian of science Mario Biagioli has put it in his recent study of Galileo, the 'focus on processes of self-fashioning may help bypass some of the deadlocks of the so-called externalists-versus-internalists debate that has characterized much of recent and not so recent science studies.' One can view Galileo's insights, that is, not exclusively as the consequence of external social and political factors impinging on the scientific imagination nor as merely the result of developments within Renaissance mathematics and astronomy, but rather as the outcome of Galileo's own efforts to navigate courtly culture and its patronage expectations in relation to late Renaissance or baroque science. The Galilean revolution is thus a result neither of social change per se nor purely of developments intrinsic to science but of the way these two spheres intersected in Galileo's studied 'self-fashioning.' [See page 322 below.]

Especially significant, however, is Greenblatt's insistence on a new notion of the human person – one that would have been wholly alien to Burckhardt. For while its title seems to suggest a kind of independence on the part of the self, or, as one critic has trenchantly observed, while Greenblatt seems at times to invite us 'to read "self-fashioning" as free, expressive self-making,' *Renaissance Self-Fashioning* is in fact a study *not* of the way in which human subjects fashioned themselves but rather of the way in which certain political and religious forces in the Renaissance created the fiction of individual autonomy. For, in the end, Greenblatt's *Renaissance Self-Fashioning* offers a view of the self as a cultural artifact, a historical and ideological illusion generated by the economic, social, religious, and political upheavals of the Renaissance. Greenblatt's project, in short, has contributed in decisive ways to a new historiography of the self. Earlier histories – grounded in the liberal and conservative myths of the gradual but heroic emancipation of the individual – have given way to histories that explore the varied constructions of the self in different time periods and different cultures. Not only is it no longer possible to view its history as one of continuous development, but individualism, [. . .] is itself not a uniquely Western phenomenon.

This new understanding of the history of individualism is explicit in the structure of *Renaissance Self-Fashioning* in which the various 'authors' – Thomas More, William Tyndale, Thomas Wyatt, Edmund Spenser, Christopher Marlowe, and William Shakespeare – are each viewed as shaped above all by the social, cultural, religious, and political tensions of Tudor England. Thus identity is not a given; rather, it is a cultural or political artifact, or, as Greenblatt pithily remarks, 'we may say that self-fashioning occurs at the point of encounter between an authority and an alien.' More's self-fashioning, for example, is portrayed as taking place in the interplay of his submission to the authority of the church and his opposition to heresy and the monarchy, while Tyndale's self is depicted as developing out of the tensions between his opposition to the church, on the one hand, and his submission to Scripture as authority, on the other. Or, as Greenblatt observes, in an eloquent comparison of the processes of self-fashioning that shaped the identities of More and Tyndale, 'The Bible . . . provides for Tyndale what the Church provides for More: not simply a point of vantage but a means to absorb the ambiguities of identity, the individual's mingled egotism and self-loathing, into a larger, redeeming certainty.' [. . .]

To be sure, there are moments in *Renaissance Self-Fashioning* and elsewhere in his work when Greenblatt seemingly longs for a more resilient self – moments that come close to reifying the concept of selfhood that he elsewhere unrelentingly deconstructs. At one point, he characterizes the Renaissance self as 'brittle and inadequate'; at another, [. . .] finally and most poignantly, in the final sentence to *Renaissance Self-Fashioning*, after offering an anecdote, Greenblatt explains his need to tell a personal story – a story about himself – because, as he puts it, 'I want to bear witness at the close to my overwhelming need to sustain the illusion that I am the principal maker of my own identity.' Nonetheless, such passages are fleeting, and for the most part Greenblatt maintains or implies that even the most substantial selves are egos built on fictions. In one of his most revealing discussions of Renaissance selfhood, for example, Greenblatt, after citing a famous passage from *Leviathan* in which Thomas Hobbes offered his definition of 'person,' notes that

> in Hobbes, the 'natural person' originates in the 'artificial person' – the mask,
> the character on a stage 'translated' from the theater to the tribunal. There is
> no layer deeper, more authentic, than theatrical self-representation. This con-
> ception of the self does not deny the importance of the body ... but it does
> not anchor personal identity in an inalienable biological continuity. The crucial
> consideration is ownership: what distinguishes a 'natural' person from an 'arti-
> ficial' person is that the former is considered to *own* his words and actions. Con-
> sidered by whom? By authority. But is authority itself then natural or artificial?
> In a move that is one of the cornerstones of Hobbes's absolutist political phi-
> losophy, authority is vested in an artificial person who represents the words and
> actions of the entire nation. All men therefore are impersonators of themselves,
> but impersonators whose clear title to identity is secured by an authority irrev-
> ocably deeded to an artifical person. A great mask allows one to own as one's
> own face another mask.

Or, as Greenblatt concludes in the epilogue to *Renaissance Self-Fashioning*, 'the human subject itself began to seem remarkably unfree, the ideological product of the relations of power in a particular society.' Greenblatt, in short, is power-fully historicist in his argument. Like other historicists, he sees the self not as a free, autonomous subject but rather as subjected to (because generated by) the codes of culture and power, or what Greenblatt calls 'the cultural poetics' of a particular set of cultural, political, and social relations. Identity is shaped from the outside. [. . .]

Thus from the vantage point of much new literary criticism, Burckhardt's self-creating individual is largely myth. This is so much the case, in fact, that among New Historicists and other scholars influenced either by Greenblatt or other post-structuralist and postmodern discourses, *The Civilization of the Renaissance in Italy* now serves as a canonical market of a paradigm surpassed. [. . .]

The tide has shifted, then, from Burckhardt's notion of the discovery of the individual to a New Historicist analytics of self-fashioning. Certainly many aspects of the notion self-fashioning are, as I have tried to suggest, compelling at both a descriptive and a heuristic level. But how are historians to make sense of this transformation in the radically altered understanding of the construction of the self in Renaissance Europe? Are we simply to accept the view that the self, in the Renaissance as in all periods, is a mere cultural artifact, and that the humanist self was (and remains) no more than an illusion – something 'remark-ably unfree' or merely 'the ideological product of the relations of power in a par-ticular society'? Was the individual, in fact, 'continually made and remade'? In short, does the concept of self-fashioning provide an adequate description of the production of subjectivities or, more prosaically, of the discovery of the individ-ual in the Renaissance?

One of the most striking features of Renaissance notions of the self was an explicitly layered quality, which represented a sense not only of inwardness or interiority but also of mystery about what Renaissance writers, drawing on a long tradition, imagined as their inner selves. This concern was manifest as early as the fourteenth century in Petrarch's writings, especially the *Secretum* [what is secret] in which, under the influence of Augustine, Petrarch examined the depth and the shortcomings of his own soul. In the sixteenth century, however, this concern reached a new level of intensity. The Venetian reformer Gasparo Contarini conveyed a sense of this inwardness in a celebrated letter, his epistle to Tommaso Giustiniani of April 1511: 'if you were to know me from within [*nell'intrinseco*], as I really am (but even I do not know myself well), you would not make such a judgment about me.' In a similar vein, John Calvin, in language that substantially expanded the topography of interiority, encouraged his readers to look more deeply into themselves: 'The human heart has so many crannies where vanity hides, so many holes where falsehood lurks, is so decked out with deceiving hypocrisy, that it often dupes itself.' Montaigne, one of the preeminent architects of inwardness in the sixteenth century, made a similar observation: 'I, who make no other profession, find in me such infinite depth and variety, that what I have learned bears no other fruit than to make me realize how much I still have to learn.' And the works of Wyatt, the Tudor poet, as Greenblatt himself notes, are marked both by their 'inwardness' and their 'intensely personal' nature.

Indeed, one can point not only to author after author from the Renaissance – Petrarch, Erasmus, Luther, More, Montaigne, Shakespeare – who made issues of interiority central to his discussion of the human situation but also to the way in which this dimension of experience was registered beyond the realm of great letters. An especially poignant series of examples derives from the inquisitorial records and the martyrologies of this period. *The Acts and Monuments* of the English martyrologist John Foxe, for instance, are filled with Protestant saints who vacillate over the question of whether or not they should reveal their beliefs and convictions to the Catholic prelates who examined them, before finally electing to make their 'inner' convictions known. Inquisitorial archives provide similar cases, the most celebrated of which was that of the Italian lawyer Francesco Spiera, who struggled with the question of whether or not to dissimulate his beliefs as he was led into the tribunal in Venice, only to abjure his convictions before the Inquisitor and later to regret it so deeply that he starved himself to death, convinced he was going to Hell. Calvin, who was familiar with this case, raised the possibility that Spiera was hardly an isolated example. The Catholic lands, he wrote in a series of treatises and letters, were filled with those he called Nicodemites (in reference to the early Christian Nicodemus, who, according to the Gospel of John, had come to Jesus 'by night') – men and women, that is, who were Protestant by belief but who continued to attend Mass and make a show of being Catholic to protect themselves and their families from persecution. And, in the Renaissance court as well, the issue of the representation of the self was a central dimension of the life of the elites. The very popularity of Baldassare Castiglione's *Book of the Courtier* not only in Italy but throughout

Europe provides evidence of this. The Italian humanist and historian Francesco Guicciardini gave simultaneous expression to courtly and religious concerns when he observed in his *Ricordi* [*Diaries*]: 'And yet the position I have filled under several Popes has obliged me for personal reasons [*per el particulare mio*] to desire their greatness. But for this I should have loved Martin Luther as myself.'

The experience of personhood in the Renaissance world was, in short, often the experience of a divided self, of a person who was frequently forced to erect a public façade that disguised his or her convictions, beliefs, or feelings. In the Renaissance generally and the sixteenth century in particular, we see a new emphasis on inwardness or the idea of an interior self as the core of personal identity. To be sure, there was nothing new about the notion of interiority per se. Medieval society, especially in the wake of the cultural and monastic revivals of the late eleventh and the twelfth centuries, had numerous writers and theologians who fashioned a deep sense of inwardness and interiority. Bernard of Clairvaux's mystical theology, which was even distributed in vernacular translations, elaborated the most complex psychology of the soul since Augustine. Peter Abelard's ethics shifted the attention of moral judgment away from deed to the intention that lay behind it. Aelred of Rivaulx underscored the importance of inwardness in his celebrated treatise on spiritual friendship. And medieval penitential theory and practice began to stress contrition – genuine sorrow for one's sins – over external acts of penance. But there was something significantly new about the way in which men and women in the Renaissance began to conceptualize the relation between what they saw as the interior self on the one hand and the expressions of one's thoughts, feelings, or beliefs on the other. Indeed, it is by carefully analyzing this shift from medieval to Renaissance notions of the relation of the interior self to such expressions that we can both better grasp what has come to be called the Renaissance discovery of the individual along with the new sense of subjectivity (both in the sense of ownership of and agency behind one's speech, thoughts, and actions) that it entailed. Here my analysis shall be limited, as I noted earlier, to two relatively well-focused developments: the Renaissance refashioning of the virtue of prudence and the rather more sudden emergence in sixteenth-century discourse of the ideal of sincerity.

Prudence, unlike sincerity, is an ancient virtue, with classical roots. It played a central role for Aristotle, who viewed prudence (*phronesis*) as the practical reason that guided one's choice in the process of ethical decision-making. In late antiquity, a number of authors – most notably, Augustine – linked this classical ideal to the Christian concept of Providence. Indeed, the two terms *prudentia* and *providentia* both derived from the Latin *providere* ('to foresee,' 'to take precaution,' 'to provide for'). As a result, throughout most of the Middle Ages, prudence was viewed as Christian wisdom and took its place alongside temperance, fortitude, and justice as one of the four cardinal virtues. For instance, the twelfth-century theologian Alan of Lille stated in his *De virtutibus* [*On the virtues*], 'prudence is the discernment of those things that are good, evil, or mixed, with the avoidance of evil and the election of the good.' In Thomas Aquinas's *Summa theologiae* [*The Essentials of Theology*], prudence is represented as a principle of order, one that is decisive, when properly developed, in holding the passions and the appetites in check when these threaten one's ability to obtain happiness or salvation. 'Prudence,' Thomas wrote, 'is a virtue most necessary for human life. For a good life consists in good deeds. Now in order to do good deeds, it matters not only what a man does but also how he does it; to wit, that he do it from right choice and not merely from impulse or passion.'

Yet this ideal underwent a significant shift in the Italian Renaissance, especially in the late fourteenth and fifteenth centuries, when humanists began reading and interpreting Aristotle's works – above all, his *Nicomachean Ethics* – outside a strictly theological context. In the hands of such humanists as Coluccio Salutati, Leonardo Bruni, Giovanni Pontano, and Lorenzo Valla, prudence was no longer the equivalent of providence but rather an ethical strategy that gave new emphasis to the individual's will. And in the early sixteenth century, in the work of Machiavelli, prudence was divorced entirely from ethics. As Machiavelli argued in a famous passage of *The Prince*, 'a wise ruler [*uno signore prudente*] cannot, nor should he, keep his word when doing so would be to his disadvantage and when the reasons that led him to make promises no longer exist . . . But one must know how to disguise this nature well, and how to be a fine liar and hypocrite [*simulatore e dissimulatore*]; and men are so simple-minded and so dominated by their present needs that one who deceives will always find one who will allow himself to be deceived.' In Castiglione's *Book of the Courtier*, the humanist Pietro Bembo states that one should never trust anyone, not even a dear friend, to the extent of 'communicating without reservation all one's thoughts to him,' while the diplomat Federico Fregoso, the primary speaker of Book II, explicitly recommends 'a certain studied dissimulation' in one's conversation. Although other voices are presented as objecting to the opinions of these speakers, the overall thrust of Castiglione's dialogue is to view conversation as an art, in which nothing is said that has not previously been thought through. As Federico remarks at the beginning of Book II, 'One should consider carefully whatever one does or says, attending to the place where one does it, in whose presence, at what time, and the motive for one's actions, one's own age, profession, the ends one is striving for, and the means that can lead there, and thus, with these things having been taken into account, let him accommodate himself discreetly for all he wishes to do or to say.'

This new understanding of prudence was widespread. [. . .]

A prudential rhetoric was, moreover, an increasingly important dimension of the everyday. In a variety of venues, great emphasis was placed on the importance of cultivating a certain ambiguity about one's beliefs in daily interactions. Renaissance books – from Paolo da Certaldo's *Libro di buoni costumi* to Leon Battista Alberti's *Della famiglia* to Francesco Guicciardini's *Ricordi* – recommended a certain caution in revealing one's convictions or feelings. To a large degree, it is not surprising that the demands of everyday life, both in the cities and the courts of Renaissance Europe, tended to collapse the traditional distinction between prudence and dissimulation. Although historical sources are limited, we do have some sense of the history of the self in urban contexts. In their efforts to maintain their honor in the eyes of their neighbors and fellow workers or to negotiate the demands of their own sexuality against a backdrop of seemingly impossible religious demands, for example, it is evident that lay people in the late Middle Ages often viewed the self as a complex entity. For the early Renaissance, evidence is most persuasive in such settings as Florence, where merchants, bankers, and affluent artisans began keeping diaries (*ricordi*) that often provide revealing glimpses of these internal conflicts. And a recent study of sexuality in Renaissance Venice has made it clear that adult Venetians, while posing publicly as moral members of a Christian society, often self-consciously engaged in a variety of sexual practices beyond the expected boundaries of proper behavior – evidence that self-fashioning was an aspect of the lives of townspeople as well as those of courtiers.

The Renaissance refashioning of prudence indicates a significant shift in the understanding of the self. Both the emphasis on deliberation – as, for example, in the popularity of dialogues in which the interlocutors debate issues from different perspectives – and the practical divorce of prudence from ethics placed new emphasis on the human subject. To be sure, there was much in Aquinas's thought that had invested the self (whether understood as intellect or will) with a significant role in decision-making, but Aquinas's emphasis consistently fell on the need to bring the appetites and the will into conformity with properly determined ends. In the Middle Ages, it was the role of the virtues both to hold the passions in check and to encourage thoughtful deliberation about the proper ends of one's actions. From the fifteenth century on, by contrast, the will was seen as increasingly free of these external (and internal) constraints and more emphasis was placed on the feelings, emotions, and expressiveness of what we might describe as the individual subject.

This new emphasis on the self as subject is even more apparent in the Renaissance invention of sincerity. Like many words that eventually gained a wide currency, sincerity had many significations. Before the Renaissance, the word 'sincere' had generally referred to something (often a material substance such as a liquid or a metal) that was pure or unadulterated, but in the sixteenth century, as the eminent literary historian Lionel Trilling argued in a famous essay, sincerity became a moral category, referring, as Trilling put it – concisely but usefully – 'to a congruence between avowal and actual feeling.'[3] That is, in the midst of the sixteenth century (although there is some evidence that this new moral meaning of sincerity had begun to appear in earlier Renaissance writers such as Petrarch and Valla), we discover a growing moral imperative to make one's feelings and convictions known. Indeed, I would argue that this is a characteristically modern concern: to state that someone is sincere or not sincere, to see particular utterances and works of art and literature as essential expressions of individual selves, above all, to desire to connect speech with feeling. The sixteenth and seventeenth centuries explored many facets of this ideal. '[L]ooke in thy heart, and write' – as Sir Philip Sidney's muse encouraged him – might be seen as an epigram of the age, as might the Shakespearean imperative from Polonius, 'to thine own self be true.' But the struggle for the sincere ideal began earlier, among the Italian humanists, though it was the early Protestant reformers who elevated sincerity to a defining virtue.

Medieval authors had also developed an ideal of the proper relation between what they described as the internal self (*homo interior*) and one's words and actions. But, significantly, they did not use the term 'sincerity' to describe this relation. Turning to language that had in fact developed much earlier, within early medieval monasticism, they cultivated the ideal of *concordia* (harmony or agreement) and related expressions [. . .] to describe the proper interplay between self and one's words and deeds. A key text was the *Rule of St. Benedict*, in which the interior self was to be fashioned to correspond to the language of the psalms that punctuated the monk's daily life, as when Benedict counseled monks to pray in such a way 'that our mind be in agreement with our voice.' In the twelfth century, this ideal took hold. Hugh of St. Victor, in his commentary on the *Rule of St. Augustine*, for example, cited Benedict when he wrote: 'of those chanting in church, . . . their mind should be in agreement [*concordare debet*] with their voice.' In his *Life of Aelred*, the Cistercian Walter Daniel praised the way in which Aelred's teachings were in harmony with his life and his works: 'he did not live differently than he taught, but his work was in agreement [*concordabat*] with his voice, and what he taught in words, he put forth with examples.' *Concordia* was the central thread of the universe in Bernard of Sylvester's neo-Platonic *Cosmographia*. It bound the earth to the heavens and the soul to the body. [. . .]

Indeed, over and over again in the texts from the Middle Ages, *concordia* was viewed as the ideal around which one should structure language and life in relation to beliefs and convictions. In the early thirteenth century, St. Francis wrote that one should pray in such a way that 'one's voice was in agreement with one's mind,' and the ideal of *concordia* or *consonantia* persisted through Dante and Thomas à Kempis. In the late fifteenth century, we find it as well in the Platonic writings of Marsilio Ficino. 'No harmony gives greater delight than that of heart and tongue' is the title Ficino gives to one of his letters. Like the other neo-Platonic writers Bernard of Sylvester and Alan of Lille before him, Ficino too made it clear that the concord between heart and tongue was only one aspect of a larger divine plan. As he wrote in his letter on music, 'a man is not harmoniously formed who does not delight in harmony . . . for God rejoices in harmony to such an extent that he seems to have created the world especially for this reason, that all its individual parts should sing harmoniously to themselves and to the whole universe.' As an ethic, then, *concordia* or harmony placed the greatest emphasis on the agreement of one person with another in relation to the worship of God. But the shift to the ideal of *sinceritas* was not merely the result of shifts in social and economic structures, with the consequences these new arrangements had for collective life. It was primarily the outgrowth of an intellectual revolution central to the rise of Protestantism.

Like many other dimensions of medieval life, the ideal of *concordia* had rested on the assumption, widespread in the monastic and Catholic culture of this period, that the human person was fundamentally similar to God. [. . .] Medieval writers – especially beginning in the twelfth century – strove to model themselves on Christ. They viewed the spiritual life as preeminently a quest for the recovery of the image of God within themselves. The Delphic Oracle's pronouncement 'Know Thyself' became, in their understanding of the human person, not a command to discover a unique personality but rather an ideal to recover the image of God within the self. [. . .]

In the late Middle Ages, beginning with William of Ockham, nominalist theologians began to develop arguments that eventually eroded, especially in the work of Martin Luther, the anthropology on which this ideal of *concordia* had been based. For, unlike earlier medieval theologians and mystics, Luther could not accept the principle that man was essentially similar to God. To the contrary, Lutheran anthropology was based on a principle of dissimilarity. The human person was fundamentally sinful, a concept that was reiterated with special force in Calvin's recurrent emphasis on the majesty of God and the depravity of man. The implications of this shift to a new anthropology were manifold, but at the very least they undermined the possibility of *concordia*. The human person was no longer viewed as in a (potentially) harmonious relation to God, the cosmos, and to him or herself but as an inevitably sinful portion of Creation, whose value in God's eyes was largely a mystery.

But if the ideal of *concordia* had begun to lose its force, how were men and women to conceive of the ideal relation between what they viewed as their internal selves (their thoughts, their feelings, and their convictions) and the broader world? In the sixteenth century, this relation began to be described in terms of sincerity. Crucially, the terms *concordia* and sincerity were not fully synonymous. Whereas *concordia* was based on a complex assumption about the potentiality of harmony throughout the universe – a harmony that ideally would be reflected in the way the individual Christian modeled him or herself on the image of God, the sincere ideal could not appeal, at least not for long, to the image of God within the individual person. To be sure, for Luther, grace to some degree substituted – at least in the elect – for the medieval ideal of *similitudo* (likeness). But, in general, the sincere ideal could not appeal to a common notion of the internal self. Once the idea of similarity or likeness between God and the human person had been ruptured, it became increasingly difficult to express a common Christian ideal. A particular person's actions and words were viewed as expressing something far more limited: the internal, particular, and even unique self within. However, not all writers held that one's words and deeds should be a genuine representation of one's beliefs or feelings at all times. As we have seen, the Renaissance period is largely defined by the ascendancy of a doctrine of prudence that held the contrary: that there were numerous occasions on which particular men and women should conceal what is in their minds and hearts. Nonetheless, in both discussions of sincerity and counsels of prudence, a new understanding of the human person emerged – one that placed greater stress on the internal self as agent or subject, as director of one's words and deeds. And although the Protestant attack on the medieval view of the human as a representation, however flawed, of the divine was only one factor in the discovery of the individual, it is nonetheless clear that the development of the individual in the Renaissance had little to do with the cultivation of a sense of interiority per se. What was novel about sixteenth-century views of the self was the new under-standing of the relation of one's thoughts and feelings to one's words and actions. On the one hand, Renaissance writers, especially by the sixteenth century, placed new emphasis on differences between individuals. On the other, in overturning the medieval ideal of prudent restraint on one's emotions, Protestant reformers gave a new legitimacy to the expression of one's emotions – an expressiveness of feelings that would, increasingly, be subsumed under the ideal of sincerity.

Luther, Calvin, and other early Protestant reformers played a pivotal role in articulating this new concern with sincerity. Luther was especially forceful in his praise of this virtue in his 'Preface to the Psalms,' which he published in his German Bible of 1528. The Book of Psalms, Luther argued, far surpassed the lives of saints and other moral tales because it 'preserves, not the trivial and ordinary things said by the saints, but their deepest and noblest utterances, those which they used when speaking in full earnest and all urgency to God. It not only tells us what they say about their work and conduct, but also lays bare their hearts . . . [I]t enables us to see into their hearts and understand the nature of their thoughts.' Especially noteworthy is the degree to which Luther's endorsement of sincerity is linked to a new valuing of the human passions:

> The human heart is like a ship on a stormy sea driven about by winds blowing from all four corners of heaven. In one man, there is fear and anxiety about impending disaster; another groans and moans at all the surrounding evil. One man mingles hope and presumption out of the good fortune to which he is looking forward; and another is puffed up with a confidence and pleasure in his present possessions. Such storms, however, teach us to speak sincerely and frankly, and make a clean breast. [*Solche sturmwinde aber leren mit ernst reden und das herss öffenen, und den grund eraus schütten.*] For a man who is in the grip of fear or distress speaks of disaster in a quite different way from one who is filled with happiness; and a man who is filled with joy speaks and sings about happiness quite differently from one who is in the grip of fear. They say that when a sorrowing man laughs or a happy man weeps, his laughter and his weeping do not come from the heart. In other words, these men do not lay bare, or speak of things which lie in, the bottom of their hearts.

Clearly, Luther's view of the proper relation of the emotions to human action and expressiveness marks a radical departure from Aquinas's ethics, which had appealed to prudence and reason to restrain the passions and emotions in the shaping of human acts and speech. To Luther, earnest speech found its model in the David of the Hebrew Psalms – an ideal reiterated in the writings of Calvin. [. . .]

The refashioning of the ideal of prudence and the emergence of the sincere ideal were both woven – as two threads among many – into the complex web of causes that led, in the Renaissance period, to the discovery of the individual, although the emergence of sincerity is particularly revealing. For, unlike *concordia*, which insisted on identity or similitude between God and the human person, on the one hand, and between the heart and the tongue, on the other, sincerity was an ethic of difference. To be sure, it preserved the ideal of harmony between the heart and the tongue, but the heart was now viewed not as a micro-cosm of a greater whole but rather as an individual entity, which, while perhaps similar to other hearts in its proclivity to sin and to self-deception, was above all characterized by its own irreducible individuality, its particular desires and affec-tions that set it apart from other persons. Luther's image of the diverse passions (fear, anxiety, hope) of men at sea, tossed about 'by winds blowing from all four corners of heaven,' underscores this new sense of individuality. In *Loci communes* [*Common places*], Melanchthon was more explicit: 'we see that in some characters, some affections rule, and that in other persons, others hold sway. Each is drawn by his own desire.' Similarly, Montaigne emphasized that he was writing not of men in general but of 'a particular one.' In a world cut off both from a communion based on similitude with God and an implicit anthropolog-ical identity with other Christians, even the most sincere individual could appeal to no truth greater than that based on his or her feelings, emotions, passions, or affections. As an ideal, therefore, sincerity may have seemed to preserve some-thing of the traditional medieval concern with the need to bring expression and behavior into harmony with one's internal beliefs. In reality, this harmony was profoundly limited, or individualistic. It reached out precariously from an indi-vidual speaker's or writer's heart. One's language, therefore, may have resonated with the feelings of a friend or lover, or perhaps, fleetingly, with those of one's readers. Writing of his friendship with La Boétie, for example, Montaigne observed that their very souls had communicated with one another 'to the very depths of our hearts.' But ultimately, no matter how sincere one was, such expres-sions, precisely because they were based on feelings and emotions, were unable to establish consensus or a sense of community. Where God once was, the indi-vidual now stood alone, faced with an increasingly complex dilemma of not knowing if those whom one addressed would ever understand one's deepest feel-ings, concerns, or hopes.

The discovery of the individual was to a large degree, therefore, the result of fun-damental shifts in the ethical visions of Renaissance humanists and Protestant reformers. In fashioning their religious, social, even personal identities, Renais-sance men and women could draw on two distinct, even opposed virtues. On the one hand, there were those who embraced what I have been describing as a Renaissance notion of the prudential self (a rhetorical posture that subordinated honesty to decorum); on the other, there were those who favored the ideal of sin-cerity (which subordinated decorum to honesty). Guicciardini exposed the con-flict between these two virtues in his *Ricordi*: 'Frank sincerity,' he wrote, 'is a quality much extolled among men and pleasing to everyone, while simulation [*simulazione*], on the contrary, is detested and condemned. Yet for a man's self, simulation is of the two by far the more useful; sincerity [*realitá*] tending rather to the interest of others.' To be sure, for the overwhelming majority, life was lived in the gray areas between, as Polonius's counsel in *Hamlet* suggests. Polonius not only reminded Laertes to be true to himself but also to 'give [his] thoughts no tongue.' But this tension between two conflicting ethical models points, in my view, to a vital and dynamic aspect of the understanding of the human self that was new in the sixteenth century. For, despite the very real differences between them, both prudentialism and the sincere ideal played pivotal roles in shaping the Renaissance notion of the self as an individual and expressive subject. It was only such a self that could be called upon, as circumstances shifted, to project a faithful representation of its concerns, its feelings, its beliefs to the outside world or to hold them in check, concealing them. This is not to say that what contemporaries imagined as the inner self was, as we are often inclined to believe, 'truer' than the ways one chose to represent it, either in the city or the court. Rather, the new sense of the self views the human being as agent, subject, or author – as someone responsible for his or her actions and assertions. Moreover, the very existence of such a duality (between prudence and sincerity) in Renaissance discourse is itself revealing. It provided a kind of ethical field on which many men and women in this period negotiated the demands of everyday life. And, over time, it sharpened contemporary notions of the self as a unique, complex entity.

This sense of particularity or individuality emerges with special clarity in the case of Montaigne. Much of the scholarship on Montaigne has connected his emphasis on self-knowledge and on the individual with his decision in 1571, at the age of thirty-eight, to retire from public life and devote his leisure to the study of himself – a project he ultimately realizes in the *Essays*. To be sure, there is much that lends support to this connection. Montaigne memorialized his retirement with a Latin inscription engraved on the wall of his study; he only rarely returned to public service (twice as mayor and briefly in 1588 as a go-between in the negotiations between the king and Henri of Navarre in the course of the French wars of religion); and, in his *Essays*, he reiterated the value the private sphere had assumed in the course of his life. Indeed, he is perhaps best known for the image he created of the individual cultivating freedom entirely apart from others. 'We must reserve a back shop [*arriereboutique*] all our own, entirely free, in which to establish our real liberty and our principal retreat and solitude.' 'Here,' Montaigne continues,

> our ordinary conversation must be between us and ourselves, and so private that no outside association or communication can find a place . . . We have a soul that can be turned upon itself; it can keep itself company; it has the means to attack and the means to defend, the means to receive and the means to give: let us not fear that in this solitude we shall stagnate in tedious idleness: *In solitude be to thyself a throng* [Tibullus]. Virtue, says Antisthenes, is content with itself, without rules, without words, without deeds.

Not surprisingly, Greenblatt makes much of this passage, which he cites from John Florio's 1603 translation. Like many other commentators, Greenblatt is drawn to the back room, the *arriereboutique*, the place that Florio had translated as 'storehouse' and the commercial connotations it unleashes. This word, Greenblatt writes, 'conjures up a world of *negotium* [business], in effect a world of private property. If Montaigne counsels a retreat from this world, he is, at the same time, assuming its existence; that is, his sense of self is inseparable from his sense of the *boutique* and all it represents.' For Greenblatt, in short, Montaigne's individualism or self-fashioning is primarily a consequence of the dynamics of an emerging capitalism; the self is implicated in the structures of an economy that would place a supreme value on separating one's private from one's public life.

Yet the emphasis that Greenblatt and other commentators have placed on the split between the public and the private in Montaigne's writings misses an equally fundamental tension in his thought, namely, Montaigne's deeply felt desire to be both prudent and sincere. Indeed, we can also read the *Essays* and therefore Montaigne's own self-fashioning as an effort to negotiate the tensions between these two ideals. Montaigne's praise of sincerity applies to both spheres, just as his own sense of the importance of prudence does. This does not prevent him from condemning prudence in the sense of needless dissembling and dissimulation (though he more often uses this term in the more traditional sense of a kind of practical reason), nor does it mean that he is himself fully sincere. But it does imply that Montaigne's sense of self is largely shaped by his consciousness of the degree to which the pressure to dissemble can conflict with the ideal of sincerity.

The desire for, as well as the impossibility of, sincere speech can be seen as one of the threads that ties the *Essays* together. This work gave poignant expression to a widely felt need, in the age of the court, to find certain spaces – in one's own room, or library, or friendships, or writings – to provide a comparatively honest or sincere account of oneself and one's feelings. Yet this virtue is not only to be practiced in private, among friends, but in public as well. Of course, Montaigne himself is anything but private. He writes his book for a broad public. He never really retreats to the back room. And he tells us again and again that he rejects dissimulation. Contrasting his own temperament with others who served, as Montaigne did, as a facilitator in the political negotiations, he writes, 'I have an open way . . . I do not refrain from saying anything, however grave or burning . . . This is what makes me walk everywhere head high, face and heart open.' 'It is painful for me to dissemble,' he remarks, noting that this ability is not in his nature. Repeatedly, he lashes out against dissimulation ('among the most notable qualities of this century'). He favors a more direct, a more sincere speech. But 'as for this new-fangled virtue of hypocrisy and dissimulation, which is so highly honored at present,' he writes, 'I mortally hate it; and of all vices, I know none that testifies to so much cowardice and baseness of heart. It is a craven and servile idea to disguise ourselves and hide under a mask, and not to dare to show ourselves as we are . . . A generous heart should not belie its thoughts; it wants to reveal itself even to its inmost depths [*jusques au dedans*].'

Unlike the Protestant theologians who connected sincerity (*sincérité, ernst reden, sinceritas, Aufrichtigkeit*) with the need to express one's emotions, the Catholic and stoic Montaigne based his ethic of sincerity on the need to be true to one's nature or temperament. In doing so, he took some pleasure in critiquing the courtly ethos of the Renaissance:

Now for my part I would rather be troublesome and indiscreet than flattering and dissembling. I admit that a touch of pride and stubbornness may enter into keeping me sincere and outspoken [*entier et descouvert*] without consideration for others; and it seems to me that I restrain myself a little less whenever it would be appropriate to restrain myself more, and that I react against the respect I owe by growing more heated. It may be, too, that I let myself follow my nature for lack of art. When I display to great men the same extreme freedom of tongue and bearing that I exercise in my own house, I feel how much it inclines toward indiscretion and incivility. But besides the fact that I am made that way, I have not a supple enough mind to sidestep a sudden question and escape it by some dodge, or to invent a truth, or a good enough memory to retain something thus invented, and certainly not enough assurance to maintain it; and I put on a bold face because of weakness. Therefore I give myself up to being candid and always saying what I think, by inclination and by reason, leaving it to Fortune to guide the outcome.

Thus his project – especially in the essays written before 1580 – may have had the stamp of self-fashioning, but as Montaigne grew older, he was less confident in his ability to shape himself. 'Others form man,' he wrote in an essay of 1585, 'I tell of him, and portray a particular one, very ill-formed, whom I should really make very different from what he is if I had to fashion him over again. But now it is done.' To be sure, the tension in this sentence is enormous. Montaigne does not form or fashion himself, he tells us – only to add that this is something he has already done. But we need not conclude a contradiction or an inconsistency. Montaigne's understanding of self allows for a complex interplay between nature and culture; indeed, it was part of Montaigne's humanist strategy to link his understanding of individualism with his view of nature. 'Natural inclinations,' he observed, 'gain assistance and strength from education; but they are scarcely to be changed and overcome.' 'We do not root out these original qualities,' he continued, 'we cover them up, we conceal them.' And then he provides – perhaps somewhat disingenuously – a compelling (though equally contradictory) example: 'Latin is like a native tongue to me; I understand it better than French; but for forty years I have not used it at all for speaking or writing. Yet in sudden and extreme emotions, into which I have fallen two or three times in my life – one of them when I saw my father, in perfect health, fall back into my arms in a faint – I have always poured out my first words from the depths of my entrails in Latin; Nature surging forth and expressing herself by force, in the face of long habit.' Here, of course, the contradiction lies in the fact that a particular language is not a part of nature but rather of culture, something taught and instilled. But Montaigne's point is rather obvious. There are multiple layers in the make-up of a particular person: a natural temperament, a cluster of (often conflicting) emotions, a primary language, a particular family and education, as well as broader political, social, and cultural forces – all of these go into shaping us, making us who we are. Accordingly, we are never purely the roles we play, though there is the possibility, which Montaigne himself acknowledges, that we can become our roles. '*The whole world plays a part*,' he writes, citing Petronius, and adds: 'We must play our part duly, but not as the part of a borrowed character. Of the mask and appearance we must not make a real essence, nor of what is foreign what is our very own. We cannot distinguish the skin from the shirt. It is enough to make up our face, without making up our heart [*poictrine*].

The construction – above all, Montaigne's insistence that our mask need not shape our interior self – is sharply at odds with Greenblatt's view that, in the Renaissance period, 'there is no layer deeper, more authentic, than theatrical self-representation.' To be sure, Montaigne's *Essays* often point to the prevalence of such self-fashioning in Renaissance culture. But he also managed to suggest the existence of a complex array of other forces that shape our identities – forces often inevitably in tension or in conflict with the roles we choose to play. That he was able to do so stems, I believe, from the growing importance placed on the questions of prudence and sincerity in the Renaissance. For both these virtues emphasized the need for the individual to fashion the public self *from within*, to know when it was most appropriate to present in one's expressed life a reflection of 'true' feelings (as in the case of the Protestants) or 'true' nature (as in the case of Montaigne) or when, by contrast, it was more appropriate to project or to wear a mask, to dissemble – in short, to exercise prudence in one's affairs, whether public or private.

Although a precise identification of the forces that led to the invention of sincerity and the refashioning of prudence lies beyond the scope of this essay, it is clear that historical discussions of the emergence of the self as subject – what Burckhardt long ago called 'the development of the individual' – cannot and should not be confined to one particular historical moment or context, especially when such a framework is conceptualized as a monolithic, closed, or totalizing system. Indeed, if we stand back from New Historicist theories about self-fashioning, we see clearly that their analyses are too often developed in precisely such a limited fashion, with insufficient attention to broader ideas and vocabularies within European culture. This is not to say that More's arguments with Tyndale, for example, or Shakespeare's dramas do not command our attention. Much recent historical scholarship has benefited from renewed attention to the event and the anecdote, reinvigorating historical writings that had become, all too often, bland and rather predictable social-scientific reconstructions of the past. But we ought not to allow a fascination with great works or even with the unusual, the strange, and the anecdotal to obscure the underlying complexities of longer-term historical changes and their relation to the moral or the cultural life. This is not merely a theoretical claim. To the contrary, the evidence I have presented concerning both the refashioning of prudence and the invention of sincerity – albeit preliminary and necessarily tentative – points to a gradual tendency, beginning in the fifteenth but accelerating in the sixteenth century, to view the self as an agent or subject and in increasingly individualized terms. The ideals of prudence and sincerity, that is, were not fashioned at one particular moment or even in one particular context but developed gradually over the course of several generations. [. . .] From this perspective, the identities of such figures as More and Tyndale were not simply functions of specific, relatively easily identifiable cultural and political forces such as the church or the monarchy in a particular society. To the contrary – even in the absence of direct evidence – their views of the self and its *relative* autonomy must have emerged through their expo-sure – in their education, their reading, their conversation – to new vocabularies that had, in the Renaissance period, begun to invest the self with a new sense of subjectivity and, above all, in an increasingly fragmented culture, with a height-ened sense of individualism.

To be clear, there is nothing about this approach that is necessarily incompat-ible with that of the New Historicists, whose writings have done much to illu-minate the salient role that political, social, and cultural institutions played in shaping the self. But the individual so shaped was not a blank tablet or text on which such institutions or indeed certain fundamental tensions or conflicts in the culture (political and religious) were 'inscribed.' To the contrary, the context of selfhood in the Renaissance world ensured that the notion of person was any-thing but blank. Increasingly widely diffused humanist educational practices, evolving child-rearing theories that stressed a sensitivity to each particular child's emotions and feelings, a developing model of companionate marriage, Protestant sermons that gave warrant to both expressiveness and plain speaking, the increas-ingly broad diffusion of books, new practices of reading, and even the com-modification of the mirror – these and many other factors, none of which can be reduced to one unifying cultural or social explanation, were part of the complex set of interactions through which Renaissance men and women were shaped with a new awareness of the self as subject, as an individual. The fash-ioning of selves in the Renaissance world, as indeed the fashioning of selves in other times and places, is overdetermined, and is not reducible to one particular matrix or dialectic, no matter how powerful or persuasive.

The emphasis on the broader cultural climate in the shaping of the self is crucial also for our understanding of the remarkable resiliency of certain aspects of self-hood in the Renaissance. The Renaissance experience of selfhood appeared to transcend social and cultural experience. 'Someone says to me, "You don't express yourself as if you were Cicero." "What of it? I am not Cicero. I express myself,"' Angelo Poliziano wrote in the late fifteenth century, demonstrating the degree to which the self was seen as something independent, strong, even God-given. One's past, one's experiences, one's memories, and one's inner life all mat-tered. Despite growing anxieties about selfhood or perhaps because of them, men and women in the Renaissance were more than likely to embrace the humanist anthropologies that viewed the self as something autonomous and willful, indeed, as a fundamental, underlying essence or as a building block of human society. The language of prudence and sincerity points to a sense of interiority, albeit constructed, that cannot be viewed purely reflectively in relation to the cultural poetics of a particular place and period but was in fact relatively immune to the sort of ideological forces and totalizing pressures of the church or the monarchy that Greenblatt and other New Historicists have seen as determining if not as wholly hegemonic in the formation of Renaissance identities.

In particular, this broadening of our conception of the forces that shaped Renaissance selves allows for a far clearer understanding of the possibility of agency, dissent, and opposition [. . .]. The Renaissance self was something greater than the sum of one's social roles. Indeed, the growing importance of the ideals of prudence and sincerity – as well as the tensions between them – made it increasingly possible in the Renaissance and in the early modern period generally to view a particular person as a complex individual, who was self-conscious about the degree to which the inner self, now viewed as largely cut off from God, directed the outer, public self in its daily interactions with one's fellow citizens, subjects, or courtiers. At the time of the French Revolution, the republican opponents of the Old Regime self-consciously celebrated the sincerity (or the transparency) of their speech and actions.

A historical account of the Renaissance discovery of the individual, therefore, does not need to embrace either the essentialism of Burckhardt or the narrowly synchronic and totalizing historicism of Greenblatt. The primary cultural factors in the making of Renaissance individualism were the emergence of humanism and the development of Protestantism, both of which deeply problematized the relation of what contemporaries viewed as the internal self to one's words and actions. The primary social factors were the rapid expansion of urban life and the burgeoning size of the courts. The demise of the ideal of *concordia* and the emergence of a new understanding of prudence, as well as the construction of the sincere ideal, point to a major historical shift in Renaissance Europe. It was, in fact, a religious or ethical revolution that played a pivotal role in fostering an emerging ethic of individualism, at least in the sense that the individual came to see him or herself as a unique entity, largely responsible for his or her words and deeds, and capable of either concealing or revealing his or her feelings and beliefs as circumstances dictated. To be sure, such an individual was capable of assuming many guises, from the benevolent humanism of Juan Luis Vives to the aggressive individualism of Renaissance despots. That such an individual could take on narrowly self-interested, self-aggrandizing, or even destructive attributes should surprise no one. Burckhardt himself was deeply ambivalent about the consequences of 'the development of the individual' and should not be seen – as he too often is – as celebrating it.

Finally – though a proper investigation of these issues must be done elsewhere – it is clear that the questions Burckhardt raised about the discovery of the individual are not exclusively a matter for intellectual or literary history. To the contrary, a grasp of the shifting nature of the self in Renaissance Europe should be at the heart of our studies of the social, political, economic, and cultural histories of the period. This is not to claim that the self was prior to larger structural forces or that the self can be viewed in isolation from them. Nor is it to claim that the Renaissance self always entailed a sense of subjectivity and a related sense of individualism. The Renaissance world was profoundly diverse, and it is likely that we can locate many different constructions of identity within it. But it is my hope that this essay will enliven debate about the enduring significance of Burckhardt's questions. For merely to ask them is to refuse to flatten the self out, to efface it, even to erase it – as it were – by viewing it as the function of one particular context, an approach that results, inevitably, in a distorted if not an impoverished picture of the past. [. . .] The history of the making of our modern identities is, after all, far from a trivial matter; it goes to core questions of ethics, literature, philosophy, and religion – questions that have emerged as central in many of the current discussions of both the value and the limits of individualism.

NOTES

1   The key text is Stephen J. Greenblatt, *Renaissance Self-Fashioning: From More to Shake-speare* (Chicago, 1980).
2   Michael Mascuch, *Origins of the Individualist Self: Autobiography and Self-Identity in England, 1591–1791* (Stanford, Calif., 1996), 14.
3   Lionel Trilling, *Sincerity and Authenticity* (Cambridge, Mass., 1971), 2. Trilling's observations on the history of this word derived from his reading of the entries 'sincere' and 'sincerity' in the *Oxford English Dictionary*. Nonetheless, my preliminary research into the history of this term (in English, German, Latin, and the Romance languages) largely confirms Trilling's point.

3   Albert Rabil Jr **'The Significance of "Civic Humanism" in the Interpretation of the Italian Renaissance'**

Source: from *Renaissance Humanism: Foundations, Forms and Legacy*, Volume 1, *Humanism in Italy*, ed. Albert J. Rabil, Jr, University of Pennsylvania Press, Philadelphia, 1988, chapter 7, pp. 141–79.

In his still classic analysis of the Renaissance, Jacob Burckhardt asserted that both republics and despotic states indifferently produced 'the individual' who emerged for the first time in fourteenth-century Italy: for these men were characterized above all else by their learning, their indifference to politics, and their cosmopolitanism. The class of men known as humanists, intended by this description, were devoted above all to classical – Greek and Latin – languages and literature. In classical culture they found all they needed for the expression of their many-sided personalities. Burckhardt admitted that it was above all others the Florentines 'who made antiquaria n interests one of the chief objectives of their lives' and that 'they were of peculiar significance during the period of transition at the beginning of the fifteenth century, since it was in them that humanism first showed itself practically as an indispensable element in daily life.'

For several generations after Burckhardt, interpretation of Renaissance humanism emphasized it as an antiquarian movement more or less diffused throughout Italy. The fact that it first expressed itself most forcefully in Florence around the turn of the fifteenth century and that Florence was a republic rather than a princely state did not lead anyone to raise the question of whether there might be some connection between humanism and Florentine polity and, if so, whether the definition of humanism as a movement indifferent to politics might not need to be modified. [. . .] The most powerful representatives of civic humanism belong to Florence, which was the cradle of humanism and its most brilliant light throughout the period of humanism's ascendancy. But the spirit

evoked by civic humanism was not confined to Florence. It spread with the
humanist movement throughout the cities and courts of Italy, breathing a new
ethos into an old world.

The new spirit began with Petrarch and continued until the rise of Platonism
(roughly from 1350 until 1475), when it was replaced by new impulses – the
Florence of Savonarola was not at all the Florence of Leonardo Bruni. But even
as humanist culture and the conditions that had given rise to it were dying, the
spirit it had generated continued to be diffused. In the fifteenth century it found
expression in art, history, and education. In the sixteenth, it flowered in science
and religion.

What does the glorification of civic life and the construction of an earthly city
by man mean? It means the validation of human activity of all kinds and, with
this validation, the belief that activity takes precedence over contemplation inasmuch as it keeps human beings rooted in practical human concerns. [. . .] [T]he
prologue of Leon Battista Alberti's *Della famiglia* [*On the Family*] asks the question whether human failure or success depends on fortune or on human character. His answer is unequivocal: fortune triumphs only over those who submit
to it. The Romans, he argues, did not triumph over many barbarous nations by
luck but by the strength of their own virtues. These virtues were, primarily,
concern to do good works and keep the traditions of their fatherland, and 'as
long as they possessed lofty and pious spirits, grave and mature counsel, perfect
faith and loyalty toward the fatherland – as long as concern for the public
good outweighed with them the pursuit of private ends, as long as the will of
the state overruled the individual's desires' – so long did Rome prosper. But 'as
soon as unjust desires counted for more in Italy than good laws and the hallowed
habits of restraint, the Latin empire grew weak and bloodless.' Fortune cannot
rob us of our character, and as long as we possess nobility of soul we can ascend
to the highest peaks of human achievement and glory. Alberti goes on to say that
what is true of empires is true also of families, and he wishes to exhort his own
kinsmen to maintain the traditions that enabled the family to rise to greatness
in the past.

Individual greatness is part of cultural greatness. And cultural greatness is the
product of many generations working always with the future in view. [. . .]
Human beings achieve personal greatness by having in mind the greatness of the
community of which they are a part.

The source of this new attitude was the *studia humanitatis* [studies of the
humanities]. Through their labors in philological criticism, humanists for the
first time discovered a distance between the past and the present. It was this
humanist discovery that brought to awareness the fact that a break had occurred
and gave rise to the need to define the present as against the past. The sense of
separation created the need to build anew – on the past but differently from the
past. [. . .] 'Thanks to *litterae* [letters] the mind unfolds and enlarges itself. And
while it enriches itself with untold treasures, it learns to respect the value of other
minds and to live in human society. Wisdom, far from incarcerating itself in an
ivory tower "lives in cities, flees solitude and longs to be of help to as many men
as possible."'

[H]umanism is much more than an antiquarian movement, it represents an alliance between the man of thought and the man of action, . . . this alliance finds its fullest expression in Florence where scholarship was joined with a republican civic spirit, . . . this civic humanism spread throughout the cities and courts of Italy during the Quattrocento, and . . . as it did so it profoundly affected attitudes and developments in the arts and sciences. [. . .] Hans Baron has made the question of civic humanism the central preoccupation of his scholarly career.[1] [. . .] And it is Baron's formulation that has been so widely discussed in the interpretation of Renaissance humanism during the past generation.

Baron begins with two important assumptions. First, as he says, 'we have learnt to interpret the coming of the early Renaissance also as a fundamental transformation in *Weltanschauung*.' This view, articulated in a general way by Wilhelm Dilthey, reinforces Burckhardt's contention that there is a fundamental discontinuity between the Middle Ages and the Renaissance. Something must therefore account for it. Second, as Vasari long ago recognized, there were two Renaissances in art, but only the second of them, in early Quattrocento Florence, established the new Renaissance *Weltanschauung* [world view]. But if the Renaissance really began in Florence at the beginning of the Quattrocento there must be some connection between this beginning and humanism.

Baron discovered the connection in 'civic humanism,' which appears in his earliest writings in German and English. In his edition of Bruni's works in 1928 he argued that from Salutati to Ficino humanists in Florence were identified with the wealthy ruling families, shared their interests, and developed a positive evaluation of social activity. Such a development was only possible in a republic; humanists who patronized the courts of despots were contemptuous of the business enterprises of the Florentine burgher and extolled the life of leisure. Thus civic humanism cannot be separated from Florence's republican political tradition, for it could have developed in no other environment.

The actual transition he traces in two articles published in English in 1938. In one, entitled 'Franciscan Poverty and Civic Wealth as Factors in the Rise of Humanistic Thought,' he demonstrates that in the thought of all Trecento humanists – above all in Petrarch, but also in his Florentine disciples – the attitude toward wealth and the active political life is ambivalent. Petrarch extolled poverty when he lived at Vaucluse but not after he moved to the court of Milan. Petrarch cites Cicero and Seneca in whose writings the Stoic wise man eschews riches in favor of a life of solitude and independence, and he finds these views echoed in writer after writer. Such an attitude was out of step with the feeling of the Florentine citizens, who could not be reconciled to a humanism of this kind. In fact a new view emerged in 1415 in Francesco Barbaro's treatise *On Wifely Duties*, 'the first time that we meet with expressions of the genuine civic spirit in humanistic literature.' In it he describes possessions as useful for many purposes, especially for our descendants. Shortly afterward, Bruni's apology for wealth rediscovered the civic character of Aristotle's *Politics* and the positive evaluation of wealth in Aristotle's *Ethics*. Humanists in Florence and elsewhere began to echo these views, to rediscover Xenophon's *Oeconomicus* – the most kindly disposed of all classical works toward the acquisition of wealth – and to discover more positive attitudes in Seneca and Cicero as well.

In another article, 'Cicero and the Roman Civic Spirit in the Middle Ages and the Early Renaissance,' Baron examines still another side of the attitude toward Cicero that helps to mark the transition. In the Middle Ages Cicero was seen as the Stoic sage removed from the world (corroborated by the medieval view of Cicero's attitude toward wealth), a perspective affirmed in part by Petrarch, who was repelled by his discovery (in 1345 in the *Letters to Atticus*) of Cicero the political figure. The civic humanists of the early Quattrocento, by contrast, found in Cicero's combination of literary and political activity a view of him congenial to themselves.

Baron thus established his thesis that the transformation we call the Renaissance that occurred in early Quattrocento Florence applied not only to the history of art but also to the humanist movement. But the question remains: What caused the transformation? Why was there suddenly a new appreciation for the positive values of wealth and of Cicero the philosopher-statesman? Whence arose civic humanism? In his major work on the subject, published in 1955, Baron ascribed the cause to Florence's conflict with Milan, culminating in a war fought between 1400 and 1402 in which Florence avoided Milanese conquest.

The possibility of conquest by Milan posed a threat to Florentine autonomy almost continually after 1350. Milan was ruled by Ghibellines, men who had been appointed by the emperors and who made themselves tyrants when Hohenstaufen rule came to an end (1254 in Germany, 1266 in Sicily). The leading force against the Ghibellines was the papacy, now in exile at Avignon, allied with Guelf (bourgeois) cities like Florence. More often than not (though not consistently) Florence saw itself as a defender of the church and supporter of its policies. In 1377, however, the papacy, preparing to return to Rome from its extended exile at Avignon, sent legates ahead to assert strong leadership (in effect tyrannies) in the areas surrounding Rome. Florence soon found itself at the head of a central-Italian league fighting in the 'War of the Eight Saints' against the dangers of attack from the papal state. The outcome of this war was to strengthen the tendency of the Florentines to regard themselves as the leaders of the free city-states.

During the 1380s Milan continued to expand southward and to incorporate smaller city-states into its orbit of power. Neither Rome nor Venice would aid Florence but were content to let Florence bear the burden of opposition to Milan. Florence did so – between 1390 and 1392 and again between 1397 and 1398. The latter struggle ended in a treaty that did not, however, guarantee the safety of the city-states allied with Florence, and within two years Milan had annexed them all. In 1400, therefore, Florence was isolated; only Bologna stood as a buffer between Milan and Florence. With a sense of desperation, Florence hired a mercenary army of German knights, led by Rupert of the Palatinate, the newly elected pretender to the imperial throne. The Visconti, however, defeated Rupert in October 1401, before he could make his way very far into Italy. Milan was now at the height of its power, and Florence seemed doomed. In the spring of 1402 (when the armies could once again campaign), the Milanese entered Bologna. By

June nothing lay between the Milanese army and Florence. The Florentines expected to see the enemy before the gates any day. Yet the signal for attack was not given, probably because the Visconti had defeated its other enemies by a show of might and by propaganda, waiting for treachery and defection to undermine a city. But the moment came and went. For the plague erupted in northern Italy, carrying off the Milanese tyrant, Giangaleazzo Visconti, on 3 September. Milanese expansion was altogether halted, at least for a time, by his death.

The Florentines 'credited their almost miraculous salvation more to the brave stand which they alone had made than to the sudden removal of the tyrant from the scene.' The fact that Florence had met the crisis alone was decisive for the climate of that city. 'When the crisis had passed, the real issue of the Floren-tine–Milanese contest stood revealed: out of the struggle had come the decision that the road was to remain open to the civic freedom and the system of inde-pendent states which became a part of the culture of the Italian Renaissance.'

The effects of this event on the humanists were immediate and decisive. In a *History of Florence, 1380–1406*, written in 1407, Gregorio Dati asserted that 'all the freedom of Italy lay in the hands of the Florentines alone, that every other power had deserted them.' To the humanists, Florence had become the city of freedom. This view is nowhere more evident than in Leonardo Bruni's *Panegyric to the City of Florence* (which Baron dates 1403–4 rather than, as previously believed, 1400) and his second *Dialogue to Peter Paul Vergerius* (which Baron dates 1405 rather than 1401). In the latter he raised for the first time questions about Dante's inter-pretation of Caesar and his assassins Brutus and Cassius. Dante had placed Caesar in limbo and his assassins in the depths of hell. Now Dante had long been the pride of Florence, but his monarchical views were contrary to the republican sen-timents of those who had just lived through a crisis threatening their liberty. Bruni sought a solution that would both exalt republican sentiments and save Dante. He argued that Dante had used historical figures only to serve the ends of his poetical imagination without actually taking sides with Caesar's tyranny against the last defenders of civic freedom in Rome. This new republican view of Dante had been unknown during the Trecento. So congenial was it to the feeling of the humanists that it was repeated by humanists throughout the century.

Bruni also argued in dialogue 2 that the republic had given rise to men of great talent in many fields but that 'after the republic had been subjected to the power of one man [i.e. the Roman emperor], those brilliant minds vanished as Cor-nelius Tacitus says.' This judgment was new, both because no one had consis-tently maintained it in the past and because it rested on a new historian, Tacitus, who had only recently been rediscovered through the manuscript at Monte Cassino brought to Florence by Boccaccio. In Tacitus himself the judgment quoted by Bruni had been a secondary one, for he had accepted the imperial monarchy as a historical necessity and, indeed, became a guide for monarchical publicists in the sixteenth and seventeenth centuries. Bruni selected a facet of Tacitus congenial to his new point of view.

In his *Panegyric* Bruni maintained further, following the lead of Salutati, that Florence had been founded during the days of the Roman Republic, before the corruption of the empire had set in. It was the Roman army under Sulla in the first century B.C. that founded Florence. By the time Bruni came to write his history of Florence some years later, he added to his arsenal of reasons for Florence's establishment during the Roman Republic the discovery of the part the Etruscan city-states played in pre-Roman times. Thus Florence had originally been a city with free blood running in its veins. To the argument that Vergil, Horace, and other great writers lived during the reign of Augustus, Bruni replied that they had been raised under the Republic. (Poggio was to make the same reply to Guarino during the next generation in the same dispute.) Finally, the freedom of these city-states was stifled by the Roman Empire and reemerged after its fall. Thus the resurgence of Florence in contemporary times has its roots in the earlier energy of the city in republican Rome. Machiavelli developed this conception of Bruni's that a wealth of human energies had been stifled by the Roman Empire but came to the fore again with the rise of free city-republics. Not until the triumph of monarchic absolutism in the latter part of the sixteenth century was this republican interpretation of Roman history in Florence challenged.

Baron argues further that this change in political preference from monarchy to republic involved at the same time a deeper underlying change in intellectual vision, in other words, that the humanism that emerged in Florence could only have emerged under the conditions of a free city-state. Not only so, but this new civic humanism became determinative for the whole of humanism during the Quattrocento: the essence of Italian humanism in general during the Quattrocento was Florentine civic humanism.

In order to appreciate these larger claims, the nature of the change in consciousness must first be explored. Baron sees it preeminently in Bruni's *Dialogues*. In dialogue 1 Bruni argues, through Niccolò Niccoli, that classical learning is dead in his own time (Salutati excepted) and that this fact is reflected in the myriad deficiencies of the 'three crowns of Florence,' Dante, Petrarch, and Boccaccio. Dialogue 2 rehabilitates the three Florentine writers and asserts that far from being dead, learning is everywhere being revived. The reversal of historical judgment is profound. Instead of seeing the classical past as something to which the present can never measure up, it is regarded as something to be equaled and surpassed. In other words, the classical ideal is no longer to be viewed only as an intellectual tradition but is fused with civic aspirations. Civic humanism is the result of this fusion.

Baron finds evidence of this new civic humanism in the transformation of humanist attitudes toward the vernacular. In 1435 a debate took place between Bruni, Biondo, and other humanists working in the Roman curia, which was exiled at the time in Florence. Biondo argued that the Italian vernacular had been created by a fusion of Latin with the languages of the Germanic invaders of the Roman Empire. Bruni opposed Biondo's view, contending that there had always existed both a popular and a learned way of speaking and that popular speech was the Italian vernacular, even in the days of Terence and Cicero. Biondo's theory is the more historically correct and was judged so even by his contemporaries. But Bruni may not have been affirming a rigid classicism that finds no value in the vernacular, as previous interpreters have largely maintained. Indeed, in Biondo's account of the debate itself, it is evident that he regarded the vernacular as inferior. Bruni instead may have been attributing a higher value to the vernacular, and so giving a higher status to popular culture. This interpretation is suggested more strongly by his *Life of Dante* written during the following year (1436) in which he asserted that *every* language has its own perfection, even its own way of speaking scientifically, thus explicitly placing the vernacular on a level with Latin and Greek. This judgment coincides with the earliest use of the vernacular as a literary language by humanists in the 1430s, notably by Palmieri and Alberti. After Bruni, one finds in Alberti, Lorenzo de' Medici, and Cristoforo Landino affirmations of the equality of the vernacular with the classical languages. This alliance indicates a new type of classicism, one 'willing to employ the ancient model as a guide in building a new literature with a new language in a new nation.'

The fusion between the civic spirit and Christianity is evident in a different way. In the Trecento there had been a tendency to fuse pagan and Christian literature. The tendency is evident in Petrarch and Boccaccio; Petrarch had argued that the pagan poets were really monotheists and Boccaccio that they were the first theologians. Salutati did not at first accept this position, apologizing in a letter of 1378 for reading pagan poets in spite of their errors. But in the late 1390s he developed the earlier position of his predecessors, maintaining that the pagan poets were genuine seekers after piety. Thereafter he used this idea as a key to interpreting classical mythology. He did not, for all that, identify pagan gods with Christian saints. But a number of humanists were led to make this identification. Francesco da Fiano, for example, a Roman humanist writing at the turn of the century, argued in his enthusiasm for antiquity, that even theologically there was little difference between paganism and Christianity. Salutati was drawn back from this tendency by the emergence of civic humanism. In other words, civic humanism arrested the movement of humanism toward paganism and brought it closer to Christianity. No longer glorifying classical culture as an ideal, humanists were free to use their classicism in the interest of elevating their own culture without confusing the two.

As one would expect, civic humanists assumed different attitudes toward their own world. Both Petrarch and Boccaccio extolled the ideal of the aloofness of the sage and expressed contempt for marriage and civic responsibility. In his *Life of Dante* Boccaccio viewed Dante's family life and his worries about administration of the city-state as the causes of his unhappiness. This attitude persisted among a number of Quattrocento humanists. The most outstanding example among many who could be cited is Niccolò Niccoli, Bruni's spokesman in his *Dialogues*. He sought neither marriage nor public office, but lived solely for his studies, as his eulogists said after his death. Baron characterizes him as 'the type of citizen turned socially irresponsible man of letters,' and cites in this connection Niccoli's opposition to Florentine efforts to resist tyranny. A purely scholarly attitude that seeks to avoid identification with civic life – exemplified chiefly in marriage and service to the state – was a strong tendency among *literati*, which the emergence of civic humanism in Florence short-circuited.

   These new attitudes, Baron believes, were not confined to Florence. When, in the 1420s, Milanese expansion once again brought Florence into conflict with the Visconti, Florence was badly defeated on the battle-field and was saved from being overrun only by the intervention of Venice. Venetian humanists, deeply influenced by Florentine civic humanism after 1402, spoke of themselves as protectors of Italy's liberty. Their hope for permanent cooperation between the 'free peoples' of Italy became an inspiring political ideal among Venetians as well as among Florentines. Other smaller city-states were subsequently added to this alliance. Genoa broke away from Milan in 1435–36 and joined Florence and Venice. Lucca followed suit in 1438. All four were then joined in an alliance of the 'free peoples' of Italy. It was in this atmosphere that the Florentine Poggio Bracciolini (in 1435) and the Venetian Pietro del Monte (in 1440) defended the 'Respublica Romana' against Caesar [i.e. a republic against a dictator].

   The high point of this republican sentiment was reached in the late 1440s. In 1447 the last Visconti died and the Milanese proclaimed a 'Respublica Ambrosiana.' Because of its lack of republican tradition, Milan was unable to establish a firm republican regime. Instead, in the ensuing chaos, Venice was persuaded to take over some of the smaller city-states formerly under Milan. This event led Milan to turn once again to dictatorship, this time to the Sforzas. The ensuing Treaty of Lodi pitted Florence in an alliance with Milan against Venice and Naples. The absence of a republican tradition in Milan halted the progress of republicanism and hence also of civic humanism. Neoplatonism replaced humanism as the dominant thought current in Florence. But by then the civic spirit had left its place of birth and had spread throughout Italy. Baron summarizes this period as follows:

> Humanism, as molded by the Florentine crisis, produced a pattern of conduct and thought which was not to remain limited to Florentine humanists. From that time on there would exist a kind of Humanism which endeavored to educate a man as a member of his society and state; a Humanism which refused to follow the medieval precedent of looking upon the Rome of the emperors as the divinely guided preparation for a Christian 'Holy Empire' and the center of all interest in the ancient world; a Humanism which sought to learn from antiquity by looking upon it not melancholically as a golden age never again to be realized, but as an exemplary parallel to the present, encouraging the moderns to seek to rival antiquity in their vernacular languages and literatures and in many other fields. Whereas such an approach to the past and to the present had nowhere been found before 1400, it became inseparable from the growth of Humanism during the Renaissance.

These qualities of civic humanism became the chief contributions of humanism to the subsequent development of the West. Baron continues, 'Renaissance Humanism would by no means occupy the place in the growth of the modern world that is rightly attributed to it had those traits ever disappeared again after they had emerged from the early-Quattrocento crisis.' For 'although this type of socially engaged, historically-minded, and increasingly vernacular Humanism far from exhausts the rich variety of the humanistic movements of the Renaissance, in many respects it was the salt in the humanistic contribution to the rise of the modern world.'

To state this point in the strongest possible way, Baron wants to maintain that without civic humanism, which grew on Florentine soil – and could only have grown in a republican atmosphere – the western world would not now have as part of its heritage political pluralism in both thought and form, an orientation toward the future rather than toward the past, or vernacular literatures. It is in these senses, rather than in 'the discovery of the world and of man,' as Burckhardt would have it, that the Italian Renaissance represents the birth of the modern world.

There have been a number of critical responses to the idea of civic humanism in the form in which Baron states it. One kind of critique raises questions about the adequacy of his methodology. Others, focusing on his conclusions, arrive at various judgments. One critic denies the existence of civic humanism altogether. Others believe that Baron has effectively demonstrated the existence of a civic humanism but that many of the larger conclusions he wishes to draw from his demonstration are not warranted. Still others, accepting the establishment of a Florentine civic humanism, raise the question – as Florentine historians – whether alternative explanations do not clarify or augment the theory in important respects. I shall discuss each of these types of response in turn.

An Italian critic, Gennaro Sasso, in a review essay of the first edition of the *Crisis*, suggests that Baron is guilty of exalting Florence's struggle with Milan into an eternal moment of the human spirit. He cites the passage in which Baron asserts that Florence's relation to Milan in 1402 was analogous to that of Britain to Germany at Dunkirk in 1940: in both cases a historic moment came and went, and unforeseen developments upset the apparently inevitable course of fate. Baron believes that only from this perspective can we grasp adequately the psychological significance of the crisis of 1402 for the history of Florence. Unfortunately, Sasso maintains, this methodological flaw – seeing the Florentine–Milanese struggle as an eternal moment – permeates Baron's study. For instead of investigating concretely the question of the internal nature and vitality of the Florentine and Milanese governments with a view to establishing the concrete ways in which they embodied political ideals, he has made them 'ideal types.' For although Baron has clearly demonstrated that the political sentiment of liberty is embodied in the writings of the humanists, he has not demonstrated that these sentiments find expression in the real political life of Florence. Rather he has assumed that the government of Florence must have embodied the sentiments expressed by the humanists (thus taking the humanists' assessment at face value) and was therefore 'good.' Milan, as a tyrannical government, was 'bad.' The ideal types are not themselves established by concrete analysis but set up as the basis for the analysis that takes them for granted. This flaw raises the question: Why is Florence judged good in this schema? The answer is the cultural results it achieved. Cultural results that have contributed to the democratic development of the West have grown out of the Florentine Renaissance, and these results justify Florentine politics. But in making such an assumption, Baron has left the plane of political-historical analysis entirely.

Sasso has raised an important question. The methodological issue is a critical one. It is important to recall that Baron's thesis began to emerge in the 1920s, when he first used the phrase 'civic humanism,' and that he documented its presence during the 1930 while he was fleeing Hitler's Germany first for Italy and subsequently for the United States. It is not surprising that the way in which he finally formulated his thesis has an intrinsic relation to the rise of tyranny before his eyes and its opposition by the political democracies. Doubtless the attempt to demonstrate that political democracy and cultural pluralism were the hallmarks of the humanism that marks the real birth of the Renaissance and that this humanism was not, as earlier interpreters had believed, indifferent to politics or more intimately related to tyrannical than to republican politics, was an important motivation. The most problematic aspects of Baron's thesis rest on it.

It is difficult to believe that the growth of political democracy, the rise of vernacular literatures, and an attitude that looks toward future achievement rather than toward an ideal past would never have developed if they had not been bequeathed to the western world by republican Florence in the transition from the medieval to the modern worlds. It is one thing to say that humanism may have had a connection with all these things, another to say that humanism is responsible for them in the sense that without it they would not have come into being. In Baron, this thesis is asserted without being demonstrated. Nor could it very well be demonstrated, even on a superstructure much greater than the one Baron constructs. The rise of nation-states and their various political forms, the development of vernacular literatures, and the emergence of modern science with its explosive view of knowledge are much too complex to rest solely on the foundation of Renaissance Florence. But if these larger claims are problematic, what of the notion of civic humanism itself?

Jerrold Seigel denies that civic humanism ever existed.[2] [. . .] According to this older view, humanists were professional rhetoricians and their interests were determined by that fact. They were never inspired by political considerations.

Since Baron's thesis rests principally on his interpretation of Leonardo Bruni and his new dating of Bruni's *Dialogues* and his *Panegyric to the City of Florence*, Seigel focuses his attention on these aspects of Baron's thesis. He argues that Bruni's *Dialogues* were not, as Baron believes, conceived and written at different times (the second after Giangaleazzo's death) but at the same time (both prior to his death). His 'most powerful argument' in this connection is that Bruni follows very closely, in both the form and substance of his arguments, book 2 of Cicero's *De oratore* [*On the Orator*]. There Cicero was addressing himself to the relation between knowledge and the ability to speak well. Bruni shows himself – and in the same way as Cicero – concerned with this question. Cicero's book is obviously of a piece; since Bruni imitates Cicero his two dialogues must also be of a piece. And since, further, it is acknowledged that dialogue 1 was written in 1401, that is, prior to the climax of the crisis with Giangaleazzo, the same must also be true for dialogue 2. Neither dialogue, in fact, had anything to do with the birth of a new civic spirit but both had to do with rhetoric, of which Bruni was a professional practitioner.

Seigel likewise finds the dating of the *Panegyric* in 1403 rather than 1400 unconvincing. The *Panegyric* refers to Giangaleazzo's capture of a number of cities. F. P. Luiso demonstrated years ago that this passage refers to the years 1397 to 1400 and not to 1402. But what of the fact that Bologna is included in this list, when it did not fall until 1402? The reference, Seigel maintains, is not to the historical event of 1402 but to rumors that were rife in Florence in 1400 when the city was on edge, rumors to which Bruni himself later referred in his history of Florence. Even more decisive is the fact that if the *Panegyric* had been written in 1403 it would surely have mentioned the death of Giangaleazzo, which it does not do.

Baron responded one year later . . . to Seigel's critique. Regarding Bruni's use of Cicero's *De oratore*, he maintains that even if everything Seigel says about his use of it is true (though there is much about is that could be disputed), the question would still remain to what extent he made use of it and, more importantly, when. Bruni could have used *De oratore* for dialogue 1 and then returned to it years later. However, Baron concludes, neither Seigel's contention nor this rejoinder is testable by reference to the texts, and the debate should turn on what the texts themselves tell us. What do they tell us?

Regarding the *Panegyric*, the critical passage contested by Seigel in his reference to Luiso reads as follows: 'In Tuscany, he [Giangaleazzo] held Pisa, Siena, Perugia, and Assisi in his grip, and eventually he had even occupied Bologna.' This list, Baron points out, proceeds chronologically. Pisa fell in 1399, Siena later that year, Perugia at the beginning of 1400, Assisi in May. Since Bologna is placed at the end of this list the time referred to must be subsequent to the fall of Assisi. The text itself thus supports the later dating. And if one accepts the post-1402 date of the *Panegyric*, the later date of dialogue 2 is also confirmed, since the latter cites the former.

What does the life of Bruni subsequent to the writing of these treatises indicate about his allegiances? Seigel attempts to show that throughout the remainder of his life Bruni's preoccupations were rhetorical and not political; Baron, to the contrary, that Bruni's biography reveals a Florentine patriot whose principal intellectual occupation was the writing of a history of Florence that embodied a new political outlook in relation to past histories of the city.

Baron's analysis appears to have more textual support than Seigel's effort to dislodge it. But at this level the debate does not illuminate the broader issues involved.

Other intellectual historians have accepted some aspects of Baron's thesis, offering various qualifications. Kristeller, for example, whose interpretation of humanism Seigel would prefer to that of Baron, has written:

Hans Baron in a series of studies has forcefully described this civic humanism which flourished in Florence during the first half of the fifteenth century, and it certainly deserves attention as one of the most impressive phases of

Renaissance humanism, even though it would be quite mistaken to identify Renaissance humanism as a whole with this Florentine civic humanism. There was a good deal of 'despotic humanism' even in fifteenth-century Italy, and it would be quite impossible to compare under the heading of 'civic humanism' the entire political literature of the Renaissance period, let alone the large body of humanist literature that was not concerned with political problems at all.[3]

Charles Trinkaus suggests that to state the issue in terms of civic versus despotic humanism is to miss the central point, namely, that the real influence of humanism lies in a different area altogether – that referred to by Kristeller as not concerned with political problems at all. He writes:

a weakness in the concept of a 'civic humanism,' as both Hans Baron and Eugenio Garin have conceived it, is that it stresses the political and even the republican aspects of the idea too exclusively. The well-known fact that human-ists with similar moral philosophies have served at both despotic and republican centres with equal praise for the ruling power has given rise to the facetious sug-gestion that there was also a 'despotic humanism.' May I suggest that the entire question has been too narrowly conceived, and that it is in the humanists' affir-mation of an activist, constructivist, industrious view of man's nature, within a societal rather than a political nexus, that their significance may be discovered. The true significance of the Renaissance and of the humanist movement as a central part of it lies more in what Burckhardt and Michelet called 'The Dis-covery of the World and of Man' than in a poorly founded, premature vision of political democracy.[4]

Eugene Rice sums up what is accepted and what questionable in the view of many intellectual historians while relating it to his study of changes in the idea of wisdom:

The civic enthusiasm of Bruni, Palmieri, Manetti, and Alberti is only one facet of Italian humanism in the fifteenth century; and it would be misleading to suppose that ideas of wisdom which got their special flavor from this civic emphasis on active life were necessarily typical either of Italy or of the century as a whole. They appear, indeed, to have been limited both in time and place: to Florence, with the occasional exception of the Venetian Republic and to the first three-quarters of the century. Outside of Florence, the ideals of humanism and the burgher class were less closely allied, and speculation on the meaning of wisdom tended to reflect, not the novel interests of the *bourgeoisie*, but the traditional attitudes of princely or ecclesiastical governments or the more per-sonal, often pessimistic sentiments of individual humanists. The important con-sequence was a tendency to renew – or simply perpetuate – the traditional emphasis on contemplative and religious elements in the idea of wisdom, an attitude as typical of the period as the more original position of Bruni.[5]

Wallace K. Ferguson raises another issue: the priority of Petrarch as a founder of humanism, put into question by Baron's thesis. He finds compelling the older and almost universal judgment that Petrarch inaugurated a new age and sees

Dante as the transitional figure rather than Petrarch, Petrarch as the seminal figure rather than Salutati or Bruni. Baron, in a friendly debate with Ferguson, replied that he considers Petrarch neither medieval nor Renaissance but rather like Moses, who was allowed to see the promised land but not to enter it. For intellectual historians, the question of Petrarch's place remains fundamental in assessing the new consciousness of the Renaissance.

The presence of a new form of humanism in Florence raises the question: What is its source and meaning? A number of Florentine social historians have focused on this question during the generation after the first appearance of Baron's thesis and have thrown a different light on his interpretation.

Marvin Becker accepts the connection between culture and politics that Baron wishes to establish but finds the connection in economic and political developments internal to the Florentine state rather than in the impact of external events on Florence.[6] Moreover, the critical events that congealed a 'civic humanism' he attributes to the years after 1343, when a good many indexes point to profound changes within Florence itself. The key to all change was the increased need for money to finance wars of expansion in which Florence was engaged throughout Tuscany. Until the 1320s the public treasury was more or less in balance. Communal debts could still be met by noble families who regarded the city more or less as their fief. But from that time forward the debt progressively increased until, by the 1340s, it had reached sizable proportions. The establishment of the *Monte*, or floating communal debt, in 1345 symbolized a turning point. 'The *Monte* came to be so imbedded in civic life that it was to assume the role of determinant in the formulation of public policy.' Although contemporaries believed that the conditions creating it would pass away, the debt never thereafter decreased but instead grew rapidly with each passing decade. As a result, government spending and borrowing played an increasingly decisive role in Florentine politics. Guilds, the *Parte Guelfa* [the bourgeoisie supporting the pope against the Holy Roman Emperor], wealthy families, and other corporate bodies within the commune to which people had previously given as great or greater allegiance as to the commune itself, were now replaced by the commune as the object of allegiance, for every Florentine family with any wealth invested its money in the communal debt. When the debt was established in 1345 less than one hundred families had large-scale *Monte* holdings; by 1427 the number had increased twenty-fold, and in most instances the amounts involved were thirty and forty times greater than earlier. The management of such great sums of money required a large, professional bureaucracy. The Florentine bureaucracy increased fivefold between 1343 and 1393; and crucial positions within it having to do with the management of money came to be filled by appointment (that is, by professionals) rather than by lot or popular election.

The wars against the Visconti near the end of the Trecento further intensified the tendencies that had emerged in the 1340s. In 1390 Florence resorted to forced loans (*prestanze*) which might be exacted several times a year, thus increasing the public debt even further. In 1427 the *catasto* or direct tax on the value of individual goods was introduced. It is hardly surprising that Leonardo Bruni, chancellor of Florence at this time (1427–44), asserted that wealth is to the city as blood is to the individual.

So also with other expressions of Florentine civic humanism: when Bruni extolled equality before the law, he was praising a much tighter state control over the lives of every citizen. The *vita civile* was an expression of the stake each citizen had in the survival of the Florentine state. Civic humanism, there-fore, did not arise out of the wars with the Visconti, but out of the economic conditions brought on by Florentine expansion much earlier in the Trecento, which in turn caused a tightening of state control over and intervention in the life of each citizen. The ideas of the civic humanists followed and reinforced an economic reality.

Becker's analysis raises the question of whether external political factors can be given the weight that Baron gives them in his interpretation of civic humanism.

Lauro Martines has examined the problem from yet another perspective.[7] He studied the family backgrounds and the political and literary activities of eleven Florentine humanists: Salutati, Niccoli, Bruni, Poggio, Manetti, Marsuppini, Palmieri, Rinuccini, Alberti, and Pieruzzi. He found that all these men were born to wealth or acquired it, that is, that they belonged to the ruling class. This ruling class had increased its power in Florence after the revolt of the woollen workers – the so-called Ciompi Revolution – in 1382. Again in 1387 and in 1393 they took more and more power away from the minor guilds until the lower middle class was left with only one-fourth of the seats in the legislative councils.

In view of the relation of the humanists to the ruling class, it was natural that they should have established an alliance between service to the state and humanistic studies. It is true, as Baron says, that during most of the Trecento the humanists lacked a definite connection with the public sphere. This con-nection was established by a group of *literati* who found themselves in the 1380s and especially in the 1390s belonging to the ruling oligarchy. This fact is not to deny that something decisive happened that affected the outlook of at least one group of these humanists in the crisis of 1400 to 1402, but it is to say that the social and political environment had already formed them to some extent, even if the crisis re-formed their intellectual vision. Moreover, Baron leaves very much in the background the oligarchic nature of the Florentine repub-lican spirit and does not emphasize nearly as much as a modern historian should that when these men wrote extolling Florence's republican virtues, they were writing ideologically, that is, out of their own class interest. These virtues were what supported them in power. It is only natural that they should have been drawn to them.

The Florentine oligarchical republic ended in 1434 when the city came under the rule of one family, the Medicis. Martines asks what brought about this transformation in the conduct of the political class. He suggests two reasons, one political and the other economic.

Politically, one family had been prevented from gaining too much power through the fostering of equality among the ruling families. But after 1434 sus-picion within this group grew so great that this equality was upset and the balance gravitated to one family, the Medicis. By the time Piero di Cosimo died in 1469 the Medicis could dispense with any one family or group of families if they chose, while they themselves became indispensable. The expulsion of Piero di Lorenzo in 1494 (after which Florence returned for a time to republican government) shows that these families could have done as much even in the 1460s. But their mutual suspicion prevented them from acting.

Economically, Florence had begun to decline by the 1450s. Many skilled workers were fleeing the city. The reason was that the wealthy class did not invest in business but instead turned Florence itself into a kind of business, loaning the city money (especially for war) and seeing this money returned with high interest. The Medicis, instead of developing policies to stimulate trade, 'raised taxes on goods and increased interest rates on war loans so as to benefit the ruling clique.' These practices meant that the lower orders of citizens were continually drained, while the higher ranks rapidly accumulated money. The money accumulated by the wealthy, not being spent on business, was spent on lavish display: new family palaces, furnishings, works of art, clothing, jewelry, and dowries. Until around 1400 Florence had received an influx of new business families (who, until that time, often made their way into the political arena as well); but the failures after 1450 were not balanced by the rise of new businesses or by the penetration of businessmen into the ruling classes, where their presence might have acted as a force for more enlightened economic policy. The direction of economic change was toward agriculture. Martines concludes:

> An end to the large-scale rise of new men, commercial and industrial hard times, the concomitant pursuit of safer investment outlets, the pressure to spend lavishly as a mark of social rank – these trends made for a ruling class that had lost or was losing its political nerve. The upper classes became more exclusive and class conscious, and the oligarchy turned ever more sectarian, restricted and servile.

This world provided the context for the decay of civic humanism. As politics became the privilege of an ever-diminishing number of families, less and less was left to action in real life. Thought became otherworldly; contemplation became once again an ideal, and much that had previously been ascribed to the actions of men now once again came under the goddess Fortuna. This otherworldliness can be seen in the paintings of Botticelli and Filippino Lippi, in the contrast between the early and late writings of Alberti, and in the *Disputationes camaldulenses* [Debates at the Benedictine Congregation of Camaldoli] of Cristoforo Landino (1475). The contemplative ideal of Neoplatonism is a hallmark here, as it is in Giovanni Pico della Mirandola's *Oration* (1486). It is no accident, therefore, that civic humanism was replaced in Florence by the Platonic Academy of Marsilio Ficino. This intellectual transformation had its counterpart in the political arena and in the economic activities of the oligarchs that aggravated the political situation.

In 1494 the Medicis were overthrown and Florence returned once again for a few years to republican government, showing that that spirit had not died in the city. The question arises: Why did civic ardor in Florentine humanism fade between 1434 and 1494 if the republican spirit was still alive? The conclusion must be that more is required for civic humanism than desire; the reality itself is needed, that is, a political situation in which men can see a close relation between the civic life that actually exists and the sort of life they want, between what is and what they hope to attain. As Martines argues:

> The result was that men like Salutati and Bruni, Poggio and Manetti were as much at home with philological and literary questions as with political and historical ones. But in the second half of the century, when interest in political and historical reflection could no longer draw on the resources of a vigorous civic life, a convenient change ensued: subject matter of this sort was gradually purged from the program of humanism, and the *studia humanitatis* became more thoroughly literary, or much more purely concerned with idealistic and abstract questions.

With the expulsion of the Medici, things that had been forbidden were suddenly possible again, and the republican spirit surged back. For a generation new intellectual energies were released in the social and political spheres. This generation produced Machiavelli, Guicciardini, and Giannotti. Moreover, 'if something noteworthy was to be accomplished, it must be the work of specialists, of men who would bend all their energies and passion to the political and social problems of the hour and whose study of history, ancient and modern, would bear the stamp of that ardor.' Such ardor existed in these historians and political writers of the first decades of the sixteenth century. They were, Martines concludes, as different from Salutati and Bruni as were Weber [social scientist, 1864–1920] and Mannheim [sociologist, 1893–1947] from Burckhardt.

Gene Brucker, in a recent study of the history of Florence between 1378 and 1430,[8] maintains that the civic thesis of Baron, the statist thesis of Becker, and the class thesis of Martines do not fit well together or explain other facets of Florentine life. He believes, however, that a close study of Florentine government during these years, and especially of the *Consulte e pratiche* [record of political deliberations] provides a frame of reference that unites many otherwise loose strands.

In an earlier study Brucker had argued (contrary to Becker) that between 1343 and 1378 Florence was still controlled by its corporate bodies, until the Ciompi Revolution [a rising by the lowest class of day labourers in Florence in 1348] revealed their weakness. In his sequel he recognizes the fact that constitutionally Florence did not change after 1382, but nonetheless profound changes took place both in the nature of the leadership and in the leadership's conception of politics.

The first change was the emergence during the 1380s of a group of upper-class merchant families into a position of political power. These families constituted 'the most cohesive force in Florentine society through the Renaissance and beyond.' Through their rise to power Florence was transformed from a 'corporate' to an 'elitist' state. But the elite served as a new corporation, so to speak. The families that gained power came to a consensus among themselves regarding most issues of domestic and foreign policy. They could not control the political deliberations of the larger state assemblies, but as long as their inner cohesion remained unbroken there was continuity and stability in Florentine politics. Brucker thus disagrees with Becker's thesis that the elitist state appeared in the 1340s, arguing that even as Florence was developing its new polity in the 1380s, corporate loyalties of all kinds continued to express themselves, including above all the loyalty of the ruling families to one another.

The new regime reached the height of its power in the defeat of Giangaleazzo Visconti in 1402 and the conquest of Pisa in 1406. There is no indication, however, that the struggle with Giangaleazzo had the importance that Baron attributes to it. There was no panic, even after Bologna fell in June. Merchants continued to complain about heavy taxes and the stagnation of trade, but no more than usual. Florence did not attempt to attract new allies by some bold new policy. Diplomats were in Rome and Venice discussing terms of an alliance, and these overtures were supported by citizens who spoke in the *pratiche*, but with no sense of urgency or overwhelming need for an alliance. No agreement had been concluded when a report reached Florence on 12 September of Giangaleazzo's death. 'The reaction to this news was muted, with no discernible sign of jubilation. . . . Neither the struggle nor the sacrifices ended with Giangaleazzo's death.' Public records for the year 1402 'reveal uncertainty and vacillation, doubt and disagreement, and abrupt shifts in attitude and policy that do not relate logically to events or circumstances.' If the Florentines 'sensed that they were living through an historic 'moment of decision,' their demeanor did not indicate this awareness.'

Before the end of the decade, however, there is strong evidence in the public debates of a significant change in Florentine outlook, as seen in the style and content of the debates themselves.

In seeking to persuade each other as well as the rank and file, the leaders systematically employed the skills of the logician and the rhetorician. Speeches became longer and more analytical; they were studded with allusions to historical precedents and references to classical authors. These innovations were not simply rhetorical gambits, but signs of a basic shift in historical outlook. Florentines were being taught, in these debates, to view their past as a unique experience, filled with challenges and ordeals, but also with triumphs. If they did not yet link their origins directly with republican Rome, as the humanists were beginning to do, they did see the relevance of Roman history to their own problems. Though they still referred to divine grace as essential for Florence's prosperity, they placed increasing emphasis upon themselves as the makers of their destiny. They were proud of their demonstrated ability to maintain their freedom and their republican regime, and they looked with scorn and pity upon their neighbors, the Pisans and Pistoiese, who had contributed to their own downfall by failing to achieve civic unity.

Brucker rejects the explanation that cultural lag accounts for the introduction into public debate of humanist ideas that had appeared some years earlier, for he finds 'that internal developments were as important as threats from abroad in changing Florentine perceptions and points of view.' Moreover, even in foreign affairs, one cannot look exclusively at the struggle against Giangaleazzo but must consider, as the Florentines themselves did, the whole spectrum of their struggles with the church and with King Ladislas [a belligerent and expansionist king of Naples, d. 1414] as well. Nonetheless, the evidence of these debates 'does lend support to Baron's major thesis about the emergence in Florence of a new view of history and politics in the first decade of the Quattrocento.' The public debates were an ideal forum for introducing humanist attitudes. He suggests that 'Bruni may have received some stimuli for the development of his ideology by listening to the debates in the palace.' However that may be, 'ideas that had been nurtured in private by Salutati and his circle were being spread, through the medium of the *pratiche*, to a large group of citizens, whose minds must have been influenced by their exposure to humanist propaganda.'

Was this humanist propaganda simply the ideological standpoint of a ruling class, as Martines maintains? Brucker does not believe so. For he finds in the public debates, perhaps as another dimension of the new humanist ideas, greater concern for the general public good and a growing sophistication about the nature and functions of government. There is an ever stronger effort to consult, to persuade one's opponents. to exercise patience and seek moderate solutions. The records reveal an increasing capacity for analytical thinking and preoccupation with budgetary projections to determine whether and to what extent Florence could carry on its foreign wars. At the same time the government revised its policy in relation to the *contado* or rural districts around the city: whereas these had been exploited in the preceding century, efforts were now made to treat them more equitably. The same policy was instituted in Florence itself with the introduction of the *catasto* or direct tax in 1427.

Nonetheless, despite its growing professionalism and increasing tendency to think of the good of the state as a whole, the regime gave way to Medici rule in 1434. Its failure was due to the costly wars with Ladislas and Genoa between 1409 and 1414 – the crises that had caused the larger-minded responses just mentioned – and, even more, the confrontation with Milan between 1423 and 1430. These conflicts led to an increase in the tax burden beyond what could be borne and to a scramble for public office as a means of offsetting losses incurred through taxation. These tensions produced rifts within a ruling elite that had until then managed to present a united front.

Even though the regime collapsed and was replaced by Medici rule, there were no constitutional changes. Moreover, rule by an elite group of families continued to be the norm, even though the families themselves changed and Cosimo himself exercised more direction on policy than anyone had done previously. The professionalism and sophistication of the bureaucracy also were not lost but continued in a direction that led to Machiavelli and Guicciardini. Thus it can be said that in some respect the civic humanist contribution to Florentine polity ran through the Quattrocento and into the Cinquecento.

The most recent contribution to this debate, Quentin Skinner's history of political thought in the Renaissance, has placed Florentine civic humanism –

whatever its impetus – within the larger framework, both spatial and temporal, of writings about polity.[9]

Skinner's analysis goes back to the century between 1200 and 1300, when many Italian communes developed republican institutions as the *popolani* [artisans] in commune after commune rose against the nobility and set up rival administrations in the cities. A great deal of civil violence resulted, leading, after 1300, in the emergence of *signori*, strong political leaders who could enforce order. In order to protect against abuses of power, there began to appear many different kinds of defenses of republican liberty. There were two sources of these defenses: one was the rhetorical tradition of the *ars dictaminis*, whose practitioners were the direct forebears of the humanists; the other the tradition of scholastic philosophy.

In the manuals of letter writing (*ars dictaminis*) composed by a number of prehumanists after 1200, model speeches on political matters are included, which, in turn, led a number of *dictatores* [practitioners of the art of letter writing] to write about politics in the form of civic chronicles, advice books to guide city magistrates, even a play, Albertino Mussato's *Ecerinis* (1314), lamenting tyranny. Whatever the form, the writers all ask why *signori* are advancing in so many cities, and they all agree that the free cities are weakened by internal factions. They also attribute loss of civic liberty to the increase of private wealth (which some believe causes political factiousness). Baron contends that this bias is due to Franciscan influence on thirteenth-century writers. But the prehumanists were expressing Stoic rather than Franciscan beliefs, to wit, that those who covet wealth destroy the virtues.

How do these writers believe that republican values can be preserved? Through the abolition of personal and sectional interests and the equation of private good with the good of the city as a whole. But how is unity between individual and civil interests to be achieved? They give an answer that was to be developed by the humanists of the Quattrocento: if men are corrupt the best institutions will not work, and if they are virtuous the health of institutions is of secondary importance (a position later defended by Machiavelli and Montesquieu). They therefore ask how to promote men of virtue to serve as leaders, and respond that the traditional nobility must be bypassed and men from all classes be made eligible.

Scholastic writers base their ideas on Aristotle's *Ethics* and *Politics*, which were translated fully into Latin between 1240 and 1250. The scholastic theorists no less than the rhetorical writers were committed to an ideal of political independence and republican self-government. In so doing they hark back to Rome's republican period rather than to the empire as the age of Rome's greatest excellence, and they adopt a new attitude toward Cato and Cicero, leading figures in the republic. Formerly they were viewed as Stoic sages aloof from political life; now they are praised as great patriots and paragons of civic virtue. Baron is thus wrong, Skinner maintains, in arguing that this attitude appeared only in the early Quattrocento. Rather, 'the main elements in this humanist historical consciousness were in fact formed with the arrival of scholastic political theory in Italy nearly a century before.' But scholastic writers are aware of the fragility of republican institutions and ask why they are so vulnerable. They do not believe, as the prehumanists do, that private wealth corrupts politics, but they do agree on the evil of factiousness. The relation between faction and tyranny they take from Aristotle, and the conclusion they draw is that civil discord is the principal danger to the liberty of city republics.

How can faction be avoided and peace secured? With the rhetorical theorists they agree that sectional interests must be set aside and the good of each individual equated with the good of the city as a whole. But how is this unity to be achieved? Here the scholastic writers diverge sharply from the prehumanists, emphasizing not a 'true nobility,' in other words virtuous individuals, but efficient institutions. To avoid factions or rival parties the ruler should be the whole body of the people, so that no such internecine fighting can in principle arise. In defending this view the scholastics (particularly Marsilio of Padua in his *Defender of Peace*) argue that in delegating their authority to a ruler the people do not alienate it but remain the sovereign legislators at all times. Ultimate authority always remains in the hands of the people, though a ruler may exercise it for a particular time. But how is sovereignty that is delegated retained by the people? Through the imposition of three restraints: election, forcing rulers to govern according to law rather than their own discretion, and a system of checks.

By reviewing both the prehumanist and the scholastic traditions of political thought Skinner has shown that what Baron believed to be new in the early Quattrocento was in fact inherited from the city republics of medieval Italy. This view also does greater justice to the continuity between Petrarch and his successors than Baron is able to do.

Skinner then turns his attention to the relation between the humanists of the Quattrocento and this earlier thought of the *dictatores* and scholastics. Because Florence was politically stable (internally) by the beginning of the Quattrocento, the humanists no longer saw faction as the great problem but rather the use of mercenary troops. Their solution was the revival of an armed and independent citizenry (as in Aristotle's *Politics*, 3). Like the *dictatores* the humanists prefer republican Rome to the empire, but Bruni adds an original element: the connection between freedom and the greatness of commonwealths. Florence is great, he says, because its citizens are all engaged in the cultivation of the virtues. But this idea is fully in accord with the earlier notions of the *dictatores* that the health of a republic depends on developing the spirit of its citizens (not on perfecting the machinery of government) and that a citizen's worth is measured by his talent rather than by his lineage or wealth. Moreover, the latter idea requires a positive view of human nature or dignity and a rejection of Augustine's repudiation of the cardinal virtues. By reconstructing the classical image of human nature that Augustine had tried to obliterate, they argue that although the human capacity for action is limited, the controlling factor is not providence but the caprices of fortune. This led some (such as Poggio) to be pessimistic but others (notably Alberti in his preface to *On the Family*) to be strongly assertive of the power of human will.

At the same time, however, Quattrocento civic humanism was discontinuous with the Middle Ages. Humanists attacked scholastic method, especially its interpretation of Roman law. Moreover, they exalted activity (*negotium*) above leisure (*otium*). Baron has rightly stressed that this argument was first wholeheartedly embraced by the Florentine humanists of the early Quattrocento (Dante still thought of wisdom as purely intellectual rather than as a moral virtue). Finally, as a result of their attack on scholasticism, the humanists developed a new view of history, inventing the notion of the Middle Ages and regarding it as having come to an end in their own time through their own innovations.

If Skinner has shown the richness of political thought relevant to Baron's thesis prior to the crisis of 1400–1402, J. G. A. Pocock, looking at the problem from the end point of Florentine republicanism (1494–1512 and 1527–30), especially with a view to illuminating the originality and genius of Machiavelli, proposes to reveal the consequences of that republicanism in the larger western (English and American) political tradition in the seventeenth and eighteenth centuries. He thus supports – though in his own way – Baron's most controversial contention, that Florentine republicanism was essential to the development of western democratic polity.[10]

What is of interest here is not the later permutations of the Machiavellian moment but only what was involved in its emergence. In order to grasp the innovations of the civic humanists it is necessary to understand the patterns of thought they inherited from the past, which provided the matrix of their ideas. One of the most compelling features of Pocock's complex treatment is the way in which he builds the context, so that the reader can see the sets of ideas with which the Florentine civic humanists were working and how their minds grappled with – in some cases transforming – these sets of ideas in relation to the political reality of the Florentine republic during its last years. There were four: first, the Augustinian Christian frame of reference; second, the Roman civic humanist modification of it by Boethius; third, the medieval view of the relation between the universal and the particular; and fourth, the Aristotelian political tradition, including Roman history as well.

Augustine rejected the idea that any fulfillment of human life was possible in political terms (the earthly city) and enjoined Christians to set their sights on the heavenly city, the city of God, in which alone justice (the preeminent political virtue) could be realized. History itself has no meaning; its meaning is given to it by the purposes of God, which lie outside history itself.

Yet Christians continued to be concerned with political history, and this concern expressed itself through the Greek notion of *arete* (civic excellence) and the Latin notion of *virtus* (virtue). Boethius, in his influential *Consolation of Philosophy*, written while he was in prison and as a reflection on his own downfall, inquires of God how He, who is perfect virtue, could allow virtue to become subject to fortune (as in his own case). Augustine would simply have responded that anyone who participates in the fallen city must expect injustice. But Boethius wants to understand how the heavenly city permits the earthly city to stand. Philosophy leads him to the view of the eternal now (*nunc-stans*), the view that to

God all things are visible as a unity, so that the problem of historical succession does not exist. All Boethius can know is that the *nunc-stans* exists; he cannot share its vision. Redemption comes only through the grace of God, and although philosophy, faith, and virtuous practice might solicit it, they can never command it. History thus has only a private meaning. Its public meaning was restored through the papal church, which institutionalized the *nunc-stans*. The only means of giving significance to time in this context was apocalyptic prophecy, through which it was claimed that redemption was to be found in the fulfillment of prophecy rather than in a timeless institution. Not surprisingly, most medieval heretics were apocalyptic.

To the medieval mind the true is the universal, which is not timebound; the particular cannot be true precisely because it is circumstantial, accidental, and time-bound. The problem this concept raises for political thought is illustrated in Sir John Fortescue's *In Praise of the Laws of England* (1468–71), in which he sets out to discover the universal principles on which English law is based, only to run up against his own presupposition that since 'England' is a particular, there can be no body of universals concerning it. Thus English laws cannot be shown to be universal by any rational criterion, but only by virtue of their longevity, that is, by custom. This notion makes legislation difficult, for it takes a long time to establish a consensus. We find ourselves, in fact, in the paradoxical situation that when usage is well established a ruler does not really need to govern, he only needs to apply the law as built up through consensus (*jurisdictio*); but when an unprecedented event occurs, he actually does govern, inasmuch as there is no collective wisdom to tell him what to do; but in this case he does not govern by law but in the absence of it (*gubernaculum*).

These patterns of political thought were the ones inherited by Renaissance humanists, and the problem they all present has to do with time; it is to find universal significance in the particular. It was this problem that led the humanists away from reading Aristotle's *Politics* in relation to the theme of natural law (through which people perceive the values inherent in nature and pursue them in society). Their orientation was rather the relation of the citizen to the city-state. Different groups of citizens in the Italian republics pursued many different ends. The problem was how to distribute power in such a way that the pursuit of individual ends (the particular) could also be related to the good of the republic as a whole (the universal). Aristotle's delineation of governments into monarchies (the one), aristocracies (the few), and democracies (the many) was crucial for their resolution of this problem. The one, the few, and the many were each to be entrusted with particular functions of government; thus each would rule and be ruled and no one group would predominate. Based on this analysis, it became usual to visualize society as a blend of the one, the few, and the many.

Polybius, who was translated from Greek into Latin between 1510 and 1520, set himself the task in book 6 of his *Histories* to explain Rome's military success. He did so by relating that success to its internal stability, achieved through balancing the one, the few, and the many. All cities, he asserted, must pass through Aristotle's sixfold classification (monarchy/tyranny, aristocracy/oligarchy, polity/democracy) if they were to escape instability. To his later readers (but not to Polybius) it seemed that if such a balance could be effected, then a regime that could last forever might be created. Guicciardini held out such a hope; Machiavelli radically departed from it.

The myth of Venice came to be identified with the account of Polybius: Venice was a stable regime because it was a perfect blend of the one, the few, and the many – a myth as much of Florentine as of Venetian making. Though at variance with the idea that Venice was an aristocracy of well-balanced elements (a view the Venetians apparently had of themselves), it came to predominate in Florence after the overthrow of the aristocratic Medici regime and the institutionalization, under Savonarola, of a constitution that included a consiglio grande [great or grand council], a signoria [governing council] and a gonfaloniere [standard bearer] – which contemporaries identified with the many, the few, and the one of classical theory.

Machiavelli transforms all these inherited paradigms: he gives priority to time over eternity, to change over stasis, and to Rome (a republic based on change) over Venice. He accepts Boethius's notion of virtue and his contrast between virtue and fortune, and builds his new political paradigm upon it.

In *The Prince* Machiavelli is concerned with innovators and the ways in which (through their virtue) they have imposed their will upon their *fortuna*. In the spectrum between *institutio* [stable society, ruled by law] and *gubernaculum*, he is interested in the extreme form of *gubernaculum*, the moment that the ruler must rule without norms from the past to guide him, without legitimacy, as an innovator.

What Machiavelli does for the ruler in *The Prince* he does for the republic in *The Discourses*. There are two daring and arresting hypotheses at the foundation of the latter (both of which Guicciardini was to reject). The first is 'that the disunion and strife among nobles and people was the cause of Rome's attaining liberty, stability, and power – a statement shocking and incredible to minds which identified union with stability and virtue, conflict with innovation and decay.' The second is that the ideal of stability is not the only value to be pursued. Stability was pursued by Sparta and Venice, both of which lasted longer than Rome, but its pursuit assumes that the sole purpose of the state is to maintain itself. Rome, by contrast, created an empire, a choice that involved a preference for a more popular, as opposed to aristocratic, form of government. Thus Rome is 'the 'new prince' among republics, and Machiavelli would rather study Rome than Venice as he would rather study the new prince than the hereditary ruler: the short view is more interesting than the long, and life in it more glorious.' 'The Roman path does not guarantee against ultimate degeneration, but in the present and foreseeable future – in the world of accidental time, in short – it is both wiser and more glorious.'

This conclusion leads Machiavelli, in *The Art of War*, to link warrior and citizen in an inextricable bond. The citizen dedicates his life, the warrior his death to the state; both thus perfect human nature by sacrificing the particular to the universal. The enemy of the republic is corruption, for it creates inequality among citizens. Indeed, 'the concept of corruption is tending to replace that of the mere randomness of *fortuna.*' In the citizen as warrior, will replaces intelligence, action replaces prudence. Although Machiavelli's contributions to republican theory were extraordinarily original, they were based on and limited to his decision that 'military dynamism was to be preferred before the search for stability.'

In all his arguments Machiavelli carried out a drastic secularization of political consciousness: he established that civic virtue and the *vivere civile* [living in accordance with civic virtue] may develop in the dimension of contingency. Citizens move toward the goal of stability through their own time-bound wills. But if they do not need the superhuman in order to become citizens, instead achieving citizenship in the world of time and fortune, the earthly and heavenly cities have once again split apart, and civic ends are divorced from the ends of redemption. This suggestion is Machiavelli's most subversive one.

In grappling with politics in terms of the vicissitudes (particularities) of time – and in putting to rest the orientation of human life toward the eternal, the universal, and the wholly rational – the civic humanists introduced a historical consciousness that has ever since characterized western thinking. They were the first historicists in the western tradition (and perhaps in this sense the first 'modern men'). When they began to write, words like stability, immobility, monarchy, authority, eternity, hierarchy, and universality dominated political writing; in their own works and subsequently (as a result, in important respects, of their influence) these had been replaced by republicanism, secularism, progress, patriotism, equality, liberty, and utopia. Only the terms reason, virtue, and experience survived from the earlier tradition of political thought. Insofar as this is the case, civic humanism must be regarded as one of the most enduring contributions of Italian humanists generally to modern western culture.

Baron's hypothesis has proved to be a rich one indeed; it has led to a battery of new inquiries regarding the origin, nature, development, and influence of Italian humanism. All aspects of the thesis have been attacked, defended, and expanded in various ways. Although nothing like a synthesis can be said to have emerged, the result is certainly a more richly detailed picture of humanism than we have earlier possessed. As in the case of most other historical paradigms of equal power, this one is not likely to lead to a unanimous conclusion. But it has profoundly altered and enriched the study of humanism, and whatever the outcomes of continuing study prove to be, the terrain will forever look quite different as a result of the identification of civic humanism.

NOTES

1   For a complete bibliography of the writings of Hans Baron, see *Renaissance Studies in Honor of Hans Baron*, ed. A. Molho and J. A. Tedeschi (Dekalb, IL, 1971), lxxi–lxxxvii. See also the two appreciations of his work, which open that volume, by Denys Hay (xi–xxix) and August Buck (xxxi–lviii).

2   J. E. Seigel, '"Civic Humanism" or Ciceronian Rhetoric?' *Past and Present* 34 (1966): 3–48.

3   P. O. Kristeller, *Renaissance Thought II: Papers on Humanism and the Arts* (New York, 1965) pp. 46–47.

4   C. Trinkaus, *In Our Image and Likeness: Humanity and Divinity in Italian Humanist Thought*, 2 vols. (Chicago, 1970), 1:283. Trinkaus had made these same points earlier, in a review of the first edition of *Crisis* in *Journal of the History of Ideas* 17 (1956): 426–32.

5   E. F. Rice, Jr., *The Renaissance Idea of Wisdom* (Cambridge, MA, 1958), 49.

6   See his *Florence in Transition*, 2 vols. (Baltimore, 1967–68), esp. vol. 2, *Studies in the Rise of the Territorial State*. His thesis is succinctly stated in 'The Florentine Territorial State and Civic Humanism in the Early Renaissance,' in *Florentine Studies*, ed. N. Rubinstein (Evanston, IL, 1968), 109–39.

7   L. Martines, *The Social World of the Florentine Humanists, 1390–1460* (Princeton, 1963).

8   G. Brucker, *The Civic World of Early Renaissance Florence* (Princeton, 1977).

9   Q. Skinner, *The Foundations of Modern Political Thought*, vol. 1, *The Renaissance* (Cambridge, 1978). Chapters 1–4 are most relevant to the present discussion.

10 J. G. A. Pocock, *The Machiavellian Moment: Florentine Political Thought and the Atlantic Republican Tradition* (Princeton, 1975); idem, '*The Machiavellian Moment* Revisited: A Study in History and Ideology,' *Journal of Modern History* 53 (1981): 49–72, which focuses on the debate surrounding the transition between the Florentine republican tradition and the Atlantic tradition of the seventeenth and eighteenth centuries (not addressed in my discussion). See also the excellent review essay of the book by J. H. Hexter in *History and Theory* 16 (1977): 306–37, esp. 318–23, for a description of the central Machiavellian moment.

4   Elizabeth L. Eisenstein **The emergence of print culture in the West: 'Defining the Initial Shift'**

Source: from *The Printing Revolution in Early Modern Europe*, Elizabeth L. Eisenstein, Cambridge University Press, Cambridge, 1993, chapter 2, pp. 12–41.

We should note the force, effect, and consequences of inventions which are nowhere more conspicuous than in those three which were unknown to the ancients, namely, printing, gunpowder, and the compass. For these three have changed the appearance and state of the whole world.

Francis Bacon, *Novum organum*, Aphorism 129

To dwell on the reasons why Bacon's advice ought to be followed by others is probably less helpful than trying to follow it oneself. This task clearly outstrips the competence of any single individual. It calls for the pooling of many talents and the writing of many books. Collaboration is difficult to obtain as long as the relevance of the topic to different fields of study remains obscure. Before aid can be enlisted, it seems necessary to develop some tentative hypotheses relating the shift from script to print to significant historical developments.

This task, in turn, seems to call for a somewhat unconventional point of departure and for a reformulation of Bacon's advice. Instead of trying to deal with 'the force, effect, and consequences' of a single postclassical invention that is coupled with others, I will be concerned with a major transformation that constituted a large cluster of changes in itself. Indecision about what is meant by the advent of printing has, I think, helped to muffle concern about its possible consequences and made them more difficult to track down. It is difficult to find what happened in a particular Mainz workshop in the 1450s. When pursuing other inquiries, it seems almost prudent to bypass so problematic an event. This does not apply to the appearance of new occupational groups who employed new techniques and installed new equipment in new kinds of workshops while extending trade networks and seeking new markets to increase profits made from sales. Unknown anywhere in Europe before the mid-fifteenth century, printers' workshops would be found in every important municipal center by 1500. They added a new element to urban culture in hundreds of towns. To pass by all that, when dealing with other problems, would seem to be incautious. For this reason, among others, we will skip over the perfection of a new process for printing with movable types and will not pause over the massive literature devoted to explanations of Gutenberg's invention. We will take the term 'printing' to serve simply as a convenient label, as a shorthand way of referring to a cluster of innovations (entailing the use of movable metal type, oil-based ink, wooden handpress, and so forth). Our point of departure will not be one printing shop in Mainz. Instead, we will begin where many studies end: after the first dated printed products had been issued and the inventor's immediate successors had set to work.

The advent of printing, then, is taken to mean the establishment of presses in urban centers beyond the Rhineland during an interval that begins in the 1460s and coincides, very roughly, with the era of incunabula [the earliest printed books]. So few studies have been devoted to this point of departure that no conventional label has yet been attached to it. One might talk about a basic change in a mode of book production or about a communications or media revolution or perhaps, most simply and explicitly, about a shift from script to print. Whatever label is used, it should be understood to cover a large cluster of relatively simultaneous, interrelated changes, each of which needs closer study and more explicit treatment – as the following quick sketch may suggest.

First of all, the marked increase in the output of books and the drastic reduction in the number of man-hours required to turn them out deserve stronger emphasis. At present there is a tendency to think of a steady increase in book production during the first century of printing. An evolutionary model of change is applied to a situation that seems to call for a revolutionary one.

A man born in 1453, the year of the fall of Constantinople, could look back from his fiftieth year on a lifetime in which about eight million books had been printed, more perhaps than all the scribes of Europe had produced since Constantine founded his city in A.D. 330.

The actual production of 'all the scribes of Europe' is inevitably open to dispute. Even apart from the problem of trying to estimate numbers of books that went uncatalogued and then were destroyed, contemporary evidence must be handled with caution, for it often yields false clues to the numbers of books involved. Since it was customary to register many texts bound within one set of covers as but one book, the actual number of texts in a given manuscript collection is not easily ascertained. That objects counted as one book often contained a varying combination of many provides yet another example of the difficulty of quantifying data provided in the age of scribes. The situation is similar when we turn to the problem of counting the man-hours required to copy manuscript books. Old estimates based on the number of months it took forty-five scribes working for the Florentine manuscript book dealer, Vespasiano da Bisticci, to produce two hundred books for Cosimo de Medici's Badia library have been rendered virtually worthless by recent research.

Thus the total number of books produced by 'all the scribes of Europe' since 330 or even since 1400, is likely to remain elusive. Nevertheless, some comparisons are possible and they place the output of printers in sharp contrast to preceding trends. 'In 1483, the Ripoli Press charged three florins per quinterno [five sheets of paper] for setting up and printing Ficino's translation of Plato's *Dialogues*. A scribe might have charged one florin per quinterno for duplicating the same work. The Ripoli Press produced 1,025 copies; the scribe would have turned out one.' Given this kind of comparison, it seems misguided to suggest that 'the multiplication of identical copies' was merely 'intensified' by the press. Doubtless, hand copying could be quite efficient for the purpose of duplicating a royal edict or papal bull. Sufficient numbers of copies of a newly edited Bible were produced in the thirteenth century for some scholars to feel justified in referring to a Paris 'edition' of a manuscript Bible. To turn out one single whole 'edition' of any text was no mean feat in the thirteenth century, however. The one thirteenth-century scribal 'edition' might be compared with the large number of Bible editions turned out in the half-century between Gutenberg and Luther. When scribal labor was employed for multiplying edicts or producing a whole 'edition' of scripture, moreover, it was diverted from other tasks.

Many valued texts were barely preserved from extinction; untold numbers failed to survive. Survival often hinged on the occasional copy being made by an interested scholar who acted as his own scribe. In view of the proliferation of 'unique' texts and of the accumulation of variants, it is doubtful whether one should refer to 'identical copies' being 'multiplied' before print. This point is especially important when considering technical literature. The difficulty of making even one 'identical' copy of a significant technical work was such that the task could not be trusted to any hired hands. Men of learning had to engage in 'slavish copying' of tables, diagrams, and unfamiliar terms. The output of whole editions of sets of astronomical tables did not merely 'intensify' previous trends. It reversed them, producing a new situation which released time for observation and research.

The previous introduction of paper into thirteenth-century Europe, it should be noted, did not have anything like a 'similar' effect. Paper production served the needs of merchants, bureaucrats, preachers, and literati; it quickened the pace of correspondence and enabled more men of letters to act as their own scribes. But the same number of man-hours was still required to turn out a given text. Shops run by stationers or *cartolai* multiplied in response to an increasing demand for tablets, notebooks, prepared sheets, and other supplies. In addition to selling writing materials and schoolbooks as well as book-binding materials and services, some merchants also helped book-hunting patrons by locating valued works. They had copies made on commission and kept some for sale in their shops. But their involvement in the book trade was more casual than one might think. 'The activities of the *cartolai* were multifarious . . . Those who specialized in the sale and preparation of book materials or in bindings were

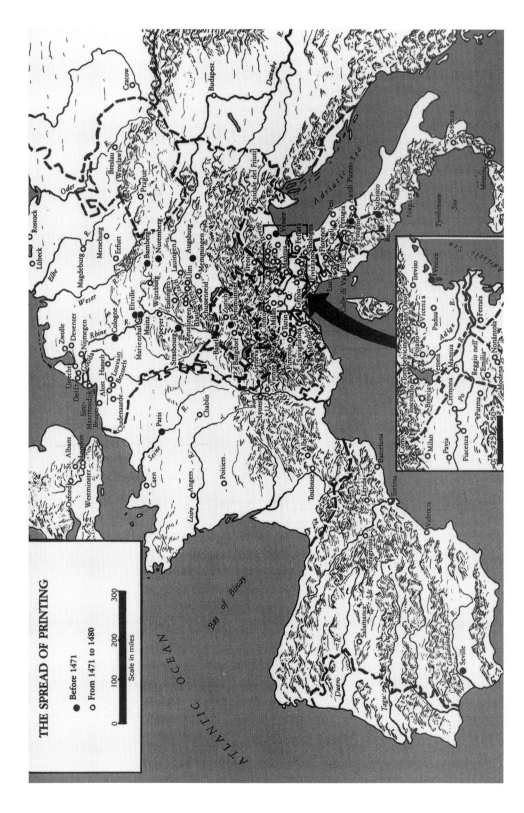

THE SPREAD OF PRINTING

- Before 1471
- From 1471 to 1480

Scale in miles

0   100   200   300

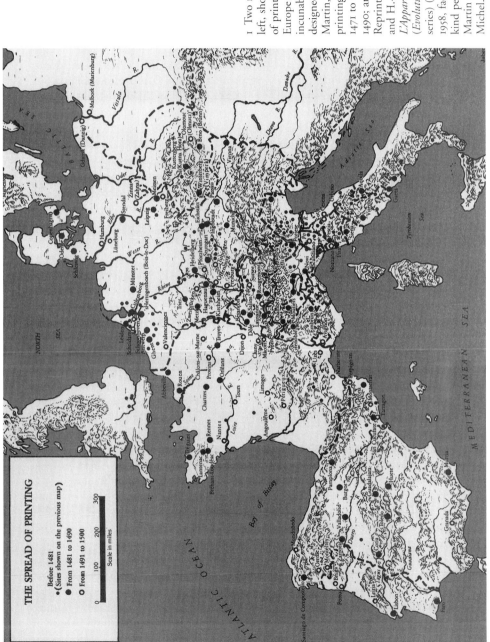

1 Two maps above and left, showing the spread of printing in Western Europe during the age of incunabula. These maps, designed by Henri-Jean Martin, show the spread of printing before 1471; from 1471 to 1480; from 1481 to 1490; and from 1491 to 1500. Reprinted from L. Febvre and H.-J. Martin, *L'Apparition du livre* (*Evolution de l'humanité* series) (Paris: Albin Michel, 1958, facing p. 272), with kind permission of H.-J. Martin and Editions Albin Michel.

THE SPREAD OF PRINTING

Before 1481
• (Sites shown on the previous map)
● From 1481 to 1490
○ From 1491 to 1500

Scale in miles
0   100   200   300

probably concerned little if at all, with the production or sale of manuscripts and (later) printed books, either new or secondhand.'

Even the retail book trade that was conducted by Vespasiano da Bisticci [1421–98], the most celebrated Florentine book merchant, who served prelates and princes and 'did everything possible' to attract patrons and make sales, never verged on becoming a wholesale business. Despite Vespasiano's unusually aggressive tactics in promoting sales and matching books with clients, he showed no signs of ever 'having made much money' from all his transactions. He did win notable patrons, however, and achieved considerable celebrity as 'prince of publishers.' His shop was praised by humanist poets along lines which were similar to those used in later tributes to Gutenberg [1400–68] and Aldus Manutius [*c.* 1450–1515]. His posthumous fame – achieved only in the nineteenth century after the publication of his memoirs and their use by Jacob Burckhardt – is perhaps even more noteworthy. Vespasiano's *Lives of Illustrious Men* contains a reference to the beautifully bound manuscript books in the Duke of Urbino's library and snobbishly implies that a printed book would have been 'ashamed' in such elegant company. This one reference by an atypical and obviously prejudiced bookdealer has ballooned into many misleading comments about the disdain of Renaissance humanists for vulgar machine-made objects. Actually, Florentine bibliophiles were sending to Rome for printed books as early as 1470. Under Guidobaldo da Montefeltro, the ducal library at Urbino acquired printed editions and (shamelessly or not) had them bound with the same magnificent covers as manuscripts. The same court also sponsored the establishment of an early press in 1482. That Vespasiano was indulging in wishful and nostalgic thinking is suggested by his own inability to find sufficient support from princely patrons to persist in his exclusive trade. His chief rival in Florence, Zanobi di Mariano, managed to stay in business right down to his death in 1495. 'Zanobi's readiness to sell printed books – a trade which Vespasiano spurned – explains his survival as a bookseller in the tricky years of the late fifteenth century. Vespasiano dealing exclusively in manuscripts was forced out of business in 1478.'

One must wait for Vespasiano to close shop before one can say that a genuine wholesale book trade was launched.

As soon as Gutenberg and Schoeffer had finished the last sheet of their monumental Bible, the financier of the firm, John Fust, set out with a dozen copies or so to see for himself how he could best reap the harvest of his patient investments. And where did he turn first of all to convert his Bibles into money? He went to the biggest university town in Europe, to Paris, where ten thousand or more students were filling the Sorbonne and the colleges. And what did he, to his bitter discomfiture find there? A well organized and powerful guild of the booktrade, the Confrérie des Libraires, Relieurs, Enlumineurs, Ecrivains et Parcheminiers . . . founded in 1401 . . . Alarmed at the appearance of an outsider with such an unheard of treasure of books; when he was found to be selling one Bible after another, they soon shouted for the police, giving their expert opinion that such a store of valuable books could be in one man's possession through the help of the devil himself and Fust had to run for his life or his first business trip would have ended in a nasty bonfire.

This story, as told by E. P. Goldschmidt, may be just as unfounded as the legend that linked the figure of Johan Fust with that of Dr. Faustus. The adverse reaction it depicts should not be taken as typical; many early references were at worst ambivalent. The ones that are most frequently cited associate printing with divine rather than diabolic powers. But then the most familiar references come either from the blurbs and prefaces composed by early printers themselves or from editors and authors who were employed in printing shops. Such men were likely to take a more favorable view than were the guildsmen who had made a livelihood from manuscript books. The Parisian *libraires* may have had good reason to be alarmed, although they were somewhat ahead of the game; the market value of hand-copied books did not drop until after Fust was dead. Other members of the *confrérie* could not foresee that most bookbinders, rubricators, illuminators, and calligraphers would be kept busier than ever after early printers set up shop. Whether the new art was considered a blessing or a curse, whether it was consigned to the Devil or attributed to God, the fact remains that the initial increase in output did strike contemporary observers as sufficiently remarkable to suggest supernatural intervention. Even incredulous modern scholars may be troubled by trying to calculate the number of calves required to supply enough skins for vellum copies of Gutenberg's Bible. It should not be too difficult to obtain agreement that an abrupt rather than a gradual increase did occur in the second half of the fifteenth century.

Scepticism is much more difficult to overcome when we turn from consideration of quantity to that of quality. If one holds a late manuscript copy of a given text next to an early printed one, one is likely to doubt that any change at all has taken place, let alone an abrupt or revolutionary one.

> Behind every book which Peter Schoeffer printed stands a published manuscript . . . The decision on the kind of letter to use, the selection of initials and decoration of rubrications, the determination of the length and width of the column, planning for margins . . . all were prescribed by the manuscript copy before him.

Not only did early printers such as Schoeffer try to copy a given manuscript as faithfully as possible, but fifteenth-century scribes returned the compliment. As Curt Bühler has shown, a large number of the manuscripts made during the late fifteenth century were copied from early printed books. Thus handwork and presswork continued to appear almost indistinguishable, even after the printer had begun to depart from scribal conventions and to exploit some of the new features inherent in his art.

That there were new features and they were exploited needs to be given due weight. Despite his efforts to duplicate manuscripts as faithfully as possible, the fact remains that Peter Schoeffer, printer, was following different procedures than had Peter Schoeffer, scribe. The absence of any apparent change in product was combined with a complete change in methods of production, giving rise to the paradoxical combination of seeming continuity with radical change. Thus the temporary resemblance between handwork and presswork seems to support the thesis of a very gradual evolutionary change; yet the opposite thesis may also be supported by underlining the marked difference between the two

2 The similarity of handwork and presswork is demonstrated by these two pages, one taken from a hand-copied Bible (the so-called Giant Bible of Mainz), and the other from a printed Bible (the celebrated Gutenberg Bible). Reproduced by kind permission of the Rare Book and Special Collections Division of the Library of Congress, Washington, DC.

different modes of production and noting the new features that began to appear before the fifteenth century had come to an end.

Concern with surface appearance necessarily governed the handwork of the scribe. He was fully preoccupied trying to shape evenly spaced uniform letters in a pleasing symmetrical design. An altogether different procedure was required to give directions to compositors. To do this, one had to mark up a manuscript while scrutinizing its contents. Every manuscript that came into the printer's hands, thus, had to be reviewed in a new way – one which encouraged more editing, correcting, and collating than had the hand-copied text. Within a generation the results of this review were being aimed in a new direction – away from fidelity to scribal conventions and toward serving the convenience of the reader. The highly competitive commercial character of the new mode of book production encouraged the relatively rapid adoption of any innovation that commended a given edition to purchasers. Well before 1500, printers had begun to experiment with the use 'of graduated types, running heads . . . footnotes . . . tables of contents . . . superior figures, cross references . . . and other devices available to the compositor' – all registering 'the victory of the punch cutter over the scribe.' Title pages became increasingly common, facilitating the production of book lists and catalogues, while acting as advertisements in themselves. Hand-drawn illustrations were replaced by more easily duplicated woodcuts and engravings – an innovation which eventually helped to revolutionize technical literature by introducing 'exactly repeatable pictorial statements' into all kinds of reference works.

The fact that identical images, maps, and diagrams could be viewed simultaneously by scattered readers constituted a kind of communications revolution in itself. This point has been made most forcefully by William Ivins, a former curator of prints at the Metropolitan Museum. Although Ivins's special emphasis on 'the exactly repeatable pictorial statement' has found favor among historians of cartography, his propensity for overstatement has provoked objections from other specialists. Repeatable images, they argue, go back to ancient seals and coins, while *exact* replication was scarcely fostered by woodblocks, which got worn and broken after repeated use. Here as elsewhere, one must be wary of underrating as well as of overestimating the advantages of the new technology. Even while noting that woodcuts did get corrupted when copied for insertion in diverse kinds of texts, one should also consider the corruption that occurred when hand-drawn images had to be copied into hundreds of books. Although pattern books and 'pouncing' techniques were available to some medieval illuminators, the precise reproduction of fine detail remained elusive until the advent of woodcarving and engraving. Blocks and plates did make repeatable visual aids feasible for the first time. In the hands of expert craftsmen using good materials and working under supervision, even problems of wear and tear could be circumvented: worn places could be sharpened, blurred details refined, and a truly remarkable durability achieved.

It is not so much in his special emphasis on the printed image but rather in his underrating the significance of the printed text that Ivins seems to go astray. Although he mentions in passing that 'the history of prints as an integrated series' begins with their use 'as illustrations in books printed from movable types,' his analysis elsewhere tends to detach the fate of printed pictures from that of printed books. His treatment implies that the novel effects of repeatability were confined to pictorial statements. Yet these effects were by no means confined to pictures or, for that matter, to pictures and words. Mathematical tables, for example, were also transformed. For scholars concerned with scientific change, what happened to numbers and equations is surely just as significant as what happened to either images or words. Furthermore, many of the most important pictorial statements produced during the first century of printing employed various devices – banderoles, letter-number keys, indication lines – to relate images to texts. To treat the visual aid as a discrete unit is to lose sight of the connecting links which were especially important for technical literature because they expressed the relationship between words and things.

Even though block print and letterpress may have originated as separate innovations and were initially used for diverse purposes (so that playing cards and saints' images, for example, were being stamped from blocks at the same time that hand illumination continued to decorate many early printed books), the two techniques soon became intertwined. The use of typography for texts led to that of xylography for illustration, sealing the fate of the illuminator along with that of the scribe. When considering how technical literature was affected by the shift from script to print, it seems reasonable to adopt George Sarton's strategy of envisaging a 'double invention; typography for the text, engraving for the images.' The fact that letters, numbers, and pictures were *all* alike subject to repeatability by the end of the fifteenth century needs more emphasis. That the printed

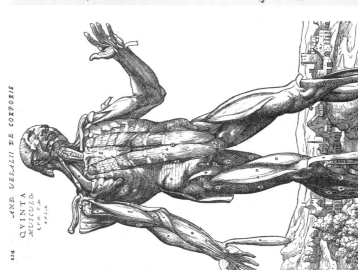

3 This example of a visual aid keyed to a text comes from Andreas Vesalius, *De humani corporis fabrica libri septem* (Basel: Johann Oporinus, 1555, pp. 224–5). Reproduced by kind permission of the Folger Shakespeare Library.

book made possible new forms of interplay between these diverse elements is perhaps even more significant than the change undergone by picture, number, or letter alone.

The preparation of copy and illustrative material for printed editions also led to a rearrangement of book-making arts and routines. Not only did new skills, such as typefounding and presswork, involve veritable occupational mutations, but the production of printed books also gathered together in one place more traditional variegated skills. In the age of scribes, book making had occurred under the diverse auspices represented by stationers and lay copyists in university towns; illuminators and miniaturists trained in special ateliers; goldsmiths and leather workers belonging to special guilds; monks and lay brothers gathered in scriptoria; royal clerks and papal secretaries working in chanceries and courts; preachers compiling books of sermons on their own; humanist poets serving as their own scribes. The advent of printing led to the creation of a new kind of shop structure; to a regrouping which entailed closer contacts among diversely skilled workers and encouraged new forms of cross-cultural interchange.

Thus it is not uncommon to find former priests among early printers or former abbots serving as editors and correctors. University professors also often served in similar capacities and thus came into closer contact with metal workers and mechanics. Other fruitful forms of collaboration brought together astronomers and engravers, physicians and painters, dissolving older divisions of intellectual labor and encouraging new ways of coordinating the work of brains, eyes, and hands. Problems of financing the publication of the large Latin volumes that were used by late medieval faculties of theology, law, and medicine also led to the formation of partnerships that brought rich merchants and local scholars into closer contact. The new financial syndicates that were formed to provide master printers with needed labor and supplies brought together representatives of town and gown.

As the key figure around whom all arrangements revolved, the master printer himself bridged many worlds. He was responsible for obtaining money, supplies, and labor, while developing complex production schedules, coping with strikes, trying to estimate book markets and lining up learned assistants. He had to keep on good terms with officials who provided protection and lucrative jobs, while cultivating and promoting talented authors and artists who might bring his firm profits or prestige. In those places where his enterprise prospered and he achieved a position of influence with fellow townsmen, his workshop became a veritable cultural center attracting local literati and celebrated foreigners, providing both a meeting place and message center for an expanding cosmopolitan Commonwealth of Learning.

Some manuscript bookdealers, to be sure, had served rather similar functions before the advent of printing. That Italian humanists were grateful to Vespasiano da Bisticci for many of the same services that were later rendered by Aldus Manutius has already been noted. Nevertheless, the shop structure over which Aldus presided differed markedly from that known to Vespasiano. As the prototype of the early capitalist [. . .], the printer embraced an even wider repertoire of roles. Aldus's household in Venice, which contained some thirty members, has recently

OFFICINÆ TYPOGRA-
PHICÆ DELINEATIO.

EN Thymii fculptoris opus,quo prodidit unâ
Singula chalcographi munera ritè gregis.
Et correctorum curas,operasq; regentum,
Quasq; gerit lector, compofitorq; vices.
Ut vulgus fileam. tu qui légis ifta, libello
Fac iteratâ animi fedulitate fatis.
Sic meritæ cumulans hinc fertilitatis honores,
Ceu pictura oculos, intima mentis ages.

L. I. L. F.

This cut, the work of Thymius' accurate hand
Shows all at once how printing shops are manned:
The masters' duties, the correctors' chores,
The work of readers and compositors.
To this small book then you'll apply your mind
Good reader, if you're not the vulgar kind,
So that a picture in your mind may rise
To match this picture that's before your eyes.

L. I. L. F.

4 A master printer in his shop. The Latin verse and woodblock first appeared in Jerome Hornschuch, *Orthotypographia* (Leipzig: M. Lantzenberger, 1608). The English translation comes from a facsimile edition, edited and translated by Philip Gaskell and Patricia Bradford (Cambridge University Library, 1972, p. xvi). Reproduced by kind permission of the Syndics of Cambridge University Library.

been described by Martin Lowry, as an 'almost incredible mixture of the sweat shop, the boarding house and the research institute.' A most interesting study might be devoted to a comparison of the occupational culture of Peter Schoeffer [*c.* 1449–1502], printer, with that of Peter Schoeffer, scribe. Unlike the shift from stationer to publisher, the shift from scribe to printer represented a genuine occupational mutation. Although Schoeffer was the first to make the leap, many others took the same route before the century's end.

[. . .] [M]any of Schoeffer's pioneering activities were associated with the shift from a retail trade to a wholesale industry. 'For a while the trade in printed books flowed within the narrow channels of the manuscript book market. But soon the stream could no longer be contained.' New distribution outlets were located; handbills, circulars, and sales catalogues were printed; and the books themselves were carried down the Rhine, across the Elbe, west to Paris, south to Switzerland. The drive to tap markets went together with efforts to hold competitors at bay by offering better products or, at least, by printing a prospectus advertising the firm's 'more readable' texts, 'more complete and better arranged' indexes, 'more careful proofreading' and editing. Officials serving archbishops and emperors were cultivated, not only as potential bibliophiles and potential censors, but also as potential customers who issued a steady flow of orders for the printing of ordinances, edicts, bulls, indulgences, broadsides, and tracts. By the end of the century, Schoeffer had risen to a position of eminence in the city of Mainz. He commanded a 'far-flung sales organization,' had become a partner in a joint mining enterprise, and had founded a printing dynasty. His supply of types went to his sons upon his death, and the Schoeffer firm continued in operation, expanding to encompass music printing, through the next generation.

As the foregoing may suggest, there are many points of possible contrast between the activities of the Mainz printer and those of the Paris scribe. Competitive and commercial drives were not entirely absent among the stationers who served university faculties, the lay scribes who were hired by mendicant orders, or the semi-lay copyists who belonged to communities founded by the Brethren of the Common Life. But they were muted in comparison with the later efforts of Schoeffer and his competitors to recoup initial investments, pay off creditors, use up reams of paper, and keep pressmen employed. The manuscript bookdealer did not have to worry about idle machines or striking workmen as did the printer. It has been suggested, indeed, that the mere act of setting up a press in a monastery or in affiliation with a religious order was a source of disturbance, bringing 'a multitude of worries about money and property' into space previously reserved for meditation and good works.

As self-serving publicists, early printers issued book lists, circulars, and broadsides. They put their firm's name, emblem, and shop address on the front page of their books. Indeed, their use of title pages entailed a significant reversal of scribal procedures; they put themselves first. Scribal colophons had come last. They also extended their new promotional techniques to the authors and artists whose work they published, thus contributing to new forms of personal celebrity. Reckon masters [professional arithmeticians] and instrument makers along with professors and preachers also profited from book advertisements that spread their fame beyond shops and lecture halls. Studies concerned with the rise of a lay intelligentsia, with the new dignity assigned to artisan crafts, or with the heightened visibility achieved by the 'capitalist spirit' might well devote more attention to these early practitioners of the advertising arts.

Their control of a new publicity apparatus, moreover, placed early printers in an exceptional position with regard to other enterprises. They not only sought ever larger markets for their own products, but they also contributed to, and profited from, the expansion of other commercial enterprises. What effects did the appearance of new advertising techniques have on sixteenth-century commerce and industry? Possibly some answers to this question are known. Probably others can still be found. Many other aspects of job printing and the changes it entailed clearly need further study. The printed calendars and indulgences that were first issued from the Mainz workshops of Gutenberg and Fust, for example, warrant at least as much attention as the more celebrated Bibles. Indeed, the mass production of indulgences illustrates rather neatly the sort of change that often goes overlooked, so that its consequences are more difficult to reckon with than perhaps they need be.

In contrast to the changes sketched above, those that were associated with the consumption of new printed products are more intangible, indirect, and difficult to handle. A large margin for uncertainty must be left when dealing with such changes. [. . .]

In view of the fragmentary evidence that is available and the prolonged fluctuations that were entailed, it would seem prudent to bypass vexed problems associated with the spread of literacy until other issues have been explored with more care. That there are other issues worth exploring – apart from the expansion of the reading public or the 'spread' of new ideas – is in itself a point that needs underlining [. . .]. When considering the *initial* transformations wrought by print, at all events, changes undergone by groups who were already literate ought to receive priority over the undeniably fascinating problem of how rapidly such groups were enlarged.

Once attention has been focused on the already literate sectors, it becomes clear that their social composition calls for further thought. Did printing at first serve prelates and patricians as a 'divine art,' or should one think of it rather as the 'poor man's friend'? It was described in both ways by contemporaries and probably served in both ways as well. When one recalls scribal functions performed by Roman slaves or later by monks, lay brothers, clerks, and notaries, one may conclude that literacy had never been congruent with elite social status. One may also guess that it was more compatible with sedentary occupations than with the riding and hunting favored by many squires and lords. In this light, it may be misguided to envisage the new presses as making available to low-born men products previously used only by the high born. That many rural areas remained untouched until after the coming of the railway age seems likely. Given the large peasant population in early modern Europe and the persistence of local dialects which imposed an additional language barrier between spoken and written words, it is probable that only a very small portion of the entire population was affected by the initial shift. Nevertheless, within this relatively small and largely urban population, a fairly wide social spectrum may have been involved. In fifteenth-century England, for example, mercers and scriveners engaged in a manuscript book trade were already catering to the needs of lowly bakers and merchants as well as to those of lawyers, aldermen, or knights. The proliferation of literate merchants in fourteenth-century Italian cities is no less notable than the presence of an illiterate army commander in late sixteenth-century France.

It would be a mistake, however, to assume that a distaste for reading was especially characteristic of the nobility, although it seems plausible that a distaste for Latin pedantry was shared by lay aristocrat and commoner alike. It also remains uncertain whether one ought to describe the early reading public as being 'middle class.' Certainly extreme caution is needed when matching genres of books with groups of readers. All too often it is taken for granted that 'low-brow' or 'vulgar' works reflect 'lower-class' tastes, despite contrary evidence offered by authorship and library catalogues. Before the advent of mass literacy, the most 'popular' works were those which appealed to diverse groups of readers and not just to the plebes.

Divisions between Latin and vernacular-reading publics are also much more difficult to correlate with social status than many accounts suggest. It is true that the sixteenth-century physician who used Latin was regarded as superior to the surgeon who did not, but also true that neither man was likely to belong to the highest estates of the realm. Insofar as the vernacular-translation movement was aimed at readers who were unlearned in Latin, it was often designed to appeal to pages as well as apprentices; to landed gentry, cavaliers, and courtiers as well as to shopkeepers and clerks. In the Netherlands, a translation from Latin into French often pointed away from the urban laity, who knew only Lower Rhenish dialects, and toward relatively exclusive courtly circles. At the same time, a translation into 'Dutch' might be aimed at preachers who needed to cite scriptural passages in sermons rather than at the laity (which is too often assumed to be the only target for 'vernacular' devotional works). Tutors trying to educate young princes, instructors in court or church schools, and chaplains translating from Latin in response to royal requests had pioneered in 'popularizing' techniques even before the printer set to work.

But the most vigorous impetus given to popularization before printing came from the felt need of preachers to keep their congregations awake and also to hold the attention of diverse outdoor crowds. Unlike the preacher, the printer could only guess at the nature of the audience to which his work appealed. Accordingly, one must be especially careful when taking the titles of early printed books as trustworthy guides to readership. A case in point is the frequent description of the fifteenth-century picture Bible, which was issued in both manuscript and then blockbook form, as the 'poor man's' Bible. The description may well be anachronistic, based on abbreviating the full Latin title given to such books. The *Biblia pauperum praedicatorum* was aimed not at poor men but at poor preachers who had a mere smattering of Latin and found scriptural exposition easier when given picture books as guides. Sophisticated analysts have suggested the need to discriminate between actual readership as determined by library catalogues, subscription lists, and other data (with due allowance made, of course, for the fact that many book buyers are more eager to display than to read their purchases) and the more hypothetical targets envisaged by authors and publishers. All too often, titles and prefaces are taken as evidence of the actual readership although they are nothing of the kind.

> Information on the spread of reading and writing . . . must be supplemented by analysis of contents; this in turn provides circumstantial evidence on the composition of the reading public: a cookbook . . . reprinted eight or more times in the XVth century was obviously read by people concerned with the preparation of food, the *Doctrinal des Filles* . . . a booklet on the behavior of young women, primarily by 'filles' and 'mesdames.'

Such 'circumstantial evidence,' however, is highly suspect. Without passing judgment on the audience for early cookbooks (its character seems far from obvious to me), booklets pertaining to the behavior of young ladies were probably also of interest to male tutors or confessors or guardians. The circulation of printed etiquette books had wide-ranging psychological ramifications; their capacity to heighten the anxiety of parents should not go ignored. Furthermore, such works were probably also read by authors, translators, and publishers of other etiquette books. That authors and publishers were wide-ranging readers needs to be perpetually kept in mind. Even those sixteenth-century poets who shunned printers and circulated their verse in manuscript form took advantage of their own access to printed materials. It has been suggested that books describing double-entry bookkeeping were read less by merchants than by the writers of accountancy books and teachers of accountancy. One wonders whether there were not more playwrights and poets than shepherds who studied so-called *Shepherd's Almanacks*. Given the corruption of data transmitted over the centuries, given the false remedies and impossible recipes contained in medical treatises, one hopes that they were studied more by poets than by physicians. Given the exotic ingredients described, one may assume that few apothecaries actually tried to concoct all the recipes contained in early printed pharmacopeia, although they may have felt impelled to stock their shelves with bizarre items just in case the new publicity might bring such items into demand. The purposes, whether intended or actual, served by some early printed handbooks offer puzzles that permit no easy solution. What was the point of publishing vernacular manuals outlining procedures that were already familiar to all skilled practitioners of certain crafts? It is worth remembering, in any event, that the gap between shop-room practice and classroom theory was just becoming visible during the first century of printing and that many so-called practical handbooks and manuals contained impractical, even injurious, advice.

While conjectures about social and psychological transformations can be postponed, certain points should be noted here. One must distinguish [. . .] between literacy and habitual book reading. By no means all who mastered the written word have, down to the present, become members of a book-reading public. Learning *to read* is different, moreover, from learning *by reading*. Reliance on apprenticeship training, oral communication, and special mnemonic devices had gone together with mastering letters in the age of scribes. After the advent of printing, however, the transmission of written information became much more efficient. It was not only the craftsman outside universities who profited from the new opportunities to teach himself. Of equal importance was the chance extended to bright undergraduates to reach beyond their teachers' grasp. Gifted students no longer needed to sit at the feet of a given master in order to learn a language or academic skill. Instead, they could swiftly achieve mastery on their own, even by sneaking books past their tutors – as did the young would-be astronomer, Tycho Brahe [1546–1601]. 'Why should old men be preferred to their juniors now that it is possible for the young by diligent study to acquire the same knowledge?' asked the author of a fifteenth-century outline of history.

As learning by reading took on new importance, the role played by mnemonic aids was diminished. Rhyme and cadence were no longer required to preserve certain formulas and recipes. The nature of the collective memory was transformed. [. . .]

Not only did printing eliminate many functions previously performed by stone figures over portals and stained glass in windows, but it also affected less tangible images by eliminating the need for placing figures and objects in imaginary niches located in memory theaters. By making it possible to dispense with the

use of images for mnemonic purposes, printing reinforced iconoclastic tendencies already present among many Christians. Successive editions of Calvin's
Institutes elaborated on the need to observe the Second Commandment. The
favorite text of the defenders of images was the dictum of Gregory the Great that
statues served as 'the books of the illiterate.' Although Calvin's scornful dismissal
of this dictum made no mention of printing, the new medium did underlie the
Calvinist assumption that the illiterate should not be given graven images but
should be taught to read. In this light it may seem plausible to suggest that
printing fostered a movement 'from image culture to word culture,' a movement
which was more compatible with Protestant bibliolatry and pamphleteering than
with the baroque statues and paintings sponsored by the post-Tridentine Catholic
church.

Yet the cultural metamorphosis produced by printing was really much more
complicated than any single formula can possibly express. For one thing,
engraved images became more, rather than less, abundant after the establishment
of print shops throughout Western Europe. For another thing, Protestant propaganda exploited printed image no less than printed word – as numerous cari-
catures and cartoons may suggest. Even religious imagery was defended by some
Protestants, and on the very grounds of its compatibility with print culture.
Luther himself commented on the inconsistency of iconoclasts who tore pictures
off walls while handling the illustrations in Bibles reverently. Pictures 'do no more
harm on walls than in books,' he commented and then, somewhat sarcastically,
stopped short of pursuing this line of thought: 'I must cease lest I give occasion
to the image breakers never to read the Bible or to burn it.'

If we accept the idea of a movement from image to word, furthermore, we
will be somewhat at a loss to account for the work of Northern artists, such as
Dürer or Cranach or Holbein, who were affiliated with Protestantism and
yet owed much to print. As Dürer's career may suggest, the new arts of printing
and engraving, far from reducing the importance of images, increased opportunities for image makers and helped to launch art history down its present
path. Even the imaginary figures and memory theaters [. . .] did not vanish
when their mnemonic functions were outmoded, but received a 'strange new
lease on life.' They provided the content for magnificent emblem books and for
elaborate baroque illustrations to Rosicrucian and occult works in the seventeenth
century. They also helped to inspire an entirely new genre of printed literature –
the didactic picture book for children. Leipzig boys in Leibniz's day 'were
brought up on Comenius' picture book and Luther's Catechism.' In this
form, the ancient memory images reentered the imagination of Protestant
children. [. . .] Surely the new vogue for image-packed emblem books was no
less a product of sixteenth-century print culture than was the imageless 'Ramist'
textbook.

Furthermore, in certain fields of learning such as architecture, geometry, or
geography, and many of the life sciences as well, print culture was not
merely incompatible with the formula offered above; it actually increased
the functions performed by images while reducing those performed by
words. Many fundamental texts of Ptolemy, Vitruvius, Galen, and other ancients

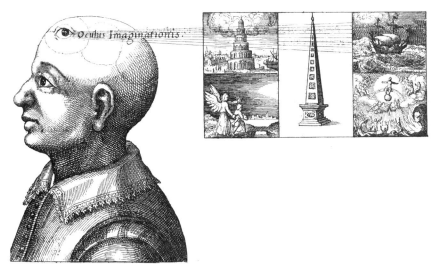

5 Seeing with a 'third eye' in the seventeenth century. After their original functions were outmoded, ancient memory arts acquired an occult significance and received a new lease on life in printed form. From Robert Fludd, *Utriusque cosmi maioris . . .* (Oppenheim: Johan-Theodor de Bry, typis Hieronymi Galleri, 1621, II, 47). Reproduced by kind permission of the Folger Shakespeare Library.

had lost their illustrations in the course of being copied for centuries and regained them only after script was replaced by print. To think in terms of a movement going from image to word points technical literature in the wrong direction. It was not the 'printed word' but the 'printed image' which acted as a 'savior for Western science'. [. . .] Within the Commonwealth of Learning it became increasingly fashionable to adopt the ancient Chinese maxim that a single picture was more valuable than many words. In early Tudor England, Thomas Elyot expressed a preference for 'figures and charts' over 'hearing the rules of a science' which seems worth further thought. Although images were indispensable for prodding memory, a heavy reliance on verbal instruction had also been characteristic of communications in the age of scribes. To be sure, academic lectures were sometimes supplemented by drawing pictures on walls; verbal instructions to apprentices were accompanied by demonstrations; the use of blocks and boards, fingers and knuckles were common in teaching reckoning; and gestures usually went with the recitation of key mnemonics. Nevertheless, when seeking rapid duplication of a given set of instructions, words simply had to take precedence over other forms of communication. How else save by using words could one dictate a text to assembled scribes? After the advent of printing, visual aids multiplied, signs and symbols were codified; different kinds of iconographic and nonphonetic communication were rapidly developed. The fact that printed picture books were newly designed by educational reformers for the purpose of instructing children and that drawing was considered an increasingly useful accomplishment by pedagogues also points to the need to think beyond the simple formula 'image to word.'

As these comments may suggest, efforts to summarize changes wrought by printing in any one statement or neat formula are likely to lead us astray. Even while acknowledging that there was an increased reliance on rule books and less on rules of thumb or that learning by reading gained at the expense of hearing or doing, one must also consider how printing encouraged new objections to bookish knowledge based on 'slavish' copying and how it enabled many observers to check freshly recorded data against received rules. Similarly, one must be cautious about assuming that the spoken word was gradually silenced as printed words multiplied or that the faculty of hearing was increasingly neglected in favor of that of sight. Surely the history of Western music after Gutenberg argues against the latter suggestion. [. . .]

The purpose of this preliminary discussion has been simply to demonstrate that the shift from script to print entailed a large ensemble of changes, each of which needs more investigation and all of which are too complicated to be encapsulated in any single formula. But to say that there is no simple way of summarizing the complex ensemble is not the same thing as saying that nothing had changed. To the contrary!

5   Peter Burke **'Learned Culture and Popular Culture in Renaissance Italy'**

Source: from *Varieties of Cultural History*, Peter Burke, Polity Press, Cambridge, 1997, Chapter 8, pp. 124–35.

The study of the Italian Renaissance continues to flourish. The history of popular culture continues to expand. Recent studies of popular culture have argued, reasonably enough, that it is more fruitful to study interactions between learned culture and popular culture than to attempt to define what separates them. All the same, studies of the Italian Renaissance have little to say about popular culture, and studies of Italian popular culture even less to say about the Renaissance. To consider whether the gap should be filled and how it might be filled is the purpose of this chapter.

It is understandable that the two cultures should have been studied separately, since a number of barriers excluded ordinary people from the world of Renaissance art and literature. In the first place, there was the barrier of language. Much of high culture was Latin culture, but the vast majority of the population did not study Latin. Ordinary people spoke their regional dialect, and outside Tuscany only the upper classes knew the reformed Tuscan which was on its way to becoming standard literary Italian. In the second place, there was the barrier of literacy. Reading and writing were skills possessed by only a minority of the population, even if that minority was a large one in the case of urban males. In the third place, there was the economic barrier preventing ordinary people from buying books or paintings.

However, all these obstacles could be surmounted. According to a recent history of Italian education in this period, 'almost all the vernacular schools taught the rudiments of Latin grammar.' The dialect of Tuscans, especially Florentines, gave them access to the literary language. Inhabitants of large towns such as Venice, Florence, Rome and Milan had relatively easy access to schools, and also to works of art displayed in public places – frescoes in churches, statues on the piazza, and so on.

Historians of Italian culture of this period have therefore to deal with a two-way process. On one side, there is the spread of the forms and ideas of the Renaissance from the elites to the people, their social as well as their geographical diffusion. For convenience – using a simple spatial metaphor – we may call this a movement 'downward'. On the other side, there is movement 'upward', in which Italian artists and writers drew on the heritage of popular culture.

This essay will therefore be divided into two parts. All the same, it has a common theme. On both sides of the interaction, we must look not only for appropriation but also for reception and assimilation. Ariosto, for example, transformed the traditional romances of chivalry he read into something very different in tone and spirit. On the other side, Menocchio the miller, a long-forgotten figure restored to history by Carlo Ginzburg, read the *Golden Legend*, the *Travels* attributed to Sir John Mandeville, Boccaccio's *Decameron* and so on, but what he found in these texts was rather different from what was seen by the inquisitors who interrogated him.

THE POPULARIZATION OF THE RENAISSANCE

In Italy in the sixteenth and seventeenth centuries, some ordinary people were familiar with a part of the classical tradition. For example, works by Cicero, Ovid and Virgil were translated into the vernacular at this time. The story about the Roman matron Lucretia and her suicide following her rape by King Tarquin appears to have been quite well known. A version quoting 'Livy of Padua' as its source (though it probably drew more directly on Boccaccio) was turned into an Italian ballad which was printed in Venice by Agostino Bindoni, whose family of printers specialized in cheap popular texts.

A relatively clear-cut example of movement downwards is that of the popularization of Ariosto's *Orlando Furioso* [1516]. The poem was of course written by a noble for nobles, and in its published form it was quite expensive. However, the 'laments' of characters from the poem such as Bradamante, Isabella, Rodomonte, Ruggiero and so on, as well as other verse paraphrases, supplements and summaries, were available in chap-book form in the sixteenth century. Some of these texts were anonymous, but one – an attempt to compress the 'beauties' of the poem into sixteen pages – was the work of the Bolognese poet Giulio Cesare Croce, a well-known mediator between learned and popular culture.

It cannot be assumed that these paraphrases and summaries were intended for ordinary people alone. The library of Henri III of France contained a book entitled *Bellezze del Furioso*, almost certainly selections from Ariosto. However, Ariosto's popular appeal was noted by some contemporary observers. According to the poet Bernardo Tasso, the *Furioso* was read by craftsmen and children. According to the Venetian publisher Comin dal Trino, it appealed to common people (*il volgo*). Unusually for the sixteenth century, this modern text was taught in some schools alongside the Latin classics. There is also evidence from the archives, mainly from heresy trials, for interest in Ariosto on the part of ordinary people. In Venice a swordsmith's apprentice, a silk merchant and a prostitute all confessed to reading *Orlando Furioso*. In Calvin's Geneva an Italian once found himself in trouble because he had described the book as his 'Bible'.

Montaigne's journal of his visit to Italy offers us further evidence of Ariosto's penetration of popular culture. At a spa near Lucca, for example, he met a poor peasant woman named Divizia, who could not read or write but had often heard Ariosto read aloud in her father's house, thanks to which she had become a poet herself. Near Florence, and elsewhere in Italy, Montaigne tells us that he was surprised to meet peasants and shepherdesses who knew Ariosto by heart. In the eighteenth century, visitors to Naples sometimes described the professional storytellers who read, or more exactly performed Ariosto's poem in the streets and squares of the city, with the text at hand to assist their memory if it failed.

The poems of Torquato Tasso also seem to have entered popular culture. His epic *Gerusalemme liberata* [1575] was translated into a number of dialects – Bolognese in 1628, Bergamask in 1670, Neapolitan in 1689, Venetian in 1693, and so on. Joseph Addison's *Remarks on Several Parts of Italy* (1705) noted the custom 'of the common people of this country, of singing stanzas out of Tasso', a point which would be repeated by Rousseau and Goethe in the case of the Venetian gondoliers.

One would of course like to know much more about these incidents – how faithfully the peasants, storytellers and gondoliers remembered the texts, and, still more important, what the epics of Ariosto and Tasso meant to them. My own hypothesis would be that ordinary people read or heard *Orlando Furioso* and *Gerusalemme liberata* as examples of romances of chivalry – or as they called them, 'books of battles' (*libri di battagie*) – which were widely available in chap-book form in sixteenth-century Italy and were sometimes used in elementary schools to encourage boys to learn to read. Menocchio the miller also enjoyed this kind of literature.

In the case of the visual arts, the relation between learned and popular is considerably more complicated, because the 'high' art of the Italian Renaissance was generally produced by men with the training and status of craftsmen. They produced religious paintings without the opportunity to study theology, and scenes from classical mythology without being able to read Latin, let alone Greek. It follows that works like Botticelli's *Primavera*, or Titian's *Sacred and Profane Love*, which appear to refer to Neoplatonic ideas, must have been the outcome of a complex process of mediation between learned and popular culture, in which the participants included not only artists and patrons but also humanists, such as

Angelo Poliziano and Marsilio Ficino, and popularizers, such as the Venetian professional writers or *poligrafi*.

Paintings of this kind, secular in subject-matter, were not widely seen during the Renaissance. They belonged to the 'private' rather than the 'public' circuit. It was, however, possible for a wider public to see graphic versions of some of them, notably the engravings after Raphael by Marcantonio Raimondi. The work of art had already entered the age of mechanical reproduction. Like printing, engraving was a great popularizer, at least in the sense that it allowed many more people to see images, and probably more kinds of people as well.

Ceramics offered another means of diffusing images more widely, since the raw material was cheap. The majolica plates and jugs produced in Faenza, Urbino, Deruta and elsewhere were frequently decorated with scenes from classical mythology and ancient history. Some were based on the Raimondi engravings after Raphael. Some of these ceramics were made for wealthy patrons, but others were simple drug-pots for the shops of apothecaries. The painted terracotta images produced by the Della Robbia family workshop in Florence might be regarded as the poor man's sculptures. The workshop produced some large expensive altarpieces for churches, but also small images for wayside shrines or private individuals. It would be an exaggeration to speak of 'mass-production' but signs of hasty work can be found, and it is not uncommon for a particular image (an Adoration, say, or a Madonna and Child) to survive in eight, nine, ten, or even twenty almost identical copies.

The problem is of course to discover how people who were not members of a cultural elite perceived these objects, and especially whether or not they were interested in the styles as well as the stories. In the case of Florence, at least, there is evidence of a sophisticated popular visual culture. Some ordinary people, craftsmen and shopkeepers, were not only familiar with the names of the leading artists of their city, past and present, but they were not afraid to offer opinions – often critical opinions – about the value of particular works. Some of the evidence for this statement comes from Vasari's *Lives of the Artists* (1550), which from time to time discusses popular reactions to particular works of art or artists. Particularly interesting in this respect is Vasari's discussion of Florentine responses to Perugino, beginning with enthusiasm and ending with satire. Vasari's testimony to popular interest in aesthetics may be supplemented by that of Antonfrancesco Grazzini, a man of the shopkeeper class (probably an apothecary), whose poems, or more exactly songs (*madrigalesse*), sometimes mention works of art. Two of these songs comment critically on Vasari's decision to paint the cupola of the cathedral of Florence, declaring 'the fault was George's, ('Giorgin fece il peccato') and that it showed 'little sense and less judgement' ('poco senno e men giudizio').

POPULAR INSPIRATION IN THE RENAISSANCE

It is time to turn from the popularization of the Renaissance to the importance of 'low' elements in 'high' culture. The presiding genius over this section of the chapter is of course Mikhail Bakhtin, whose *World of Rabelais* (written in the

1930s, but not published until 1965) argued that the author of *Gargantua and Pantagruel* drew heavily on the 'culture of folk humour', in particular the grotesque and the carnivalesque. This work, which is a *tour de force* of the historical imagination, has been taken as a model for recent studies of Breughel, Shakespeare and other artists and writers of the Renaissance.

The World of Rabelais has also been criticized by Renaissance specialists. On the assumption that Bakhtin claims that *Gargantua and Pantagruel* belongs wholly to popular culture, critics have pointed out that Rabelais was a learned man and that his work would not have been fully comprehensible to ordinary people. Unfortunately, Bakhtin's account of the relation between 'high' and 'low' culture was neither precise nor explicit. At times the contrast or opposition with which he is concerned seems to be that between the culture of two social groups, the elite and the people. At other times the two opposed cultures are defined in functional terms as the 'official' and the 'unofficial'. These distinctions may overlap but they do not coincide. The students of Montpellier, for example, whose festivities Bakhtin describes, belonged to a social elite, but participated in unofficial culture.

Another important distinction which remains blurred in Bakhtin's work is that between appropriating (and transforming) elements from popular culture (which Rabelais certainly does) and participating fully in that culture. I have argued elsewhere that sixteenth-century European elites were 'bicultural'. They had a learned culture from which ordinary people were excluded, but they also participated in what we now call 'popular' culture. Would these elites have participated in the same way as people for whom popular culture was all the culture they had? Or did they associate popular culture with particular times and places of relaxation? The concept of 'participation' is itself somewhat elusive. Despite these ambiguities, and the need to draw more careful distinctions, Bakhtin's study both could and should inspire future research on the various cultures and subcultures of Renaissance Italy, encouraging us to ask exactly what artists and writers took from popular traditions, as well as what they did with what they appropriated.

There have been relatively few studies of this kind. Before Bakhtin, Domenico Guerri had already examined what he called 'the popular current in the Renaissance', but he virtually limited himself to the subject of jokes and comic verses in Florence. The art historian Eugenio Battisti published a wide-ranging study of what he called the 'Anti-Renaissance', a fascinating collection of essays on medieval, mannerist, grotesque, occult and other themes in art and literature. However, Battisti tried to pack too much into his category of 'anti-Renaissance'. His chapters range from self-conscious rejections of classicism to medieval survivals which might be better described as 'non-Renaissance'.

In the case of art, one might begin the study of the interaction between high and low with certain grotesque or comic sculptures, already mentioned in the chapter on humour. It might be unwise to assume that whatever is comic is necessarily popular, but it is worth remembering that Aristotle – as interpreted by Italian humanists – argued that comedy was concerned with 'low' people. Take for example the statue by the sculptor Valerio Cioli representing Grand Duke Cosimo de' Medici's favourite dwarf, nicknamed 'Morgante' after the giant in

Pulci's poem of that name. The statue was placed in the Boboli gardens, a place of relaxation which has been described as a kind of sixteenth-century 'fun house'. In similar fashion the famous gardens of Bomarzo, created for the Roman aristocrat Vicino Orsini, might be described as a kind of sixteenth-century Disneyland. The huge stone monsters, the leaning tower, and the hell mouth all play on a popular taste for the grotesque, whatever layers of learned meaning have been superimposed on it.

The Commedia dell'Arte also deserves study from the point of view of this essay, with special reference to the fascinating and perplexing problem of the relation between the characters or masks of this apparently popular art form – the boastful soldier, the foolish old man, the cunning servant – and those of ancient Greek and Roman drama. Did the extemporizers owe their knowledge of these masks to the humanists? Or did the classical masks survive 'underground' in popular culture, to emerge in the sixteenth century, and inspire 'high' Renaissance drama?

The paragraphs which follow concentrate on literature, and especially on four writers: Boccaccio, Folengo, Ariosto and Aretino (at the expense of Burchiello, Berni, Pulci, Ruzante, Calmo and other examples of mediators between the two cultures). These four writers will be discussed in chronological order, which also happens to be a logical order, an order of increasing complexity in the relation between learned and popular culture. The increase in complexity over time is probably no accident, but the result of a process which may be described as the 'withdrawal' of elites from participation in popular culture.

The obvious place to start is of course Boccaccio's *Decameron* [1353]. As in the case of Rabelais, Boccaccio is remembered today for his 'vulgarity', so that it needs to be emphasized that he too was a learned man, a university teacher who wrote treatises in Latin and lectured on Dante. His Tuscan was 'canonized' in the sixteenth century (along with Dante's and Petrarch's) as a model of pure Italian. All the same, it is clear that many of the stories in the *Decameron* were taken from popular oral tradition, from what nineteenth-century scholars called 'folktales', and also that they illustrate some of Bakhtin's favourite themes.

The place of the carnivalesque in Boccaccio's work is clear enough, above all in the story of Frate Alberto (day 4, story 2), which ends with a ritualized hunt of the 'wild man' on Piazza San Marco in Venice. A number of the stories include episodes of what Bakhtin calls 'grotesque realism' or 'degradation'. This would, for example, be a plausible way of reading the first story in the collection, the tale of the wicked notary who managed to trick posterity into venerating him as a saint. Tricks recur in Boccaccio's *novelle*, as they do in those of other storytellers of the Renaissance (such as Sacchetti, Masuccio Salernitano, Bandello, and Grazzini), who draw on the popular tradition of the *beffa* [hoax, jest, prank]. For example, Bruno and Buffalmaco persuade the painter Calandrino, who is portrayed as a simpleton, to look for a magic stone which is supposed to make whoever carries it invisible, or they steal his pig and then 'prove' to him that he stole it himself.

The Benedictine monk Teofilo Folengo also drew on the tradition of the *beffa* in the twelfth section of his poem *Baldus*, describing a sea voyage with the owner of a flock of sheep, in which the trickster buys the ram and immediately throws it into the sea, where it is inevitably followed by the rest of the flock. Rabelais later appropriated this episode for his own purposes (in his *Fourth Book*, chapter 6). However, *Baldus*, published in 1517 under the pseudonym 'Merlin Cocaio', is essentially an example of the grotesque, a mock romance of chivalry narrated in a mock epic style. The poem tells the story of a young nobleman, a descendant of the paladin Rinaldo, who is raised among peasants but has his head as full of romances as Don Quixote's would be later in the [next] century. Baldus, together with two companions, a giant called Fracassus and a trickster called Cingar, becomes involved in a series of comic adventures which draw on popular traditions. Bakhtin himself drew attention to the episode in which someone is resurrected from the dead by a drenching in urine.

The subject of Folengo's poem is a hybrid, at once bucolic and chivalric, and the style, appropriately enough, is also hybrid. The language is a form of Latin which often behaves as if it were Italian or dialect – a mixture of two or three codes, or better, a product of their interaction. In a battle scene, for example, the rhetoric of the 'high' style, appropriate for epic encounters, is constantly pulled down to earth by the use of crudely Latinized technical terms such as *alebardae* (halberds), *banderae* (banners), *lanzae* (lances), *partesanae* (partisans), *picchiae* (pikes), *stendardi* (standards) and so on, or by words imitating the sound of drums and trumpets:

> Stendardique volant, banderae; timpana pon pon continuo chioccant; sonitan-tque tarantara trombae.

The epic begins with an invocation not to the muses, but to plump country girls, fattened on polenta [pearl barley] and macaroni (or gnocchi [dumplings]). Hence the style is now known as 'macaronic' Latin. Folengo was the greatest master of this language but he was not its inventor. It was a literary elaboration of the language of notaries, who wrote it for convenience, and of students, who spoke it for fun.

The first example, that of Boccaccio, shows a learned man drawing on a popular tradition in which he participated. The second, that of Folengo, is more complex, since it shows a learned man making a self-conscious synthesis of learned and popular traditions, or at least playing with the tensions between them.

The example of Ariosto is still more complicated. Like the *Baldus*, *Orlando Furioso* is a romance of chivalry, or a mock romance of chivalry – it is difficult to choose between these alternatives because Ariosto deliberately hovers on the edge of parody. The romance of chivalry was originally a high-status genre: stories about nobles, written for nobles, and in some cases (including that of Ariosto himself) written by nobles. However, as we have seen, this genre was also part of Italian popular culture in the sixteenth century. It took the form of printed chapbooks and also of oral performances by wandering singers of tales, or *cantimbanchi*, who sang or recited the stories on the piazza, asking for money at the end of each instalment, thus leaving the audience in suspense till they had made their contribution. The printed versions and the oral versions influenced each other.

Like other men of letters, Ariosto enjoyed these oral performances and his poem owes something to them. For example, although he wrote to be read, the author took over some of the popular formulas telling the audience to listen – 'as I shall continue the story in the next canto' ('come io vi seguirò ne l'altro canto'), and so on. Ariosto thus exemplifies a complex process of reappropriation, that of an educated man borrowing and transforming popular themes which had earlier been borrowed from high culture. When the *Furioso* was itself popularized, as we have seen it was, we are confronted with a case of double reappropriation. Circularities of this kind are not unknown today. For example, a novel by the Brazilian writer Jorge Amado, *Tereza Batista* (1972), draws on a chapbook by Rodolfo Coelho Cavalcanti (these booklets were and perhaps still are circulating in the northeast of Brazil, at least in the areas most remote from towns and television). Cavalcanti drew in turn on the traditional theme of the *donzela guerreira* or warrior maiden which goes back to the romances of chivalry – and of course to Ariosto's heroine Bradamante.

The last example to be discussed here is that of Pietro Aretino. Aretino made his reputation in Rome as a composer of biting pasquinades [satires, lampoons]. The *pasquinata* was a genre on the frontier between learned and popular culture. The practice of attaching satiric verses to the mutilated classical statue on Piazza del Pasquino in Rome goes back to the later fifteenth century, and at that time the verses were in humanist Latin. In the early sixteenth century, it became common to write the verses in a vernacular which everyone could understand. Aretino went on to write *Il Marescalco*, the carnival comedy built around a *beffa*.

However, the best example of the mixture or interaction of learned and popular elements in Aretino's work is surely his *Ragionamenti*, dialogues in which an old prostitute instructs a young one in the skills of the profession. The dialogues offer a series of scenes from low life in early sixteenth-century Rome, apparently faithful to the colloquial language and the slang of that social milieu. At the same time, humanist readers would have been aware that the dialogues borrow from and allude to a classical Greek text, Lucian's *Dialogues of the Courtesans.* The dialogues also may be read as a parody of Renaissance treatises on good manners, and especially of Castiglione's famous *Book of the Courtier.* Here as elsewhere Aretino exploits the similarities between the terms *cortegiano*, 'courtier', and *cortegiana*, 'courtesan'.

Aretino [1492–1556] was the son of a craftsman, he grew up in the world of popular culture, and to the end of his life he appreciated street singers. He was a friend of Andrea, one of the court fools to Pope Leo X. Like the painters already discussed, he lacked the opportunity for a conventional humanist education in Latin and Greek (it was presumably a more learned friend who drew Lucian to his attention). He came to high culture as an outsider and he rejected some of it as artificial and affected, notably the conventions for the Petrarchan love sonnet and the rules for spoken Italian laid down by Castiglione's friend Pietro Bembo (rules which are mocked in the *Ragionamenti*). Like his friend the artist Giulio Romano, Aretino liked to break rules. In this sense he was a self-conscious 'mannerist' or 'anti-classicist'. Low culture, the culture in which he grew up, was his instrument to subvert high culture, or at least those parts of it which he disliked.

One might say that he drew on the non-Renaissance for the purposes of an anti-Renaissance.

Cultural historians are surely right to shift, as they have been doing, from concern with popular culture in itself to a study of the long process of interaction between learned and popular elements. If we focus on the interaction between high and low, however, we need to recognize the variety or polymorphism of this process. The examples cited in this chapter do not exhaust the range of possibilities, but they may at least be sufficient to suggest the remarkable range of possible relationships between high and low, the uses of popular culture for Renaissance writers, the uses of the Renaissance for ordinary people, and finally, the importance of the 'circular tour' of images and themes, a circular tour in which what returns is never the same as what set out.

6   Jill Kraye **'The transformation of Platonic love in the Italian Renaissance'**

Source: from *Platonism and the English Imagination*, ed. Anna Baldwin and Sarah Hutton, Cambridge University Press, Cambridge, 1994, chapter 8, pp. 76–85.

One of the most serious obstacles to the reception and adoption of Platonism by Italian scholars of the early fifteenth century was the theory of Platonic love. Yet by the middle of the sixteenth century this doctrine had become the most popular element of Platonic philosophy and was playing a significant role in the development of Italian literature. The transformation of Platonic love from an embarrassing liability into a valuable asset was a key episode in the history of Plato's reemergence during the Renaissance as a major influence on Western thought.

Through their knowledge of Greek, Italian humanists became familiar with a wider range of Platonic dialogues than had been known in the Middle Ages; but they did not always like what they read. Among the things they found particularly offensive was the homosexual and pederastic orientation of Platonic love. Leonardo Bruni, the most prominent early translator of Plato, felt obliged to bowdlerise his Latin versions of the *Phaedrus* (1424) and the *Symposium* (1435). In Bruni's translation, for instance, Alcibiades' attempted seduction of Socrates (*Symposium* 215a–22a) becomes a high-minded quest for philosophical enlightenment, with Alcibiades describing himself as 'inflamed with the desire for learning'. Fascinated though he was by the concept of divinely-inspired amatory fury, as expounded in the *Phaedrus*, Bruni was simply unable to accept Plato's explicit treatment of homosexuality.

Bruni's contemporary in Florence, the Camaldulensian monk Ambrogio Traversari, had similar scruples. These led him to delete from his Latin version of Diogenes Laertius' *Lives of the Philosophers* (1433) the homosexual love poems attributed to Plato (III.29–32), including the lascivious epigram about kissing Agathon. Virtually the only humanist to express appreciation of these poems was Antonio Panormita, author of a scabrous verse collection entitled

Hermaphroditus (1425). The 'wanton' and 'effeminate' love poetry which Plato addressed to young men provided Panormita with classical precedent for his own pornographic efforts. Rather than bolstering Panormita's case, however, this claim served to undermine further Plato's moral credibility. And worse was in store.

George of Trebizond published his *Comparatio Aristotelis et Platonis* [*Comparison of Aristotle and Plato*] (1458) as part of a one-man campaign to save Christendom from the irreligious and immoral doctrines of Platonism. He therefore went out of his way to portray Plato as a purveyor of sexual depravity and an unashamed pederast. Aristotle, whom George regarded as the bulwark of Western civilisation, may have been over fond of women, but at least he had not indulged in unnatural vice nor inflamed grown men with a desire for the youthful beauty of adolescent boys. In his lurid account of the *Symposium* – pointedly referred to as *De cupidine* ('On Desire') rather than by its customary title *De amore* ('On Love') – George deliberately distorted the speech of Aristophanes (189c–93d) so as to equate Platonic love with continuous sexual fulfilment, achieved when the two masculine halves of the original male creature were reunited.

The aim of Cardinal Bessarion's *In calumniatorem Platonis* [*Against the Calumniators of Plato*] (1469) was to defend Plato against George's allegations, especially the damaging accusations of sexual misconduct. Bessarion did not deny that Platonic love was essentially homosexual in outlook, but he did insist that Socrates' attachment to young men such as Phaedrus was entirely honorable and chaste, and that it had nothing to do with lust. To reinforce this point, Bessarion stressed the similarity between Plato's concept of love and that praised in the Song of Solomon and the letters of St Paul. He also associated it with the cosmic love described by Dionysius the Areopagite in chapter 4 of *De divinis nominibus* [*The Names of God*], which had God as both its source and its goal. Contrary to what George had claimed, Plato's spokesman in the *Symposium* was not the raffish Aristophanes but the wise and noble Socrates. As for the amatory verses to Agathon and other boys, Bessarion maintained that Diogenes Laertius had wrongly attributed to Plato poems which were actually written by the voluptuary Aristippus of Cyrene.

FICINO

Marsilio Ficino, equally anxious to discredit George of Trebizond's attack on Plato's character, had one of the characters in his *Symposium* commentary (1469) state, with obvious reference to George, that those who dared to slander Plato because 'he indulged too much in love' should be ashamed of themselves, 'for we can never indulge too much or even enough in passions which are decorous, virtuous and divine'. Like Bessarion, Ficino too attempted to defend Socrates' reputation for moral probity. After noting that even in his trial Socrates had not been charged with immoral love affairs, Ficino asked: 'Do you think that if he had polluted himself with a stain so filthy, or rather, if he had not been completely above suspicion of this charge, he would have escaped the venomous tongues of such detractors?' He also followed Bessarion's lead in reassigning to Aristippus the homosexual poems traditionally attributed to Plato.

Ficino likewise took over Bessarion's tactic of associating Platonic discussions of love with those found in the Bible. He maintained, for instance, that the burning desire Socrates says he feels upon glimpsing Charmides' torso (155d) should be interpreted, like the Song of Solomon, allegorically. Ficino, however, carried the Christianisation of Platonic love much further than Bessarion, even managing to impose a Thomist interpretation on the salacious speech of Aristophanes. Another way in which Ficino made Platonic love more palatable was to emphasise its place within an elaborate system of Neoplatonic metaphysics. Relying heavily on Plotinus, *Enneads* I.6 ('On Beauty') and III.5 ('On Love'), Ficino turned Diotima's ladder (*Symposium* 210a–12a) into an ontological ascent from Soul, the hypostasis to which man belonged, through the Angelic Mind and ultimately to the One, the Neoplatonic equivalent of the Christian God.

But Ficino's efforts to accommodate the theory to the values of a fifteenth-century audience did not include concealing or denying – it would hardly have been possible in a commentary on the *Symposium* – that the virtuous love practised by Socrates and promoted by Plato was homoerotic. Indeed, Ficino completely accepted the idea that Platonic love involved a chaste relationship between men, as can be seen from his dedication of the work to his friend Giovanni Cavalcanti. Giving Cavalcanti credit for having inspired the commentary, Ficino stated that although he had learned the definition and nature of love from Plato, 'the power and sway of this god was hidden from me for thirty-four years, until a certain divine hero, beckoning to me with heavenly eyes, demonstrated . . . how powerful love is'. Further corroboration of the strictly masculine context of Ficino's conception of Platonic love comes from a contemporary biography of him, which states that 'he was enraptured by love just as Socrates was, and he used to discuss and debate the subject of love in the Socratic manner with young men'.

Ficino differed from Plato in his outright condemnation of consummated homosexual love, which he described as 'against the order of nature'. But this did not stop him from endorsing Plato's belief that the soul's spiritual ascent to ultimate beauty was fuelled by love between men. The man who follows the lower sort of love, which seeks mere physical 'conception and generation' (*Symposium* 206e), desires, according to Ficino, a 'beautiful woman' to procreate 'handsome offspring'; but the man who pursues the higher and heavenly love, which pertains to the soul rather than the body, desires to teach 'men who are handsome', seeing in their external appearance a reflection of internal virtue. On the heavenly journey, Ficino wrote to Cavalcanti, we should have god as our guide and a male friend as our companion.

One of Ficino's followers, Girolamo Benivieni, was inspired by his *Symposium* commentary to produce an elegant but obscure Italian *canzone*. The poem was itself commented upon, in 1486, by the young Giovanni Pico della Mirandola, who used this form to put forward his own interpretation of Platonic love, which differed in some respects from that of Ficino. But Pico shared Ficino's conviction that while 'earthly love, that is, the love of corporeal beauty, is more properly directed towards women than towards men, the reverse is true of heavenly love', citing as his authority the speech of Pausanias (*Symposium* 180c–5c). In Pico's opinion, sexual love, which led to copulation, was less unseemly with the feminine sex than with the male. Heavenly love, on the other hand, was directed entirely towards the spiritual beauty of the soul or intellect, a beauty that was 'much more perfect in men than in women, as is true of any other attribute'. It was with this 'chaste kind of love', wrote Pico, that Socrates loved not only Alcibiades, but 'almost all of the cleverest and most attractive young men in Athens'. Pico was by no means proof against female beauty – earlier in 1486 he had caused a scandal by attempting to abduct the wife of a government official from Arezzo – but, for him as for Ficino, what prompted the soul to start on its arduous spiritual ascent to God was the masculine beauty 'of Alcibiades, or Phaedrus, or some other attractive body'.

Following in the footsteps of Bessarion and Ficino, Pico linked Platonic love to the Song of Solomon, adding, however, a new dimension by drawing on the Cabbalistic doctrine of the *mors osculi*, 'the death of the kiss'. This death, symbolised by a kiss, occurred 'when the soul, in an intellectual rapture, unites so completely with incorporeal things that it rises above the body and leaves it altogether'. Pico stated that the opening verse of the Song of Solomon: 'Kiss me with the kisses of thy mouth', alluded to this sort of kiss. Even more audaciously, he accepted the Platonic authorship of the poem about kissing Agathon, denied by Bessarion and Ficino, and asserted that it too referred to *mors osculi*.

Through their interpretive skills, Bessarion, Ficino and Pico had removed from Platonic love the immoral connotations which had threatened to hinder the reception of Plato's philosophy by Renaissance thinkers. But while they expunged any taint of carnal homosexuality from Platonic love, they did not question its homoerotic nature, nor its relegation of heterosexual love to an inferior status on the grounds that love between the sexes resulted in physical procreation, whereas love between men led to spiritual perfection. This distinction is clearly enunciated in the writings of Lorenzo de' Medici, the unofficial ruler of Florence and the patron of both Ficino and Pico. In 1474 Lorenzo wrote a series of Platonic love letters to Ficino, demonstrating that he had thoroughly absorbed the lessons taught in his *Symposium* commentary. Lorenzo was well aware that the spiritual love which he felt for Ficino was more exalted than the human love, directed towards women, which he celebrated in his poetry. In his *Comento* on his own poems, Lorenzo stated that they were not concerned with the love praised by Plato, which is 'the means for all things to find their perfection and to rest ultimately in supreme beauty, that is, in God'. His poetry dealt instead with a love, which, although not the supreme good, was nevertheless good in itself and natural, because it was necessary for the propagation of the species. Yet despite his recognition of the difference between the two sorts of love, Lorenzo allowed himself to borrow certain Platonic themes from both Ficino and Pico, using them, alongside motifs taken from Ovid, Petrarch and the *Stil nuovo* [New Style] poets, to elaborate the story of his love affair with his mistress.

BEMBO

Lorenzo's appropriation of the language of Platonic love to describe some aspects of the romance between a man and a woman prepared the way for works such as Pietro Bembo's *Gli Asolani* [*The Lovers of Asolo*] (1505), in which both human and divine love were presented as unequivocally heterosexual. In this dialogue, set in the court of Asolo, a group of men and women gather together to converse on the subject of love. The inclusion of women is defended on the grounds that they 'as well as men have minds' and therefore have the right to seek knowledge of 'what one ought to flee from or pursue'; the love being discussed is clearly as relevant to them as the men in the group. Lavinello, attempting to strike a balance between the attack on love by Perottino and the overpraise of it by Gismondo, portrays an elevated, spiritual love, which obviously derives from the Platonic theory. But here, unlike previous treatments, women are envisaged as the object of Platonic love:

> Who can fail to see that if I love some gallant, gentle lady, and love her rather for her wit, integrity, good breeding, grace, and other qualities than for her bodily attractions, and love those attractions not for themselves but as adornments of her mind – who can fail to see my love is good because the object of my love is likewise good?

Most of the central ideas set out in Ficino's *Symposium* commentary are echoed by Bembo, but he transforms the latter's abstract, philosophical terminology into vivid, poetic metaphors. Ficino's doctrine that the beauty which provokes love can be perceived by the eyes and the ears alone of the five senses is expressed by Bembo through an image of love spreading and beating its wings: 'And on its flight two senses guide it: hearing, which leads it to the mind's attractions, and sight which turns it to the body's'. While Ficino – and, for that matter, Plato (*Symposium* 201d) – provided only a perfunctory description of Diotima, Bembo carefully sets the scene for Lavinello's encounter with his guide to the mysteries of love: from a little grove on a charming mountaintop, surrounded by silvan quietude, emerges 'a solitary figure, a bearded white-haired man clothed in material like the bark of the young oaks surrounding him'. Although the message this hermit conveys is taken from Ficino, he speaks straightforwardly, avoiding any overtly philosophical language. Instead of erudite discourse on the Neoplatonic hypostases [i.e. enduring essences underneath externals], the hermit explains to Lavinello that 'beyond this sensible, material world . . . there lies another world which is neither material nor evident to sense, but completely separate from this and pure . . . a world divine, intelligent and full of light'. The aged hermit tells Lavinello that he now regards the sensual delights which he desired in his youth in the same light as a man, restored to health, might regard his fevered fancies. It is only when we grow older, he says, that 'our better part, namely the soul' is able to rule our worse part, the body, and that our reason is able to control our senses. For Bessarion, Ficino and Pico, there was a complete separation between physical love, which had women as its object, and spiritual love, which was shared between men. By contrast, Bembo's version of Platonic love is unified and evolutionary, with male-female relationships gradually progressing, as one grows older, from a sexual to a spiritual plane.

CASTIGLIONE

Although *Gli Asolani* [*The Lovers of Asolo*] was widely read and influential, the new style of Platonic love formulated by Bembo reached its largest audience when his friend Baldesar Castiglione chose to cast him as one of the main characters in his hugely popular *Il libro del cortegiano* [*The Book of the Courtier*] (1528). Castiglione sets out a vision of the perfect courtier and uses Bembo's speech, which is the culmination of the book, to describe what his attitude towards love should be. As in *Gli Asolani*, there is a progression from the sensual love of youth to the spiritual love of old age, both directed exclusively towards women. Moreover, Plato's pederastic ideal of an older and wiser man educating his young lover in virtue is given a novel heterosexual twist by Castiglione's Bembo, who states that the courtier should be at pains to keep his lady 'from going astray and by his wise precepts and admonishments always seek to make her modest, temperate and truly chaste'. Much of the philosophical content of the speech is taken over from Ficino, but Castiglione gives these doctrines even more literary embellishment than Bembo had done. The Ficinian doctrine that beauty can be perceived only through sight and hearing becomes, in Castiglione, an admonition to the lover to 'enjoy with his eyes the radiance, the grace, the loving ardour, the smiles, the mannerisms and all the other agreeable adornments of the woman he loves' and to 'use his hearing to enjoy the sweetness of her voice, the modulation of her words and, if she is a musician, the music she plays'. Castiglione carried on the trend, initiated by Bessarion, of giving Platonic love a strongly religious colouring. He has Bembo end his speech with a hymn, which is full of Biblical imagery, and in which love is identified with the 'searing power of contemplation' that ravished the souls of 'ancient Fathers', taking them from their bodies and uniting them with God. And from Pico, Castiglione takes the idea that the Song of Solomon refers to 'the death of the kiss'; but while he too alludes to the poem about kissing Agathon, unlike Pico he does not name the male dedicatee of these verses.

   Where Castiglione differs from all his predecessors is in the scepticism about Platonic love which he permits his characters to voice. Morello complains that he cannot understand the sort of love described by Bembo because in his view 'to possess the beauty he praises so much without the body is a fantasy'. Morello also does not believe that beauty is always as good as Bembo says, for he remembers 'having seen many beautiful women who were evil, cruel and spiteful . . . beauty makes them proud, and pride makes them cruel'. Bembo firmly denies that this is so and, dutifully toeing the Platonic line, affirms that 'one cannot have beauty without goodness' since 'outward beauty is a true sign of inner goodness'. None the less, by introducing the down-to-earth objections of Morello, Castiglione raises doubts about the extreme idealism of the Platonic theory.

The combination of literary skill and psychological insight which Castiglione brought to the topic of Platonic love was the high point of the tradition. Now that Platonic love was safely in the heterosexual camp, its themes were taken up in a stream of *trattati d'amore* (treatises on love). The inevitable price of such popularity was a drastic reduction in philosophical content and an increasing staleness, as once lively motifs became hackneyed through continual repetition. A notable exception to this dreary picture is the *Dialoghi d'amore* [*Dialogues, on Love*] of Leone Ebreo, written around 1501–2, but not published until 1535. Leone, a Portuguese-Jewish physician who emigrated to Italy after 1492, put forward his ideas on love in the form of a playful, but extremely erudite, conversation between the female Sofia (wisdom) and her male admirer, Filone (love). From the opening lines, Sofia's flirtatious teasing of the besotted Filone leaves the reader in no doubt as to the heterosexual nature of the love they speak about. Like other writers on Platonic love, Leone pointed out its compatibility with the tenets of religion: but, in his case, the religion was Judaism rather than Christianity. Again and again he noted that Plato's ideas derived from Moses and the Cabbalists: Aristophanes' myth of the androgyne, for instance, turned out to be nothing more than the Genesis account of the creation of Adam and Eve, amplified and polished 'after the manner of Greek oratory'.

One of the last Italian Platonic love treatises was Giordano Bruno's *Eroici furori* [*Heroic frenzies*] (1585), written during his sojourn in England. In some respects this work – a series of sonnets written and commented on by Bruno – was quite conventional. There was the by now obligatory reference to the Song of Solomon, 'which under the guise of lovers and ordinary passions contains . . . divine and heroic frenzies, as the mystics and cabalistic doctors interpret it'. And in the dedication to Sir Philip Sidney, Bruno, like most authors of such treatises, attacked sensual love, calling it 'witless, stupid and odiferous foulness . . . worthy of pity and laughter'. But Bruno's polemic took an unexpected turn towards misogyny: 'and all this for those eyes, those cheeks, for that breast . . . that scourge, that disgust, that stink, that tomb, that latrine, that menstruum, that carrion, that quartan ague, that distortion of nature, which with . . . a shadow, a phantasm, a dream, a Circian enchantment put to the service of generation, deceives us as a species of beauty'. This contempt for women was philosophically, not psychologically, motivated. Throughout the *Eroici furori* [*Heroic frenzies*], Bruno deliberately subverts the metaphors of love poetry, bending them to his own metaphysical purposes. Thus, for him, female beauty is a symbol of the allure of the perceptible world; by downgrading it, he was indicating the immeasurable distance between sensible and intelligible beauty, between physical desire and heroic love – man's doomed but noble desire to understand the infinity of God. His aim was to recover the profound philosophical significance which Platonic love had had for Ficino and Pico, not to return to their homoerotic conception of it. That conception had been superseded by a notion of Platonic love which was better suited to the social, cultural and literary concerns of the Renaissance: a non-sexual, spiritually uplifting love between the sexes.

7   Letizia Panizza '**Valla's *De voluptate ac de vero bono* [*Of the True and False Good*] and Erasmus' *Stultitiae Laus* [*In Praise of Folly*]: Renewing Christian Ethics'**[1]

Source: from Erasmus of Rotterdam Society Yearbook 15, 1995, pp. 1–25.

In making comparisons and contrasts, one needs a fixed point of reference. In this Phillips lecture for the Erasmus of Rotterdam Society, the fixed point is of course Erasmus. I must confess, however, that I come to Erasmus as an outsider, from fifteenth-century Italian humanism. While this may put me at a disadvantage, it also gives me a very different perspective on Erasmus. Features are highlighted that would not be so noticeable were one merely moving back from Erasmus to Valla or to a general study of Erasmian sources. In this lecture, furthermore, I shall be limiting my focus to only two works of these authors: Valla's dialogue on pleasure, and Erasmus' praise by a personified Folly of herself. What has struck me on this journey has been a desire to reform ethics by means of the new rhetorical and philological skills developed by Italian humanists; a dislike for scholastic theology as well as for that other major discipline in medieval universities, canon law; and a resolve to return to a simplified teaching, derived from the New Testament, about a comprehensible, attractive, and coherent ethical life for clergy and laity alike.

Studies of Erasmus' interest in Valla are not new; one could easily conclude from the ample literature that there was nothing left to say. From an early age (Valla died in 1457, a decade before Erasmus' birth) Erasmus was impressed by Valla, extensively and profoundly. In the 1991 Bainton Lecture, 'Erasmus and Valla: The Dynamics of a Relationship', now printed in this *Yearbook* for 1992, Richard Schoeck has brought together the already considerable research, going back to Preserved Smith's biography of 1923, about just what Erasmus gained from his sympathetic reading of Valla. Schoeck provides ample proof of Erasmus' assimilation of Valla's reforms of the Latin language (of grammar, rhetoric, and dialectic, and of methods of textual analysis) on the one hand, and his equally radical reform of New Testament studies on the other. Erasmus did not introduce Valla to the Low Countries; he drew on and greatly augmented an admiration for Valla that was already there. Even before Erasmus' mid-life stay in Italy from 1506 to 1509, he had already adapted Valla's *Elegantiae* [*Refinements*], published Valla's *Collatio Novi Testamenti* [*Collation of the New Testament*], and studied Valla's *Dialecticae Disputationes* [*Dialectical Disputations*]. He was also acquainted with Valla's key ethical work, the dialogue *De voluptate ac de vero bono* [*Of the True and False Good*], which he may have been instrumental in getting printed.

What can bear further examination is the specific role Valla's *De voluptate* played in determining the form and content of Erasmus' *Praise of Folly*, composed right after Erasmus left Italy in 1509. Similarities have been remarked (mainly to do with Epicurean themes, such as the praise of pleasure). But as far as I can tell, there has been no close textual comparison of the two, noting in detail not just the criticism and rejection of Stoic elements, and the defense of

Epicurean ones, but also the contrast of these with Christian values. Some other minor pieces of Erasmus' have been said to display *De voluptate*'s inspiration. But while *De contemptu mundi* [*on Scorn for the World*] and the colloquy *Epicureus* [*The Epicurean*] are sympathetic to Epicurean pleasure, they are not tied specifically to Valla's *De voluptate* in the way that *Praise of Folly* is. There may also be more affinities between Valla's *De libero arbitrio* [*On Free Will*] and Erasmus' diatribe on the same subject than have been recorded. Valla meant *De libero arbitrio* to complete and complement the ethical discussions in *De voluptate*. Might not Erasmus have gained at least a few insights from Valla? In the early version of his *Dialecticae disputationes*, in the chapter to do with the virtues, Valla had even boldly asserted: 'Indeed, together with Christ I both affirm and believe without reservation that good works are sufficient for eternal life.' If that was so, then ethics was central to salvation.

A grasp of the ethical issues of Valla's dialogue should make more apparent both the nature and the significance of Erasmus' borrowings. For Valla, the question that needed addressing most of all was, Why be ethical? – a question about the role of motivation in making ethical choices. Neither exclusive ancient philosophies by themselves – the humanist preference – nor a gloomy, pessimistic Christian devotion emphasizing a purposeless renunciation, punishment and hell could supply a satisfactory answer. Motivation, Valla saw, presupposes that the ethical goal, the *bonum* [good], is both desirable and attainable; otherwise, who would strive for it? who would be moved by it? Valla perceived the need for reviving a Christian ethics that would offer people happiness, if not in this life, then certainly in the next.

Insistence on motivation went hand in hand with a concern on Valla's part that ethics should be for all, on the grounds that the Christian *evangelium* [gospel] preached salvation for all (in contrast again not only with pagan philosophies, directed at a few initiates, but also with much contemporary preaching about few being saved and many damned). The most important Christian virtue, Valla recognized, was charity [i.e. love], which all can practice, and which is the main reason for the superiority of New Testament ethics over Old Testament and pagan ones. Precisely because founded on charity, which requires sharing with others, the Christian ethical life is a communal not a solitary one. Valla went so far as to condemn the contemplative religious ideal as antisocial and un-Christian. His understanding of charity also lay at the root of his fierce denunciation of the self-claimed moral superiority of religious orders, and of his denial of established distinctions between clergy and laity based on the intrinsic moral superiority of one state of life over the other. All three 'states of life' – virginity or celibacy, marriage, and widowhood – could be equally meritorious.

An attractive ethics went hand in hand also with cleaning up God's image, so to speak, among contemporary believers. If the vast majority of the human race is doomed to perdition because it is unable to be good, questions arise about the creation of a human nature inclined to evil, and therefore about the Creator himself. And if God is presented as behaving like a capricious, implacable father/tyrant who created the human race only then to torment and destroy it, how can be also be good, just and loving? Valla spends much time defending the goodness of nature and human nature, including the senses and the body, as a way of restoring confidence in a good Creator.

Finally, Valla took as axiomatic that there could be no ethics without free will, for if everybody had some measure of choice, then all could perform good works and be saved. Free will, furthermore, was part of our human nature, not a supernatural gift. It could be persuaded, instructed, and educated to pursue one course of action rather than another – hence the supreme importance of reforming the art of preaching according to classical rhetoric. With free will, Christians could practice the various acts of charity so necessary to distinguish them from pagans.

VALLA'S 'DE VOLUPTATE' [OF THE TRUE AND FALSE GOOD] AND ETHICAL REFORM

Valla chose to argue about ethics and motivation by means of a dialogue with many voices, in which Stoic ideals were cast down and Epicurean ones raised up. For Valla to have reversed the usual position of these two classical sects, and in particular to praise Epicurean pleasure as the only natural ethical goal, represented at best paradoxical, at worst scandalous, attitudes to his contemporary fifteenth-century readers. The Stoics were almost universally admired by Christians for their love of righteousness for its own sake (called *honestum*), and their hatred of *voluptas* (meaning base sense pleasures only) and *stultitia* (the madness of those abdicating reason for a life of the senses). The Epicureans were almost universally despised for their materialism (they denied the immortality of the soul and a purposeful order in nature) and alleged crass hedonism. Indeed, the goals of the two sects were drastically opposed, and expressed by the mutually exclusive opposites *virtus* and *voluptas* – one noble, the other base. *Voluptas*, furthermore, was indistinguishable both from madness (*stultitia*) and vice.

Yet Valla proclaimed that he would call his treatise *De voluptate*, 'a pleasant not odious title, rather than *De vero bono* . . . for throughout this work I dispute about the true good, which is the same as pleasure.' Imagining an objection, Valla retorts: 'Indeed, I myself state and affirm, and affirm again that my thesis is this – there is nothing else besides this good.'

By means of speakers who themselves play roles, Valla did far more than discuss classical ethics. His speakers are not genuine attackers or upholders of Stoic and Epicurean morals; their allegiance is to Christianity (as Dame Folly's is as well). The 'Stoic' in particular gives an exaggerated, distorted and inconsistent account of his sect (he attacks nature as harmful to the human race, while genuine Stoic doctrine preaches theories of divine providence), which nevertheless captures contemporary tendencies. Neither is the 'Epicurean' authentic (as with Erasmus, Epicurean denial of immortality is temporarily ignored). Neither Valla nor Erasmus was trying to 'revive' pagan philosophies *in toto*. Valla was attacking contemporary Christians who imagined that dour Stoic asceticism and the Christian way of life were one and the same thing. Their illusion was fed, as Valla understood, first by a long tradition within the church of a holy alliance between the two (especially between Seneca and St. Paul) going back to St. Jerome himself; and second, by Petrarch and later humanists who elaborated a renewed

Christian ethics based on Roman Stoicism, especially Seneca. In Valla's own life-time, the legend of Seneca's supposed secret conversion to Christianity flourished. Valla was the first to denounce as a fraud the St. Paul–Seneca correspondence that supported the conversion; and Erasmus followed suit in the next century in his editions of Seneca. Erasmus' targets, however, were not quite the same as Valla's. While both maintained that a renewed Christian ethics must be founded on Scripture, Erasmus saw his contemporary university scholastics as pompous, hypocritical, self-sufficient 'Stoics' who turned people away from a Christian life; but he did not include humanists.

The Christian speaker in book 3 reveals Valla's new message: Christianity offers the best motivation for ethical behavior, promising a reward that everyone wants, and that everyone has the power to win, namely pleasure – or any other synonym like happiness, paradise, charity, enjoyment. Righteousness is a means to an end. 'For us,' specifies the Christian speaker, 'the [Stoic] *honestum* is not to be sought for its own sake, nor for the sake of earthly advantages, but because it is a step towards that beatitude which our spirit or soul, delivered from its mortal body, enjoys with its creator from whom it came forth.' Supremely confident of his philological skills, and in opposition to medieval theology, Valla abolished all distinction between the experience of physical and spiritual pleasures, represented by the words *voluptas* on the one hand and *delectatio* [pleasure] and *beatitudo* [happiness] on the other. Scripture was his proof:

> Who doubts that there is any better name for *beatitudo* than *voluptas*? I find the latter term both in Genesis [2:18]: 'A Paradise of pleasure,' and in Ezekiel [31:9]: 'The fruit and tree of pleasure,' and likewise whenever divine blessings are spoken of. And in the Psalms [36:8] as well: 'You will give them to drink from pleasure's torrent,' [. . .]

Valla draws as well on the New Testament, especially St. Paul's Epistles, to stress that the Christian ethical life, lived in the hope of good things to come, is full of joy. Therefore, the Christian speaker concludes, 'Nothing is done rightly without pleasure, nor is there any merit for those who fight in the army of the Lord patiently but not gladly. It is said: "The Lord loves a cheerful giver" [2 Cor. 9:7]; and elsewhere: "Rejoice in the Lord" [Ps. 37:4] . . . which can also be translated as "Take pleasure in the Lord."'

Christians who take the Stoic 'virtue for its own sake' as a maxim, and take as a model the self-sufficient Stoic sage who must have all the virtues or none, stand condemned by Scripture and argument. The first 'Stoic' speaker can thus deliver a mock eulogy of the Stoic good, showing it to be ridiculous, repulsive, unnatural, and full of contradictions – just as Dame Folly will do. Stoic ethics is said to be so difficult to follow that nobody can be ethical. The speaker gloomily bemoans the depravity of Nature herself inclining mankind more to vice – i.e. pleasure – than to harsh virtue. In sheer number, furthermore, the vices outweigh the virtues (a parody of the Stoic association of all pleasure with vice, and their view that unless you had all the virtues you had none). [. . .]

One of the most unusual features of Valla's ethics, taking up the bulk of the 'Epicurean' speech in book 2, is the replacement of Aristotelian virtue as a mean between two extremes with single virtues opposing single vices: justice opposed to injustice, chastity to unchastity, fortitude to cowardice and so on. With an equal number of virtues and vices, the moral scales are not weighed against the human race. Valla also denies that there *are* Stoic virtues. Roman heroes, held up as *exempla* of Stoic fortitude, did not perform great deeds 'for their own sake.' Base, self-seeking and hypocritical, they craved glory, which is a kind of pleasure. Roman justice, praised by Cicero, did not really exist. Prudence is not even a virtue, but a form of practical knowledge based on experience. As for Stoic temperance and renunciation, that too was a fiction.

Both the 'Epicurean' and the Christian spokesmen attack the Stoics for depriving human beings of their emotions. 'They frequently denounce nature and strive to reform her,' points out the 'Epicurean,' 'as with the disturbances and emotions of the soul, which they wish to uproot, and they argue that there's nobody who isn't out of his mind, mad – and whatever else that's more insulting.' Stoic *apatheia*, freedom from emotional disturbance, was especially important for the *sapiens*, the Stoic sage, whose qualities – he was aloof, morally self-sufficient, emotionally detached – had become absorbed into descriptions of the contemplative; and through Petrarch, also constituted the Christian scholar and humanist. The 'Stoic' spokesman's boast that the contemplative life made men divine was for Valla, and later Erasmus, a denial of Christian love of neighbor, and of charity's supremacy as the only virtue that mattered.

The 'Epicurean' parodies the series of rhetorical questions in Aristotle about the absurdity of imagining the gods to be performing acts of virtue rather than merely contemplating (*Nicom. Ethics* 10.8.1178b) with a contrary set of rhetorical questions. What is the value in becoming like gods who are no more than tree trunks? who show no love or feeling for one another? who might as well be asleep? These are thoughts unworthy of a brutish one-eyed Cyclops, let alone a philosopher, he mocks, and especially Aristotle, who encourages us to imitate such gods while at the same time declaring humans to be political animals. 'If I had to choose one of the two lives [of action or contemplation] for the gods,' concludes the 'Epicurean,' 'I would prefer to represent them acting rather than contemplating, so that first of all they might celebrate their assembly and ranks, keep the laws, as it were, and behave like citizens holding office': in other words, like busy committee members of the medieval Italian city-state republics!

Valla's dynamic concept of Christian virtue leads to a relentless undermining of the sense of moral superiority that contemplative religious orders, as well as scholastic philosophers and theologians, liked to claim for themselves. Everybody, on the other hand, can practice charity, the cornerstone for a renewed Christian ethics, equated with *fortitudo* [moral courage] in this life – the one virtue to which the four Stoic cardinal virtues had been reduced by the 'Epicurean,' though understood now in a different sense – and with *voluptas* in the next. Pauline quotations devastate Stoic (and Christian neo-Stoic) pretensions about virtue for its own sake and the wise man's imperturbability, about hypocritical preaching of poverty and renunciation, and contempt for the masses. 'Those who have lacked faith, hope and charity have not had any virtue,' declares the Christian speaker. And without charity, the mistress of all the virtues, even if someone distributes all his goods among the poor, and gives his body over to be burned – as St. Paul points out–it profits him nothing. The words seem tailormade not only for [. . .] Stoic misanthropic poverty, [. . .] but also for an entire medieval ascetic tradition of ethics with no *voluptas*. Even the pleasure of Paradise is increased by sharing with others. Neither God nor nature, God's creation, wished humans to be solitary or self-sufficient in doing good. From the very beginning, God said: 'It is not good for man to be alone; I will make him a help like himself (*adiuto-rium simile sibi*)' (Gen. 2:18). With great audacity, contradicting the traditional interpretation of *adiutorium* [help mate] as a female subordinate, Valla has his Christian interlocutor gloss: 'Although this was said about the woman, it must be understood also about the man. For just as a wife is a help to her husband, so is the husband to his wife, and likewise other people to each other – this is the nature of charity.' Once again, an ethical life is for all, regardless of state in life, education or sex.

ERASMUS' 'STULTITIAE LAUS' [IN PRAISE OF FOLLY] AND VALLA'S 'DE VOLUPTATE' [OF THE TRUE AND FALSE GOOD]

While the Greek title, *Encomium Moriae*, punning on Thomas More's name, binds Erasmus' paradoxical eulogy to the two friends' love of the Greek master of the genre, Lucian, the Latin title, *Stultitiae laus*, makes clearer the ties with Stoic madness, delirium and folly – and thence to Valla. Erasmus' impersonation of Lady Folly (an example of high rhetorical artifice typical of the declamation [. . .] has never ceased to delight but also to perplex readers since it first appeared. In the Prefatory Letter to More the appeal to Lucian and Apuleius, to the tradi-tion of mock eulogy and the ambiguities of 'serious joking' [. . .] put us on guard: there is much more than meets the eye. By means of *Stultitia* disarmingly per-sonified, Erasmus holds up to ridicule the proud, self-satisfied 'sages' of early 16th-century northern Europe.

   If Erasmus is careful about the matching of light style and serious but pleasant content, so had Valla been. In his proemium [introduction], Valla had promised a mixture of 'some amusing features, and if I may say so, almost licen-tious ones.' The praise of pleasure required an appropriate style, 'one that was more pleasant and cheerful' rather than 'sad and harsh,' Valla had specified. Erasmus, under the inspiration of Lucian, takes the serious jesting even further: 'For just as there is nothing more amusing than to treat serious matters in a light-hearted way, so there is nothing more entertaining than to treat amusing matters in such a way that one seems to be nothing less than a light-hearted person oneself!'

   The continual anti-Stoic, and in particular anti-Seneca strand weaving its way through Erasmus' declamation (Seneca is explicitly named at least ten times), with a corresponding pro-Epicurean strand, is difficult to make sense of without Valla. Erasmus' praise of *stultitia*, to my mind, resembles in particular the 'Epicurean's' praise of *voluptas* in the second part of book 1 in Valla's dialogue. The very words are interchangeable in Stoic moral philosophy, and both are anathema, in that those who follow pleasure are mad, and the mad, bestial life of sense pleasure is diametrically opposed to Stoic reason and virtue.

The parodoxical and polemical praise of *voluptas* and *stultitia* by Erasmus, in opposition to the goals of *honestum* and *sapientia* [wisdom] admired by the learned, follows a strategy initiated by Valla. Valla had already linked the two despised goals: 'Not only do we prefer the Epicureans, wretched and contemptible men, to the custodians of *honestum*, but we will also prove that these very followers of *wisdom* have pursued not virtue but virtue's shadow, not righteousness but vanity, not duty but vice, *not wisdom but madness* – and that they would have been better if they had given themselves over to *pleasure*, if they didn't do just that!' (emphasis mine). Even more, Erasmus follows another semantic strategy originating with Valla, that of continually playing on the double senses and ambiguities of the four terms, so that we move from pagan to sometimes antithetical Christian meanings.

Lady Folly loves exposing Stoic hypocrisy, just as Valla had done before. The cream of society and the academics, who despise her for praising her own stupidity, shamelessly seek flattery from others. 'And yet not even these Stoics spurn pleasure,' Folly declares as if fresh from reading Valla, 'although they carefully dissemble and denounce it among the crowd with a thousand reproaches, so that, not surprisingly, they themselves may enjoy it all the more having deterred others.' 'Unless you include pleasure, which is the seasoning of *stultitiae*,' she spells out, 'what part of life is not sad, gloomy, unappealing, boring and irksome?'

Lady Folly and pleasure, just as the Stoics would have it, are twin sisters; praise one and you praise the other. *Stultitia* is surrounded by none but the most pleasurable companions (including Pleasure personified): Self-satisfaction, Flattery, Oblivion, Wantonness, and Intemperance. Her very parents are Pluto, the underworld god of affluence, and a beautiful young nymph – parents who would do for pleasure as well. Venus, the very personification of sexual pleasure (forever denounced in Cicero's and Seneca's Stoic moral philosophy), is nothing without Folly, we are told. Rounding on all Stoic recommendations of abstinence from *voluptas* – part of Folly's continual jibes at 'unnatural' Stoics – she dismisses poverty, ugliness, old age, and harsh virtue from her company. In their place are (Epicurean) *hedone* (the Greek word for *voluptas*), madness, wantonness, intemperance, and good fortune. For Seneca, ignorance, moral turpitude, and pleasure extinguished the moral spark in the human race. But Folly persuades us that these so-called defects are advantages because natural. Even the solemn Stoics, she points out, who think of themselves as next to the gods, must 'cast aside their ironclad dogmas, and rave and become silly for a while' if they want to reproduce themselves. The sage may condemn natural pleasures, but she insists, 'It's me, me, I say, that the sage will have to summon if he wishes to become a father!'

Folly reminds her audience that laughter, merriment, festivity, and play are hers by right. Since Nature, pleasure, and herself are all one, the traditional union of Stoic wisdom (or *honestum*) and *Natura* is thereby rejected. But Valla's 'Epicurean,' defending nature and hence natural feelings and instincts, had already accused the Stoics of ingratitude, of departing from the customs of normal social life, and of condemning laughter, that peculiarly human quality.

Folly attacks the four Stoic virtues of temperance, fortitude, justice and prudence, just as the Epicurean spokesman had done in book 2 of Valla's dialogue, and for the same underlying reason: they have never been pursued 'for their own sake,' but have been sought for satisfaction, self-interest, one's advantage, or glory – all of them kinds of pleasure. Folly, furthermore, takes over one of Valla's most original points about the number of Stoic vices, passions, defects, and faults far exceeding the virtues, with the consequence that the human race can never be ethical. For Folly, this is what it means to be human; for Jupiter himself 'has bestowed upon us far more emotion than reason.' Indeed, reason is confined to a tiny corner of our brain while the passions are all over, so numerous as to rule us almost entirely. [. . .]

Those who reject Nature's gifts, whether beauty, youth, health and the like, show contempt for Nature and hatred for themselves, Folly reveals. They regard Nature not as a good parent but as a stepmother – the same phrase as Valla's 'Stoic' speaker, and another clue to Erasmus' close reading – who has placed evil within them so that they prefer another condition to their own. 'Desire to be what you are,' also the gist of Valla's message as delivered by the 'Epicurean,' is now Folly's advice to sour misanthropes. Among such antisocial people how can there be friendship, argued by both Cicero and Seneca as the fruit of Stoic virtue and wisdom? 'It either is not formed at all among those gods, the sages, or turns out to be gloomy and unpleasant, and then only among the few.' Friendship belongs to the followers of laughter and pleasure.

The above remarks undermine Stoic temperance and ascetic abstinence; Valla's speakers had also found the other Stoic virtues, fortitude and prudence, wanting. Valla's 'Epicurean' had attacked Stoic military and civic heroes who, far from exercising fortitude 'for its own sake,' desired glory, a form of *voluptas*, and their own self-interest, or *utile* [benefit]. The suicides Cato and Lucretia and the conquerer Scipio Africanus feared more their own dishonor and are not, therefore, *exempla* [examples] of fortitude. [. . .]

Folly too is not be outdone in the general debunking, and she has her lists of heroic Romans resembling Valla's. [. . .] They were unfit for leadership as they could not share their life with ordinary men and women, converse with others, or conduct everyday activities. Better for each and every Stoic misanthrope to be banished to some desert to enjoy his wisdom all by himself!

Valla had tied glory not to fortitude but to pleasure. Folly places glory firmly under *her own* dominion, and even asserts herself as its parent. From her, not from Stoic fortitude, 'sprang all the great deeds of mighty heroes which the writings of so many eloquent men have praised to the skies. Folly is the one who has brought forth cities. By her are empires, legal institutions, religion, policy, and public laws maintained; neither is human life anything other than Folly's toy.' And as for the world of scholarship and learning – Erasmus engages in one of his delightful pieces of self-mockery – it owes its existence to nothing else but 'a thirst for glory. The most truly foolish men have thought to purchase I don't know what sort of fame for themselves (there can be nothing more futile) with

their long night vigils, and their tormented labors.' Thus motivation for the performance of Stoic virtue is to be found neither in 'virtue for its own sake,' nor
glory, an empty word, but in pleasure.

Valla had even removed prudence from the virtues because he deemed it a kind
of knowledge. Erasmus takes up precisely this point with absurd effect: our Lady
Folly, *Stultitia* (which can mean crass stupidity and ignorance), brings prudence
into her family! [. . .] The possibility of doing good is thus brought within ordinary people's reach. Prudence depends on experience, Folly asserts, which the
sage doesn't have. Stoic contempt for the man of affairs, the *occupatus*, so manifest in Seneca and Petrarch, is thus also overturned. It is the fool, now identified
with the ordinary man and woman, who 'gathers the fruit, unless I am mistaken,
of true prudence by going forth and taking risks in society's affairs.' [. . .]

Folly quotes approvingly St. Paul's words stating that 'God has chosen the
foolish things (*stulta*) of this world . . . so that the world might be saved by foolishness, since it could not be restored by wisdom.' Therefore, Folly explains, children, old men, women, and fools are the most devout in a Christian ethics. The
very founders of the Christian religion were plain, simple people, and 'the bit-
terest enemies of learning.' The separation of ethics from erudition could not be
more complete, but as in Valla, it was done by opposing St. Paul to the Stoics.
[. . .]

Valla's Christian speaker had homed in on markedly inhuman and unchristian
aspects of Stoic doctrine: the *apatheia* or emotional impassibility of the sage, his
uprooting of all feeling, and his rejection of human infirmities. Lady Folly does
exactly the same, but in my opinion Erasmus more than Valla develops the
Pauline paradox of Christian folly (charity, humility, self-effacement, and gen-
tleness) being the highest wisdom. She also pokes more fun than Valla at the traditional Stoic paradoxes. As Folly puts it: 'If some wise man, dropped for me
from heaven as it were, were to rise up and shout out that this creature whom
all men accept as a god and master is not even a man, that like beasts he is driven
by his passions and is a slave of the worst sort, for he willingly serves so many
and such sordid masters . . . what else might he have done, I ask you, than seem
to all to be out of his mind, a madman?' The passage reverses Stoic paradoxes
about the wise (and virtuous) Stoic sage to show that he is not wise but mad,
and that the rest of humankind, forever damned as *stulti* [fools] because given to
voluptates [pleasures], is wise. True wisdom or prudence means living as a mortal
among mortals: 'As nothing is more stupid than a wisdom turned the wrong way
around, so nothing is more imprudent than a misguided prudence,' sums up
Lady Folly, showing off not just a flourish of very clever rhetorical antitheses, but
also a parody of precisely the Stoic paradox. [. . .]

The Christian [. . .] is glad to acknowledge his infirmities in keeping with the
'new' virtue of humility, unheard of in antiquity. Valla's preacher had adopted the
Pauline theme of boasting of weakness, a good antidote to arrogant Stoic self-
satisfaction. Lady Folly insists that she, not false wisdom, can alleviate our mis-
eries and burdens by spreading honey-like *voluptates* in life and stimulating the
hope of good things to come. A pleasurable goal, supplying motivation for living,
is part of a truly natural ethics, and just the opposite of the Stoic one suppress-

ing emotions, vituperating human nature, and despising natural limitations. Ordinary human activities – folly for the Stoic – are also natural. In fact, 'The happiest people are farthest removed from dealings with the arts and sciences, and follow nature alone as their leader,' says Folly, once again reversing Stoic doctrine about only the wise man being happy and virtuous. The wise are doubly fools because, 'forgetting that they were born into the human condition, they strive to lead the lives of immortal gods, and like the giants of old wage war on nature with academic disciplines for war engines.' [. . .]

The two humanists' interpretation of contemporary 'Stoic' targets shows interesting variations. Valla had aimed his sarcasm at contemporaries who preferred mainly Stoic but also Aristotelian pagan ethics to Christian humility and charity. 'What else is this, I ask, than to imagine that Christ has come in vain, indeed to confess that he has not come at all!' Folly savagely attacks scholastic logicians and dialecticians, university authorities, who are consumed with their logic-chopping [. . .] Erasmus is not, of course, preaching an unlearned or anti-intellectual morality in exalting folly and madness. 'That great doctor of the Gentiles,' explains Folly, 'not unwillingly called himself foolish.' The reason was not ignorance; Paul was concerned 'lest his words offend his listeners' ears as rather arrogant, and so forearmed himself with the pretext of folly – "I speak as one not at all wise" – because he knew that it was the privilege only of fools to speak the truth without giving offence.' [. . .]

A small detail, inserted by Erasmus in his diatribe against the falsely-wise, which had also been employed by Valla, illustrates how closely Erasmus sometimes adapts the Italian humanist. Both authors make use of Christ's long invective against the doctors of the old law (Matt. 23:13–33), 'Woe to you, scribes and Pharisees,' where they are accused of pedantry, hypocrisy, legalism, vanity, and greed; they are 'whitened sepulchers,' both blind and stupid. [. . .] All are declared heretics, followers of bankrupt moral systems.

Erasmus has Stultitia apply Christ's condemnation of the scribes and Pharisees and doctors of the law [. . .] to the self-appointed sages of his day, at the very end of a sarcastic invective against just about every form of theologian (Realists, Nominalists, Thomists, Albertists, Occamists, Scotists), or religious order (Franciscans, Bernardines, Benedictines, Augustinians, Colettines), or professional office (preacher, priest, teacher, professor, judge or lawyer). All are charlatans, condemned by Paul, and now by Christ, who has hidden the mystery of salvation from the wise (*sapientes*) and revealed it to fools (*stulti*): 'Concerning this issue, you will find throughout the gospel that Christ condemns the scribes, Pharisees and doctors of the law, but carefully protects the uneducated multitude. For what else does "Woe to you, scribes and Pharisees" mean than "Woe to you sages"?' Christian charity, far from being the exclusive prerogative of a few touchy men, can be found in uneducated children, women, and fishermen. [. . .]

Folly, however, not only introduces Platonic teaching about the most excellent divine madness, love, but allies it with Paul's *raptus* [being carried away] to the third heaven, and with the ecstasy of the ultimate mystical experience, union with God. In the *Phaedrus*, Plato had Socrates distinguish between a higher, divinely inspired madness – identified with ecstasy – and a lower, merely bodily, if not bestial, one – madness in the ordinary but also the medical sense. Folly denounces the latter as coming from hell and the Furies, lumps it together with Stoic *stultitia* – the final insult – but proudly asserts, now completely transformed, that ecstasy comes 'from me!' Within ecstasy is found the fullness of *voluptas*: 'That happiness which Christians pursue with such struggle is nothing else but a kind of madness and folly.' [. . .]

Both Valla's and Erasmus's works are superficially so different that a detailed comparison might have seemed fruitless; yet Erasmus, I hope to have shown, made Valla's ethical program his own. Both writers felt that New Testament doctrine was meant to reach a wide audience: men, women, even children. In their opinion, Christianity proposed a new ethics with compelling motivation, the hope of happiness shared by a community; and placed at the center a virtue, charity, no classical pagan sect had thought of. Both authors felt that Christianity's precious message had been buried, disfigured, and betrayed by a bundle of ethical counsels best represented by the Stoics. And both used as an agent of reform a new kind of humor, 'playful seriousness,' to draw us to an appreciation of charity and a refined *voluptas* as our goal. As a final remark, let me say that I have not wished by this study to perform a 'reductionist' critique on Erasmus' *Stultitiae laus*, to give the impression that everything Erasmus wrote in it can be sucked back into Valla's dialogue. The two works stand on their own; and as in all great works of art, the whole is greater than the sum of its parts. I have wished, on the contrary, to enhance Erasmus' composition, to illuminate yet another aspect of its amazing complexity that still defies centuries of interpretation, and to show how Valla enables us to arrive at a deeper understanding of Erasmus than before.

NOTE

1   This article is based on the Fifth Annual Margaret Mann Phillips Lecture held at the Union Theological Seminary, New York, 13 July 1992, and I am grateful to Richard DeMolen for his kind invitation. The first part, concentrating on issues, has preserved more than the rest the flavor of a spoken address.

8   Maureen Ramsay **'Machiavelli's political philosophy in *The Prince*'**

Source: from *Niccolo Machiavelli's* The Prince: *New interdisciplinang essays*, ed. Martin Coyle, Manchester University Press, Manchester, 1995, chapter 8, pp. 174–93.

Trying to place Machiavelli's *The Prince* in the history of political thought involves confronting a bewildering array of conflicting interpretations of his political views. This can be all the more perplexing when what is initially striking about *The Prince* is its brevity, clarity and, though intense and dynamic, its *ad hoc* nature, its lack of philosophical rigour. Although there are those who imply the opposite, by claiming that Machiavelli was the founder of political science, it is now generally agreed that he was not a systematic, analytic political thinker. His methodology was consistent only in so far as it yielded a number of artistic, intuitive generalisations made by reflection on personal experience and observation, and supplemented by the inaccurate and selective use of historical evidence. As Isaiah Berlin writes:

> Machiavelli's theories are certainly not based on the scientific principles of the seventeenth century. He lived a hundred years before Galileo and Bacon, and his method is a mixture of rules of thumb, observation, historical knowledge and general sagacity, somewhat like the empirical medicine of the pre-scientific world. He abounds in precepts, in useful maxims, practical hints, scattered reflections, especially historical parallels, even though he claims to have discovered general laws. [. . .]

The fact that Machiavelli bases his conclusions on observation and experience is not sufficient to describe him as a political scientist. His methodology was not systematic or intellectually coherent enough to be afforded such a title, but it would not be seriously misleading to see in Machiavelli an embryonic form of more modern methods of political analysis. Machiavelli certainly saw himself as an innovator, radically breaking with medieval and ancient thought and with its theological and metaphysical underpinnings. In chapter XV he defiantly announces that in departing from 'the methods of others' he is blazing a new trail of philosophical analysis in order to reach the truth of practical politics. This new approach aims to apply directly to the problems of the real world. His purpose is to 'write something useful to him who comprehends it'. For this reason he writes that 'I have decided that I must concern myself with the truth of the matter as facts show it rather than with any fanciful notion' (chapter XV). Machiavelli claimed the novelty of his work lay in talking about 'man' and the state as they exist in reality, as they are, not as they ought to be. And it is the content of these observations and conclusions deduced from the way in which 'men' actually behave that have led to the rival interpretations on the significance of their import.

The political reality described by Machiavelli helped foster the idea in popular imagination that he was the author of the doctrine that 'the end justifies the means'. Although Machiavelli never articulates his descriptions or prescriptions in this formulation, the means–end relationship and the relationship between politics and morality are the central issues which have inspired most interest in his political philosophy.

If any means can justify any end, then it is not difficult to see why many writers from Machiavelli's own time onwards have castigated him variously as a man inspired by the devil, as an immoral writer and a teacher of evil. This was the view of most of the Elizabethan dramatists and was shared by Cardinal Pole, Bodin and Frederick the Great. [. . .] For other commentators, however, assessment of the Machiavellian dictum is tempered by consideration of the morality or desirability of the end to be justified. These have been held to be those of a passionate patriot, a democrat and a believer in liberty. According to Spinoza and Rousseau it is this fact that makes *The Prince* not an immoral work, but a satire on princes written to forearm and forewarn the people on what rulers actually did and could do.

For [some] commentators it is precisely the applicability of the doctrine that 'the end justifies the means' which marks Machiavelli's greatest contribution to a philosophy of politics. It was he who recognised the 'autonomy of politics'. Such a doctrine is appropriate and necessary to the realm of politics where evaluations of actions must be made without reference to extra-political or moral factors. Ends–means considerations are especially relevant to the political sphere in its proper concern with the interests of the state. [. . .]

Other writers have taken a slightly different approach and have seen Machiavelli's portrayal of means and the ends they were designed to achieve as accurate descriptions of the political practice of his own time and of ours, and as key insights into the nature and realities of political power. The means–end dichotomy has also been interpreted not as justificatory or descriptive but as a hypothetical, technical imperative of the form – if you want X, do Y. It is neither moral nor amoral. The ends themselves are not justified as rational or good, the means to achieve them are neither praised nor blamed. They are advocated only as what is necessary to achieve the end in question. Thus Machiavelli is ethically neutral and politically uncommitted. Since this technical imperative can apply to a variety of political actors – princes, tyrants, democrats, republicans – it follows that it can be put to the service of many ideologies in justifying or achieving a variety of ends – liberatory, revolutionary, democratic, nationalistic or despotic.

The purpose of this chapter is to attempt to clarify Machiavelli's position on the means–end relationship and the relationship between politics and morality. In particular the chapter will examine the originality and uniqueness of Machiavelli's views in relation to past and present political and ethical thought, and argue that, despite their notoriety, his ideas and their attendant problems are a common feature both of political thought and practice and also of personal and political life.

ENDS AND MEANS, POLITICS AND MORALITY

Whether or not Machiavelli conceived of the means–end relationship as justificatory, as descriptive or as a technical imperative is a matter of dispute. In a sense, his glaring illustration that there is no escape from the weight of means and ends combines all three aspects of the relationship. This is because this is the way people do behave: people constantly act as though the end justifies the means, and, without judging any particular end to be good or bad, practical necessity dictates that certain means will be required to achieve them. Whether there are some means so evil that they should never be used, or whether there are some ends so good that they justify any means, is a separate question, but not one Machiavelli avoided. In fact, it is precisely his testament to these permanent questions that generates interest in Machiavelli.

For Machiavelli, the ends of political life were the acquiring and holding down of power, the stability of the state, the maintenance of order and general prosperity. To say that Machiavelli was a scientist or a technician of political life because he was not concerned with whether such ends were rational or good is to overstate the case. He never explicitly justified these ends, but simply accepted them as given, because he assumed that order and security were universal ends that all human beings aspire to, and that these were necessary for human welfare. If this is so, then it is plausible to see Machiavelli as implicitly concerned with ends, the moral purpose of which is to secure the good for human beings, given what he took to be in human interests and the context of human desires. However, if the ends of order and stability are to be achieved, what means are morally permissible as well as practically expedient?

Machiavelli was not concerned to define moral rules and explain why they should be obeyed, or to define the rights, duties and obligations of princes or citizens. Rather he was concerned in *The Prince* with those qualities (capacities and dispositions) rulers must have to establish, restore or maintain order and stability. These qualities were psychological and social rather than traditional moral traits. In chapter XV he lists some of the qualities that normally bring praise or blame and admits that it would be praiseworthy for a prince to exhibit those qualities which are considered good. Machiavelli here is not denying that liberality, mercy, honesty, kindness, chastity, reliability and tolerance are virtues. He is, though, drawing attention to the fact that no ruler can possess or fully practise them because the realities of the human condition dictate behaviour which by normal standards would be condemned as immoral. The irony of the political situation is such that 'when we carefully examine the whole matter, we find some qualities that look like virtues, yet if the prince practises them – they will be his destruction, and other qualities that look like vices, yet – if he practises them – they will bring him safety and well-being' (chapter XV). Chapters XVI–XVIII illustrate in detail this point, that morally good human actions can lead to evil results, and immoral actions may have beneficial consequences. The classical virtue of liberality is considered to be a good, yet the consistent practice of it can be damaging. A liberal prince may use up all his resources and be forced in the end to tax his people excessively and so make him hateful to his subjects. His liberality injures the many and rewards the few as well as bringing ruin to himself. Whereas if a prince is mean initially, he will have enough income to carry out his enterprises without harming the people or becoming extortionate. Similarly with cruelty and mercy. In chapter XVII, Machiavelli writes:

Cesare Borgia was thought cruel; nevertheless that well-known cruelty of his reorganised the Romagna, united it, brought it to peace and loyalty. If we look at this closely, we see that he was more merciful than the Florentine people, who, to escape being called cruel, allowed the ruin of Pistoia. A wise prince, then, is not troubled about a reproach for cruelty which keeps his subjects united and loyal because, giving a very few examples of cruelty, he is more merciful than those who, through too much mercy, let evils continue, from which result murder or plunder, because the latter commonly harm a whole group, but those executions that come from the prince harm individuals only.

Here Machiavelli is making three points. First, as in the case of liberality, he is not denying that mercy is a virtue. Just as in order to be liberal the Prince might have first to be mean, so in order to be merciful the Prince might have to be cruel. What is valued here is still the traditional virtue. Second, the selective use of cruelty can bring about the benefits of unity, peace and loyalty, whereas too much mercy can lead to ruin. This is not simply an appeal to the good consequences cruelty might promote *per se*, but a recognition that well-intentioned failure to act may have consequences far more cruel than the original inaction was designed to avoid. Where omissions have worse consequences, then cruelty is the preferable course of action. The aim is to avoid cruelty, not to promote it. This is obvious in the third point, that the lesser evil consists in harm to individuals rather than to a whole group. In political situations where choices between two evils have to be made, it is more morally responsible to act to choose the lesser evil. Machiavelli is not just simply saying that good ends outweigh immoral means; that moral squeamishness in abstaining from immoral means does not absolve responsibility for the bad consequences which result from omissions; or that in some situations the best course of action is that which avoids the worst excesses of violence and cruelty; or even that the Prince cannot conform to conventional moral standards if the interests of the state or the common good are to be preserved. He is also saying that sometimes, in employing immoral means, the Prince will be closer to displaying the virtues of conventional morality than those who, by embodying these virtues, achieve the opposite. The quality of mercy might be cruelty in disguise – we may have to be cruel in order to be kind.

Machiavelli does not disregard conventional morality as such. He exhorts his Prince to act according to the accepted virtues of truth, charity, humanity and religion when he can. That is, when the political situation is stable and secure. In these circumstances public and conventional morality are identical. However, the Prince must be adaptable and 'have a mind ready to turn in any direction as Fortune's winds and the variety of affairs require yet, . . . he holds to what is right when he can and knows how to do wrong when he must' (chapter XVIII). This is because politics poses questions for which conventional morality is inappropriate. In times of necessity the Prince must be unconstrained by normal ethical ideals and adopt methods which, though contrary to these ideas, will lead to beneficial consequences. Here there seems to be a split between private and public morality, so that, in certain circumstances, the latter has its own distinctive ethic.

However, there are passages where Machiavelli seems to indicate that the distinction he is making is not between private and public morality itself but rather between conventional morality and what people actually do in both the public and the private sphere. This is seen in his comments on human nature and human behaviour. These suggest it is partly because people do not act according to the dictates of conventional morality in the daily business of their lives that the Prince must behave in a similar fashion. In chapter XVIII, for instance, he argues for the breaking of promises on two grounds. The first is with reference to a consequentialist ethic, for experience shows that princes who do break their promises have done great things. The second is with reference to the corrupt nature and behaviour of human beings in general. A prudent prince cannot keep his word, first, when it works against him and, second, 'when the reasons that made him promise are annulled. If all men were good, this maxim would not be good, but because they are bad and do not keep their promises to you, you likewise do not have to keep yours to them' (chapter XVIII). Here, the Prince is not to act as he ought, according to abstract, conventional virtues, but as other people act. Similarly, when discussing cruelty and mercy, and whether it is better to be loved than feared, Machiavelli advises it is safer to be feared, given the nature of human beings (chapter XVII):

> Because we can say this about men in general: they are ungrateful, changeable, simulators and dissimulators, runaways in danger, eager for gain; they offer you their blood, their property, their lives, their children . . . when need is far off; but when it comes near you, they turn about. A prince who bases himself entirely on their words, if he is lacking other preparations, fails; because friendships gained with money, not with greatness and nobility of spirit are purchased but not possessed, and at the right times cannot be turned to account. Men have less hesitation in injuring one who makes himself loved than one who makes himself feared, for love is held by a chain of duty which, since men are bad, they break at every chance for their own profit; but fear is held by a dread of punishment that never fails you.

'Men' in general do not exhibit the qualities of conventional morality. The Prince can deceive because he 'always finds men who let themselves be deceived' (chapter XVIII). The Prince need only appear to have the conventional virtues of mercy, faith, integrity and religion 'because in general men judge more with their eyes than with their heads, since everybody can see but few can perceive' (chapter XVIII). It seems, too, that the Prince must adopt a consequentialist ethic because it is the case that 'as to the actions of all men and especially those of princes, against whom charges cannot be brought in court, everyone looks at their result' (chapter XVIII).

In order to bring about beneficial results the Prince must cultivate not conventional virtue but Machiavellian *virtù*. There is much scholarly dispute as to whether Machiavelli attached a precise or consistent meaning to *virtù*. Russell Price has shown that Machiavelli used *virtù* as a complex cluster concept which includes traditional, Christian moral virtue, military *virtù*, political *virtù*, a combination of military and political *virtù*, an instrumental *virtù*, cultural virtue as well as ancient and modern *virtù*. It is clear, though, that princely *virtù* for Machiavelli was a consistent concept in so far as it embodied those qualities, capacities and dispositions necessary for the Prince to establish, restore or maintain the stability of the state, to win honour and glory for himself and to overcome the blows of fortune. The quality of *virtù* is displayed in a mode of conduct which Geerken argues underlies the plurality of meanings and has three components: '(a) suitability to prevailing circumstances, (b) adequate deliberation regarding options, priorities and consequences, and, finally, (c) timely and successful action'.

Virtù, then, will consist of different qualities at different times given what is necessary to attain goals in particular circumstances. Qualities which manifest *virtù* include fortitude in adversity, foresight and insight, willingness to take risks, resourcefulness and firmness of purpose. The qualities of *virtù* can be displayed in evil actions as well as good. Hence Machiavelli's admiration for Cesare Borgia who, though cruel, was an exemplar of these qualities.

However, Machiavelli did not admire all actions simply because they were bold, resolute and effective. When discussing Agathocles [361–289BCE], the tyrant of Sicily, in chapter VIII he makes the distinction between cruelty 'well' and 'ill' used. 'Well-used' cruelties are those that are necessary and constructive, those which a conqueror must carry out and 'then does not persist in' and which he then 'transmutes into the greatest possible benefit to his subjects' (chapter VIII). 'Ill-used' cruelties are those which persist with time and which are unnecessary and destructive. Agathocles showed fortitude in adversity and was bold, resolute and resourceful, but his 'outrageous cruelty and inhumanity together with his countless wicked acts do not permit him to be honoured among the noblest men'. Acting in this manner may bring success and 'sovereignty but not glory' (chapter VIII). The difference between the deeds of Agathocles and Borgia was that if Borgia had succeeded his deeds would have resulted in a strong state and so the common good (whether or not the latter was his intention). Agathocles' deeds involved uneconomic and gratuitous cruelty and led to a worse state of affairs than before. Machiavelli is reluctant to admit that Agathocles' deeds were worthy of the name *virtù*. *Virtù* is ascribed to actions consistent with the acquisition of glory, when dictated through necessity and where they serve common interests and the needs of the public realm.

When evaluating the relationship between means and ends and between politics and morality in *The Prince*, it is necessary to see the problematic against the backdrop of Machiavelli's pessimistic assumptions about the timeless and unchanging nature of human motives and aspirations. Machiavelli's view of human beings as natural egotists with a lust for domination and power led him to see history as an arena of conflict involving deceit, treachery and violence. The roots of this conflict were psychological, but the solution was social and political. The ends of political life were to achieve the order and stability necessary to secure the fundamental human desires of self-preservation and security. Therefore political morality must be one designed to achieve these ends. Conventional morality in many circumstances is inappropriate and seems to defeat these purposes. This is because the consistent practice of traditional virtues may lead to outcomes which are not virtuous, even according to that tradition's own standard, and because observing these virtues may not lead to good consequences. Conventionally immoral actions may bring beneficial results, whereas an action done for a good motive or a well-intentioned inaction may have bad or worse consequences than the supposed immoral action. Failing to act for reasons of moral purity does not lessen the responsibility for bad consequences which result from the omission. At certain political conjunctions, it is morally necessary to employ evil means to achieve the desired result. This is not because conventional virtues are not good in themselves or desirable for both public and private practices but because people are not by nature good and do not live according to these abstract virtues in either the public or the private sphere. In order for people to live according to the virtues, certain conditions of political security and stability must pertain. When this is the case moral questions can be raised and moral virtues can be pursued within the accepted values of the established and stable community. When this is not the case, conventionally immoral actions are necessary to establish the conditions for morality and what is politically and ultimately personally valuable depends on prudential calculation. Here conventional values are questioned against the criteria of human interests and desires and the result is a consequentialist ethic. An effective political morality must be one designed for human beings as they are, in the circumstances they find themselves in, in order to create a situation where human beings will be fit for morality.

ORIGINALITY AND UNIQUENESS OF MACHIAVELLI'S VIEWS

Precursors

The question arises as to how far Machiavelli's views on the relationship between ends and means, morality and politics is all that unique to either past or present political thought. Since ancient times political writers had been concerned with princes and princedoms. In the princely literature from the Middle Ages to the Renaissance, political theorists compiled a list of cardinal and princely virtues which it was the duty of a good ruler to acquire. The prince, like his subjects, was advised to be liberal, generous, merciful, truthful, kind, chaste, reliable, tolerant and devout. It was assumed that it was rational to act morally; that public virtue was identical to private virtue; that ethics and politics were interrelated and inseparable. Since these abstract virtues were delineated and endorsed without reference to the social or political context in which they were to be cultivated, Machiavelli complained that such advice applied to perfect princes living in perfect states, neither of which exists in reality. Machiavelli's unique contribution to princely literature was his discussion of actual political situations with the aim of formulating rules for political conduct useful for those who govern the state. As we have seen, in chapters XV to XIX he forcefully overturns the idealised conception of the virtues found in traditional humanist catalogues. He begins by tacitly agreeing that it would be admirable for the Prince to have such virtues, and that in times of stability their practice was possible. However, he shows that necessity forces rulers to commit deeds which are not by conventional standards moral. In this he rejects the humanist conception that moral means achieve desirable ends. In order to attain the ends of political life, it cannot be rational to adopt moral means when this will defeat ultimate purposes. Practical rationality demands that the Prince must act according to necessity, regardless of abstract moral imperatives. In real life, force of circumstances are such that political morality must be divorced from conventional morality and from what would be desirable in private moral behaviour.

Although earlier writers did not directly anticipate Machiavelli's views, all but the most naive and utopian could not help but be aware of the moral problems and the element of expediency involved in successful political action. Sidney Anglo has argued:

> That Machiavelli has come to be particularly identified with the divorce of politics from private morality, with the doctrine of expediency in political actions, and with the mode of justifying all political means on grounds of reasons of state, is less due to his uniqueness than to the dynamic way in which he expressed these ideas.

Other writers have shown that the kind of issues Machiavelli's political theory raises had been aired at least since the time of Aristotle and were raised more explicitly in the princely literature of the fifteenth-century Italian humanists. In chapter III of *The Politics*, Aristotle describes how the problem of immoral means necessary for political survival concerns all forms of government, whether or not they adopt such policies to further their own interests or for the common good. Here there is a clear awareness of the realities of political action and a suggestion that there may be different moral criteria for judging public and private affairs. In the same chapter Aristotle writes that 'the virtues of the good citizen and the virtue of the good man cannot be always the same, although in some cases (i.e. in the perfect state) they may'. Aquinas in his *Commentary on Politics* took this directly to mean that 'it follows, therefore, that the virtue of the good citizen and the good man are not the same'. Aristotle and his followers, in their accounts of the means used by tyrants to maintain their position, outlined the methods Machiavelli took to be essential, not just for the tyrant but also for the Prince. So, for example, in the fifth book of *The Politics*, the tyrant, like Machiavelli's prince, is advised to cultivate a reputation for the virtues, to appear to be religious, and to produce the impression that he acts in the character of a statesman if he wishes to maintain his power to rule.

The political realism reflected in the internal and external affairs of the medieval state highlighted the problem of justification. This had not escaped the notice of medieval theologians and legal theorists who had frequently used the notion 'necessity has no laws' to justify extraordinary means in exceptional circumstances. The problem was accentuated by the changing politics of Europe and demonstrated in the practices of emerging states, if only because they were more powerful. It was acknowledged by the fifteenth-century Italian humanists, whom Gilbert views as forerunners to the more explicit formulations of the problem by Machiavelli. These writers, though they endorsed the traditional princely virtues, recognised that beneficial political consequences may necessitate or excuse immoral means. Gilbert quotes Pontano:

> It is the act of a wise man, when two ills are put before him, always to choose the smaller one. Hence it is permissible, for the sake of the State and of a king who is father of his people, sometimes to tell falsehoods; though when time and circumstance require silence about the truth, especially when the safety of the king, the kingdom, and the fatherland is in question, he who prudently keeps still certainly does not seem to be a liar. Or if he uses deception he does not seem straight away to be a liar, since he acts like a prudent man who balances utilities and necessity with the true and the false.

Other writers, too, had indicated that the standard of public utility was at stake when the breaking of promises was permissible. Platina allows for breaches of faith in abandoning foreign treaties when the interests of the native subjects are threatened by common enemies or the threat of war. He suggests that in these circumstances even the private citizens commit no fraud if they breach agreements. Patricius implies the public interest when he commends those times when a ruler must simulate and dissimulate. The Prince must not appear gloomy and morose because this makes his subjects anxious. Since it would be disastrous to let the subjects know of some impending disaster, for the ruler 'it is proper that by simulation and dissimulation he should often show the contrary to the truth'. The importance of the ruler appearing to preserve religious and other virtues had been recognised by Aristotle. Egidio, Beroaldus and Campanus, too, demonstrated the necessity of simulating the appearance of being good to win the respect and admiration of the people. When a ruler could not be loved because of the unpopular measures he imposed, Carafa advises that, to avoid being hated, the ruler should make it clear to his subjects that 'necessity and not desire, induces you to do it'.

Therefore, within the political and theoretical context in which Machiavelli wrote, there already existed an awareness of expediency when faced with political realities. But for earlier writers these questions usually had been touched upon with reference to extraordinary situations and they had never fully articulated a specific doctrine, justificatory, explanatory or descriptive of political necessity and morality. For Machiavelli, expediency was not just a feature of abnormal situations but was generally the norm of political activity, given the nature of human beings and the uncertainty which prevailed in human affairs. In order to ensure the good life for human beings a stable, political order was required. To the realisation of this end, and with it the very possibility of the merging of morality and politics, the practice of traditional moral virtues was obsolete.

Machiavelli is unique, then, in that he took the suggestions, hesitations and implications in other political thinkers' advice to princes to their logical and most extreme conclusion. He shamelessly and powerfully 'blurted out' what they had whispered and what any reflecting person must have known, but did not dare or care to admit.

OTHER TRADITIONS IN POLITICAL AND ETHICAL THOUGHT

If Machiavelli was the first political theorist explicitly to endorse a prudential and consequentialist ethic based on beliefs about human nature and society, he certainly was not the last. Two dominant traditions in the history of both political and ethical thought take on board, albeit in more sophisticated form, certain features of Machiavelli's assumptions and conclusions.

Aspects of Machiavelli's ideas pave the way for the rise of liberal thought which opens up with the development of capitalism and which begins in a systematic, theoretical form with Hobbes. In this tradition, the abstract pre-social individual is the most fundamental and important social unit, while power and stability are the ultimate goals of social and political life. For Machiavelli, and the liberal tradition, the individual stands apart from society. Society is the backdrop against which individuals, separated from their social relationships and roles, act to achieve their own ends. Human beings, their motives and aspirations are defined independently of the specific social context in which these are formulated and experienced. They are essentially the same at all times and places because they are motivated by the same insatiable passions. Human beings are self-assertive, self-preserving, infinitely desirous and endlessly ambitious in a world of scarcity and limited satisfactions. The realisation of the most fundamental human desires for self-preservation and security can be achieved by creating a strong and stable state. Human psychology thus becomes the cause of external conflict and the remedy for social cohesion. Self-preservation is the overriding motivational factor in creating or maintaining political arrangements which promote human desires. It follows, then, that if human beings are solely motivated by such desires, morality can be imposed by force, derived from fear of sanctions or observed only because doing so leads to their satisfaction. Moral injunctions now take the form of technical imperatives and become factual statements about the means necessary to achieve the given and required end. Reasoning in moral matters is concerned not with questioning or revising these ends but with prudential calculation, assisting human beings to attain their ends – the most basic of which is security. In brief, notwithstanding the differences in and the developments of political and moral thought, the liberal tradition continues to have at its core the key dichotomies and assumptions found in Machiavelli: the separation of the individual and society and also of the private and public sphere; the sovereignty of the individual; the pre-social, pre-political notion of an unchanging human nature; the instrumental nature of rationality and morality.

Continuities with the issues Machiavelli raises, however, are nowhere more apparent than in traditions of ethical justification and their ongoing problems. It would be absurd to attribute to Machiavelli a systematic ethical theory, but in so far as the doctrine of political expediency embodies his views on politics and morality, this has parallels with all forms of normative and political theories which rely on a utilitarian or consequentialist ethic. For Croce and his followers to argue that Machiavelli divorced morality from politics is to make a false antithesis. Isaiah Berlin suggests that what Machiavelli distinguishes is not moral from political values but two incompatible ways of life and therefore two moralities. For Berlin, these are the morality of the pagan and heroic world versus Platonic–Hebraic–Christian morality, each with its own values and claims to ultimacy. Machiavelli was not rejecting Christian values but showing the need 'to choose either a good, virtuous private life or a good, successful social existence, but not both'. Dante Germino has proposed that Machiavelli's position can be seen as similar to the contrast made by Weber (in *Politik als Beruf* [*Politics as a Profession*]) between 'ethics of responsibility' and 'ethics of intention', in which it is irresponsible in politics to act out of pure motives of individual conscience, without weighing the consequences which actually result. But, broadly speaking, the legacy of Machiavelli is the contrast not between the political and the moral but between consequentialist ethics and all other forms. Consequentialist ethics contrast with Christian, traditional and Kantian ethics; any kind of moral purism or idealism; any ethic that has as its source and criterion of value the word of God, eternal reason or the dictates of conscience; ethics which focus on the salvation of the individual soul or the individual as an end in themselves; ethics which stress intentions, or which embody abstract conceptions of justice, fairness and rights. In short, consequentialist ethics conflict with any ethic that, in formulating rules governing how people should be treated, places restrictions on the means no amount of good consequences would sanction or permit. Machiavelli demonstrates and highlights the incompatibility of consequentialist ethics from other systems of value, and it is this collision which persists between rival ethical positions.

Though Machiavelli justified public morality on grounds of reasons of state, and though varieties of utilitarianism may differ on what ends are justified, all moral theories which justify actions according to outcomes suffer from the problems of condoning means that on other standards are bad or undesirable. The problem of means and ends is not unique to Machiavelli but is relevant to all justifications which rely on a consequentialist ethic. These range across and pervade diverse ideological frameworks and apply to all areas of public and private life. This is seen in theological and Christian formulations of just war theory; defences of *raison d'état*, imperialist and populist, Catholic and Protestant; Marxist justifications for revolution, defences of the market economy and in arguments for and against a variety of issues such as legal punishment, discrimination, abortion, infanticide and euthanasia. Consequentialist calculation is also an intimate feature of our daily lives, since in all the small lies we tell and the promises we break we constantly act as if the end justified the means. Moreover, in practical politics there has always been the problem of adopting anything other than a version of utilitarianism, when ends that are judged good (on whatever grounds) cannot be achieved without recourse to means, which, judged according to the principles of alternative moral traditions, would be impermissible but which, if adhered to, would make the end unrealisable. Even regimes which stress the importance of individual rights and liberties have been more than ready to sacrifice these to achieve a desired outcome. Such acts as the bombing of Hamburg and Dresden, Hiroshima and Nagasaki and American involvement in Vietnam could be justified only by appeal to their consequences, despite the fact that the perpetrators of such deeds did not subscribe to a consequentialist ethic.

The pervasiveness of means–end reasoning in moral and political, private and public life illustrates the diverse situations in which moral demands or principles conflict and the frequency with which choice has to be made between one or the other. Action directed to outcomes can involve sacrificing moral principles, but the case against moral purity does not deny that this is a sacrifice. Machiavelli acknowledges that it cannot be called good to lie, cheat, be cruel and faithless. He, like many Marxist and revolutionary thinkers following him, thought such actions were necessary to achieve a better, more humane future, but he did not deny the contradiction of achieving moral ends through immoral means. In his poem 'To Those Born Later', Brecht says that living in dark times he cannot live 'wisely', according to the morality of the 'old books', 'shun the strife of the world', 'get along without violence' or 'return good for evil'; but he laments this and makes a plea to future generations who have escaped this contradiction:

> And yet we know:
> Hatred, even of meanness
> Contorts the features.
> Anger, even against injustice
> Makes the voice hoarse. Oh, we
> Who wanted to prepare the ground for friendliness
> Could not ourselves be friendly.
>
> But you, when the time comes at last
> And man is a helper to man
> Think of us
> With forbearance.

Actions which involve the sacrifice of moral values may be necessary in an imperfect world, but the efficacy of such actions does not obscure their anti-moral and inhuman nature. James Connolly reiterates this point: 'No, there is no such thing as humane or civilised war! War may be forced upon a subject race or subject class to put an end to subjection of race, of class, or sex. When so waged it must be waged thoroughly and relentlessly, but with no delusions as to its elevating nature, or civilising methods'.

Trotsky confirms this view of both the necessity and the immorality of the means to liberatory ends:

Nevertheless do lying and violence in themselves warrant condemnation? Of course, as does the class society which generates them. A society without contradictions will naturally be a society without lies and violence. However, there is no bridge to that society save by revolutionary, that is violent means. The revolution is itself a product of class society and of necessity bears its traits. From the point of view of 'eternal truths' revolution is of course anti-moral. But this means that idealist morality is counter revolutionary, that is, in the service of the exploiters.

It is not, though, just the acknowledgement of the necessity of immoral means which forms the case against idealist morality in Machiavelli or in other consequentialist justifications. The case against moral purism argued for in contemporary literature, and found in embryonic form in Machiavelli, depends on a rejection of the acts and omissions doctrine to show that there is no escape from the dilemma of dirty hands. The acts and omissions doctrine states that failure to perform an act with certain foreseen consequences is morally less bad than to perform an act with the same foreseen consequences. Machiavelli shows, like others who reject this doctrine, that certain omissions are as blameworthy as certain acts and sometimes more so, because those who fail to act, whatever their good intentions, are causally responsible for harm they could have prevented. If an action which employs violent, cruel or otherwise immoral means is the only way to change the world's destiny for the better, then those who fail to act will be responsible for maintaining the evil of the status quo and for allowing worse consequences to result. As Machiavelli noted, it is not the most moderate and morally pure who have provided the fewest victims in history. At certain political conjunctions there can be no ethical neutrality in decision-making – 'all roads lead to the mire'. In these circumstances, abstaining from immoral means is at best self-deception, at worst immoral.

It is not a particularly Machiavellian idea, nor exclusively a Marxist one, that the end justifies the means or that it is impossible to apply in politics the same moral standards that are appropriate to the private sphere. Whatever ideology they are informed by, all practical politics at some time or other involves actions which would be condemned if performed by private citizens or if judged with regard to other moral considerations. Though the Anarchist tradition has argued against this and for the inseparability of means and ends, requiring that political action should be judged by personal standards, in contemporary times the emergence of radical feminism marks the sharpest break with Western political thought in this respect by questioning the legitimacy of the distinction between the private and public spheres of action. The radical feminist claim that the 'personal is political' exposes the idea that male power is not confined to the public world of politics but also extends to areas of personal life, such as the family and sexuality, which are normally seen as private and non-political. But for many radical feminists, personal politics also means that women's experience of intimate relations provides a fund of values which should inform, inspire and regulate political life.

It is easy to see, though, why an 'ethic of care' arising from women's experience of connection and responsiveness, and informed by love, empathy, compassion and responsibility, would be as inappropriate to politics as Machiavelli thought traditional and princely virtues were. This is because, in the world as it is, with 'men' as they are, politics is about power, albeit in both political and private life. Change depends not on the personal reflected in the political but on the transformation of social structures which no amount of princely, personal or female virtue alone can transform or maintain.

We may agree that feminism provides insights into what is morally good. We may also agree that the mode of morality which dominates the public sphere embodies typical male views of human nature as abstract, universal and self-interested which are false to the experience of women. Though the feminist alternative virtues may be desirable in themselves, it is surely Machiavelli's point that we are involved in a world where any such morality is impossible and undesirable. Without the deceit, violence, fraud and ruthlessness that would be psychopathic in personal relations, ends cannot be achieved which make the practice of virtue possible.

We need not be committed either to a view of human nature as universal and unchanging and of conflict as endemic, nor to a view that endorses male values and conceptions to see that, in the world as it is, a consequentialist ethic and the dilemmas this brings are unavoidable if political goals are to be achieved.

And when the time comes at last and 'man is a helper to man' it will still be the case that, despite the flourishing of personal virtues and their reflection in public life, there will still be occasions when these have to be sacrificed for the sake of the common good or for their very preservation itself. There will always be decisions to be made in both personal and public affairs which require prudential calculation and which will justify means which contradict those most cherished values. Traditional male conceptions of what constitute the political sphere is not the only arena in which it would be fair to say that we will still be faced with the problem of Machiavelli who has left us with 'an enigma that perhaps will never be resolved'.

Section Two
Courts, Patrons and Poets

9   Evelyn S. Welch **'Sight, sound and ceremony in the chapel of Galeazzo Maria Sforza'**

Source: from *Early Music History*, volume 12, Cambridge University Press, Cambridge 1993, pp. 151–78.

Bernardino Corio's late fifteenth-century history of Milan covers the city's past from its foundations to the collapse of the Sforza dynasty.[1] Following the historiographic traditions established by Leonardo Bruni, its essential outlines are founded on careful use of sources and, for more recent events, contemporary memories and impressions. It is, however, also characterised by judicious revisionism and anecdotal invention. The careful reader always needs to ask why digressions have been included and what hidden points are being made. It is therefore well worth inquiring why Corio, a member of Duke Galeazzo Maria Sforza's court, chose to link his master's assassination on 26 December 1476 with a passage on his chapel choir and musical taste.

Literary conventions demanded warnings of impending disaster and Corio provided a series of portents leading up to the fateful day. There were the traditional signs: falling stars, flying crows, unexplained fires and an atypical desire on Galeazzo Maria's part to see his children. But the clearest evidence of a death foretold was the duke's own order that his chapel singers should put on mourning garments and insert a section from the Office for the Dead into the daily mass: *Maria mater gratiae, mater misericordiae* [Mary, Mother of Grace, Mother of Pity]. Whether genuine or not, this bizarre anecdote permitted a short description of Galeazzo Maria's musical enthusiasms: 'The duke took great delight in song, for which he kept about thirty northern singers, honourably paid, and among whom there was one called Cordiero, to whom he gave a salary of 100 ducats a month. And the ornaments in his chapel were such that they could be valued at 100,000 ducats.' Corio pointedly ended this description of the Sforza chapel with the seemingly unconnected information that during the Christmas festivities of 1476, 'all the duke's feudatories and courtiers had come from his dominions to Milan to await his arrival, and all were malcontent since he had not made any payments'. In Corio's conjunction, the contrast between the enormous riches heaped on the singer, Jean Cordier, and the relative disenfranchisement of the Milanese aristocracy had its effect at the end of the month. With the support of a significant section of the city's Ghibelline nobility, three of Galeazzo Maria's courtiers stabbed the duke to death in the church of S. Stefano.

Was the duke's fondness for music responsible, even indirectly, for his murder? Scholars have long recognised the importance of his short-lived court chapel. Yet it has received surprisingly little detailed attention in its own right, remaining as a backdrop to the excellent studies devoted to the fifteenth-century court chapels of Ferrara and Naples. The duke himself has been perceived primarily as a poor counterpart of Ferrante of Aragon, Ercole d'Este and Pope Sixtus IV. It is now time to reverse the comparison and examine Galeazzo Maria's own reasons for establishing one of the greatest collections of singers and composers of the period, and the political implications of his patronage.

The simultaneous creation of polyphonic court chapels in Italy in the 1470s has usually been explained in terms of princely rivalry. Much of the relevant correspondence accuses Galeazzo Maria and his ambassadors of preventing singers from arriving at their posts or of suborning musicians contracted elsewhere. The diplomatic stakes could be high, creating tensions between major Italian and non-Italian powers. In 1475, for example, the Duke of Burgundy, Charles the Bold, was forced to intervene in the dispute between King Ferrante of Naples and Galeazzo Maria over Jean Cordier's employment. Yet such arguments reveal less about the individual ambitions of particular patrons than they do about the limited availability of the finest singers. Like precious gems or classical coins, renowned musicians were prestige objects which rulers fought to obtain. But competitive or acquisitive instincts do not fully explain the sums which Galeazzo Maria was willing to invest in his chapel. *Magnificentia* had many aspects; yet the Duke of Milan was singularly uninterested in antiquities, made no effort to obtain well-known painters or sculptors, and, having dismissed the humanists resident at his father's court, commissioned little prose or poetry in either Latin or the vernacular. Music was the only area in which he could claim international renown for the quality and sophistication of his patronage. Why?

His early education offers only a partial explanation for this specialised interest. At the age of six Galeazzo Maria found his life transformed when his father, Francesco Sforza, accepted the surrender of Milan's republican government in 1450. No longer the son of a stateless *condottiere* [mercenary captain], the boy, now the Count of Pavia, was heir to one of Italy's most powerful dominions. Every care was taken over his upbringing. With a personal retinue of almost forty men (who were ordered to keep him under continual surveillance) and the best tutor in Milan, no moment or opportunity was lost in his training. While his younger brothers and sisters were permitted a degree of freedom, Galeazzo Maria was expected to undergo extensive preparations for his inheritance. This included musicianship, and even if he never achieved the standards of Ercole d'Este, Galeazzo Maria emerged with some crucial skills. A well-known letter of 1452 from his tutor reported that the eight-year-old boy had just begun Latin but was still learning French songs with 'great pleasure' and that his riding was improving daily. He also learned to play the organ, becoming a keen collector of instruments in later life.

Such training had many merits. Songs were an obvious means of teaching a foreign language and even tiny children could put on performances for distinguished guests. Another letter, from 1450, describes a display by the five-year-old Ippolita Maria Sforza before the French ambassador:

Yesterday, around the 22nd hour, the ambassador of the King of France, the magnificent lord Baylis de Senis arrived. Wishing to execute the orders which your lordship had written to me, I sent our son, Count Galeazzo Maria, to meet him two miles out accompanied by all my gentlemen with four trumpets . . . who accompanied [the ambassador] to the castle . . . after lunch he came to visit me. And I, having been advised, arranged to meet him with the most magnificent lady my mother at the head of the hall, and with my ladies and many others of this territory, all well arranged, and with my children next to me, I most pleasantly received him. Having taken him into the beautifully prepared hall, I had him sit down between my mother and myself. And as he was speaking of many pleasurable matters [cose da piacere], I had our children and the other youths and ladies perform a number of dances. And then he had his perform some, which were most attractive. And thus was carried out until the hour for dinner, and I also had our daughter Ippolita sing him a few pretty songs. Then he and I went to supper. Having dined, that is he in his room and I in mine, we returned to the said hall, where more and more similar dances, most lovely, were performed with the greatest pleasure of the said Monsignore who, considering their young age, marvelled at the excellent dancing and singing of our children.

Such performances impressed guests at home. Cultivating the ability to listen with discernment proved equally important when travelling abroad. The count's early state visits were all punctuated with musical events. As an adolescent in Venice in 1455, he was, among other amusements, treated to the singing of an English woman. His tutors and courtiers reported that:

Today the *signoria* sent, according to its custom, many most notable gentlemen to pick up your son, the illustrious Count Galeazzo, and accompany him to the Darsena [wet dock, basin], where first they showed him all those galleys, rope-making and the other artefacts they make. Secondly, in order to give him greater delight and pleasure, they had some birds boiled up according to the custom here. Thirdly, they conducted him and the rest of us into the room of the Arsenale [naval dockyard] where they had arranged an elegant luncheon of confections of many different types. And to ensure that he had even greater pleasure, they arranged for the arrival of some most notable singers, among whom there was a young English woman who sang so sweetly and pleasantly that it seemed not a human voice, but divine. Then, with the arrival of evening, they accompanied us to the house with great honour and kindness, striving continuously, besides the company they offered, to give us all those pleasures which were possible.

Such delights were designed to appeal to a young guest and are recorded wherever Galeazzo Maria travelled in his youth. The ballad performance in 1459 by Cosimo de Medici's professional *improvisatori* which took place when the Count of Pavia arrived in the villa at Careggi have been widely reported. But a more informal type of performance also took place within the household, as a letter by Galeazzo Maria to his father reveals:

I went to visit the magnificent Cosimo who had one of his son Piero's daughters play a pipe organ, which was a lovely thing to hear. But he did the same thing every day after I arrived, and he also arranged for some of his singers to sing. This gave us singular pleasure; but a much greater pleasure was the familiarity extended to me, in arranging for me to stay with the women, where I am. By this act, he has shown me that he wishes me well as a good servant. Then having heard these instrumental pieces and songs, in which master Hector, who was always present and sang and had one of his sons play an accompaniment, I went for my pleasure through the city with master Sigismondo and him.

The examples could be multiplied. Providing pleasure, *piacere*, was an essential item in fifteenth-century state visits; whether at home or abroad, music was an expected part of this entertainment. Sforza *feste* were characterised by 'balli et canti' [dances and songs]. Players were invited to perform while guests dined or during the evening after the party had returned from a long day's hunting. By the mid-Quattrocento, an ability to enjoy, understand and perform music was a necessary element of any aristocratic child's education. This was particularly true for marriageable young girls, for whom the ability to sing and dance brought decorous opportunities for public display. Bona of Savoy, for example, danced a moresca [Moorish dance] for the Sforza ambassador in order to show her fine physique; that of Dorotea Gonzaga (suspected of an inherited back disorder) was demonstrated by her dancing in a thin gown. While similar male performances were rarely commented upon in such detail, older men also shared these popular musical enthusiasms. The burdens of state did not prevent the Sforza's chief secretary, Cicco Simonetta, from collecting the music of Lorenzo Giustinian. Yet it is significant that in his letter requesting not only the songs but also an adolescent singer and lute player for his household, Simonetta made it clear that the boy and the music were not for his personal pleasure. They were destined for his children's education. Learning and listening to secular music was still perceived as an adjunct to youth, not as an appropriate occupation for an elder statesman.

In procuring a lutenist for his household this secretary, an immigrant from Calabria, was imitating the educational and social expectations of the Milanese court. But in emphasising the ubiquity of the culture to which Simonetta aspired it is possible to overstress its importance. Good horsemanship and an understanding of the finer points of falconry were as important as an ability to sing or play the lute. Music was only one part of an aristocratic child's education; for a future prince it had to take second place to more 'serious' matters. This was particularly problematic in Milan. If Galeazzo Maria's abilities as a hunter or lover of music were never in doubt, his interest in Latin and the examples of antiquity was always questionable. It became a cliché that the count was reluctant to read classical literature, and as he entered adolescence the *piacere* that he so enjoyed was increasingly viewed as an impediment to his preparation for rulership. The conflict is best documented during the count's trip to Ferrara in 1457. On that journey, as is well known, the young boy asked for French romances to read on the hot summer journey, 'to give pleasure to the assembled company'. The request was couched, however, in such a way as to suggest that he would also read his Latin texts. At thirteen, Galeazzo Maria was no longer a child and, as a little tract his father prepared for him pointed out, it was time to put aside childish ways and take up serious matters. The dispute over how much Latin Galeazzo Maria was required to read over the summer raged in correspondence between Milan and Ferrara, with his tutor, Guiniforte Barzizza, complaining that his charge, aided and abetted by Borso d'Este, would not scan his daily passages. To the deep disapproval of the humanist and his parents, he preferred the pleasures of hunting, dining and dancing. Barzizza noted with annoyance that Borso d'Este was spending all his time indulging Galeazzo Maria's youthful desires and that the time given over to *piacere* prevented the Ferrarese leader from attending to state matters and, indeed, caused him to lose all dignity.

The arguments continued as Galeazzo Maria grew older. In 1459 his uncle Lancilloto del Maino noted with satisfaction that the count had left a dancing party in Dorotea Gonzaga's honour to meet an ambassador (he also noted with similar pleasure the young man's ability to get his hand down the front of Dorotea's dress). But that year Galeazzo Maria's behaviour in Florence gave rise to concern, with the Mantuan ambassador reporting Francesco's fears that 'Count Galeazzo . . . doesn't seem to have grown up yet'. Six years later matters had still not improved and the duke refused to allow his son to visit either the Gonzaga or Este courts, saying that Galeazzo Maria's inclinations to *piacere*, particularly that of hunting birds, were interfering with his future role: 'It was necessary for [Galeazzo Maria] to leave the birds alone and to devote himself to, and be of assistance in, important matters in order to learn the style and the practice of rulership and governing.' Sforza's despair at his son's seeming immaturity was conveyed in one of the last letters he wrote before his death in March 1466: 'Galeazzo, I want you from now on to apply your brain and your mind to military matters and to what makes a soldier . . . I want you from now on to put aside boys' concerns and turn to those of men . . .'

Although not specifically singled out for comment, music and dancing, as well as hunting, seem to have been included in the pleasures Galeazzo Maria was expected to place to one side. For rulers of the mid-Quattrocento the decorum of musical entertainment was clear: it could not be allowed to distract from more weighty matters. The humanist Panormita had commented approvingly that King Alfonso of Aragon 'sometimes dismissed his trumpeters in order to concentrate on his reading of Livy, and . . . occasionally became so absorbed in his reading that he seemed not to hear the music of flutes and the sounds of dancers around him'. Galeazzo Maria's desire to present a newly matured image after his father's death in 1466 did not extend this far; but in the early years he was willing to concentrate on military and diplomatic responsibilities. Thus, the transition from Francesco, a soldier with little formal education, to the new, carefully trained duke initially brought little change to Milan's cultural patronage. Even when he deposed his mother from joint rule in late 1467, there was considerable continuity in their patterns of musical employment. Francesco and Bianca Maria had already made considerable changes during their sixteen-year reign. The previous duke, Filippo Maria Visconti, had, according to his somewhat astonished contemporary biographer, been totally indifferent to *spettacoli* [spectacular entertainments] and had refused to hire musicians. In introducing a steady succession of performers, including the famous Pietrobono himself, to whom they sent their own protégés for training, Francesco and Bianca Maria had returned the Milanese court to the intellectual and social mainstream. In general, however, they maintained a modestly-sized group of instrumentalists and singers whose primary function was secular entertainment, the 'cose da piacere' with which they had enticed the French ambassador in 1450. The cathedral choir, numbering around seven singers, could be called upon for important ceremonial occasions and the court itself contained men well versed in musical matters. With some advance notice, an impressive display could be put on by joining these amateur and professional musicians with those of neighbouring courts. The continuing ad hoc arrangement of such occasions emerges from a letter of 15 June 1468 when Vincenzo de' Medici (a member of the important Lombard as opposed to Florentine clan of the same name) wrote to Galeazzo Maria concerning the duke's forthcoming wedding to Bona of Savoy.

> In talking of the arrival of the most illustrious and excellent lady your wife, I seem, with reverence, to have understood that your lordship has made and is making provisions for many virtuous persons, such as citizens and courtiers and others of whatever rank, as is worthy and accustomed. But I don't believe that your lordship has had time, being occupied in so many diverse things, to consider my role. Therefore I thought I would suggest that your lordship deign to use me in some way as one who has always been brought up and has exercised his profession in the court in many things, above all in singing. Now I have found a good singing companion called Lanceloto dala Croce, a gentleman of worth. He and I are almost of the same age and well matched in our singing, and perhaps, indeed without any perhaps, we will shame the young ones, as you will see when we are put to the test. Again, as the French are arriving, they will see and understand that in Lombardy there are those who know how to sing songs in their language just as well as them and better. Your lordship is well informed and knows how many virtues God on high has endowed me with. Do not forget me in this festival as I will bring it honour.

While Vincenzo's fate is unknown, Galeazzo Maria did borrow musicians in order to put on a convincing performance of some magnificence for his bride and her French followers. The Marquis of Monferrato's trumpeters and an English soprano were, for example, called in for the ceremonies. These difficulties may have convinced him of the need for a more permanent group of performers. A few months after Bona's arrival the Sforza ambassador in Naples engaged two singers from Alfonso of Aragon's chapel, Raynerio de Precigneyo and the Frenchman Antonio Ponzo. This does not, however, indicate any major expansion. The duke was perfectly happy to let yet another singer, Filipeto Romeo, leave Milan. Only in 1469, after the death of his mother and the birth of a son, was Galeazzo Maria able to break free of previous inhibitions. At the age of twenty-five he finally consigned the school books still in his personal possession (including a 'librazolo in vulgare de balli et canti' [little book of dances and songs written in Italian] and the 'librazolo de diversi soneti facti per Donato Cagnola musico ducale' [little book of various sonnets composed by Donato Cagnola, ducal musician]) to the library in the castle at Pavia before embarking on a period of extraordinary grand gestures.

These ranged from painting the city walls of Vigevano in the Sforza colours of red and white, through redecorating the castles of Pavia and Milan, beginning new fortresses and palaces, repaving the urban centre of Milan, and commissioning large-scale medallion portraits of his wife and himself in pure gold, to – perhaps most startling to his contemporaries – opening negotiations for the title of King of Lombardy. Much of his attention, however, was focused on the reorganisation of his personal retinue, which quadrupled in the 1470s. But it was still another year before music came to the fore. With their experience of the Neapolitan royal chapel, Raynerio and Antonio Ponzo might have been expected to be influential in convincing Galeazzo Maria that such regal aspirations required regal music. But in late 1470 there was still no suggestion of a court choir and sacred music was not yet a priority. When, after an aborted attempt to travel to either France or Rome, the young duke and his wife proceeded to Florence under the guise of a vow to Ss Annunziata, they took a small number of singers. Passing through Emilia Romagna and Tuscany the retinue, numbering in the hundreds, awed the locals with their lavish gold and silver brocades. Although a substantial group of trumpeters was used on the trip, there were only four unnamed *cantori*, the same number recorded in Francesco Sforza's court, suggesting that early efforts to locate musicians had been limited. Indeed the list of participants in the abortive French trip hints that it may have been difficult to muster even these four. While every other court position was filled, the spaces for singers on the administrative lists included only Raynerio's name, leaving blank lines for his, as yet unknown, companions. Thus even if the duke had had long-term plans for a major chapel, he had still not acted upon them.

When he did, however, the innovations were startling in their scope. Between 1471 and 1472, the choir of four became one of almost thirty. This decision, as Lewis Lockwood has pointed out, was taken at the same time as the Duke of Ferrara, Ercole d'Este, put his plans for a new court chapel into motion. It is unlikely, if not impossible, that having made no move to establish sacred music within his court for over five years, Galeazzo Maria chose purely by coincidence to establish a chapel just before Ercole began recruiting singers himself. Milanese soldiers and informants had been camped on the Mantuan borders during the period of the Ferrarese succession, and although no documentation survives, Sforza spies within the Este court may well have reported on the new musical plans. But while the connection is clear, the relationship between the two initiatives may be more complex than straightforward competition. As a mature, internationally respected figure, Ercole gave licence to the younger, much less well-established Galeazzo Maria. With the nascent Ferrarese choir as his example, the Duke of Milan could follow his own instincts and transfer music from the traditional category of court entertainment to the realm of a serious state interest; *cose da piacere* [things of delight] could now become *cose di stato* [things of state].

The Milanese chapel's establishment was closely connected to other changes underway in the Sforza court. Many events once reserved for semi-private enjoyment had become increasingly public in their presentation and importance. The large-scale performance of sacred and secular music at the Milanese court joined a series of new ceremonies already underway, such as the processions of the feast of St George and the Christmas ceremony of the Yule Log. These annual festivals and other celebratory events such as baptisms and betrothals were designed to ensure that independent vassals and difficult members of the Lombard aristocracy would be drawn to the Sforza centres of Pavia and Milan. After 1469 feudatories had to attend Galeazzo Maria's court on major feast days such as Christmas and Easter in order to maintain their standing and privileges. Foreign dignitaries and ambassadors would also be invited to attend. In this way each group would, despite the Sforza dynasty's lack of legal title to the duchy of Milan, ritually acknowledge the family's standing. It was, indeed, just this imposition in Christmas 1476 which provided the chance for Galeazzo Maria's assassination.

The duke was murdered while attending mass but piety, the traditional formula for expressing an interest in sacred music, played a relatively small role on these occasions. Galeazzo Maria was perfectly aware of the need to appear in the guise of a Christian prince, founding at least one monastery and several chapels. Nevertheless, the language of secular pleasure dominated discussions concerning the new choir. When writing to the Bishop of Novara on 29 January 1473, for example, he made the association clear: chapels were being founded because song gave him more delight than any other pleasure. Like Ercole d'Este and the King of Naples, the Duke of Milan would be regularly observed while attending mass. But in following and improving on these examples, he could enjoy what was otherwise a tedious state duty.

To those close to the court, this attitude lacked decorum. In describing the duke's newly acquired habit of listening to Lenten preachers, the Mantuan ambassador could barely restrain himself:

This time I have little to write to your lordship as I have not heard anything new from any side. This illustrious lord [Galeazzo Maria Sforza] attends to his confessions and sermons. He has arranged for preaching in the castle every day since Sunday; he calls for preachers, now one, now another, from those who are preaching in this land and has had many new confessors come. And, during one sermon, he spoke with me and asked me whether your lordship would confess and take communion this Easter. I replied, yes, and that it was your custom to take communion at Easter. He then asked me if you would leave off women this time. I replied no, because as you had none there were none to leave off. His lordship laughed and said, 'the Marquis [Ludovico Gonzaga] has many more sins than I do . . . Undoubtedly I am a bit pompous, but that is no great sin in a lord. I am not proud. I have only the sin of sensuality [luxuria], and that I have in all perfection. I have adopted it in all the types and forms that one can have, but I have no other sins, certainly I have few.' My lord, if I had the authority I would have hit His Excellency for having made me such an appalling confession.

Galeazzo Maria's attitude that pomp was no sin in a great lord reached its logical conclusion in his court chapel. No effort and little expense were spared on its recruitment and construction. On 15 October 1471, six months after his return from Florence and two months after he got back from an extended hunting trip in the *monlavano*, the duke wrote to King Edward of England [Edward IV] explaining that Raynerio 'musico nostro' [our musician] and his courtier Aloysio would be arriving to search out new singers. Near-death in November did not lessen his determination, nor did it slow down his incessant acquisition of other Italian rulers' musicians. Although Galeazzo Maria continued to seek musicians from Naples, Savoy, closer and more vulnerable to Sforza pressure, quickly became his favourite poaching ground. A close connection between the Savoyard chapel and its new Milanese counterpart can be demonstrated in a variety of ways. In December 1471 he asked Yolanda of Savoy to send her entire choir to meet him in Novara, a request repeated on two occasions the following year when he specified she need send only the 'adult singers and not the little ones'. That same year he acquired the duchess's choirmaster, the tenor Antonio Guinati, and made the well-known request for the song 'Robineto notato su l'ayre de Ros-abella' [Robineto to the tune of Rosabella]. Yolanda's irritation at this audition-ing at her expense is clear from her comments two years later that, while she did not blame the duke, her singers had left her without licence and were required to return. This did not, however, stop Galeazzo Maria from demanding the loan of her organ-maker in 1474.

The continual search for singers from 1471 until 1476 is extensively documented in the magisterial nineteenth-century study of Emilio Motta. Galeazzo Maria scooped up the available musicians within Milan itself, and by promising high wages threatened the stability of the Aragonese and Estense choirs. Italy alone could not provide the necessary talent. France was a favourite source, and in 1472 and again in 1473 Gaspar van Weerbeke returned to his native Flanders to preach the benefits of a move to Milan. Galeazzo Maria's broadcasting of the fact that he wished, as he put it, to 'breathe new life into music in Italy' (*suscilare la musica in Italia*) by establishing chapels throughout his dominions had rapid effects. Even rulers and ambassadors who had not had the privilege of listening to his choir remarked upon it. It quickly became public knowledge that the introduc-tion of a good singer or a piece of music would ensure Galeazzo Maria's grati-tude. The Mantuan ambassador, Zaccaria da Pisa, acted as an informal adviser and procurement officer; ecclesiastics like the Bishop of Como, Branda Cas-tiglione, began recommending artists. In introducing the French singer Tomaso Leporis, the bishop, a close political ally of the Sforza, was careful to flatter the duke, noting that 'every day the news that your lordship wishes to found a notable and worthy chapel is spreading'.

The result was that by 1474 Galeazzo Maria's choir contained, on either full or temporary contracts, some of the most renowned names of music history, including Loyset Compère, Josquin Desprez, Alexander Agricola and Jean Cordier. Motta published several lists of these singers to which a further docu-ment from the end of Galeazzo Maria's lifetime can now be added. The lists were not, however, originally compiled for musicological purposes. The rapidly increasing court required a large chancery, and these papers formed an integral part of the Sforza court's financial and administrative bureaucracy. The 1474 register of singers, for example, was included in Cicco Simonetta's notebooks as one of many documents concerning the court's expansion and related salary payments. Lists of singers from 1475 have been extracted from the names of ducal householders who were given special outfits for the feast of St George and from other salary records. The last, previously unpublished, list of 1476, which includes thirty-three singers and three organists, is a register of those members of the court who would receive stabling when they travelled with the duke in 1476.

Removing this information from its bureaucratic context disguises the fact that the information was rarely exclusively concerned with either music or the chapel itself. The singers formed part of a much larger vision of court spectacle, whereby sound, vision and ceremonial reverence combined to ensure both the duke's private pleasure and dramatic public performances. Singling out singers' names does a disservice to an understanding of this more general role and conceals the fact that Galeazzo Maria's decision to expand his choir did not take place in isolation. In 1472–3 Galeazzo Maria embarked on an unprecedented expansion of all of his courtiers. Just as Weerbeke was sent out to find additional tenors and sopranos in Flanders, so too did other officials leave Milan for their homelands to encourage their compatriots to move to the Sforza court. In October 1472, for example, one of the duke's under-chamberlains arrived from Naples with twelve young Neapolitans to serve as *camerieri del signore* [gentlemen valets, grooms of the lord's chamber]. Young men of good family, preferably tall and good-looking, were sought in Cremona, Bologna, Piacenza and Milan itself. This was not just a display of luxurious indulgence. Lacking a legitimate title, Galeazzo Maria hoped to integrate potential opponents into his court, and considerable political skill went into the choice of new courtiers. Despite the financial strains which had imposed cut-backs the previous year, the 1476 list of those 'appointed to follow the court of our illustrious prince and excellent signore to whom accommodation must be given' suggests that Galeazzo Maria's retinue must have been remarkably impressive.

Even this document, however, represents only a small fraction of those with court connections. In order to save money, many courtiers were non-resident. The travelling court, therefore, consisted of those members whose presence was considered worth paying for. Putting the singers into context the document reveals that Galeazzo Maria moved with ten professional hand-ball players, five barbers, forty dog-handlers and thirty staff to supervise the hunts and the hawks. His summary of expenses for the year in question indicates that the same sum, 5000 ducats, was spent on both his singers and his dog-handlers. The list's compilers were quite straightforward in their assessment of an individual's worth, measuring status purely in terms of the number of horses he was permitted to stable at ducal expense. Thus the duke's younger brothers were each allowed thirty-two, while the most senior *cameriere da camera* [groom of the chamber], Francesco de Petrasanta, had to make do with twelve. The leading *cameriere da guardacamera* [groom of the antechamber], Giovanni Francesco Pallavicino, and the singer Pietro da Holi or Daule were permitted four horses each; the under-chamberlains had no allowance at all. This document suggests that Daule's standing surpassed that of his fellow singers, who were paired according to criteria which are still unclear and given a mutual stabling allowance. Even Jean Cordier, the most highly paid member of the choir, was expected to share seven horses with a singer named Rolando, while the choir leader, Antonio Guinati, and his

friend Bovis had four horses between them. The most famous composer of
Galeazzo Maria's chapel, Josquin Desprez, did particularly badly, sharing a single
pair of horses with Michael of Tours. Scholars have correctly noted that, as singers
often relied on benefices, Josquin's low salary did not necessarily indicate a lower
estimation of his talents. But in this impartial indicator, Josquin was still down
at the bottom of the list at a time when he was already producing music for the
court.

   Instead it was Pietro Daule and Antonio Guinati, now relatively unknown,
who prospered. Although the former's position in 1476 as *cameriere da guardacamera* represents a demotion it is still superior to that of most other members
of the court. Four years earlier, as a *cameriere da camera* – one of the duke's inner
circle of associates – he had been even more elevated. A list of expensive garments
given to the twenty-two chamberlains in 1472 carefully noted his dual status as
courtier and musician. While the other *camerieri da camera* were given half-length
gold brocade garments, Pietro Daule received 'A long gown of smooth red velvet,
lined with fox fur . . . which should be made in the French fashion, and five
tunics of smooth crimson velvet also in the French style, and these are in addition to the garments which he been given along with the other singers'.

   Guinati, usually referred to as L'Abbé, was never given a courtier's status but,
as choirmaster, wielded considerable power. His voice obviously pleased the duke,
for when Galeazzo Maria made his request for the 'Robineto/Rosabella' combination he specified that the words should be those normally used by Guinati.
Guinati's organisational skills were also at a premium. He did not always join the
choir when the duke demanded its presence, but he was responsible for selecting and sending the required singers. With a degree in law, and a long history of
service in the Savoyard chapel, Guinati was able to take advantage of the wealth
and patronage his position offered. His brother, originally a bombardier (he continued to offer advice on canonry to Galeazzo Maria), soon joined the choir and
he also was able to bring at least one close associate from Savoy, Pietro Alardi,
known as Bovis. The latter had been an important member of Yolanda's choir
and was heavily promoted at the expense of earlier arrivals. As Guinati and Bovis's
powers increased the two singers who had arrived from Naples in 1469 felt particularly hard done by. In 1473 Raynerio, whose comparatively low salary had
been stopped, sent three Spanish songs, 'scripti et notati' [with words and music],
to the duke, complaining that malicious tongues, particularly those of the choirmaster and Bovis, had been working against him. The letter, published by Motta
in 1887, is worth republishing in full both for its evidence of Galeazzo Maria's
continued fascination with secular music and for the details of the choir's
internal intrigues:

   Along with the present letter, I am sending you three Spanish songs which I am
   sure will be good and sweet. If you enjoy them I will send you others, and if
   there you find anything lacking or faulty in the said songs, your excellency
   should not blame me, who have written and notated them. Have them sung
   sweetly, *sotto voce* [as in a whisper], and slowly, then I am sure they will please
   you.

I should also advise your illustrious lordship that I am very badly out of pocket. I do not have a penny to spend and I find myself with debts: I have no means of satisfying and paying my creditors if not through your help. My debts amount to about 46 ducats. And I have to satisfy them at all costs by the feast of St Martin next November. I wish to appear a man of worth, my lord, and to pay that which I owe and to maintain faith and credit as any worthy man should do, so that your lordship need not be ashamed of my deeds. Only one thing saddens me greatly, my lord, for after the many pleasures and services which I have done for master l'Abbé [Guinati] and master Bovis, they wish at present to do me harm in return for this goodness. Praise God and let his will be done in all. Our Lord God forgive them, for they have no excuse. But I am certain and have no doubt that our Lord God is just and patient and will show the truth in all things. The evil tongues have done me enough harm, and I am certain that they have had my provision taken away, and they do nothing every day with your lordship but assault your ears with evil tales of me . . . God forgive them, for certainly, my lord, it is not the act of a virtuous and good man to speak badly of anyone. But I am comforted by one fact, that they and I have a good schoolteacher. When one thinks well, illustrious lord, there has never been a time when envy has not reigned among equals. If we all had the intellect and understanding to know our common good, we would live together honestly as good men, and eat the bread of your lordship in peace and with happiness. But it seems to me that we go seeking more bread than grain; I believe that when we have looked everywhere, we will not find any bread more flavoursome than that of your lordship. But this cursed envy destroys everything.

I do not believe, nor can I believe, that master l'Abbé and master Bovis could be so cruel and iniquitous against me, that they wish to kill me in this way. I would sooner have the fever for an entire year, than have even thought of doing them the smallest displeasure, even to the lowest of their servants. And if I have offended them in some way I humbly ask for a good pardon, and if I have failed in some way I offer myself up to any reproof which would please them and, please God, to your lordship to whom I humbly and continually commend myself.

With this fascinating description of the in-fighting taking place in the Milanese choir, Raynerio's letter suggests that the struggle for position and prominence was as acute among the musicians as it was among other gentlemen of the court. While Weerbeke and Tomaso Leporis may have had the tasks of selecting singers from abroad, Guinati and his Savoyard compatriots controlled their promotion in Milan. Along with Pietro Daule, their access to the duke and his duchess (who was, of course, originally from Savoy herself) gave them considerable powers. Guinati personally benefited from Milanese citizenship, two houses in Milan, water rights (which he sublet to another singer) and an extraordinary three-year concession for the exploitation of the duchy's mineral rights. These were the rewards for personally supervising both the singers and the preparation of Galeazzo Maria's secular and sacred choir manuscripts. This may have involved the purchase of choirbooks for the duke's new [Franciscan] observant monastery of S. Maria degli Angeli outside Abbiategrasso and certainly included the 1472 acquisition of four volumes of French and Spanish songs (which cost 40 ducats in total) and a songbook which Pietro Daule had personally purchased from the Duchess of Savoy. Another undated note from around the same time reveals that at least some of these items were being manufactured for Galeazzo Maria's private chamber: 'libro uno de canzone spagnole et franzose per tenire in camera' [book one of Spanish and French songs kept securely].

While the expansion of sacred music had clearly not diminished Galeazzo Maria's interest in the chanson, Guinati's main concern in 1472 and 1473 revolved around the new chapel being constructed in the duke's Milanese residence, the Castello di Porta Giovia. The choirmaster was responsible for providing cloth for the priests' robes, lecterns and four extremely expensive Graduals [an antiphon sung between the Epistle and the Gospel of the Eucharist at the steps of the altar], From the documentation it emerges that the lettering was done 'ala parexina' [in block lettering?], and that each book had an illuminated frontispiece and elaborate bindings. Although none of the Graduals survive, two other sumptuous religious texts from the same period, the 'Great Hours of Galeazzo Maria Sforza' and an Italian New Testament, indicate the scale of investment involved in these commissions. With gilt borders, and two large-scale miniatures on almost every page by the painter Cristoforo dei Predis, the latter was a highly prized object. It is impossible to determine the extent of Guinati's responsibility for any of the artistic decisions concerning the chapel and its furnishings. In March 1473 he purchased a *pace*, the image kissed during the mass, and made arrangements for its redesign. The metal plate would be incised with a scene of the Resurrection, the theme that dominated the frescoed chapel ceiling.

In this instance, Guinati may have been passing on ducal instructions, rather than acting independently. Artistic and architectural matters were generally the jealously guarded province of the supervisor of ducal works, another ex-bombardier, Bartolomeo Gadio da Cremona, who with his colleague, the Florentine architect Benedetto Ferrini, produced three new palace chapels in Pavia and Milan between 1469 and 1473. How Galeazzo Maria was seen listening to the music seems to have been as important as what he heard. The Visconti castle in Pavia already had a large double-vaulted chapel on the ground floor. In 1469, however, during an extensive scheme of redecoration, the duke took the opportunity to designate the single-vaulted room which led from the great hall into his private apartments (a space which had previously served as his father's courtiers' dining-room) as a second chapel, the *cappella di camera*. Only the *camerieri da camera* had permission to enter the ducal suite regularly, and the physical distinction between the upper and lower chapels, mirrored in the later construction in Milan, may have contributed to the division of Sforza singers into *cantori di cappella* and *cantori di camera*.

The transformations in the Milanese and Pavian chapels were not designed to offer fine acoustics. They were undertaken to ensure that the visual impact of Galeazzo Maria's choir was as splendid as its sound. Signorial magnificence would touch both senses simultaneously. By 1471 Galeazzo Maria had decided to place an elaborate carved polyptych housing the Visconti's most precious sacred relies in the upper chapel at Pavia. The sum of 2000 ducats was assigned to complete the work, half of which was taken up by the carved woodwork. Three of Milan's most prominent painters – Vincenzo Foppa, Bonifacio Bembo and the portraitist Zanetto Bugatto – were given the commission to paint 200 saints on the doors, a job which occupied their attention from 1473 to 1476. During that period Galeazzo Maria was equally preoccupied with his Milanese chapels. The architects had just finished work on a second chapel in the Sforza castle and were already planning a third for the newly extended south wing. The most important of these was, once again, that sited on the *piano nobile* leading into the duke's private apartments. The use of a chapel as an entry point into a signorial suite was not Galeazzo Maria's innovation. He himself had been received by Cosimo de' Medici in the as yet unfrescoed palace chapel of Via Larga in 1459. But he had noted how unsuitable the small private space was for large crowds and how quickly the group had had to vacate the room. He would not repeat the mistake. His new chapels were dramatically enlarged. Unlike their Medici or Montefeltro counterparts, these Milanese rooms were not spaces for private prayer and contemplation but areas of public performance. Even when the throngs invited for special feasts could not get into the lower chapel they could watch from the adjacent *camera delle columbine* [chamber of the doves] (so called because of the dove motif with which it was decorated) through a large grated window.

This chapel still survives today and gives some impression of the effect the duke intended to convey. Its lower walls, now left bare, were probably covered in tapestries or brocade. The upper section is still covered with large figures of saints standing against a background of raised gold gesso [plaster]. The lunettes carried an image of the Annunciation along with Galeazzo Maria's arms, monograms and *imprese* [heraldic devices], while the ceiling, completed by the artist Stefano dei Fedelis, was filled with two separate scenes from the Resurrection. More than four artists were involved in the decoration, which had to be done rapidly and to a tight budget. Nonetheless, the lavish use of azure and gold tends to blur the stylistic distinctions, creating an overall sense of grandeur at a reasonable cost.

The Milanese castle's upper chapel, which led into Galeazzo Maria's private suite, has disappeared. The documentation suggests that access to this space was more restricted, and that the room was split by a *tramezzo* [partition] wall, a pattern the ducal supervision of works suggested should be imitated in Pavia using a 'transverse wall like that in Milan with a door in the centre and a window on each side, through which those in the chapel might be able to follow the Mass and also see the altarpiece'. A door connected the chapel to the bedroom used by either the duke or his most distinguished guests. It was particularly appropriate that its first occupant after the chapel's completion was Cardinal Pietro Riario the nephew of the other great fifteenth-century musical patron Pope Sixtus IV. On 12 September 1473 the Mantuan ambassador Zaccaria da Pisa, gave a full description of the visit:

> In the castle courtyard all the trumpets of his lordship were arrayed, and playing they accompanied him inside; they went up on horseback to the hall where, dismounting, they went towards the rooms where your lordship had stayed. At

the head of this hall there was a chapel, newly built above the other one below. Gathered here were all the chapel singers [cantori di cappella], who immediately began singing the *Te Deum laudamus* [We praise thee, O God]. The chapel was completely adorned with brocade cloths, and the ceiling above was painted, the altar in the middle with the usual ornaments and so too the rest of the ornaments of the chapel. From this chapel one enters the room where your lordship had stayed without returning to the hall since at the side of the chapel, to the left, a double door has been built which serves as two exits. One leads into the above-mentioned room, the other into another room on the left which is above our lord's room below – the one which is panelled . . . They are all beautifully decorated and in his [Pietro Riario's] there is a set of white-gold brocade hangings and the walls around are covered with tapestries as are all the rest of the rooms.

Riario was undoubtedly impressed by both the visual and aural wealth displayed for his benefit. His own ninety-three-strong retinue included two musicians, and some of his time in Pavia was spent admiring and listening to the instruments of the famed organ-maker Isaac Argyropoulos. It is again undoubtedly no coincidence that Galeazzo Maria put on a dramatic presentation of choral skill in the same year that Sixtus IV began recruiting singers for the Sistine chapel. Indeed, the duke hoped to take his choir to Rome the following year to impress Della Rovere personally. But music was not the primary reason for these exchanges; it provided a highly effective backdrop to serious diplomacy. Galeazzo Maria had already forged a strong alliance with the Savonese pope; by the end of the 1473 visit Riario's brother, Girolamo, was the new owner of the contested city of Imola with Caterina Sforza as his newly betrothed fiancée. The singers, therefore, were only one part, albeit a very important one, of the court scenery, which assured the pope's representatives of the high value of a Milanese alliance. The publicly strengthened tie to the papacy, in turn, convinced doubting Sforza courtiers, citizens and feudatories that any internal opposition would be fruitless.

In his final assessment of Galeazzo Maria's reign, Bernardino Corio described him as 'above all, most liberal, eager for glory and to be feared. He held it dear that one could say with truth that his court was one of the most splendid in the universe. He was most magnificent in his trappings and in his lifestyle and in his court was above all most splendid'.

The concentration on the court and personal display has often been seen by modern scholars as a sign of the weakness and vanity which led to his death. But, as Riccardo Fubini has shown, the assassination was not the isolated act of impetuous youths outraged at Galeazzo Maria's excesses. It seems rather to have been a well-coordinated attempt undertaken by resentful members of the Milanese nobility. For a group once accustomed to real political influence, the sight, sounds and ceremonies devised by the duke had worked all too well. The rituals of court life were replacing the possibilities of genuine power. Confined by Galeazzo Maria to rigidly defined court roles, starved of the privileges and funds they had come to accept as their due, the families who sponsored the plot hoped to regain their influence under a more compliant regime. Galeazzo Maria's singers alone did not, therefore, draw him to his death. But when, in 1477, Bona of Savoy dismissed many of the choir members and refused to complete the vast polyptych in the Pavian chapel she was doing much more than saving money. If music had become a symbol of Galeazzo Maria's signorial ambitions, its reduction was a sign that the new regent had recognised the limitations of magnificence.

NOTE

1   B. Corio, *Storia di Milano*, ed. E. De Magri (Milan, 1857; rept, Milan, 1975). On history writing in Milan see G. Ianziti, *Humanistic Historiography under the Sforzas: Politics and Propaganda in Fifteenth-Century Milan* (Oxford, 1988).

10   Michael Baxandall **'Painting and Experience in Fifteenth Century Italy'**

Source: from *Painting and Experience in Fifteenth Century Italy*, Michael Baxandall, Oxford University Press, Oxford, second edition, 1988, pp. 36–46. © Oxford University Press 1972, 1988. By permission of Oxford University Press.

Renaissance people were, as has been said, on their mettle before a picture, because of an expectation that cultivated people should be able to make discriminations about the interest of pictures. These very often took the form of a preoccupation with the painter's skill, and [. . .] this preoccupation was something firmly anchored in certain economic and intellectual conventions and assumptions. But the only practical way of publicly making discriminations is verbally: the Renaissance beholder was a man under some pressure to have words that fitted the interest of the object. The occasion might be one when actual enunciation of words was appropriate, or it might be one when internal possession of suitable categories assured him of his own competence in relation to the picture. In any event, at some fairly high level of consciousness the Renaissance man was one who matched concepts with pictorial style.

This is one of the things that makes the kind of culturally relative pressures on perception we have been discussing so very important for Renaissance perception of pictures. In our own culture there is a class of over-cultivated person who, though he is not a painter himself, has learned quite an extensive range of specialized categories of pictorial interest, a set of words and concepts specific to the quality of paintings: he can talk of 'tactile values', or of 'diversified images'. In the fifteenth century there were some such people, but they had relatively few special concepts, if only because there was then such a small literature of art. Most of the people the painter catered for had half-a-dozen or so such categories for the quality of pictures – 'fore-shortening', 'ultramarine at two florins an ounce', 'drapery' perhaps, and a few others we shall be meeting – and then were thrown back on their more general resources.

Like most of us now, his real training in consciously precise and complex visual assessment of objects, 'both natural ones and those made by man's art', was not on paintings but on things more immediate to his well-being and social survival:

6 Pisanello. *Studies of a Horse.* Paris, Louvre (Cod. Vallardi 2468). Pen, wash and chalk.
Photo: R.M.N.-J.G. Berizzi

The beauty of the horse is to be recognized above all in its having a body so broad and long that its members correspond in a regular fashion with its breadth and length (Figs 6 and 7). The head of the horse should be proportionately slender, thin and long. The mouth wide and sharply cut; the nostrils broad and distended. The eyes should not be hollowed nor deeply recessed; the ears should be small and carried like spears; the neck long and rather slender towards the head, the jaw quite slender and thin, the mane sparse and straight. The chest should be broad and fairly round, the thighs not tapering but rather straight and even, the croup short and quite flat, the loins round and rather thick, the ribs and other like parts also thick, the haunches long and even, the crupper long and wide. . . . The horse should be taller before than behind, to the same degree a deer is, and should carry its head high, and the thickness of its neck should be proportionable with its chest. Anyone who wants to be a judge of horses' beauty must consider all the parts of the horse discussed above as parts related in proportion to the height and breadth of the horse. . . .

But there is a distinction to be made between the general run of visual skills and a preferred class of skills specially relevant to the perception of works of art. The skills we are most aware of are not the ones we have absorbed like everyone else in infancy, but those we have learned formally, with conscious effort: those which we have been taught. And here in turn there is a correlation with skills that can be talked about. Taught skills commonly have rules and categories, a terminology and stated standards, which are the medium through which they are teachable. These two things – the confidence in a relatively advanced and valued skill, and the availability of verbal resources associated with them – make such skills particularly susceptible to transfer in situations such as that of a man in front of a picture.

This raises a problem. We have been moving towards a notion of a Quattrocento cognitive style. By this one would mean the equipment that the fifteenth-century painter's public brought to complex visual stimulations like pictures. One is talking not about all fifteenth-century people, but about those whose response to works of art was important to the artist – the patronizing classes, one might say. In effect this means rather a small proportion of the population: mercantile and professional men, acting as members of confraternities or as individuals, princes and their courtiers, the senior members of religious houses. The peasants and the urban poor play a very small part in the Renaissance culture that most interests us now, which may be deplorable but is a fact that must be accepted. Yet among the patronizing classes there were variations, not just the inevitable variation from man to man, but variation by groups. So a certain profession, for instance, leads a man to discriminate particularly efficiently in identifiable areas. Fifteenth-century medicine trained a physician to observe the relations of member to member of the human body as a means to diagnosis, and a doctor was alert and equipped to notice matters of proportion in painting too. But while it is clear that among the painter's public there were many subgroups with special visual skills and habits – the painters themselves were one such subgroup – this book will be concerned with more generally accessible styles of discrimination. A Quattrocento man handled affairs, went to church, led a social life; from all of these activities he acquired skills relevant to his observation of painting. It is true that one man would be stronger on business skills, another on pious skills, another on polite skills; but every man had something of each of these, whatever the individual balance, and it is the highest common factor of skill in his public that the painter consistently catered for.

To sum up: some of the mental equipment a man orders his visual experience with is variable, and much of this variable equipment is culturally relative, in the sense of being determined by the society which has influenced his experience. Among these variables are categories with which he classifies his visual stimuli, the knowledge he will use to supplement what his immediate vision gives him, and the attitude he will adopt to the kind of artificial object seen. The beholder must use on the painting such visual skills as he has, very few

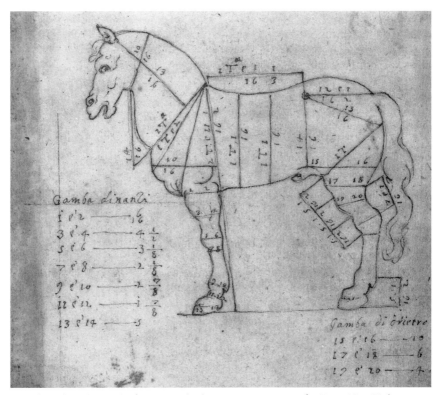

7 Carlo Urbino (1553–85) after Leonardo da Vinci. *Dimensions of a Horse.* New York, Pierpont Morgan Library, MS. M.A., 1139, fol. 82 r. Pen, wash and chalk. Photo: Art Resource, New York.

of which are normally special to painting, and he is likely to use those skills his society esteems highly. The painter responds to this; his public's visual capacity must be his medium. Whatever his own specialized professional skills, he is himself a member of the society he works for and shares its visual experience and habit.

We are concerned here with Quattrocento cognitive style as it relates to Quattrocento pictorial style. This chapter must now exemplify the kinds of visual skill a Quattrocento person was distinctively equipped with, and try to show how these were relevant to painting.

Most fifteenth-century pictures are religious pictures. This is self-evident, in one sense, but 'religious pictures' refers to more than just a certain range of subject matter; it means that the pictures existed to meet institutional ends to help with specific intellectual and spiritual activities. It also means that the pictures came within the jurisdiction of a mature body of ecclesiastical theory about images. There is no sign of the more academic elaborations of this theory being active in many people's minds during the fifteenth century, though they were quite often rehearsed by the theologians, but a few of the basic principles still set standards for the pictures much more real for the public mind than some of the artistic theory we make so much of now.

What was the religious function of religious pictures? In the Church's view the purpose of images was threefold. John of Genoa's late thirteenth-century *Catholicon,* still a standard dictionary of the period, summarized them in this way:

Know that there were three reasons for the institution of images in churches. *First*, for the instruction of simple people, because they are instructed by them as if by books. *Second*, so that the mystery of the incarnation and the examples of the Saints may be the more active in our memory through being presented daily to our eyes. *Third*, to excite feelings of devotion, these being aroused more effectively by things seen than by things heard.

In a sermon published in 1492 the Dominican Fra Michele da Carcano gives an orthodox Quattrocento expansion of this:

. . . images of the Virgin and the Saints were introduced for three reasons. *First*, on account of the ignorance of simple people, so that those who are not able to read the scriptures can yet learn by seeing the sacraments of our salvation and faith in pictures. It is written: 'I have learned that, inflamed by unconsidered zeal, you have been destroying the images of the saints on the grounds that they should not be adored. And we praise you wholeheartedly for not allowing them to be adored, but we blame you for breaking them . . . For it is one thing to adore a painting, but it is quite another to learn from a painted narrative what to adore. What a book is to those who can read, a picture is to the ignorant people who look at it. Because in a picture even the unlearned may see what example they should follow; in a picture they who know no letters may yet read.' St. Gregory the Great wrote these words to Serenus, Bishop of Marseilles. *Second*, images were introduced on account of our emotional sluggishness; so that men who are not aroused to devotion when they hear about the histories of the Saints may at least be moved when they see them, as if actually present, in pictures. For our feelings are aroused by things seen more than by things heard. *Third*, they were introduced on account of our unreliable memories. . . . Images were introduced because many people cannot retain in their memories what they hear, but they do remember if they see images.

If you commute these three reasons for images into instructions for the beholder, it amounts to using pictures as respectively lucid, vivid and readily accessible stimuli to meditation on the Bible and the lives of Saints. If you convert them into a brief for the painter, they carry an expectation that the picture should tell its story in a clear way for the simple and in an eye-catching and memorable way for the forgetful, and with full use of all the emotional resources of the sense of sight, the most powerful as well as the most precise of the senses.

Of course, the matter could not always be as simple and as rational as this; there were abuses both in people's responses to pictures and in the way the pictures themselves were made. Idolatry was a standing preoccupation of theology: it was fully realized that simple people could easily confuse the image of divinity or sanctity with divinity or sanctity itself, and worship it. There were

widely reported phenomena that tended to go with irrational responses to the
images; a story in Sicco Polentone's *Life of St. Anthony of Padua* printed in 1476:

> Pope Boniface VIII . . . had the old and ruinous Basilica of St. John Lateran at
> Rome rebuilt and redecorated with much care and expense, and he listed by
> name which saints were to be depicted in it. The painters of the Order of Minor
> Friars were preeminent in this art and there were two particularly good masters
> from this Order. When these two had painted up all the saints the Pope had
> ordered, on their own initiative they added in a blank space pictures of Sts.
> Francis and Anthony. When the Pope heard about this he was angered by their
> disrespect of his orders. 'I can tolerate the St. Francis,' he said, 'as it is now done.
> But I insist on the St. Anthony being removed completely.' However all the
> people sent by the Pope to carry out this command were thrown down to the
> ground, fiercely knocked about and driven away by a terrible, resounding,
> gigantic spirit. When the Pope heard of this, he said: 'Let the St. Anthony alone,
> then, since we can see he wants to stay; in conflict with him, we can only lose
> more than we gain.'

But idolatry never became as publicly scandalous and pressing a problem as it
did in Germany; it was an abuse on which theologians regularly discoursed, but
in a stereotyped and rather unhelpful way. Lay opinion usually felt able to dismiss
it as an abuse of pictures that did not constitute a condemnation of the institution of images itself; as the humanist Chancellor of Florence Coluccio Salutati
had described it:

> I think [an ancient Roman's] feelings about their religious images were no dif-
> ferent from what we in the full rectitude of our faith feel now about the painted
> or carved memorials of our Saints and Martyrs. For we perceive these not as
> Saints and as Gods but rather as images of God and the Saints. It may indeed
> be that the ignorant vulgar think more and otherwise of them than they should.
> But one enters into understanding and knowledge of spiritual things through
> the medium of sensible things, and so if pagan people made images of Fortune
> with a cornucopia and a rudder – as distributing wealth and controlling human
> affairs – they did not deviate very much from the truth. So too, when our own
> artists represent Fortune as a queen turning with her hands a revolving wheel,
> so long as we apprehend that picture as something made by a man's hand, not
> something itself divine but a similitude of divine providence, direction and
> order – and representing indeed not its essential character but rather the
> winding and turning of mundane affairs – who can reasonably complain?

The abuse was agreed to exist in some measure but did not stimulate churchmen
to new thoughts or action on the problem.

As for the pictures themselves, the Church realized there were sometimes faults
against theology and good taste in their conception. S. Antonino, Archbishop of
Florence, sums up the three main errors:

> Painters are to be blamed when they paint things contrary to our Faith – when
> they represent the Trinity as one person with three heads, a monster; or, in the

8 Matteo di Giovanni. *The Assumption of the Virgin* (1474). London, National Gallery.
Panel. Reproduced by permission of the Trustees of the National Gallery.

9 Gentile da Fabriano. *The Adoration of the Magi* (1423). Florence, Uffizi. Panel. Photo: Alinari-Anderson.

Annunciation, an already formed infant, Jesus, being sent into the Virgin's womb, as if the body he took on were not of her substance; or when they paint the infant Jesus with a hornbook, even though he never learned from man. But they are not to be praised either when they paint apocryphal matter, like midwives at the Nativity, or the Virgin Mary in her Assumption handing down her girdle to St. Thomas on account of his doubt (Fig. 8), and so on. Also, to paint curiosities into the stories of Saints and in churches, things that do not serve to arouse devotion but laughter and vain thoughts – monkeys, and dogs chasing hares and so on, or gratuitously elaborate costumes – this I think unnecessary and vain.

Subjects with heretical implications, apocryphal subjects, subjects obscured by a frivolous and indecorous treatment. Again, all three of these faults did exist. Christ was erroneously shown learning to read in many paintings. The apocryphal story of St. Thomas and the Virgin's girdle was the largest sculptured decoration on S. Antonino's own cathedral church at Florence, the Porta della Mandorla, and appears in numerous paintings. Gentile da Fabriano's *Adoration of the Magi* (Fig. 9), painted for the Florentine merchant and humanist Palla Strozzi in 1423, has the monkeys, dogs and elaborate costumes S. Antonino considered unnecessary and vain. But, also again, the complaint is not new or particularly of its time; it is just a Quattrocento version of a stock theologian's complaint, voiced continually from St. Bernard to the Council of Trent. When S. Antonino looked at the painting of his time he might well have felt that, on the whole, the Church's three functions for painting were fulfilled: that most pictures were (1) clear, (2) attractive and memorable, (3) stirring registrations of the holy stories. If he had not, he was certainly the man to say so.

So the first question – What was the religious function of religious paintings? – can be reformulated, or at least replaced by a new question: What sort of painting would the religious public for pictures have found lucid, vividly memorable, and emotionally moving?

The painter was a professional visualizer of the holy stories. What we now easily forget is that each of his pious public was liable to be an amateur in the same line, practised in spiritual exercises that demanded a high level of visualization of, at least, the central episodes of the lives of Christ and Mary. To adapt a theological distinction, the painter's were exterior visualizations, the public's interior visualizations. The public mind was not a blank tablet on which the painters' representations of a story or person could impress themselves; it was an active institution of interior visualization with which every painter had to get along. In this respect the fifteenth-century experience of a painting was not the painting we see now so much as a marriage between the painting and the beholder's previous visualizing activity on the same matter.

So it is important before all else to know roughly what sort of activity this was. One handbook that is usefully explicit is the *Zardino de Oration,* the *Garden of Prayer,* written for young girls in 1454 and later printed in Venice. The book explains the need for internal representations and their place in the process of prayer:

> The better to impress the story of the Passion on your mind, and to memorise each action of it more easily, it is helpful and necessary to fix the places and people in your mind: a city, for example, which will be the city of Jerusalem taking for this purpose a city that is well known to you. In this city find the principal places in which all the episodes of the Passion would have taken place for instance, a palace with the supper-room where Christ had the Last Supper with the Disciples, and the house of Anne, and that of Caiaphas, with the place where Jesus was taken in the night, and the room where He was brought before Caiaphas and mocked and beaten. Also the residence of Pilate where he spoke with the Jews, and in it the room where Jesus was bound to the Column. Also the site of Mount Calvary, where he was put on the Cross; and other like places. . . .
>
> And then too you must shape in your mind some people, people well-known to you, to represent for you the people involved in the Passion the person of Jesus Himself, of the Virgin, Saint Peter, Saint John the Evangelist, Saint Mary Magdalen, Anne, Caiaphas, Pilate, Judas and the others, every one of whom you will fashion in your mind.

When you have done all this, putting all your imagination into it, then go into your chamber. Alone and solitary, excluding every external thought from your mind, start thinking of the beginning of the Passion, starting with how Jesus entered Jerusalem on the ass. Moving slowly from episode to episode, meditate on each one, dwelling on each single stage and step of the story. And if at any point you feel a sensation of piety, stop: do not pass on as long as that sweet and devout sentiment lasts. . . .

This sort of experience, a visualizing meditation on the stories particularized to the point of perhaps setting them in one's own city and casting them from one's own acquaintance, is something most of us now lack. It gave the painter's exterior visualizations a curious function.

11   Clifford Geertz 'Art as a Cultural System'

Source: from *Local Knowledge: Further Essays in Interpretative Anthropology,*
Clifford Geertz, Basic Books Inc., New York, 1983, chapter 5, pp. 94–5, 102–9,
117–20.

Art is notoriously hard to talk about. It seems, even when made of words in the literary arts, all the more so when made of pigment, sound, stone, or whatever in the nonliterary ones, to exist in a world of its own, beyond the reach of discourse. It not only is hard to talk about it; it seems unnecessary to do so. It speaks, as we say, for itself: a poem must not mean but be; if you have to ask what jazz is you are never going to get to know. [. . .]

But, of course, hardly anyone, save the truly indifferent, is [. . .] silent, artists included. On the contrary, the perception of something important in either particular works or in the arts generally moves people to talk (and write) about them incessantly. Something that meaningful to us cannot be left just to sit there bathed in pure significance, and so we describe, analyze, compare, judge, classify; we erect theories about creativity, form, perception, social function; we characterize art as a language, a structure, a system, an act, a symbol, a pattern of feeling; we reach for scientific metaphors, spiritual ones, technological ones, political ones; and if all else fails we string dark sayings together and hope someone else will elucidate them for us. The surface bootlessness of talking about art seems matched by a depth necessity to talk about it endlessly. And it is this peculiar state of affairs that I want here to probe, in part to explain it, but even more to determine what difference it makes. [. . .]

For Italian painting, I will mainly rely on Michael Baxandall's recent book, *Painting and Experience in Fifteenth Century Italy* [Text 10], which takes precisely the sort of approach I here am advocating. Baxandall is concerned with defining what he calls 'the period eye' – that is, 'the equipment that a fifteenth-century painter's public [that is, other painters and "the patronizing classes"] brought to complex visual stimulations like pictures.' A picture, he says, is sensitive to the kinds of interpretive skill – patterns, categories, inferences, analogies – the mind brings to it:

A man's capacity to distinguish a certain kind of form or relationship of forms will have consequences for the attention with which he addresses a picture. For instance, if he is skilled in noting proportional relationships, or if he is practiced in reducing complex forms to compounds of simple forms, or if he has a rich set of categories for different kinds of red and brown, these skills may well lead him to order his experience of Piero della Francesca's *Annunciation* differently from people without these skills, and much more sharply than people whose experience has not given them many skills relevant to the picture. For it is clear that some perceptual skills are more relevant to any one picture than others: a virtuosity in classifying the ductus [drawing, making strokes with a pen] of flexing lines – a skill many Germans, for instance, possessed in this period . . . would not find much scope on the *Annunciation*. Much of what we call 'taste' lies in this, the conformity between discriminations demanded by a painting and skills of discrimination possessed by the beholder.

But what is even more important, these appropriate skills, for both the beholder and the painter, are for the most part not built in like retinal sensitivity for focal length but are drawn from general experience, the experience in this case of living a quattrocento life and seeing things in a quattrocento way:

. . . some of the mental equipment a man orders his visual experience with is variable, and much of this variable equipment is culturally relative, in the sense of being determined by the society which has influenced his experience. Among these variables are categories with which he classifies his visual stimuli, the knowledge he will use to supplement what his immediate vision gives him, and the attitude he will adopt to the kind of artificial object seen. The beholder must use on the painting such visual skills as he has, very few of which are normally special to painting, and he is likely to use those skills his society esteems highly. The painter responds to this; his public's visual capacity must be his medium. Whatever his own specialized professional skills, he is himself a member of the society he works for and shares its visual experience and habit.

The first fact [. . .] to be attended to in these terms is, of course, that most fifteenth-century Italian paintings were religious paintings, and not just in subject matter but in the ends they were designed to serve. Pictures were meant to deepen human awareness of the spiritual dimensions of existence; they were visual invitations to reflections on the truths of Christianity. Faced with an arresting image of the Annunciation, the Assumption of the Virgin, the Adoration of the Magi, the Charge to St. Peter, or the Passion, the beholder was to complete it by reflecting on the event as he knew it and on his personal relationship to the mysteries it recorded. 'For it is one thing to adore a painting,' as a Dominican preacher defending the virtuousness of art, put it, 'but it is quite another to learn from a painted narrative what to adore.'

Yet the relation between religious ideas and pictorial images (and this I think is true for art generally) was not simply expositive; they were not Sunday school illustrations. The painter, or at least the religious painter, was concerned with inviting his public to concern themselves with first things and last, not with providing them with a recipe or a surrogate for such concern, nor with a transcription of it. His relation, or more exactly, the relations of his painting, to the wider culture was interactive or, as Baxandall puts it, complementary. Speaking of Giovanni Bellini's *Transfiguration*, a generalized, almost typological, but of course marvellously plastic, rendering of the scene, he calls it a relic of cooperation between Bellini and his public – 'The fifteenth-century experience of the *Transfiguration* was an interaction between the painting, the configuration on the wall, and the visualizing activity of the public mind – a public mind with different furniture and dispositions from ours.' Bellini could count on a contribution from the other side and designed his panel so as to call that contribution out, not to depict it. His vocation was to construct an image to which a distinctive spirituality could forcibly react. The public does not need, as Baxandall remarks, what it has already got. What it needs is an object rich enough to see it in; rich enough, even, to, in seeing it, deepen it.

There were, of course, all sorts of cultural institutions active in forming the sensibility of quattrocento Italy which converged with painting to produce the 'period eye,' and not all of them were religious (as not all the paintings were religious). Among the religious ones, popular sermons, classifying and subclassifying the revelatory events and personages of the Christian myth and setting forth the types of attitude – disquiet, reflection, inquiry, humility, dignity, admiration – appropriate to each, as well as offering dicta [sayings] as to how such matters were represented visually, were probably the most important. 'Popular preachers . . . drilled their congregations in a set of interpretive skills right at the centre of the fifteenth-century response to painting.' Gestures were classified, physiognomies typed, colors symbologized, and the physical appearance of central figures discussed with apologetical care. 'You ask,' another Dominican preacher announced,

Was the Virgin dark or fair? Albertus Magnus says that she was not simply dark, nor simply red-haired, nor just fair-haired. For any one of these colours by itself brings a certain imperfection to a person. This is why one says: 'God save me from a red-haired Lombard,' or 'God save me from a black-haired German,' or 'from a fair-haired Spaniard,' or 'from a Belgian of whatever colour.' Mary was a blend of complexions, partaking of all of them, because a face partaking of all of them is a beautiful one. It is for this reason medical authorities declare that a complexion compounded of red and fair is best when a third colour is added: black. And yet this, says Albertus, we must admit: she was a little on the dark side. There are three reasons for thinking this – firstly by reason of complexion, since Jews tend to be dark and she was a Jewess; secondly by reason of witness, since St. Luke made the three pictures of her now at Rome, Loreto and Bologna, and these are brown-complexioned; thirdly by reason of affinity. A son commonly takes after his mother, and vice versa; Christ was dark, therefore . . .

Of the other domains of Renaissance culture that contributed to the way fifteenth-century Italians looked at paintings, two which Baxandall finds to have been of particular importance were another art, though a lesser one, social dancing, and a quite practical activity he calls gauging – that is, estimating quantities, volumes, proportions, ratios, and so on for commercial purposes.

Dancing had relevance to picture seeing because it was less a temporal art allied to music, as with us, than a graphic one allied to spectacle – religious pageants, street masques, and so on; a matter of figural grouping not, or anyway not mainly, of rhythmic motion. As such, it both depended upon and sharpened the capacity to discern psychological interplay among static figures grouped in subtle patterns, a kind of body arranging – a capacity the painters shared and used to evoke their viewer's response. In particular, the *bassa danza*, a slow paced, geometrized dance popular in Italy at the time, presented patterns of figural grouping that painters such as Botticelli, in his *Primavera* (which revolves, of course, around the dance of the Graces) or his *Birth of Venus*, employed in organizing their work. The sensibility the *bassa danza* represented, Baxandall says, 'involved a public skill at interpreting figure patterns, a general experience of semi-dramatic arrangement [of human bodies] that allowed Botticelli and other painters to assume a similar public readiness to interpret their own groups.' Given a widespread familiarity with highly stylized dance forms consisting essentially of discrete sequences of *tableaux vivants*, the painter could count on an immediate visual understanding of his own sort of figural tableaux in a way not very open in a culture such as ours where dance is a matter more of movement framed between poses than poses framed between movement and the general sense for tacit gesture is weak. 'The transmutation of a vernacular social art of grouping into an art where a pattern of people – not gesticulating or lunging or grimacing people – can still stimulate a strong sense of . . . psychological interplay, is the problem: it is doubtful if we have the right predispositions to see such refined innuendo at all spontaneously.'

Beyond and behind this tendency to conceive of both dances and paintings as patterns of body arrangement carrying implicit meaning lies, of course, a wider tendency in the whole society, and particularly in its cultivated classes, to regard the way in which men grouped themselves with respect to one another, the postural orderings they fell into in one another's company, as not accidental but the result of the sorts of relationships they had to one another. But it is in the other matter Baxandall takes to have had a forming impact on how the people of the Renaissance saw paintings – gauging – that this deeper penetration of visual habit into the life of society, and the life of society into it, is apparent.

It is an important fact of art history, he notes, that commodities have come regularly in standard-size containers only since the nineteenth century (and even then, he might have added, only in the West). 'Previously a container – barrel, sack, or bale – was unique, and calculating its volume quickly and accurately was a condition of business.' And the same was true of lengths, as in the cloth trade, proportions, as in brokerage, or ratios, as in surveying. One did not survive in commerce without such skills, and it was merchants who, for the most part, commissioned the paintings, and in some cases, like Piero della Francesca, who wrote a mathematical handbook on gauging, painted them.

In any case, both painters and their merchant patrons had a similar education in such matters – to be literate was at the same time to have command of the sorts of techniques available to judge the dimensions of things. So far as solid objects were concerned these skills involved the ability to break down irregular or unfamiliar masses into compounds of regular and familiar, and thus calculable, ones – cylinders, cones, cubes and so on; for two-dimensional ones, a similar ability to analyze ununiform surfaces into simple planes: squares, circles, triangles, hexagons. The heights to which this could rise is indicated in a passage Baxandall gives from Piero's handbook:

> There is a barrel, each of its ends being 2 bracci in diameter; the diameter at its bung is $2\frac{1}{4}$ bracci and halfway between bung and end it is $2\frac{2}{9}$ bracci. The barrel is 2 bracci long. What is its cubic measure?
>
> This is like a pair of truncated cones. Square the diameter at the ends: $2 \times 2 = 4$. Then square the median diameter $2\frac{2}{9} \times 2\frac{2}{9} = 4\frac{76}{81}$. Add them together [giving] $8\frac{76}{81}$. Multiply $2 \times \frac{2}{9} = 4\frac{4}{9}$. Add this to $8\frac{76}{81} = 13\frac{31}{81}$. Divide by 3 = $4\frac{112}{243}$. . . . Now square $2\frac{1}{4}$ [giving] $5\frac{1}{16}$. Add it to the square of the median diameter: $5\frac{1}{16} + 4\frac{76}{81} = 10\frac{1}{129}$. Multiply $2\frac{2}{9} \times 2\frac{1}{4} = 5$. Add this to the previous sum [getting] $15\frac{1}{129}$. Divide by 3 [which yields] 5 and $\frac{1}{3888}$. Add it to the first result . . . = $9\frac{1792}{1888}$. Multiply this by 11 and then divide by 14 [that is, multiply by pi/4]: the final result is $7\frac{23600}{54432}$. This is the cubic measure of the barrel.

This is, as Baxandall says, a special intellectual world; but it is one in which all of the educated classes in places like Venice and Florence lived. Its connection with painting, and the perception of painting, lay less in the calculational processes as such than in a disposition to attend to the structure of complex forms as combinations of simpler, more regular, and more comprehensible ones. Even the objects involved in paintings – cisterns, columns, brick towers, paved floors, and so on – were the same ones that handbooks used to practice students in the art of gauging. And so when Piero, in his other hat as painter, renders *The Annunciation* as set in a columned, multilevel, advancing and receding Perugian portico, or the Madonna in a domed, half-rounded cloth pavillion, a framing dress to her own, he is calling upon his public's ability to see such forms as compounds of others and thus to interpret – gauge, if you will – his paintings and grasp their meaning:

> To the commercial man almost anything was reducible to geometrical figures underlying surface irregularities – that pile of grain reduced to a cone, the barrel to a cylinder or a compound of truncated cones, the cloak to a circle of stuff allowed to lapse into a cone of stuff, the brick tower to a compound cubic body composed of a calculable number of smaller cubic bodies, and . . . this habit of analysis is very close to the painter's analysis of appearances. As a man gauged a bale, the painter surveyed a figure. In both cases there is a conscious reduction of irregular masses and voids to combinations of manageable geometric bodies. . . . Because they were practised in manipulating ratios and in analysing the volume or surface of compound bodies, [fifteenth-century Italians] were sensitive to pictures carrying the marks of similar processes.

The famous lucid solidity of Renaissance painting had at least part of its origins in something else than the inherent properties of planar representation, mathematical law, and binocular vision.

Indeed, and this is the central point, all these broader cultural matters, and others I have not mentioned, interworked to produce the sensibility in which quattrocento art was formed and had its being. (In an earlier work, *Giotto and the Orators*, Baxandall connects the development of pictorial composition to the narrative forms, most especially the periodic sentence, of humanist rhetoric; the orator's hierarchy of period, clause, phrase, and word being consciously matched, by Alberti and others, to the painter's one of picture, body, member, and plane.) Different painters played upon different aspects of that sensibility, but the moralism of religious preaching, the pageantry of social dancing, the shrewdness of commercial gauging, and the grandeur of Latin oratory all combined to provide what is indeed the painter's true medium: the capacity of his audience to see meanings in pictures. An old picture, Baxandall says, though he could have omitted the 'old,' is a record of visual activity that one has to learn to read, just as one has to learn to read a text from a different culture. 'If we observe that Piero della Francesca tends to a gauged sort of painting, Fra Angelico to a preached sort of painting, and Botticelli to a danced sort of painting, we are observing something not only about them but about their society.'

The capacity, variable among peoples as it is among individuals, to perceive meaning in pictures (or poems, melodies, buildings, pots, dramas, statues) is, like all other fully human capacities, a product of collective experience which far transcends it, as is the far rarer capacity to put it there in the first place. It is out of participation in the general system of symbolic forms we call culture that participation in the particular we call art, which is in fact but a sector of it, is possible. A theory of art is thus at the same time a theory of culture, not an autonomous enterprise. And if it is a semiotic theory of art it must trace the life of signs in society, not in an invented world of dualities, transformations, parallels, and equivalences. [. . .]

'Art,' says my dictionary, a usefully mediocre one, is 'the conscious production or arrangement of colors, forms, movements, sounds or other elements in a manner that affects the sense of beauty,' a way of putting the matter which seems to suggest that men are born with the power to appreciate, as they are born with the power to see jokes, and have only to be provided with the occasions to exercise it. As what I have said here ought to indicate, I do not think that this is true (I do not think that it is true for humor either); but, rather, that 'the sense of beauty,' or whatever the ability to respond intelligently to face scars, painted ovals, domed pavillions, or rhymed insults should be called, is no less a cultural artifact than the objects and devices concocted to 'affect' it. The artist works with his audience's capacities – capacities to see, or hear, or touch, sometimes even to taste and smell, with understanding. And though elements of these capacities are indeed innate – it usually helps not to be color-blind – they are brought into actual existence by the experience of living in the midst of certain sorts of things to look at, listen to, handle, think about, cope with, and react to; particular varieties of cabbages, particular sorts of kings. Art and the equipment to grasp it are made in the same shop.

For an approach to aesthetics which can be called semiotic – that is, one concerned with how signs signify – what this means is that it cannot be a formal science like logic or mathematics but must be a social one like history or anthropology. Harmony and prosody [science of versification] are hardly to be dispensed with, any more than composition and syntax; but exposing the structure of a work of art and accounting for its impact are not the same thing. [. . .]

If we are to have a semiotics of art (or for that matter, of any sign system not axiomatically self-contained), we are going to have to engage in a kind of natural history of signs and symbols, an ethnography of the vehicles of meaning. Such signs and symbols, such vehicles of meaning, play a role in the life of a society, or some part of a society, and it is that which in fact gives them their life. Here, too, meaning is use, or more carefully, arises from use, and it is by tracing out such uses as exhaustively as we are accustomed to for irrigation techniques or marriage customs that we are going to be able to find out anything general about them. [. . .]

To be of effective use in the study of art, semiotics must move beyond the consideration of signs as means of communication, code to be deciphered, to a consideration of them as modes of thought, idiom to be interpreted. It is not a new cryptography that we need, especially when it consists of replacing one cipher by another less intelligible, but a new diagnostics, a science that can determine the meaning of things for the life that surrounds them. It will have, of course, to be trained on signification, not pathology, and treat with ideas, not with symptoms. But by connecting incised statues, pigmented sago palms, frescoed walls, and chanted verse to jungle clearing, totem rites, commercial inference, or street argument, it can perhaps begin at last to locate in the tenor of their setting the sources of their spell.

12 Meyer Schapiro **'Style'**

Source: from *Theory and Philosophy of Art: Style, Artist and Society: Selected Papers*, Meyer Schapiro, George Baziller, New York, 1994, pp. 51–8.

[I]

By style is usually meant the constant form – and sometimes the constant elements, qualities, and expression – in the art of an individual or a group. The term is also applied to the whole activity of an individual or society, as in speaking of a 'life style' or the 'style of a civilization.'

For the archaeologist, style is exemplified in a motif or pattern, or in some directly grasped quality of the work of art, which helps one to localize and date the work and to establish connections between groups of works or between cultures. Style here is a symptomatic trait, like the nonaesthetic features of an artifact or sign. It is studied more often as a diagnostic means than for its own significance as an important constituent of culture. For dealing with style, the archaeologist has relatively few aesthetic and expressive physiognomic terms.

To the historian of art, style is an essential object of investigation. He studies its inner correspondences, its life history, and the problems of its formation and change. He, too, uses style as a criterion of the date and place of origin of works, and as a means of tracing relationships between schools of art. But the style is, above all, a system of forms with a quality and a meaningful expression through which the personality of the artist and the broad outlook of a group are visible. It is also a vehicle of expression within the group, communicating and fixing certain values of religious, social, and moral life through the emotional suggestiveness of forms. It is, besides, a common ground against which innovations and the individuality of particular works may be measured. By considering the succession of works in time and space and by matching the variations of style with historical events and with the varying features of other fields of culture, the historian of art attempts, with the help of common-sense psychology and social theory, to account for the changes of style or specific traits. The historical study of individual and group styles also discloses typical stages and processes in the development of forms.

For the synthesizing historian of culture or the philosopher of history, the style is a manifestation of the culture as a whole, the visible sign of its unity. The style reflects or projects the 'inner form' of collective thinking and feeling. What is important here is not the style of an individual or of a single art, but forms and qualities shared by all the arts of a culture during a significant span of time. In this sense one speaks of Classical or Medieval or Renaissance Man with respect to common traits discovered in the art styles of these epochs and documented also in religious and philosophical writings.

The critic, like the artist, tends to conceive of style as a value term; style as such is a quality and the critic can say of a painter that he has 'style' or of a writer that he is a 'stylist.' Although 'style' in this normative sense, which is applied mainly to individual artists, seems to be outside the scope of historical and ethnological studies of art, it often occurs here, too, and should be considered seriously. It is a measure of accomplishment and therefore is relevant to understanding of both art and culture as a whole. Even a period style, which for most historians is a collective taste evident in both good and poor works, may be regarded by critics as a great positive achievement. So the Greek classic style was, for Winckelmann [1717–68] and Goethe [1749–1832], not simply a convention of form but a culminating conception with valued qualities not possible in other styles and apparent even in Roman copies of lost Greek originals. Some period styles impress us by their deeply pervasive, complete character, their special adequacy to their content; the collective creation of such a style, like the conscious shaping of a norm of language, is a true achievement and is transmitted to successive generations of artists. Correspondingly, the presence of the same style in a wide range of arts is often considered a sign of the integration of a culture and the intensity of a high creative moment. Arts that lack a particular distinction or nobility of style are often said to be style-less, and the culture is judged to be weak or decadent. A similar view is held by philosophers of culture and history and by some historians of art.

Common to all these approaches are the assumptions that each style is peculiar to a period of a culture and that, in a given culture or epoch of culture, there is only one style or a limited range of styles. Works in the style of one time could not have originated in another. These postulates are supported by the fact that the connection between a style and a period, inferred from a few examples, is confirmed by objects discovered later. Whenever it is possible to locate a work through nonstylistic evidence, this evidence points to the same time and place as do the formal traits, or to a culturally associated region. The unexpected appearance of the style in another region is explained by migration or trade. The style is therefore used with confidence as an independent clue to the time and place of origin of a work of art. Building upon these assumptions, scholars have constructed a systematic, although not complete, picture of the temporal and spatial distribution of styles throughout large regions of the globe. If works of art are grouped in an order corresponding to their original positions in time and space, their styles will show significant relationships which can be coordinated with the relationships of the works of art to still other features of the cultural points in time and space, and often found in the pictured material aspects of the time and place.

[II]

Styles are not usually defined in a strictly logical way. As with languages, the definition indicates the time and place of a style or its author, or the historical relation to other styles, rather than its peculiar features. The characteristics of styles vary continuously and resist a systematic classification into perfectly distinct groups. It is meaningless to ask exactly when ancient art ends and the medieval begins. There are, of course, abrupt breaks and reactions in art, but study shows that here, too, there is often anticipation, blending, and continuity. Precise limits are sometimes fixed by convention, for simplicity in dealing with historical problems or in isolating a type. In a stream of development the artificial divisions may even be designated by numbers – Styles I, II, III. But the single name given to the style of a period rarely corresponds to a clear and universally accepted characterization of a type. Yet direct acquaintance with an unanalyzed work of art will often permit us to recognize another object of the same origin, just as we recognize a face to be native or foreign. This fact points to a degree of constancy in art that is the basis of all investigation of style. Through careful description and comparison and through formation of a richer, more refined typology adapted to the continuities in development, it has been possible to reduce the areas of vagueness and to advance our knowledge of styles.

Although there is no established system of analysis and writers will stress one or another aspect according to their viewpoint or problem, in general the description of a style refers to three aspects of art: form elements or motifs, form relationships, and qualities (including an all-over quality which we may call the 'expression').

This conception of style is not arbitrary but has arisen from the experience of investigation. In correlating works of art with an individual or culture, these three aspects provide the broadest, most stable, and therefore most reliable criteria. They are also the most pertinent to modern theory of art, although not in the same degree for all viewpoints. Technique, subject matter, and material may be characteristic of certain groups of works and will sometimes be included in definitions; but more often these features are not so peculiar to the art of a period as the formal and qualitative ones. It is easy to imagine a decided change in material, technique, or subject matter accompanied by little change in the basic form. Or, where these are constant, we often observe that they are less responsive to new artistic aims. A method of stone-cutting will change less rapidly than the sculptor's or architect's forms. Where a technique does coincide with the extension of a style, it is the formal traces of the technique rather than the operations as such that are important for description of the style. The materials are significant mainly for the textural quality and color, although they may affect the conception of the forms. For the subject matter, we observe that quite different themes – portraits, still lifes, and landscapes – will appear in the same style, and in the works of a single artist.

It must be said, too, that form elements or motifs, although very striking and essential for the expression, are not sufficient for characterizing a style. The pointed arch is common to Gothic and Islamic architecture, and the round arch to Roman, Byzantine, Romanesque, and Renaissance buildings. In order to distinguish these styles, one must also look for features of another order and, above all, for different ways of combining the elements in a search for a new effect or solution of a new problem.

Although some writers conceive of style as a kind of syntax or compositional pattern, which can be analyzed mathematically, in practice one has been unable to do without the vague language of qualities in describing styles. Certain features of light and color in painting are most conveniently specified in qualitative terms and even as tertiary (intersensory) or physiognomic qualities, like cool and warm, gay and sad. The habitual span of light and dark, the intervals between colors in a particular palette – very important for the structure of a work – are distinct relationships between elements, yet are not comprised in a compositional schema of the whole. The complexity of a work of art is such that the description of forms is often incomplete on essential points, limiting itself to a rough account of a few relationships. It is still simpler, as well as more relevant to aesthetic experience, to distinguish lines as hard and soft than to give measurements of their substance. For precision in characterizing a style, these qualities are graded with respect to intensity by comparing different examples directly or by reference to a standard work as an impressive model, or where conflicting proposals arise, one resorts to a concensus of local and foreign architects and other professionals. Where quantitative measurements have been made, they tend to confirm the conclusions reached through direct qualitative description. Nevertheless, we have no doubt that, in dealing with qualities, much greater precision can be reached.

Analysis applies aesthetic concepts current in the teaching, practice, and criticism of contemporary art; the development of new viewpoints and problems in the latter directs the attention of students to unnoticed features of older styles. But the study of works of other times also influences modern concepts through discovery of aesthetic variants unknown in our own art. As in criticism, so in historical research, the problem of distinguishing or relating two styles discloses unsuspected, subtle characteristics and suggests new concepts of form. The postulate of continuity in culture – a kind of inertia in the physical sense – leads to a search for common features in successive styles that are ordinarily contrasted as opposite poles of form; the resemblances will sometimes be found not so much in obvious aspects as in fairly hidden ones – the line patterns of Renaissance compositions recall features of the older Gothic style, and in contemporary abstract art one observes form relationships like those of Impressionist painting.

The refinement of style analysis has come about in part through problems in which small differences had to be disengaged and described precisely. Examples are the regional variations within the same culture; the process of historical development from year to year; the growth of individual artists and the discrimination of the works of master and pupil, originals and copies. In these studies the criteria for dating and attribution are often physical or external – matters of small symptomatic detail – but here, too, the general trend of research has been to look for features that can be formulated in both structural and expressive-physiognomic terms. It is assumed by many students that the expression terms are all translatable into form and quality terms, since the expression depends on particular shapes and colors and will be modified by a small change in the latter. The forms are correspondingly regarded as vehicles of a particular affect (apart from the subject matter). But the relationship here is not altogether clear. In general, the study of style tends toward an ever stronger correlation of form and expression. Some descriptions are purely morphological, as of natural objects – indeed, ornament has been characterized, like crystals, in the mathematical language of group theory. But terms like 'stylized,' 'archaistic,' 'naturalistic,' 'mannerist,' 'baroque,' are specifically human, referring to artistic processes, and imply some expressive effect. It is only by analogy that mathematical figures have been characterized as 'classic' and 'romantic.'

[III]

The analysis and characterization of the styles of primitive and early historical cultures have been strongly influenced by the standards of recent Western art. Nevertheless, it may be said that the values of modern art have led to a more sympathetic and objective approach to exotic arts than was possible fifty or a hundred years ago.

In the past, a great deal of primitive work, especially of representation, was regarded as artless even by sensitive people; what was valued were mainly the ornamentation and the skills of primitive industry. It was believed that primitive arts were childlike attempts to represent nature – attempts distorted by ignorance and by an irrational content of the monstrous and grotesque. True art was admitted only in the high cultures, where knowledge of natural forms was combined with a rational ideal which brought beauty and decorum to the image of man. Greek art and the art of the Italian High Renaissance were the norms for judging all art, although in time the classic phase of Gothic art was accepted. Ruskin, who admired Byzantine works, could write that in Christian Europe alone 'pure and precious ancient art exists, for there is none in America, none in Asia, none in Africa.' From such a viewpoint careful discrimination of primitive styles or a penetrating study of their structure and expression was hardly possible.

With the change in Western art during the last seventy years, naturalistic representation has lost its superior status. Basic for contemporary practice and for knowledge of past art is the theoretical view that what counts in all art are the elementary aesthetic components, the qualities and relationships of the fabricated lines, spots, colors, and surfaces. These have two characteristics: they are intrinsically expressive, and they tend to constitute a coherent whole. The same tendencies to coherent (well-ordered) and expressive structure are found in the arts of all cultures. There is no privileged content or mode of representation (although the greatest works may, for reasons obscure to us, occur only in certain styles). Perfect art is possible in any subject matter or style. A style is like a language, with an internal order and expressiveness, admitting a varied intensity or delicacy of statement. This approach is a relativism that does not exclude absolute judgments of value; it makes these judgments possible within every framework by abandoning a fixed norm of style. Such ideas are accepted by most students of art today, although not applied with uniform conviction. [. . .]

13 Earl Rosenthal 'The Diffusion of the Italian Renaissance Style in Western European Art'

Source: from *Sixteenth Century Journal*, IX.4, 1978, pp. 33–45.

The problematic aspects of the subject became apparent to me while studying individual instances of the diffusion of the style from Italy to Spain, specifically Italian sculptors who worked in Spain and Spanish architects and sculptors who returned from study in Italy to work in the Renaissance style. In this way I came to appreciate the difficulties they faced and the special talent for synthesis required of converts to the new style who returned to work in their native lands. I became increasingly curious about the process of the diffusion of the Renaissance style in Europe. Of course, there are scholars who assume that the Renaissance style emerged spontaneously and somewhat anonymously all across Europe out of the cultural conditions or, simply, the spirit of the age. Foremost among those favoring a pan-European genesis of the style are historians of painting, in great part because of the extraordinary development of spatial illusion in the painting of Flanders in the early fifteenth century. Most of these scholars seem to assume that what is true of painting, which is generally accepted as the leading art of the period, is also true of the other arts; but, as we shall see, that is not the case. Historians who specialize in sculpture occasionally cite isolated instances of late fourteenth-century naturalism in northern Europe as anticipatory of the Renaissance, but few challenge the primacy of Italians in the formulation of the Renaissance style. Historians of architecture unanimously credit Brunelleschi with the inventive revival of classical forms and recognize that two generations of Italian architects expanded and elaborated the style before any tell-tale classical orders appeared in the rest of Europe. Clearly, therefore, historians of the three major arts have very different ideas of the genesis of the Renaissance style. One way out of this impasse, it seemed to me, was to gain more concrete evidence of the process of the diffusion of the Renaissance style in architecture and sculpture. Hence I shall present some preliminary evidence concerning that process in architecture and, more briefly, in sculpture and, finally, I shall offer some speculations on what happened in painting.

As most architectural historians see it, the process of diffusion began in Florence early in the fifteenth century when Brunelleschi, largely in the context of ecclesiastical commissions, formulated his idea of Roman architecture on the basis of ancient ruins in Rome and Romanesque buildings in Florence. These he obviously accepted as surrogates for classical models. The severity and restraint of his architectural forms would seem to be in accord with the admiration of contemporary Florentine humanists for Republican Rome, partly because Florence was founded during that period and partly because its authors provided philosophical support for the Republican government of Florence now endangered from within and without. Despite these political implications, the first Italian centers to adopt the new architectural style were those ruled by *signori*, specifically Lionello d'Este of Ferrara, Federico da Montefeltro in Urbino, Alfonso I of Aragon, the King of Naples, and the princely pope, Nicholas V in Rome. While these centers adopted the new style before 1450, several others followed shortly, including the principalities of Rimini, Mantua and Milan and the republics of Siena and Venice (though in the latter two the style was intruded rather than adopted officially). From these centers, the style in architecture was diffused over Italy in the last quarter of the century.

In the principalities of the early adopters, notably Ferrara, Urbino, Naples, Mantua and the Vatican, the new style was used primarily to renovate their medieval castles by adding classical frames to doors and windows, garden loggia and porticoed courtyards with arcades on classical columns. At times classical elements were painted on facades and interior walls. Restricted by the fortress function and the medieval dispositions of their castles, the lords of Italy more readily displayed their knowledge of the architecture of the ancients in temporal structures of wood, canvas and plaster erected for official festivities, triumphal entries and receptions and performances of various kinds. Of course, these are lost to us, and so are the conversations of these lords with architectural theorists such as Alberti, Filarete and Francesco di Giorgio Martini, all of whom made the rounds of the major courts of Italy. These conversations and ephemeral decorations for court festivals played a major role in the conversion of the ambassadors of European princes to the new style. Quite understandably, in the service of the lords of Italy, Tuscan theorists and designers were inclined to suppress Republican Roman models in favor of the more appropriate imperial motives. Thus the style that had been formulated by Brunelleschi largely in the context of ecclesiastical architecture, under the guidance of Republican ideals, was first accepted outside the territory of Florence by pseudomonarchs who used it primarily for seignorial functions and favored imperial Roman sources. As we shall see, this redirection of the style by the *signori* at mid-century facilitated its diffusion to the rest of Europe.

A style is diffused not as a total configuration but, rather, in the fragments experienced by aliens of varied backgrounds who visited different Italian centers for various lengths of time at different stages of the development of the style. Inevitably, each visitor came away with a different and very personal idea of the new style. In spite of all these variables in the diffusion of the style from 1450 to 1600, some general patterns are revealed by the charting of the chronological and geographical distribution of concrete data: (1) the several architectural genres commissioned in the Renaissance style outside Italy; (2) the social class of the patrons; and (3) the nationality of the architect, specifically Italians working abroad and artists from other cultural areas who visited Italy and returned to their homelands to work in the Renaissance style.

The earliest architectural works reflecting the new style outside Italy are centered around Buda in Hungary, where Mattias Corvinus, the King of Hungary, began renovating several of his residences in the 1460s. Corvinus, the first European ruler to adopt the Renaissance style in architecture, was quickly followed by the King of Poland in the 1470s and the Bohemian court at Prague in the 1490s. The precocious Renaissance in eastern Europe was unfortunately interrupted by the incursions of the Turks. In western Europe, aside from the modest chapel designed in the 1470s by Francesco Laurana for Rene d'Anjou in the cathedral of Marseilles, the first building to reflect the Renaissance style was the palace of the [Mendoza] in Cogolludo in Castile, designed by Lorenzo Vazquez, a Spanish architect who returned from study in Italy about 1488. In the Loire valley in France, little more than ornament recalls Charles VIII's importation of Italian artisans to Amboise in 1495. Though western patrons adopted the style a generation after those of eastern Europe, there was a steady expansion of the style until it was firmly established in most of western Europe by the middle of the sixteenth century. In England most of the buildings in the Renaissance style were erected after 1550 and they were predominantly country houses. Of course, in England and elsewhere in northern Europe the style continued to expand well after my terminal date of 1600, but here we are primarily concerned with the process of the infusion of the style, not its full scope in any one area.

It is evident that throughout transalpine Europe, the overwhelming majority of works in the Renaissance style were seignorial residences, concentrated around the leading court centers of Europe. In Hungary, Bohemia and Poland, previous to 1550 there are eighteen seignorial residences as against only three civic buildings; and of the ten ecclesiastical works, eight are seignorial burial chapels. In France previous to 1550, thirty-four royal residences and chateaux were built or renovated in the environs of Paris, the Loire valley and Normandy. Of the four civic buildings known to me in this period, the town hall in Paris and the exchange in Lyon were designed by architects in the service of Francis I and a third, at Beaugency, was commissioned by the Duke of Orleans. It would seem, therefore, that many civic buildings owed their Renaissance style to princely

patrons rather than civic authorities. Seignorial residences and patronage also predominate in the Austro-German area, the Lowlands and England.

In Spain, the picture is quite different. Ecclesiastical commissions outnumber
residential or civic buildings throughout the sixteenth century. Works in the new
style are not concentrated at court centers alone because they were executed for
both ecclesiastical and secular patrons in most of Spain. The Catholic monarchs,
who initiated many buildings, did not adopt or encourage the Renaissance style
in royal residences. In the few cases in which they renovated royal castles, the
decoration was carried out in the Mudejar style. Around 1500, when they ordered
the building of four hospitals following the cruciform plan in Santiago de Com-
postela, Toledo, Granada and Valencia, they followed the general disposition of
Filarete's hospital for the Sforza in Milan, but that Italian model was probably
suggested by the archbishop of Toledo, Pedro Gonzalez de Mendoza, a leading
evangelist of the new style. Not until the 1530s, when Charles V ordered the renovation of the castles at Madrid, Toledo and Granada was the Renaissance style
employed for a royal residence in Spain, but by then the style had been firmly
established, primarily by members of the Mendoza and Fonseca families, many
of whom had held ambassadorial posts in Italy. One of them, Inigo Lopez de
Mendoza, while in Rome around 1505 sent a plan for the church of San Antonio
in Mondejar in Castile. Although it was never completed, it has the distinction
of being the first church with classical pilasters and ornament in western Europe.
But it was only in the 1520s that the Renaissance style was generally accepted for
church architecture in Spain with the design of the Hieronymite church in
Granada by a Florentine, Jacopo Torni l'Indaco and the cathedral in the same
city by Diego Siloe who had studied for an extended period in Italy. Their Renaissance ideas were developed in the cathedrals of Malaga, Jaen, and Baeza and, ultimately, in far off Mexico and Peru. In France in the 1520s evidence of the
Renaissance style in churches is limited to ornament applied to the Gothic piers
of St. Eustache in Paris and a few finials in the form of a candelabra on the chevet
of St. Pierre at Caen. The first church to be designed in the new style was the
chapel of the royal chateau at Anet designed by Philibert de l'Orme in 1549. In
the rest of Europe, the acceptance of the Renaissance style for church architecture, apart from seignorial burial chapels, occurs even later.

It is also evident that princes and their highest ministers commissioned most
of the architectural works in the Renaissance style outside Italy. Not only the
seignorial residences and burial chapels, which make up the greater part of architectural commissions, but also many of the ecclesiastical and civic genres in architecture were executed in the Renaissance style owing to the intervention of the
ruling class. Also indicative of the distinctly seignorial associations of the style in
the early sixteenth century is the fact that some grand prelates did not initiate
residences in the Renaissance style until they were appointed to high government
posts. This was true of cardinals George d'Amboise, who became governor of
Normandy in 1499, and Thomas Wolsey, who was appointed Lord Chancellor
by Henry VIII in 1515.

In charting the nationalities of the architects involved in the process of diffusion, that is, Italians working abroad and native-born architects who had studied

in Italy and returned to work in the Renaissance style, Buda in the 1460s is again the earliest court in Europe to have invited Italian architects working in the Renaissance style, with Vienna and Graz following by the end of the century. In the West, Italian designers are recorded at Marseilles, Amboise and Lisbon. In the case of the latter, the Italian was Andrea Sansovino, the best architect and sculptor to go abroad in the fifteenth century. None of his works there, however, have been identified, and he had little evident effect on Portuguese architecture in spite of his being there the better part of a decade. We should note that late fifteenth-century Italians who went to Hungary, Poland, Bohemia and even to Germany, France and England, were often invited primarily for their expertise in fortifications, not because they worked in the Renaissance style, but then they were sometimes asked to make designs for non-military projects.

Numerous Italian architects are recorded in the latter half of the sixteenth century at the courts of eastern Europe, the Austro-German area, and Portugal, while there are none recorded in England, the Lowlands and France, and only one in Spain. This reveals the relative independence of the West and the continued dependence of the East on Italians for works in the Renaissance style.

An important variable in the tabulation of Italians abroad is the length of time they stayed in any one center. For example, in 1509 Michele Carlone went to La Calahorra in southern Spain just long enough to install a courtyard that he had executed in Genoa; while Primaticcio arrived at Fontainebleau in 1532 and continued to work for the French Crown for more than thirty years. Also some Italian architects customarily went to Austro-German centers as *gastarbeiter* [guest workers], arriving in the spring and leaving before the chill of autumn, and thus inevitably called "the swallows of spring" by envious German masons. Incidentally, it is often suggested that the diffusion of the Renaissance style in all the arts was due to a surplus of trained artisans in Italy who went abroad to seek work, but I have found little evidence of this. In most cases, architects were sent abroad by an Italian lord at the request of a foreign prince.

Thus far I have found no record of native architects who went to Italy from Hungary, Poland, Bohemia, Austria, Germany, Switzerland or Scandinavia. From England, only John Shute is known to have gone to Italy, where he was sent by the Duke of Northumberland in 1550 for the express purpose of studying ancient Roman and modern Italian architecture; and some of what he learned was included in a treatise finished in 1563. French architects first went to Italy in the 1530s, when Nicolas Bachelier accompanied the Bishop of Rodez to Venice and Philibert de l'Orme went to Rome, while Ducerceau and, possibly, Jean Bullant followed in the 1540s. Apparently a Spanish architect, Lorenzo Vazquez, has the distinction of being the first alien architect to study in Italy and to return (in 1488) to work in the Renaissance style in his native land. More than a generation passed before several other Spaniards (Alonso Berruguete, Bartolome Ordonez, Diego Siloe and Pedro Machuca) went to Italy for extended periods of study and, on their return in 1517–1519, made architectural designs in the new style. This group played a more active role than any of the Italians in the introduction and spread of the Renaissance style in Castile and Andalusia. At least four other Spanish architects studied in Italy before travel abroad required official permission in 1559, but after that time Spaniards continued to utilize Italian architectural treatises, such as those of Serlio and Vignola. In contrast to the active role of Spanish architects, the French remained dependent on Italians for the first forty years of the assimilation of the style. Fortunately for the French architectural tradition, the Italian designers who worked there (Fra Giocondo, Leonardo, Primaticcio and Serlio) were of higher caliber than those invited to the rest of Europe in the sixteenth century. These Italians were the ones who accommodated traditional French architectural types to the new Renaissance style, whereas in Spain and England that task was accomplished less surely and more slowly by natives. It must be recognized, however, that in the design of country houses, English architects also benefited from the Italians' accommodation of the classical orders to the pavilion-and-corridor format common to both the French and English traditions.

The information gathered thus far makes possible the plotting of the diffusion of the Renaissance architectural style from Italian to tertiary centers in the rest of Europe. In the earliest instance of diffusion, the King of Hungary, who wanted an Italian architect to renovate his castle at Buda in the 1460s, quite naturally contacted princely rulers, the dukes of Ferrara and Milan. Shortly after, Rene d'Anjou made arrangements with the King of Naples for Francesco Laurana to come to Marseilles, and that was the port in which Charles VIII loaded two ships with works of art and Italian artisans to introduce the new style to France. Naples may also be the center in which Lorenzo Vazquez acquired architectural repertory that he employed in the very early palace in Cogolludo, begun in 1492. Around 1500, Milan and Pavia increased in importance. Reflections of the Lombard style are found in George d'Amboise's residence at Gaillon in Normandy, begun in 1501, and in the chateaux of the Loire valley; and, around the same time, Lombards working in the port of Genoa made portals and courtyards that were shipped to La Calahorra and Valencia in southeastern Spain. At the same time, Emperor Maximilian I at Innsbruck began to look to Milan, though he never had enough income to support grand scale architectural projects, and later Vienna, Graz and Dresden depended almost equally on Milan and Venice. Florentines, especially those working in Rome in the early sixteenth century, became important for Spain. The Torni brothers came from that ambience at the end of the second decade and so did the several returning Spaniards mentioned earlier, Berruguete, Machuca and Siloe, though the latter certainly worked with Ordonez in Naples and probably in Carrara. Florentines were increasingly important to Francis I, but of those who went to France, only Leonardo is known to have made architectural designs, while Primaticcio and Serlio, who were firmly rooted in the Florentine–Roman tradition, were Bolognese by birth. Hence, while Florence didn't at first play as important a role as the secondary centers of Milan, Genoa, Ferrara, Rome and Naples, she was always in the background as the fountainhead of the style, and she became a more active participant in the process of diffusion in the first third of the sixteenth century.

From these Italian cities the task of diffusion was passed on to northern European centers. Of those in eastern Europe, only Buda was of international importance; while in the west, Gaillon was quickly succeeded as a radial center of the style by the Loire valley around 1515 and then by the royal works in Paris and Fontainebleau after 1530. The distinctive style in architecture and interior decoration formed there had extraordinary diffusion, not only in France but also in the Lowlands, England, Scandinavia and Germany. An offshoot of the Fontainebleau School is the center of Antwerp, which in the 1560s became important for the publication of pattern books of architectural ornament like that of Hans Vredeman de Vries. No center in the Austro-German area came to play an international role comparable to those in France and the Lowlands, but that is probably due, in part, to the proximity of Milan and Venice and, in part, to the division of income in prosperous Germany among eight princelings, about one hundred and fifty dukes and counts, and numerous free imperial cities. While there were many Italians in the Austro-German area in the latter half of the sixteenth century, they were almost exclusively occupied with the renovation and decoration of the interiors of princely residences rather than in architectural design. In Spain there were many centers of nearly equal importance locally. From the 1530s, the nation as a whole carried the Renaissance style to the New World, but in the 1550s court architects in Madrid had to approve all projects for major buildings in the colonies.

The essential mechanism of the diffusion of the Renaissance style is now clear. The initial agents of diffusion were, in the main, diplomats at Italian and then other European courts, and the early adopters (in transalpine Europe) were the princes they served. This is described as "social-group diffusion," in that it took place within a supra-national governing class that had regular channels of communication through diplomacy, war and also intermarriage. These princes and their ministers employed the new style primarily for their residences and funerary chapels and for temporary festive architecture, while other classes of society (even those with international contacts) generally refrained from using the style even after examples were scattered about Europe for more than a generation. This suggests that architecture in the Renaissance style had a value other than the aesthetic one for European princes and their ministers and, presumably, for other potential patrons of the day. Speculation on that value can be made more confidently after a brief review of the diffusion of the Renaissance style in sculpture.

Several problems in the charting of sculptural works should be noted. Many of its smaller genre, notably bust portraits, reliefs and statuettes migrate from the places in which they were made and they are seldom well documented. Also, we have lost more sculpture than architecture, because of the iconoclasm that accompanied the religious strife of the period, especially in Bohemia, Germany, Switzerland and the Lowlands, while in Hungary even more was destroyed by the Turks. Moreover, problems are posed for some scholars by the affinity of some northern schools with aspects of Italian Renaissance sculpture, especially the serene sculptural forms of the Detente Style in fifteenth-century France and instances of the marked naturalism in anatomical detail in the statuary of the Netherlandish-German tradition; but none of these have been included in my charts of the diffusion of the Italian Renaissance style because both schools are wholly understandable within their own art traditions.

The primary sculptural genre involved in the diffusion of the Renaissance include funerary monuments, fountains, ecclesiastical sculpture of various kinds, portraits, and ornament. The earliest evidence of the style in sculpture outside Italy is found in Valencia where, in 1418, Juliano Florentin executed reliefs that repeat motives from Ghiberti's first doors; but nothing came of this precocious intrusion of the new Florentine style in Spain. In the East, the King of Hungary in the 1460s began importing sculpture by Verrocchio, Benedetto da Maiano and other Florentines for his residences in and around Buda. In the 1470s, Francesco Laurana, who was brought to France by Rene d'Anjou, made Passion reliefs at Avignon; but French sculptors seem not to have responded to them. Only from the 1490s, in the familiar architectural centers of Toledo, Avila and Burgos and in the Loire valley and in Paris, was the new style gradually assimilated. In 1499 Maximilian I called a Lombard to Innsbruck to design an equestrian statue, which was never executed, and he initiated work on a huge free-standing sepulchre for the court chapel which was to include about forty over life-size statues in bronze, executed by German sculptors.

In sculpture, as in architecture, the new style was again sustained by continuous patronage through the sixteenth century and firmly established in western countries, while in the East, only Poland continued the style, almost exclusively in funerary monuments. In much of northern Europe, especially in Bohemia, Germany, Switzerland, and the Lowlands, reform movements disrupted the sculptural tradition for more than a quarter century, but Germany came back vigorously in the last third of the sixteenth century, particularly in fountain sculpture and statuettes in bronze.

Also evident from these tabulations is the predominance of one sculptural genre – funerary monuments. Sepulchres made up about 85 percent of the sculptural commissions in England and Poland, about half in France and the Lowlands. In Spain, thirty-one funerary monuments were commissioned in the Renaissance style previous to 1550, but the genre does not predominate because of the extraordinary number of polychrome wood altarpieces and religious statuary that reflect the Italian Renaissance style. Polychrome wood was also the primary medium in transalpine Europe, but few altarpieces in the new style were made there. That medium in the North proved to be a major obstacle to the infusion of the Renaissance style, which had been developed primarily in marble and bronze, usually free of polychromy or even gilding. Another obstacle was the lack of coincidences in the sculptural genre of Renaissance Italy and northern Europe where there was virtually no secular sculpture.

The early patrons of sculpture in the Renaissance style were also princes and their courtiers though the percentage in sculpture may be closer to 70 percent in contrast to the near 90 percent in architecture. Even the Catholic monarchs, who had not fostered the Renaissance style in architecture, began in 1511 to commission a series of family tombs from Domenico Fancelli, a Florentine who worked in Carrara; but, not surprisingly, the Mendozas had employed him earlier for the same purpose.

Italian sculptors in northern Europe were concentrated even more exclusively at princely courts than were Italian architects, and there were fewer major centers for sculpture, although Augsburg and Nuremberg were important additions in Germany. In the latter half of the sixteenth century in Germany and Austria, many Italian sculptors were at work, but they were usually limited to figural decoration in plaster.

Surprisingly few European sculptors other than Austro-Germans and Spaniards went to Italy to study Renaissance or ancient sculpture. While Michel Pacher must have visited Padua and Mantua previous to executing his paintings of the St. Wolfgang altarpiece in the 1470s, the trip left his sculptural form unaffected. A generation later, in the first decade of the sixteenth century, a few young German sculptors (the Vischer brothers and Hering Loy) made brief trips to Italy; and a few more went in the last third of the century with the break explained by the disruptive religious disputes of the intervening years. Before 1500 Vasco de la Zarza returned from Italy to Avila and Damian Forment, to Valencia, and in the years 1517–1519, three major Spanish sculptors (Siloe, Ordonez and Berruguete) returned to Spain after extended periods of study in Italy. Between that time and the restrictions on travel abroad, four other sculptors are known to have studied in Italy. Thus Spain maintained a fairly steady contact with the Italian developments in sculpture.

In sum, the patterns of diffusion in the two arts have much in common. In both cases the patrons were primarily princes and a seignorial art genre predominated in each. Those genre – palatial residences and funerary monuments – were sufficiently complex in form to embody the primary design principles and a fair part of the characteristic motives of each medium and also to display the feeling for form peculiar to the style. A palatial residence is the best of all possible genres for the diffusion of the Renaissance style in architecture, whereas lesser works such as isolated portals, loggia, staircases or private chapels would not in themselves be sufficient to adequately reveal the essentials of the style. In sculpture, the free-standing tumba (which was favored over the wall tomb in most of Europe) was the most complex of genres in the sculptural medium, with the possible exception of monumental fountains. The tomb usually included a recumbent effigy and praying figures of the deceased as well as allegorical statuary in niches or placed along the sides of the sepulchre and, on the stylobate, narrative reliefs. Lesser sculptural genres, such as bust portraits, reliefs of the Madonna and Child, or even equestrian monuments are too limited in form. Perhaps, indicative of the importance of the primary vehicle in the diffusion of the style is the fact that there was a long delay in the diffusion of an important Italian sculptural type not included in the tomb, that is, the statue standing free of an architectural framework and designed to be of almost equal interest from all angles of view – surely the most important achievement of Italian Renaissance sculptors. A few fountains with free-standing (but not necessarily plurifacial) statues were brought from Florence to Buda in the 1470s and to Gaillon from Genoa and Venice around 1510, and Cellini made a project for a gigantic fountain for Francis I in the early 1540s, but non-Italians remained oblivious to the problem of plurifacial design in statuary. Even the south German sculptors who began to make statuettes in wood and bronze around 1510 did not design them to be seen from more than a shallow frontal arc until the last third of the century, when the formal problem was posed in a series of monumental fountains in bronze commissioned for the main squares of south German cities.

The sculptural and architectural genres that served as primary vehicles for the diffusion of the Italian Renaissance style in Europe were supported by princely patronage in a few interrelated court centers, and there was a sense of competitiveness among them. These conditions encouraged the continued exploration of the potential of the style in each genre, and they may even be requirements for the rapid and successful diffusion of a style. If patronage in an imported style is discontinuous and uncompetitive, and if the works commissioned pertain to lesser art genres and are scattered in unrelated centers, diffusion is not likely to take place.

The predominance of the seignorial class as patrons and the princely palace and funerary monument as the genres they commissioned in the new style suggests that its initial value was symbolic rather than aesthetic. Of course, the choice of the Renaissance style for seignorial functions was prepared for by humanists, who had delineated the configuration of the Renaissance prince largely on the basis of Roman models and, in their panegyrics, made lavish use of heroic metaphors derived from antiquity. These persistent references to ancient Rome, together with the architectural theorists' formulations of a hierarchy of increasingly geometric residential plans for social groups from the artisan to the prince, led to dissatisfaction with the irregular and even accidental aggregation of structures that usually made up the fortified castles inherited from feudal forebears. Also, humanists fostered architecture along with literature as the most princely kind of patronage and the best suited to attain glory in their own day and enduring fame through the ages. Once convinced of the propaganda value of magnificent palaces and funerary monuments for themselves and their dynasties, princes inevitably employed the most rhetorical of architectural styles, that of ancient Rome. Its grand scale conveyed an idea of strength and security free of the tyrannical associations of the out-dated fortress, and its strict symmetry and pervasive proportionality embodied the ideal of stability and order and even foresight (virtues generally claimed for the principality over the republic). And, of course, the magnificence associated with rulership was best expressed in the humanistic ambience of these courts by the costly materials and rich ornament of imperial Rome as revived by Renaissance architects. These associations also pertain to the architectural and sculptural components of the funerary monument which was increasingly concerned with the commemoration of the heroic deeds of the triumphant ruler. While much more could be said of these associations, the essential point to be made is the essentially symbolic value of the new style used for the seignorial genre that served as the primary vehicles for the diffusion of the new style in architecture and sculpture.

The first evidence of the Italian Renaissance style in painting is somewhat earlier than that for the other arts in each cultural area (the 1440s in Flanders, 1450s in France and the 1470s in Austria and Spain), but its progress was a good deal slower than that of the other arts. Painting also differs in that the seignorial class played no greater role in its patronage than the clergy or the upper middle class, and the subjects of early examples of the style are not secular but overwhelmingly religious. We are confronted with the anomalous conclusion that painting, which is usually considered the leading art of the period, was not in the vanguard of the diffusion of the style in Europe, and this would seem to be due, at least in part, to the relative lack of princely patronage. That, too, is odd because the *signori* of Italy were early and enthusiastic patrons of monumental mural decorations for the great halls, courtyards and even facades of their residences. The subjects were usually historical or mythological narratives and, at times, events in the life of the lord himself; but in all cases the themes were metaphoric references to his courage, wisdom, power, and magnificence.

Why, we must ask, didn't the princes of Europe emulate the *signori* of Italy in the use of propagandistic murals in their palaces? One might be inclined to suspect a technical obstacle, because there were few practitioners of true fresco outside Italy at this time, but European princes could have followed the Venetians who painted narrative cycles on huge canvases, first in a stain technique and then in oil. In fact, the obstacle was not technical but generic. The figured tapestry, a highly developed representational art in the Franco-Flemish area, served to decorate the interiors of the castles of most of Europe; and it had the added advantage of contributing to the warmth of northern interiors. Even after Francis I's gallery at Fontainebleau popularized murals within elaborately modeled plaster frames in the 1530s, the progress of the genre was slow because northerners continued to favor tapestries. Monumental murals had even less of a chance in northern churches, because windows were larger and wall areas smaller than in Italy and sacred imagery was executed in the splendor of stained glass. Other than monumental murals, the ideal genre for the diffusion of the Renaissance style in painting, narrative subjects might have been executed on panels or canvases for altarpieces, which were attaining gigantic proportions in late fifteenth-century Italy; but that prospect was blocked by another obstacle. Transalpine Europe and Spain continued to prefer carved altarpieces in polychrome wood.

Hence the two genres that would have served best to display the essential features of the new style in painting were not of use to either princely or ecclesiastical patrons during the late fifteenth and early sixteenth centuries, and the infusion of the style into the North was left to lesser pictorial genres that had no sustained patronage or important social function. There was no primary vehicle comparable to the palatial residence and the funerary monument in the other major arts, and thus the diffusion took place willy-nilly with Italian Renaissance ideas infused almost imperceptibly at times into northern pictorial genres.

While painting faced more obstacles than other major arts, there is no reason to deny that diffusion took place, and that the Renaissance style in painting, as in architecture and sculpture, was formulated by a small group of artists and patrons in Florence in the early fifteenth century and that from the 1440s it was extended and elaborated in secondary centers in Italy and then in tertiary centers abroad. The new social system of Europe, rather than giving rise to the style, provided institutional channels for its diffusion. While thus denying a pluralistic genesis of the Renaissance style, we can properly describe it as pluralistic in achievement in that individual converts all over Europe extended the potential of the style.

14 C. A. Macartney **'The Foreign Kings of Hungary'**

Source: from *Hungary: a Short History*, C. A. Macartney, Edinburgh University Press, Edinburgh, 1962, chapter 3, pp. 38–63.

The extinction of the old national dynasty with Andrew III's death altered its conditions of existence for the Hungarian state. Under its own interpretation of the position, the right of electing its new king had now reverted to the nation, whose freedom of choice was in theory unlimited; there was no theoretical bar to its setting one of its own members over it. But a firmly-implanted European usage had by this time come to limit the enjoyment of royal dignity to those who could show some hereditary title to it, most of these persons belonging to a small clique – into which the Árpáds themselves had levered themselves – of interrelated families of, as it were, professional royalties. It would have required a strong man, with a united nation behind him, to defy a well-supported claim from a member of one of these families, and the Hungarians, too, admitted the compulsive virtue of the blood-tie. They themselves confined their search to persons in whose veins the blood of the Árpáds ran, at least through some maternal forbear, who could continue the line – the line, not an individual, for the choice once made, the principle of legitimacy came into operation again; it was the singular misfortune of the country that for over two centuries after 1301, only one king died leaving behind him legitimate male issue. This meant that except in the one case in question, and in the two others where peculiar circumstances resulted, after all, in the election of a national king, their chosen ruler always came from some foreign, and foreign-based, dynasty. In fact, until the sixteenth century, when the Crown became permanently vested in the Habsburg dynasty, it was worn (transitory and disputed cases apart) by two Angevins, one Luxemburger, one Habsburg and three Jagiellos; with, intervening, two national kings, one of whom ruled only in part of the country.

To have a foreign king was by no means always an unmixed disadvantage for Hungary. Fresh ideas and institutions were sometimes brought in which fructified and enriched the political, social, cultural and economic life of the country, and without which it might well have failed to keep pace with the general advance of the contemporary Europe towards a higher level of civilisation. It is true that the Hungarians did not always relish these innovations, and often bound the monarch of their choice by strict capitulations to respect their own hardly-won and cherished national institutions. Their ability to do this – an outcome, strictly speaking, of the electoral nature of the Crown, not of the fact that the candidate was usually a foreigner – was a main reason why, for good or ill (and the advantages did not lie all on one side), Hungary throughout her history was able to preserve her native features in a larger degree than most other European countries. But the central issue was nearly always that of power, in relation to the international situation. A monarch disposing of resources of his own could be hoped to use them for the country's benefit, and especially for its defence; it was this calculation which more than once determined the national choice. On the other hand, a too powerful monarch, the centre of whose power and interests alike lay outside Hungary, might too easily use those resources, not to develop the country's national life, but to crush it, and to squander its own resources in the pursuit of his private, extra-Hungarian, objectives. The balance of advantage and disadvantage, in this respect, swayed uneasily throughout the centuries with the fluctuations of the international power-position and the personality of the ruler. Under many of its foreign rulers, and almost continuously after the Crown became stabilised in the house of Habsburg, the central problem of the country's whole political life was whether the benefits brought by foreign rule outweighed its disadvantages; and on this question opinion in the country was eternally divided, up to the last day of Habsburg rule.

These considerations were not yet apparent in the first years after Andrew's death. What happened then was simply that the dynastic rivalry of ten years before broke out again in modernised form, the Angevin candidate, whom the Pope supported, being now Charles Martell's son, the boy, Charles Robert; the Czech, another boy, Wenceslas III, for whom his father stood sponsor. This time Albrecht of Habsburg did not claim the throne for himself, contenting himself with supporting Charles Robert. Charles Robert, Wenceslas and Otto of Bavaria all had their partisans inside Hungary, and at first Charles Robert's party was the weakest of all. Both Wenceslas and Otto were in turn crowned, and Charles Robert's supporters could only give him a symbolic coronation, with a substitute crown.[1] But in a few years his rivals gave up the struggle in disgust. On 20 August 1310 he was crowned again, this time in due form, and thereafter his rule was not seriously opposed from abroad. He still, indeed, had many opponents among the 'kinglets', but he was able to win most of them over by diplomacy, and in 1312 won a crushing victory at Rozgony over the chief of the remaining malcontents, the Amadés and the Csáks. This victory re-established the royal authority on a firm footing; the only internal trouble which he had to face thereafter was in reality only half internal, fomented by Venice.

Charles Robert was undoubtedly favoured by the international situation, which, with Germany distraught by the conflict between Empire and Papacy, the Tatars grown passive in the east and the power of Byzantium in full decay, was more favourable than ever before or since to the independent development of the states of east-central Europe; it is no accident that Poland, Bohemia, Hungary and Serbia should all look back on the fourteenth century as the age of their greatest glory. As these conditions favoured Hungary's neighbours, as well as herself, Charles Robert's attempts at expansion were only moderately successful. He made Bosnia his friend and client, but Venice snatched South Dalmatia from him, Serbia, the Bánát of Macsó, and the newly-founded 'Voivody' of Wallachia disputed Szörény with him and in 1330 inflicted a heavy defeat on his arms. Against this, he drove the Austrian and Czech marauders out of his land, and, on the whole, preserved friendly relations with Poland, Bohemia and Austria.

The latter part of his reign was in the main peaceful and marked by a steadily increasing prosperity, the lion's share of which accrued to the king himself.

One of the chief props of his power was the wealth which he derived from the gold mines of Transylvania and north Hungary, the production of which he stimulated by a number of sensible devices. Eventually it reached the remarkable figure of 3,000 lb. of gold annually – one third of the total production of the world as then known, and five times as much as that of any other European state. Some 35–40 per cent of this accrued to the Crown as revenue and enabled Charles Robert, first of all Hungarian kings, to introduce a systematic fiscal policy. He renounced the *lucrum camerae*, or profit on the coinage, on which many of his predecessors had largely depended, introduced a stable currency based on gold, and reformed the system of direct taxation, basing it on a house-tax levied on every *porta* or peasant household.[2] He still had enough to maintain a sumptuous and refined court, the cultural influences at which were, incidentally, French rather than German.

Not the least of the benefits conferred by Charles Robert on Hungary was to leave behind him, in the person of his son Louis (Lajos) an heir whose succession (*jure legitimo* [by legal right]) was not questioned either inside or outside Hungary. Conventional historians reckon the reign of Louis (the only one of its kings on whom the nation has conferred the name of 'Great') as marking the apogee of Hungarian history. Louis was, of course, fortunate in that the favourable European constellation continued to prevail, and, at home, he could build on the foundations laid firmly by his father; but in addition, he was a man of remarkable qualities of both head and heart. Charles Robert had been more respected than loved, especially after one curious incident in which he took an extraordinarily barbarous revenge on the family of a man who had tried to assassinate him; Louis was generally loved. 'I call God to witness', the Venetian envoy wrote of him, 'that I never saw a monarch more majestic or more powerful, nor one who desires peace and calm so much as he.' 'There was no other', wrote another contemporary, 'so kind and noble, so virtuous and magnanimous, so friendly and straightforward.' He was indeed a true paladin, distinguished not least for his extraordinary physical courage in battle.

It was chiefly his international triumphs that earned him the name of 'Great'. Keeping the peace with his western neighbours, he resumed Béla III's policy of expansion in the south and east. Venice was forced to re-cede Dalmatia. The Bánáts in the northern Balkans were restored. The Ban of Bosnia and the Voivodes of Wallachia and Moldavia (where a second Vlach principality had come into being when the Tatars were driven out of it) acknowledged him as their suzerain, as did, for shorter periods and more formally, the rulers of Serbia, northern Bulgaria and, for a few years, Venice itself. Galicia and Lodomeria were recovered in 1354. Over this ring of dependencies, Hungary presided as *Archiregnum* [dominant power]. The climax of Louis' glory came in 1370, when, by virtue of a dynastic compact concluded in 1354 with Casimir of Poland, he ascended the Polish throne.

At home, the gold flowed in an undiminished stream into Louis' coffers, enabling him to keep a court even more splendid than his father's. And the whole country, spared for two generations from serious invasion or civil war, blossomed with a material prosperity which it had never before known. By the end of Louis' reign its total population had risen to some three millions, and it contained 49 royal boroughs, over 500 market towns and more than 26,000 villages. The economy was still predominantly agricultural, but as these figures show, the towns, which the Angevins favoured especially, granting many of them extensive charters of self-government, prospered. Craftsmen began to practise their trades and to organise themselves in guilds. International commerce, favoured by the continued stability and high repute of the currency, began to make headway.

The arts, too, flourished. A university, one of the earliest in Europe, was founded in Pécs in 1367 (it is true that it proved short-lived). The first comprehensive national chronicle, one copy of which is one of the most magnificent illuminated codices in Europe, dates from about the same period.

This prosperity, and not less the order which the two Angevins were able to enforce, allowed the nation to accept, without serious resentment, the fact that their reigns constituted what to modern eyes would appear a period of political reaction. Even the memory of Andrew III's constitutional innovations (which had, indeed, never been put into practice) vanished, it seems, even from memory, under their rules. They made appointments according to their pleasure, legislated as they pleased, and when (occasionally) they convoked a Diet, it was simply to inform it of decisions taken. Their absolutism was, however, not the old patrimonial absolutism of St Stephen and his successors, which was foreign to their eyes, but a much more hierarchical structure which embodied many features of west European feudalism. Even after Charles Robert had broken the power of the kinglets, he did not attempt to destroy the magnates as a class, but bestowed a large part of the confiscated estates on a new set of great families. Louis continued this policy, and by the end of his reign about fifty of these families owned between them one-third of the soil of Hungary. The status and importance of the magnates was enhanced by the new military system introduced by the Angevins. Military service was still the obligation of all noblemen, who, when their services were required, were mustered under the 'banners' of the king, the queen, or one of the great officials (the Voivode of Transylvania, etc.), smaller contingents following the Ispáns of their counties. But the lords were now required to bring contingents of heavily-armed cavalry from among their own followers; if a force numbered fifty men, it served under its lord's banner, and was known as his *banderium*. Many small nobles took service in these private *banderia*. It was at this time, and largely through this innovation, that the class of *familiares* – small nobles who took service, military or other, under a magnate, becoming his henchmen and retainers, while he in practice, although not in theory, was their feudal superior, became numerous.

This growth of the magnates' power was, indeed, partially compensated by another development, in the opposite direction. It was not everywhere that a magnate's authority quite eclipsed that of the county in which he had his estates, and under the Angevins' system of delegating power, rather than exercising it directly through their own officials (they were no bureaucrats) the control of the administration and justice in each county passed during their reigns increasingly into the hands of the *universitates* [the whole body] of the local nobles, who exercised it through their own elected representatives. These 'noble counties', which now began to replace the old 'royal counties', were from the first the special preserve and stronghold of the richer common nobles. They were, of course, still subject to the ultimate control of the king's representative, the Ispán, and the most common effect of the development, at least during its early stages, was to strengthen the king's authority by providing him, in the lesser nobles, with a counter-weight against the magnates, such as the rulers of economically more developed countries found in the burgesses of their towns. This consideration led several of the kings to allow the counties to develop a very extensive autonomy, which at a later stage, when the magnate class had allied itself with the Crown, became the defence of the smaller men and, the crown being worn by foreign rulers, the defence also of the national cause, which they came to represent against both the other forces.

In 1351 Louis also confirmed the Golden Bull, adding an explicit declaration that all nobles enjoyed 'one and the same liberty', a provision which, it appears, besides re-affirming the rights of the noble class as a whole, including the *familiares* [household retainers], also enlarged its ranks by bringing full noble privileges to a further class of border-line cases. Other provisions of the law stabilised land tenure by universalising the system of *aviticitas* [lit. inheritance through the grandfather] under which all land was entailed in the male line of the owner's family, collaterals succeeding in default of direct heirs; if the line died out completely, the estate reverted to the Crown. The daughters of a deceased noble were entitled to a quarter of the assessed value of his property, but this had to be paid them in cash.

At the same time, Louis standardised the obligations of the peasant to his lord at one-ninth of his produce – neither more nor less. As he also had to pay the tithe to the church and the *porta* to the state, the peasant's obligations were thus not inconsiderable, but do not appear to have been crushing in this age of prosperity; his right of free migration was specifically re-affirmed.

Some Hungarian historians do not count the two Angevins as foreign kings at all, and it is true that both of them, especially Louis, who was born and bred in Hungary, regarded themselves completely as Hungarians. Charles Robert had no other throne, and did not try to acquire another for himself. Louis treated all his acquisitions, except perhaps that of Poland, as appendices to Hungary, and even Poland he ruled through Hungarians. But it is easily arguable that his Balkan enterprises brought Hungary, on balance, more loss than profit, even if the large expense of them be left out of account, for few of the vassals proved loyal when a crisis came. Rather they regarded Hungary as an oppressor and hastened to make common cause with her enemies.[3] She certainly got nothing at all, except a little reflected glory, out of Louis' acquisition of Poland. In south Italy Louis and his mother, carrying out plans laid by Charles Robert, embarked on purely dynastic enterprises which brought positive and real damage to Hungary. The object was to secure the throne of Naples for Charles' younger son, Andrew, who, under a compact between Charles and Robert of Sicily, had married Robert's granddaughter, Joanna, on the understanding that he should succeed to the throne on Robert's death (her father, Charles, having predeceased Robert). But Andrew's accession was unpopular in Naples. To get him recognised at all cost enormous sums of money in bribes, and, after a short and insecure reign, he was murdered. Louis undertook two campaigns in Italy to avenge his brother and secure the throne for the latter's little son. Both were unsuccessful, and cost Hungary money which, spent in the country, would have transformed the face of it.

Matters took a sharp turn for the worse when Louis died in 1382. He had left no son, but two daughters, of whom he had destined the elder, Maria, then a girl of eleven, and betrothed to Sigismund, younger son of the Emperor Charles IV and himself Marquis of Brandenburg, to succeed him on both his thrones. The Poles refused to continue the union with Hungary, and although they ended by accepting Maria's younger sister, Hedwig or Jadwiga, as queen, they married her to Jagiello of Lithuania, under whom Poland's ways diverged from Hungary's. The Hungarians themselves were divided on the question of the female succession, and a party of them crowned the girls' cousin, Charles of Durazzo, only to see him assassinated a month later. Another party had already crowned Maria, but her rule was only nominal: Sigismund, after marrying his bride, got himself crowned as her consort in 1387 and, after her death in 1395, ruled alone until his own death in 1437.

Sigismund was at first extremely unpopular, not only for the cruelty with which, in breach of his pledged word, he put Charles' leading supporters to the sword, but also as an intruder and a foreigner. 'By God', one of his victims flung in his teeth, 'I am no servant of thine, thou Czech swine.' In 1401 a group of nobles actually held him in prison for several weeks, and two years later malcontents called in another anti-king, who, however, failed to establish himself, although he retained possession of Dalmatia, which he then sold to Venice. Later, passions cooled somewhat, but when Sigismund was elected German king in 1410, and still more when he succeeded his brother in Bohemia in 1420, the nation complained with acerbity that he neglected its affairs.

His reign had its redeeming features. The momentum imported by the Angevins was still carrying the country forward, economically and culturally, and Sigismund himself, although extravagant and – at least in his youth – silly, was an intelligent enough man, with a European outlook. He introduced a number of useful administrative and military reforms, the latter including the institution of a *militia portalis*, or second-line army of peasant soldiers, and not the Angevins themselves did more than he to promote the prosperity of the towns and to raise their status. He encouraged manufacture, and was the true father of Hungary's international trade, which he advanced by abolishing internal duties, regulating tariffs on foreign goods and standardising weights and measures throughout the country. Records show that Hungary in his day was importing cloth, linen, velvet, silks and spices and southern delicacies; her chief exports were linen goods, cloth, metal and iron goods, livestock, skins and honey. The memory of this well-being survives in the many fine buildings, dating from his reign, still to be seen in Hungary's towns. An unintentional benefit conferred by him on his country was that his repeated and prolonged absences from Hungary, and his extravagances, both enabled and compelled his subjects to recover some of the constitutional ground which they had lost to his predecessors. He found himself obliged to consult Diets, if not regularly, at least frequently, and to defer to the principle, then generally recognised in central Europe, that their consent was necessary when a subsidy, or new taxation, was required. It was during his reign that the office of the Palatine, who was head of the administration during the king's absence, developed (this was, indeed, formally legalised only under his successor) from that of the king's representative to that of intermediary between the king and the nation, whose function and duty it was to 'represent law and justice for the inhabitants of the country *vis-à-vis* the king's majesty, and for the king's majesty *vis-à-vis* them'.

Under the same influences there now began to emerge the famous and peculiar mystic doctrine, formulated in classical form in the sixteenth century by the jurist Werbőczy, of the Holy Crown: to wit, that the true political being of Hungary resided in the mystical entity (of which the physical crown was the incorporate symbol) of the Holy Crown, of which the king was the head and the nation, or corporate aggregate of nobles, the body; each member being incomplete without the other, and complementary to it, in that the king was the fount of nobility and the nobles, in virtue of their right to elect their king, the fount of kingship.

But the debit side of Sigismund's all too long reign was also very heavy. He never succeeded in recovering Dalmatia, and in his efforts to do so, he pledged the valuable counties of Szepes, a main source of the king's wealth, to Poland. The nation was perfectly justified in its complaints over his long absences, and by reason of them, and for other causes, partly personal, he was never truly master in the country. The new big families whom the Angevins had promoted had on the whole remained loyal to their benefactors, but they had yet acquired an unhealthy predominance in the country, and an excess of power in their own preserves, and towards Sigismund, as we have seen, they showed no such loyalty. He did not willingly promote their power, but in fact he increased it by the lavish sale, to meet his extravagant expenditure, of crown lands, which by the end of his reign were reduced to 5 per cent of the area of Hungary. Unable to cope with his most powerful subjects as a class, he could do no more than play off some of them against the rest. This he did by organising a group of them in a chivalric league, known as 'the Order of the Dragon', of which he was himself President. Offices and favours were shared out among the members of this group, but even they were not always reliable; cases occurred when the Order itself defied the king.

The smaller men suffered, especially the peasants, whose condition deteriorated substantially, less owing to any aggravation of their legal burdens (peasants serving in the *militia portalis* were exempt from the *porta* tax) than from increases in the tax itself, illegal exactions, and perhaps most of all, under the increasingly rapid transition to a money economy, with which they could not easily cope. The consequent unrest was fanned by the spread from Bohemia of Hussite doctrines, which took hold especially in north Hungary, and was embittered by the cruelty with which the heretics were persecuted. The first serious specifically peasant revolt which Hungary had ever known broke out in the very last months of Sigismund's reign, as the result of the action of a bishop in Transylvania in claiming the tithe in money. It spread over much of Transylvania, and gained considerable temporary successes before it was put down. A consequence of this revolt was the birth of an institution destined later to become important, the 'Union of the Three Nations', under which the Hungarian nobles of the Transylvanian coun-ties, the Saxons and the Szekels formed a league for the mutual defence of their interests against all parties, save only the king.

This grievous event occurred at a moment when Hungary was most sorely in need of all her strength and all her unity, for her old unthreatened state was over. In 1352 the Osmanli Turks had crossed the Straits and established themselves in Gallipoli. In 1362 they took Adrianople. In 1388 they made Sisman's Bulgaria tributary; in 1389 they annihilated the power of Serbia on the field of Kossovo.

Sigismund, to do him justice, had early recognised the reality of the Turkish danger (to which Louis had been curiously blind) and in 1395 had led an expe-dition into the Balkans which had met with some success. He had followed this up the next year with a larger expedition in which crusading contingents from many European countries had taken part; but this time the Christian armies had been disastrously defeated at Nicopolis in north Bulgaria (22 September 1396), the Hungarian contingent, which had formed the bulk of the army, being anni-hilated, and Sigismund himself barely escaping with his life. Hungary, and all central Europe, lay open to the invaders, and were only respited, not by their own efforts, but by the intervention of Timur's Mongols, who were now threat-ening the Turks' rear and in 1402 actually took the Sultan Bayazid himself pris-oner, after a pitched battle outside Ankara. For some time after this the Turks' operations on their European front were on a reduced scale, but they recom-menced in 1415. The Voivode of Wallachia submitted, Bosnia repudiated Hungary's suzerainty, and her only remaining Balkan client was a fragmentary Serbia under the 'Despot', George Branković. South Hungary itself and Transyl-vania suffered repeated raids.

In 1437 the Sultan Murad was preparing for a grand attack on Hungary itself, and at this most inauspicious juncture Sigismund died, having crowned his dis-services to Hungary by leaving no son, but only a girl, Elizabeth, the issue of his second marriage, with the daughter of the Count of Cilli, who was married to Albrecht, head of the Albertinian line of the Habsburgs and ruler of Austria Above and Below the Enns.[4] Sigismund had designated Albrecht to succeed him in both Hungary and Bohemia, and the Hungarians duly elected him, while stipulating that he should defend the country with all his forces (also, that he should not accept the Imperial crown). All might have turned out well, for Albrecht, who was both conscientious and able, was prepared to fulfil his promise and in fact set about organising an army for a campaign against the Turks; but dysentery carried him off before he had reigned two full years and another dynastic crisis broke out. Elizabeth was big with child, and claimed at least the regency, but a majority of the Hungarians were unwilling to wait for the birth of a child who might not even be a boy, and in any case to endure a long regency under a woman. They elected the young king of Poland as Wladislav V. Immediately after, Elizabeth was delivered of a boy, whom she succeeded in getting crowned, calling in to support her the Czech war-lord, Giskra, who occupied north-western Hungary. The position of the young Ulászló (as the Hungarians called him) was thus threatened from the rear at the moment when he most needed security.

In this most critical hour Hungary was saved principally by the genius of a single man, János (John) Hunyadi, one of the most interesting and attractive figures in the national history. He had risen from small beginnings; son of a lesser noble of Vlach origin (it is true that his ascent to position and wealth had been so meteoric as to give rise to rumours that he was Sigismund's own natural son), he had begun life as a professional condottiere, but had shown such extraordinary talent in that capacity that Sigismund had given him high command, and Albrecht even higher, appointing him Ban of Szörény. Ulászló, whose cause he had supported, promoted him to Captain-General of Belgrade and Voivode of Transylvania. He was now the most important man in Hungary, after the young king himself, and also in a fair way to becoming the richest, for he was as great a money-maker as he was soldier; by not long after this, his private estates were estimated to have covered nearly six million acres. In Transylvania, in 1442, Hunyadi brilliantly defeated a Turkish army, then in 1443 persuaded Ulászló to undertake a campaign in the Balkans, this being the first time for many years that the Turks had had the offensive taken against them on that front. This was so signally successful that the Sultan agreed to a peace which liberated all Serbia from his rule. Unhappily, the Papal Legate, who had been organising a crusade which was frustrated by Hunyadi's action in concluding the peace, persuaded Ulászló that a word given to an infidel need not be kept. The next year he and Hunyadi accordingly led a new army into the Balkans, where the enraged Sultan, meeting them outside Varna on 10 November, defeated them disastrously. The young king himself perished, with the flower of his army, while Hunyadi barely escaped with his life.

He managed, however, to get back to Hungary, where he performed a service hardly less valuable than his feats in the field, in mediating a solution of the dynastic question. For Elizabeth had meanwhile died, leaving her little boy, Ladislas (known as Ladislas Postumus), with the Holy Crown, in the charge of his uncle, the Emperor Frederick, and the easy-going Frederick was content to leave Hunyadi in charge of Hungary as 'governor' or 'regent' until the child should have grown up.

During the next years Hunyadi was by no means always successful; Giskra defeated him in 1447 and had to be left master of north-western Hungary, and in the same year he suffered another heavy defeat at the hands of the Turks in Serbia. He did, however, succeed in holding them back as no European had done before him. His crowning achievement came in 1456, when he so heavily routed a Turkish army which was besieging Belgrade that it was seventy years before the danger recurred in so acute a form.

The relief of Belgrade, for which the Pope ordered all the church-bells of catholic Europe to ring daily at noon, that the faithful might pray in unison for it, was also Hunyadi's last victory, for he died a few weeks later of a fever contracted in the camp. And at first it seemed as though he was to be ill repaid. In 1452 the Austrian and Bohemian Estates had forced Frederick to release Ladislas from tutelage, and the next year he was solemnly reinstated as King of Hungary. The boy-king allowed Hunyadi to remain *de facto* regent, but himself fell under the influence of his maternal uncle, the Count of Cilli, who distrusted the Hunyadi family, a feeling reciprocated by Hunyadi's brother-in-law, Mihály (Michael) Szilágyi. On Hunyadi's death, Ladislas nominated his uncle as the new Captain-General of Hungary, passing over Hunyadi's elder son, another Ladislas. Soon after, the king and his uncle visited Belgrade, then in Szilágyi's hands, the Szilágyi's partisans murdered Cilli. The king then treacherously seized Ladislas Hunyadi and put him to death; his younger brother Mátyás (Matthew) Hunyadi, then a boy of sixteen, he took to Prague, where he threw him into prison; only to die himself, still unmarried, a year later.

For the first time in Hungarian history there was now no candidate for the throne able to put forward a claim based even tenuously on heredity. There were, of course, pretenders enough, including the evergreen Emperor Frederick, but this time the nation was tired of foreign kings. The name of Hunyadi was magical among the small nobles, and it was easy for Szilágy to organise them to favour the surviving bearer of the name. On 24 January 1458, while the great men were still debating, a huge multitude of common nobles, assembled on the ice of the frozen Danube, proclaimed Mátyás king. Emissaries having with some difficulty extracted him from the keeping of George Podiebrad, in Prague (for the Czechs, too, had decided in favour of a national king), he was brought to Buda and enthroned amid scenes of national rejoicing.

Mátyás Corvinus, as he is commonly known from his crest, a raven, is, with the somewhat qualified exception of John Zápolyai, the only completely 'national' king to have worn the Holy Crown after the extinction of the old dynasty, and it is natural that Hungarian historians should have seen his reign, in retrospect, through something of a golden haze. The remarkable glamour of his personality is undeniable. He was, as his panegyrists never tire of repeating, a true Renaissance prince. He was exceedingly talented in every respect: a brilliant natural soldier, a first-class administrator, an outstanding linguist, speaking with equal fluency half a dozen languages, a learned astrologer, an enlightened patron of the arts and himself a refined connoisseur of their delights. His library of 'Corvina' was famous throughout Europe. Besides the illuminated MSS of which this mainly consisted (many of which he had specially wrought for him by Italian craftsmen), his collections, on which he spent vast sums, included pictures, statues, jewels, goldsmiths' work and other *objects d'art*. Under his patronage, architecture and the arts flourished in Hungary. Scholars of European repute lived and worked at his court and in the circle of the Archbishop-primate, János Vitéz. Some of them produced elaborate and scholarly works, still valuable in parts, on Hungarian history. The first book printed in Buda antedated Caxton. Sumptuous buildings sprang up in the capital and in other centres. Most of these were destroyed in the subsequent Turkish invasion, which also dispersed the remnants of his collections, but those which have survived, notably the magnificent Coronation church of Buda, show that Mátyás'

Hungary could challenge comparison with most European states of the day. His reign saw the foundation of Hungary's second university – unfortunately, another short-lived creation.

The word 'Renaissance' is to be taken exactly, for especially after Mátyás had married, as his second wife, Beatrix of Aragon, daughter of the King of Naples, the influences of the early Italian Renaissance dominated his court. They brought with them the absurdities of the day. The cult of Attila and his Huns, at that time held to be the Magyars' ancestors, flourished. The historian Bonfinius traced the Hunyadi's own ancestry back to a Roman consul, himself the descendant of Zeus and the nymph Taygeta. But the classical trappings were used to enhance the national glory. When Mátyás' father-in-law sent him a Spanish horse-master, he replied:

'For centuries we have been famed for our skill in horsemanship, so that the Magyar has no need to have his horses dance with crossed legs, Spanish fashion.'

Seen unromantically, his reign, of course, appears as the usual mixture of good and bad. His first years were necessarily spent in consolidating his position, for he had many opponents, both abroad and at home. Even Podiebrad had demanded a heavy ransom for releasing him, and although the Emperor Frederick did not press his claim by arms, he, too, demanded a big price for suspending them, and for restoring the Holy Crown. The Czechs were still installed in north-western Hungary, the Turks still dangerous in the Balkans. Many of the magnates were very hostile to the young upstart, as they regarded him, and he soon became involved in a dispute with his own uncle and sponsor, Szilágy, who had hoped to rule for him till he grew older.

Mátyás overcame all these difficulties with energy and skill. Podiebrad was paid off, Frederick bought off, through the mediation of the Pope; the Czechs were mopped up, an accommodation having been reached with Giskra. Szilágy was sent on an expedition into the Balkans, which ended in his death, and the other magnates brought to heel. Two successful expeditions were carried out against the Turks, a chain of fortresses built along the southern frontier, and Hungarian suzerainty re-established, if in somewhat shadowy form – it was worth little unless enforced by garrisons, which could not be spared – over Bosnia, Serbia and Wallachia, and later, also over Moldavia.

It is by his acts after he had really become master of his country that Mátyás is to be judged. His electors had bound him stringently to observe constitutional forms, and this he always did, hearing the views of the Council and admitting the principle that the Diet should meet annually. He actually enlarged the autonomous powers of the counties. Nevertheless, the whole bent of his mind was towards the fashionable 'princely' absolutism of his age, and his respect for constitutional institutions was largely formal. In practice, he disregarded the Council; his real instruments were his secretaries, a body of men picked by himself, generally young and often of quite obscure origin. When the Diet proved recalcitrant, he bent it to his will, ruthlessly enough. His rule was in fact a near-absolutism, and the touchstone of it is, whether or no it was enlightened and beneficial.

In some respects, it was certainly both these things. He simplified the admin-

istration and made it more efficient, and carried through a grandiose reform of
the entire judicial system, abolishing many anachronisms and abuses and introducing a simplified and accelerated procedure which was of particular benefit to
the small man. He encouraged the towns, especially the smaller market towns,
and while not alleviating the legal position of the serfs, in fact greatly improved
their condition by the even-handed justice which he enforced, so that when he
was dead they mourned: 'King Mátyás is dead, justice is departed.'

The central controversy of his day turned round his defence policy and the
financial burdens which he imposed on the nation in support of it. He trebled
the size of the *militia portalis*, following this up by the most famous of all his
'innovations', the creation of a standing army, some 30,000 strong, which ranked
as part of the king's *banderium*. This force, which was drawn largely from the
defeated Hussites, and was known, after its commander, 'Black' John Haugwitz,
as the 'Black Army', was his most powerful weapon against all enemies, abroad
or at home.

Since the upkeep of this force, supervening on the cost of his sumptuous court
and his collections, involved an expenditure far beyond what could be met out
of ordinary revenue, Mátyás reorganised the tax system in ways which cut at the
root of the national tradition. He screwed up the profits from the regalia,[5] introduced a *tributum fisci regalis* [tax of the royal exchequer] from which none of his
subjects was exempt, and frequently – in the latter half of his reign, regularly –
imposed a special *porta* tax of a florin per *porta*. Although he conceded the right
of the Diet to vote this, yet in 1470, when that body objected, he dissolved it
and had the tax collected by his servants. By these means he raised the royal
revenue to the unprecedented figure of 6–800,000 forints; although in some years
his expenditure far exceeded even this sum.

In the first years, the nation was prepared to accept extraordinary financial
burdens to redeem the Holy Crown, rid north Hungary of the Czechs, and above
all, to secure its defences against the Turks. But after his good beginning in the
last-named field, Mátyás allowed his attention to be distracted to the west. He
had then some excuse: the Austrians and Czechs were proving worse neighbours
than the Turks, who remained passive for some ten years after their defeats. But
Mátyás let himself be drawn into an ever-widening circle of campaigns in the
Lands of the Bohemian Crown and Austria, in pursuit for himself of the
Bohemian Crown, the dignity of Roman King and the succession to the Imperial Crown itself, after Frederick should die. In fact, he succeeded in 1469 in
making himself master of Moravia, Silesia and Lusatia, with the title of King of
Bohemia (although this was also borne simultaneously by Podiebrad) and, in
1478, in forcing Frederick to cede him Lower Austria and Styria. To his subjects,
he justified these campaigns, and the taxes which he levied to finance them, by
the argument that Hungary alone was no match for the Turks; that the sovereign
princes of Austria and Bohemia would not help him and could not be trusted
not to stab him in the back; and that he could therefore only organise the great
crusade if he had at his disposal the resources of the Bohemian and Imperial
Crowns. There was perhaps something in this argument, for the only source
which sent Mátyás any help against the Turks was the Holy See, which sent some

rather jejune subsidies. But the Hungarians, although probably not oppressed by conscience-pricks over the blatant aggressiveness of Mátyás' wars, saw no profit in them, had no ambition to become the nucleus of a multi-national empire, and believed that Mátyás was simply gratifying personal ambition at the expense of the security of Hungary's southern frontier – which, in fact, the Turks raided again in 1474 and 1476, doing much damage. There was much grumbling, and in 1470 a party which included some of Mátyás' oldest supporters conspired to set Casimir of Poland on the throne, and next year Casimir actually crossed the Carpathians at the head of an army.

He found few supporters and the enterprise collapsed easily enough; but it cannot be said that in his lifetime Mátyás was ever beloved as Stephen I or Louis the Great had been.

Mátyás might nevertheless have established a new, native dynasty; but neither of his two wives bore him an heir. His only issue, a boy called John, was his illegitimate son by a bourgeoise of Breslau. One of Mátyás' main preoccupations as he grew older was to ensure this boy's succession, and he eventually reached agreement in principle with Maximilian of Austria whereby John was to marry Maximilian's daughter; Hungary was to hand back Austria and Styria to Maximilian; and Maximilian was to renounce his father's old claims on Hungary and recognise John as its sovereign. But on 6 May 1490, when actually on his way to the meeting which should have made the agreement definitive, Mátyás died suddenly, and the whole house of cards collapsed. The smaller nobles would have liked another ruler of the Hunyadi stock, but John's illegitimacy was a real objection, and he himself was of too peaceable and unambituous nature to press his claim hard. Maximilian was another candidate, but the magnates were afraid of him; what they wanted was, as one of them put it cynically, 'a king whose plaits they could hold in their fists'. Such a man was to hand in Wladislas Jagiello (Ulászló II in Hungarian history), whom the Bohemians had chosen as their king in 1471 precisely for his negative qualities, a choice which he had thereafter justified so amply as to earn from his subjects the name of 'King Dobře' (King O. K.) from his habit of assenting without cavil to any proposal laid before him.

In the event Maximilian contented himself with the restoration of the Austrian provinces and with an agreement that if Ulászló died without heirs, Maximilian himself, or his heirs, should succeed. Thereafter he exercised an increasingly close, although friendly, protectorate over Hungary, which was not altered when Ulászló, after many curious adventures, eventually married and, in 1506, became father of a boy. Another agreement was concluded in 1515 under which this boy, Louis, married Maximilian's granddaughter, Mary, while his sister, Anne, was betrothed to Maximilian's younger grandson, Ferdinand, who was to succeed to Louis's thrones if Louis died without issue.

During these years Maximilian built up for himself a considerable party in Hungary, especially in the west of the country, but he also had many opponents. The national party, strong among the smaller nobles, refused to recognise the validity of the dynastic compacts, and a Diet in 1505 actually passed a resolution never again to receive a foreign king. This party's candidate, should Ulászló's line die out, was one John Zápolyai, whose uncle and father had risen from small beginnings to hold successively the office of Palatine under Mátyás, while John himself was Voivode of Transylvania and the biggest landowner in Hungary.

Meanwhile, under King Dobře's rule, conditions in Hungary plunged downhill with Gadarene rapidity. His electors had forced him to repeal all Mátyás' 'innovations', including his extraordinary taxation. This involved the dissolution of the Black Army, the chief instrument of Mátyás' personal power; for defence, the nation now reverted to the *banderial* system. The king had also to promise to convoke the Diet regularly, giving advance notice of the subjects which he proposed to lay before it, and agree that no decree issued by him was legal without the Council's confirmation. He fell entirely into the hands of the clique round him, who plundered the royal revenues so ruthlessly that only a fraction of them reached the treasury. The annual revenue fell to under 200,000 florins. The king himself was reduced to selling off Mátyás' collections. Sometimes he had literally to beg for food and drink for his court. At one carnival the king's own estates could produce only eight turkeys.

The power of the magnates, which at the same period became almost total in Bohemia, was to some extent limited in Hungary by the resistance of the lesser nobles, who succeeded in asserting a right to a share in the membership of the Council, as also to attendance at the Diet. In 1514, too, they achieved a remarkable paper reaffirmation of their position in the shape of a codification of the Customary Law of Hungary, drawn up by the jurist Werbőczy. This work, known as the 'Tripartitum', which, although never formally promulgated, was ever after universally treated as authoritative, laid down in explicit terms the complete legal equality of all nobles, as enjoying 'one and the same liberty'. In practice, this helped them little politically: even in the Diet the magnates could always get their way by prolonging the debates until the small men could stay away from their farms no longer.

It did, however, help to reaffirm the cardinal distinction between the free and the unfree population, and the most unhappy feature of the period was the swift deterioration of the position of the latter class. The phenomenon was not a specifically Hungarian one; it was occurring simultaneously in Germany, Bohemia and Poland, and even set in rather later in Hungary than in the neighbouring countries. But here, too, the peasants found their burdens progressively increased and their liberty, especially that of escaping from a tyrannous landlord, progressively restricted. The Diet of 1492, while confirming their right to change their masters, reduced their inducement to do so by making it illegal for any lord, including the king and the Free Districts (the prohibition was extended to the boroughs in 1498) to exact less than the minimum legalised dues and services. This Law was a serious blow to the market towns and the Districts, which under Mátyás had achieved a half-free condition, compounding their obligations for a relatively small annual sum. In 1504 peasants were forbidden hunting or fowling.

Then, in 1514, there came an extraordinary and terrible episode. The Cardinal Primate, Támás Bakócz, aspired to the Papacy. He was not elected, but as consolation and diversion, entrusted with the organisation of a crusade. None of the big men volunteered, but a huge army of peasants and masterless men did so. Bakócz put them under the command of a Szekel professional soldier named Dózsa. Left without proper leadership or supplies, the wretched crusaders grew restive and presently Dózsa turned them not against the Turks but against the lords. The movement expanded into an almost nation-wide jacquerie [peasant uprising]. There was savage fighting in which fearful atrocities were committed on both sides. Then the revolt was put down. Dózsa was put to death by inde-scribable tortures. A Diet intoxicated by a spirit of almost inconceivable vindic-tiveness ordered the most savage reprisals against all leaders and all perpetrators of any atrocities, and their kinsfolk, and condemned the entire class of peasants, with certain exceptions, to 'real and perpetual servitude'. They became irrevo-cably bound to the soil, in which they were explicitly declared to have no own-ership whatever – they were wage-earners pure and simple. Their *corvée* [unpaid labour] was raised to fifty-two days in the year, and their other dues and pay-ments increased. This savage law, too, was enshrined in the Tripartitum.

Louis succeeded his father in 1516, but, a boy of nine, naturally could bring no remedy. Meanwhile the defences of the country went from bad to worse. The frontier garrisons were left without pay, the fortresses fell into ill-repair. The king disbanded his own *banderium* for lack of funds, and several of the magnates fol-lowed his example. Then, in 1520, the Turkish threat grew acute again. Suleiman the Magnificent succeeded to the Sultanate and at once sent Louis a demand for tribute; when this was rejected, he marched on Belgrade and took it. The country awoke to the danger and agreed to a general tax for establishing a permanent mercenary army, but this was to replace, not supplement, the existing system. The lords were relieved of the obligation of maintaining *banderia* and the lesser nobles from obeying the levée. The proceeds of the tax were embezzled and the army never raised.

Hungary was given a brief respite by the Sultan's decision to reduce Rhodes before turning north again, but in 1525 attack was again imminent. Messengers scoured Europe appealing for help, but hardly any came; the Empire was occu-pied with France, Poland with the Tatars, Bohemia was indifferent. When, in 1526, the Sultan commenced his advance in earnest, it was at first almost unop-posed. The levée was, after all, proclaimed and the *banderia* re-activated, but when, in July, Louis set out from Buda he had at first only 3,300 men with which to meet the Sultan's 70–80,000 regulars and half as many irregulars. By the time the two armies made contact at Mohács, Louis' army had swollen to 25,000, but the detachments from Transylvania and Croatia had not yet arrived. Disregard-ing advice to wait for these, the Hungarians attacked on 29 August. The army was almost utterly destroyed and the king himself perished by some fatal mishap in the rout.

NOTES

1   By this time the tradition had grown up that coronation was invalid unless performed with the Holy Crown.
2   Strictly, the *porta* was the gate through which a peasant's waggon passed into his yard. It was thus not an exact measure, since two or three peasants might share one yard.

3   The resentment was particularly strong where religious considerations reinforced purely
     political ones, as among the Bogumils of Bosnia.
4   A tributary of the River Danube.
5   The royal right of enjoying the revenues of vacant bishoprics and abbacies.

15 Andrew Gurr 'Physical conditions of the London stage'

Source: from *Playgoing in Shakespeare's London*, Andrew Gurr, Cambridge
University Press, Cambridge, second edition, 1996, chapter 2, pp. 13–21.

(A) THE AMPHITHEATRE PLAYHOUSES

There were two quite different types of commercial London playhouse, one
beginning in 1567, the other in 1575. The 'public' playhouses or open amphitheatres, the first of which seems to have opened in 1567, were versions of the animal-
baiting houses and galleried inn-yards. The 'private' playhouses or halls were built
in large rooms on the model of the banqueting halls in the royal palaces and great
houses where plays were provided for banqueting guests. The terms 'public' and
'private' were not used to differentiate the two types until about 1600, and they
indicate more about the social antecedents of each type than any difference of
commercial function. The terms 'amphitheatre' and 'hall' are better indications
of their character. The value of the terms 'public' and 'private' lies chiefly in the
way they indicate the social snobbery which separated the two kinds.

   The 'public' amphitheatres were built in the suburbs. The first of them (so far
as we know) was the Red Lion, built in Whitechapel in 1567, and replaced in
1576 by the Theatre in Shoreditch, on one of the main roads north out of the
city. The dimensions of the Red Lion's stage are known, but nothing about its
auditorium. Much of what we know about the Theatre and its near neighbour,
the Curtain, built in the following year, has likewise to be inferred from the evidence for the later playhouses, which are rather better documented. The Theatre
was dismantled in 1598 so that its timbers could be used as the frame for the
Globe. In its basic layout and audience capacity the later playhouse must have
closely resembled it. Much more is known about the Rose, built in 1587, on evidence in Philip Henslowe's records and from its foundations, partly uncovered
in 1989. We also know something of the Swan, built in 1595 near the Rose on
Bankside in Surrey, close to Paris Garden, which was the chief bear-baiting-house.
We know about the Swan largely thanks to the drawing which the Dutchman
Johannes De Witt made of its interior on a visit in 1596. Different kinds of evidence, including builder's instructions and lawsuits, give information about the
last five major amphitheatres, the Globe (1599) on the Bankside, the Fortune
(1600) to the north, the Boar's Head (1601) in Whitechapel to the east, the Red
Bull (1604) in Clerkenwell to the north-west, and the Hope, built on the Bankside to double as a baiting-house and playhouse in 1614. The main features of
the auditorium seem to have been basically similar in all the amphitheatres, and
it is possible to identify something like a typical setting for seeing a play at any
of the 'public' venues. John Brayne, who built the Red Lion playhouse in 1567,
partnered James Burbage in building what was probably its replacement, the

10 A map of London showing its playhouses built between 1567 and 1629. Braun and Hogenberg's *Civitates Orbis Terrarum*, first ed. 1572. The playhouses and inns used for playing are marked in their approximate locations, with the date of the building where known. In the seventy years from 1572 London expanded to cover most of the periphery shown here. Map in Guildhall Library, Department of Prints, London, annotations reproduced

Boar's Head 1602

Red Lion 1567

Theatre 1576

Curtain 1577

Bull Inn

Cross Keys Inn

Bell Inn

LONDINVM FERACISSIMI AN GLIAE REGNI METROPOLIS

Fortune 1600

Red Bull 1604

Paul's

Bel Savage Inn

Blackfriars

Salisbury Court 1629

Cockpit 1616

Hope 1614

Rose 1587

Globe 1599

Swan 1595

THE TOWN

Theatre, in 1576. Most likely all of these earliest amphitheatres had an auditorium similar in structure to the galleried animal-baiting rings which had stood on the south bank of the Thames for the previous forty or more years. They probably also resembled the great coaching inns, which had square yards and surrounding galleries. In fact two later play-houses, the Boar's Head and the Red Bull, were converted from inns, and the square-built Fortune may have been similar to them. The 1576 edition of William Lambarde's *Perambulation of Kent* describes playgoing at the Bel Savage Inn in Ludgate, and the 1596 edition adds the Theatre to the account without otherwise altering what is described. The arrangements for playgoing at the two venues were evidently similar. The inns and amphitheatres provided standing-room in the 'yard' around the stage, an area obviously not available to audiences at the baiting-houses, but apart from that extra space the auditorium layout probably did not differ in any fundamental way. The playhouses certainly copied their three levels of galleries from the baiting-houses.

Samuel Kiechel, a German merchant visiting London in 1584, reported that both of the playhouses then had three levels of galleries. These served as the chief accommodation for playgoers, offering seating on wooden 'degrees' or steps, and a roof to fend off the London weather. The stage itself, jutting from one side into the middle of the yard, was also protected by a cover or 'heavens', but the yard itself was open to the sky, and the playgoers who gathered there closest to the stage had nothing but their legs to uphold them. This minimal provision – no seating, and no protection from the rain – helps to explain one of the curious features of the earliest playhouses which seems to have been altered when the new generation appeared in the 1590s. Admission to the earliest playhouses was a gradual progression from the minimal comfort of the yard to the better and more sheltered places in the galleries. As Lambarde put it in his 1596 edition (p. 233): such as goe to *Parisgardein*, the *Bell Savage*, or *Theatre*, to beholde Beare baiting, Enterludes or Fence play, can account of any pleasant spectacle, [if] they first pay one pennie at the gate, another at the entrie of the Scaffolde, and the thirde for a quiet standing.

Thomas Platter, a young Swiss visitor in 1599, described the same system with the added detail that the best seats were cushioned. You went in by the entrance doors directly to the yard, as you would entering a coaching inn-yard through its great double gates. Once in the yard you could choose to enter the galleries for a seat, and if you wanted more privacy and a cushion you could pay once again for a room in the galleries closest to the stage. This arrangement, a sequence of choices, may have owed something to the design of the inns, and it must have been acceptable to the players familiar with the traditions of the booth stages in market squares, where the entire audience simply stood around the booth stage. It can hardly have been used in the baiting-houses, where the yard became the baiting arena, but in the playhouses it was an arrangement which must have seemed entirely natural to those who assumed that a normal audience would principally be a crowd of men and women clustered on their feet around the stage platform. So you were admitted to the yard, and could go elsewhere only if you chose to separate yourself from the principal audience, the crowd standing around the stage platform. If it rained, you had the choice of getting wet or paying a second penny for the shelter of the galleries.

The second generation of playhouses, including possibly the Rose (1587), and the Swan (1595) and certainly the Globe and Fortune, seem to have been designed with a less clumsy system of admission which acknowledged from the start that the gallery sitters were different from the standers of the yard. De Witt's drawing of the Swan has caused some debate about this, because the openings marked 'ingressus' in the gallery walls surrounding the yard seem to mark the same cumbrous sequential system as the Theatre, where the first penny gaining entrance to the yard required the gallery-goer to push his or her way through the crowd before surrendering another penny for a seat and a roof. But the Globe and the Fortune, built as exact rivals – James Burbage transported the timbers of his Theatre from the northern suburb to the Bankside near to Philip Henslowe's Rose, and Henslowe promptly built the Fortune in the north not far away from the old Theatre site, using as his builder the man who had just completed the Globe – had a more sophisticated admission system. Access to the galleries in these playhouses did not entail passing through the yard. Once in one of the two entrance-ways you chose either to enter the yard or to mount the stairs which rose in towers above the entrance-ways directly into the galleries. The 'twopenny galleries' in fact could accommodate more than twice as many playgoers as the yard, so it is understandable that the players eventually came to feel that gallery patrons deserved better treatment than to be siphoned through the crowd who were paying least for their pleasure.

The 'two small doors', which were all that the audience at the Globe had to escape by in 1613 when a performance of *Henry VIII* set the thatching over the galleries alight and destroyed the playhouse, could admit more than three thousand people in all. When the house was full, the crowding was intense. At the Fortune, built in an 80-foot square, probably out of an existing building, the yard measured 55 feet along each side, with the stage jutting into the centre from a tiring-house front occupying 43 of the 55 feet on the side opposite the entry gates. It thus gave the standers in its yard a total space of 1,842 square feet. The Boar's Head playhouse, converted from an inn-yard in 1599, had rather less than that, and only two levels of gallery. The Globe, built on a circular or polygonal frame almost exactly 100 feet in outside diameter, and with a yard about 70 feet in diameter, offered nearly 2,500 square feet. There is no firm evidence about how many people this space could hold, and it would not have been really packed very often. But it could be enough of a squeeze to be an uncomfortable experience, if we are to judge by Marston's reference to being 'pasted to the barmy Jacket of a Beer-brewer', and Dekker's frequent mentions of garlic breathed stinkards. The only actual figures we have allocating a set number of standing spectators to a fixed space come from documents about the king's visit to Oxford in 1605 and the play performed for him at Christ Church. There 400 square feet were allowed for 130 standers. But that ratio – 3 square feet each – was actually more than the average gentleman or lady was allowed for sitting at the same play ($2\frac{1}{4}$ square feet), and cannot bear much relation to the level of crowding acceptable at the Globe or Fortune. Calculations of 600 or 800 in the yard at these playhouses probably rather underestimate the maximum capacity. At the nine per-

formances of *A Game at Chesse* at the rebuilt Globe in 1624 the squeeze must have
been fearsome, and there could hardly have been less than a thousand people in the
yard for each performance, since the Spanish Ambassador claimed that there were
'more than 3,000 persons there on the day that the audience was smallest'.

The change in the admission system for the later playhouses probably indicates
a shift in priorities to favour the gallery audience over the 'understanders' in the
yard. The wealthiest patrons most likely always had separate access to their places,
since the 'lords' rooms which were on the balcony immediately over the stage
must have been reached through the tiring-house. The sixpence which a lord's
room cost would have been paid at the tiring-house door at the back of the playhouse. The revised entry system devised for the Globe and Fortune went some
distance towards giving comparably separate access for the gallery patrons. This
system, a major stairway with doors leading off to each gallery level, may have
been devised for the Rose. Sir John Harington wrote an epigram, about a lady
who was caught on the stairs by a pair of thieves, which dates from the 1590s and
clearly indicates that access to the galleries at that time was no longer through
the yard. We need not assume that the anecdote in the epigram really happened,
since Harington is clearly developing a bawdy pun on the stock term for
stealing, 'cony-catching' (catching rabbits), but the material circumstances of the
stairway must be genuine.

> A lady of great Birth, great reputation,
> Clothed in seemely, and most sumptuous fashion
> Wearing a border of rich Pearl and stone,
> Esteemed at a thousand crowns alone,
> To see a certaine interlude, repaires,
> To shun the press, by dark and privat staires.
> Her page did heare a Torch that burnt but dimly.
> Two cozening mates, seeing her deckt so trimly,
> Did place themselves upon the stayres to watch her,
> And thus they laid their plot to cunny-catch her:
> One should as 'twere by chance strike out the light;
> While th'other that should stand beneath her, might
> Attempt (which modestie to suffer lothes)
> Rudely to thrust his hands under her clothes.
> That while her hands repeld such grosse disorders,
> His mate might quickly slip away the borders.
> Now though this act to her was most unpleasant
> Yet being wise (as womens wits are present:)
> Straight on her borders both her hands she cast,
> And so with all her force she held them fast.
> Villaines, she cryde, you would my borders have:
> But I'll save them, tother it selfe can save:
> Thus, while the Page had got more store of light,
> The coozening mates, for fear slipt out of sight.
> Thus her good wit, their cunning over-macht,
> Were not these conycatchers conycatchd?

If this anecdote relates to an amphitheatre, as its dating indicates it must, then it suggests a few additional points about gallery audiences. Wealthy noblewomen could expect to see plays there unescorted except by their pages. Cutpurses were regularly in attendance. Nor did crowds come to the playhouse so thick and so fast that a gallery-goer might not climb the stairs alone. This last point fits in with the implications of Philip Henslowe's takings from the galleries of the Rose. His average income was less than half the maximum. Overcrowding, except at new plays and exceptionally scandalous events like *A Game at Chesse*, was not usually the playgoer's main problem.

By John Orrell's calculations, allowing an 18-inch spread and also 18 inches fore and aft for each person on the 'degrees', the Globe's galleries could hold almost 1,000 on each of the two lower levels, and on the third level where sight lines would have required a steep rake and less depth of degrees, about 750. By the same criterion the Fortune galleries could hold 880 in the lower galleries and 660 in the upper tier. The allocation of space for the Christ Church performance in 1605 which Orrell uses to obtain his figures in fact allocated 18 inches in width for everyone, but gave a relatively generous 30 inches fore and aft for lords and 24 inches fore and aft for Court ladies and the king's servants. The gentlemen in the upper tier were confined to 18 inches each way. It seems plausible to assume that the public amphitheatres would provide the minimum spacing for all their customers, though of course Lambarde's third penny 'for a quiet standing' (i.e. a seat) might have given access to a more spacious arrangement, like the Oxford allocation for Court ladies, close to the stage. If so, the totals for the lower galleries would be less than a thousand each. The lords' rooms must have been spacious, with benches or stools. On the Swan's balcony De Witt sketched not more than two people to a room. A reference from about 1609 to a gallant who 'Plays at Primero over the stage' indicates that there could easily be space for a card-game in the lords' rooms. Primero was a gambling game rather like poker involving three or more players.

This disposition, with space for about 800 in the yard and over 2,000 in the various galleries, matches the contemporary estimates for the total capacity of the amphitheatres. The Spanish Ambassador reckoned over 3,000 at the second Globe, which being built on the same foundations as the first must have had a similar total capacity. De Witt gave the same total for the Swan in 1596.

16   C. L. Barber **'The Merchants and the Jew of Venice: Wealth's communion and an intruder'**

Source: from *Shakespeare's Festive Comedy: A Study of Dramatic Form and its Relation to Social Custom*, C. L. Barber, Princeton University Press, Princeton, New Jersey, 1959, chapter 7, pp. 163–91.

> Should I go to church
> And see the holy edifice of stone
> And not bethink me straight of dangerous rocks,

> Which, touching but my gentle vessel's side,
> Would scatter all her spices on the stream,
> Enrobe the roaring waters with my silks,
> And, in a word, but even now worth this,
> And now worth nothing? [Act I, sc ii, 39–46]

When Nashe, in *Summer's Last Will and Testament*, brings on a Christmas who is a miser and refuses to keep the feast, the kill-joy figure serves, [. . .] to consolidate feeling in support of holiday. Shakespeare's miser in *The Merchant of Venice* has the same sort of effect in consolidating the gay Christians behind Portia's 'The quality of mercy is not strained.' The comic antagonist as we get him in Nashe's churlish Christmas, uncomplicated by such a local habitation as Shakespeare developed for Shylock, is a transposed image of the pageant's positive spokesmen for holiday. Summer reminds him, when he first comes on, of the role he ought to play, and his miserliness is set off against the generosity proper to festivity:

Summer. Christmas, how chance thou com'st not as the rest,
Accompanied with some music, or some song?
A merry carol would have grac'd thee well;
Thy ancestors have us'd it heretofore.
Christmas. Aye, antiquity was the mother of ignorance: this latter world, that sees but with her spectacles, hath spied a pad in those sports more than they could.
Summer. What, is't against thy conscience for to sing?
Christmas. No, nor to say, by my troth, if I may get a good bargain.
Summer. Why, thou should'st spend, thou should'st not to care to get. Christmas is god of hospitality.
Christmas. So will he never be of good husbandry. I may say to you, there is many an old god that is now grown out of fashion. So is the god of hospitality.
Summer. What reason canst thou give he should be left?
Christmas. No other reason, but that Gluttony is a sin, and too many dunghills are infectious. A man's belly was not made for a powdering beef tub: to feed the poor twelve days, and let them starve all the year after, would but stretch out the guts wider than they should be, and so make famine a bigger den in their bellies than he had before. . . .
Autumn. [Commenting on Christmas]
A fool conceits [imagines] no further than he sees,
He hath no sense of aught but what he feels.
Christmas. Aye, aye, such wise men as you come to beg at such fool's doors as we be.
Autumn. Thou shut'st thy door; how should we beg of thee? . . .
Christmas. Liberalitas liberalitate perit [generosity dies from generosity]; . . . our doors must have bars, our doublets must have buttons. . . . Not a porter that brings a man a letter, but will have his penny. I am afraid to keep past one or two servants, lest, hungry knaves, they should rob me: and those I keep, I

warrant I do not pamper up too lusty; I keep them under with red herring and poor John [salt dried fish, poor fare] all the year long. I have damned up all my chimnies. . . .

Here is the stock business about denying food and locking up which appears also in Shylock's part, along with a suggestion of the harsh ironical humor that bases itself on 'the facts' – 'aye, such wise men as you come to beg at such fool's doors as we be' – and also a moment like several in *The Merchant of Venice* where the fangs of avarice glint naked – 'if I may get a good bargain.' Shylock, moreover, has the same attitude as Nashe's miser about festivity:

> What, are there masques? Hear you me, Jessica.
> Lock up my doors; and when you hear the drum
> And the vile squealing of the wry-neck'd fife,
> Clamber not you up to the casements then,
> Nor thrust your head into the public street
> To gaze on Christian fools with varnish'd faces;
> But stop my house's ears – I mean my casements.
> Let not the sound of shallow fopp'ry enter
> My sober house.
>   (II.v.28–36)

Lorenzo's enterprise in stealing Jessica wins our sympathy partly because it is done in a masque, as a merriment:

> *Bassanio.*   . . . put on
> Your boldest suit of mirth, for we have friends
> That purpose merriment . . .
>   (II.ii.210–212)

> *Lorenzo.* Nay, we will slink away at supper time,
> Disguise us at my lodging, and return
> All in an hour.
>   *Gratiano.* We have not made good preparation.
>   *Salerio.* We have not spoke us yet of torchbearers.
>   *Solanio.* 'Tis vile, unless it may be quaintly ordered. . . .
>   (II.iv.1–6)

The gallants are sophisticated, like Mercutio, about masquerade; but this masque *is* 'quaintly ordered,' because, as Lorenzo confides to Gratiano,

> Fair Jessica shall be my torchbearer.
>   (II.iv.40)

The episode is another place where Shakespeare has it come true that nature can have its way when people are in festive disguise. Shylock's 'tight' opposition, 'fast bind, fast find' (II.v.54) helps to put us on the side of the 'masquing mates,' even though what they do , soberly considered, is a gentlemanly version of raiding the Lombard quarter or sacking bawdy houses on Shrove Tuesday.

MAKING DISTINCTIONS ABOUT THE USE OF RICHES

The Merchant of Venice as a whole is not shaped by festivity in the relatively direct way that we have traced in *Love's Labour's Lost* and *A Midsummer Night's Dream*. The whirling away of daughter and ducats is just one episode in a complex plot which is based on story materials and worked out with much more concern for events, for what happens next, than there is in the two previous comedies. This play was probably written in 1596, at any rate fairly early in the first period of easy mastery which extends from *Romeo and Juliet, A Midsummer Night's Dream*, and *Richard II* through the Henry IV and V plays and *As You Like It to Julius Caesar* and *Twelfth Night*. At the opening of this period, the two comedies modeled directly on festivities represent a new departure, from which Shakespeare returns in *The Merchant of Venice* to write a comedy with a festive emphasis, but one which is rather more 'a kind of history' and less 'a gambold.' The play's large structure is developed from traditions which are properly theatrical; it is not a theatrical adaptation of a social ritual. And yet analogies to social occasions and rituals prove to be useful in understanding the symbolic action. I shall be pursuing such analogies without suggesting, in most cases, that there is a direct influence from the social to the theatrical form. Shakespeare here is working with autonomous mastery, developing a style of comedy that makes a festive form for feeling and awareness out of all the theatrical elements, scene, speech, story, gesture, role which his astonishing art brought into organic combination.

Invocation and abuse, poetry and railing, romance and ridicule – we have seen repeatedly how such complementary gestures go to the festive celebration of life's powers, along with the complementary roles of revellers and kill-joys, wits and butts, insiders and intruders. What is mocked, what kind of intruder disturbs the revel and is baffled, depends on what particular sort of beneficence is being celebrated. *The Merchant of Venice*, as its title indicates, exhibits the beneficence of civilized wealth, the something-for-nothing which wealth gives to those who use it graciously to live together in a humanly knit group. It also deals, in the role of Shylock, with anxieties about money, and its power to set men at odds. Our econometric age makes us think of wealth chiefly as a practical matter, an abstract concern of work, not a tangible joy for festivity. But for the new commercial civilizations of the Renaissance, wealth glowed in luminous metal, shone in silks, perfumed the air in spices. Robert Wilson, already in the late eighties [1580s], wrote a pageant play in the manner of the moralities, *Three Lords and Three Ladies of London*, in which instead of Virtues, London's Pomp and London's Wealth walked gorgeously and smugly about the stage. Despite the terrible sufferings some sections of society were experiencing, the 1590s were a period when London was becoming conscious of itself as wealthy and cultivated, so that it could consider great commercial Venice as a prototype. And yet there were at the same time traditional suspicions of the profit motive and newly urgent anxieties about the power of money to disrupt human relations. Robert Wilson also wrote, early in the eighties, a play called *The Three Ladies of London*, where instead of London's Wealth and Pomp we have Lady Lucar [lucre] and the attitude towards her which her name implies. It was in expressing and so coping with these anxieties about money that Shakespeare developed in Shylock a comic antagonist far more important than any such figure had been in his earlier comedies. His play is still centered in the celebrants rather than the intruder, but Shylock's part is so fascinating that already in 1598 the comedy was entered in the stationer's register as 'a book of the Merchant of Venice, or otherwise called the Jew of Venice.' Shylock's name has become a byword because of the superb way that he embodies the evil side of the power of money, its ridiculous and pernicious consequences in anxiety and destructiveness. In creating him and setting him over against Antonio, Bassanio, Portia, and the rest, Shakespeare was making distinctions about the use of riches, not statically, of course, but dynamically, as distinctions are made when a social group sorts people out, or when an organized social ritual does so. Shylock is the opposite of what the Venetians are; but at the same time he is an embodied irony, troublingly like them. So his role is like that of the scapegoat in many of the primitive rituals which Frazer [see *The Golden Bough*] has made familiar, a figure in whom the evils potential in a social organization are embodied, recognized and enjoyed during a period of licence, and then in due course abused, ridiculed, and expelled.

The large role of the antagonist in *The Merchant of Venice* complicates the movement through release to clarification: instead of the single outgoing of *A Midsummer Night's Dream*, there are two phases. Initially there is a rapid, festive movement by which gay youth gets something for nothing, Lorenzo going masquing to win a Jessica gilded with ducats, and Bassanio sailing off like Jason to win the golden fleece in Belmont. But all this is done against a background of anxiety. We soon forget all about Egeus' threat in *A Midsummer Night's Dream*, but we are kept aware of Shylock's malice by a series of interposed scenes. Will Summer said wryly about the Harvest merrymakers in *Summer's Last Will and Testament*, 'As lusty as they are, they run on the score with George's wife for their posset.' We are made conscious that running on the score with Shylock is a very dangerous business, and no sooner is the joyous triumph accomplished at Belmont than Shylock's malice is set loose. It is only after the threat he poses has been met that the redemption of the prodigal can be completed by a return to Belmont.

The key question in evaluating the play is how this threat is met, whether the baffling of Shylock is meaningful or simply melodramatic. Certainly the plot, considered in outline, seems merely a prodigal's dream coming true: to have a rich friend who will set you up with one more loan so that you can marry a woman both beautiful and rich, girlishly yielding and masterful; and on top of that to get rid of the obligation of the loan because the old money bags from whom your friend got the money is proved to be so villainous that he does not deserve to be paid back! If one adds humanitarian and democratic indignation at anti-semitism, it is hard to see, from a distance, what there can be to say for the play: Shylock seems to be made a scapegoat in the crudest, most dishonest way. One can apologize for the plot [. . .] by observing that it is based on a fairy-story sort of tale, and that Shakespeare's method was not to change implausible story material, but to invent characters and motives which would make it acceptable and credible, moment by moment, on the stage. But it is inadequate to praise the play for delightful and poetic incoherence. Nor does it seem adequate to say, [. . .] that things just do go this way in comedy, where old rich men are always baffled by young and handsome lovers, lenders by borrowers. [. . .] but the question is whether Shakespeare has done something more than merely appeal to the feelings any crowd has in a theater in favor of prodigal young lovers and against old misers. As I see it, he has expressed important things about the relations of love and hate to wealth. When he kept to old tales, he not only made plausible protagonists for them, but also, at any rate when his luck held, he brought up into a social focus deep symbolic meanings. Shylock is an ogre, [. . .] but he is the ogre of money power. The old tale of the pound of flesh involved taking literally the proverbial metaphors about money-lenders 'taking it out of the hide' of their victims, eating them up. Shakespeare keeps the unrealistic literal business, knife-sharpening and all; we accept it, because he makes it express real human attitudes:

> If I can catch him once upon the hip,
> I will feed fat the ancient grudge I bear him.[1]
>   (I.iii.47–48)

So too with the fairy-story caskets at Belmont: Shakespeare makes Bassanio's prodigal fortune meaningful as an expression of the triumph of human, social relations over the relations kept track of by accounting. The whole play dramatizes the conflict between the mechanisms of wealth and the masterful, social use of it. The happy ending, which abstractly considered as an event is hard to credit, and the treatment of Shylock, which abstractly considered as justice is hard to justify, *work* as we actually watch or read the play because these events express relief and triumph in the achievement of a distinction.

   To see how this distinction is developed, we need to attend to the tangibles of imaginative design which are neglected in talking about plot. So, in the two first scenes, it is the seemingly incidental, random talk that establishes the gracious, opulent world of the Venetian gentlemen and of the 'lady richly left' at Belmont, and so motivates Bassanio's later success. Wealth in this world is something profoundly social, and it is relished without a trace of shame when Salerio and Salanio open the play by telling Antonio how rich he is:

> Your mind is tossing on the ocean;
> There where your argosies with portly sail –
> Like signiors and rich burghers on the flood,
> Or, as it were, the pageants of the sea –
> Do overpeer the petty traffickers,
> That curtsy to them, do them reverence,
> As they fly by them with their woven wings.
>   (I.i.8–14)

[. . .] Elizabethan auditors would have thought not only of the famous Venetian water ceremonies but also of 'colorfully decorated pageant barges' on the Thames or of 'pageant devices of huge ships which were drawn about in street shows.' What is crucial is the ceremonial, social feeling for wealth. Salerio and Salanio do Antonio reverence just as the petty traffickers of the harbor salute his ships, giving way to leave him 'with better company' when Bassanio and Gratiano arrive. He stands at ease, courteous, relaxed, melancholy (but not about his fortunes, which are too large for worry), while around him moves a shifting but close-knit group who 'converse and waste the time together' (III.iv.12), make merry, speak 'an infinite deal of nothing' (I.i.114), propose good times: 'Good signiors, both, when shall we laugh? say, when?' (I.i.66). When Bassanio is finally alone with the royal merchant, he opens his mind with

> To you, Antonio,
> I owe the most, in money and in love.
> (I.i.130–131)

[. . .] [T]hese lines summarize the gentleman's world where 'there is no incompatibility between money and love.' So too, one can add, in this community there is no conflict between enjoying Portia's beauty and her wealth: ' her sunny locks / Hang on her temples like a golden fleece.' When, a moment later, we see Portia mocking her suitors, the world suggested is, again, one where standards are urbanely and humanly social: the sad disposition of the county Palatine is rebuked because (unlike Antonio's) it is 'unmannerly.' Yet already in the first scene, though Shylock is not in question yet, the anxiety that dogs wealth is suggested. In the lines which I have taken as an epigraph for this chapter, Salerio's mind moves from attending church – from safety, comfort and solidarity – through the playful association of the 'holy edifice of stone' with 'dangerous rocks,' to the thought that the sociable luxuries of wealth are vulnerable to impersonal forces:

> rocks,
> Which, touching but my gentle vessel's side,
> Would scatter all her spices on the stream,
> Enrobe the roaring waters with my silks . . .
> (I.i.31–34)

The destruction of what is cherished, of the civic and personal, by ruthless impersonal forces is sensuously immediate in the wild waste of shining silk on turbulent water, one of the magic, summary lines of the play. Earlier there is a tender, solicitous suggestion that the vessel is the more vulnerable because it is 'gentle' – as later Antonio is gentle and vulnerable when his ships encounter 'the dreadful touch / Of merchant-marring rocks' (III.ii.270–271) and his side is menaced by a 'stony adversary' (IV.i.4).

When Shylock comes on in the third scene, the easy, confident flow of colorful talk and people is checked by a solitary figure and an unyielding speech:

Shylock. Three thousand ducats – well.
Bassanio. Ay, sir, for three months.
Shylock. For three months – well.
Bassanio. For the which, as I told you, Antonio shall be bound.
Shylock. Antonio shall become bound – well.

Bassanio. May you stead me? Will you pleasure me? Shall I know your answer?

Shylock. Three thousand ducats for three months, and Antonio bound.

(I.iii.1–10)

We can construe Shylock's hesitation as playing for time while he forms his plan. But more fundamentally, his deliberation expresses the impersonal logic, the mechanism, involved in the control of money. Those *well*'s are wonderful in the way they bring bland Bassanio up short. Bassanio assumes that social gestures can brush aside such consideration:

Shylock. Antonio is a good man.
Bassanio. Have you heard any imputation to the contrary?
Shylock. Ho, no, no, no, no! My meaning in saying he is a good man, is to have you understand me that he is sufficient.

(I.iii.12–17)

The laugh is on Bassanio as Shylock drives his hard financial meaning of 'good man' right through the center of Bassanio's softer social meaning. The Jew goes on to calculate and count. He connects the hard facts of money with the rocky sea hazards of which we have so far been only picturesquely aware: 'ships are but boards'; and he betrays his own unwillingness to take the risks proper to commerce: 'and other ventures he hath, squand'red abroad.'

. . . I think I may take his bond.

Bassanio. Be assur'd you may.
Shylock. I will be assur'd I may; and, that I may be assured, I will bethink me.

(I.iii.28–31)

The Jew in this encounter expresses just the things about money which are likely to be forgotten by those who have it, or presume they have it, as part of a social station. He stands for what we mean when we say that 'money is money.' So Shylock makes an ironic comment – and [it] *is* a comment, by virtue of his whole tone and bearing – on the folly in Bassanio which leads him to confuse those two meanings of 'good man,' to ask Shylock to dine, to use in this business context such social phrases as 'Will you *pleasure* me?' When Antonio joins them, Shylock (after a soliloquy in which his plain hatred has glittered) becomes a pretender to fellowship, with an equivocating mask:

Shylock.   This is kind I offer.
Bassanio. This were kindness.
Shylock.   This kindness will I show.

(I.iii. 143–144)

We are of course in no doubt as to how to take the word 'kindness' when Shylock proposes 'in a merry sport' that the penalty be a pound of Antonio's flesh.

In the next two acts, Shylock and the accounting mechanism which he embodies are crudely baffled in Venice and rhapsodically transcended in Belmont. The solidarity of the Venetians includes the clown, in whose part

Shakespeare can use conventional blacks and whites about Jews and misers without asking us to take them too seriously:

> To be ruled by my conscience, I should stay with the Jew my master, who (God bless the mark) is a kind of devil. . . . My master's a very Jew.
>
> (II.ii.24–25)

Even the street urchins can mock Shylock after the passion which 'the dog Jew did utter in the streets':

> Why, all the boys in Venice follow him,
> Crying his stones, his daughter, and his ducats.
> (II.viii.23–24)

TRANSCENDING RECKONING AT BELMONT

The simplest way to describe what happens at Belmont is to say that Bassanio is lucky; but Shakespeare gives a great deal of meaning to his being lucky. His choosing of the casket might be merely theatrical; but the play's handling of the age-old story motif makes it an integral part of the expression of relations between people and possessions. Most of the argument about gold, silver, and lead is certainly factitious, even tedious. It must necessarily be so, because the essence of a lottery is a discontinuity, something hidden so that the chooser cannot get from here to there by reasoning. Nerissa makes explicit a primitive notion of divination:

> Your father was ever virtuous; and holy men at their death have good inspirations. Therefore the lott'ry that he hath devised in these three chests of gold, silver, and lead, whereof who chooses his meaning chooses you, will no doubt never be chosen by any rightly but one who shall rightly love.
>
> (I.ii.30–36)

The elegant phrasing does not ask us to take the proposition very seriously, but Nerissa is pointing in the direction of a mystery. Part of the meaning is that love is not altogether a matter of the will, however willing. Portia recognizes this even when her heart is in her mouth as Bassanio is about to choose:

> Away then! I am lock'd in one of them.
> If you do love me, you will find me out.
> Nerissa and the rest, stand all aloof.
> Let music sound while he doth make his choice . . .
> (III.ii.40–43)

The song, 'Tell me, where is fancy-bred,' serves to emphasize the break, the speechless pause while Bassanio chooses. The notion that it serves as a signal to warn Bassanio off gold and silver is one of those busy-body emendations which eliminate the dramatic in seeking to elaborate it. The dramatic point is precisely that there is no signal: 'Who chooseth me must give and hazard all he hath' (II.vii.16).

If we look across for a moment at Shylock, thinking through opposites as the play's structure invites us to do, his discussion with Antonio about the 'thrift' of Jacob and the taking of interest proves to be relevant to the luck of the caskets. Antonio appeals to the principle that interest is wrong because it involves no risk:

> This was a venture, sir, that Jacob serv'd for;
> A thing not in his power to bring to pass,
> But sway'd and fashion'd by the hand of heaven.
>
> (I.iii.92–94)

One way to get a fortune is to be fortunate: the two words fall together significantly at the conclusion of the opening scene:

> *Bassanio.* O my Antonio, had I but the means
> To hold a rival place with one of them,
> I have a mind presages me such thrift
> That I should questionless be fortunate!
> *Antonio.* Thou know'st that all my fortunes are at sea . . .
>
> (I.i.173–177)

Antonio's loan is venture capital. It fits with this conception that Bassanio, when at Belmont he goes 'to my fortune and the caskets,' turns away from money, from 'gaudy gold, / Hard food for Midas,' and from silver, the 'pale and common drudge / 'Tween man and man' (III.ii.101–104). Money is not used to get money; that is the usurer's way:

> *Antonio.* Or is your gold and silver ewes and rams?
> *Shylock.* I cannot tell; I make it breed as fast.
>
> (I.iii.96–97)

Instead Bassanio's borrowed purse is invested in life – including such lively things as the 'rare new liveries' (II.ii.117) that excite Launcelot, and the 'gifts of rich value' which excite Nerissa to say

> A day in April never came so sweet
> To show how costly summer was at hand
> As this fore-spurrer comes before his lord.
>
> (II.ix.93–95)

With the money, Bassanio invests *himself*, and so risks losing himself – as has to be the case with love. (Antonio's commitment of his body for his friend is in the background.) It is a limitation of the scene where he makes his choice that the risk has to be conveyed largely by the poetry, since the outward circumstances are not hazardous. Portia describes Bassanio as

> young Alcides when he did redeem
> The virgin tribute paid by howling Troy
> To the sea monster. . . . Go, Hercules!
> Live thou, I live.
>
> (III.ii.55-61)

Of course we know that these are lover's feelings. But the moment of choice is expressed in terms that point beyond feelings to emphasize discontinuity; they convey the experience of being lost and giddily finding oneself again in a new situation. The dramatic shift is all the more vividly rendered in the language since gesture here can do little. Portia speaks of an overwhelming ecstasy of love when 'all the other passions fleet to air' (III.ii.108). Bassanio likens himself to an athlete

> Hearing applause and universal shout,
> Giddy in spirit, still gazing in a doubt
> Whether those peals of praise be his or no.
>   (III.ii.143–145)

He describes in a wonderful way the experience of being disrupted by joy:

> Madam, you have bereft me of all words,
> Only my blood speaks to you in my veins;
> And there is such confusion in my powers
> As, after some oration fairly spoke
> By a beloved prince, there doth appear
> Among the buzzing pleased multitude,
> Where every something, being blent together,
> Turns to a wild of nothing, save of joy,
> Express'd and not express'd.
>   (III.ii.175–183)

This poetry is remarkable for the conscious way that it describes being carried beyond expression, using words to tell of being beyond them. The lines in which Portia gives herself and her possessions to Bassanio make explicit, by an elaborate metaphor of accounting, that what is happening sets the accounting principle aside:

> You see me, Lord Bassanio, where I stand,
> Such as I am. Though for myself alone
> I would not be ambitious in my wish
> To wish myself much better, yet for you
> I would be trebled twenty times myself,
> A thousand times more fair, ten thousand times more rich,
> That, only to stand high in your account,
> I might in virtues, beauties, livings, friends,
> Exceed account. But the full sum of me
> Is sum of nothing, which, to term in gross,
> Is an unlesson'd girl, unschool'd, unpractic'd. . . .
>   (III.ii.149–159)

This is extravagant, and extravagantly modest, as fits the moment; but what is telling is the way the lines move from possessions, through the paradox about sums, to the person in the midst of them all, 'where I stand,' who cannot be added up. It is she that Bassanio has won, and with her a way of living for which his humanity, breeding, and manhood can provide a center:

> Happiest of all is that her gentle spirit
> Commits itself to yours to be directed,
> As from her lord, her governor, her king.
> (III.ii.163–165)

The possessions *follow* from this human, social relation.

COMICAL/MENACING MECHANISM IN SHYLOCK

But the accounting mechanism which has been left behind by Bassanio and Portia has gone on working, back at Venice, to put Antonio at Shylock's mercy, and the anxiety it causes has to be mastered before the marriage can be consummated,

> For never shall you lie by Portia's side
> With an unquiet soul.
> (III.ii.305–306)

Historical changes in stock attitudes have made difficulties about Shylock's role as a butt, not so much in the theater, where it works perfectly if producers only let it, but in criticism, where winds of doctrine blow sentiments and abstractions about. The Elizabethans almost never saw Jews except on the stage, where Marlowe's Barabas was familiar. They did see *one*, on the scaffold, when Elizabeth's unfortunate physician suffered for trumped-up charges of a poisoning plot. The popular attitude was that to take interest for money was to be a loan shark – though limited interest was in fact allowed by law. An aristocrat who like Lord Bassanio ran out of money commanded sympathy no longer felt in a middle-class world. Most important of all, suffering was not an absolute evil in an era when men sometimes embraced it deliberately, accepted it as inevitable, and could watch it with equanimity. Humanitarianism has made it necessary for us to be much more thoroughly insulated from the human reality of people if we are to laugh at their discomfiture or relish their suffering. During the romantic period, and sometimes more recently, the play was presented as a tragi-comedy, and actors vied with one another in making Shylock a figure of pathos. I remember a very moving scene, a stock feature of romantic productions, in which George Arliss came home after Bassanio's party, lonely and tired and old, to knock in vain at the door of the house left empty by Jessica. How completely unhistorical the romantic treatment was. [. . .]

To insert a humanitarian scene about Shylock's pathetic homecoming prevents the development of the scornful amusement with which Shakespeare's text presents the miser's reaction in Solanio's narrative:

> I never heard a passion so confus'd,
> So strange, outrageous, and so variable,
> As the dog Jew did utter in the streets.
> 'My daughter! O my ducats! O my daughter!
> Fled with a Christian! O my Christian ducats! . . .'
> (II.viii.12–16)

Marlowe had done such a moment already with Barabas hugging in turn his money bags and his daughter – whom later the Jew of Malta poisons with a pot of porridge, as the Jew of Venice later wishes that Jessica 'were hears'd at my foot, and the ducats in her coffin' (III.i.93–94). But the humanitarian way of playing the part develops suggestions that are *also* in Shakespeare's text:

> I am bid forth to supper, Jessica.
> There are my keys. But wherefore should I go?
> I am not bid for love; they flatter me.
> But yet I'll go in hate, to feed upon
> The prodigal Christian.
>
> (II.v.11–15)

Shakespeare's marvelous creative sympathy takes the stock role of Jewish usurer and villain and conveys how it would feel to be a man living inside it. But this does not mean that he shrinks from confronting the evil and the absurdity that go with the role; for the Elizabethan age, to understand did not necessarily mean to forgive. Shylock can be a thorough villain and yet be allowed to express what sort of treatment has made him what he is:

> You call me misbeliever, cutthroat dog,
> And spet upon my Jewish gaberdine,
> And all for use of that which is mine own.
> (I.iii.112–114)

We can understand his degradation and even blame the Antonios of Venice for it; yet it remains degradation:

> Thou call'dst me dog before thou hadst a cause;
> But, since I am a dog, beware my fangs.
> (III.iii.6–7)

Shylock repeatedly states, as he does here, that he is only finishing what the Venetians started. He can be a drastic ironist, because he carries to extremes what is present, whether acknowledged or not, in their silken world. He insists that money is money – and they cannot do without money either. So too with the rights of property. The power to give freely, which absolute property confers and Antonio and Portia so splendidly exhibit, is also a power to refuse, as Shylock so logically refuses:

> You have among you many a puchas'd slave,
> Which, like your asses and your dogs and mules,
> You use in abject and in slavish parts,
> Because you bought them. Shall I say to you,
> 'Let them be free, marry them to you heirs! . . .'
>   You will answer,
> 'The slaves are ours.' So do I answer you.
> The pound of flesh which I demand of him
> Is dearly bought, 'tis mine, and I will have it.
> (IV.i.90–100)

At this point in the trial scene, Shylock seems a juggernaut that nothing can stop, armed as he is against a pillar of society by the principles of society itself: 'If you deny me, fie upon your law! . . . I stand for judgement. Answer. Shall I have it.' Nobody does answer him here, directly; instead there is an interruption for Portia's entrance. To answer him is the function of the whole dramatic action, which is making a distinction that could not be made in direct, logical argument.

Let us follow this dramatic action from its comic side. Shylock is comic, so far as he is so, because he exhibits what should be human, degraded into mechanism. The reduction of life to mechanism goes with the miser's wary calculation, with the locking up, with the preoccupation with 'that which is mine own.' Antonio tells Bassanio that

> My purse, my person, my extremest means
> Lie all unlock'd to your occasions.
>
> (I.i.138–139)

How open! Antonio has to live inside some sort of rich man's melancholy, but at least he communicates with the world through outgoing Bassanio (and, one can add, through the commerce which takes his fortunes out to sea). Shylock, by contrast, who breeds barren metal, wants to keep 'the vile squeeling of the wryneck'd fife' out of his house, and speaks later, in a curiously revealing, seemingly random illustration, of men who 'when the bagpipe sings i'th'nose, / Cannot contain their urine' (V.i.49–50). Not only is he closed up tight inside himself, but after the first two scenes, we are scarcely allowed by his lines to feel with him. And we never encounter him alone; he regularly comes on to join a group whose talk has established an outside point of view towards him. This perspective on him does not exclude a potential pathos. There is always potential pathos, behind, when drama makes fun of isolating, anti-social qualities. Indeed, the process of *making fun of* a person often works by exhibiting pretensions to humanity so as to show that they are inhuman, mechanical, not validly appropriate for sympathy. With a comic villain such as Shylock, the effect is mixed in various degrees between our responding to the mechanism as menacing and laughing at it as ridiculous.

So in the great scene in which Solanio and Salerio taunt Shylock, the potentiality of pathos produces effects which vary between comedy and menace:

> *Shylock.* You knew, none so well, none so well as you, of my daughter's flight.
> *Salerio.* That's certain. I, for my part, knew the tailor that made the wings she flew withal.
>
> (III.i.27–30)

Shylock's characteristic repetitions, and the way he has of moving ahead through similar, short phrases, as though even with language he was going to use only what was his own, can give an effect of concentration and power, or again, an impression of a comically limited, isolated figure. In the great speech of self-justification to which he is goaded by the two bland little gentlemen, the iteration conveys the energy of anguish:

– and what's his reason? I am a Jew. Hath not a Jew eyes? Hath not a Jew hands, organs, dimensions, senses, affections, passions? fed with the same food, hurt with the same weapons, subject to the same diseases, healed by the same means, warmed and cooled by the same winter and summer as a Christian is? If you prick us, do we not bleed? If you tickle us, do we not laugh? If you poison us, do we not die? And if you wrong us, shall we not revenge? If we are like you in the rest, we will resemble you in that.

(III.i.60–71)

Certainly no actor would deliver this speech without an effort at pathos; but it is a pathos which, as the speech moves, converts to menace. And the pathos is qualified, limited, in a way which is badly falsified by humanitarian renderings that open all the stops at 'Hath not a Jew hands, etc. . . .' For Shylock thinks to claim only a *part* of humanness, the lower part, physical and passional. The similar self-pitying enumeration which Richard II makes differs significantly in going from 'live with bread like you' to social responses and needs, 'Taste grief, / Need friends' (*R.II* III.ii.175–176). The passions in Shylock's speech are conceived as reflexes; the parallel clauses draw them all towards the level of 'tickle . . . laugh.' The same assumption, that the passions and social responses are mechanisms on a par with a nervous tic, appears in the court scene when Shylock defends his right to follow his 'humor' in taking Antonio's flesh:

> As there is no firm reason to be rend'red
> Why he cannot abide a gaping pig,
> Why he a harmless necessary cat,
> Why he a woollen bagpipe – but of force
> Must yield to such inevitable shame
> As to offend himself, being offended;
> So can I give no reason, nor I will not,
> More than a lodg'd hate and a certain loathing
> I bear unto Antonio . . .

> (IV.i.52–61)

The most succinct expression of this assumption about man is Shylock's response to Bassanio's incredulous question:

> *Bassanio.* Do all men kill the things they do not love?
> *Shylock.* Hates any man the thing he would not kill?

> (IV.i.66–67)

There is no room in this view for mercy to come in between 'wrong us' and 'shall we not revenge?' As Shylock insists, there is Christian example for him: the irony is strong. But the mechanism of stimulus and response is only a part of the truth. The reductive tendency of Shylock's metaphors, savagely humorous in Iago's fashion, goes with this speaking only the lower part of the truth. He is not cynical in Iago's aggressive way, because as an alien he simply doesn't participate in many of the social ideals which Iago is concerned to discredit in self-justification. But the two villains have the same frightening, ironical power from moral simplification.

Shylock becomes a clear-cut butt at the moments when he is himself caught in compulsive, reflexive responses, when instead of controlling [the] mechanism he is controlled by it: 'O my daughter! O my ducats!' At the end of the scene of taunting, his menace and his pathos become ridiculous when he dances like a jumping jack in alternate joy and sorrow as Tubal pulls the strings:

> *Tubal.* Yes, other men have ill luck too. Antonio, as I heard in Genoa –
> *Shylock.* What, what, what? Ill luck, ill luck?
> *Tubal.* Hath an argosy cast away coming from Tripolis.
> *Shylock.* I thank God, I thank God! – Is it true? is it true?
> *Tubal.* I spoke with some of the sailors that escaped the wrack.
> *Shylock.* I thank thee, good Tubal. Good news, good news! Ha, ha! Where? in Genoa?
> *Tubal.* Your daughter spent in Genoa, as I heard, one night fourscore ducats.
> *Shylock.* Thou stick'st a dagger in me. I shall never see my gold again. Fourscore ducats at a sitting! Fourscore ducats!
> *Tubal.* There came divers of Antonio's creditors in my company to Venice that swear he cannot choose but break.
> *Shylock.* I am very glad of it. I'll plague him; I'll torture him. I am glad of it.
> *Tubal.* One of them show'd me a ring that he had of your daughter for a monkey.
> *Shylock.* Out upon her! Thou torturest me, Tubal. It was my turquoise; I had it of Leah when I was a bachelor. I would not have given it for a wilderness of monkeys.
> *Tubal.* But Antonio is certainly undone.
> *Shylock.* Nay, that's true, that's very true.

(III.i.102–130)

This is a scene in the dry manner of Marlowe, Jonson, or Molière, a type of comedy not very common in Shakespeare: its abrupt alternations in response convey the effect Bergson describes so well in Le Rire,[2] where the comic butt is a puppet in whom motives have become mechanisms that usurp life's self-determining prerogative. Some critics have left the rhythm of the scene behind to dwell on the pathos of the ring he had from Leah when he was a bachelor. It is like Shakespeare once to show Shylock putting a gentle sentimental value on something, to match the savage sentimental value he puts on revenge. There *is* pathos; but it is being fed into the comic mill and makes the laughter all the more hilarious.

THE COMMUNITY SETTING ASIDE ITS MACHINERY

In the trial scene, the turning point is appropriately the moment when Shylock gets caught in the mechanism he relies on so ruthlessly. He narrows everything down to his roll of parchment and his knife: 'Till thou canst rail the seal from off my bond . . .' (IV.i.139). But two can play at this game:

> as thou urgest justice, be assur'd
> Thou shalt have justice more than thou desir'st.
> (IV.i.315–316)

Shylock's bafflement is comic, as well as dramatic, in the degree that we now see through the threat that he has presented, recognizing it to have been, in a degree, unreal. For it is unreal to depend so heavily on legal form, on fixed verbal definition, on the mere machinery by which human relations are controlled. Once Portia's legalism has broken through his legalism, he can only go on the way he started, weakly asking 'Is that the law?' while Gratiano's jeers underscore the comic symmetry:

> A Daniel still say I, a second Daniel!
> I thank thee, Jew, for teaching me that word.
> (IV.i.340–341)

The turning of the tables is not, of course, simply comic, except for the bold, wild and 'skipping spirit' of Gratiano. The trial scene is a species of drama that uses comic movement in slow motion, with an investment of feeling such that the resolution is in elation and relief colored by amusement, rather than in the evacuation of laughter. Malvolio, a less threatening kill-joy intruder, is simply laughed out of court, but Shylock must be ruled out, with jeering only on the side lines. The threat Shylock offers is, after all, drastic, for legal instruments, contract, property are fundamental. Comic dramatists often choose to set them hilariously at naught; but Shakespeare is, as usual, scrupulously responsible to the principles of social order (however factitious his 'law' may be literally). So he produced a scene which exhibits the limitations of legalism. It works by a dialectic that carries to a more general level what might be comic reduction to absurdity. To be tolerant, because we are all fools; to forgive, because we are all guilty – the two gestures of the spirit are allied, as Erasmus noted in praising the sublime folly of following Christ. Shylock says before the trial 'I'll not be made a soft and dull-ey'd fool' by 'Christian intercessors' (III.iii.14–15). Now when he is asked how he can hope for mercy if he renders none, he answers: 'What judgement shall I dread, doing no wrong?' As the man who will not acknowledge his own share of folly ends by being more foolish than anyone else, so Shylock, who will not acknowledge a share of guilt, ends by being more guilty – and more foolish, to judge by results. An argument between Old Testament legalism and New Testament reliance on grace develops as the scene goes forward. (Shylock's references to Daniel in this scene, and his constant use of Old Testament names and allusions, contribute to the contrast.) Portia does not deny the bond – nor the law behind it; instead she makes such a plea as St. Paul made to his compatriots:

> Therefore, Jew,
> Though justice be thy plea, consider this –
> That, in the course of justice, none of us

> Should see salvation. We do pray for mercy,
> And that same prayer doth teach us all to render
> The deeds of mercy.
>
> (IV.i.97–102)

Mercy becomes the word that gathers up everything we have seen the Venetians enjoying in their reliance on community. What is on one side an issue of
principles is on the other a matter of social solidarity: Shylock is not one of the
'we' Portia refers to, the Christians who say in the Lord's Prayer 'Forgive us our
debts as we forgive our debtors.' All through the play the word Christian has
been repeated, primarily in statements that enforce the fact that the Jew is outside
the easy bonds of community. Portia's plea for mercy is a sublime version of what
in less intense circumstances, among friends of a single communion, can be conveyed with a shrug or a wink:

> Dost thou hear, Hal? Thou knowest in the state of innocency Adam fell; and
> what should poor Jack Falstaff do in the days of villany?
>
> (*1 H.IV* III.iii.185–188)

Falstaff, asking for an amnesty to get started again, relies on his festive solidarity
with Hal. Comedy, in one way or another, is always asking for amnesty, after
showing the moral machinery of life getting in the way of life. The machinery
as such need not be dismissed – Portia is very emphatic about not doing that.
But social solidarity, resting on the buoyant force of a collective life that transcends particular mistakes, can set the machinery aside. Shylock, closed off as he
is, clutching his bond and his knife, cannot trust this force, and so acts only on
compulsion:

> *Portia.*   Do you confess the bond?
> *Antonio.* I do.
> *Portia.*   Then must the Jew be merciful.
> *Shylock.* On what compulsion must I? Tell me that.
> *Portia.* The quality of mercy is not strain'd;
> It droppeth as the gentle rain from heaven
> Upon the place beneath. It is twice blest –
> It blesseth him that gives, and him that takes.
>
> (IV.i.181–187)

It has been in giving and taking, beyond the compulsion of accounts, that Portia,
Bassanio, Antonio have enjoyed the something-for-nothing that Portia here summarizes in speaking of the gentle rain from heaven.

SHARING IN THE GRACE OF LIFE

The troth-plight rings which Bassanio and Gratiano have given away are all that
remain of plot to keep the play moving after the trial. It is a slight business, but
it gives the women a teasing way to relish the fact that they have played the parts
of men as they give up the liberty of that disguise to become wives. And the play's

general subject is continued, for in getting over the difficulty, the group provides one final demonstration that human relationships are stronger than their outward signs. Once more, Bassanio expresses a harassed perplexity about obligations in conflict; and Portia gayly pretends to be almost a Shylock about this lover's bond, carrying the logic of the machinery to absurd lengths before showing, by the new gift of the ring, love's power to set debts aside and begin over again.

No other comedy, until the late romances, ends with so full an expression of harmony as that which we get in the opening of the final scene of *The Merchant of Venice*. And no other final scene is so completely without irony about the joys it celebrates. The ironies have been dealt with beforehand in baffling Shylock; in the moment of relief after expelling an antagonist, we do not need to look at the limitations of what we have been defending. So in *Summer's Last Will and Testament*, when Summer is confronted by a miserly Christmas, he comes out wholeheartedly for festivity, whereas elsewhere, confronting spokesmen for festivity, he is always wry about it. He dismisses Christmas with

> Christmas, I tell thee plain, thou art a snudge [miser],
> And wer't not that we love thy father well,
> Thou shouldst have felt what 'longs to Avarice.
> It is the honor of nobility
> To keep high days and solemn festivals –
> Then to set their magnificence to view,
> To frolic open with their favorites,
> And use their neighbors with all courtesy,
> When thou in hugger-mugger spend'st thy wealth.
> Amend thy manners, breathe thy rusty gold:
> Bounty will win thee love, when thou art old.

The court compels Shylock to breathe his gold and give bounty to Lorenzo. He is plainly told that he is a snudge – and we are off to noble magnificence and frolic at Belmont. No high day is involved, though Shakespeare might easily have staged the solemn festival due after Portia's wedding. Instead Lorenzo and Jessica feel the harmony of the universe and its hospitality to life in a quiet moment of idle talk and casual enjoyment of music. There is an opening out to experience in their exquisite outdoor poetry which corresponds to the openness stressed by Nashe in contrast to miserly hugger-mugger.

> The moon shines bright. In such a night as this,
> When the sweet wind did gently kiss the trees
> And they did make no noise – in such a night
> Troilus methinks mounted the Troyan walls
> And sigh'd his soul towards the Grecian tents,
> Where Cressid lay that night.
>
> (V.i.1–6)

The openness to experience, the images of reaching out towards it, or of welcoming it, letting music 'creep in our ears,' go with the perception of a gracious universe such as Portia's mercy speech invoked:

> How sweet the moonlight sleeps upon this bank!
> Here will we sit and let the sounds of music
> Creep in our ears. Soft stillness and the night
> Become the touches of sweet harmony.
> Sit, Jessica. Look how the floor of heaven
> Is thick inlaid with patens of bright gold.
> There's not the smallest orb which thou behold'st
> But in his motion like an angel sings . . .
>
> (V.i.54–61)

Lorenzo is showing Jessica the graciousness of the Christian world into which he has brought her; and it is as richly golden as it is musical! Jessica is already at ease in it, to the point of being able to recall the pains of famous lovers with equanimity, rally her lover on his vows and turn the whole thing off with 'I would out-night you did no body come, / But hark, I hear the footing of a man.' That everybody is so perfectly easy is part of the openness:

> *Lorenzo.* Who comes so fast in silence of the night.
> *Messenger.* A friend.
> *Lorenzo.* A friend? What friend? Your name, I pray you, friend? . . .
> Sweet soul, let's in, and there expect their coming.
> And yet no matter. Why should we go in?
> . . . bring your music forth into the air.
>
> (V.i.25–27, 51–54)

As the actual music plays, there is talk about its Orphic power, and we look back a moment toward Shylock

> The man that hath no music in himself
> Nor is not mov'd with concord of sweet sounds,
> Is fit for treasons, stratagems, and spoils . . .
>
> (V.i.82–84)

A certain contemplative distance is maintained by talking *about* perception, *about* harmony and its conditions, even while enjoying it. Portia comes on exclaiming how far the candle throws its beams, how much sweeter the music sounds than by day. There are conditions, times and seasons, to be observed; but the cosmo-logical music, which cannot be heard directly at all, is behind the buoyant decorum of the people:

> How many things by season season'd are
> To their right praise and true perfection!
> Peace ho! The moon sleeps with Endymion
> And would not be awak'd
>
> (V.i.107–110)

At the end of the play, there is Portia's news of Antonio's three argosies richly come to harbor, and the special deed of gift for Lorenzo – 'manna in the way / Of starved people.' Such particular happy events are not sentimental because

Shakespeare has floated them on an expression of a tendency in society and nature which supports life and expels what would destroy it.

I must add, after all this praise for the way the play makes its distinction about the use of wealth, that *on reflection*, not when viewing or reading the play, but when thinking about it, I find the distinction, as others have, somewhat too easy. While I read or watch, all is well, for the attitudes of Shylock are appallingly inhuman, and Shakespeare makes me feel constantly how the Shylock attitude rests on a lack of faith in community and grace. But when one thinks about the Portia-Bassanio group, not in opposition to Shylock but alone (as Shakespeare does not show them), one can be troubled by their being so very very far above money:

> What, no more?
> Pay him six thousand, and deface the bond.
> Double six thousand and then treble that . . .
> (III.ii.298–300)

It would be interesting to see Portia say no, for once, instead of always yes: after all, Nashe's miser has a point, '*Liberalitas liberalitate perit.*' One can feel a difficulty too with Antonio's bland rhetorical question:

> when did friendship take
> A breed of barren metal of his friend?
> (I.iii.134–135)

Elizabethan attitudes about the taking of interest were unrealistic: while Sir Thomas Gresham built up Elizabeth's credit in the money market of Antwerp, and the government regulated interest rates, popular sentiment continued on the level of thinking Antonio's remark reflects. Shakespeare's ideal figures and sentiments are open here to ironies which he does not explore. The clown's role just touches them when he pretends to grumble

> We were Christians enow before, e'en as many as could well
> live by one another. This making of Christians will raise the
> price of hogs.
> (III.v.23–26)

[. . .] [W]e shall see, in *As You Like It*, a more complete confronting of ironies, which leaves, I feel, a cleaner after-taste. Shakespeare could no doubt have gone beyond the naïve economic morality of Elizabethan popular culture, had he had an artistic need. But he did not, because in the antithetical sort of comic form he was using in this play, the ironical function was fulfilled by the heavy contrasts embodied in Shylock.

About Shylock, too, there is a difficulty which grows on reflection, a difficulty which may be felt too in reading or performance. His part fits perfectly into the design of the play, and yet he is so alive that he raises an interest beyond its design. I do not think his humanity spoils the design [. . .] for audiences who assumed that to be human was to be ipso-facto good. But it is true that in the small compass of Shylock's three hundred and sixty-odd lines, Shakespeare provided material that asks for a whole additional play to work itself out. [. . .]

The figure of Shylock is like some secondary figure in a Rembrandt painting, so charged with implied life that one can forget his surroundings. To look sometimes with absorption at the suffering, raging Jew alone is irresistible. But the more one is aware of what the play's whole design is expressing through Shylock, of the comedy's high seriousness in its concern for the grace of community, the less one wants to lose the play Shakespeare wrote for the sake of one he merely suggested.

NOTES

1   It is striking that, along with the imagery of the money-lender feeding on his victims, there is the complementary prohibition Shylock mentions against eating with Christians; Shakespeare brings alive a primitive anxiety about feasting *with* people who might feast *on* you. And when Shylock violates his own taboo ('But yet I'll go in hate, to feed upon / The prodigal Christian.' II.v.14–15) it is he who is caught upon the hip!

2   Henri Bergson, *Laughter: An Essay on the Meaning of the Comic*, 1911.

17   Ruth Nevo **'Jessica's monkey; or The Goodwins'**

Source: from *Comic Transformations in Shakespeare*, Ruth Nevo, Methuen and Co. Ltd, London and New York, 1980, chapter VII, pp. 128–40.

Most modern discussions of Shylock have understandably turned upon or implied the question whether Shakespeare was anti-Semitic, whether and to what degree he shared the anti-Semitic stereotypes of folk-lore and popular culture.

It would seem to me as hard to prove from the text of *The Merchant* that Shakespeare was anti-Semitic as it would be to prove him a republican on the grounds that his kings are not always all they should be. It would seem to me possible on the grounds of what Coleridge called the 'omni-humanity' of his imagination, as well as the power of his intellect, to dismiss the case out of court. But we are not therefore to suppose him incapable of creating an anti-Semite. The 'rush from word to world', from character to author, obscures a vital distinction. Shakespeare may not have been an anti-Semite, but Antonio certainly is – undisputedly, and by self-confession. And one will go far to find in any literature a representation of the dynamic tension of the relation between anti-Semite and Jew more profound and comprehensive than this.

The Jew, says Sartre

finds arraigned against him the irrational powers of tradition, of race, of national destiny, of instinct . . . values accessible only to intuition . . . the Jew demands proof for everything that his adversary advances because thus he proves himself. He distrusts intuition because it is not open to discussion and because, in consequence, it ends by separating men. If he reasons and disputes with his adversary, it is to establish the unity of intelligence.[1]

The parable has been, in a sense, Shylock's bid 'to establish the unity of intelligence'. In a moment of expansion he makes a bid for friendship, for social recognition at least, for confirmation of himself as a person through an appeal to a shared scripture. There is a certain intimacy in his view of the biblical patriarchs and he is inviting Antonio's participation in it. When this is repudiated he is deeply offended, and thrown back as ever into his own defensive-aggressive postures. Hence his famous outburst:

> Signior Antonio, many a time and oft
> In the Rialto you have rated me
> About my moneys and my usances.
>   (I. iii. 106–9)

'The merry bond', half ingratiating, half menacing is preposterous, absurd, improbable in the highest degree. But there is bitter enmity between the Merchant and the Usurer and Antonio is too ready to trust his luck. The bond encapsulates the antagonism between these two, the alienation which characterizes their relations. And there is a displaced eroticism in

> an equal pound
> Of your fair flesh, to be cut off and taken
> In what part of your body pleaseth me.
>   (I. iii. 149–51)

The Jew, if he cannot be at one in love with these others, will devour them. Thus he himself feeds fat not only the ancient grudge he bears them, but also that figment of their own ancient blood-libel paranoia that he is. They reciprocally reinforce each other's antagonism in a self-perpetuating spiral. Where the one sees a fawning Jew, the other sees a fawning publican [tax gatherer], and each is determined his view shall prevail. To this ancient contention, however, Shakespeare adds the vividly realized, specific motivation of betrayal, bereavement and revenge, and thereby definitively forecloses comic possibilities by actualizing the very human harm, the human suffering, which comedy exists to circumvent.

Shylock's response already quoted to Jessica's flight, – to Jessica's monkey – in Act III, scene i, is significant and expressive in the highest degree. The fury, the outrage, the pain, the incomprehension are rendered with that command of nuance, of rhythm, of immediacy which marks a totally imagined individual utterance. It is truly 'language in action', [. . .] and it completes and fills out one of the scenes on which we ground our perception of the dynamic realism of *The Merchant of Venice*. This is important. For if Shylock is seen as craftily, and stereotypically, planning the death of Antonio from the start it will be easier to assimilate the play to its fairytale pole. But this is precluded by the realism of the portrayal. Consider the whole scene which follows Jessica's flight; the whole painful exchange with the Venetians. For instance, 'My own flesh and blood to rebel', mutters Shylock. 'Out upon it, old carrion, rebels it at these years?' (III. i. 36) is the contribution of the wit Salanio. And Shylock, dogged, obdurate: 'I say, my daughter is my flesh and my blood' (III. i. 37). As they bait him and he snarls back, and as he oscillates between fury and exasperation, lamentation and self-pity, grief and vindictive rejoicing at Antonio's losses, and renewed anguish at his own 'loss upon loss'; and as this tumult of emotion crystallizes upon the dream of revenge and the taste of power – 'Let him look to his bond' – we, who come to this play from the timeless universe of the whole Shakespearean canon, may well hear echoes from the lives and deaths of other fathers and other daughters: 'According to my bond' . . . 'a carbuncle in my blood' . . . 'these pelican daughters'. . . . Be this as it may, it is the father's grief that is presented as engendering the thirst for revenge, the determination to *seek* revenge. [. . .]

> When I was with him I have heard him swear
> To Tubal and to Chus, his countrymen,
> That he would rather have Antonio's flesh
> Than twenty times the value of the sum
> That he did owe him . . .
>
> (III. ii. 284–8)

But, even leaving aside the question of the reliability of Jessica as reporter, these critics surely overlook the optative mode of this reported speech. A desire, wishful thinking, a dream, is different from an action, even from a plan. And it is worth noting in this connection that Launcelot Gobbo's parodic function appears to be mainly directed to underscoring the desertion of Shylock the father.

He first appears, with his conscience and *his* father, immediately after Morocco's arrival in Belmont and immediately before the domestic scene between Shylock and Jessica. His burlesque conflict of conscience anticipates that of both the daughters – the faithful and the faithless; but where he leaves the rich Jew for the poor but noble Bassanio, thus vindicating by implication Portia's intuitive choice of suitor, he also debases in anticipation the abandonment of Shylock by Jessica, not for a poor Bassanio, but for a Lorenzo enriched by stolen goods. Launcelot counts his future blessings with comic gusto, but old Gobbo's affection, and unintentional ironies from Launcelot like 'it is a wise father that knows his own child', together with expressions of disenchantment like Gratiano's on the 'strumpet wind' (II. vi. 19), all draw together as by magnetic attraction to foreground and enhance the father's loss, rather than the daughter's escape. It is the father's point of view which is given dominance, and which is directly expressed in Act III, scene i. Jessica's flight therefore presents itself as betrayal in contrast with the other daughter's good choice. And Launcelot is again choric commentator upon her defection when he announces that her one hope of not being damned is that she may be a bastard and not the Jew's daughter at all. And if that casts an aspersion upon her mother (as Jessica points out) why truly then, Launcelot fears 'she is gone both ways'. For when he shuns Scylla her father, 'he falls into Charybdis her mother' and so she is damned by both (III. v. 15–17).

Moreover, there is the impact of the Jew himself. In the climax of the scene between Shylock and the Christians after Jessica's desertion, when Shylock makes his famous plea for consideration as a member of the human race, it will be noticed that he, as it were dismembers himself to do so:

Hath not a Jew eyes? Hath not a Jew hands, organs, dimensions, senses, affections, passions; fed with the same food, hurt with the same weapons, subject to
the same diseases, heal'd by the same means, warm'd and cool'd by the same
winter and summer, as a Christian is?

(III. i. 59–64)

And as the speech reaches its end it is as if he consolidates his disintegrated, fragmented self upon the will to revenge. In this he will better his instruction, outdo
them even at their own game of hate. If we do not see the weight Shakespeare is
giving the birth and growth of this obsession in Shylock we will lose a large part
of the dramatic agon [contrast, struggle] of the trial scene; just as we will if we
do not give due weight to a further inference we are invited to make: that
Antonio's melancholy is triggered and exacerbated by Bassanio's determination
to woo Portia, and to win thereby both a wealthy wife and clearance of his debt
to Antonio.

   Three wills are in asymmetrical conflict in that great scene. Shylock's, Antonio's,
and Portia's, and the amazingly dramatic thing is that the wills of Shylock
and Antonio are not opposed in the matter of the bond but secretly consonant.
This perception has been carefully prepared for, particularly by the parallel
reports from Salanio and Solarino of the Jew's discovery of Jessica's flight and of
Antonio's parting from Bassanio. From the one we have the burlesquing of
Shylock's outcry:

> My daughter! O my ducats! O my daughter!
> Fled with a Christian! O my Christian ducats!
>
> (II. viii. 15–16)

What we have at first hand, be it noted, in Act III, scene i, is subtly but significantly different.

> The curse never fell upon our nation till now, I never felt it till now. Two thou-
> sand ducats in that, and other precious, precious jewels. I would my daughter
> were dead at my foot, and the jewels in her ear! Would she were hears'd at my
> foot, and the ducats in her coffin! No news of them? Why, so – and I know not
> what's spent in the search. Why, thou loss upon loss! the thief gone with so
> much, and so much to find the thief, and no satisfaction, no revenge, nor no
> ill luck stirring but what lights a' my shoulders, no sighs but a' my breathing,
> no tears but a' my shedding.
>
> (III. i. 85–96)

This is Lamentations itself, a 'woe is me', a curse, a Jeremiad which consigns both
thief and theft – all that was precious – to the grave in a transport of grief at the
'loss upon loss' that has befallen him.

   On the other hand, there is the account of Antonio's farewell, which must
surely strike us as excessively sentimental. It is before there is any real danger,
remember:

> And for the Jew's bond which he hath of me,
> Let it not enter in your mind of love.

> And even there, his eye being big with tears,
> Turning his face, he put his hand behind him,
> And with affection wondrous sensible
> He wrung Bassanio's hand, and so they parted.
>
> (II. viii. 41–2; 46–9)

If the Jew is in love with his daughter/ducats, Antonio it seems, is in love with Bassanio. Beautiful feelings, beautiful sentiments, are pitched against mercenary and demeaning utilities. So the Venetians view it. And we are invited to bring the same perspective to the trial scene.

Antonio expresses a disinterested, fastidious altruism:

> I do beseech you
> Make no more offers, use no farther means,
> But with all brief and plain conveniency
> Let me have judgment and the Jew his will.
>
> (IV. i. 80–3)

But his exhibitionistic desire (expressed in his letter in III. ii. 315–22) for Bassanio to witness his self-sacrificial death is again made manifest in

> when the tale is told, bid her be judge
> Whether Bassanio had not once a love.
>
> (IV. i. 276–7)

He is driven by a positive compulsion to self-immolation. Antonio's *imitatio dei* [imitation of God] is the ultimate aestheticizing of his protest at the loss of Bassanio's exclusive love. The strange 'I am a tainted wether of the flock,/Meetest for death;' (IV. i. 114–15) thus acquires a further meaning. He will be martyred sacrifice and high priest of magnanimity, and so legitimize and even enhance his love for Bassanio. Thus not only is Antonio's life at stake, but his self-esteem in his own eyes, the worth or value he holds himself to possess.

No less is this true of Shylock. The Jew exhibits an absorbing and undissimulated passion. 'Do all men kill the things they do not love?' asks Bassanio and Shylock flashes back, 'Hates any man the thing he would not kill?' But not only his revenge is at stake. The Jew's demand for law has a validity of its own and an inner compulsion of its own. This is why his argument is so trenchant on the one hand – the argument from slavery, for instance – and so defiantly, perversely arbitrary on the other:

> But say it is my humor, is it answer'd?
> What if my house be troubled with a rat,
> And I be pleas'd to give ten thousand ducats
> To have it ban'd? What, are you answer'd yet?
>
> So can I give no reason, nor I will not,
>
> (IV. i. 43–6; 59)

His rage to have his own back is a burning need to be recognized as a man more sinned against than sinning, as an aggrieved victim of injustice and betrayal. By his demand for justice he will force them to recognize his humanity, coerce the Venetian polity into accepting his membership of it. He will prove his claim to dignity, worth and value, thrust it down their throats, so to speak, in all its maddened extremity.

> What judgment shall I dread, doing no wrong?
> The pound of flesh which I demand of him
> Is dearly bought as mine, and I will have it.
> If you deny me, fie upon your law!
>
> (IV. i. 89; 99–101)

His cry of joy when he thinks that Portia endorses his bond: 'A Daniel come to judgment' is, it will be noticed, not the Daniel of the lion's den, but the Daniel – defender and justifier – of the wronged and libelled Susanna. For both contenders the fulfilment of the bond is a desperate act of self-assertion.

To these violent compulsions Portia's speech is tangential, irrelevant; but it lifts the issues at stake onto an impersonal plane where they can be resolved, as Pauline doctrine demands they be resolved, in terms of the age-old debate between the Christian and the Pharisee, the New and the Old Law, mercy and justice, spirit and letter. In this context the pound of flesh acquires still further symbolic power. Shylock's 'pound of flesh' is the letter of the old law. The blood, the invisible blood he may not spill, is the free-flowing, transcendent and unquenchable life of the spirit. 'Blood' has already acquired related connotations in Morocco's boast:

> Bring me the fairest creature northward born,
> Where Phoebus' fire scarce thaws the icicles,
> And let us make incision of your love,
> To prove whose blood is reddest, his or mine.
>
> (II. i. 4–7)

and Bassanio's courtship:

> Only my blood speaks to you in my veins,
>   all the wealth I had
> Ran in my veins . . .
>
> (III. ii. 176; 254–5)

Portia's *coup de théâtre* is of course a triumph – casuistry against casuistry in the name of equity. The Pharisee is crushed. And Portia drives her point home. He shall have justice and nothing but justice. As he undoes step by step his previous repudiations of all their offers in lieu of the forfeiture, he is exposed, stripped, dispossessed and ridiculed. His humiliation is complete. Finally his life and all his possessions lie at their mercy and it is graciously forthcoming: his fine reduced by half, the other half in trust for his daughter, provided he become a Christian and leave all in his will to his son-in-law and daughter. The Venetian world of commerce is purged of its mercenary demon and redeemed by its merciful angels. The antinomy between beauty and utility dissolves in grace embodied in the gracious Portia. And the inner meaning of her magnificent remedy – that the spirit giveth life – will be played out again in the ring episode, where final recognitions are brought about, actions are reversible, and giving and taking transformed into giving and forgiving.

What could be a more triumphant comic resolution? Evil has not only been exorcized, it has been seen to have been exorcized, positively, literally, in the scapegoat figure. And it has been writ large, since he is offered redeeming baptism, that what is cast out is his carnal and vindictive sinful self, a sin-offering for all Venice. And so, indeed, the play has been taken by its apologizers, with the moonlit ending as lyric and festive dénouement. But we must truncate our imaginations in order to collaborate with this view.

Because there are two Shylocks in *The Merchant of Venice*. The burlesque ogre [. . .] and the human being possessing a gloomy and savage dignity. The two alternate bewilderingly and never cohere. They are distinguishable and inseparable, two incompatible images held in solution; yet another (perhaps the chief) evidence of the self-division, the self-alienation of the play. The older, naive, personified vice or humour level of the characterization gives us the stereotype figure about whom everything is known. It is also the figure others tell Shylock he is, and it is what he finally becomes, defeated in his desperate self-assertive effort to circumvent their reduction of him, even if it must be as one even more villainous than they think him. The other Shylock [. . .] unfolds, is unpredictable, responds in unforeseen ways to circumstances. And being a person, he has the dignity of human personality, the dignity that is grounded in pain and passion, irrespective of virtue or vice, of good or evil. The benign offer of conversation is the ultimate cruelty of alienation, of denial of that essential being which has just made itself so palpably manifest. Therefore it is counterfeit mercy.

By the same token, a *pharmakos* [a burlesque ogre], if he is really to carry away his community's sins, must not stand there jeering at his sacrificers, must not disconcert them with the trenchant rationality of his argument, or challenge and defy them. Nor must he have a scamp of a faithless servant, and a runaway daughter whom he mourns with an exacerbated, irascible, impatient and totally undissimulated grief. He must not, in short, if we are to rejoice at his casting forth, impose upon us his alien and alienated vision in language which is uniquely, inviolably, uncompromisingly his own. Shakespearean comedy is not reducible to ritual comic origins. Shakespeare has trained us, and continually invites us, through the web of language and the play of depth and surface, to expect real recognitions rather than ritual gestures. Shylock the scapegoat may leave the stage as he will – totter or shuffle or creep – his experience, his exposure, seen as it has been seen, from within, precludes all possibility of *comic* exorcism and throws a long shadow across the moonlit garden of Belmont in Act V.

In Shakespeare's other dual-location comedies, *A Midsummer Night's Dream*, for instance, or *As You Like It*, or *The Shrew*, the benign comic dialectic of wisdom and folly dissolves in mockery the antinomies and disjunctions and impossible choices which generate tragedy. What is finally celebrated in them is a right seeing which is born of the lived-through delirium of wrong seeing; or wisdom bred of the experiencing of some liberating and remedial folly. And these saving higher follies are exactly what they are: figments of an imagination irradiated by its adventures in another, but available, realm of the psyche where extravagant, irrational, lunatic or preposterous possibilities are entertained. Bassanio's choice does partake of the nature of a higher folly, as does Shylock's of the preposterous, but Belmont is no such realm of transformation; only of an uneasy evangelicalism.

Morocco, Aristotle's magnanimous man – 'a golden mind stoops not to shows of dross' (II. vii. 20) – chooses gold because 'never so rich a gem/Was set in worse than gold' (II. vii. 54–5). Aragon, the fastidious, who

> will not choose what many men desire,
> Because I will not jump with common spirits,
> And rank me with the barbarous multitudes.
>
> (II. ix. 31–3)

chooses silver for its motto – 'Who chooseth me shall get as much as he deserves' – as an emblem of 'the stamp of merit'. While to Bassanio goes the prize for his refusal to be 'deceived by ornament': specious rhetoric, decorous piety, outward marks of virtue, artificial cosmetics; in other words for his choice of '-plainness' rather than eloquence, of a higher utility before an apparent beauty.

> Therefore then, thou gaudy gold,
> Hard food for Midas, I will none of thee;
> Nor none of thee, thou pale and common drudge
> 'Tween man and man; but thou, thou meagre lead,
> Which rather threaten'st than dost promise aught,
> Thy paleness moves me more than eloquence,
>
> (III. ii. 101–6)

This choice is in accordance with the evangelical role the figure in the casket is to play, but the casket choice exhausts too soon the function of a comic device to precipitate and exacerbate follies, errors, or fantasies, the exhibition of which will generate remedy in the therapeutic comic process of enlightenment. What it boils down to is that there is no true comic device. Shakespeare has tossed away this trump card, so that the maskings and unmaskings and reconciliations of the rings episode become mere comedy-game flourishes upon the theme of letter and spirit, inner meaning and outer manifestation. He has left the living to be done, in another world, by his scapegoat.

The Belmont of Act V is the way the Christians would like to see themselves – rid now of vulgar money cares. We do not feel that they are wiser than they were. Only that they have what they wanted. Portia's disguise has not been a device whereby her own self-discovery was extended, a means whereby she can be herself and not, or more than, herself at once and, we believe, for ever. Bellario vanishes, and the recognitions of Act V are merely technical.

According to the intuitions of inherited wealth, because these Venetians are beautiful, because they have beautiful feelings, they are also good. And happy. Belmont magnetizes all of the play's aestheticism, isolating Shylock as 'the man that hath no music in himself,/Nor is not moved with concord of sweet sounds'; and is therefore 'fit for treasons, stratagems and spoils'. But the moonlit lovers' duet 'On such a night', though it subdues to what it works in its remembered tales of tragic women, treacherous or betrayed – Cressida, Dido, Thisbe, Medea – echoes ominously. Though Jessica is carefully distinguished from her father, and saved for Belmont music lovers by her 'attentive' spirits, the motions of *his* spirit, Lorenzo tells us, 'are dull as night,/And his affections dark as [Erebus]' (v. i. 86–7).

But this time, the story of the night is irremediably troubling.

Once again at the end, for closure, Antonio stands surety for Bassanio, for good behaviour this time, not hard cash. He offers his 'soul' as forfeit for Bassanio's good faith where once his body had been forfeit for Bassanio's 'wealth' (v. i. 249ff). The duplication emphasizes the duality arising from the uneasy split between the two *topoi*. The play remains dichotomized between its two places, their polarity unresolved, its comic potential unfulfilled. [. . .]

NOTE

1   Jean-Paul Sartre, *Anti-Semite and Jew* (1948), trans. George J. Becker (New York: Schocken, 1948), pp. 112–14. Sartre's brilliant analysis is worth comparing at many points with Shakespeare's dramatization; see particularly pp. 126–9.

Section Three

Challenges to Authority

18   Jeffrey Chipps Smith **'Art or Idol? Religious Sculpture'**

Source: from *German Sculpture of the Later Renaissance,* Jeffrey Chipps Smith
c.1520–1580, Princeton University Press, Princeton, New Jersey, 1994, pp. 39–41,
111–16.

AUGSBURG

In Augsburg, both an imperial free city and an episcopal seat, the situation
was considerably more complex. The populace included Catholics, Lutherans,
and Zwinglians, each of whom came to have their own churches. By 1530 the
Lutherans occupied St. Anna and the preaching houses – not churches – of St.
Georg, St. Ulrich and Afra, and Heilig Kreuz; the Zwinglians had services in the
Barfüsserkirche; and the Catholics used the cathedral and the remaining
churches. Periodic damage to art prompted the council to issue a decretal [eccle-
siastical law] on 19 March 1529 forbidding the destruction or disfiguring of objects
in churches and cemeteries.

Local religious tensions resulted in several interesting encounters. In 1533 a
controversy arose in the Catholic church of St. Moritz between Anton I Fugger
a wealthy parishioner, and Marx Ehem, the Protestant warden of this church. To
prevent the celebration of mass, Ehem ordered the church's sacristy locked. At
his own expense Fugger, a Catholic and one of the principal patrons of the
church, quickly supplied another set of liturgical objects so the masses could continue. On Good Friday, 11 April, Ehem had the holy sepulchre with its sculptural
Entombment group sealed up so the Catholics could not lay the body of Christ,
in the form of a carved crucifix, in the tomb. Next, Ehem removed all of the
items used for the Ascension day ceremony including the liturgical vessels and
the image of Christ seated on a rainbow with its accompaning angels and Holy
Spirit. When Fugger secretly had a new, more expensive set of vessels and images
made, Ehem secured with timbers and iron the hole in the vault through which
Christ rose in the ceremony. Fugger somehow managed to have the hole reopened
and the ceremony was progressing as normal before a full audience when Ehem
and a group of supporters, with knives drawn, stormed into the church. After
the congregation fled, Ehem lowered the Christ figure and when it was about six
meters from the ground he let it go. The statue of Christ and the rest of the
ensemble smashed. Ehem had successfully if violently disrupted the Catholics'
service. This incident illustrates the passions and strengths of conviction on both
sides of the image controversy. It also points out the delicate position of Augsburg's city council that admonished both Ehem and Fugger yet barely punished
either for fear of offending the Protestant and Catholic camps.

On 29 July 1534 the city council ruled that Catholic masses were henceforth
limited to the cathedral, St. Moritz, St. Ulrich and Afra, and five other churches.
This was a significant reduction. Martin Bucer, the Strasbourg preacher, came
to Augsburg and spoke against images. As a precaution the cathedral chapter
removed many precious works and shipped them to the bishop's residence in
Dillingen. Several clerics even transferred their personal stone epitaphs from

Augsburg to more secure locales between 1534 and 1537. For instance, in 1537 Konrad Adelmann ordered his epitaph that had been carved in the 1520s by Hans Daucher, Augsburg's leading sculptor, to be moved from the cathedral cloister to Holzheim bei Dillingen.

On 17 January 1537 Augsburg's government abolished Catholicism within the city. The very next day, as the cathedral chapter left for Dillingen, the cathedral and St. Ulrich and Afra were 'gereinigt' [cleaned]. Similar cleansings of images occurred in Heilig Kreuz on 22 January and, two days later, in St. Moritz and St. Georg. In the case of the cathedral, many of the sculptures and paintings were placed in the crypt rather than being destroyed outright. The stone tombs and epitaphs of former bishops and clerics in the church and the cloister were liter-ally defaced: noses and ears were knocked off or entire heads were smashed though the accompanying coats of arms were rarely damaged. These desecrations were directed against individuals who symbolized the institution of the Catholic church. The Reformers felt that these clerics in death, as in life, should not pray to idols. Interestingly, these Protestant iconoclasts were very selective in the mon-uments they defaced. Several adjacent epitaphs of private individuals in the clois-ters, such as that of the city doctor Adolph Occo, were left unscathed. Within the church, the Protestants slashed the lower landscape of the giant mural paint-ing of St. Chrisopher while the upper portions, apparently out of their reach, were unharmed. Nearby, the stone Ölberg on the south wall was totally obliter-ated. Stained-glass windows and the portal statues were left untouched since these were difficult to use for purposes of veneration.

Bishop Christoph von Stadion, writing from Dillingen, complained bitterly about this destruction in a letter to Emperor Charles V. While strongly defend-ing the pious use of images, the bishop lamented the paganism emerging in Augs-burg. Specifically, he contrasted the besieged depiction of St. Ulrich that long had appeared on the Perlach tower, next to the Rathaus, with the very recently erected Neptune fountain. Von Stadion worried about the spiritual health of his flock because under the Protestants pious Christian statues were being replaced by heathen idols. Fortunately, not all of the churches in Augsburg were disturbed. Several powerful patrician families, including the Fuggers and Welsers, protected St. Anna and the Dominikanerkirche.

Protestant domination of Augsburg did not last long. Charles V and his allies defeated the Schmalkaldic League at the battle of Mühlberg in April 1547. The victorious emperor settled in Augsburg and convened an imperial Reichstag from 2 September 1547 to May 1548. Cardinal Otto Truchsess von Waldburg, the young and militant new bishop of Augsburg, returned in 1547 where he celebrated mass in the cathedral on 5 August. Although the bishop smashed the cathedral pulpit that had be constructed for the use of a Zwinglian preacher, he sought an accommodation with the city by requesting the council's approval to use one 'Götzenaltar' with appropriate vessels and art works. On 2 August 1548 a resti-tution edict between the cardinal-bishop and the city council was signed. Protes-tant and Catholic services were both to be tolerated. All churches converted to Protestantism between 1534 and 1537 reverted to Catholic use. Furthermore, Truchsess von Waldburg ordered that the redecoration of the cathedral be relatively spare. One crucifix was erected in the choir. The new sacrament house was made of wood rather than of a more costly material. Gradually many of the other statues and altars that had been placed in the crypt in 1537 were cleaned and reset. Even late in his reign, the cardinal-bishop issued decretals that all objects that could be considered idolatrous should be removed from churches within the diocese. He sought to minimize the potential for conflict.

Thereafter both Protestants and Catholics were permitted to worship in Augsburg. In spite of the occasional Catholic-perpetuated incidents of iconoclasm, the local religious accommodation held. The Peace of Augsburg of 1555 subsequently made a similar recognition of the religious status quo within the rest of the imperial German-speaking lands. As the century progressed and new artistic commissions were given to redecorate the Catholic churches, considerable care was taken to select themes that also would be acceptable to local Protestants, specifically to the Lutherans. Only from the 1570s, in the aftermath of the Council of Trent, were important new artistic projects, including the conscious revival of older sculptural programs, commissioned by Augsburg's Catholics. [. . .]

The Catholic revival's impact upon art manifest[ed] itself differently in each city, bishopric, and princely territory. To demonstrate this, I wish next to examine five instances in which new religious sculpture did result from a reassertion of strong Catholic authority. The situations in Augsburg, an imperial free city, Trier, an archepiscopal city, Würzburg, a prince-bishopric retaken by the Catholics, Ingolstadt, the university city ruled by the dukes of Bavaria, and Innsbruck, where Ferdinand of Tirol built a private chapel, offer different responses to the religious situation. Yet in each case, the artistic commissions may be linked with a new militant Catholicism that emerged especially in southern Germany. This militancy expressed itself peacefully in the classrooms and parishes rather than on the battle fields as it had in the 1540s.

AUGSBURG

Augsburg, more than any other city, served as the focal point for the skirmishes between the Protestant and Catholic camps. In Chapter Two we witnessed the city's iconoclastic struggles and saw that significant groups of both confessional faiths continued to reside within its walls. Amid the seeming chaos of the period. Otto Truchsess von Waldburg was elected bishop of Augsburg in 1543. Within a few years, Otto, who became a cardinal in 1544, emerged as Germany's strongest Catholic cleric and an ardent advocate of church reform. The bishop took full advantage of Charles V's victory over the Protestants at Mühlberg and the emperor's presence at diets in Augsburg in 1547–48 and 1550–51 to reassert Catholic authority. He celebrated his inaugural mass in Augsburg cathedral on 5 August 1547. Over the next year Otto demanded civic reimbursement for destroyed church ornaments and restitution of all churches seized by the Protestants between 1534 and 1537. Under his direction a few new artistic commissions were given to replace significant works that had been destroyed in 1537. For instance, in 1554 Christoph Amberger painted a new high altar for the cathedral. Its design and iconography carefully replicate the essential traits of the former high or Mary Altar that Hans Holbein the Elder had painted in 1508–9. Since all traces of the altar had likely disappeared, Holbein's drawing, today in Danzig (Stadtmuseum), must have served as Amberger's model. This selective recreation of certain paintings and sculptures illustrates a conscious desire to re-establish the Catholic church's bonds with its recent past. As we shall see shortly, Amberger's altarpiece is but one of several examples of this practice. The bishop was, however, sensitive to Protestant complaints about idols so he restricted the amount of decorations permitted in other churches in the diocese.

Bishop Otto championed the Catholic faith while being politically savvy in his dealings with Augsburg's strong Protestant community. During his long reign from 1543 to 1573, he established an accommodation between Augsburg's Catholics and Protestants. Both sides could worship in relative peace and educate their children without interference. Otto strengthened the quality both of priests and public preaching in the diocese. In 1549 he established a Catholic college in Dillingen, site of his official residence; five years later the school was elevated to a university that specialized in training priests. The bishop enlisted Jesuit Peter Canisius, an eloquent moralist and reformer, to be his cathedral's preacher from 1559 to 1567. Bishop Otto, active at the various sessions of the Council of Trent, published its decrees in 1565 and organized meetings to explain the points to Catholic delegates attending the 1566 imperial diet in Augsburg. Except for his periods of residence in Rome. Bishop Otto provided firm leadership and much needed stability to Augsburg's Catholic community.

Another strong reforming cleric, Abbot Jakob Köplin (1548–1603), restored Augsburg's other major church, the imperial Benedictine monastery of St. Ulrich and Afra (Fig. 11). Decimated during the upheavals of the 1530s, little remained of the church's artistic decorations when it was returned to the Catholics in 1548. For the next twenty years Köplin focused upon his primary task of rebuilding the monastery's clerical community. Only when this was accomplished did the abbot begin plans for the artistic enrichment of his church. Inspired by the Council of Trent's reaffirmation of religious art, Köplin ordered local sculptor Paulus II Mair to carve a monumental new high altar. When consecrated in 1571, Mair's Mary Altar must have astounded many since at 16.5 meters high it was the largest Catholic altarpiece in Germany since the 1520s, with the sole exception of Hans Mielich's new high altar (1560–72) in Ingolstadt. The design of the winged retable with its corpus, predella, and superstructure (Auszug) are intentionally archaic. Mair and his patron consciously looked beyond the prevailing Renaissance style to the altar forms of the later fifteenth and early sixteenth centuries. The standing Virgin and saints in the corpus, the half-length predella figures of Sts. Simpertus, James Major, and Narcissus, and the Gothic-style tracery of the upper sections of the altar recall works such as the *Blaubeuren Altar* (1493–94) by Michael Erhart, Mair's great grandfather, or Jörg Lederer's St. Blasius Altar in Kaufbeuren of 1518.

Rasmussen correctly labelled the Mary Altar as a major example of the Catholic *restauratio*. The appearance of the original high altar of St. Ulrich and Afra is unknown. It is possible that Mair purposefully evoked the memory of this earlier altar much as Amberger's 1554 High Altar for the cathedral paid homage to Holbein's destroyed masterwork. Rasmussen suggests that this reusing of Gothic forms is part of the Counter-Reformation Catholic church's desire to re-establish a tie with the historical traditions of the past that had been severed by icono-clasm. That is, historicism provided a means of continuity. In our discussion of Münster following the suppression of the Anabaptists, we observed the some phe-nomenon as the bishop and cathedral chapter quickly restored and replaced select statues, such as that of Paul, their patron saint. To the Catholic clergy and laity alike, religious sculpture represented a physical embodiment of their beliefs. Works, such as Mair's altar, bridge the intervening dislocation caused by the Reformation back to a time when art piously served a single Christian church. The altars in St. Ulrich and Afra and in the cathedral anticipare the widespread seventeenth-century practice of re-using and incorporating late medieval and early Renaissance sculpture in new altarpieces.

Interestingly, Mair's Mary Altar was replaced only a generation later. Was the change prompted by a shift in aesthetic values or by qualms over the quality of Mair's work. In 1601 Köplin's ambitious successor, Abbot Johann Merk (1600–32), built a new sacristy and, above it, the Marienkapelle (Schneckenkapelle). In the same year he transferred the Mary Altar to this chapel. The church had no high altar until Hans Degler's magnificent St. Narcissus (or Adoration of the Shep-herds) Altar was dedicated in 1604. By 1600 the German Catholic church was much stronger than it had been thirty years earlier. Merk desired a new high altar that better expressed the church's more confident spirit. When comparing the two altarpieces, Mair's figures seem static and strangely lifeless. Each statue or group of statues dutifully fills its assigned niche; everything is clearly and appro-priately arranged. Nevertheless, the Mary Altar is devoid of the fervent spiritu-alism that characterizes the best pre-Reformation altars. Admittedly, Mair might have been compelled to copy certain features of the original altarpiece destroyed by the iconoclasts. Degler, on the other hand, is a worthy successor to Hans Lein-berger or Veit Stoss. He emulated the emotionalism inherent in their finest creations. This is hardly accidental since Degler too studied older altars for both the structure of the frame and his narrative vocabulary. Degler's figures use bold, overstated gestures to animate the telling of the holy story. He offers a brilliant realization of the Counter-Reformation's *theatrum sacrum* [i.e. emphasis on dra-matic engagement during religious rites], which would come to dominate German sculpture throughout much of the seventeenth and eighteenth centuries. With Degler, one experiences a creative borrowing of the best features of late Gothic and early Renaissance art which are then combined with the zeal of the resurgent German Catholic church.

Although Mair's altar was moved from its original location, it remained tremen-dously popular with worshippers seeking the Virgin's assistance. Romanus Kistler, writing in 1712 on the occasion of the monastery's 700th anniversary, observed that a large number of votive pictures hung on the walls adjacent to the altar in acknowledgment of the miracles performed by 'Maria Trost' (Mary the consoler). The tenor of his text and the implied power of the Virgin as

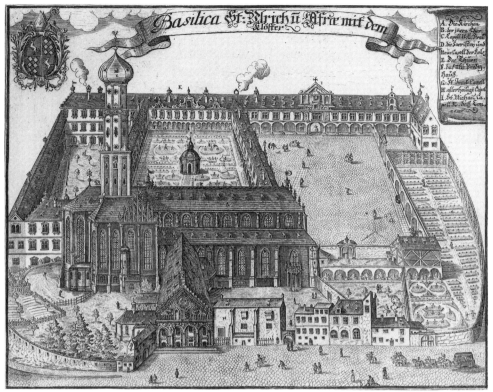

11 Daniel Mannasser, *View of St. Ulrich and St. Afra in Augsburg*, 1626, engraving, Munich, Staatliche Graphische Sammlung.

manifest through the altarpiece are strikingly similar to the attitudes discussed in Chapter One.

In addition to Paulus Mair's Mary Altar, Abbot Köplin ordered the restoration of the tomb of St. Simpertus in 1579. Damage to Michel Erhart's recumbent effigy was repaired and a new stone base, marked with the abbot's coat of arms, was added, Köplin also permitted several members of the Fugger family to assume responsibility for the maintenance and re-decoration of five of the side chapels of the nave. Although most of the resulting artistic commissions postdate 1580, it demonstrates how the wealthy laity were once again eager to secure the spiritual and social gains associated with church donations.

St. Ulrich and Afra was not the only Augsburg church that gradually added new sculptural decorations. The Dominikanerkirche, which had not been sacked in 1537 due to the strong pressure of the Fuggers and other leading Catholic patricians, received several modest commissions. Antwerp sculptor Willem van den Broecke (Guilielmus Paludanus) carved a series of alabaster reliefs for one or, more likely, two projects for the church. Four typological scenes (*Crucifixion– Sacrifice of Abraham, Last Supper–Offering of Melchizedek*), dated 1560, one bearing the arms of the May and Rembold families of Augsburg, hung originally in a red marble frame on the fifth column of the nave. A second, higher quality Crucifixion relief of 1562 was also made for this church. These reliefs are export

12 Hubert Gerhard, *Altar of Christoph Fugger*, detail of *Prophet*, 1581–84, formerly in Augsburg, Dominikanerkirche, now London, Victoria and Albert Museum. Photo: V & A Picture Library.

products. Van den Broecke is documented throughout this period in Antwerp, so trips to Augsburg in 1562 or to Schwerin in 1563, where other carvings were delivered to the Schlosskirche, are unlikely. In January 1581 the heirs of Christoph Fugger (d. 1579) commissioned Paulus Mair, the master of the Mary Altar, to make a frame and several sketches for a new altar destined for the sixth column of the nave. The bronze Resurrection, prophets, and other elements of this once grand altar went, however, to Hubert Gerhard and Carlo Pallago, two young masters only recently arrived in Augsburg who would soon reinvigorate the city's sculptural tradition (Fig. 12). While this particular project was not completed until 1584, it again illustrates the gradual renewal of interest in religious sculpture and the engagement of patricians as well as clerics in the rebeautification of Augsburg's Catholic churches. [. . .]

19 Susan Karant-Nunn **'Progress toward Reform'**

Source: from *Zwickau in Transition 1500–47: The Reformation as an Agent of Social Change*, Susan Karant-Nunn Ohio State University Press, Columbus, 1987, pp. 121–5, 127–36.

Despite small and temporary divisions in the ranks, the council proceeded to create a Lutheran church for the entire city [of Zwickau]. Disagreement does not appear to have slowed it. Civic interest triumphed over the compunctions of councillors who otherwise tended either to the Catholic right or to the radical left. Even the dullest councillors were glad of an opportunity, provided by the Reformation, to hasten and facilitate the city's accumulation and consolidation of jurisdiction over all persons and properties within the walls and many without. For decades the council had struggled to acquire more power, at the expense of nearly every other type of corporation. The Reformation represented to all the city fathers a chance not just to punish Catholic moral and fiscal abuses but indeed to eliminate this mighty institution entirely and to absorb its functions. This was a gigantic windfall of power for ambitious men.

It has been customary to give Hermann Mühlpfort most of the credit for orchestrating the Reformation from within the council. Mühlpfort had first entered the governing circle as an electoral appointee in 1510. He was burgomaster during that crucial year from Saint Michael's Day (29 September), 1521 until Saint Moritz's Day (28 September), 1522. He held the same office in 1523–24, 1525–26, 1527–28, 1529–30, 1531–32, and 1533 until his death. His was no small part in Zwickau's ecclesiastical 'purification.' He worked hand in hand, however, with his counterpart in alternate years, the Paris master of arts Laurentius Bärensprung, first a councillor in 1504. In these years the council in office and the council theoretically out of office strove together to build a Lutheran church polity.

How Bärensprung became attracted to Lutheran teaching is unfortunately not known. Very likely he was first drawn to humanism and disapproval of the institutional Catholic church; when Egranus, whom Bärensprung admired, made his final exit, the councillor found his personal evolution into an advocate of Lutheranism quite natural within Zwickau's setting. Bärensprung was ruling burgomaster in 1520–21 and was clearly as decisive as any of his colleagues in moving toward civic control of the local church. He died on 19 April 1533. The man was laden with debts, but Johann, first as duke, then as elector [of Saxony] insisted that his colleagues tolerate his precarious financial state.

The year 1522 was a turning point for the Catholic church in Zwickau. In most respects, at year's beginning church structure was unchanged. By year's end the church, though still alive, was a shadow of its former self. The changes were overwhelmingly the doing of the council, whose larger, often worldly purposes coincided with Nicolaus Hausmann's spiritual ones. For a time council and pastor were allies. Nevertheless, it would be shy of the mark to say that the Lutheran Reformation had been carried out.

In the early weeks of 1522, the populace was still in turmoil as a consequence of Müntzer's, Storch's, and others' work of marshalling public opinion against the council, not a difficult task. The council's burdens, partly self-made, became at once so enormous that any notion of half the councillors being out of office in alternate years now became and remained ludicrous. The council took on, for example, the hearing of all cases of slander among the citizens, which, it admitted, had become so frequent that 'the council has practically enough to do every day with these matters.' Of course, it made hardly any difference whether the council *qua* council presided over slander hearings or whether it assigned them to the courts: the judges and jurymen were all councillors.

Citizens daily harangued the councillors to their faces. Even though sixteen student supporters of Müntzer/Storch had been dismissed from the grammar school in January, some students or their families apparently sassed Burkhard Waldauff, one of the two councillors appointed to oversee the academy. Some citizens did not take pride in the school, regarding it as a perpetrator of humanist intellectualism, which was alien to them and linked to the city councillors. In August 1523 the council had to arrest people who stood outside the school and mocked the students.

In spite of all the council could do, Zwickau knew little peace in these days. There were three leading factions. First was the party of the city council and Pastor Hausmann, which labored not only for law and order but for the confinement, if not the abolition, of Catholic institutions, to the advantage of the city government. It is probable but not presently demonstrable that many of Zwickau's better educated, humanistically inclined citizens were sympathetic to this group and that Egranus's admirers might have felt more at home here after their leader's departure than in association with the other parties. Second were the so-called sectarians, sometimes referred to as Storchites, but who in fact continued to identify strongly with Thomas Müntzer. These were mainly artisans and their families, but they ran the gamut in their economic status from exceedingly comfortable to poor. They shared a deep resentment of the council's usurpations at their expense, an attraction to less authoritarian religion, and a cultural orientation not toward southwest German humanism but toward the environs of Zwickau itself. Third were the Catholics, clergy and laity. This is the group that has been largely overlooked by scholars, yet evidence of its existence and of its strength is considerable. One reason that the council launched a veritable campaign against the secular priests, the Franciscans, and the Cistercians early in 1522 was that their hold on the people was strong. Numerous persons of unidentified socioeconomic condition went regularly to the Franciscans to confess, to hear mass, and to listen to sermons that were becoming intensely political. When on 20 March 1524 communion in both kinds was first offered to the laity, only twenty citizens received it. The council found that moderate measures did not adequately discourage members of this tradition-bound Catholic sector, and, as we shall see, it quickly turned to concerted action.

A minority of Zwickau's residents actively involved themselves in these controversies that so arouse our interest. They no doubt had their opinions, but they did not take to the streets or join conventicles. Even if, as was rumored, Müntzer or Storch had succeeded in enlisting 'twelve apostles and seventy-two disciples,' it is to be remembered that eighty-four is not a high percentage of approximately 7,500. Zwickau's main industry was woolweaving; and if indeed many of the city's religious radicals were affiliated with this craft, this was only to be expected. Most of the councillors themselves throughout the first half of the sixteenth century were woolweavers or wool merchants by profession. It is perhaps remarkable that two of the three Zwickau Prophets were not associated with cloth production at all. Certainly conditions in Zwickau do not lend credibility to the widely held belief today that there has ever been a strong link between weaving and religious nonconformity. None of this lessens the significance of the Zwickau radicals' appeal, but it may help to keep that appeal, and the nature of the Reformation for that matter, in proper perspective.

Against this background of partisan strife, the council proceeded undaunted against the Catholic church in Zwickau. So far as the secular priests were concerned, of which Zwickau's churches and chapels had several dozen, the council gave Hausmann permission to bring them to order and delegated a councillor to assist him. It took measures to retain Johann Zeidler, Egranus's successor, as preacher in Saint Mary's Church. It also at this time wished to keep Wolfgang Zeiner as preacher at Saint Katherine's. By June, evidently with Duke Johann's approval, the council instructed its secretary to write to every benefice holder and tell him that if he did not reside in the city and personally carry out the duties of his office, he would no longer receive income from 'his' endowment. Fortunately for the council, Johann regarded Lutheranism in general and reform of clerical abuses in particular far more favorably than did his conservative brother Frederick the Wise. The council, in consultation with Hausmann, forbade Zwickau's several lay fraternities to receive further moneys from testaments, but it specifically exempted the hospitals and churches from this provision. Here again it encountered no resistance from Duke Johann.

Dealing with the regular clergy was more challenging. The Franciscans and the Cistercians were corporations of literate and determined men who had behind them not merely their local colleagues but the authority and tradition of the Catholic hierarchy. They were not so easily divided and conquered. They met the propagandistic and legal maneuvers of the council with like ploys. Thus, without the condonation of the princes, it is not certain that the council would have been victorious.

The princes, however, had nothing to do with the way in which the council's problems with the Cistercians in the Grünhainer Hof were solved. This was a case in which the common folks' proclivity toward violence served the council's own purposes. Indeed, according to Peter Schumann, whose father took part, some councillors themselves joined right in. For unknown reasons the Cistercians imprisoned a peasant in March 1522. The people were incensed. If any element bound the majority of Zwickau's residents throughout the Reformation era, it was disgust and anger at the corrupt, arrogant, self-serving behavior of the clergy, particularly of monks and friars. Popular resentment easily ignited. [. . .]

The effects of this uprising constituted for the council a giant step toward gaining control of the urban church. The city fathers' implicit, if not explicit, approval of the riot is borne out by the total lack of discussion of it in the minutes. Indeed, few minutes on any subject were taken during the second half of March and all of April, suggesting that whatever was talked about was ultra-secret in nature. Normally, whenever widespread popular dissatisfaction threatened to erupt into violence, the council's secretary took up much space in the minutes book recording the discussions. In March 1522 this was strikingly not the case. Public ire had coincided with conciliar ambition, and mob action achieved what might have taken the bureaucracy years. A master glazier, Hans Wimmer, who had personally smashed all the monks' windows (had he installed them?), enjoyed lasting renown for his boldness, not just among ordinary citizens.

The council hastened to try to obtain the vacated monastery and the Cistercians' rural jurisdictions near Zwickau. The prince did not match their haste. Elector Johann Friedrich conceded the building in Zwickau to the council only in October 1542. Even so the council was obliged to pay the elector four hundred florins for this property. The Hof was thenceforth to house the city grammar school. The city failed to gain the rural jurisdictions.

During April 1522 the council had its hands full. Having seen the masses in action against the Grünhainer Hof, and feeling daily the barbs of the Franciscans, the gentlemen worried about further riots. On the evening of 8 April, someone assaulted a friar with a tankard. A spirit of rebellion lay very near the surface. On hearing that Luther was in the vicinity and aware how effective his sermons had been in restoring order in Wittenberg, the council enthusiastically invited him to detour to Zwickau. He arrived the very next day and stayed at the home of Burgomaster Hermann Mühlpfort. Between 29 April and 2 May, Luther preached four times: twice at the Franciscan friary, once at city hall, and once at Schloss Zwicker, in that order. The first location no doubt galled the Franciscans, who were powerless to prevent him from speaking on their premises.

The reformer's sermons were on the following subjects: (1) that good works flow from faith; (2) good works and marriage; (3) the true way (Christ) and the false way, Christ's atonement for the sins of mankind; (4) faith and love, the duties of the priest (to preach and to pray), baptism, and prayers for the dead. In view of conditions in Zwickau, it is to us nothing short of astonishing that Luther failed to address the matter of civic unrest. It is unlikely that he had not been apprised of the enthusiasm for Müntzer/Storch that persisted in the city. Rather, he was still convinced that the word of God itself would convert and pacify. Simply summarizing his beliefs, based in scripture as he saw them to be, would reform and tranquilize the population.

Peter Schumann, who got the information from his father, states that fourteen thousand people turned out to hear Luther speak at the city hall. Such a figure is not unthinkable: Zwickau's resident population was about half that, and an additional seven thousand could well have come in from the surrounding countryside and neighboring towns. The *Geleitsmann* of Borna, one of the officials who were to oversee and facilitate the movement of people and goods on the highways, told the elector that there had been twenty-five thousand in the audience. Some sort of outburst occurred among the listeners as Luther delivered his sermon from city hall. [. . .] The council paid Luther an honorarium of ten gold florins.

The quelling of public display against the council was owing less to Luther's appearance than to the absence in Zwickau of a leader for the sectarians. Among the partisans of Müntzer and Storch feeling ran strong against Luther as well as against humanism and those attracted to it. In late November 1522, the council had one Christoff Burghard (or Bernfuhrer) apprehended and questioned about his '*ratio fidei.*' [reason for his faith] He was accused of being inclined toward religious enthusiasm (*schwirmmherrey*) and the ill-behavior 'of the spirits' and of being a member of Müntzer's sect. He was supposed to have written a song against Luther and Erasmus, and others were rumored to be in complicity with him. He was banished early the next year for five years, a very severe punishment designed to set an example.

The council now concentrated on the Franciscans. Earlier in the year it had backed away from its half-hearted attempt to assume governance of the friars. The brothers had refused to hand over a key, but to resort to force at this point would have produced princely reprobation. As the spring wore on, the gentlemen found intolerable the hold of the friars on a number of residents who went to them for spiritual ministration. In early June two councilmen went to the monastery and told the 'guardian' that 'Werner' was not to preach any more. The result was less than satisfactory, for the scribe remarked just two weeks later that the Franciscans would have to elect another custodian and another guardian because the behavior of the current ones 'will lead to a riot.' Finally, at the end of June the entire council solemnly walked to the cloister, removed the guardian 'and others' and imposed its own member upon the brothers. Who this was is not stated, but it could have been Herr Michel Sangner, whom the friars had rejected earlier. The council intended to put the old guardian out of the city. This did not produce harmony. The Franciscans labored all the harder to arouse the public against the magistrates, who finally appealed to Duke Johann. Technically, Johann permitted them only to reprimand the friars; nevertheless, in October they banned from the city a friar who had preached 'hard' against Hausmann. A debate between the Franciscans and the reformed clergy in the presence of the Rat on 21 November 1524 was for show only, giving the council a chance formally to excoriate the brothers.

At some point in its various discussions of ecclesiastical matters with Duke Johann and Elector Frederick the Wise in 1522, the council obtained formal jurisdiction over priestly endowments. [. . .] Regarding the All Souls benefice, a member of the council was to go to the administrator or to the testamentaries and tell them that the interest from the endowment would be better used by the hospital or the school. The council also began to put pressure on the Calend Fraternity, whose wealth it wished to use for the city's philanthropic purposes. The prior and elders of that brotherhood were to be made to render an account to the council so that the money could later be diverted from financing masses for members to maintaining the poor 'etc.' Such a radical change required princely assent, and the council sought it. It did not obtain final permission to dissolve the organization until 1527.

During the fall of 1521, Hausmann wrote an 'Ordinance for Priests.' This work is evidently not extant, but his broader, more comprehensive assessment of the church in Zwickau, probably composed early in 1523 at the behest of Duke Johann, is. Hausmann considered the first order of business to be circumscribing, if not wholly eliminating, the participation of dozens of altarists [catholic priests] in the life of the parish. In this the council could hardly have agreed more fully, and vowed its cooperation.

Hausmann worked closely with the councillors during this period. He went to

Zeitz several times in the company of one or more of the gentlemen to inform diocesan authorities of what the council and he were doing in Zwickau. This cannot have been a pleasant task, but it was one that Frederick the Wise's reluctance to permit innovation made necessary. The councilmen's sense of comradery with Hausmann is given expression by the patricians' invitation to him and the two preachers, Johann Zeidler and Wolfgang Zeiner, to join them in their private Mardi Gras festivities. [. . .]

It is virtually impossible to assess the impact of the sermon on the people of the city. The preaching position was instrumental in many German cities in starting reform. In Zwickau, where the Rat called for reform before anyone else, the burghers were not so keen to espouse the movement. Preachers of every variety passed through town, from the erudite, humanist Egranus to the inflammatory Müntzer; from the blunt, anti-popular Conrad Cordatus to the weak-voiced Christoff Ering. The people judged them more than anything else by the sheer theater of their delivery, and, secondarily, by the degree of their antipathy for the council. The theological convictions of the homilists counted as a distant third factor, remarkably behind the first two. The council's best hope for calming and converting the people lay in attracting absolutely spell-binding preachers of Lutheran doctrine, of peace and respect for the law. [. . .]

During the autumn of 1522, the council named a committee from its own ranks to suggest how school and parish might be financially sustained. The members were Mühlpfort, Vogt Wolff Schicker, Schultheiss Gotthard Büttner, and Burkhard Waldauff. Inspired by Luther's outline of a community chest for the city of Leisnig in 1523, the committee evidently suggested adopting such a mechanism. The first pertinent reference in the council minutes is to 'dy gemayne Buchsen' [i.e. common box] on 8 August 1523, and the second to 'der gemeyne kasten' [i.e. community chest] on 19 August. All church funds were to be channeled into this chest.

Beginning in 1523 the council actively sought to remove tax exemptions from clerical properties. The secretary expressed the monetary motive quite freely, along with other reasons. The council opened negotiations with the Dominicans of Plauen to shut their depot in Zwickau. It offered to buy their house for a fair price or to let them sell it to a burgher. In any case, the black friars were to be informed, their property would no longer be free of tax. In contrast to the Franciscans, the Dominicans did not undertake the cure of souls in Zwickau. Their purpose there was exclusively economic. On 6 April 1524, the Dominicans sold their house to the council for two hundred florins.

At the time of the 1533 visitation, there were still twenty-three occupied priests' houses in the city. The unanswered question is whether their inhabitants were working clergymen, former priests, or people whom the council had allowed to reside in them. [. . .] A conciliar decree of October 1524 that altarists [catholic priests] did not have to be paid at all unless they deserved to be, that is, unless they submitted to the reformed church, was unrealistic. The council had to find ways of maintaining those who stayed even though, private and individual masses being more and more restricted, the men could render only small service to the church over which Hausmann presided. A few who were not averse to

cooperating with the Lutheran-minded authorities were given elementary clerical tasks to perform and were generally accorded better treatment. Most were not
turned out of their homes in any event. In this regard both pastor and council
conceded that a complete transition from old to new would take time. Yet the
need to sustain so many priests was one factor hindering smooth operation of
the community chest.

There were other, more telling ones. Although the council minutes for 29
September 1523 to 28 September 1524 are missing, it is apparent from other
sources that during this period the councillors intensified their efforts to buy out
or confiscate ecclesiastical endowments and to concentrate all their incomes in
the new community chest. Only in early 1524 did Egranus, now in Joachimsthal,
stop receiving income from a Lehen [living] in Saint Mary's Church, for example;
and the excuse for denying it to him was 'because he does not reside.' The School
and Corpus Christi fraternities met their doom in 1523 along with a number of
endowed masses. Problems arose because principal sums were not returned either
to members or heirs of endowers. This produced a certain ambivalence, particularly in well-to-do quarters. [. . .]

Many [. . .] endowers or their heirs appealed attempts to deny them income
from benefices. The Römer descendants won some concessions in 1529 and 1545.
In 1545 Burgomaster Oswald Lasan apparently succeeded, with the help of Luther,
Bugenhagen, and Melanchthon, in having a portion of the revenue from the
Jacob and Laurence endowment, established by his forebears, earmarked for the
support of student members of his family. Some claimants on benefices even tried
to take back the principal.

We do not know what percentage of all revenues from pre-Reformation endowments was diverted as a result of such efforts. As usual, much documentation is
missing. More important – a second affliction of the community chest from its
inception – accounting practices in connection with these moneys were severely
flawed. From the start a councillor served as administrator (*fursteber*) of the community chest, and he was obligated to present an annual account to the council.
But the council itself – and this constitutes a third impediment to the success of
the fund – came to view the chest as a source of loans to its members and their
friends and relatives. Previously the gentlemen had borrowed chiefly from the
'new councillors' money,' which every man elected to the city council for the first
time had to pay before taking his seat.

A fourth obstacle to the smooth functioning of the community chest was the
fact that Zwickau citizens were no longer as free with their alms as they had been
under Catholicism. The council repeatedly deliberated the question of how to
get the people to continue the level of donation that they had made before.
Luther finally perceived the magnitude of the problem when he took part in the
general visitation of 1528–29. He wrote, 'Under popery the people were charitable and gave gladly; but now under the gospel, nobody gives anything but only
fleeces his neighbor. Each person wants to have everything for himself alone. And
the longer the gospel is preached, so much more do the people drown in greed,
arrogance, and luxury, just as if the poor begger's sack was supposed to stay there
forever. The devil has indeed made two inroads among the people.'

Table 15
Some Religious Changes in Zwickau, 1523–1545

1521		Priests, monks, and friars may not beg from house to house.
1523	4 June	Corpus Christi procession moved from afternoon to morning, severely curtailed; sermon in St. Mary's churchyard.
	2 July	*Salve Regina* [Hail Mary, Queen . . .] eliminated.
	8 July	St. Mary's Church, Host no longer borne around.
	16 July	St. Katherine's Church, Host no longer borne around.
1524	Lent	Several couples wed; citizens privately eat meat though Rat forbids sale, confiscates two slaughtered calves.
	22 March	Hausmann has *Frühmesser* [early Mass] altar and choir screen removed from St. Katherine's Church.
	24 March	Mass said in German; communion offered in both kinds.
	25 March	Passion sermon eliminated.
	26 March	Reformed baptismal ceremony introduced; Old Testament readings in German.
	25 December	New Testament readings in German.
1525	30 April	Entire service in German.
1526	Lent	Meat may be freely sold.
1529	January	Visitors permit Latin mass and vespers on high feast days; Saturday bell ringing for souls of dead eliminated.
1545	5 August	On Luther's order, elevation of Host and Chalice ceases.

The years 1523 and 1524 were particularly full ones for the reformers of the church in Zwickau. Working closely together, the city council and Pastor Hausmann had virtually concluded the process of establishing Lutheranism and eliminating Catholicism before the outbreak of the Peasants' War in their area. The power of most Catholic corporations had been broken, and a new ecclesiastical administration with the council at its top had been created. The council met every expression of opposition with decisive suppressive measures. Nonetheless, opposition remained. Even if they did not exactly flourish, both Müntzerites and Catholics were still present.

The single major goal that the council had failed to attain was the abolition of the Franciscan community. Success was soon to come, but its achievement was an accompaniment to the Peasants' War and must be described in its proper context. So long as the Franciscans remained, even though they no longer enjoyed any formal authority, they constituted a symbol of traditional religion that could arouse antipathy toward the council in some quarters.

By the death of Frederick the Wise in early May 1525, a great many details remained to be worked out, but the city council had made those major revisions in policy and practice that lay at the heart of the Lutheran Reformation. Working with Hausmann they had eliminated male (but not female) monasticism and were treating with their prince to obtain monastic holdings and jurisdictions. They had accepted Hausmann's 'Ordinance of Priests' and reduced Saint Mary's staff to a pastor, a preacher, and two deacons. Saint Katherine's clergy, always less numerous, was similarly reduced. The council had only to buy out, or await the deaths of, a few priests. The preachers in both Saint Mary's and Saint Katherine's churches were committed to Lutheran teaching. Hausmann had markedly reduced the number and purposes of masses, though negotiations with some endowers remained in progress. Hausmann and others had finally convinced Luther of the need for a German mass. A short version (1524) and a longer version (1526) were finally forthcoming and were adopted by Zwickau's pastor, as were Luther's other revised rituals as they came off the printing presses of Wittenberg and then of Zwickau itself. A community chest now existed, out of which clergy, teachers, the poor, and the ill were to gain sustenance. This community chest was never the fiscal success that it might have been in better, more honest managers' hands, but it was not a total failure either. The destitute could no longer beg from house to house or in the marketplace, but if they appeared on Sunday after the sermon, they got their dole.

Governance of the church by mid-1525 lay in the hands of the city council. The councillors thought that it did, and for the time being, at least, they were not wrong. Pastor Hausmann had to seek their consent for every sort of innovation. The gentlemen so readily gave it that the pastor quickly came to think of himself as the highest local authority in church affairs. These differing views of the source of power would soon lead to a collision between council and pastor, and in turn between elector and city, as we shall see. Unmistakably, however, the Catholic church was finished in Zwickau before the summer of 1525. The council had put widespread popular antipathy toward Catholic clergy to its own use, had seized control of religious institutions, and had imposed its political as well as its theological will upon a people that had not entirely anticipated the outcome. The years of flux, during which persons with widely varying opinions on religion were bold enough to speak out, now came abruptly to an end. The Peasants' War so frightened those in power, of every sort at every level, that it ultimately reinforced an already growing authoritarianism in ruling circles.

The Reformation came far sooner to electoral cities like Zwickau than it did to outlying hamlets and villages. Zwickau compelled the peasants directly under its rule to accept pastors to the council's liking, that is, Lutheran. Yet it could not alter overnight the common people's own private convictions. Nor could it affect independent congregations or parishes within noble domains. Fully another decade would elapse before the elector, through his appointed representatives and in his name, would end Catholicism in the countryside. In 1533 the parish visitors commented about peasants in 'the council's villages': 'Because some are still papists and have not been to the sacrament in many years, they are supposed to improve their ways or not be tolerated in the community any longer.' Convert and conform or get out of the elector's lands!

Pockets of quiet resistance lived on within Zwickau itself. The visitors had to ordain 'that no one who would not receive the Lord's Supper under both kinds may henceforth serve as anyone's godparent nor may he be buried with the customary ceremonies.' Blasius Walter, an impecunious weaver, died on 25 January 1540. He had refused ever to receive communion in both kinds and had openly decried the practice. He was buried in Saint Moritz's cemetery, which lay outside the walls, '*sine crux, dux, et lux et sine Campana*' (without cross, procession, light or knell). The city was moderate by sixteenth-century standards: it did not force all recusants into exile.

20   Robert W. Scribner **'Luther Myth: A Popular Historiography of the Reformer'**

Source: from *Popular Culture and Popular Movements in Reformation Germany*, R. W. Scribner, Hambledon Press, London, 1987, chapter 14, pp. 301–3, 306–22.

The life and career of Martin Luther must be one of the best known stories of the modern period. Less well known is what we might call the 'popular historiography' of the Reformer – how he was regarded by his contemporaries and by later generations, before our modern biographies came to be written. In order to explain the nature of this 'popular historiography' I want to discuss here certain 'myths' about Luther that can be found in sixteenth-century sources, and in folktales recorded during the nineteenth century. 'Myth' is used here both in a narrow sense to mean an individual narrative, and in a broader sense to designate the genre constituted by a number of similar tales. Let us establish the meaning of the term by concentrating on sixteenth-century examples, beginning with one of the most striking individual narratives. This was first published as a broadsheet in 1617, and is known as the Dream of Frederick the Wise (Fig. 13). It relates a threefold dream experienced by the Elector Frederick the Wise of Saxony on the evening of 30 October, 1517 – the eve of the day on which Luther is said to have posted his Ninety-five Theses in Wittenberg.

Frederick fell asleep in his castle at Schweinitz, pondering how he could assist the holy souls in Purgatory to attain blessedness, and he dreamed that God had sent him a monk of fine and noble features, a natural son of the Apostle Paul. As companions God had given the monk all the dear saints, who assured Frederick that if he would permit the monk to write on his castle church at Wittenberg he would not regret it. Since this request was affirmed by such powerful witnesses, Frederick agreed. The monk now wrote in such great letters that they could be read all the way from Wittenberg to Schweinitz, and the quill with which he wrote stretched all the way to Rome, where it pierced the ear of a lion, and began to topple the papal throne. The scene recurred in a second dream, and now all the Estates of the Holy Roman Empire ran to the pope, who beseeched their protection from this evil. In the third dream, some attempted to break the monk's quill, but could not. When asked whence he had such a quill, the monk replied that it came from a one-hundred-year-old goose. Then the monk's quill

13 The Dream of Elector Frederick the Wise, 1617, woodcut. Photo: Germanisches National Museum, Nürnberg.

produced others, which were taken up by other learned folk, whose quills became as long and as hard as the monk's. On awakening, Frederick sought an interpretation of his dream, but was advised that God alone could interpret its mysteries and it was best left to see what the future might bring.

Characteristic of this tale is its double legitimation, through its alleged historicity and its overtly prophetic nature. In 1617, the year of the first Reformation Jubilee, it was presented to the reader as an historical event with a well-attested provenance. The editor of the broadsheets claimed that the story had been narrated to Frederick's chaplain, Georg Spalatin, who passed it on to Antonius Musa, later Superintendent of Rochlitz, who had written it down. The editor of 1617, identified only by the initials D.K. (but who was probably David Krautvogel, Superintendent of Freiberg in Saxony), claimed to have read this manuscript in 1591, when it was in the possession of the pastor of Rochlitz, Batholomeus Schönbach. All these details, attested by prominent Lutheran churchmen, bear witness to the historical truth of the tale, which is then confirmed by its prophetic character.

This prophetic character is found not simply in the accuracy with which the dream foretells historical events – Frederick pondering on indulgences as Luther is about to attack their basis, Luther's Pauline theology, the posting of the Theses, the shaking of the power of Rome, the inability of secular princes to defend the papacy, and the continuation of Luther's work by other Reformers. It is also found in its allusion to a prophecy said to have been uttered by John Hus at the stake in 1415: that he, a goose, may be burned (in Czech 'husa' means 'goose'), but in a hundred years a swan (Luther) would come, which could not be burned. The broadsheet makes this reference more explicit in the engraving illustrating its text, showing a goose burning on a pyre. Further prophetic confirmation is found in the structure of the narrative: Luther is sent by God, recommended by the saints, and the dream recurs three times, thus attesting its prophetic validity.

All these features make the story easily recognizable as myth: that is, a historical narrative of events embodying some sacred or supernatural quality, intended as a symbolic form of communication, and to do with origins or transformations. It is the end-product of a process of myth-building around Luther's person which began almost as soon as he became a public figure. This process can be traced in the propaganda pamphlets of the early 1520s and in visual depictions of Luther. Its substantial content is best summarized in a 1520 pamphlet which argues that Luther instructs the people by virtue of his office as a monk, a doctor and a preacher. As monk, he exemplifies a pious Christian life; as doctor, he is a pious teacher; as preacher, he proclaims the saving doctrine of the Word of God. This corresponds to three visual images of Luther: Luther as friar with a tonsure, Luther in his doctor's cap, and Luther holding the Bible. Taken together, they present him as a 'holy man', as the 'man of God'. His stature was immeasurably increased beyond this, however, by attributing to him the status of sainthood. [. . .]

To depict Luther as a living saint of Christ-like stature seems paradoxical for a movement which rejected the cult of the saints because it placed mere humans on the same level as God. The contradiction with the Reformer's basic doctrines was so great that it was hardly likely to become an overt constituent element in Luther myth. However, it was always present as an undertone in the view of him as an exemplary Christian, a man of exceptional piety, and a chosen tool of God's purpose in showing the true way to salvation. More acceptable motifs were found in the Old Testament. A 1524 broadsheet shows Luther leading Christian believers out of Egyptian darkness towards the light of the crucified Christ. The scene has certain similarities with Christ's harrowing of Hell, but its overt purpose is to present Luther as a modern Moses, a divinely chosen prophet, teacher and leader who shows the way to God. But even here traditional elements are not eliminated. Luther appears in the role of a mediator, shown in the woodcut by the way in which he shows a kneeling woman the way to the crucified Christ. The printed text is even more explicit, offering thanks to God, 'that you have, O gentle Lord, redeemed us from the gates of Hell, through Martin Luther, with your Word, and opened Heaven to us'. However, it was the Moses comparison that was to be taken up, and it was developed at some length in sermons by Johann Mathesius in 1562, which became in print what was effectively the first Luther biography. He justified the comparison with the tag: 'The deeds are the same, only the persons are different' (*Res sunt eadem, personae mutantur*).

A 1524 pamphlet claimed that the peasants in the inns hailed Luther as a prophet sent by God, and the motif of the prophet was the one most easily reconciled with Reformation belief. The popular propaganda of the 1520s applied many prophetic labels to Luther. He was a Daniel awakened among the people, an Elias or John the Baptist. The last two were especially appropriate as typological models. Elias, who slew the idolatrous priests of Baal, was the prime example of a preaching prophet whose mission was to lead the people to repentance. John the Baptist, himself spoken of as a 'second Elias', attacked the hypocrisy of the Pharisees and showed the way to Christ. In a funeral sermon delivered in Eisleben shortly after Luther's death, Michael Colius praised him as a 'true Elias und John the Baptist for our age', and it thereafter became a commonplace to refer to Luther as the 'third Elias'.

Luther was also set within the framework of apocalyptic prophecy. He was identified with the angel in Apocalypse 14, 8 and 18, 1 who is sent to proclaim the fall of Babylon, to overthrow the whore and to break the cup of abomination from which all the kings and peoples of the earth have drunk. [. . .]

Two other prophecies of the later Middle Ages were applied to Luther. One was published in 1488 by the astrologer Johann Lichtenberger, predicting the birth in 1484 of a 'minor prophet', who would bring wondrous exposition of Scripture, alteration of laws and the introduction of new ceremonies which the people would take as divine doctrine. He would be a monk in a white cowl, followed by another monk, and the devil would perch on his shoulder. Many specific features of this prophecy could be applied to Luther only with great difficulty, although his birthdate in 1483 stood close enough to that of the 'minor prophet'. Luther's Catholic critics did apply it to him, interpreting the devil on his shoulder as proof of his satanic inspiration, and one sixteenth-century reader penned into his copy the names 'Luther' and 'Melanchthon' on the woodcut illustration of the prophet and his attendant monk. In 1527 Luther wrote a preface to a German edition of Lichtenberger's prophecy, denouncing it as ungodly and a fantasy. Perhaps for this reason it had no wider resonance during the course of the sixteenth century, although it did turn up again as late as 1718, as one of several prophecies said to have foretold Luther's divine mission. The second prophecy was published in 1527 by Andreas Osiander, the Nuremberg Reformer. This was a reworking of an Italian pseudo-Joachimite work which Osiander transformed into a pictorial prophecy of Luther's reform, which was depicted as inaugurating the dawn of the last age before the Second Coming of Christ.

The Luther prophecy which most fascinated the sixteenth century, however, was that attributed to Hus, about the burning of the goose and the swan to come which could not be burned. In 1531 Luther applied this prophecy to himself (to do so involved not a little distortion of the historical tradition!), and in 1537 it was popularized in Johann Agricola's *Tragedy of John Hus*. Thereafter it became a firm part of Luther myth, highlighted in every Luther biography. Justus Jonas and Bugenhagen both repeated it in their funeral sermons for Luther, and it featured prominently in Mathesius's influential 1562 sermons. Mathesius mentioned it as one of three authentic prophecies concerning Luther, a choice of some significance, for it was the threefold recurrence of such forecasts which attested their validity. One of the others was the prediction of an old monk to the young Luther that he would not die of an illness which he was suffering at the time, but would survive to become a great man. The third was a prophecy attributed to Johann von Hilten, a Franciscan imprisoned in Eisenach in 1483 for heterodox views. He had prophesied that in 1516 another monk would appear to reform the church.

All these prophecies led contemporaries to the firm conclusion that Luther was without doubt a divinely ordained prophet. As early as 1529 Friedrich Myconius was addressing him as 'a prophet of the Lord to the Germans', a title Luther accepted himself, and by the time of his death his identity as *the* German prophet was firmly established. Thereafter the number of prophecies around Luther mushroomed with alarming speed. These included not just prophecies about Luther, but the Reformer's own prophecies. Indeed, Mathesius saw the ability to prophesy as fundamental evidence of Luther's divine mission. Within six years of Luther's death these prophecies had been collected and published, and five such collections appeared between 1552 and 1559. That published in 1557 by Peter Glaser, a pastor in Dresden, listed 120 prophecies of Luther, and when Glaser reissued the work in 1574, the number had grown to 200. The 1559 collection published by Georg Walther, preacher of Halle in Saxony, was also reissued in 1576, and that same year Johann Lapaeus, pastor of Langenberg near Einbeck, published an extensive list of witnesses to Luther's status as a prophet, including the direct testimony of over a dozen eminent Reformers such as Bugenhagen, Johannes Brenz, Nikolaus von Amsdorf, Urbanus Rhegius, Erasmus Alberus and Andreas Musculus. [. . .]

The Luther myth of the sixteenth century was a complex construct, built from several mythic images of Luther: the German prophet, the man of God, the church father, the evangelist, the Third Elias, the saint and 'Wonder Man', and the worker of miracles. Its individual attributes were borrowed from Christian history – from a stock repertoire of images of church fathers, evangelists, lives of the saints, typological models from the Old and New Testaments, from pious anecdotes and the creations of propaganda and polemics. They added up to create a mythical rather than a historical Luther, establishing a language in which his followers could speak of him and express what he meant to them. This is the tradition which produced such a splendid individual myth as the Dream of Frederick the Wise, and which laid down the bounds within which the history of the Reformation and Luther's role within it were written until the mid-eighteenth century. Luther was set within the framework of salvation history as seen through the eyes of his followers, and this was essentially a prophetic and eschatological framework. It presupposed a world in which the divine will was manifested in divinely ordained events and persons, who could display supernatural power.

For several reasons, however, the Luther myth could never quite rid itself of the image of Luther as saint. The view of him as *Wundermann*, capable of *Wunderzeichen* [miraculous signs], persisted, although it was often explained in merely allegorical terms. It was given fresh life by the Reformation jubilees of 1617 and 1717, and by the religious passions of the Thirty Years' War. Sceptical voices were raised around the beginning of the eighteenth century, Gottfried Arnold complaining in 1699 of a 'subtle idolatry' of Luther, while the Göttingen theologian

Christian August Heumann challenged the Dream of Frederick the Wise as a fable. Nonetheless, belief in Luther's thaumaturgic power [wonder working] remained strong enough for an apprentice in 1708 to cut a splinter from Luther's bed in Eisleben as a relic, while splinters from the Eisleben Luther-house were believed to heal toothache and other ills. Indeed, that was long believed to be miraculously immune to fire and plague – at least until 1689, when it was finally consumed by fire. There were several miraculous Luther images. The most famous was that in Oberrossla, which sweated as a portent of imminent disaster, exactly in the manner of a Catholic miraculous image. All this ensured the persistence of many of the features of the sixteenth century Luther myth well into the nineteenth century, even into the twentieth. Indeed, the nineteenth century even saw three further editions of Luther's prophecies: one in 1829, a new edition of Lapaeus in 1846 (the three-hundredth anniversary of Luther's death), and a third in 1853.

Let me now turn to Luther folktales. Again I would like to begin with a striking example. This tale concerns Castle Singerberg, which lay on a high peak between Ilmenau and Stadtilm in Thuringia. It had once been used by a ne'er-do-well young nobleman, who imprisoned the kinsman who was rightly lord of the castle and used it as a base from which to waylay travellers. One day this nobleman seized a group of monks from Erfurt, among whose number was Dr Martin Luther. Luther was held hostage and the others sent off to fetch a ransom. In the evening Luther was asked to entertain the noble and his boisterous companions. He complied, and sang in Latin a song containing a formula of such secret power that they all fell asleep. Luther released the other captives and led them from the castle. As he left, he sang another of his songs and placed a spell upon it: as high as the castle stands upon the mountain, so deep shall it disappear within it, and no one shall set eye upon it again until the same melody is heard once more upon the peak. Once a shepherd grazing his flocks on the Singerberg chanced to play this melody upon his flute. To his amazement, a castle appeared before him, with all its doors open and all within still and slumbering. He filled his flask with its wine, and left to see to his sheep, whereupon the castle disappeared. Unaware of the role of the melody in materializing the ghost castle, he was unable ever to make it reappear. To this day, the Singerberg stands deserted and empty, the peak regarded as the haunt of evil spirits. [. . .]

The Luther folktales can be divided into six different types. The first is the 'Great Man' tale, reflecting anecdotal interest in the doings of a famous historical figure. Some in this category represent the desire to achieve fame by association, for example through a 'Luther slept here' story, attached to several otherwise insignificant places, such as Castle Krottdorf in Siegerland, where the bed in which he allegedly slept was still on show at the beginning of this century. Others combine this desire for reflected glory with sentimental tales of the foibles of the great, such as those which tell of Luther drinking at an inn and forgetting to pay the bill as he left. Sometimes the tale may merely record that he passed that way on some historic occasion, for example, on his way to the Diet of Worms.[1]

The second type is the aetiological tale, explaining the origins and names of things. There are several 'Luther-springs' and numerous 'Luther-beeches' or 'Luther-lindens', all deriving their name from some alleged connection with the Reformer. The Luther-linden in Mohra in Thuringia, the ancestral home of the Luther family, was so called because Luther preached under the tree in May 1521, since the nearby chapel was too small to hold all those who wished to hear him. The Luther-springs have similar tales explaining their origins, such as that about the Luther spring at Tambach near Gotha. In 1537 Luther was taken ill at Schmalkalden, and since there was fear for his life, he was sent back to Weimar. At Tambach he was too overcome with pain to continue his journey, but took water from a nearby spring and immediately recovered. Thenceforth the spring was called the Luther-spring and regarded as healing water.

Such attempts to supply a mythic tradition for a local landmark (perhaps also to encourage tourism!) sometimes bear traces of a christianization of popular culture. There was an old pagan cultic spring near Jena, which Luther was said to have visited to drink its waters, after which it was called the Luther-spring. Clearly, association with Luther was seen to be more advantageous to its reputation than any dimly remembered pagan origin. A similar case is the Luther-linden at Naschhausen in the Saale valley, under which Luther is said to have preached against the errors of Carlstadt. It stood at the entrance to a pagan 'sacred grove', and so had its special quality preserved by a christianizing aetiology.

The third type is a more specific kind of aetiological tale, explaining the origins of local customs. Nordhausen explained its manner of celebrating St Martin's Day through two Luther folktales. In the first, Luther arrives by chance at the town, having broken a wheel on his wagon. He is taken in by a poor shoemaker's family, who feed him roast goose and cabbage with wine, so that these dishes were henceforth eaten on St Martin's Day. When the townsfolk learned of his presence, they ran out excitedly, rang the church bells and sang his hymn 'A mighty fortress', a practice which then became an annual custom. In the second tale, Luther is invited to dine with the Mayor of Nordhausen on his birthday. Lutherans who recalled the Catholic custom of lighting candles in each window on St Martin's eve decide to do the same in Luther's honour, as a Lutheran event. These tales supply an explanation for the survival of a Catholic custom, the Martin's goose and the Martin's lights, in a Protestant town. They establish a mythic origin for what was in fact a very recent custom, for Luther was never in Nordhausen in November, and St Martin's Day had been celebrated as a Protestant feast only since 1835.

A fourth type of tale presents Luther as an exemplary Christian. He gives alms, prays for sick friends and by his piety and strength of personality converts opponents of the Reformation. As such, he is a man specially favoured by God, who hears his prayers by restoring the sick to health, such as Melanchthon and Myconius. Luther even prays successfully for the relief of drought, beseeching God not to punish the people for their sins in this way. This group of stories, which go back to sixteenth-century sources, include those about Luther as prophet, both the subject of prophecy and himself a prophet.

The fifth type of tale is close to this, showing a Luther who wields supernatural powers himself, especially the ability to bless or curse. In one group of tales Luther speaks a fire-blessing which protects a town from fire. Sometimes the town is reputed as a consequence not to have been visited by fire from that day to this, as in Wertheim in Baden. The number of tales about his ability to curse is slightly larger. In one tale from Orlamünde, where he was given a hostile reception by supporters of Carlstadt in 1524, he cursed the town wells, so that they were forever dry or bitter, and water had to be hauled uphill from the river. Another tale recounts how the citizens of Orlamünde stoned Luther at the instigation of the devil, and in anger he uttered the curse: 'May the stones stick in your godless throats' – for which reason the people of Orlamünde suffer excessively from goitres. In two tales about Rudolstadt he was said to have been so displeased by the bad weather on his arrival that he cursed the town to suffer rain throughout its annual fair (in the second version, the rain curse was occasioned by his dislike of the watery beer!).

The last type of tale features Luther as the worker of miracles and magic, powers not too far removed from his ability to bless or curse. A tale from Altenstein in Saxony tells how he was seized on his return from Worms and carried off by his unknown captors. Terrified, angry and suffering from thirst, he sat down to rest, and in displeasure struck the ground with his staff. Water immediately issued forth, to form yet another 'Luther-spring'. When he became too tired to be led on further by his captors, he refused to budge from the spot, and miraculously the imprints of his feet were left in the stone on which he stood. In some stories such miraculous results involve the use of magic. One tale from the Spreewald in the Mark Brandenburg tells how Luther is fleeing from his pursuers when he comes upon a peasant sowing his crop. Luther tells him to go home for his sickle, and the newly sown oats will be ready for him when he returns. The farmer obeys, and comes back to find the crop ready to harvest. At that point the pursuers arrive, and ask if the peasant has seen their quarry. Truthfully he replies that Luther came that way as he was sowing the crop, so that they give up the chase, thinking Luther has long since escaped. In other stories, Luther uses magical incantations, as in the tales of how he stilled a fire in Possneck in 1525. The tale of the Singerberg is the most striking of the incantation tales, although it bears close resemblance to a traditional fairy tale. The fire-blessings mentioned earlier are also close to incantations, and resemble the kind of incantations circulating in popular books of magic during the nineteenth century.

How should we regard this rather disparate collection of stories? The tales of the magical harvest from the Spreewald and of the Singerberg are so similar to fairy tales that it is tempting to regard them as merely good yarns. They could simply be examples of the *Schwank* or 'merry tale' so popular in German litera-ture. Their entertainment value may be more important than any message they might communicate about Luther. Indeed, the Reformer might be seen in many ways as peripheral in them. The Singerberg is one of a number of 'magic moun-tains' in Thuringia, and there are other tales of a ghost castle inside it, into which someone occasionally finds his way. Its name is said to be derived from the sounds of singing heard to issue from it, suggesting singing as the cause of its enchant-ment. Luther's magical powers may simply derive from his appearance in the story, rather than from any quality intrinsic to his person. It could, perhaps, have been any other figure with local associations and sufficient charismatic appeal to feature in folklore, such as Faust, who had strong links to Thuringia.

We could argue, then, that the folklore figure of Luther has simply been assimilated to typological models of the folktale. This would appear to be the case with the aetiological tales. Those about Luther in Rudolstadt, when he cursed the town to endure bad weather during the summer fair, are simply a folk explanation for the notoriously bad weather in that part of Thuringia. This explanation gains likelihood from the fact that Luther never visited Rudolstadt, and the earliest version of this tale was recorded in 1853, set to an old folk tune, for which it is suspected that a local worthy wrote the words.

The same absorption of the mythic Luther into wider patterns of folklore can be seen in the case of the various 'Luther-springs'. There are numerous German folktales locating the origins of local landmarks in the mythic past, either supplying a plausible historical account for them, or else a metaphysical explanation for their existence. Thus, associating a spring with Luther provides it with a local history of its own. Or its existence may be traced to some non-natural deed of the Reformer, as in the story of Luther producing a spring by striking the ground with his staff. There are tales about the footprints of other 'supernatural' figures, in some cases the footprints of the Devil (and in one case, not his footprints, but the impression of his rump). Here we could speak of a two-way process of assimilation. The mythic Luther has been assimilated into a pre-existing literary tradition; but at the same time a traditional popular form – the aetiological tale – itself becomes the bearer and transmitter of the Luther myth.

Nonetheless, it says too little about such tales to see them merely as a matter of literary form. We can see this through two further examples. The first relates how Luther invented the *Bratwurst*, or German sausage. Luther and St Nicholas stage a contest to prove which is the true belief, Protestantism or Catholicism. Equipped with only a staff, they are to climb the Blocksberg from opposite sides, the winner being the first to reach the top. St Nicholas faints from hunger, but Luther arrives fresh and victorious, with three-quarters of his staff missing; miraculously, this has been transformed into a *Bratwurst*, which he has eaten. This is an excellent 'merry tale', but makes a number of indirect polemical points. St Nicholas was associated with the *Schlachtfest*, a day of merrymaking on which a pig was slaughtered and no doubt sausages eaten. His feast day, on 6 December, competed with that of St Martin on 11 November as an autumnal-winter feast. In the Luther tale, there is a double symbolic replacement: Protestantism displaces Catholicism, and the Protestant saint replaces the Catholic. It was also a Catholic legend that Luther had forgotten to pay for his *Bratwurst* when drinking in an inn, and this tale can also be seen as both a reply to, and a satire upon Catholic slanders of the Great Man as a toper and a glutton.

The polemical purpose is more overt in the second tale. This relates that on Luther's death the story was spread around that his remains had been removed from the coffin by the Devil and carried off to Hell. To refute the slander, the coffin was officially exhumed, and there was indeed no corpse inside. Instead, three white mice leapt out. One ran to the nearest church, where it devoured the host in the monstrance; the second ran to a nearby abbey, where it gnawed off all the locks and bolts, so releasing all the monks and nuns inside; the third ran to Hell, where it put out the fires of Purgatory (delicacy prevents me from saying how this was done). Meanwhile, Luther's body had been taken up into heaven, like Elias, in a fiery chariot. This tale cleverly depicts three of Luther's attacks on Catholic doctrine, against the Mass, monastic vows and Purgatory. It also jokingly refuted a Catholic jibe about the exact whereabouts of Luther's remains, a subject of some concern to Lutherans, who agonized about it in both the eighteenth and nineteenth centuries.

Could we suggest, then, that the Luther folktales fulfil a historical and polemical purpose? They provide historical legitimation for important Protestant events, and they serve a propagandist function in the ongoing confessional antagonism with Catholicism. G. S. Kirk has suggested that myths fulfil three functions: they are *operative, iterative* and *validatory*. By this he means that they tend to be repeated regularly on ritual and ceremonial occasions (*operative*); that they confirm and maintain memory (*iterative*); and that they provide authority for customs and institutions (*validatory*). We can certainly discern all three both in Luther folktales and in the Luther myth of the sixteenth century. The upsurge of hagiography which followed Luther's death, an essential stage in the creation of the sixteenth-century myth, recalled and reaffirmed the purpose of the religious schism at a time when it had not only lost its leader, but seemed to have achieved little in the way of lasting reform.

The Dream of Frederick the Wise probably arose as a consequence of internal disputes within Lutheranism, when the normative value of Luther's theology was being called into question. It was an iterative attempt to confirm and maintain the memory of the Reformer's allegedly divine mission. The use of the Luther myths on Reformation anniversaries such as that in 1617 both confirmed and maintained memory, and validated the confession.

The folktales can be seen to follow the same pattern. They fulfilled a validatory function for Nordhausen's newly-minted nineteenth-century Protestant celebrations of St Martin's Day. It speaks for itself that the first collection of Luther folktales was published in 1917. This view gains further support if we consider the *polemical* aspect of the folktales. Wolfgang Brückner compares the corpus of nineteenth-century Luther folklore to the traditional genre of the saint's life, and Gruppe's catalogue is laid out along these lines: the personal history of the saint, his temptations and dangers endured, his struggles with the Devil, his power of intercessory prayer, his prophecies, blessings and curses, his miracles and his relics. Thus, Luther folktales can be seen as a mirror image of Catholic attempts to denigrate Luther. Where Catholics attempted – as they did until well into our own century – to present him as wicked, evil and an agent of the Devil, Protestant propaganda presented him as divinely favoured and as the ideal Christian. In the same way, there emerged various 'Reformation folktales', found alongside those about Luther. These Protestant tales are mirror images of Catholic tales

asserting supernatural proofs for the validity of Catholic belief. They tell of supernatural intervention on behalf of the Lutheran faith, which withstands the attacks
and trials of Satan, and which is confirmed by stories of ghosts, spirits and
miracles. We should especially call attention to the *expressive* nature of such tales,
which could be seen pre-eminently as manifestations of Lutheran piety. It is piety
which provides an explanation for the popularity of miraculous Luther-images
during the seventeenth and eighteenth centuries, and for the continuing use of
Luther images in German churches right up to the 1970s.

Let me come to my last point. How far did the Luther myths of the sixteenth
to nineteenth centuries represent a genuinely popular tradition? They could be
seen as similar to the Christian legends of the Middle Ages. It was pointed out
quite some time ago that such legends bear witness to a continual desire for
believers to see an exemplary model of the ideal relationship between God and
ordinary Christians. This ideal relationship is expressed through the person of
some 'bearer of salvation' who achieved this union to an exceptional degree. Thus,
legends such as the lives of the saints portray not the life-histories of actual individuals, but a popular Christian ideal, raised to an appropriately supernatural
level. According to this view, myths, legends, folktales provide ideal models for
imitation, created by the people themselves. Such an argument is difficult to
prove or disprove with any degree of certainty. But wherever I have been able to
trace the provenance and historical development of the nineteenth-century
Luther myths, and especially their roots in earlier ages, I have encountered not
the idealizing activity of a Protestant populace, but the hand of a pious Lutheran
pastor, who recorded and transmitted the folktales, and in some cases may even
have created them a priori. The Luther myth was popular in the sense that it was
intended for popular consumption, and perhaps its very survival is evidence of
some kind of minimal popular reception. But I suspect that the Luther folktales,
and the Luther myth in general, represent not popular culture, but an attempt
to 'Lutheranize' popular culture, another example of the process Peter Burke calls
the 'Reformation of popular culture'. [Text 5]

This opens up a good deal of questions we cannot embark upon here, for it
would lead a good deal further than Luther myths. It is better to conclude with
another folktale which provides a salutory warning about clever attempts at interpretation. In the early nineteenth century a teacher in the Luther-School in
Eisleben decided to drop Luther's *Small Catechism* from the curriculum as no
longer suited to modern needs. As he entered the classroom with the replacement text, the book was violently knocked from his hand, and he received a stun-
ning cuff on the ear. As he tried to clear his ringing head, he saw in the doorway
the lifesize figure of Luther, wagging an admonitory finger. If your head buzzes
when you finish reading this, please attribute it to him and not to me.

NOTE

1   The Diet of Worms in 1521 was a meeting of the Diet of the Holy Roman Empire.
     Luther attended and defended his views and works on grounds of conscience and
     scripture.

21 Henry Kamen 'Excluding the Reformation'

Source: from *The Spanish Inquisition: an historical revision*, Henry Kamen,
Weidenfeld and Nicolson, London, 1997, Chapter 5, pp. 83–101.

We live in such difficult times that it is dangerous either to speak or be silent.

Juan Luis Vives to Erasmus, 1534

In the early dawn of the European Reformation many intellectuals in Spain were foremost in their support for change. At the 1520 Diet of Worms, when Luther had to defend himself publicly, 'everybody, especially the Spaniards, went to see him', admitted the humanist Juan de Vergara. 'At the beginning everybody agreed with him', Vergara went on, 'and even those who now write against him confess that at the beginning they were in favour of him.'

Spaniards of that generation were excited at the new horizons opened up by Renaissance scholarship. Scholars who went to Italy, such as Antonio de Nebrija who returned from there to take up a chair at Salamanca in 1505, were in the vanguard of the drive to promote learning. From Italy Peter Martyr of Anghiera came in 1488 to educate the young nobles of Spain, preceded four years before by Lucio Marineo Siculo, who joined the ranks of the professors at Salamanca. A key figure in the advancement of learning was Cisneros, archbishop of Toledo from 1495 and Inquisitor General from 1507. He founded the university of Alcalá, which became the centre of humanist studies in Spain. Its first chancellor, Pedro de Lerma, had studied at Paris. Nebrija was, as Erasmus wrote to the Valencian humanist Luis Vives in 1521, its 'principal ornament'. Among its professors were the converso [convert] brothers Juan and Francisco de Vergara. The latter was described by Lucio Marineo Siculo as the greatest classical scholar in Spain. One of the key tasks that Cisncros set the professors of the university was the pro-duction of a critical edition of the Bible which would remain a classic of con-temporary scholarship. The great Polyglot Bible that resulted from this enterprise consisted of six volumes, with the Hebrew, Chaldean and Greek originals of the Bible printed in columns parallel to the Latin Vulgate. The Complutensian (from Compluto, the Latin name for Alcalá) Polyglot was finally published in 1522.

The accession of Charles I of Spain to the Imperial title (as Charles V of Germany) in 1519 also generated enthusiasm among scholars in the peninsula. It seemed as though Spain was about to participate in a great European enterprise. From Charles's own homeland, the Netherlands, the influence of Erasmus began to penetrate the open frontiers of Spain. In 1516 the name of Erasmus was first traced by a Spanish pen, and in 1517 Cisneros unsuccessfully invited him to come to Spain. By 1524 a number of intellectuals in the peninsula had rallied to the doctrines of Erasmus, to whom Vives wrote in June 1524, 'our Spaniards are also interesting themselves in your works'. The wit and satire directed by Erasmus against ecclesiastical abuses, and particularly against lax standards in the mendi-cant orders, found a ready hearing in a country where the highest Church offi-cials had themselves led the movement in favour of reform. The presence of prominent intellectuals and literary men in the entourage of Charles V ensured protection for the new ideas at court. Finally, the two principal prelates in the

Church – the archbishop of Toledo, Alonso de Fonseca, successor to Cisneros, and Alonso Manrique, the Inquisitor General – were enthusiastic Erasmians. The success of Erasmus was confirmed with the translation of his *Enchiridion* [*Handbook of the Christian Soldier*] undertaken in 1524 by Alonso Fernández, archdeacon of Alcor. Published towards the end of 1526, it was greeted by widespread enthusiasm. The translator wrote to Erasmus in 1527:

> At the emperor's court, in the cities, in the churches, in the convents, even in the inns and on the highways, everyone has the *Enchiridion* of Erasmus in Spanish. Till then it had been read in Latin by a minority of Latinists, and even these did not fully understand it. Now it is read in Spanish by people of every sort, and those who had formerly never heard of Erasmus have learned of his existence through this single book.

The publisher of the *Enchiridion*, Miguel de Eguía, was printer to the university of Alcalá and brought out about a hundred books of humanist orientation. Erasmus, by far the best seller, was informed in 1526 that 'though the printers have produced many thousands of copies, they cannot satisfy the multitude of buyers'. There were many personal contacts between friends of the humanist who came to Spain and Spaniards who went north to see him. Among the latter the most significant was young Juan de Vergara, who left the peninsula with the emperor in 1520 and spent two years with Erasmus in the Netherlands. On his return, starry-eyed, he wrote to Vives: 'The admiration felt for Erasmus by all Spaniards is astonishing.' This was not quite true. Many Spanish scholars were critical of the northerner's methods of exegesis. Others were uneasy at similarities between Erasmus and Luther. Some of the mendicant orders in particular were smarting under the satirical attacks of Erasmus, and pressed for a debate on his 'heresies'. A conference presided over by Manrique, and including some thirty voting representatives of the orders, eventually met at Valladolid in the summer of 1527. The deliberations were inconclusive, with half the representatives coming out in favour of the Dutchman. The failure of the attack appeared as a victory for the humanists. On 13 December Charles V himself wrote to Erasmus, asking him not to worry over controversy in Spain:

> as though, so long as we are here, one could make a decision contrary to Erasmus, whose Christian piety is well known to us . . . Take courage and be assured that we shall always hold your honour and repute in the greatest esteem.

The triumphs of Spanish humanism were, inevitably, exaggerated by contemporaries. No more than a fraction of the elite (notable among them the grandee Mendoza family) were active patrons of the arts, and only a small number of clergy and scholars were devoted to classical studies. Few lasting advances were made in education or literacy, and the popular tradition in literature [. . .] was still predominant. The learned aspects of humanism always took second place to the influence of scholastic theology. The new learning and Erasmianism were largely phenomena of the emperor's court. Beyond its confines, even among the nobles and elite, Latin was virtually a dead tongue, studied but never spoken.

The Florentine ambassador Guicciardini in 1512 made an observation that other foreigners were to echo throughout the century. The Spaniards, he said, 'are not interested in letters, and one finds very little knowledge either among the nobility or in other classes, and few people know Latin'. Regular contact with the Netherlands and Italy had by the early 1500s introduced some literate Spaniards to the art and spirituality of the North and the literature of the Renaissance. The impact was significant but small. The study of Greek never caught on. When some years later in 1561 Cardinal Mendoza y Bobadilla of Burgos was asked to suggest scholars with knowledge of Greek who might suitably represent Spain at the Council of Trent, he could name only four people in the whole country.

The opening of intellectual horizons in Spain was soon threatened from within by the growth of illuminism and the discovery of Protestants, and from without by the limitations imposed throughout Europe on free thought by political events.

The spiritual and devotional movements in Castile in the late fifteenth century were warmly patronized by Cisneros, and produced a literature of which the most outstanding example was the *Spiritual ABC* (1527) of the Franciscan friar Francisco de Osuna. Adepts of the Franciscan school believed in a mystical method known as *recogimiento*, the 'gathering up' of the soul to God. Those who practised it were *recogidos*. Out of this mystical school there grew up a version (condemned by the general chapter of the Franciscans in 1524) emphasizing the passive union of the soul with God. The method was known as *dejamiento* (abandonment), and adepts were called *dejados* or *alumbrados* (illuminists). Mystical movements and the search for a purer interior religion were common coin in Europe at this time. In Spain there was powerful patronage of mystics by the great nobility. One alumbrado group was patronized by the Mendoza Duke of Infantado in his palace at Guadalajara. It consisted of the *beata* [saintly or devout woman] Isabel de la Cruz, Pedro Ruiz de Alcaraz, and María de Cazalla and her Franciscan brother Juan, auxiliary bishop of Ávila. Alcaraz was also connected with another group at Escalona, patronized by the Marquis of Villena. Meanwhile a parallel group of mystics emerged in Valladolid. The chief influence here was the beata Francisca Hernández, whose fame as a holy woman attracted into her circle Bernardino Tovar, a brother of Juan de Vergara, and the Franciscan preacher Francisco Ortiz.

In 1519 Isabel de la Cruz was denounced to the Inquisition by a servant-girl of the Mendozas. There had been fusses before about other beatas – the beata of Piedrahita (1512) was a famous example – and little may have come of this denunciation. But investigations happened to coincide with alarm over Lutheranism in Germany. The inquisitors quickly realized that elements of heresy were involved. One by one, in a slow and patient enquiry that stretched over several years, the illuminist leaders were detained on the orders of Inquisitor General Manrique. Isabel and Alcaraz were arrested in April 1524. On 23 September 1525 Manrique issued an 'edict on the alumbrados', a list of forty-eight propositions which gives a valuable summary of their doctrine and leaves little doubt that their beliefs were indeed heretical. Isabel and Alcaraz were sentenced to appear in an auto de fe [a public act to confirm the faith] at Toledo on 22 July 1529. The attention of the inquisitors now shifted to Valladolid, where Francisca Hernández had gathered around her a group of adepts who practised recogimiento in opposition to the method of the Guadalajara mystics. Her most devoted admirer was the well-known preacher Francisco Ortiz, and she lived for a while with the rich Cazalla family, relatives of María de Cazalla. Her fame spread: great lords and clergy visited her, and Erasmians such as Eguía and Tovar frequented the house. Her imperious character brooked no rivalry, however, and she quarrelled first with the Cazallas, then with the Erasmians. When she was arrested by the Inquisition in March 1529, the indignant Francisco Ortiz went into his pulpit and denounced the Inquisition for its 'public and open' sin in detaining her, but was himself immediately arrested and sentenced to reclusion in a monastery.

In August 1529 Manrique fell into disfavour and was confined to his see of Seville. At the same time the protecting hand of the emperor was withdrawn: Charles left in July for Italy and took with him some of the most influential Erasmians. This made it possible for the traditionalists, who had been biding their time after the defeat at Valladolid, to take the offensive.

One of the first prosecutions for Erasmian ideas was that of Diego de Uceda, chamberlain to a high official in the Order of Calatrava [a military religious order]. A deeply religious Catholic, Uceda was also an Erasmian who shared the Dutchman's scepticism about superstitions and miracles. Journeying in February 1528 from Burgos to his native city of Córdoba, he fell in with a travelling companion to whom he talked too earnestly and freely about religion, particularly about Luther. He was denounced to the Inquisition by his companion, arrested, tortured, and sentenced despite all the evidence that he was blameless in his religious beliefs and practices. He finally abjured his 'errors' at the Toledo auto de fe of 22 July 1529.

The mingling of mystical, Erasmian and heretical influences made the late 1520s a unique period of both freedom and tension. The inquisitors sought Lutheran ideas everywhere, and located them in the views of some of the alumbrados. More significant for them, perhaps, was the fact that nearly every person implicated in the groups of these years was a converso [convert from Judaism or Islam]: Isabel, Alcaraz, Hernández, Ortiz, Tovar, the Cazallas. It was as though conversos were seeking to reject formal Catholicism by interiorizing their religion. The tendency had a long history among them. Completely at home neither in Judaism nor in Christianity, many of them at all social levels had demonstrated signs of scepticism, unease and Nicodemism [an ascetic life of contemplative prayer]. As far back as the reign of King Juan II of Castile (d. 1454), there had been the reputed case of the converso Alfonso Fernández Samuel, who in his will had requested that when laid out in his coffin, he should have the cross placed at his feet, the Koran at his breast, and the Torah, 'his life and light', at his head. In the early years of the Inquisition, considerable evidence came to light not simply of judaizing but also of messianism on one hand and irreligious scepticism on the other. Many conversos, indeed, were ironically condemned for beliefs that orthodox Judaism would have regarded as heretical, such as denying the immortality of the soul. Spiritual dissent among the conversos did not, therefore, necessarily imply any drift towards Judaism. There was nothing remotely Jewish about the beliefs of the alumbrados: the root influence was Franciscan spirituality, the environment was the comfortable patronage afforded by Old Christian nobility.

From the moment she was detained, Hernández attempted to save her skin by incriminating all those against whom she bore a grudge. Tovar had persisted in following her despite the warnings of Vergara. It was no doubt knowledge of Juan de Vergara's hostility that moved Hernández, at her trial in 1530, to denounce him as a Lutheran, a claim that was supported by other disciples of hers. Tovar was already in prison. He was followed there by his brother in June 1530. Finally in April 1532 María de Cazalla was imprisoned and tortured and accused of the various heresies of Lutheranism, illuminism and Erasmianism. Her trial dragged on until December 1534, when she was fined and ordered not to associate again with illuminists. Her brother the bishop had opportunely died in 1530. The Inquisition had not yet finished with their family, however, for from them sprang the circle of Protestants that alarmed Valladolid two decades later. Although the circle had closed round the mystics, they emerged comparatively unscathed. Hernández was by 1532 living in freedom in Medina del Campo; Isabel and Alcaraz, condemned to 'perpetual' prison, were released after a few years; María de Cazalla was fined and had to express her repentance.

The attack on the alumbrados, though of short duration and with few serious casualties, had consequences of lasting importance. This can be seen clearly in the case of the famous preacher Juan de Avila. Active in the mission field in Andalusia in the late 1520s, Avila was denounced as an alumbrado and spent nearly a year (1532–3) in the cells of the Inquisition. He used his idle hours to think out the shape of a book of spiritual guidance, the *Audi, Filia* [listen, O daughter], which was not in fact presented for publication until 1556. An innocent victim of the alumbrado scare in the 1530s (Avila was a converso), in the 1550s he fell foul not only of the Protestant scare but also of an Inquisitor General, Valdés, who was suspicious of all mystical writings ('works of contemplation for artisans' wives' was how he saw them, according to Luis de Granada). Valdés banned the book in his 1559 Index, and Avila in despair burnt a large number of his manuscripts. Though the *Audi, Filia* circulated in manuscript for several years, it was not until after its author's death in 1569 that the Inquisition allowed it to be published again, at Toledo in 1574. A whole generation of spirituality – we shall come across the case of Luis de Granada – fell under suspicion because of the supposed danger from illuminism.

The most direct threat, however, seemed to come from Lutheranism. An Old Christian, the Basque priest Juan López de Celaín, who had links with the alumbrados of Guadalajara, was arrested in 1528 and burnt as a 'Lutheran' in Granada in July 1530. Lutheranism was also one of the allegations made against Juan de Vergara. Secretary to Cisneros and later to his successor as archbishop of Toledo, Alonso de Fonseca, Vergara was one of the foremost classical scholars in Spain. He had collaborated in the Polyglot Bible, had held the chair of philosophy at Alcalá, and had proposed offering the chair of rhetoric there to Vives. Arrested in 1530, tried and imprisoned, Vergara was obliged to abjure his errors in an auto at Toledo on 21 December 1535, and to pay a heavy fine of 1,500 ducats. After this he was confined to a monastery, from which he emerged in 1537. Like others who completed their allotted penance, he was able to resume his old position in society. We encounter him once more in 1547 at the centre of the great controversy in Toledo over the proposed statutes to exclude conversos from office in the cathedral [laws to exclude those of 'unclean' blood]. He died, still honoured, in Alcalá in May 1566.

Alonso de Virués, a Benedictine and preacher to Charles V, was the first of several eminent preachers to the emperor to be accused of heresy, presumably because of contacts that he, like Vergara, had made abroad, Arrested in 1533 and confined in prison by the Inquisition of Seville for four long years, he pleaded in vain that Erasmus had never been condemned as unorthodox. Finally in 1537 he was made to abjure his errors, condemned to confinement in a monastery for two years, and banned from preaching for another year. Charles V made strenuous efforts to save Virués, and in May 1538 obtained from the pope a bull annulling the sentence. Virués was restored to favour and appointed in 1542 as bishop of the Canary Islands, where he died in 1545.

Another outstanding case, sometimes connected with the origins of Protestantism in Spain, was Juan de Valdés, also of the university of Alcalá, who in the fateful year 1529 published his theological study *Dialogue of Christian Doctrine*, which was closely based on some of Luther's early writings. It was immediately attacked by the Inquisition despite the testimony of Vergara and others. The controversy over the book took so dangerous a turn that in 1530 Valdés fled to Italy, just in time to avoid the trial that was opened against him. His treatise was thereafter distinguished by its appearance in every Index of prohibited books issued by the Inquisition. In 1533 Mateo Pascual, former rector of the Colegio Mayor of San Ildefonso at Alcalá University, and at the time vicar general of the see of Saragossa, fell under suspicion for his links with Juan de Valdés. He was detained for a while in the Inquisition of Toledo, then released to return to Saragossa. Some years later he left Aragon and went to live in Rome, where he died in 1553.

A further casualty of the alumbrado trials was the printer to Alcalá University, Miguel de Eguía, denounced by Francisca Hernández for Lutheranism. He was imprisoned in 1531 and spent over two years in the cells of the Inquisition at Valladolid, but was released at the end of 1533 and was fully absolved. Less fortunate was Pedro de Lerma. Former chancellor of Alcalá University, former dean of the theological faculty at the Sorbonne, canon of Burgos cathedral, he fell under the influence of Erasmus and publicized it in his sermons. He was denounced to the Inquisition, imprisoned, and finally in 1537 was made to abjure publicly, in the towns where he preached, eleven propositions he was accused of having taught. In shame and resentment the old man shook the dust of Spain off his feet and fled to Paris where he resumed his position as a dean of the faculty, dying there in August 1541. According to his nephew Francisco de Enzinas (famous in the history of European Protestantism as Dryander), people in Lerma's home city of Burgos were so afraid of the possible consequences of this event that those who had sent their sons to study abroad recalled them at once. Such a reaction shows an awareness among some Spaniards of the problems involved. Erasmianism and the new humanism were being identified with the German heresy, and for many the only protection was dissociation.

In December 1533 Rodrigo Manrique, son of the Inquisitor General, wrote from Paris to Juan Luis Vives, on the subject of Vergara's imprisonment:

> You are right. Our country is a land of pride and envy; you may add: of bar-barism. For now it is clear that down there one cannot possess any culture without being suspected of heresy, error and Judaism. Thus silence has been imposed on the learned. As for those who take refuge in erudition, they have been filled, as you say, with great terror . . . At Alcalá they are trying to uproot the study of Greek completely.

Erasmus's links with his friends in Spain were affected by the reaction. His last surviving letter to that country is dated December 1533. Three years later he died, still highly respected in the Catholic world, so much so that in 1535 the pope had offered him a cardinal's hat. In Spain his cause (as we shall see) survived, but was restricted to a few learned circles. His works remained on sale to the Spanish public for much of the century. But the tide now turned against him.

The decline of interest in Erasmianism, and the suspicions directed against liberal humanism, seemed to be justified by the apparent links between Erasmus and the growing Protestant menace. In our time, Bataillon has shown how the Protestant stream which sprang from illuminism between 1535 and 1555 adapted Erasmianism to its own purposes and moved towards the Lutheran doctrine of 'justification by faith alone' without ever formally rejecting Catholic dogma. Many leading humanists, such as Juan de Valdés, were Erasmians whose defec-tions from orthodoxy were so significant as to give cause for the belief that they were crypto-Protestants. Vigilance against radical Erasmianism was therefore strengthened.

The Lutheran threat, however, took a long time to develop. In 1520 Luther had probably not been heard of in Spain. Lutheran books were first sent to the penin-sula, with what result we do not know, by Luther's publisher Froben in 1519. The first Spaniards to come into contact with his teachings were those who accom-panied the emperor to Germany. Some of them, seeing in him only a reformer, were favourable to his ideas.

However, a full generation went by and Lutheranism failed to take root in Spain. There was, in those years, no atmosphere of restriction or repression. Before 1558 possibly less than fifty cases of alleged Lutheranism among Spaniards came to the notice of the inquisitors. In most of them, it is difficult to identify specifically Protestant beliefs.

There was some curiosity about the heresies that Luther was propounding, but little sign of any active interest. What explanation can we offer for this aston-ishing inability of Protestant ideas to penetrate the peninsula? With its unre-formed Church, backward clergy and mediaeval religion, Spain was surely ripe for conquest by the Reformation. In one major respect, however, the country was peculiarly unfertile ground. Unlike England, France and Germany, Spain had not since the early Middle Ages experienced a single significant popular heresy. All its ideological struggles since the Reconquest [of Muslim Spain] had been directed against the minority religions, Judaism and Islam. There were consequently no native heresies (like Wycliffism in England) on which the German ideas could build. Moreover, Spain was the only European country to possess a national institution dedicated to the elimination of heresy. By its vigilance and by coordinating its efforts throughout the peninsula, the Inquisition may have checked the seeds of heresy before they could be sown. In the 1540s, possibly the only Spanish intellectuals to come directly into contact with Lutheranism were those in foreign universities (at Louvain, for example, where Philip II was shocked by the views of some of the Spaniards in 1558; or in France, where Miguel Servet was educated); those accompanying the emperor's court in Germany; and those who, with the opening of the Council of Trent (1546), were obliged to read Lutheran books in order to combat the errors in them. Among the labouring classes, Spaniards occasionally came into touch with immigrant workers from France or the Netherlands who had direct experience of the new beliefs. Ideas transmitted at this level, however, were confused, distorted, and unlikely to strike root anywhere.

The area most vulnerable to the penetration of foreign ideas was Seville, centre of international commerce. In 1552 the Inquisition there seized some four hundred and fifty Bibles printed abroad. As archbishop of Seville, Manrique had encouraged the appointment of scholars from Alcalá to be canons and preachers in the cathedral. But times were changing, both in Spain as a whole and in Seville. In 1546 the city obtained a new archbishop who was also made Inquisitor General, Fernando de Valdés, a ruthless careerist who saw heresy everywhere. One of the cathedral preachers, Juan Gil, commonly known as Egidio, was nominated by Charles V in 1549 as bishop of Tortosa. The appointment was quashed when Egidio was accused of heresy and in 1552 made to retract ten propositions. 'In truth', commented a member of the disciplinary committee, Domingo de Soto, 'apart from this lapse he is a very good man, and his election [as bishop] was a good decision'. Egidio died in peace at the end of 1555. In 1556 Valdés objected to the appointment as cathedral preacher of Constantino Ponce de la Fuente, an Alcalá humanist and converso who had been chaplain to Charles V in Germany. His writings were examined for heresy; arrested by the Inquisition, he died in its cells two years later. Neither Egidio nor Constantino can be considered Lutherans. They were humanists who believed in a strongly spiritual religious life and none of their views appears to have been explicitly heretical.

There were, certainly, Protestant sympathizers in Seville. International trade links brought together in the city a broad range of people and opinions that could not fail to influence some Spaniards. Heretical books were imported in quantity. The Spanish 'Protestants' in Seville probably totalled around one hundred and twenty persons, including the prior and members of the Jeronimite monastery of San Isidro, together with several nuns from the Jeronimite convent of Santa Paula. The group managed to exist in security until the 1550s, when some monks from San Isidro opportunely fled. The exiles included Cipriano de Valera,

Casiodoro de Reina, Juan Pérez de Pineda and Antonio del Corro, who played little part in Spanish history but were glories of the European Reformation.

Meanwhile, in northern Castile, another circle of Protestant sympathizers had come into existence. The founder was an Italian, Carlos de Seso, who had turned to Protestantism after reading Juan de Valdés, and who from 1554 had been corregidor (civil governor) of Toro. His missionary zeal soon converted an influential and distinguished circle centred on Valladolid and numbering some fifty-five persons, most of noble status and some with converso origins. The most eminent of the converts was Dr Agustín Cazalla, who had been to Germany as chaplain to Charles V and had also accompanied Prince Philip there. Cazalla was influenced by his brother Pedro – parish priest of Pedrosa, near Valladolid – and with him the whole Cazalla family, led by their mother Leonor de Vivero, fell into heresy. Their beliefs were no simple extension of the illuminist or Erasmian attitudes of the previous generation. In their clear rejection of most Catholic dogma the Valladolid heretics were true Protestants. They also included scions of impeccably Old Christian nobility. A leading member of the group, Fray Domingo de Rojas, son of the Marquis of Poza, recruited young Anna Enríquez, daughter of the Marquesa of Alcanices. He told her 'that there were only two sacraments, baptism and communion; that in communion Christ did not have the part attributed to him; and that the worst of all things was to say mass, since Christ had already been sacrificed once and for all'.

The Seville group was exposed in 1557, when Juan Ponce de León, eldest son of the Count of Bailén, was arrested together with others for introducing books from Geneva. His chief accomplice was Julián Hernández, who had spent a considerable time in the Reformed churches of Paris, Scotland and Frankfurt, and who specialized in smuggling Protestant literature into his native country. The Inquisition collected information and in 1558 made a wave of arrests, including the whole Cazalla family in April and Constantino in August. A merciless repression was set in train by Fernando de Valdés, who was concerned to exaggerate the menace in order to regain the favour he had recently lost with the court in Spain.

Commenting on the high social origins of many of the accused, Valdés told Charles V that 'much greater harm can follow if one treats them with the leniency that the Holy Office has shown towards Jewish and Muslim conversos, who generally have been of lowly origin'. The emperor did not need to be alerted. The sudden emergence in Spain's two principal cities of a contagion from which everyone felt the country had been free, sent shock waves through the nation. Charles, in retirement at his villa beside the monastery of Yuste in Extremadura, saw to his horror the rise within Spain of the very menace that had split Germany apart. For him there could be only one response: ruthless repression. His historic letter of 25 May 1558 to his daughter Juana, regent in Spain during Philip II's absence in the Netherlands, appealed to her to follow the tough policy that he himself had used against heresy in Flanders.

I am very satisfied with what you say you have written to the king, informing him of what is happening about the people imprisoned as Lutherans, more of whom are being daily discovered. But believe me, my daughter, this business has caused and still causes me more anxiety and pain than I can express, for while the king and I were abroad these realms remained in perfect peace, free from this calamity. But now that I have returned here to rest and recuperate and serve Our Lord, this great outrage and treachery, implicating such notable persons, occurs in my presence and in yours. You know that because of this I suffered and went through great trials and expenses in Germany, and lost so much of my good health. Were it not for the conviction I have that you and the members of your councils will find a radical cure to this unfortunate situation, punishing the guilty thoroughly to prevent them spreading, I do not know whether I could restrain myself [from] leaving here to settle the matter. Since this affair is more important for the service of Our Lord and the good and preservation of these realms than any other, and since it is only in its beginnings, with such small forces that they can be easily put down, it is necessary to place the greatest stress and weight on a quick remedy and exemplary punishment. I do not know whether it will be enough in these cases to follow the usual practice, by which according to common law all those who beg for mercy and have their confession accepted are pardoned with a light penance if it is a first offence. Such people, if set free, are at liberty to commit the same offence, particularly if they are educated persons.

One can imagine the evil consequences, for it is clear that they cannot act without armed organization and leaders, and so it must be seen whether they can be proceeded against as creators of sedition, upheaval, riots and disturbance in the state. They would then be guilty of rebellion and could not expect any mercy. In this connection I cannot omit to mention what was and is the custom in Flanders. I wanted to introduce an Inquisition to punish the heresies that some people had caught from neighbouring Germany and England and even France. Everyone opposed this on the grounds that there were no Jews among them. Finally an order was issued declaring that all people of whatever state and condition who came under certain specified categories were to be *ipso facto* burnt and their goods confiscated. Necessity obliged me to act in this way. I do not know what the king my son has done since then, but I think that the same reason will have made him continue as I did, because I advised and begged him to be very severe in dealing with these people.

Believe me, my daughter, if so great an evil is not suppressed and remedied without distinction of persons from the very beginning, I cannot promise that the king or anyone else will be in a position to do it afterwards.

This letter really marks the turning point in Spain. From now on, thanks to the fears of Charles and the policy laid down for Inquisitor General Valdés, heterodoxy was treated as a threat to the state and the religious establishment. Writing to the pope on 9 September the same year, Valdés affirmed that 'these errors and heresies of Luther and his brood which have begun to be preached and sown in Spain, threaten sedition and riot'.

Sedition and riot, armed organization and leaders – how far from the dreams of Cazalla and Constantino! Yet once again well-meaning men were prey to the tensions gripping Europe, and the result was a series of autos de fe that burnt out Protestantism in Spain. The first significant auto was held at Valladolid on Trinity Sunday, 21 May 1559, in the presence of the regent Juana and her court. Of the thirty accused, fourteen were burnt, including Cazalla and his brother and sister. The only one to die unrepentant was Francisco Herrero, from Toro. All the rest died repentant after professing conversion, among them Agustín Cazalla, who blessed the Holy Office and wept aloud for his sins. The next auto at Valladolid was held on 8 October in the presence of Philip, who had now returned to Spain and for whom an impressive ceremony was mounted. Of the thirty accused, twenty-six were considered Protestants, and of these, twelve (including four nuns) were burnt at the stake. Carlos de Seso was the showpiece. The inquisitors had for days attempted to make him recant and, in fear for his life, he had shown every sign of repentance. But when at last he realized that he was to be executed regardless, he made a full and moving statement of belief: 'in Jesus Christ alone do I hope, him alone I trust and adore, and placing my unworthy hand in his sacred side I go through the virtue of his blood to enjoy the promises that he has made to his chosen'. He and one other accused were burnt alive as impenitents. 'How could you allow this to happen?', he is said to have called out to the king during the auto. 'If my own son were as wicked as you', Philip is said to have replied indignantly, 'I myself would carry the wood with which to burn him!' The exchange, not documented in any reliable source, was probably apocryphal.

It was now the turn of Seville, where sympathy for Constantino and hostility to the actions of the Inquisition were widespread. A Jesuit reported in 1559 of the former that 'he was and still is highly esteemed', and that 'there are a great many of these murmurings [against the Inquisition]'. The first great auto there was held on Sunday, 24 September 1559. Of the seventy-six accused present, nineteen were burnt as Lutherans, one of them in effigy only. This was followed by the atuo held on Sunday, 22 December 1560. Of the total of fifty-four accused on this occasion, fourteen were burnt in person and three in effigy; in all, forty of the accused were Protestants. Egidio and Constantino were two of those burnt in effigy, while those actually burnt included two English sailors, William Brook and Nicholas Burton, and a native of Seville, Leonor Gómez, together with her three young daughters. This auto de fe was followed by one two years later, on 26 April 1562, and by another on 28 October. The whole of that year saw eighty-eight cases of Protestantism punished; of these, eighteen were burnt in person, among them the prior of San Isidro and four of his priests.

With these burnings native Protestantism was almost totally extinguished in Spain. For contemporaries in 1559, it was the start to an emergency without precedent in Spanish history. That very August the primate of the Spanish Church, Archbishop Carranza of Toledo, was arrested by the Inquisition on charges arising in part out of allegations made by Cazalla and Seso. Threatened, as it seemed, by the incursions of heresy, the inquisitors stretched their resources to check the contagion wherever it might appear. In Toledo in September 1559 placards were found posted up on houses and in the cathedral itself, attacking the Catholic Church as 'not the Church of Jesus Christ but the Church of the devil and of

Antichrist his son, the Antichrist pope'. The culprit, apprehended in 1560 and burnt, was a priest, Sebastian Martínez. At the same time, in Seville pamphlets circulated attacking 'these thieves of inquisitors, who rob publicly and who burnt the bones of Egidio and of Constantino out of jealousy'. The leaflets also asked the public to 'pray to God for his true Church to be strong and constant in the truth and bear with the persecution from the synagogue of Satan' (that is, the Inquisition).

The great autos de fe up to 1562 served to remind the population of the gravity of the crisis and taught them to try to identify Lutherans in their midst. As a consequence the tribunals of the Inquisition in the 1560s devoted themselves to a hunt for Lutheran heresy, and drew into their net scores of Spaniards who in an unguarded moment had made statements praising Luther or attacking the clergy. In Cuenca, for instance, no sooner had one resident heard the news from Valladolid than he zealously denounced one of his neighbours to the Inquisition for reading a certain book of whose contents he – being illiterate – knew nothing. In those same weeks the archbishop of Tarragona (Fernando de Loazes, who had some years before been inquisitor in Barcelona) stopped over in Cuenca on his way to his diocese. He was asked about the Carranza case, and replied: 'If the archbishop was a heretic, we are all heretics'. He too was denounced to the Inquisition. In both cases, the inquisitors sensibly took no action.

These years helped the old and ailing Inquisitor General Valdés to save his career for a while longer. He attempted to convince Philip II that a major crisis was in the making, and that only the Inquisition could resolve it. In May 1558 he wrote informing Philip, then in Brussels, of Lutheran books in Salamanca and many other places, of problems with the Moriscos, of the discovery of judaizers in Murcia, and of the Lutherans in Valladolid and Seville. The Murcia cases, in which a large number of people were executed on very flimsy evidence, was in fact a local phenomenon of passing importance. The Protestant cases were serious enough, on the other hand, to encourage Valdés to ask, virtually, that the country be put into the hands of the Inquisition. He suggested that new tribunals be set up immediately in Galicia, Asturias and the Basque country; that a second tribunal be set up in Valladolid; that special vigilantes be set up everywhere; that no book should in future be printed without the permission of the Inquisition; that no books should be sold without prior examination by the inquisitors; and so on. Fortunately, the new king took no notice of these suggestions.

The Protestant scare was in any case never as grave as Valdés made out. After the anti-Lutheran repression of these months, the Inquisition was in reality over the hump. From the 1560s Judaism was no longer an issue, and the Reformation no longer a threat. Autos de fe were wound down. When held they were more showy and ceremonious, in the manner of the great autos of 1559, to make up for the lack of penitents. In perspective, the Protestant crisis in Spain, often presented as a singularly bloody period of repression, seems almost humane when compared with the ferocity of religious persecution in other countries. In all Spain probably just over a hundred persons were condemned to death by the Inquisition between 1559 and 1566. The English authorities under Queen Mary had executed nearly three times as many heretics as died in Spain in the years just after

1559, the French under Henry II at least twice as many. In the Netherlands ten times as many had died. In all three countries, very many more died for religious reasons in the years that followed. 'The healthiest of all is Spain', Philip II observed with some justice to the Inquisitor General.

Protestantism never developed into a real threat in Spain. Several cases, from all over the peninsula, are known to us because they appear in the records of the Inquisition. Three men appeared on suspicion in an auto in Saragossa on 17 May 1560. In an auto of 20 November 1562 two were burnt alive for Protestantism. The total number of Spaniards accused of 'Lutheranism' (as the inquisitors insisted on labelling all varieties of Reformation belief) in the last decades of the century totalled about two hundred. Most of them were in no sense Protestants. The majority of these cases demonstrated in reality the ignorance of the inquisitors rather than any real Lutheran threat. They recall the equally indiscriminate persecution that the tribunal had directed against conversos a half-century before. Irreligious sentiments, drunken mockery, anticlerical expressions, were all captiously classified by the inquisitors (or by those who denounced the cases) as 'Lutheran'. Disrespect to church images, and eating meat on forbidden days, were taken as signs of heresy. A hapless uneducated woman of Toledo who claimed in 1568 that 'all those who die go straight to heaven', was accused of the heresy of denying the existence of purgatory. It is clear that in such cases, of which there were very many, the agents of the Holy Office were reacting to unofficial beliefs among the people rather than to any infiltration of heresy.

There were of course a few convinced heretics to be found – among them the nobleman Gaspar de Centelles, burnt in Valencia in 1564, and Fray Cristóbal de Morales, burnt in Granada in 1571 – but fewer than a dozen Spaniards were burnt alive for Lutheranism in the later part of the century outside the cases tried at Valladolid and Seville. Others – like the slightly crazy Friar Pedro de Orellana, who spent twenty-eight years in the prisons of the Holy Office – were arrested for offences that included suspicion of 'Lutheranism', but had no identifiable Lutheran beliefs.

Much of the potential Spanish Reformation had emigrated abroad. Since the mid-sixteenth century Spaniards sympathetic to the Reformation could be found dotted around intellectual groups in western Europe. Rather than refugees, they were part of the well-worn tradition of wandering scholars. True emigration commenced with the discovery of the Protestant cells in Seville and Valladolid. A small stream of refugees made their way into the Reformation communities abroad.

Many in Spain were alarmed by the trend. In some cases, there were fears of the dishonour that could be brought on families by heresy. This provoked at least one murder, that of Juan Díaz in Germany [. . .]. The government, for its part, tried to repatriate Spaniards who fell under suspicion. Philip II was convinced by his officials that it would be a useful policy. In 1560 his ambassador in London, Quadra, reported that several Spanish Protestants were turning up in that city. 'They arrive every day with their wives and children and it is said that many more are expected'. Philip's father had in the 1540s condoned the occasional seizure outside Spain of Castilians who became active Protestants. They were packed off home and made to face the music there. The intention was not, as a subsequent ambassador of Philip in England explained, to eliminate them but to keep an eye on them and hope that others would take the hint and mend their ways. Under Philip II, the selective kidnapping was carried out by two agents based in the Netherlands, one of them the army paymaster Alonso del Canto. They were sponsored by the king's secretary Francisco de Eraso. With the help of special funds, a little network was set up to spy on Spanish émigrés living in England, the Netherlands and Germany. Their most notable success was in persuading the famous humanist Furió Ceriol to return to Spain in 1563. In the process, they collected valuable information on Spanish Protestants abroad. Canto in the spring of 1564 was able to inform Madrid of the preparation by Juan Pérez de Pineda of a new version of the Bible in Spanish.

The real brunt of the attack on so-called 'Lutheranism' was borne by foreign visitors, such as traders and sailors, and by foreigners resident in Spain. The heresy scare intensified xenophobia among many sections of the population. It made Spain, at least for a while, unsafe for foreigners. The Holy Office had been active against them from as early as the 1530s. Spain's extensive trade with northern Europe made contact with outsiders inevitable, especially in the ports. The first Protestant foreigner to be burnt by the Inquisition was young John Tack, an Englishman of Flemish origin, burnt in Bilbao in May 1539. Up until 1560, nine other foreigners were arrested and 'reconciled' by the inquisitors on this coastline.

In the Toledo area in the 1560s French and Flemish residents were those principally accused of heresy. Some had accompanied Philip II back from Flanders or had come with the new queen, Elizabeth Valois, from France. The 1560s were the only decade in which Flemings figured in any number. More usually, those accused were French. In Barcelona the inquisitor in 1560 felt it opportune to hold an auto de fe 'so that people are on their guard against foreigners'. Foreigners indeed constituted the bulk of prosecutions in these years, especially in frontier tribunals. In Barcelona between 1552 and 1578 there were fifty-one alleged Lutherans burnt in person or in effigy, but all were foreign. Nearly all the cases arising at Valencia from 1554 to 1598 involved foreigners, eight of whom were burnt in person or in effigy. In the tribunal of Calahorra (later transferred to Logroño), though there were as many as sixty-eight cases of suspected Lutheranism in 1540–99, the majority (82 per cent) were foreigners. 'All the people punished in this Inquisition are poor foreigners', the tribunal reported in 1565. In northern Spain, as a result of the proximity of the Calvinist areas of France, Frenchmen were singled out for suspicion. Between 1560 and 1600, the Inquisition in the provinces of the crown of Aragon and in Navarre executed some eighty Frenchmen as presumed heretics, burnt another hundred in effigy, and sent some three hundred and eighty to the galleys.

The victimization of non-Spaniards by the Inquisition brings into focus its xenophobic and racialist tendencies. As it had pointed the finger once at conversos and Moriscos [. . .], so it now pointed the finger at all foreigners, regardless of religion. The attitude, even when practised in the crown of Aragon, must be attributed mainly to the Castilian inquisitors. In the 1560s the Consellers of Barcelona reminded the inquisitors that they were unwise to pick on French people indiscriminately, since they must know that the greater part of Frenchmen were Catholic. But the inquisitors, sticking by an ideological attitude that endured into the first half of the twentieth century, persisted in describing all nations outside Spain as '*tierras de herejes*' (heretical countries).

The Castilian inquisitors looked with special suspicion on the Basques and Catalans. In 1567 the local inquisitor, who happened to be visiting San Sebastían, commented that 'the natives of this town have too much contact with the French, with whom they link up through marriage; and they always speak their language [i.e. French], rather than their own or Spanish', In Catalonia, the inquisitors were continuously suspicious of the religion of the Catalans, but failed all the same to find any heresy in the province. 'Their Christianity is such', an inquisitor reported in 1569, 'that it is cause for wonder, living as they do next to and among heretics and dealing with them every day'. There was, in effect, an open frontier between France and Catalonia. The bookshops of Barcelona were full of books printed in France. Possibly one-tenth of the population of Barcelona and one-third of that of Perpignan [now part of France], Catalonia's two main cities, were French. Despite this unimpeded contact between the two nations, Catalans made not the slightest move towards embracing heresy. In default of victims among the Catalans, the Inquisition sought them among the French.

The failure of the Protestant cause in the Mediterranean inevitably raises the question of why no Reformation occurred in Spain. Efficiency of repression is not the answer. Repression was more efficient and more brutal in other countries, notably the Netherlands, yet persecution there did not check the Reformation. Philip II was convinced that *timely* repression and continuous vigilance were the key. 'Had there been no Inquisition', he affirmed in 1569, 'there would be many more heretics, and the country would be much afflicted, as are those where there is no Inquisition as in Spain'. The king may have believed it, but it was not true.

Nor is it possible to maintain that Spain was sealed off from contact with heresy. The outdated image of an iron curtain of the Inquisition descending on the country and cutting it off from the rest of the world, has no relation to reality. Precisely in the 1550s and 1560s, very many Spaniards were travelling abroad. More Spaniards than ever before published (as we shall see) their books in foreign parts. Tens of thousands, mainly Castilians, served overseas in the army, where they rubbed shoulders with people of other faiths. The land frontier in the Pyrenees was occasionally watched, because of the danger of military intervention by French Protestant nobles and by bandits, but it could never be closed. Throughout the late sixteenth century, Spaniards drifted at will over the frontier. Some went to trade, some to be educated, some because they wished to join the Calvinists in Geneva. At the same time, many foreigners, principally artisans, came to Spain. It was a handful of these who, through carelessness on their part, fell into the hands of the Inquisition.

The difficulty in controlling the Pyrenees frontier, Spain's chief overland link with the world outside, comes through in the anxious correspondence of the ambassador to France in the 1560s, Francés de Álava. In 1564 and 1565 he sent reports to the king about booksellers from Saragossa, Medina del Campo and Alcalá who had come to Lyon and Toulouse to purchase books on law and philosophy for taking home. In one of the cases, he said, the bookseller had links with Geneva. This importation of foreign books, we may observe, was carried out in open contravention of the laws of Castile. Álava also confirmed that 'many books, catechisms and psalters in Basque' had passed through Toulouse to Spain. Basque was his own native language, so he knew of what he spoke. Books in Catalan, he reported, had also been taken into Catalonia, and other heretical books had gone to Pamplona. In those same weeks the archbishop of Bordeaux forwarded a report on a citizen of Burgos who 'had taken four or five loads of heretical books in Spanish and in Latin through the mountains of Jaca'. Despite the open frontier, heresy failed to penetrate at all. The Reformation remained, for Spaniards, a phenomenon that did not affect them.

22 Thomas Hanrahan '*Lazarillo de Tormes*: Erasmian Satire or Protestant Reform?'

Source: from *Hispania* 66, September 1983, pp. 333–9.

The author of *Lazarillo de Tormes* sought to please and instruct; most readers would acknowledge his success as an entertainer and if they were also critics, would probably differ as to his precise purpose while assigning him a general didactic intent. The disagreement about the specific intent of *Lazarillo* is as noticeable as its pervasive satire. [. . .] The present article proposes to offer a few observations on the doctrinal content of *Lazarillo* that might aid in narrowing the years of its composition and the field of author candidates.

   A useful point from which to begin would be Bataillon's contention that there is no positive doctrine proposed in the novel. [. . .] What positive doctrine or evidence of one is there in the First Treatise? Five of the masters of Lázaro were churchmen and the first, the blind man, introduced the religious criticism which would follow the basic biblical theme of the blind leading the blind; for the blind man, despite his astuteness, lacked that prime requisite of Christian living, charity. He exploits the superstition and credulity of others and lives off the proceeds. This is more than a criticism of superstition, common enough at the time, for it goes to the theological question of the efficacy of certain kinds of prayer. For every occasion the blind man has a set prayer which he will recite for a price. Erasmists were not alone in criticizing the superstition of a multiplicity of prayers and a patron saint for every calling and circumstance.[1] The Reformers, however, simply rejected the invocation of the saints as incompatible with scriptural insistence upon Christ being the only mediator between man and God. Erasmians criticized abuses in the veneration of the saints, but others intent upon a primal reform simply denied the concept of the intercession of the saints on man's behalf. Thus, in *Lazarillo* what ostensibly seems Erasmian, is in reality a statement of deep doctrinal difference.

The Second Treatise intensifies this criticism and centers not on invocation of the saints, but on the efficacy of a sacramental system, to which theologians ascribed real causality in the process of justification. Again Erasmians and others preferred to correct abuses connected with stole fees and stipends while reformers rejected the doctrine itself.[2] For them, only faith put man in direct contact with God, who would justify him and impart to him His grace. The sacraments, at best, were considered useful symbols of that faith, but had no efficacy of their own. [. . .]

In the Second Treatise the priest is shown in all his miserliness; at times the humorous description can divert the reader's attention from the theological reproach. The priest quite literally lives off the dead. He, as the blindman, receives money for praying on another's behalf, but his case is more serious, as the sacraments, which should be a source of spiritual life, are celebrated for those already dead.

There is here obvious criticism of stole fees, but the validity of praying for one already dead and judged is being questioned as well and presented with a contrapuntal life-death theme. [. . .]

When Lázaro describes the bread locked up in the trunk, the language used parodies the private adoration of the Eucharist. The reader is presented with the priest keeping under lock and key a source of life as something which cannot be used, but only adored; thus, it has ceased to be a source of nourishment. While the Reformers were of different minds regarding the doctrine of the real physical presence of Christ in the Eucharist, Luther's insistence upon the communal aspect of the Mass along with his denial of sacramental causality would have precluded private adoration of the Eucharist. In this sense the satire or parody here is certainly more Protestant than Erasmian.

It is worth nothing that the cleric of Maqueda is the quintessence of miserliness, yet he is not the favorite target of Erasmists, the mendicant friar or monk. The author opposes the term *clérigo* to that of *fraile* thus distinguishing the diocesan or secular cleric from the member of a religious order. A Mercedarian friar in need of reform would hardly have caused a contemporary reader's eyebrow to arch, but the cleric along with the Chaplain of the Sixth Treatise and the Archpriest are all members of the diocesan clergy. [. . .] The intent is not one of reforming abuses in conventual life, but of directing an animosity toward a caste set apart from the laity by virtue of the sacrament of Orders. [. . .] The *fraile* is an example of a corrupt religious who steals from his own family, but the cleric steals from the poor who have little to give. Biblical injunctions against taking from the poor in the guise of religion were well known and they indicate the more serious fault contemplated in the cleric's behavior (Lk. 11, 46). The frequent query seeking the reason for the very brief description of the Mercedarian in the Fourth Treatise possibly finds an answer in the author's desire not to confuse ordinary and accustomed Erasmian satire of religious life with his far more serious intent: to deny the validity of the clerical state. When the cleric is fleshed out in the Second Treatise, Lázaro insinuates with a pun that the avariciousness was an effect of minor orders. [. . .] The anticlerical animus becomes even clearer when one considers that casuists in questions of moral theology had for centuries used an example such as that of Zaide who steals from another to sustain life, and unanimously held that there was no guilt, since the right to existence takes precedence over that of private property. It was no accident that Zaide was not even a Christian.

Both the Archpriest and the Chaplain of the Sixth Treatise trafficked in water and wine even though secular business was forbidden to clerics by tradition and law. Again it is not the wealth of monastic institutions which is scorned. As early as 1520 Luther had in his *Babylonian Captivity* struck out at the sacramental system; in his *Appeal to the Ruling Class* he called for the abolition of the sacerdotal caste and impugned a priesthood set off from the laity. This was outright denial of the theological basis and foundation which allowed a clergy to live off stole fees or the performance of a sacramental liturgy. The Chaplain, for example, had no office which was pastoral; he was attached to the cathedral as a chantry priest. Luther had begun his attack on foundation masses and their endowment in the eighty-third of his ninety-five theses.[3] He had of course evolved in his theological position. It is not urged here that the author of *Lazarillo* was directly influenced by any one reformer, but that similar abuses evoked similar doctrinal positions.

There is the obvious thematic significance of water and wine which the priests sold: wine intimately connected to the Savior's blood in a sacramental context, and to blood and water, symbol of the crucifixion in Joannine theology. The inclination to make of these a conscious thematic technique should be resisted until a more unified study of *Lazarillo* themes can validate such a suspicion.

The sordid details of the scandalous life of the Archpriest in the last Treatise and their correspondence with certain comments of contemporary observers and chroniclers have distracted critics and fixed their attention upon the verisimilitude of the Treatise causing them to ignore the deeper theological implications, which were hinted at in the first two treatises. The blind man had taught Lázaro, and the priest of Maqueda had refused him sustenance, but the Archpriest not only fed him at his own table and gave him employment, but also arranged his marriage. Indelibly etched is the portrait of a priest whose office it was to dispense the sacraments and to guard their integrity who instead profanes Holy Orders, Matrimony and the Eucharist. Lázaro, who should have found in Matrimony a source of grace or justification, finds cause for his eventual damnation. The Archpriest should have fed Lázaro from the altar, the Lord's table, but seats him, to the shame of both, to break bread. The evil has intensified since first he lost his childhood innocence and wonder on the bridge over the Tormes. The accumulation of evil and sacrilege described in this last Treatise bring to life the arguments Luther adduces in his *Appeal to the Ruling Class*. For him the solution to these problems is the abolition of clerical celibacy and the clerical state; the author of *Lazarillo* makes no attempt to resolve his protagonist's final degradation, but his description of it parallels those of reformers who do propose radical solutions.

By 1520 Luther had evolved to where he denied indulgences, maintained that the Mass was only a commemoration, rejected the cult of the saints and the Virgin, and rejected any source of justification other than God's grace protectively covering man's intrinsically corrupt nature. This grace came from faith alone, and forgiveness was a *metanoia* [a reorientation of one's way of life], not a piece of paper to be purchased. All of these themes find a distinct resonance in the episodes of *Lazarillo*.

The language itself reveals a mentality more Reformer than Erasmian or Illuminist. It is the language of the humanist, fraught with religious significance. To comment upon pride and vanity, the author picks the example of a member of a religious order being complimented upon his final lectures prior to the conferral of his degree (Prologue). To show true love and charity he contrasts the conduct of the morisco Zaide to the petty thefts of both secular and religious clergy on behalf of their *devotas* [female followers]. His insistence upon holding up the priesthood to scorn is a crucial element of his style.

Throughout the book the author dwells upon illumination, beginning with the blind man teaching Lázaro the difference between good and evil; when a tinker comes to the door of the priest's house, Lázaro attributes his presence to an angel and his consequent stratagem to the Holy Spirit's illumination. Frequently the plays on words have a scriptural or liturgical model. [. . .] It is the congeries of detail rather than any particular item that prompts one to discern a purpose much more radical than that of Erasmian satire.

When Lázaro deals with the lay state, his comments do not seem too much different from those of contemporary Erasmists. Bataillon pointed out the frequent comic presentation of a squire as a type of male *dueña* [i.e. mother superior] by reason of his usual duties. But the squire's portrait exceeds the merely comedic; it is positive disparagement. Lázaro portrays him with sarcasm but the phrase, 'Con todo le quería bien, con ver que no tenía ni podía más' [nonetheless I loved him, seeing that he had nothing and could do no better] seems to be remembered more than the words of the squire.

From the first moment when the squire announced to Lázaro that he is the answer to the boy's prayers, modesty and humility, virtues highly esteemed in the *Enchiridion Militis Christiani* [Handbook of the Christian Soldier] are seen to be lacking. The squire proceeds to the Cathedral to hear Mass and the Canonical hours sung. A creature of habit rather than truly devout, the squire informs Lázaro that he will repeat the performance of hearing Mass and the singing of the hours on the following day. A bit later, Lázaro has the occasion to observe his master in ardent conversation with two prostitutes. Sardonically he relates the attempt of his master to captivate the two women with words not backed by coin. [. . .] The juxtaposition of the intention of hearing Mass and the conversation with the two women could illustrate the words of the *Enchiridion*: 'I think there are far too many who count up how many times they attend Mass and rely almost entirely upon this for their salvation. They are convinced that they owe nothing further to Christ. Leaving church they immediately turn to their former habits.' Lázaro also mocks the posturing and façade adopted by his famished master in his magnificent procession of one through the streets of Toledo. The squire knew the subjection and deprivation involved in serving another, but he takes from Lázaro the largest piece of bread. His selfishness is matched by his bravura. [. . .] Appearances were the main preoccupation of the squire; he would eat whatever Lázaro could beg, provided the neighbors were not aware that they both shared the same dwelling. It is this attitude that induces in Lázaro a feeling of pity and the desire that his master show less arrogance. [. . .] The impoverished squire calculates his wealth and holdings in the hypothetical conditional tense. He identifies a certain material well-being with honor; by asserting one he claims the other, a confusion resulting from his overwhelming desire to be held in esteem. Significantly he objects to the one formula of courtesy which invoked God's help for him and preferred the empty 'Besoos las manos.' [I kiss your hands]. For the squire is cynical, his sense of honor purely social, and he is prepared to lie and flatter, indeed to perpetrate injustices upon fellow retainers in order to advance his own cause. [. . .] To complete the portrait the author has the squire defraud his landlord and abandon Lázaro, leaving him to answer to the authorities for his master's debts. [. . .]

The episode of the Pardoner and his efforts to promote [. . .] spiritual privileges is usually accepted as a criticism of at least the techniques employed in the preaching of indulgences if not of indulgences themselves: a criticism which had enjoyed illustrious support. Cisneros, who never doubted the doctrinal aspect of indulgences, certainly objected to the preaching of them, perhaps because he had better plans for Spanish coin than the building of St. Peter's. In the conduct of the priest, the Second Treatise criticizes the theological underpinnings of the doctrine while in the Fifth Treatise simony and fraud in the propagation of the indulgences are satirized. The theological foundation for both indulgences, as well as for the validity of Masses offered on behalf of the dead was proclaimed by the Council of Trent and later codified in Canon Law. Thus, in the total context Lázaro does not comment simply upon the excesses which were deplored by many at the time, but his criticism reveals an antagonism to the sacramental theology of his day. The priestly caste founded upon this sacramental system is likewise question. [. . .] The reformers who rejected this doctrine adopted an alternate explanation [. . .] i.e., grace will not come from anything but individual faith and prayer. They saw therefore the Mass as a commemoration only, not an efficacious sacrifice. The efficaciousness of prayer would depend upon the virtue of faith of the one praying, not a set formula; hence living off stipends given for the Mass was scorned. *Lazarillo*, after rejecting the abuses [. . .] leaves the reader to consider the alternative.

The incident of the Buldero's [The Pardoner] false cure of the *alguacil* [constable] is placed in a context of superstition. The use of holy water, crucifix, the litany, long vocal prayers directed more to the congregation than toward God, and sermons on Christ's passion which induce tears were common themes of Reformers, Illuminists, and Erasmists. [. . .]

Thus, the author of *Lazarillo* rejects the orthodox doctrine of the intercession of the saints, the efficaciousness of vocal prayer, and the validity of indulgences. In addition, he heaps scorn upon the sacramental priesthood, the preaching of indulgences. All of these criticisms and beliefs are quite consonant, natural in fact, for someone who held a doctrine of justification similar to that of the early Reformers. They manifestly point to a mind and will well along the road of doctrinal independence from Rome.

Bataillon urged a reconsideration of the date of composition for *Lazarillo*, opting for the period between 1539 and 1550. One is tempted to incline toward this later period as being more consonant with reformation views since after Augsburg (1530) the Protestant position would have more probability of being known and distinguished in Spain from the Illuminist or Erasmist school. Yet, it is precisely the earlier writings of Luther which more exactly coincide with the doctrinal satire in *Lazarillo* than the later conciliatory and irenic formulation, largely the effort of Melanchton.

The early Reformer was much more radical and his trenchant biting sarcasm more representative of an earnest desire for ecclesiastical reform which was definitely not confined to Wittenburg. A decade later, wiser and sadder men groped across the abyss to repair a unity perceived as lost. [. . .]

Lazarillo with its insistent hammering at the very root theological issues of Reform belongs to that earlier period.

Erasmian satire took aim at vices, superstitious excesses, clerical cupidity and sought to make whole and sound the entire church, primarily by reform and healing of its members. This was frequently achieved with a smiling satire. The author of *Lazarillo* is grim and his humor should not hide the steady accumulation of details leading to the ultimate degradation and damnation of his protagonist. The causes of vices and errors which he attacks are theological; they rest upon the foundations of the existing system which will inevitably change under the increasing onslaught.

NOTES

1   Bataillon points out that Illuminism shared many of the Erasmian objections to a routine devotion and religious formalism. Indeed quite a few of the same ideas had been current in Gerson's *Contemptus Mundi* in the previous century. *Erasmo y España* (I, 202).

2   Stole fees were offerings made to the priest for administering a sacrament such as baptism, or for blessing some object. Stipends are usually associated with the celebration of Mass. While both were said to be offerings, the minimum amount would often be set by local ecclesiastical authority.

3   'Again: why should funeral and anniversary Masses for the dead continue to be said? And why does not the Pope repay, or permit to be repaid, the benefactions instituted for these purposes, since it is wrong to pray for those souls who are now redeemed?', Eighty-third thesis (1517).

23 Javier Herrero '**Renaissance Poverty and Lazarillo's Family: The Birth of the Picaresque Genre**'

Source: from 'Renaissance Poverty and Lazarillo's Family: The Birth of the Picaresque Genre', Publications of the Modern Language Association of America, vol. 94, 1979, pp. 876–86. Reprinted by permission of the Modern Languages Association of America.

When the *Lazarillo* appeared in 1554, the Renaissance artistic imagination was dominated by two colossal symbols, the Platonic shepherd and the courtly knight. Both were aesthetic projections of the dreams, aspirations, and fears of the aristocratic society that had prevailed in Europe for centuries. As Cervantes said in the first part of the *Quixote*, the *Lazarillo* meant the birth of a new genre, the picaresque novel, a genre that, with the *Quixote* itself, would give the coup de grace to these giant figures.[1] This study briefly examines how this new David, the picaresque hero, could defeat not one Goliath but two. One of them, the shepherd, could claim the highest literary nobility in Western culture: he appeared for the first time on the shield of Achilles, in Book XVIII of the *Iliad*, already playing the bucolic flute. The knight could not boast such an ancient lineage, but from the twelfth century on he rode powerfully in shining armor through the major epics and romances of European literature. [. . .]

In his victory Lazarillo had the strong support of the social and ideological trends of sixteenth-century society. Beneath the dreams of arcadia and chivalry a world was growing that was too frightening to be faced squarely. This terrifying reality, however, surfaces in the mocking outcast, the pícaro. The *Lazarillo* is, to begin with, the story of a starving family in sixteenth-century Spain, some of whose members are too weak to survive, no less succeed. Their effort to gain day-to-day sustenance meets with torture, exile, death. Lázaro, however, as he proudly tells us in the *Prólogo*, escapes from the dreadful world of the oppressed, starving poor and, through his own efforts, finds shelter in a safe harbor. From the confrontation between this helpless child and the horrifying forces that threaten him, the powerful irony of the book is born. We must, therefore, put the *Lazarillo* in its social context if we are to understand fully the way in which this conflict is artistically expressed by the anonymous Renaissance humanist who wrote it.

Poverty was a staggering social disease in sixteenth-century Europe. Historians have not been able to determine whether this evil increased considerably during the Renaissance or whether there was simply greater awareness of conditions that might not have been very different in previous centuries. Two factors, however, helped to direct the best minds of the time to the anguish of the dispossessed. On the one hand, the great urban development attracted masses of the unemployed to the cities and made their plight more widely apparent. On the other hand, the Renaissance spirit of self-reliance (coupled with the secularization of ecclesiastical property in the Reformed countries) made it seem possible, after all, to change a state of affairs that had traditionally been considered a permanent feature of a hierarchically structured universe. Although poverty may also have inspired revulsion and horror in previous centuries, these feelings now moved thinkers to search for a remedy through rationally organized activity. Several documents of the period illustrate the anxiety pervading the sixteenth century: writing about the Paris of 1596, Pierre de l'Estoile reported that 'the crowds in the streets were so great that one could not pass through: they are only masks and images of death, naked or clad in ragged robes'; a bull of Sixtus V in 1587 complains that beggars in Rome 'fill with their groans and cries not only public places and private houses, but the churches themselves; they roam like brute beasts, with no other care than the search for food.'[2] The protest against the destitution and suffering of vagrants was strongest in the Low Countries, where more thought was given to possible remedies. In the earliest social welfare proposal of the Renaissance, the *Forma Subventionis Pauperum*, proclaimed by the town of Ypres to relieve the material and moral distress of vagrancy, we read:

> Who is he that is so far wide from charity that can any longer pass by showing no benefit of charity to those poor wretches accompted in this world but as castaways, to whom whatsoever be given Christ accepts is as though it were done to Himself? Hitherto they have wandered like scattered sheep on streets and highways and uplandish places and towns, all arrayed with scurf and filthyness, pitiously punished with cold, nakedness, hunger and thirst.[3]

And William Marshall, the translator of the *Forma Subventionis*, describes in his Preface, dedicated to the queen, Anne Boleyn, the 'great multitude of poor and needy folks, which in every street and church and every man's door, yea, in every place within this realm, idly, lasciviously and dissolutely are wont and have been accustomed to go around and wander about like vagabounds'. As we shall see, the Spanish social landscape was equally grim.

The most radical proposals for social transformation came from a group of three northern humanists, related also by bonds of friendship: Erasmus, Thomas More, and the exiled Spaniard Luis Vives. Vives receives special attention here because his treatise *De Subventione Pauperum* exercised a greater influence in Spain than did the work of the others. In the ninth chapter he formally condemns the right of private property. In a program designed for the practical purpose of solving the problems of poverty in the city of Bruges through full employment of all its citizens, Vives explicitly refers to Nature, God's agent, as having destined all things to be commonly owned by all men:

> First of all Nature, by which I mean God, since Nature is nothing else but His Will . . . placed everything she had created in this house of the world without locks or bolts to be the common property of her creatures. . . . What Nature, then, liberally gave to us in common, we put away, hide, lock, forbid, enclose with hedges, walls, locks, iron, arms, and finally with laws. . . . [N]othing, in fact, belongs to anybody. A thief is, I say, a thief and a swindler, he who gambles his wealth away, keeps it in chests, squanders it on banquets or games, on excessively pompous apparel or baubles loaded with gold and silver . . . finally, he who does not share with the poor all that he has beyond the essential requirements of Nature is a thief. . . .[4]

It is not difficult to find the direct source of Luis Vives' radicalism. Sir Thomas More, in Book 1 of *Utopia*, places the responsibility for contemporary misery squarely on the shoulders of the rich and powerful. Even the crimes of those reduced to beggary are the result of a callous and corrupted nobility, and all guilt belongs to it:

> Now there is the great number of noblemen who not only live idle themselves like drones on the labors of others, as for instance the tenants of their estates whom they fleece to the utmost by increasing the returns (for that is the only economy they known of, being otherwise so extravagant as to bring themselves to beggary!) but who also carry about with them a huge crowd of idle

attendants who have never learned a trade for a livelihood. . . . Consequently, in order that one insatiable glutton and accursed plague of his native land may join field to field and surround may thousand acres with one fence, tenants are evicted. Some of them, either circumvented by fraud or overwhelmed by violence, are stripped even of their own property, or else, wearied by unjust acts, are driven to sell. By hook or by crook the poor wretches are compelled to leave their homes – men and women, husbands and wives, orphans and widows, parents with little children and a household not rich but numerous, since farm work requires many hands. . . . After they have soon spent that trifle in wandering from place to place, what remains for them but to steal and be hanged – justly, you may say! – or to wander and beg. And yet even in the latter case they are cast into prison as vagrants for going about idle when, though they most eagerly offer their labor, there is no one to hire them.[5]

The teaching of the two great Christian humanists is clear, forthright, and certainly revolutionary: God (and, as an instrument of his will, Nature) has given everything in common to all. Hungry and sick masses are invading the sixteenth-century towns like a muddy flood because the political structure of triumphant absolutism allows the powerful few to steal what rightly belongs to the many. It is true that Vives stops short of the Utopian communism of More, suggesting instead a welfare state in which the city takes care of the needs of the poor and through work and education provides the means for their rehabilitation; but the same burning thirst for justice inspires his words, and also the same indignation about a state of affairs in which men and women are deprived of their humanity and subjected to terrible suffering by a few who have created for themselves a world of gold and silver, of banquets and feasts. The progression in Vives' description of this rapacity is one of the most damning indictments ever passed on a social system: 'they enclose with hedges, walls, locks, iron [an obvious reference to the chains of the prisoners], arms and finally with laws.' [. . .]

Erasmus' thought, of course, had a decisive influence on both Vives' and More's philosophical and moral ideas. His innate moderation in purely social matters, however, limited the scope of his influence on the two radical thinkers. Erasmus held property to be legitimate only when it is used as an instrument of social welfare. This view and his studies and translations of the early fathers (especially of Ambrose, whose radicalism was as extreme as More's or Vives') were enormously influential on both humanists and, indeed, on European thought in general. Since More was soon looked on with suspicion by the Spanish Inquisition and since Vives, as a *converso* (a Jewish convert to Christianity), was an authority who was better read than quoted, the Spanish theologians tended to refer to Erasmus and the early fathers equally in their disputes on poverty. But this should not mislead us: Vives' *De Subventione Pauperum* dominated Spanish social thought throughout the century. Some later theorists, in fact, did little more than echo him. The reformer Miguel Giginta, for example, entitled his work *Tratado del remedio de pobres* [Treatise on poor relief, 1579], which is a direct translation of Vives' title. This is not the place, obviously, to explore the complex and often acrimonious discussions that raged in Spain between reformers and conservatives for a hundred years; but since these theological disputes on poverty and vagrancy permeated the intellectual and educational background from which the *Lazarillo* was born, a brief outline of the main arguments and developments is required here.

The core of the disputes is the Poor Law of 24 August 1540. Equally important are the attack on its provisions by one of the greatest theologians of the century, the Dominican Fray Domingo de Soto, in his *Deliberación en la causa de los pobres* 'Deliberation in Favor of the Poor,' published 30 January 1545, and the answer of the Benedictine Fray Juan de Medina in his *De la orden que en algunos pueblos de España se ha puesto en la limosna para remedio de los verdaderos pobres* 'Of the Ordinance Given in Some Towns of Spain with Regard to Alms for the Remedy of the True Poor.' In the last part of the title there is an obvious attack on Vives' *De Subventione Pauperum*: only the 'truly poor,' as opposed to vagrants, should be helped with alms. Medina's work appeared on 8 March 1545; the discussions, which had their climax in the 1540s, continued until the end of the century and flared up with the feverish activity of Giginta in the sixties and seventies. We can safely assert, then, that the *Lazarillo*, published in 1554, was composed at a time when the problems of poverty and vagrancy had captured the attention of most of the Spanish urban population.

This is a bold statement, and at first it might seem somewhat exaggerated. How could there be such widespread interest in legal problems when most Spaniards were illiterate? But the dispute went well beyond the written texts. The Poor Law was a brutal decree aimed at a general expulsion of the poor from the cities, as far-reaching as the expulsion of the Jews in 1492 or of the *Moriscos* in 1609. The expulsion took the form of the prohibition of vagrancy throughout the kingdom and of begging in the cities. Only the pauper who had been certified as such by the priest of his parish and had received a permit from the local authorities could beg, and then only in his hometown. Since most of the urban poor (who were the ones the aristocracy and emerging bourgeoisie wanted to get rid of) had come to the cities because of unemployment and famine in the countryside, the general expulsion meant practically the massacre, through starvation, of a considerable portion of the population. That the measure was temporally implemented as shown by Soto's comments on the absence of beggars during the Easter processions and the effect this had on the faithful, who were thus deprived of the chance to practice charity: 'tantas manadas de pobres que, so color de vagabundos, se han desterrado de las ciudades . . .' 'So many flocks of beggars who have been accused of vagrancy and have been exiled from the towns . . .'; 'ya no vemos andar pobre ninguno por las casas que ablande los corazones . . .' we no longer seen any of the poor coming to houses to soften our hearts. . . .' Soto's reaction is a direct reflection of humanist thought. Property belongs to the individual as long as he keeps only enough for his basic needs and distributes everything else to the poor; to keep more than is necessary is to steal what belongs to the poor. Anyone who tolerates the destitution of the beggars is responsible for their lives. It is true that Soto does not quote Vives (although he obviously knows him well); but the authorities he does cite, Jerome and Ambrose, are the fathers chosen by Erasmus as the models of true Christianity. He chooses, in fact, a quotation from

Ambrose that exactly phrases Vives' thought: 'Ninguno llame propios los bienes que son comunes. Lo que sobra, proveída tu necesidad, violentamente lo retienes . . .' 'Nobody should call his own the goods that are really common. What is left, after your needs are provided for, is violently taken from the others . . .' (Soto, p. 67). Soto's strong stand provoked a vehement reaction from conservative theologians; in fact, liberal and conservative positions became extremely difficult to define, since many theologians (Soto included) combined radical ideas on property with traditional approaches to the welfare of the poor. But such niceties are beyond the scope of this article. These remarks are intended to point out that the mutually fertilizing Renaissance ideas on poverty circulated widely in the Low Countries and in Paris, developed in England during the reign of Henry VIII, and ended by becoming an organic part of European humanism. From these social controversies the picaresque genre was born.

Let us now place the *Lazarillo* in this context. We have seen the world to which Lázaro belongs, and we have also briefly examined the ideologies that struggled either to change or to maintain it. The anonymous author confronts this world, not with political or ideological treatises, but with a work of art. In so doing, he breaks away from the conceptions of the pastoral and chivalric genres and writes the 'autobiography' of one of these starving beggars, getting inside Lazarillo's soul and exploring his anguish, his struggle, and finally his ironic success. The author's weapon against the oppressive forces of contemporary society is sarcasm, a sarcasm unparalleled since Lucian wrote his *Dialogues* in the declining years of classical antiquity.

The *Lazarillo* is surely one of the most intelligently structured books of the Renaissance (and indeed of Western literary tradition); no element in it, however small, should be judged devoid of significance. The name 'Lazarus' itself seems to have had an extremely rich evocative power in the sixteenth century. Its several connotations combined to suggest the character's sense of misery, degradation, and powerlessness. These are the most important meanings: (1) leper, derived probably from Lazarus, the patron saint of the lepers; the occurrence of the name in Spanish is relatively late; (2) beggar, with a deeply religious connotation, since Lazarus is the name of the beggar in the biblical parable of the miser (Luke xvi.19–31); (3) the man resurrected by Jesus (John xi.1–5), Lazarus of Bethany, who during the Middle Ages was identified with the beggar Lazarus; this misunderstanding gave an unusual dignity to this great archetype of human misery, welding the sense of poverty with the concepts of death and resurrection; (4) 'brought to the point of death by hunger,' a meaning reflected in the frequent use of the Spanish *lazerado* and *lazería* and suggested by the false etymology that derives 'Lázaro' from the Latin *lacerare*. The semantic complexity of the name would seem to fit a tragic character much better than a comic one, and in a highly ironic book like the *Lazarillo* its use points out the sad reality behind the comic treatment. But with uncanny precision the change from Lázaro to Lazarillo, and from the tragic to the comic, is backed by a folkloric tradition that had made of Lazarillo, the unfortunate par excellence, a character of popular jokes, which add to the name a note of childish naïveté, an innocence characterized by ignorance of sexual good and evil. Fittingly, Francisco Delicado's novel *La lozana andaluza* [*The sexy Andalucian girl*] (1528) contains a reference to a Lazarillo 'que cabalgó a su agüela' 'who rode [made love to] his grandmother.' The obscene allusion is clarified by relating it to proverbs about traditional Spanish fools: 'El Bobo de Coria, que empreñó a su madre y a sus hermanas, y preguntaba si era pecado', 'The fool of Coria, who made his mother and sisters pregnant and asked if it was a sin'; el Bobo de Perales 'que empreñó a todas las monjas de un convento', 'who made all the nuns of a convent pregnant,' and the like.

Let us now consider Lázaro's family in the context of the raging social polemics in sixteenth-century Europe. A comparison with a text of the Spanish canon Miguel Giginta will show the close connection between humanist ideals and the ideological background embedded in the strongly unified series of folktales and jokes that form the literary matter of *Lazarillo*. The poor, Giginta writes, need God's grace, because they are

> such unhappy wretches, that they need not a little of our Lord's help to avoid dying of despair or anger, seeing how they suffer all the extremes of misery, while the rich Christians spend their fortunes superfluously on palaces, jewels, banquets, animals, and other excesses; and, while they die of cold, their horses, housed in comfortable stables, are covered with beautiful trappings and blankets; the poor, meanwhile, are left in the streets. [. . .]

It will not be surprising, then, to find out how closely the misadventures of Lázaro's family correspond to the agonies of contemporary Spain reflected in Giginta's analysis. A world of utter misery, created by a tragically ironic 'justice,' appears through the anonymous author's account of Lázaro's family and its destruction. As we have seen, the name 'Lazarus' is significantly associated with the poor man whom Jesus had made the archetype of beggars. Cruelly treated by the arrogant rich, he shall be blessed, as the rich shall be damned. The name itself placed in this semantic soil, implies a glorification of the poor and a condemnation of the powerful.

Lázaro is born in an *aceña* 'flour mill' on the river Tormes in Tejares, a village near Salamanca. When he is eight years old, his father, who works in the mill, is accused of having 'bled' some of the bags of wheat brought to the mill. In a sardonic parody of the Gospel, the anonymous author (speaking through Lázaro, of course) narrates: 'y confesó y no negó, y padesció persecución por la justicia' 'he went ahead and confessed everything, and he suffered persecution for righteousness' sake.'[6] Punished and exiled, he tries to survive as a muleteer to a nobleman who fights against the Moors in the military expedition to Gelves, but, as his wife says later with unconscious sarcasm, he dies for the glory of his faith. Lázaro's mother, now a widow and the only support of her son, moves from their village to Salamanca to try to earn a living by approaching the 'good people.' Among other jobs, she does the laundry for some stable boys of the *comendador de la Magdalena*, a great ecclesiastical nobleman. One of them, a black slave called Zaide, begins to frequent Lázaro's house and, in time, Lázaro has a little black brother. But with the slave come (and this is important) bread, meat, and, in winter, wood for heating their little house.

This good fortune, however, does not last long. The steward of the *comendador* finds out that the slave has been feeding his wretched family and keeping them warm by stealing the horses' food and blankets and covers. The author comments coolly:

> Why should we be surprised at priests when they steal from the poor or at friars when they take rings from their monasteries to give to their lady followers, or for other things when we see how love can make a poor slave do what he did?

The author of the *Lazarillo* was certainly acquainted with the controversies over poverty and aware of the arguments against the moral and legal validity of property rights that allow the rich luxuries and ignore the needs of the poor. He emphasizes this theme by stressing Zaide's theft of the horses' possessions in order to provide for Lazarillo's family. There can be little doubt that the author chose a stable boy as his character precisely so that he could make this point. No intelligent reader can fail to see that on moral and theological grounds the real thief is the remote ecclesiastical aristocrat who, lost in the heights of his princely wealth, can only come into contact with this degraded world through the soulless steward and the thugs who support this legal crime with chains and lashes. Lázaro's father and stepfather, in accepted humanist theory, are taking what is theirs. The use of the Gospel is not all that ironic; it only seems so if we share the assumed point of view of the righteous. Lázaro's parents are persecuted for 'justice's sake' (because they do what is just: they take what is due them). It is important to observe that only two values survive the devastating sarcasm of this book: family affection, which moves Tomé González and Zaide to risk their lives for their children, and the charity and courage of the alienated – humble women in some incidents and here a black slave, the hero of the drama. That Zaide is a black and a slave is the most significant aspect of the episode: the strongest moral character of the book is not a Spaniard and has no place in the Spanish social hierarchy (except as an outcast). Thus he can be excluded from the almost universal condemnation that follows.

The main image of this narrative fits perfectly well into the urban landscape of persecuted and tortured beggars. The palace of the *comendador de la Magdalena*, the seat of aristocratic and ecclesiastical power, is lost among the peaks of a worldly greatness to which the awed gaze of Antona Pérez and her son Lázaro does not dare to rise. The lowest part of the palace, the stables, housing the great lord's horses, is still an exalted place for these two starving poor, the animals obviously having more status than they; only through a black slave can they reach that height. But not even the crumbs fallen from the rich man's table are given to them: when they try to live on what is left over from the *comendador*'s horses, they are tortured and the family unit destroyed.

After the mother is whipped and threatened with hanging if she is again seen with Zaide,[7] she takes a job as a servant in an inn. When Lázaro is about twelve or thirteen years old she decides to give him as a *lazarillo*, a guide, to a blind man. They part in tears, and Lázaro leaves the world of love and moves into a new one. In the thugs who protect the *comendador*'s property with such efficient brutality we have the poetic expression of the irons referred to by Vives and of the laws that, in More's words, maintain the power of the wealthy.

Family was the natural link by which man was chained to a certain step on the social ladder, to a station that determined his destiny in the world. In Renaissance Europe class reflected a divine order whose main example was the created universe, in which reality descended from the prime mover through the fixed stars and the spheres to the sublunar world. And in this lower sphere a descending series of animal species confirmed the concept of the cosmos as essentially an order that confers an unshakable destiny on a wide diversity of beings and unifies them by means of hierarchy and obedience. It was, finally, in the divine mind, in the Christianized version of the Platonic ideal world, that the model for such order existed in its full reality. This ideal order, then, sanctioned a class structure backed also by a secular tradition. [. . .]

To mock the hereditary bases of such an order was a task that the humanists relished. We have seen that they displace the guilt of destitution from the lower to the higher orders. In Lázaro and in his family, we find a literary interpretation of the humanists' polemic. More and Vives argue in the abstract against the destruction of the family and the corruption of the individual by the economic and social forces unleashed by absolutism. The anonymous author of the *Lazarillo* mirrors this complex intellectual, moral, and social world through the story of the de facto destruction of one such family and one such individual. Pity and laughter, not philosophical enlightenment, are the instruments of his subversive task. Under the devastating blows of his irony the complete structure of the cosmic order collapses. The links of the well-organized chain of being are transformed into the links of a chain that imprisons the impoverished and confines them to a horrifying dungeon. [. . .]

We know that a strict punitive legislation was periodically enforced during the greater part of the sixteenth century. What were the results of such a policy? Let us read Giginta's vivid description:

> There [in the streets] you will see lost boys and girls, thin, groaning, scabby, ulcered, crippled, ill in all kinds of ways, and old and younger men, with such poor color and many of deathly hue, that it seems that they are a picture of damned souls. . . . Let us go out in the morning to the hospitals at the time when they receive the sick and you will see how many arrive there from the streets that are already as good as dead; and how many must go back because there is neither bed nor food, and they must wander desolate until they throw themselves on some dung heap, or fall wherever they happen to faint, there to die in despair, abandoning all hope. . . .

One of these boys is Lázaro. In the third treatise, while still a child, Lázaro is begging in the streets of Toledo. Because the crop had been bad that year the town council had decided to apply the Poor Laws and expel the out-of-town beggars, to which number the starving Lázaro belongs. If he tries to go on begging, this is the destiny that awaits him:

The way it happened was that, since there had been a crop failure there that year, the town council decided to make all the beggars who came from other towns get out of the city. And they announced that from then on if they found one of them there, he'd be whipped. So the law went into effect, and four days after the announcement was given I saw a procession of beggars being led through the streets and whipped. And I got so scared that I didn't dare go out begging any more.

(Rudder's modern translation, pp. 67–68)

[. . .]

In the *Lazarillo*, the seat of power is no longer the castle, but the town council, as befits the bureaucratic administration of the absolute monarchy. It is an all-powerful body from which fearsome laws emerge. Such power is seen through the eyes of a beggar; in fact, the empty spaces of the meadow or the forest have been filled with an urban habitat of beggars being whipped by unspecified torturers, representing a remote authority. The beggars are called 'a procession"; the term is used here to signify directly a line or two of prisoners. But nothing is accidental in his masterpiece of sarcasm, and underlying this signification, and shadowing it with a religious evocation, we find the meaning of the Easter parades in which the suffering and passion of Christ were (and still are in Spain) commemorated. The beggars, then, whipped by the powerful, are covered with Christ's image, and in their suffering we see renewed the passion of him who said that what was done to one of these poor was done to him.

The change from the worlds of the shepherd and the knight to the world of the pícaro; from arcadia and chivalry to the desolate urban landscape of misery and hunger; from romance to irony – in fact, the Copernican revolution that produced a new genre – could only have been born of an upheaval that affected men's lives and forced educated writers to see conditions they had so far ignored. This change stemmed from an increased awareness of human misery, which the urban growth of the Renaissance had made highly visible. The genius of the Spanish author of the *Lazarillo* consists in his having found the literary voice for such a profound transformation of European society. The *Lazarillo*, of course, did not annihilate the past, but it gave artistic form to the all-pervading crisis that was destroying the basis of the traditional order.

NOTES

1   For a full discussion of Cervantes' text, see Claudio Guillén, 'Genre and Countergenre: The Discovery of the Picaresque,' in his *Literature as System* (Princeton: Princeton Univ. Press, 1971), pp. 135–58. Precedents for the *Lazarillo* can be found in classical works, such as Lucian's *Lucius: The Ass* or Apuleius' *The Golden Ass*, and in late medieval and early Renaissance descriptions of the life of beggars and vagrants, such as the *Speculum Cerretanorum* (c. 1484–86) and the *Liber Vagatorum* (1509 or 1510). Literary descriptions of low life were usual enough in the fifteenth and sixteenth centuries (*La celestina*, *La lozana andaluza*, *Eulenspiegel*, etc.), but none had the structural unity and sense of development and growth that could give birth to a genre (Guillén, 'Toward a Definition of the Picaresque,' *Literature as System*, pp. 71–106).

2   Henry Kamen, *The Iron Century* (London: Weidenfeld and Nicolson, 1971), p. 387.

3   *Forma Subventionis Pauperum Quae apud Hyperas Flandorum Urbem Viget, Universae Reipublicae Christianae Longe Utilissima.* I have quoted (modernizing the orthography) from William Marshall's English translation (1535) included in *Some Early Tracts on Poor Relief*, ed. F. R. Salter (London: Methuen, 1926), pp. 41–42. The *Forma Subventionis Pauperum* appeared in 1525; since Luis Vives' *De Subventione Pauperum* was not printed until Sept. 1526, it is impossible to prove that Vives influenced the Ypres scheme. But since that great thinker was living in neighboring Bruges, it certainly seems likely that it was he who elaborated the project, and not a group of town councillors.

4   My translation of Juan Luis Vives, *De Subventione Pauperum* (Valencia: Universidad de Valencia, 1942), pp. 84, 88–90.

5   Thomas More, *Utopia*, ed. Edward Surtz, S. J., and H. H. Hexter, *The Complete Works of St. Thomas More*, iv (New Haven: Yale Univ. Press, 1965), 63, 76. For the close relationship between Erasmus and More and for the radical character of More's thought, see the following sections in the editors' Introduction to *Utopia*: 'Christian Humanism,' 'Utopia and the Christian Revival,' and 'A Window to the Future: The Radicalism of Utopia.'

6   The Spanish text, 'y confesó y no negó y padesció persecución por la justicia,' is much more complex than expected. It is, in fact, compounded of two biblical quotations: 'confessus est et non negavit' (John i.20) and 'beati qui persecutionem patiuntur propter iustitiam, quoniam ipsorum est regnum caelorum' (Matt. v.10). The first, 'confessus est,' refers to John the Baptist facing the Pharisees, and thus, to the sixteenth-century Spanish reader, who was extremely well versed in the Gospels, it would immediately suggest the innocence of Lázaro's father and the hypocrisy of his persecutors; this impression would be reinforced by the echo of the second biblical quotation, in which *iustitiam* connotes both the righteousness of Tomé González and consequently, and ironically, the *injustice* of the official *justice* that is destroying Lázaro's family. That the Spanish Inquisition was aware of the author's sarcasm is proved by the omission of this reference from the expurgated edition of 1573.

7   With regard to Zaide, although the name is *Morisco* (Rico, p. ii) it is obvious from the text that he is a *Negro slave*. Lope de Vega calls him '*negro*' (*La Dorotea* [Valencia: Castalia, 1958], p. 67), and only his black color can explain why he and his child produce such a shocking contrast in the racially mixed society of sixteenth-century Spain. A final remark about *goodness* as an exception in the book. It is true that a few generous bystanders help the starving Lázaro, but they have an anonymous and vague existence that marks them as marginal, not only to the story but to the world itself as portrayed in the book through the great figures of the blind man, the *hidalgo*, and the ecclesiastical characters (for whom the author reserves his most venomous arrows).

24   Peter N. Dunn '*Lazarillo de Tormes:* The Case of the Purloined Letter'

Source: from Revista de Estudios Hispanicos, 22, 1988, pp. 1–14.

Lazarillo de tormes is the first of the Spanish picaresque novels, the inaugurator of a new genre in European fiction. [. . .]

Older writers on picaresque literature, such as Frank Wadleigh Chandler, refer to these novels as 'romances of roguery,' and the Spanish *pícaro* has traditionally been rendered by the English word 'rogue.' Guzmán de Alfarache, a half century after *Lazarillo*, is indeed a rogue; he becomes a cheat, a great financial swindler, a thief, a confidence trickster, and he pimps for his own wife. None of this is true of Lazarillo, who tells us that he stole only in order to avoid starvation. Obviously, stealing involves deception, and the wiles of the boy are not entirely forgotten by Lázaro the adult, in the way that he maintains appearances. Lázaro, however, faces two publics; there is the public within the fiction, the neighbors whose gossip he must suppress in defense of his newly conquered respectability; and there is the public that picks up and reads his book. One public that he sees and knows, and another public that is unknown, invisible, unidentifiable, continually expanding into a limitless future. This second public, of which we are momentarily a part, must be kept in control. Clearly, he cannot use on us the oaths and indignant gestures with which he attempts to influence the neighbors in his world, as he tells it at the end of the book. But he will have recourse to verbal gestures and rhetorical maneuvers. But more important than the public within the book is the primary *destinataire* [addressee] of his writing, a person known only by the respectful form of address, Vuestra Merced ['Your Worship']. He it is who wrote a letter to Lázaro, as we are informed in the prologue, and the *Vida* [*Life*] is the reply to that letter.

Before proceeding further, let me pause a moment to make sure that we agree on who is who in this fictional world. The title of the book is *La vida de Lazarillo de Tormes y de sus fortunas y adversidades* [*The Life of Lazarillo de Tormes and of his fortunes and adversities*]. The narrator has already reached manhood by the end of his story, but I shall distinguish between his two selves, the self that is being remembered and the self that does the remembering, the acting self and the writing self. [. . .] The former will be referred to with the diminutive form 'Lazarillo', and the latter with the plain 'Lázaro'. Since the person Lázaro addresses as 'Vuestra Merced' ('Your Worship,' or 'Your Honor') is not known by name or by any other designation, that is how I shall refer to him. The unknown author will have to be named as the unknown author.

The question of the truthfulness of Lázaro's account of his childhood is a topic that has been raised by a number of readers. [. . .] Did it all really happen as he says it did? Does he slant the story so as to gain sympathy? Is there some special guile in the manner of his self revelation? Does he seem to be counting on the indulgence of the reader? Does his story seem to have been planned with the expectation that *tout comprendre, c'est tout pardonner* [To understand everything is to forgive everything]? These are questions that I shall leave unanswered, for the good reason that they cannot be answered, and they were not meant to be answered. One can do no more than ask them, and in what follows I shall give some attention to why this is so. These questions, to the extent that they are self defeating, will make us pay attention to the way in which Lázaro, as the producer of his discourse, also asserts a pre-emptive authority over it, an authority that originally belongs to the person who commanded him to write it. If there is a sense in which Lázaro is a rogue, it is to be founded in the act by which he misappropriates his narrative, attempting to displace its original source, its own function as a letter or report, and its destination. What I have to say concerns the why and the how of this act of appropriation, the power struggle involved in it, and the consequences for the reader.

I don't need to spend time telling you what happens in the story, this deceptively simple story of a boy employed by a succession of masters until he becomes his own master. I don't need to point out that the three principal masters correspond to the medieval paradigm of the three estates, but degraded and made grotesque; or how, in the course of his training he assimilates characteristic vices from these representative figures and finally establishes himself, in his turn, as a person of self-styled honor and respectability, as a cynically complacent amalgam of all three types: a corrupt wheeler-dealer exercising public office under the protective shade, or the shady protection, of an archpriest. There are internal patterns and symmetries that have often been pointed out and commented on. [. . .] We might also note those features by means of which the text parodies chivalresque romance, the simplest and most obvious being the name of the protagonist (Lazarillo de Tormes recalls such names as Amadís de Gaula, Palmerín de Inglaterra, Cirongilio de Tracia, and so on). Structure and ideology are more complex matters, but plots of romance characteristically end by revealing a structure of familial relations that either reflects and reaffirms an implicit ideal, or repeats that which presided at the hero's origin before he set out upon his quest journey. In the case of *Lazarillo*, that common structure which unites beginning and end is anti-heroic; it is the comically ignoble one of the *ménage à trois*. Other modes of discourse are being parodied, too, but mention of chivalresque fiction and the ideal paradigms of social-historical discourse (the three estates) should suffice to show that this little text is engaged in some systematic acts of transgression against established discursive norms.

I mention these matters that (as I said) don't need to be mentioned, because they may present problems of verisimilitude in a first person narration. That forces us to ask whether we really know what he is doing when he lets us see into a life that, had it been ours, we would prefer to keep hidden. Our expectations as modern readers create their own problems, of course. We expect the first person point of view to reveal the inner world of the speaker or writer. But compared to more modern works, or to the English transformations of the picaresque nearly two centuries later, the 'I' of Lázaro looks out rather than in upon itself. I don't mean to say that it reveals no interiority at all, but that he gives the deliberate impression that he was too busy struggling to survive to be able to afford the luxury of a developed self-consciousness. His reference (in *tratado* [treatise] 1) to his little half-brother's scare at seeing his colored father offers not so much the experience of self-knowledge as a parable of it. The self in this work is an operator (in all senses of the term) rather than a consciousness to be explored; [. . .]. In other words, the lack of interiority is part of the novel's meaning. We might rephrase and remetaphorize the idea again and say that Lázaro presents himself as a lens through which he makes us view his situation, and that the lens composes the image of the situation as he would like us to see it. If we must judge, he would like us to judge not him, but his circumstance. The self that he composes in his narrative is a creature of the world in which he has grown up, and whose characteristic forms of cant and hypocrisy he has internalized. He presents himself as a quiet triumph of adaptation, in which he and his world are one. To this end, he attempts to plot his story in an exemplary, heroic mode, as a victory over adversity, at the same time as his discourse is antiheroic. This story of a boy may then be read as a device for unmasking the scandalousness of the adult world.

Readers of *Lazarillo de Tormes* in the sixteenth and seventeenth centuries evidently enjoyed it for the jokes and witty anecdotes. Recent critical readings, however, have shifted the center of interest from the boy to the man, from the actor to the writer, from the liver of his life to the artful planner and justifier of his life as representation. These shifts in critical attention have resulted from the discovery of gaps and indeterminacies [. . .] in the text. The most obvious of these are the time that has elapsed between the events of the narrative and the narrative itself and, more specifically, that between the last recorded moment and the telling of it; the mysterious identity of Vuestra Merced, the designated reader within the text; Lázaro's relation to him; and exactly what is the 'matter', *el caso*, that Lázaro is called upon to explain. As the indeterminacies multiply, so do the strings of dubious causality: was Vuestra Merced's letter a request or a command? Whose behavior is he seeking to investigate, Lázaro's or the Archpriest's, and why? What sort of authority does he wield? Is this a serious investigation, or just a way of keeping people in their place? A game of cat and mouse? Could he remove Lázaro from his public office? Is Lázaro afraid that he will do so? What sort of *reader* is this person? Does he perhaps seek nothing more than some malicious entertainment from Lázaro's story? Could he even desire Lázaro's wife for himself? Is the whole situation a bluff, and does Lázaro see through it even as he keeps up the pretence of playing the game and toeing the line? Does he write in the most objective way he knows, or does he deliberately emphasize his struggle against a cruel world? We could even ask whether he has invented Vuestra Merced as a pretext for writing. At this point it is obvious that the questions have proliferated out of control, and yet there appear to be no textual constraints that would interdict these or any other questions that an inquisitive reader might ask. We may observe, in passing, that later writers of picaresque made their texts much less open to such uninvited readings.

We now need to get back beyond the unanswered questions to the gaps and indeterminacies that generate them, and to seek to discover their function within the discourse itself. That is, not to see in how many ways we can be confused, nor even to ask why Lázaro wants us to be confused, since this question will simply send us back down the same boggy and many branching path that we have just left. Rather, it is a matter of uncovering the rhetorical strategy with which Lázaro presents his text to his readers. I should say the strategy with which he *redirects* his text, since the joke, if it is a joke, is that it was not written for the public in the first place. It was written for Vuestra Merced, and he is the only reader who could know how to read it. All we can ever know about his reading is that none of the endless possible readings that we can produce will ever be identical with it. Here, then, in the mid fifteen hundreds, is a text that, from the very moment of its writing, was predicated upon the reader's implicit understanding of the variability of reading. It incorporates within itself those very conditions that make necessary an esthetics of reception: it was intended to be read by different readers, having different kinds of interest, expecting to derive satisfactions as different one from another as fact is from fiction. This is not a matter of speculative fancy, as our string of unanswered and unanswerable but quite plausible questions has already made clear. Lázaro himself intends his text to be taken as both raw documentary fact (by Vuestra Merced), and as a work of literary art (by the rest of us). The prologue states this explicitly. The prologue indeed has an extraordinary function to perform. It is not addressed to a patron, nor does it seek to amuse the idle reader with gratuitous verbal play. It is the switch where the deviation of the text from its original *destinataire* takes place, and I will spend the rest of this paper in examining how this is done, and what are the transactions of power and authority that take place between the author and the reader.

In the prologue we find the first mention of *el caso*, the 'matter' that has attracted the attention of the personage who is to be addressed as Vuestra Merced (Your Worship) and here, too, is the *only* mention of the fact that His Worship has sent for an explanation in writing. If we skip the prologue, or read it carelessly, we miss the fact that Lázaro's text is his response to a previous text. That originating text does not exist for us, of course. Within the fictional world of the novel we may infer that it has disappeared, or that Lázaro has suppressed it, or make any other plausible supposition we like; what is important is that that letter has had consequences. It did not disappear without trace. Its trace is the text we are reading; evidently, that lost letter was a very powerful speech act.

The nature of *el caso* is another unanswerable question, one more gap in the text [. . .]. Most readers accept [. . .] that Vuestra Merced is investigating the situation of the *ménage à trois* in which the story ends, after Lázaro has married the Archpriest's mistress. Even if we accept this explanation, there is no indication of the writer's status or of his reason for making such a demand. Once again, answering that kind of question leads only to more questions of the same positive order. All such questions imply that this is a work of mimetic realism that could be pressed, under close interrogation, to yield the facts of the matter, that the gaps in a text are there to be filled rather than negotiated, that one must strive to cancel, deny, or obliterate all indeterminacies rather than respect or caress them. For us to read the text as the place where such answers must be found is to read it in the judicial spirit of Vuestra Merced.

For any reader of *Lazarillo* there are two missing terms, two glaring absences. First, the real author. His absence from the historical record has promoted more or less plausible fictions, as we might expect. Second, we may search in vain within the narrative for that invisible eminence, Vuestra Merced. So, whether we seek to examine the book in the context of the real world and within the system author-text-reader, or in the context of the fictive world and within the system narrator-text-Vuestra Merced, one necessary term is always lacking: the real author in the first instance, and the fictive reader in the second. [. . .]

In his autobiographical narrative, Lázaro succeeds in denying authority to Vuestra Merced, and does so silently. But in the prologue, this denial is its whole purpose. Let me expand this thought a little. The center of interest in the story is neither the self as source of action nor the world as determinant of the self, but rather it is the relation of the self to the world as Lázaro desires to fix it. Also, at the level of the discourse, there is another center, which is the relation of the self to its text. How, then, does he fix it, how does he sell this package of self and world and word? The answer, again, is in the prologue or, rather, it is the prologue itself. The prologue is a text of his own invention with no reference to life or history; it is pure literature, pure rhetorical strategy, and its sole function is to mediate the *Vida*, the life story to us, the readers. It is a reframing device. In mediating the life story, the prologue redefines it. By means of these few tricky paragraphs, Lázaro switches genres on us and consequently he radically trans-values his story.

A little while ago I referred to Vuestra Merced's 'lost' letter as a powerful speech act, since it resulted in Lázaro writing his life story. It will be useful, I think, to reconsider the whole text of his story as a response in the same terms, that is, as part of a verbal transaction between him and the reader.

Speech act theory recognizes that the effectiveness of an utterance depends upon its satisfying certain criteria. [. . .] It is not difficult to imagine contexts in which utterances that are formally questions, such as 'Will you close the window?', or 'When will you learn to keep your feet off the table?' function as commands. However, to treat them as questions requiring a reasoned response would be to court disaster. The point is that, since verbal transactions are encoded within a system of conventions, the hearer would have to make a conscious decision to interpret these questions literally as questions, and weigh the consequences, before replying with a predication as to how long it would take to acquire the desired degree of control over his feet. The context of an utter-ance involves power relations which are not reflected in the grammar or the syntax.

In the case of Lázaro's script, these relations are somewhat explicit, since the originator of the exchange is addressed with a title of respect, but they are also uncertain, since it is not known precisely what he asked, or why, in what terms, with what qualifiers or insinuations, on what legal or moral authority. Not knowing the conditions (verbal, gestural, and so forth) of the initiating utter-ance, we are unable to gauge the fittingness of the response. We are rendered largely incapable of judging how far he has complied. [. . .]

Even without knowing what this *caso* is, we suspect that there must be a mis-match, a lack of proportion between the request for an explanation and the response that tells the story of one's life. This lack of proportion must surely be the sign of a structural rift in the verbal exchange, a manifestation of Lázaro's desire to substitute his own agenda for that of his inquirer. This rift may be found situated within the prologue, where we observe him addressing both readers, the public and the private, us and Vuestra Merced. He first addresses us in the manner of one who has great things to impart ('cosas señaladas'), matters that deserve to be saved from oblivion. This is a topos that we commonly find in late medieval chronicles, and in romances that pretend to be chronicles – yet another discur-sive transgression. After making this proud claim, and confidently associating the arts with the impulse to honor and fame, he commits to paper that which should not even be spoken. It is a social fact, however, that honor can be ascribed only to free men and to those who serve in a noble cause; consequently, his dishonor is compounded. Now comes the brilliant, cynical maneuver of the prologue. If he must set forth the embarrassing facts of his dependency on the largesse of the Archpriest, he will project his narrative beyond the designated reader and his context of judgment to another, hypothetical reader who will read it differently. The prologue then becomes an attempt to transform what was a letter or report to a person of authority into a public text, to be read by persons who will not expect it to answer questions, but to arouse them to wonder and amusement. Citing Pliny on books, he makes a breathtaking seizure of the artistic high ground, since he obviously cannot seize the moral ground occupied by Vuestra Merced. Why write for only one person? Fame is the spur! [. . .]

What is important is that a text that has, we must suppose, fulfilled Vuestra Merced's generic expectation as a factual memo or *relación* [narrative], upon which he can proceed to form a moral and perhaps a judicial judgment, is represented as a story that will feed the new readers' curiosity and disinvite such judgments. [. . .] In Lázaro's prologue we are shown the sleight of hand by means of which he transmutes his own life story, removing it from a context of accountability to social and moral authority and relocating it in one where the consequences are of a totally different order. [. . .] By his appeal to fame and to the variability of taste, he makes a bid to place his story beyond good and evil, to detach it from the prior use that Vuestra Merced will have made of it, and from the concerns of his community. [. . .]

Within the fiction, Lázaro is accountable to Vuestra Merced in social and political, and perhaps moral, or even legal terms. As author, on the other hand, he is accountable to us in terms that are conventional, implicitly contractual, and nothing more. But as he has rigged the story, so he has also rigged the genre. What appears to us laborers in the vineyards of intertextuality to be parody of romance, must then be, from his perspective, an attempt to edit his life, to bring into view those authentic features of romance that might dignify it and make it worthy of a place on the reader's shelf. His story has been one of deprivations overcome, of hungers eventually satisfied. From the basic hunger for food, to the hunger for a place in the world, for acceptance, for honor and status. Finally he feels the hunger for immortality that can be satisfied through writing. Then, providentially, comes Vuestra Merced's letter, which generates his reply, and providence, as we know, is the mode of operation of romance. (It makes no difference whether this desire preceded or followed the arrival of that letter.) [. . .]

The discourse of insolence depends for its message on the grammar of subservience. In presenting himself, Lázaro gives the reader a key that will enable him to demystify the world of traditional values and hierarchies to which he belongs, as well as the structures of authority that sustain it. This is a world of evident dereliction and dissolution. [. . .]

25 Andrew Cunningham '**Luther and Vesalius**'

Source: from *The Anatomical Renaissance: The Resurrection of the Anatomical Projects of the Ancients*, Andrew Cunningham, Scolar Press, Aldershot, 1997, chapter 8, pp. 216–36.

Luther, it was said, hatched the egg that Erasmus had laid; in other words, he took seriously the implications of the kind of reform that Erasmus had called for

– with momentous effects for the whole of Europe. It might be said that Vesalius promoted a parallel revolution in anatomy: He taught the world to see a different body; he taught anatomists, physicians and philosophers to adopt a new ambition with respect to the Ancients. It is not particularly novel to call Vesalius a 'Luther of anatomy'. What has not been done before, however, is to look and see the ways in which his anatomical enterprise and achievement were in their own time 'Lutheran'. [. . .]

Martin Luther was a troubled Augustinian monk and professor of theology tucked away in the new little university of Wittenberg, and he had been wrestling with the implications of the fact, central to the teaching of St Augustine, of man's fallen nature. Luther took this to its logical conclusion: if man is fallen, then he is in bondage to sin and nothing he can do can justify him in the eyes of God. His sinful nature prevents man from following the law of God; yet man cannot be saved by his own efforts. Luther's solution to this, the 'blinding flash' that happened to him in the tower room in 1513 as he read the Psalms and Romans, was that justification of man was indeed possible, but only by trusting in God's 'righteousness' to save. That is to say, each individual is the potential recipient of God's abounding grace and forgiveness. All that each individual has to do is to actively accept this grace, an acceptance which can be made 'by faith alone', and then he will be 'reborn' in Christ. 'Good works' are powerless and irrelevant to salvation. Luther had found in Augustine what looked to him like a problem, and solved it through a particular reading of the Bible.

In this way of looking at the relationship of God and man, the only mediator necessary for salvation was Jesus Christ, who was himself the Son of God. Suddenly there was, for Luther, no role at all for the mediation of a special priesthood or for the apparatus of the Church, for they were presenting themselves as the essential intermediaries in a relationship which demanded that there be no intermediaries. Thus the whole Church organization, from the pope down to the parish priest, was redundant as a means to the salvation of the individual. And what is more, Luther could find no biblical warrant for the existence of a Church in the Roman Catholic form, nor for many of its practices, such as indulgences, the veneration of saints, the ritual use of relics. In his famous 95 theses of 1517 Luther challenged the Church authorities to justify in scholastic disputation – to show their textual warrant for – the practice of indulgences. Appropriately Luther pinned this challenge to dispute to the university noticeboard, which was the door of the university church of Wittenberg.

In making this resolution of his personal spiritual problems, what Luther thought and claimed he was doing was bringing back into existence the *primitive apostolic church*: the congregation of all believers. He was going back to the early church, the one that Christ intended; going back, that is, before the institution and (as he saw it) corruption of the Catholic Church. The real church was not a formally organized hierarchy of power, but one body of men, united spiritually, each with the responsibility of seeking his own salvation. To bring about this state of affairs Luther, like Erasmus, advocated the education of each individual in the articles of faith (catechizing). But Luther also insisted on *the duty of every person to read God's Word (the Bible) for himself.* Erasmus had translated the New Testament anew into what was by now the language of the learned, Latin; but Luther translated it into the language of the people, German. He published his New Testament in 1522, the complete Bible in 1534. And he saw to it that the university of Wittenberg was henceforth devoted to the creation and propagation of what was in his eyes a properly Christian curriculum of studies. Under the direction of Luther's soul-mate Philipp Melanchthon, 'the preceptor of Germany', it became the mother of Protestant universities. Thus Christianity was, for Luther, a religion of personal engagement; it is the Word of God which is (quite literally) the guide to salvation and the true Christian life, and every individual needs to read and hear it for himself. The Word, in the sense of the text of the Bible, was of central importance to him. In his confrontation with the defenders of the Catholic Church, Luther's challenge was always for them to show – to literally point out with their finger – the texts in the Bible on which their claims were built. Only this would count as authority to Luther. If they could not point to a pertinent text, their claims had no authority in Luther's eyes.

Luther and his followers had a new goal: to live the life of true apostolic Christians. The Word, the Sacrament (a reduced and redefined set of rituals), and Discipline, these were to be the keys to the new Christianity – which was, in Luther's view, the oldest form of Christianity. Catholics and Protestants now looked to the same book, the Bible, but with differing interpretations of what it taught. For the Protestants its message was that they should *be* primitive Christians, like the early Apostles.

Some of these features of the doctrine of the reformed faith can be seen dramatically in the iconography of Luther, that is, in the pictures painted of Luther and under the influence and impact of his doctrines. [. . .] Almost alone among the reformers, it appears, Luther remained favourable to the use of imagery in church. Some of the reformers of the Swiss cities, for instance, were to pursue a drastic policy of clearing out and breaking all statues, pictures and relics from their local churches, on the grounds that the worship of 'idols' was forbidden by the Commandments. Their fear was that worship of what the image represented actually became worship of the image itself, and hence idolatry. Luther, however, held the view that as we unavoidably form mental images of things that we hear described in words, so it is positively desirable to look at a pictured image which properly represents the 'thing' in question. Hence for Luther pictorial images had a useful pedagogical role in spreading the new doctrines. They are also good propaganda. Fortunately Luther's protector, the Elector Frederick the Wise of Saxony, had installed a court painter of some talent, Lucas Cranach the Elder (1472–1553), who was succeeded by his son, the Younger (1515–1586). Between them the Cranachs produced many portraits of the Wittenberg reformers and, from 1529 onwards, a number of pictures which portray several of Luther's main doctrines. So keen was Luther on the pedagogic value of illustration that he had the elder Cranach produce a number of woodcuts for his German translation of the Bible of 1522: Luther himself decided which themes should be portrayed and, to some extent, how.

A favourite theme of both Luther and the Cranachs was the Last Supper (a relatively rare theme of religious art hitherto). As Luther wrote in 1530:

> Whoever is inclined to put pictures on the altar ought to have the Lord's Supper of Christ painted, with these two verses written around it in golden letters: 'The gracious and merciful Lord has instituted a remembrance *of His wonderful works*'. Then they would stand before our eyes for our heart to contemplate them, and even our eyes, in reading, would have to thank and praise God. Since the altar is designated for the administration of the Sacrament, one could not find a better painting for it.

If we look at the altar-piece by the younger Cranach which stands today in the church at Dessau, we can see an extraordinary portrayal of this theme (see Fig. 14). For here we have Christ surrounded by the Apostles; and those 'apostles' are Luther, Melanchthon and other leaders of the Wittenberg reformation! The reformers are shown as *being* the early Apostles. And of course there is no priest acting as intermediary. Christ himself is distributing the sacramental elements directly to these apostles. What is more, communion 'in both kinds' (that is, bread and wine) is being taken, and this is another apostolic practice that Luther worked to reinstitute. Another altar-piece by the elder Cranach (see Fig. 15), still today in the church at Wittenberg, has a comparable portrayal of Luther and others as the disciples at the Last Supper. And on the wings of this there are pictures which further show the reformers as engaged in revived apostolic practices; the unordained Philipp Melanchthon as St John the Baptist, performing infant baptism; and the pastor of the church (one Johannes Bugenhagen), as St Peter holding the keys of the Church! The message about how the reformers were living out primitive apostolic practices could hardly be more direct.

It is important to appreciate the exclusiveness of the source of authority to which Luther was appealing. The practices, beliefs and behaviour of proper Christians are to be discovered only from Scripture. Scripture – written Scripture, the text of the Bible – is the arbiter, the ultimate authority. For Luther an issue is resolved when he can point to the relevant words in Scripture. This is not just a simple-minded literalism on his part. For the Word had a very special status for him. Hear him ecstatic in *The Freedom of a Christian*:

> One thing, and only one thing, is necessary for Christian life, righteousness and freedom. That one thing is the most holy Word of God, the gospel of Christ . . . 'Men shall not live by bread alone, but by every word that proceeds from the mouth of God'. Let us then consider it certain and firmly established that the soul can do without anything except the Word of God and that where the Word of God is missing there is no help at all for the soul. If it has the Word of God it is rich and lacks nothing since it is the Word of life, truth, light, peace, righteousness, salvation, joy, liberty, wisdom, power, grace, glory, and of every incalculable blessing. That is why the prophet in the entire Psalm [Psalm 19] and in many other places yearns and sighs for the Word of God and uses so many names to describe

it . . . On the other hand, there is no more terrible disaster with which the wrath of God can afflict men than a famine of the hearing of his Word . . .

The Word is, for Luther, three complementary things: it is the Scriptures, it is Christ, it is God's Law. It is all these at once – and this is the source of its authority for him. Hearing the Word, preaching the Word, reading the Word; these are central activities for a Lutheran Christian to engage in. And nothing was more powerful for Luther than the promises from the mouth of God which he could find in the written Word of God; his whole theology is based on the fulfilment of God's spoken promises. [. . .]

Luther quickly gained many adherents. [. . .] But why should the appeal of the doctrines of Luther have been so great to people who had not shared Luther's own personal dilemmas? Luther's was far from being the first heresy within the Catholic Church: why was it the most successful, both in itself and in the more extreme forms (such as Calvinism) that it spawned?

One of the positive appeals of Luther's new doctrine was that it was, in its rituals, a religion of participation. This is particularly evident in Luther's teaching on the ritual of communion. Further, each person's conscience, regulated and informed by the Word of God, was to be the final arbiter of right and wrong, not the volumes of canon law – which Luther ceremonially burnt in 1520 in response to his own books being burnt by the pope. To potential converts, therefore, 'Lutheranism' may be said to have meant a new stress on the responsibility of the individual for the fate of his own soul; a new stress, that is, on individual autonomy.

When Luther 'went public', with the 95 theses, there was great consternation in Catholic circles. Luther was ordered to be silent, but he refused. The theses were refuted in print by Johannes von Eck of Ingolstadt, defended, counter-refuted, re-defended all within the space of eight months. Then Eck challenged Luther to a public disputation, which took place at Leipzig in mid-1519. The unwillingness of Luther to disown his views at the disputation obliged Eck in 1520 to get a papal Bull excommunicating him. Seen from the perspective of the pope, Luther's message was a heresy threatening the status quo with immense social and political dangers. The emperor's support was courted by Luther, but soon the emperor too came to see the reform as a threat to social and religious order. Pope and Emperor were quickly proved right.

Now we turn to comparing the activities and claims of Luther with those of Vesalius the anatomist. We will be looking to see whether or not Vesalius undertakes new anatomizing initiatives and sees a new body *because* he has adopted Lutheran attitudes. This of course will involve establishing that Vesalius adopted Lutheran attitudes. If the comparison is successful, then it might be possible to say that just as Luther went beyond Erasmus, and followed in his own practice his understanding of what primitive Christians *did* as well as follow what they *said*, so Vesalius similarly went beyond Sylvius and Guenther and in his anatomizing followed what Galen *did* as well as what he *said* – and went even beyond that. The first thing we need to establish is whether Vesalius came into contact with reformed religious teaching.

14 Luther and his followers as the disciples of Christ at the Last Supper. Lucas Cranach the
Younger, Dessau Altar-piece, 1565, Schlosskirche, Dessau. Photo: Bildarchiv Foto Marburg.

The appeal of the reformed doctrine was primarily in the north of Europe. The
most fundamental reason for this seems to be the great shift of economic power
that was taking place at this time; a shift from the Mediterranean to the
north of Europe, from Italy to the Netherlands, from Venice to Antwerp and
Amsterdam. Though it would take another century to complete, the social and
political effects of this economic shift were already visible. It was marked by the
renewed growth of cities as centres of wealth in the north. The Lutheran reformation was to be primarily an urban phenomenon, and one could say that with
it the city people of the north put their confession where their interest was.

Vesalius was from the north. Charles of Ghent (1500–1566), was in 1519 unan-

15 Wing panels of the altar-piece by Lucas Cranach the Elder, 1547, 'Memorial of the Reformation', now in Wittenberg Stadtkirche, showing Luther's lay companions taking up what had been priestly roles. Photo: Bildarchiv Foto Marburg.

imously elected as the Holy Roman Emperor, and became Charles V. While Vesalius was an infant, his father was with the Imperial court, which at that time was in Spain (though young Vesalius may have been left at home.) Educated in the Netherlands himself, the young emperor had taken with him to Spain courtiers who were admirers of Erasmus of Rotterdam. During these years, even though the Inquisition was active in Spain, the cultivation of Erasmian ideals enjoyed an unparalleled vogue, especially at court. Charles V, though he became the hammer of the Protestants, carried his private Erasmianism with him to his grave. Vesalius's father was a member of this court.

The exciting events of Luther's rebellion against Rome were happening during Vesalius's youth in the Netherlands, and in an area relatively close by. It spilled over into the territories in which Vesalius lived. Indeed, the urgencies of the situation created by Luther and his followers intermittently recalled Charles to the northern parts of his empire for the rest of his reign.

After his time at the new humanist tri-lingual college at Louvain (1530–), where he learnt Greek and Hebrew and the best humanist Latin, Vesalius could have read the Bible in the original languages if he had wanted to. So from all this, we know that by the time he was 19 years old, Vesalius would have been aware of, and perhaps even quite familiar with, Erasmian thinking about religious reform.

In 1533 Vesalius went to Paris to study medicine. A striking feature of Paris's university at this time was that it was a bastion of religious orthodoxy. If Vesalius's parents had wanted a place for their son to learn medicine which was most likely to discourage him from the new heresy, Paris would at one time have looked ideal. For it was there that Luther's doctrines had been most thoroughly condemned in 1521. But now in 1533 the impact of Lutheran teaching was once again impossible to ignore, even at Paris. The Sorbonne and the Parlement of Paris were busily hunting out and condemning heretics: Louis Berquin had been burned alive for heresy as recently as 1529. Indeed the Syndic of the Sorbonne, Noel Beda (Bédier), seriously regarded the learning of Greek as a potentially heretical activity, summonsing the Royal Lecturers before Parlement in 1534. Among the generation of Vesalius's fellow students at Paris were Jean Calvin in the law faculty and Michael Servetus in medicine [. . .]. In November 1533 the student rector of the university, Nicholas Cop, son of the famous physician, made a notorious speech (reportedly written by Calvin) which led to both him and Calvin having to flee France for their lives. Then in October 1534 there was the 'Affair of the Placards', the outrageous attack on the mass. To have failed to notice the effects at Paris of Luther's claims, Vesalius would have had to have been a hermit; we can, I think, take it that he was familiar with them.

Was Vesalius a Lutheran, a committed follower of this new primitive Christianity? And was such a commitment on his part the source, spring and reason for his reform of anatomical practice? Did his anatomizing stem from the Reformation proper through the person of Vesalius the follower of Luther?

In the first place we have to consider the argument from silence, for there is no mention in writing by Vesalius himself, or by any of his contemporaries, of his religious persuasion. To be Catholic was to be unremarkable, and no one remarked that Vesalius was not Catholic. Secondly, after Vesalius had finished his great book, the *Fabrica* [Fig. 3], he went off and became a physician to the emperor, Charles V, refusing all offers of university posts. Charles spent his life trying to cope with the mess that Luther had created, trying to bring erring parts of his empire back to the true faith, trying to keep his empire united under one faith, Catholicism. Vesalius survived some dozen years in this court, close to the person of the Emperor. It would have been quite a feat for Vesalius, who was highly opinionated and argumentative – to keep quiet about his aberrant beliefs, if he had such beliefs. The argument from silence thus indicates that Vesalius was not a Lutheran, and indeed that he may have kept his anatomizing separate from his religious commitment, whatever it was.

On the other hand, however, there are Vesalius's actions: the pattern of what he did in his anatomizing, how he did it, and what he called on other people to do, in turn, in their anatomizing.

From his early days in Padua as an anatomical demonstrator, Vesalius, constantly placed the 'evidence of the body', acquired by personal experience of dissection or by observation of the dissected body, over the evidence of texts. As he wrote about the azygos vein in the bloodletting letter of 1539: 'No-one who has either engaged in the task of dissecting personally or who has observed a dissection will allege that [this vein] arises under the base of the heart or before the vena cava reaches the heart'. [. . .] Vesalius could make such claims because he had an unrivalled experience of and skill at dissection, greater than that of his teachers, and also because he had a strong, not to say arrogant, personality. But obviously this is not enough of an answer, for it does not account for *why* he should put the evidence of the body before the evidence of the texts that his teachers revered. It explains only how he had the technical and personality resources to maintain his position, not why he took that position. Taking that position was not easy and direct: the body did not announce itself to Vesalius as a text truer than Galen. 'I read Galen's book *On the bones* to the students at least three times,' Vesalius later wrote, 'before I dared perceive any mistake on Galen's part, although now I can't be sufficiently astonished at my own stupidity at understanding so little what was written, and thus myself deceiving my own eyes.' There had to be some impetus *outside* the body being dissected, outside the experience of dissecting, to enable Vesalius to understand 'what was written' (*quae scribebantur*). And when he did so, when he realized that Galen had made mistakes, he was aware of what kind of act it was to criticize Galen. In the bloodletting letter of 1540 Vesalius talked of criticism of Galen as being potentially 'heretical' and 'impious'; his language in this respect is quite striking, and he raises the issue several times. Although it might sound heretical to say so (he is saying), the body should be the text, and we should satisfy ourselves about what it says by dissecting personally or observing at a dissection.

With Luther, the extraordinarily explicit and repeated anthropomorphizing of 'the Word' that he went in for certainly indicates how strongly he leant on the text of Scripture. This text was, for him, alive, and not only an active agent in his struggles, working on his behalf in the cause of truth, but also the sole authority to which appeal could be made in any dispute. For Vesalius the dissected human body has this same status, as we have seen, and he repeatedly refers to it as a 'text', which can literally be read, calling it 'this true book of ours, the human body, man himself'. No other text has a remotely comparable status, not even the texts of the immortal Galen whom his teachers venerated and whose superior truth Curtius defended in that celebrated 22nd demonstration at Bologna. [. . .]

Curtius had used words and arguments, but Vesalius constantly returns to the body, to looking, showing and pointing. Only the true text, the body itself, can speak with authority, and it is the authority to be preferred in all cases over ancient written texts, whether by Galen or any other venerable Ancient. 'Show them to me' is Vesalius's challenge to Curtius, 'Galen has erred in these matters, and this is *evident here* in these subjects' (my emphasis). Vesalius is rejecting *patres istos* – those Fathers – Galen and Curtius; like Luther rejecting the authority of the pope, Vesalius the young man is rebelling against his fathers: 'It is quite true,' he scoffs at Curtius, I do not understand Hippocrates and Galen the way you do 'because I am not such an old man as you are'.

Not only does Vesalius insist on the primacy of 'the Word', that is, the body, over written text and tradition but, like Luther with the Bible, he introduces touching and pointing, into both the practice of public anatomizing and its visual representation, as aids to witnessing the truth for oneself. In the last of the Bologna demonstrations, Vesalius showed the humours of the eye. 'All these,' he said, 'anybody can see for himself at home; for surely, Domini [masters], he said, you can learn only a little from a mere demonstration if you yourselves have not taken the objects (*subjecta*) into your own hands.' The students did just this; came up and touched the parts for themselves, took them into their own hands. And in the vivisection demonstration, when pressed by the students for an answer as to the relation of the movement of the heart to the movement of the arteries, Vesalius answered: 'I do not want to give my opinion, you yourselves should feel with your own hands, and trust them.' Moreover, on the title-page of the *fabrica*, Vesalius has the students portrayed not only as close to the body, so that they can *see* it, but as actually reaching in so that they can *touch* it.

So the question recurs: *why* did Vesalius reject one authority, one text (Galen) for another (the body), why did he stress the indispensability of *personal engagement* in dissection, and the crucial importance of seeing for oneself and touching for oneself? In [. . .] doing these things he was simply following Galen, bringing Galen back to life. And the iconography of the title-page of the *Fabrica* again portrays this message: Vesalius presents himself *with* the Ancients, engaged in an ancient practice of anatomizing. It is exactly equivalent to Luther having himself presented as one of the true primitive Christians, as a disciple of Christ, in the Protestant altar-pieces painted by the Cranachs. But, again, this does not explain *why* Vesalius turned to emulating Galen, why he portrayed himself as a primitive anatomist. That impetus, I suggest, lay outside the world of anatomizing. It is in this act of trying to live out the experience of *being* Galen the anatomist that we might now be justified in seeing Vesalius as a Lutheran – or at the very least as acting here *like* a Lutheran. For this is what Luther did; he tried not just to follow the advice of Christ about how to live properly, but also to *be* a disciple of Christ in the present and to thus restore primitive Christianity.

There are some circumstances which add a little supplementary evidence to suggest that Vesalius may have been a Lutheran. There is the strange circumstance of Vesalius publishing the *Fabrica* in Basle, when Venice was so much nearer. Basle was now so reformist, so Protestant, that even Erasmus had had to leave it for a while. Yet Vesalius did not hesitate to send all the wood-blocks over the Alps in order to have them printed there. Then there is the matter of the circumstances of Vesalius's death. He died returning from pilgrimage to Palestine.

Although this could have been a quite innocent and pious journey, pilgrimages to the Holy Land were also [. . .] one of the penances meted out by the Inquisition to wanderers from the path of truth.

The connection between Vesalian anatomizing and Lutheran Protestantism is strikingly strong. Anatomy – indeed, Vesalius's anatomy – became a Lutheran Protestant endeavour, not in the medical schools but in the far larger arena of the philosophy course of universities, the basic course taken by all students at university. Anatomy was introduced in the years around the preparation of the *Fabrica* and by no less a figure than Melanchthon, Luther's soul-mate and the man who became the 'Preceptor of Germany' through his reforms of the curriculum at Wittenberg, and hence of all the universities brought into existence or reformed through the Lutheran reformation. [. . .]

That anatomy was totally God-centred. The knowledge of anatomy, Melanchthon writes (attributing the sentiment to Galen) leads us to the knowledge of God. [. . .] Melanchthon gives a quite extensive listing of the outer parts of the human body, and then turns to the inner ones:

> At this point truly you think yourself introduced into a temple and a kind of shrine; on this account you ought not to simply look at the material with particular reverence, but to take into consideration the plan and diligence of the Maker. For the scheme of the work bears witness that men do not exist by chance, but take their rise from some infinite Mind which has arranged its individual parts with astonishing care and destined them to certain goals and which has impressed knowledge and mind on it, which is the clearest mark of divinity.

Melanchthon then goes through the inner parts 'following the order of Galen', from the lower venter [stomach] through to the highest. All this was taught without performing a dissection, and it is not known whether Melanchthon used any visual representations.

Twelve years later Melanchthon issued a much revised version of this book. [. . .] In the meantime, of course, Vesalius's *Fabrica* had been published. Melanchthon acquired a copy and read it with care. At Nuremberg on 25 January 1552 he wrote a poem about the importance of the study of the human body ('De consideratione humani corporis') and placed it at the front of his personal copy of the *Fabrica*. Here it is translated:

> Think not that atoms, rushing in a senseless, hurried flight,
> Produced without a guiding will this world of novel form;
> The mind which shaped them, wise beyond all other intellects,
> Maintains and fashions everything in logical design.
> . . .
> Accordingly it follows that the body's several parts
> Came not together aimlessly as if devised by chance:
> With purpose God assigned to each its own allotted task
> And ordered that man's body be a temple to Himself
> . . .

> Wherefore, as man reflects upon the marvels in himself,
> With reverence let him venerate his Maker and his Lord,
> And keep the temple undefiled, immune from any stain,
> Lest wrath divine in vengeance come and hurl it crashing down.

In his revision of his commentary on the soul (made from June to November 1552), Melanchthon spoke about the anatomy of the human body in a way which echoed St Paul writing to the Corinthians:

> looking at this wonderful variety of work and these designs of God from without and through a thick darkness, we are struck dumb and grieve that we cannot look into nature and discern causes. But then at last when we discern the 'idea' of nature in the divine mind we shall look into that whole machine as if from the inside, and we shall understand the designs of the Maker and the causes of all the divine works. Now, through this incomplete consideration, we know that God is the Architect, and we should be inflamed with desire for that perfected wisdom.

The message is that the knowledge of anatomy is for Protestants an important means to the knowledge of God: Melanchthon is saying that through anatomy we see God 'through a glass darkly' – the best that can be obtained here on earth – 'but then face to face; now I know in part, but then shall I know even as also I am known' (Corinthians I, 13,12). Moreover, Melanchthon added a long elegy on the utility of the doctrine of the fabrication of the human body ('Elegia de utilitate doctrinae de fabrication humani corporis') by Johannes Stigelius. Melanchthon wrote in his revision that he had 'followed the best authors, *Galen*, *Vesalius* and *Leonhard Fuchs*'. [. . .]

Quite independently of any concern about the advancement or promotion of medicine, Protestantism thus had a new, more philosophical and theological role for anatomical knowledge; that this was simultaneous with the endeavours of Vesalius would seem to be more than a coincidence. For the Lutheran Protestant, the human body was the temple of God, and seeing was believing.

Thus although the evidence is not conclusive, yet because, it shows, in my view, Vesalius's work in anatomical reform replicating precisely Luther's work in religious reform, and because the Protestant leaders themselves took up Vesalian anatomy and made it central to their philosophical teaching in the Protestant cause, it points to Vesalius being a Lutheran and as coming to a new view of the body *because* he was playing out his Lutheranism into his practice of anatomy. At the very least we have Vesalius behaving here *as if* he is a Lutheran, and turning his attitudes toward reforming anatomy. And, just as Luther's work in theology can be seen as being primarily a product of the changed economic, social and political circumstances of northern Europe, so equally Vesalius's work in anatomy, though performed in the south, can be seen as a product of these same altered social and political circumstances. Indeed, neither of these intellectual revolutions were events isolated from the concerns of the real world.

Of course, it might all just be a mighty set of coincidences, all the elements that the revolutionary approaches that Luther and Vesalius had in common – the pointing, the touching, the making of the senses pre-eminent as a touchstone of faith, the promotion of new texts as authoritative, the rejecting of intellectual fathers and traditions, the making of personal experience primary, the making responsibility for one's own views a moral matter. It might just be a case of two rebellious and outspoken young men who each wished to leave their mark on history in their different spheres, and who just happened to live at much the same time. It might. But in my view it is nevertheless highly suggestive of a stronger connection of a causal nature.

Luther tried to reinstate the pure practice of the pristine church, the congregation of all believers; Vesalius tried to reinstate the pure practice of pristine anatomy, the participatory engagement in anatomizing of humans as the Alexandrians had done. Luther redefined the nature of the rituals of proper worship; Vesalius redefined the nature of the rituals of proper anatomizing. Both of them believed that a proper representation of God's wonderful works in pictures was positively desirable in order to help the memory – in altar-pieces or anatomical tables. In addition, both had themselves portrayed too – and *as* apostles, as Ancients, in the very act of reviving and living out ancient pristine practices. Both of them gave a new priority to the sacred book – the Bible in the case of Luther, the human body in that of Vesalius – which, they claimed, should be preferred over any human commentator, and which was open to be read by everyone. Neither was prepared to take as doctrine anything which could not be pointed out with the finger in the sacred book, the Word, the body. And, for what it is worth, both had bitter public rows with teacher-figures of the previous generation, who thought they had gone too far: Luther with Erasmus, Vesalius with Sylvius. Both Luther and Vesalius changed the nature of the debate. Both Vesalius and Luther sought to restore to modern life an ancient practice, and ancient beliefs: one of them tried to restore primitive Christianity, the other primitive anatomy. Both of them did these things in the same world.

26 Nancy G. Siraisi **'The old and the new'**

Source: from *The Clock and the Mirror: Girolamo Cardano and Renaissance Medicine*, Nancy G. Siraisi, Princeton University Press, Princeton, New Jersey, 1997, pp. 94–7.

[. . .] Anatomy in fact appealed to a diverse public, both erudite and popular, for many reasons. It touched on several traditional disciplines (natural philosophy, medicine, and surgery) and had a long-established, if formerly minor, place in the university curriculum in medicine. At the same time, along with botany and natural history, it was among the branches of knowledge most responsive to the general expansion of interest in collecting, inspecting, and describing particulars about the natural world. Because it drew on a significant collection of Greek texts, in which major items had been recently recovered, it shared in the contemporary prestige of medical humanism or Hellenism. It was in several ways closely linked to contemporary artistic values and activities. In addition, anatomy appealed to and strengthened existing philosophical and religious traditions of positive or negative moralizing about the human body. Dissection provided a spectacle in which moralities could be enacted as well as curiosity about 'the secrets of nature' satisfied. Indeed, the popular fascination that made some academic dissections into a public or semipublic spectacle has been plausibly related to the power of representation and theatricality in Renaissance culture. Above all, as Galen[1] had long ago proclaimed and as Vesalius echoed, human anatomy was testimony to the benevolence and design of the Creator.

Like other descriptive sciences of the period, anatomy combined observation, manipulation, verbal description, and visual representation of nature with meticulous attention to ancient texts. The striking enlargement of anatomy's practical, technical, and visual aspects is, of course, deservedly famous. As compared with its medieval predecessor, sixteenth-century anatomy was distinguished by more frequent dissections, improved techniques, more emphasis on personal observation, more attention to detail, and greatly enhanced standards of illustration. These changes involved contributions from many individuals and took place over many decades. Moreover, anatomy based on human dissection, perhaps even more than most other sciences, requires favorable social and institutional factors for its very existence as a legimate activity. Thus the extension of anatomical practice depended in many ways on developments in the broader contemporary social and cultural context – in, for example, such diverse areas as artistic style and values, attitudes to the human body, patronage and connections among rulers, courtly and professional elites, and universities, and even patterns of crime and punishment. At the same time, the entire anatomical enterprise was largely shaped by study of the texts of ancient – that is, chiefly Galenic – anatomy, the availability of which was greatly increased through the efforts of humanist scholars, editors, and printers during the first third of the sixteenth century. Sixteenth-century anatomists challenged many specifics of Galen's anatomical teaching, but his works continued to define the nature of the subject, set the terms of debate, and provide an essential point of departure. In this respect, anatomy was just as bookish and classicizing as any other branch of learned culture. Furthermore, practicing anatomists rapidly produced a large body of new Latin literature on their discipline. Hence what distinguished Renaissance anatomy from its medieval antecedents was a notable enhancement of *both* practice *and* textual foundation, the latter both ancient and modern.

Within the university faculties of medicine, where most sixteenth-century anatomical teaching took place, the status and role of anatomy in the curriculum rose significantly over the course of the century. This was so even though the level of actual institutional commitment varied greatly in different parts of Europe and was not always permanent when made. In Italy, as is well known, various universities – most notably, of course, Padua and Bologna – increased emphasis on anatomical teaching, established professorial chairs in the subject, and, late in the century, constructed permanent anatomy theaters. But even in Italy the extent to which anatomy was actually taught varied from one university to another and even in major Italian centers from decade to decade. Often, the degree to which anatomy was pursued corresponded to the presence and interest of individual anatomists and the attitude of local authorities (on whom, among other things, the supply of cadavers depended). Much anatomy continued to be taught from books and from animals. The pursuit of anatomical research and investigation, as distinct from public or private teaching or the writing and reading of anatomy books, depended entirely upon the enthusiasm and private activities of a small community of anatomists.

In part, the enhanced academic status of anatomy depended upon the perception of it as an aspect of the natural philosophical study of mankind. Vesalius himself punningly described his subject as 'the *scientia* [certain knowledge] of the parts of the human body' and 'a part [*membrum*] of [the corpus of] natural philosophy,' thus associating it not only with philosophy, but also with the branch of medicine considered nearest to philosophy, namely, medical *theoria*. Vesalius was here, implicitly, claiming the epistemological status of *scientia*, certain knowledge, for a descriptive discipline. But claims for the philosophical importance of human anatomy might also stress its significance for a religious and theological understanding of the place of man in creation; recent studies have revealed the extent to which Melanchthon's ideas of this kind influenced the formation of the Wittenberg medical curriculum. At the same time, manual techniques, suppositions about practical utility, and, often, arrangements for the actual conduct of dissections continued to connect anatomy with surgery. At Bologna, the chair of anatomy was permanently separated from the chair of surgery only in 1570, while at Padua the two disciplines were taught together for much of the century.

For both philosophical and pedagogical reasons, the subject of anatomical instruction was, as Vesalius put it, a 'canonical,' natural, and healthy human body. Essentially, this meant that a well-developed young man was taken as the ideal object of study (as the Vesalian illustrations demonstrate). In reality – as was well known to Vesalius and other anatomists who were simultaneously keenly interested in human diversity and variability – few of the actual cadavers of executed criminals, paupers, or friendless foreigners available for public dissection could have met the ideal. But various other situations called for medical practitioners to inspect the internal organs of cadavers for physical abnormalities. In sixteenth-century Italy the practice of autopsy, which first developed in the late Middle Ages, appears to have been generally accepted and relatively widespread. Respectable families, including the families of physicians, sought autopsies of deceased members (especially, according to a recent study, wives and children) in order to safeguard the health of the lineage. Individuals who died in the odor of sanctity, including Counter-Reformation Italy's two most famous saints, Carlo Borromeo and Filippo Neri,[2] were examined for physical signs of their specially favored status. Suspicion of poisoning or disagreement among physicians about the cause of death, especially where princely or eminent personages were concerned, provided yet other reasons for autopsy; such, for example, was the case with several of the eight sixteenth-century popes who were subjected to postmortem dissection. However, little was learned from most such inspections, both medical practitioners and those who engaged or permitted their services shared the belief that the postmortem appearance of the internal organs could reveal information about conditions that had affected a person in life or the cause of death. Moreover, as the sixteenth century wore on, reports of such inspections came to include increasing amounts of anatomical detail and close observation.

From about midcentury, humanistically educated physicians incorporated their awareness of recent anatomy into works on a variety of other branches of medicine. The attacks of Hellenists on anatomical works critical of Galen continued for some time, and throughout the century anatomists themselves continued to build on and criticize each other's work and to engage in vigorous controversy. But in other, general, medical works new anatomy, especially as presented by Vesalius, seems soon to have ceased to be controversial at the price of being absorbed into the mass of bookish authorities. In some respects, the process parallels the synthesis of humanistic with scholastic Aristotelian philosophy that occurred during the same period – and is indeed part of a broader movement of synthesis characteristic of many aspects of Renaissance intellectual life. In the case of anatomy, a handful of examples must suffice to illustrate developments in the milieu of the Italian universities. For Giovanni Argenterio, who taught at Pisa, Naples, and Turin in the 1550s and 1560s, Vesalian anatomy served as a model and defense for his own radical critique of Galenic pathology. But a generation later even a commentary written at Bologna on the part of Avicenna's[3] *Canon* used in teaching medical *theoria* – presumably the most conservative book in the most conservative branch of the medical curriculum – included fifty pages on the anatomy of bones and muscles, presented a Vesalian account of muscular function, and proffered the advice that the *recentiores* [the more recent, the moderns], should be followed on the division and structure of the bones. By 1596, readers of a vernacular treatise on the duties of midwives encountered the authority of the 'immortal' and 'almost divine' Vesalius, along with that of the author's teacher at Bologna, Giulio Cesare Aranzio. [. . .]

NOTES

1   Claudios Galenos d. 129 CE, Greek physician who founded experimental physiology.
2   Carlo Borromeo, 1538–84, nephew of Pope Pius IV and active in the Counter-Reformation in Italy; Filippo Neri, 1515–95, Italian priest and outstanding mystic during the Counter-Reformation and founder of the Congregation of the Oratory.
3   Ibn Sina, 980–1037, Persian physician, the most famous and influential of the philosopher scientists of Islam. The Canon of Medicine is the most famous single book in the history of medicine in both East and West. It is based for the most part on the achievements of Greek physicians of the Roman Empire.

27   Vivian Nutton 'Wittenberg anatomy'

Source: from *Medicine and the Reformation*, ed. Ole Peter Grell and Andrew Cunningham, Routledge, London and New York, 1993, chapter 1, pp. 11–12, 16–26.

The history of anatomy in the sixteenth century is frequently described in terms of the triumph of observation over book-learning, and of the penetration into Northern Europe of techniques, ideas and discoveries first formulated in Bologna and above all, Padua. It is a trail that leads inexorably from Berengario, through Vesalius, Fallopio and Fabricius, to William Harvey,[1] with, occasionally, a special mention for Leonardo da Vinci and his drawings. Statutes and university records are combed for the first references to chairs of anatomy or actual anatomical demonstrations on a corpse in order to confirm the participation of a particular institution in the march of medical progress. There is, in short, wide-spread agreement that by the end of the century Vesalian anatomy had replaced Galenic, that human dissection was both commonplace and central to any medical study, and that the message from Padua had been received swiftly and enthusiastically. Areas such as Spain, where the new anatomy does not seem to have conquered so easily, are usually forgotten or held up as dire examples of the follies of conservative academics, short-sighted administrators and religious obscurantists. From such a perspective, the history of anatomy at the Saxon University of Wittenberg becomes almost inexplicable, for here, [. . .] Vesalian anatomy was established early, held a central place in the curriculum, yet disappeared quietly in the first years of the seventeenth century, some time before the social, economic, and academic disasters of the Thirty Years' War, without, apparently, contributing much to the annals of medical discovery.

This paradox can be resolved only if we set the study of anatomy in a wider setting, as part of a broader movement for the understanding of man's place in God's creation. As the academic home of Martin Luther, the University of Wittenberg swiftly gained fame (or notoriety) for its theology, and the educational ideals formulated and put into practice there by Phillip Melanchthon (1497–1560) were adopted by many schools and universities within the Lutheran world. They aimed to produce Christian intellectuals, both learned and Lutheran. The methods of teaching employed there, whether in theology, arts, or medicine, were as modern as any in Europe, and, as we shall see, they could be adapted to changing needs and to new discoveries. But, far more than in most other universities, they were employed at Wittenberg within a specifically religious context. True, the notion that man inhabited a divinely ordered universe was commonplace, and the claim that anatomy could reveal something of the wondrous handiwork of the Creator can be found across the religious spectrum, but at Wittenberg the links were much tighter. Melanchthon, and his Lutheran followers, posited a strong interaction between body and soul, and hence a knowledge of medicine, the art of the healthy body, was essential if one was to preserve the health of the soul. Anatomy revealed not only the structures, arrangement, and purpose of the body, but also the ways in which the activities of the Christian soul were mediated in thought, imagination, or will. Such a theme was far too important to be left to the physicians or medical students alone; theologians, pastors, teachers, arts students, even pupils in the gymnasia required this information, and the Wittenberg faculty provided it for them. In lectures, books and prints, the coherent message of the Lutheran anatomists was transmitted from Wittenberg to other areas of Germany for a century or more. In this perspective, the tradition of anatomy teaching at Wittenberg was no less important, and on its own terms scarcely less successful, than that of Padua and, [. . .] deserves more than the neglect of medical and religious historians [. . .].

The formulation of the Wittenberg approach to anatomy derives from Melanchthon, theologian, educator and universal scholar, although it would be wrong to attribute it entirely to him or to see it as a totally new creation of Lutheranism. There are parallels with developments elsewhere, although Wittenberg anatomy does not fit easily into the traditional categories of medical historians. For example, Melanchthon continually stressed the importance of the Greek heritage within medicine: 'medicine is entirely Greek, and it cannot be perfectly understood without Greek'. It was a message that he had first delivered in his preface to Burchard's *Parva Hippocratis tabuia* [*Little Catalogue of Hippocrates*] in 1519 and one that he continued to repeat from then on. But it was not a case of the Greeks or nothing. Arabic authors continued to form the mainstay of the medical curriculum until the end of the century, and Melanchthon himself was perfectly willing to adopt Vesalian anatomy as an improvement on that of Galen. He obtained a copy of Vesalius' *De humani corporis fabrica* [*On the Structure of the Human Body*] soon after it appeared, reading and annotating it throughout and expressing his admiration of it in an elegant poem. The second edition of his *De anima* [*On the Soul*] carefully adapted as much as possible of the new anatomy and may have been more responsible than any other book for spreading a knowledge of Vesalian anatomy throughout north Germany. Melanchthon's criterion was truth, not Hellenism. He had sought informed advice on the best sources of anatomical information for inclusion in the first edition of the *De anima* (Wittenberg, 1540), and his choice of Galen to supplement the 'thin and babyish little book' on anatomy by Benedetti was, at the time, entirely justified. There was no book then on the market that incorporated fully the extensive anatomical discoveries of the ancient Greek physician, which had become accessible in their original Greek only after 1525. Hence, too, the need to provide detailed lexicographical equivalents for terms that would be found in the new 'Hellenic' anatomy and in the older, medieval and arabised texts. The later statutes of 1572 recommended the study of Vesalius, Fallopio or, if necessary, a suitable modern textbook of anatomy. This willingness to incorporate criticisms of Galen and new textbooks contrasts with the violent denunciations of Vesalius by such Hellenists as Cornarius, Sylvius and Caius, or with the conservative lists of set texts put out by the University of Ingolstadt and the London College of Physicians.

Nor does the anatomical tradition of Wittenberg fit easily into a schema that contrasts the written with the visual. As we have already seen, the authorities encouraged public anatomies, and dissections were performed well before they became a statutory obligation. Even if, as Friedensburg suggested, the professors themselves became less keen on public dissection, that does not mean they abandoned visual information. Melanchthon himself had praised the *Fabrica* for its remarkably beautiful illustrations (and, interestingly, for its elucidations of Galen), while a series of illustrated anatomical sheets were published by the university printer well into the next century for the benefit of those studying the *De anima* [Figs 16 and 17]. Such visual aids might well be necessary, if, as Jessen once implied, the seats in the hall were arranged in such a way that not everyone could see properly even when a public anatomy was held. Besides, this visual information supplemented that of the lecture and demonstration and served a valuable function as an aide-mémoire.

Melanchthon and his successors at Wittenberg chose their set texts and visual materials pragmatically; they incorporated the best information available into their lecture courses on anatomy without apparent concern for the controversies taking place elsewhere between Galenists and Vesalians. The reason is not far to seek: at Wittenberg anatomy was taught within a broad context that emphasized the theological and moral dimensions of the subject as much as the merely technical or therapeutic. The points that divided John Caius from Andreas Vesalius were thus relatively minor when compared with the importance of correct religious belief or of understanding the workings of the body and its relationship with the soul. It is this theological and moral emphasis that explains why, in the various prefaces, orations and books presented by Wittenberg scholars, relatively little attention is given to justifying anatomy in terms of its contribution to the understanding and cure of disease or its necessity as the basis for surgery – though these points are made – and much to its wider role.

The arguments advanced go far beyond the standard rhetoric of an exordium. To claim that anatomy revealed the majesty of God, the divine Creator, was commonplace. The idea of a purposeful designer went back to Galen, Aristotle and Plato, who all acknowledged the 'architectural Mind' that had formed man. The wonderful fabric of the human body, all were aware, provided clear and unmistakable revelations of the wisdom and foresight of its Creator. In the human body, just as in the whole theatre of nature, God had left his footprints, testimonies and evidence for man to contemplate. The handiwork of God was indeed wonderful; the way in which the foetus, which had before birth derived breath through the umbilical cord, suddenly at birth began to breathe and, simultaneously, the link that had formerly joined the foetal artery and vena cava began to disappear was nothing short of miraculous. But this whole argument was in Witteberg given a further theological twist by being directly associated with an attack on atheism and Epicurean atomism; anatomy demonstrates that man cannot be a chance concatenation of atoms but is a purposeful work of a divine Creator.

Such an argument from purpose and organization was scarcely new or unusual. But not every anatomist would assert publicly that anatomy would improve individual morality as well as health. Nor was it immediately obvious that a knowledge of the workings of the body would lead to a reduction in one's capacity for anger and to a life lived in love and charity with one's neighbours. Yet such claims were made by Melanchthon and his pupils and formed the basis for anatomical teaching within the Wittenberg tradition.

The connection between anatomy and morality was made in a variety of ways. Anatomy might serve as a meditation on death: it showed how fragile was man, how delicate his brain, how easily damaged his veins and nerves. It was thus a perpetual reminder of the transitory nature of this life and of the judgement of God to come. Alternatively, a knowledge of anatomy would reveal in man the

TABVLA EXHIBENS INSIGNIORA
MARIS VISCERA.

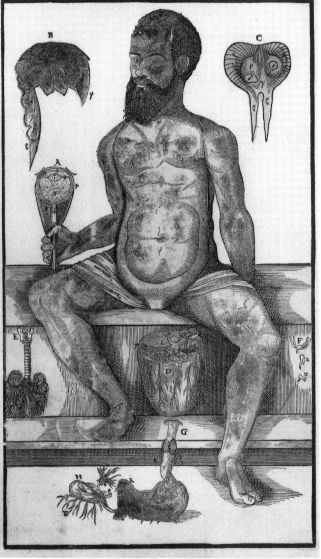

Ræfens figura Marem cum præcipuis medij atq; imi uentris organis ac uisceribus exhibet. Aperto enim abdomine primum occurrit ἐπίπλοον, quod cum undiq; cingat & uestiat infimæ cauitatis in corpore membra, pingi hoc loco non potuit. Eo dissecto, ἐπίπλοον occurrit seu omentum, quod seorsim delineatur inter uiri pedes, litera D. Sub hoc proxime locantur uentriculæ & intestina.

Ventriculi in corpore partem ac sedem anteriorem monstrant literæ E F. Atq; E quidem fundus eius est, F pars dextra uergens ad πύλωρον. Huic à parte dextra incumbit Epar litera D insignitum. A sinistra lien est, G. Intestina crassiora & κόλον repræsentat H. eiss in dextro latere, ubi è gracilibus enascitur, non omnino circunducitur, uelut hic pictura falso monstrat. L. locus est, ubi rectum intestinum descendit in anum. I. gracilium intestinorum anfractus & gyri. His omnibus in hac figura teguntur Renes, uasa urinalia & seminalia.

α γ. Vena caua, quæ dorso incumbens descendit. Huic substernitur Arteria magna ε κ, quæ deinceps uenam transcendit, prius quam, sicut & uena, in duos ramos finditur supra ossis sacri initium. Rami, qui è uena & arteria uersus Renes utrinq; excurrunt, emulgentes uocantur: Estq; ε ren dexter, δ sinister, etsi plerumq; dexter sub epate altior est sinistro sub splene.

♂♂. meatus, quo ex uena urina in uesicam ducitur, ὄυρετήρ. κ, seminalis uena, λ seminalis arteria dextram testem petens. θ. seminalis uena sinistri testis, μ. eiusdem arteria. υ. uesicæ fundus. o. o. uasa semen à testibus ad penem deferentia.

A A. portiones sunt uterarum costarum. B B notharum. C C. os lacrum. D D. os coxæ. Atq; hæc in imo uentre.

MEDII uentris membra; Pulmo, A A, & huic Cor inclusum, B. Διάφραγμα uel septum transuersum, distinguens membra medij atq; imi uentris, est C C.

PARTICVLARIVM FIGV.
RARVM DESIGNATIO.

Oculi per medium dissecti, ita ut facies eius interior in conspectum ueniat, figuram mas dextra manu gestare fingitur. Estq; 1. humor crystallinus. 2. Ab anteriore parte crystallino humori tunica obducitur, corpoream pelliculæ similis. 3. humor uitreus. 4. neruï optici subfstantia. 5. dura tunica, & crassa cerebri meninge prognata. 6. humor aqueus. 7. Vuea tunica, introrsum compressa, & perforata: pupilla. 8. Tunica ab uuea ducens initium, cilijs seu palpebrarum pilis similis. Distinguit humorem uitreum ab aqueo. 9. Musculi oculum mouentes.

A. duræ tunicæ pars, cornu instar pellucida. Huic appendices uicinæ, notant album oculi tunicam, adhærentem seu coniunctiuam.

A dextra parte capitis, cernitur integrum μεσεντέριον, à partibus connatis auulsum, ad literam B. Estq; α.α. glandulosum eius corpus, circa cuius medium est mesenterij centrum. 6, pars rectum intestinum, γ. colon dorso affigens.

A læua, exprimitur διάφραγμα, litera C. cuius substantia interior membranosa est, γ γ. Ambitus uero, α, α, carnosus. 6 6. duo ligamenta seu tendines eius, inserti uertebris lumborum. Inter has literas scissura est, qua id uertebrarum corporibus incumbit, aortam, uenamq; & χυ- γop transmittit. δ. foramen stomacho, s. uenæ caue patet.

Inter diductis uiri crura ἐπίπλοον seu omentum integrè liberatum à cohærentibus partibus reponitur, Arab. Zirbus. α, uenæ portæ caudex, ubi è iecore prodiens, inferiore omenti membranæ continetur ac fulcitur. Ei incumbit & arteria, epatis ramus & uesiculam bilis petens. s. s. omenti inferior, 3 superior membrana.

E, totius asperæ arteriæ, ab omnibus partibus liberæ anteriorem faciem exprimit. Caput eius λάρυγξ ex tribus cartilaginibus, & musculis pluribus componitur.

F, tria particularia ossa monstrat: 1. os υ referens, os linguæ uel gutturis, morsus Adam. 2. osficulum incudi, 3 osficulum malleolo comparatum.

G, anteriorem integri uentriculi & stomachi faciem exprimit, una cum uenis, arterijs, & neruis ipsius, α. stomachi pars in fauces pertingens. 6, glandulosum corpus, stomacho frequenter adnatum, qua quinte thoracis uertebræ insidet. ε γ δ. & 3 δ. nerulus sexti paris cerebri ad stomachi orificium superius, δ. exporrectus multiplici serie. θ. κ. uenæ uentriculi cum suis arterijs. κ. fundus uentriculi, quem & ipsum uenæ atq; arteriæ perreptant. λ, inferius uentriculi orificium, πύλωρος, μ, duodenum intestinum, etsi inter pingendum in posteriora reflecti debuisset. ν. bilis uesiculæ meatum in duodenum intestinum demonstrat.

H. Vesiculæ bilis receptaculum est. π. meatus uesiculæ fellis per iecoris corpus exporrecti inter ramos uenæ caue & uenæ portæ, o, uenæ portæ propagines in substantiam Epatis diffusi. ϛ. arteria & nerulus, iecori & bili uesiculæ communis.

16 Anatomical fugitive sheet: Wittenberg, 1573, coloured woodcut. Male figure, with head of Andreas Vesalius. Wellcome Institute Library, London, EPB 297.16 reproduced by permission.

'dwelling-place of God', the home of the soul, and hence impart in the observer a desire to maintain this divine temple in as neat a condition as one would a local church. Such messages were, however, far from unique to Wittenberg; they could be found, in words and pictures, in a variety of renaissance anatomy books. But few of their authors would have stressed as much as the Wittenbergers the role of anatomy in revealing the workings of the soul. In this, so Melanchthon

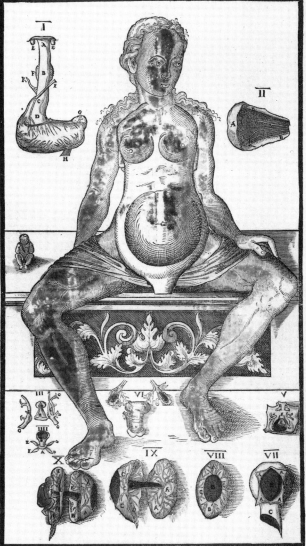

17 Anatomical fugitive sheet Wittenberg, 1573, coloured woodcut. Female figure, with hinged flap raised to show the internal organs. Wellcome Institute Library, London, EPB 298. 16 reproduced by permission.

argued, anatomy was almost as important as religion for imparting morality, a sentiment he associated with Luther, who had encouraged his son Paul to study medicine.

It was not just that contemplation of the order of the body, with its own senate and ministers, would provide a model for the ordered moral life in society or even that the body's evacuation of sooty residues through the lungs was a nice counterpart to the way in which the Christian might get rid of sin. Rather, what one gained from anatomy was a direct insight in to the way in which the faculties of the soul worked and acted together, for good or ill. To reveal this was the task of the Christian anatomist. Only by means of anatomy could one properly learn how the heart and the nerves functioned and how the various spirits (including the Holy Spirit) operated throughout the body. Anatomy would also prove that the human mind was not just a machine, but had within it free will. Indeed, only by anatomy could one really know how the mind or soul could go wrong.

This malfunctioning was expressed in two ways: in directly physical manifestations, as with madness and hallucinations, or in immorality. Melanchthon and his pupils, following a strongly Galenic line that linked soul and body closely together, made little distinction between the two types of disorder; both were disorders of the *anima* [soul]. So, just as corporal wounds could weaken, and ultimately destroy, the machine of the human body, so the soul could be also destroyed by wounds. These wounds could be physical – excessive drinking or damage to the chambers, nerves or faculties of the brain – or moral. Lust, greed, pride, 'human wounds', could not only obscure the ways of God and impede one's understanding of the mind of the creator but also block and damage in some way the 'cells' of the brain. In other words, sin had a physical effect, corrupting both soul and brain and preventing them from functioning as well as they ought. In some cases this corruption might be reversed by medicine; in others only by the aid of prayer and the gospel. Hence not only had the authorities the right and duty to lay down the appropriate religious regulations for the Christian community, they also should perform a similar function with regard to medicine, educating, upbraiding and, if necessary, removing those whose medical knowledge and practice fell short of what was needed.

Melanchthon, who was the originator of this Wittenberg programme of anatomy, did not confine himself to theoretical exhortations. He had long contemplated introducing medicine, as represented by Hippocrates and Galen, into other faculties than that of medicine, as a replacement for (or supplement to) Aristotle, since he was convinced that what they had to say about the human body gave a more accessible insight into *physice*, the world of nature. Unfortunately, it was not until 1525–6 that Greek texts of these authors were published and perhaps not for a decade or so that Latin versions of their works became widely available. For all his claims for Greek, Melanchthon's wishes could not be fulfilled for many years. Nonetheless, his influence can be detected, for example, in the anatomical information imparted at Wittenberg in the lectures on Aristotle's *Physics* by Johannes Velcurio in the early 1530s. By this date Melanchthon was already contemplating, and may even have embarked on, his exposition of the soul, ostensibly commenting upon Aristotle's *De anima* but going far beyond any commentator before or since in his introduction of anatomical material. Although he himself modestly referred to his book as a student guide, he took great pains over it. The first edition, of 1540, took him five or six years to write; the second, of 1552, perhaps a decade or more, and was substantially revised. He sought to be as up-to-date as possible. The first edition is a monument to the new Greek medicine; the second incorporates the latest Vesaliana. [. . .]

By far the most unusual feature of his exposition is Melanchthon's attention to anatomy. His original plan had not included any extensive discussion of anatomy, but he had soon come to realize that the workings of the soul could not be understood properly without a knowledge of the body. Hence his decision to devote almost half his book to a description of the body, the domicile of the soul. Besides, the newly discovered Galen included important anatomical writings of direct relevance to philosophy. The Middle Ages had known relatively little of his treatise *On the use of parts*, a treatment of anatomy in Aristotelian terms, and nothing of his *Anatomical procedures* and *On the opinions of Hippocrates and Plato*, a Platonic interpretation of the same anatomical material. All this Melanchthon read and incorporated in his own synthesis. He also devoted a considerable amount of space to lexicographical problems, recording and identifying the various terms for parts of the body found in Greek, Arabic and medieval Latin sources. This was no philological frivolity, but an essential activity at a time when nomenclature was far from settled and when considerable confusion had already arisen over the meaning of technical anatomical terms. In short, in his *De anima*, in both the first edition of 1540 and the second edition of 1552, Melanchthon provided for the studious youth of Wittenberg a work that was as modern as possible in its presentation of anatomical knowledge.

In his *De anima* Melanchthon offered to Wittenberg a pattern for the integration of anatomical instruction with philosophy and with theology. His successors in the university followed his example in a variety of ways. The publications of the medical faculty that are concerned with anatomy repeat the message of the *De anima*, and it is no coincidence that their subjects are closely related to the major theme of the book. Peucer on the brain, Johann Mathesius the younger (1544–1607) on the organ of hearing, Alberti on tears are all concerned with problems discussed at length in *De anima*. A later product of the Wittenberg school, the *Disputationes anatomicae* [*Debates on the Anatomy*] edited by Tobias Knobloch, reveals the long survival of the tradition. Its subtitle, 'explicantes mirificam corporis humani fabricam et usum' [explaining the marvellous structure and exercise of the human body], hints at God and Vesalius simultaneously, and its twenty-four chapters, each one representing a thesis by one of Knobloch's pupils, culminate in four sections on the soul in general, its faculties, the sensitive soul and the rational soul. The earlier chapters, nicely illustrated, describe the individual bones and organs and incorporate recent Italian anatomy; those in the second half, on physiology, pile up authorities in scholastic fashion as they repeat at length the doctrines of Melanchthon. They differ from contemporary theses in philosophy only in the extent to which they emphasize their shared anatomical material.

In all this there is no sense among the Wittenbergers that they are not being progressive. Mostelius, Mathesius, Alberti and Jessen all claim to be bringing into their teaching the very latest of discoveries, some made by themselves, most deriving from elsewhere. Nor should one deride as foolish their commitment to using anatomy to define and investigate the workings of the soul and its interrelationship with the body. The fact that more accurate conclusions on the anatomy and physiology of the brain were reached in the late nineteenth century is no reason to despise these attempts, which, in their own terms, are often superior to those of other contemporary anatomists. After all, when Vesalius in the later books of the *Fabrica* came to describe the workings of the body, as opposed to its structure, he was equally fallible.

SPREADING THE WORD

Looked at from another angle, however, the Wittenberg tradition of anatomy is far from negligible. Melanchthon was convinced that both moral philosophy and natural philosophy were essential for the education of the Christian; hence anatomy was too important to be left solely to the physicians. At Wittenberg, perhaps from the early 1530s, the philosophical lectures on Aristotle's *De anima* incorporated anatomical material, a tendency that became still more pronounced after the publication of Melanchthon's own textbook, *De anima*. In 1545 Melanchthon could expect all the arts students to be acquainted with the '*doctrina* on the nature of the human body, the rudiments of medicine, and the description of the faculties (*virtutes*)', and his book was again a set text in the revised statu[t]es of the mid-1550s. In the elucidation of this book philosophers and medical men collaborated to an unusual extent. In the first place, the lectures were given to students in the arts and theological faculties. They were thus central to the whole system of education at Wittenberg; they were not confined to the handful of students aiming at a higher degree in medicine. Second, by being included in the arts course, these lectures gave a preliminary orientation to the anatomy course that would be followed later on in medicine. They determined the perspective in which the good Lutheran would learn his medicine. And, third, although in the arts faculty, they were frequently given by lecturers with a more than passing interest in actual anatomy and dissection. [. . .]

   The diffusion of this synthesis did not stop at the gates of Wittenberg or at the door of the lecture-room. In 1583, Zacharias Brendel, professor of philosophy and later of medicine, was lecturing on Melanchthon's *De anima* at the Lutheran University of Jena. Thirteen years later, when the statutes of the University of Greifswald were revised, the *De anima* was among the texts set for comment in the medical faculty. It also served as a textbook in schools. At Jüterbo[r]g, on the borders of Brandenburg and Saxony, Johann Grün, the first rector of the grammar school, prepared for his young charges in 1580 a summary of the *De anima* in the form of Ramist tables, 'methodical diagrams'. According to one of the townsfolk, the new rector had succeeded admirably in encompassing so briefly the 'fabric of the human body and the vigour of the mind' (*corporis humani fabricam mentique vigorem*). At almost the same time, at the other end of Saxony, Matthaeus Dresser, rector of the gymnasium at Pirna, was preparing his own abridgement for the instruction of his pupils. He did not use Grün's trendy tables (which are by no means as easy to follow as their author had hoped), but concentrated on providing basic information, long lists of names and synonyms in Latin, Greek and German. However different their methods, both schoolmasters put forward the same justification for their books. The Christian needs to know about the ills of the body as well as of the soul: the intending physician can learn from them how evil tendencies within the soul may be corrected, while the theologian can see just how the physical body is controlled by the soul. Above all, everyone, however old, however intelligent, however industrious, can be brought by a contemplation of man to wonder at a great work of God and to find therein proofs of God's wisdom and understanding.

This theological message was not confined to books or the words of a teacher. From at least the early 1560s, the Wittenberg printers were producing cheap pairs of anatomical sheets to accompany the study of the *De anima*. By cutting out the internal organs of the male and female body and then sticking them down in order on the so-called 'Adam and Eve Figures', a student could gain a basic idea of the structure and organization of the body, which he could supplement from the brief verbal description printed around the edges of the sheets. The anatomy is crudely Vesalian; the inspiration is made plain by the close likeness of the head of the Adam figure to that of Vesalius at the front of his *Fabrica*. It is thus at one and the same time both learned and popular (for these anatomical sheets cost far less than a printed book), and it was aimed at an audience that was not confined to medicine. [. . .] The message of Wittenberg anatomy was not restricted to the specialist or to the physician.

Seen in this perspective, Wittenberg anatomy was no trivial pursuit. Its tradition was long-lasting, widespread and accessible to a broad section of the community, from schoolboys to professors, and from book-pedlars to pastors. If to modern eyes the number of 'discoveries' made by the Wittenberg anatomists is minimal, the same could be said about teachers in other areas of Europe at the same time. But, [. . .] making discoveries was not what Wittenberg anatomy was all about. What one learned through it was not only to preserve health, but also to control one's behaviour, to recognize God and to understand the doctrine of the Church. It was but one part of a plan to produce within Lutheran Saxony a learned, Christian community, free from Epicurean and atheist heresies, and firm in its knowledge of Christian principles. [. . .]

Wittenberg anatomy, then, was a joint enterprise of specialists for a common and universal purpose, the advancement of true religion through an understanding of man. It was a high aim, pursued, and in part achieved, by men of talent and learning. In their own eyes, its adherents were no conservatives, clinging to every word that Galen had ever uttered, but realists, willing to use whatever new discoveries had been made in Italy or beyond. But, if their anatomy derived from Vesalius, their outlook was focused on a different series of questions and priorities. By dissecting, and by learning from others' dissections, they were not only saving the body from disease and defeating illness in this life. More importantly, they were gaining and imparting knowledge that would save the soul and preserve it in the eternal life of heaven that they so earnestly sought. To describe or criticize the Wittenberg tradition of anatomy teaching solely in terms of this world is thus to miss the point. For Melanchthon [and his Wittenberg colleagues], the Christian life encompassed both heaven and earth, body and soul. To misunderstand the workings of the one would be to risk losing both. In this sense, anatomy, as Luther was alleged to have said, was almost as effective as religion in saving man's soul.

NOTES

1   Jacopo Berengario da Carpi (*c.*1460–*c.*1530) Italian physician and anatomist who was the first to describe the heart valves and to illustrate medical work with drawings from nature: Gabriello Fallopio (1523–62) distinguished Italian anatomist who contributed to knowledge of the ear and reproductive organs; Fabrizio Girlamo (1537–1619) Italian anatomist who studied under Fallopio, and helped to found modern embryology; William Harvey (1578–1657) pupil of Fabrizio, personal physician to James I and Charles I, famous for the understanding of the circulation of the blood.

28   Charles Webster 'Paracelsus: medicine as popular protest'

Source: from *Medicine and the Reformation*, ed. Ole Peter Grell and Andrew Cunningham, Routledge, London and New York, 1993, chapter 3, pp. 57–77.

The life of Theophrastus von Hohenheim (1493–1541), or Paracelsus as he is generally known, coincides directly with the Reformation. Indeed, at least from the time of his brief official appointment in Basle in 1527 he was sarcastically labelled as the Luther of medicine. Paracelsus occasionally mentioned Luther, and he seems to have taken seriously the parallel between their roles. With the posthumous growth of his reputation, the comparison between Paracelsus and Luther took on a more sober and less pejorative character. Paracelsus had shaken the authority of classical medicine, and Paracelsianism remained a vigorous force for more than a century. As a self-conscious movement of reform Paracelsianism constituted one of the vital ingredients of the so-called Scientific Revolution.

The academic effort has understandably been preoccupied with the natural philosophy and medical theories of Paracelsus, and with their antecedents and subsequent influence. Although Paracelsus was responsible for a not insignificant body of religious, theological, social and ethical writings, these works have attracted relatively little attention. It is therefore timely to consider the relationship of Paracelsus to the movement for religious reform and also trace connections between the medical and non-medical writings. It will be suggested that the two bodies of writing are more intimately linked than is customarily realized. Reassessment of the medical writings in the light of the protest literature of the Reformation explains some of the features which have rendered the medical work of Paracelsus uncongenial, obscure and even incomprehensible to the modern historian of science. Sensitivity to the historical circumstances of the early Reformation and Peasants' War enables us to adopt a more sympathetic response to the mission of Paracelsus. The formula which he evolved for exposition of his ideas matched the aspirations of his contemporaries and guaranteed his work a greater degree of familiarity and acceptability than would have been the case if he had adopted a dry, formal academic presentation. By adopting literary forms familiar to the reading public of his age and by presenting his scientific and medical ideas in the context of a religious and ethical framework which commanded wide assent, Paracelsus elevated the status of his mission. The reader was constantly reminded that Paracelsus was first and foremost prophet and apostle. His first priority therefore lay in defining the moral and ethical guidelines for the science and medicine of the new apostolic age. The specific scientific and technical content was secondary to this purpose, which accounts for the frequently provisional, fragmentary and unsystematic nature of the medical writings. Although Paracelsus undoubtedly sacrificed ease of accessibility to the modern reader, he successfully gauged the aspirations of his contemporaries and determined that medicine would not be excluded from the framework of reformation debate.

The maturity of Paracelsus coincided with the catastrophic decline in the standing of the Church in the German-speaking cultural area. As a young man Paracelsus personally witnessed the overturning of the authority of the Church in Basle, Nuremberg, Salzburg and Strasbourg, and his wanderings during this period familiarized him with the main territory of the peasants' uprisings of 1524 and 1525.

As a marginal figure, from a genteel but impoverished background, of uncertain social status, without firm academic credentials or ascertained civic position, Paracelsus had much in common with the alienated tradesmen, clerks and artisans who led the popular movement of social protest and religious discontent. Important among its products, this movement generated a tide of some 4,000 different pamphlets between 1500 and 1530. Pamphlets and illustrated broadsheets provided a means whereby the substance of learned academic disputations was filtered down to the lay public at large. Equally important, the pamphlets represented a buoyant, independent and heterogeneous force, constituted from a wide variety of elements blended in various combinations, perpetuating older medieval traditions of piety alongside newer influences derived from humanists such as Erasmus. The pamphlet literature became an influential vehicle of propaganda and a stimulus to defiance of authority. The pamphlets confirm the general collapse of authority of the Church hierarchy and priesthood. The Church presented an unfortunate combination of anachronism and exploitation. It was in harmony with the undeservingly affluent rather than the deserving poor. All of this contributed to the general sense of spiritual impoverishment against which the pamphlet literature reacted.

The pamphlets became an influential vehicle for anticlericalism and rehearsal of socio-economic grievances. They echoed the widespread urge for spiritual regeneration based on a return to a simple scriptural piety, modelled on the New Testament. The lex evangelica [Gospel law] and vita apostolica [Missionary life] became the watchwords of this assertive lay theology. This movement gave prominence to the idea of the universal priesthood of believers, which reinforced the status of the laity in general, but was especially important in emphasizing the worth of the common people. Hard times added to the urgency of the message of the protest literature and further intensity was provided by the eschatological perspective widely adopted in the tracts. A powerful atmosphere of expectancy was created, in which the multiple traumas of present existence constituted a final test, pending the final day of judgement and return of a beatific age.

Some indication of the intensity of eschatological speculation is provided by the publication in the period 1519–24 of some 160 tracts produced by sixty authors concerned with the conjunction of superior planets in Pisces which took place in February 1524. This literature fuelled hysteria concerning a great flood and possible end of the world. The failure of this cataclysm to materialize produced no disincentive to the prophetic literature. [. . .]

Short tracts containing prophecies concerning astrological phenomena were a potent element in the popular pamphlet literature. The title page comprising a lengthy and ominous title, together with a large woodcut burgeoning with lurid symbolism, constituted an instrument of propaganda in itself. Prophecies, prognostications, or *Practicas* brought celebrity. [. . .] Paracelsus was following the precedent of Fries, the physician of Colmar, whose dialogue in defence of astrology framed between the author and Luther, was partly instrumental in securing the sympathy of Luther and Melanchthon for astrology. Also such an intervention had the additional virtue of drawing attention to the primacy of [astrology] in the medical theory of Paracelsus, which was premised on the idea of unity between the macrocosm and microcosm. The publicity gained by Osiander, Sachs and others engaged in prophecy arguably led Paracelsus to visit Nuremberg in 1529 and use this as the base for his first publications.

The *Practica gemacht auf Europen* [Prediction for Europe] *1530–1534*, published by Frederick Peypus in Nuremberg in 1529, arguably constituted the first proper publication produced by Paracelsus and it was the first occasion on which he was described as 'Paracelsus' rather than Theophrastus von Hohenheim on a title page. Judging by conventional standards the *Practica* of 1529 was a success. The appeal of the *Practica* was undoubtedly assisted by inclusion of an elaborate woodcut on the title page (see Figure 18). Five issues of this *Practica* are recorded for the years 1529 and 1530. Paracelsus was launched into a successful career as pamphleteer. Indeed *Practicas* account for the major part of his published literary output between 1529 and his death in 1541. Prognostications account for 16 out of the 23 titles recorded in Sudhoff's bibliography for this period, which slightly underestimated the prevalence of these writings, because it does not take full account of reissues. To the general public Paracelsus was therefore primarily known as an author of disconcerting prophecies, based primarily on conjunctions, eclipses, and comets, but also incorporating evidence of other kinds. In addition, probably during his stay in Nuremberg, Paracelsus produced commentaries [. . .] and prophecies. These commentaries demonstrate the habitual tendency of Paracelsus to set himself at variance with authority. Swimming against the Lutheran tide in Nuremberg, Paracelsus disputed the claim that the Nuremberg and Lichtenberger figures sanctioned the Lutheran Reformation, instead maintaining the view stated elsewhere in his prophetic writings that schismatic reform was a vain enterprise destined to perish at the hands of a radically altered Catholic Church.

The *Practica* of 1529 contains the conventional predictions of political and civil unrest. Compared with other commentators Paracelsus paid less regard to the

18 Title page of Paracelsus: *Practica gemacht auf Europen 1530–1534*, Nuremberg: F. Peypus, 1529, Wellcome Institute Library, London, reproduced by permission.

prospects of environmental catastrophes and more to the likelihood of disintegration of the economy. The infrastructure of the *Practica* introduces many points which were to become recurrent themes in his other writings. The coincidence between a new star and the birth of Christ was seen as evidence that crucial events would be accompanied by astronomical omens, and indeed that the heavens contained the secrets of all manner of terrestrial events. Paracelsus also believed that Christ's miracles, including the healing of diseases, implied knowledge of the powers of the firmament. Therefore in order to fulfil Christ's invocation to care for the needy and the sick it was necessary to recognize the primacy of the power of the firmament. Finally, Paracelsus adopted a strong eschatological framework for his prophecies. He was sceptical about precise prophecies and warned against false prophets. Nevertheless he believed that the Day of Judgement was near and might come at any time. All the evidence suggested that after enduring terrible tribulations the new order of Christ would at last gain ascendancy over the old regimes, which, although entrenched, were at last breaking apart under the weight of their corruption.

Capitalizing on his new position as a prophet, Paracelsus published his first medical writings, two short tracts on syphilis. This represented a further effective piece of opportunism because syphilis was arousing acute anxiety, and this disease seemed totally beyond the control of the medical profession. These two tracts gave Paracelsus his chance to pay back scores against the medical elite, no doubt inspired by the humiliation he had recently suffered at their hands in Basle. He pursued the line that whatever good resided in the medicines then in use was counteracted by the incompetence and greed of medical practitioners, in whose hands all classes suffered, but the poor in particular. These tracts contained a skilful blend of medicine and social propaganda. He intermixed sensible, accessible and practical medical advice, with a strong infusion of the kind of social criticism which struck a chord with his audience and which was consistent with the message stemming from the religious and social tract literature.

Consistency between his medical and prophetic writings was emphasized by the inclusion of a large woodcut on the title page of the first of his tracts on syphilis which, like the *Practica*, was published by Frederick Peypus in Nuremberg in 1529 [Fig. 19]. The double-frame woodcut reinforced the polemical message of the tract, by contrasting the traditional and Paracelsian approaches to the sick poor. On the left the sick person crouches in an attitude of dejection, barefoot and clothed only in a shirt. By contrast the doctor's expensive attire signifies his academic status. Following established practice, the patient is being forced to eat some chicken leg before being given a concoction containing guaiacum, which is being prepared in a massive pot by a woman servant. The representative of the sick poor is casting a furtive glance at the illustration on the right which shows a comfortable hostelry scene. The windows are glazed expensively with bulls-eye panes. The anxious patient is being invited by the honest, simply-dressed proprietor, to take wine served in a cut-glass beaker before being offered a fulsome meal at a well-laid table covered by a tablecloth. Paracelsus therefore offers a form of therapy which avoids humiliating the poor with dietary prohibitions and he introduces them to a variety of simple, more effective and economical treatments, including mercurial preparations, which soon became one of the centre-pieces of Paracelsian medicine.

The utilization of a simple but effective cartoon on the title page of his first medical tract indicates the sensitivity of Paracelsus to the technique of propaganda recently developed in the popular protest literature and broadsheets. The cartoon also underlines the close association between the medical outlook and social message of Paracelsus. His medical ideas were formulated against a background of incessant writing on the religious and social questions which were preoccupying his contemporaries. In addition to producing extensive biblical commentaries, especially on the books of Psalms and Matthew, he wrote a wide variety of shorter works which were broadly compatible in style and content with the lay religious tract literature. The shorter religious, social and ethical writings of Paracelsus involved frequent reference to medicine. These shorter works provide the natural link between the more specifically theological and medical writings. Most of the social and ethical writings comprise brief essays, sometimes divided into sections commenting on biblical texts. These essays usually exist in two forms, one being a slightly abbreviated form of the other. None were published during the lifetime of Paracelsus, but most were widely copied in manuscript form after his death. If published they would have constituted tracts

Durch den hochgeler

ten herren Theophraſtum von

hochenheym beyder Artzeney Doctorem.

Vom Holtz Guaiaco gründlicher heylung / Darinn eſſen vnnd
trincken / Saltz vnd anders erlaubt vnd zu gehört.

Auch von den verfürigen vñ Irrigen büchern artzeten brauch
vnnd ordnung wider des holtz arth vnd natur auffgericht vnd
außgangen.

Vom erkantntis was dem holtz zugehört vnd was nicht / auß
welchem erſtanden dis verderben der kranckheyten.

Dergleichen wie ein almuß aus dem holtz erſtanden/ dem armen zu gut / Solchs in ein verderben gedyhen / weyter corrigirt / vnd in einen rechten weg gebracht / mehr erſprießlich.

Auch wie etlich höltzer mehr ſeind denn allein Guaiacum /
die gleich ſo wol als Guaiacum diſe krafft haben.

19 Title page of
Paracelsus: *Vom Holtz
Guaiaco gründlicher
heylung* [*Complete healing
from the wood Guaiacum*]
Nuremberg, 1529. From
Karl Sudhoff (ed.),
*Theophrastus von
Hohenheim gen.
Paracelsus. Sämtliche
Werke*, (Munich: Olms,
1923), vol. 7, 53.

varying in length between ten and twenty pages. Paracelsus produced some thirty
titles, although these involve a substantial amount of repetition.

The prevalent anticlericalism of these prospective pamphlets is well-illustrated
by the *De septem punctis idolatriae Christianae* [*The Seven Points of Christian Idolatry*]. This attack on the corruption of the clerical hierarchy provided a model
for his assault on academic medicine and the medical profession.

Paracelsus painted a portrait of a church almost totally overtaken by idolatry
and seemingly vanquished by Satan. Yet even in the prevalent darkness the word
of God carried forward the Christian message, and revelation was available to all
those amenable to the inspiration of the Holy Spirit. Through this medium
Christ himself was an active, living force, rather than merely a past historical
example.

The purity of Christ's message, Paracelsus believed, had been undermined by
the academic theologians over the centuries. This old learning, embedded in the
Old Testament and classical learning, he associated with flattery ('Schmeichelei')
and corruption. Christ, he argued, had replaced the Old Testament by the New

Testament. The new should therefore sweep away the old. Christ was therefore associated by Paracelsus with spirit, youth, vitality and power. The old religion was dead and earthbound. Paracelsus boldly announced that the tenure of the corrupt priesthood was over and he conducted a fierce diatribe against virtually every aspect of current Church practice, including most of the popular targets, such as indulgences, pilgrimages, religious orders, and taxes. The whole system was condemned because instead of faith springing from the heart it substituted trivial tokens of religious observance, which were exploited by the privileged classes to the detriment of the poor.

The frequency of intrusion of medical subject-matter is well-illustrated by *De summo et aeterno bono* [*On the utmost eternal good*] and *Liber de felici liberalitate* [*Book of happy generosity*]. These two short tracts conveniently illustrate a line of argument frequently employed in the other tracts. The following paragraphs briefly summarize the discussion of Christian brotherhood, where relevant referring to parallels from other tracts. Selective identification of biblical quotations shows the extent to which the argument of Paracelsus is constructed from biblical sources, especially from the New Testament, and the gospel of Matthew more than anything else.

The discussion of social obligation contained in *De summo bono* and *De felici liberalitate* is predictably interspersed with calls to renounce the Old Testament in favour of the New Testament order, critiques of beliefs and action reflecting adherence to the letter rather than the spirit of the new law of Christ and the apostles, and appeal to the Holy Spirit and the light of nature as guides to thought and action. In *De summo bono* the principal target of criticism is vanity, whereas in *De felici liberalitate* it is avarice. Vanity and avarice contribute similarly to the syndrome of vice.

Paracelsus opens by stressing the fundamental beneficence of the deity. Notwithstanding our fall from grace in the Garden of Eden, God had endowed the earth with ample resources to satisfy all human needs. These gifts were freely available to those pursuing their vocation in the spirit of genuine liberality.

High among God's blessings were the riches of medicine. The reader is warned not to be misled by the splendour of such Old Testament models as Solomon. The works of the old prophets were merely a trivial foretaste of the powers of Christ and the apostles. Christ undertook to feed the thousands, heal the sick and the insane, restore the sight of the blind, and indeed to raise the dead. These signs and wonders, frequently reiterated in the gospels, were guarantees of the powers allotted to the righteous.

Scientific knowledge was of course universally available, but Paracelsus argued that true insight into nature was restricted to those Christians genuinely subscribing to the apostolic faith. It was not suggested that spiritual enlightenment provided some direct revelation of the truths of natural philosophy. Post-lapsarian [i.e. after the fall of Adam] men and women were destined to live by hard work. Achievement of higher moral standing constituted a necessary precondition for determining that their labour would be rewarded by genuine knowledge, power over nature, and useful arts. Paracelsus repeatedly contrasted the dead knowledge contained in scholastic sources, signifying no more than the print from which it was composed, with the vital and productive knowledge stemming from the light of nature.

Every person was granted complete freedom, either to make responsible use of God's gifts or to abuse their privileges, by falling victim to such vices as intolerance, false pride or avarice. According to Paracelsus the human constitution contained a mixture of influences, coinciding with the attributes of the planets. The final outcome of character was not predetermined by a particular constellation of planetary attributes because moral choice could overcome any predisposition. True liberality stemmed from positive choice to renounce multifarious temptations to evil, and adoption of a discipline of service and self-sacrifice. Only the most inspired effort would prevent dissipation of precious gifts, as indicated by the scriptural warning against casting pearls before swine.

Fundamental to the expression of liberality was disinterested pursuit of the interests of the least privileged members of the community, the 'poor neighbours' as they were designated. In the eyes of God all were equal, bound together in universal brotherhood. In this context Paracelsus made repeated reference to the injunction of the Psalms: 'blessed is he that considereth the poor'. Also the gospel laid down a firm obligation of Christian duty to feed the hungry, give drink to the thirsty, clothe the naked, or take care of the prisoner, the sick and the stranger.

Paracelsus wrote particularly harshly against those who squandered their liberality on drinking and gaming in low company. He wrote at length on the improper and improvident use of God's bounty. His censure fell just as strongly on those who made signs of outward piety but were not motivated by the true evangelical spirit. They were guilty of cheating the poor by imposition of a double standard. True liberality involved the unrestricted distribution of wealth or medical knowledge according to the needs of the poor. It was for instance inadmissible for the better off to subsist on fine white bread, while consigning the poor to black bread made from coarse rye and oatmeal. The Lord was ever vigilant to detect hypocritical avoidance of Christian responsibility to the poor. Communities guilty of this vice would be deprived of the access to useful medicine, and indeed fresh plagues would be visited on them.

Any doctor taking up a court position or assuming civic office was judged guilty of betraying his obligation to use his knowledge for the common good. Fine dress and social status were regarded as pretentious surrogates for effective practice. The doctor was invited to learn from the sweaty worker or sooty miner, rather than the religious and secular orders, with all their distinctions of dress and obsession with hierarchy. Since academic education, status and wealth led to intellectual sterility and moral corruption, Paracelsus was forced to the conclusion that the greater merit resided in the lower orders, especially the skilled artisans. The common people or handworkers were held up as the model for their social superiors on both vocational and spiritual matters. The apostles were recruited from among the common people. Paracelsus believed that Christ's judgement on this matter could be taken as a sign of the intrinsically superior capacity of the common people to attain apostolic purity.

Hypocrisy served the purposes of the Devil. Neglect of the solemn obligation to serve the poor paved the way for regression into vice and ostentatious living, the ultimate expression of this tendency being relapse into idolatry. This marked the final accomplishment of the cunning wiles of the Devil.

Especially in *De felici liberalitate* Paracelsus concentrated on the Old Testament as a source for recidivism into idolatry. The living and vital images of the New Testament were forsaken in favour of images wrought from wood or silver. At the best statues and icons were minor substitutes for spiritual experience. At the worst they were the equivalent of the idols placed before the Children of Israel to mislead them. The worship of idols was associated with the corruption of values and the persecution of the saints. Corruption was detected by Paracelsus at all levels in the Church. Even the seemingly innocuous hermits wandering about in the forest, or the monks behind the thick walls of their monasteries were chastised for engaging in useless or impoverished works of mercy. Their faith and works were useless because they sprang from authority rather than the heart. Such errors were magnified with ascent in the hierarchy of the Church.

The papacy was attacked for embodying the institution of corruption. Lavish ceremonial feasts, elaborate dress, ornament, jewellery, silver, statues and paintings were castigated as manifestations of pagan idolatry. The papacy had relapsed into worshipping the goddess Diana, whose silver shrine at Ephesus was confronted by Paul. The vices of self-indulgence were intruded into the centre of religious life. Secular elites and church hierarchy had thus become united in a common way of profligate life. Religious and secular organizations were bound by rules and orders which stemmed from humans rather than from God.

In order to sustain their affluent existence the idolaters, like ants, were covetous and avaricious. Thereby they exploited rather than assisted their poor neighbours. Even their acts of charity were without real content. Even when cried up with trumpets and bells, their liberality was inspired by the Devil, as for instance the unction administered by priests, or the salves of the doctor, all of which were worthless to the poor. False prophets, false apostles and false doctors were no better than the Pharisees or Anti-Christs, all of whom would be subject to the eternal damnation at the Day of Judgement. On the other hand those who rejected the Devil, avarice and idolatry and who followed the apostolic faith would be granted fruitful knowledge and be permitted to perform genuine works of benefit, inspired by the example of Christ and the apostles as recorded in the gospels.

In *Ex libro de religione perpetua* [*From the book of everlasting religion*], Paracelsus drew out in more detail the relevance of his religious ideas to the theory of medicine. The revival of medicine was presented as a major feature of the process of renewal which would take place during the final age when the Church was reformed. In the new age of the spirit a general amelioration of life would take place. This would allow fulfilment of God's declared intention that the human race should overcome its sins and enjoy a long life. God had endowed nature with marvellous powers, but this knowledge had become neglected and lost. By following Christ's example it was now within the capacity of doctors to recover these skills and apply them for the benefit of those with the greatest need.

By this means the art of medicine would reproduce the miraculous cures recorded in the New Testament.

Paracelsus aimed to replace the prevalent 'theory' of medicine derived from the ancients with a new theory, which he also called the 'religion' of medicine. Galenic medicine is dismissed as a redundant scholastic exercise. The construction of abstract systems and discussion of recondite issues of causation was attacked by Paracelsus as a refuge from the more important priorities of medicine.

The 'highest religion' of medicine required the intensive investigation of stones, roots, plants and seeds, in order to reveal their powers. Paracelsus appealed for diseases to be treated as species with distinguishing characteristics, just as other natural species. Species of disease were to be identified and given an appropriate name. Each disease was then capable of being combated by a specific cure or arcanum [Secret remedy].

The search for arcana was by no means to be limited to the investigation of the chemical properties of natural products. Paracelsus attached great importance to the example of the wise men from the east who recognized the call of the star to visit the infant Jesus. These Magi from Saba and Tharshish were designated as ancestral natural magicians, whose experience witnessed the potency of the firmament, not only as a source of astrological omens, but as a more general source of influence on human life. Paracelsus believed that the powers of the firmament could be channelled into the service of medicine, although this was a delicate and potentially dangerous exercise because it carried the risk of trespassing into forbidden magic or superstition.

The writings of Paracelsus conventionally classified as scientific and medical are strikingly different from their counterparts produced by the medical establishment. Paracelsus avoided the commentaries, compendia, consilia [deliberations], pandectae [comprehensive treatises] or systematic expositions beloved by his medical humanist contemporaries. His writings contain few traces of the stylistic conventions cultivated in learned circles. The individual works of Paracelsus are generally short, simple in structure, impressionistic in style and wide-ranging in their coverage. Their titles pronounce bold and radical objectives. Often the title pages include a Latin short-title, sometimes making the connection with some medical classic which Paracelsus aimed to supersede, but the text is entirely in the vernacular, following the vigorous, polemical and sometimes coarse style of the pamphlet literature. Paracelsus made few concessions to humanistic refinement. He was sensitive to criticisms on this point and he conducted a stout defence of his robust and aggressive approach to medical discourse.

Although virtually none of the scientific and medical writings of Paracelsus were published during his lifetime, the works prepared for publication bear many of the hallmarks of the protest literature. It has already been noted that in physical appearance his first medical tract on guaiacum was similar to his first *Practica*. The connection with the protest literature is particularly indicated by the intrusion of religious and social comment into the scientific works. Indeed

the entire edifice of his scientific and medical writing is built on an explicit theological infrastructure, and this is emphasized by the frequency with which scientific tenets are linked to biblical quotation. Indeed the Bible is virtually the
only literary source acknowledged by Paracelsus. This overt biblicism is a further
feature of the protest tracts.

The tendency to infiltrate discussion of medical and scientific issues with religious and social allusions was prominent from the outset and it showed no
diminution in the later works. This element of continuity is conveniently indicated by reference to *De pestilitate* [*On plague*] and the Carinthian Trilogy, which
are works completed shortly before his death.

Notwithstanding its specialized title, *De pestilitate* constitutes a convenient
general review of the ideas of Paracelsus. Writings on plague, just as much as on
syphilis, were guaranteed eager reception by the reading public. Paracelsus utilized plague to defend his theories concerning the interdependence of celestial
and terrestrial events. This system of magical correspondences he identified as
the counterpart of ancient biblical magic. The key to this magic lay in the book
of Revelation. Among other things, this text contained the secret of plague. John
as the author of Revelation was drawing on a tradition of biblical wisdom
stretching back through the prophets to Moses. On this occasion Paracelsus was
kinder to the Old Testament magi than he was in some of his other writings.
These cabalists and prophets had been persecuted and their wisdom was lost. In
its place had evolved profane philosophy, which was degenerate because severed
from its biblical roots. The result was a system of lies embodied in Galenic medicine and still maintained by exploitative doctors and perpetuated by the medical
schools in Paris, Padua, Montpellier, Salerno, Vienna and Leipzig.

The following brief example indicates the manner in which the characteristic
Paracelsus argument ranges by free association over the entire subject-matter of
his discourse, generating an inextricable admixture of ingredients. He urged that
in contradistinction to the corrupt learned doctor, the natural doctor or theologian would understand that the sun possessed a hidden Evester, or 'night' spirit,
which possessed powerful hold over the Evester determining the physical
processes of human existence. Through this correspondence God was able to
punish man by infection of plague, just as the father could punish an errant child.
Planetary bodies were the hand or rod through which the father punished
humans on earth by inflicting diseases on them. The title page of the *Practica*
of 1529 provided iconographical expression of this idea. Paracelsus went on to
suggest that everything undertaken by humans, whether good or bad, was marked
down by the Evester of the sun, which acted as a chancellor or secretary. [. . .]
Sectarian misinterpreters should be warned that the moon is subservient to the
sun and its seven 'lights', a point also evident from the *Practica* woodcut. Anyone
believing that the star over Bethlehem can only be seen from Wittenberg, or the
Cross of Christ only in Rome, was guilty of leaving buried the pearl of wisdom
and thereby failing to understand the Apocalypse. It was essential to take note of
the biblical pronouncement that there would be great signs in the heavens (Revelation 12: 1). Therefore, Paracelsus warned, ignore the prattle of the schools, or
the Pharisaical pronouncements of the accursed pulpits concerning plague.

Plague is not simply an act of God, but it strikes suddenly, like a burning glass or the reflection of light, the sun using planets as its agent, each releasing a chemical poison according to its character. Such actions strike with suddenness and deadly effect, like the fatal glance of the basilisc.

De pestilitate contained a particularly concentrated attack on poly-pharmacy as practised by Galenic physicians. Paracelsus disputed the claims of the herbals that particular plants possessed 50 or over 100 virtues. He ridiculed the elaborate theoretical basis and grotesque calculations used for determining compositions and concluded that recipes, often containing as many as 40 or 50 ingredients, were useless. This approach to therapy was caricatured as an elaborate and useless religious ritual, comparing unfavourably with the simplicity of his own application of mineral remedies.

This theme provided Paracelsus with an opportunity to extol the virtues of the simple form of medicine practised by the laity. In Saxony and the towns of Braunschweig, Hildesheim and Goslar, for instance, townspeople and peasants were more skilful than all their doctors. Paracelsus acknowledged having learned from more than 80 peasants how to identify the signatures [special features] of plants and perform remarkable cures with them. This respect for the collective medical knowledge of the common people was an echo of the theme of the common people in the protest literature. The folk healers of Paracelsus were the counterpart of karsthans, the idealized wandering labourer, carrying hoe, flail or scythe, who symbolized the virtues of commonsense and simple piety. Paracelsus believed that God had chosen the simple folk, and even animals, to teach the right course of therapy. When this knowledge was guided by light (or understanding possessed by the angels, 'Engelsvernunft', equivalent to the instinctive understanding of animals, 'tierische Vernunft'), then the common people and those of low social status were capable of attaining the highest skill. Such knowledge collected into a little book would be better than all the commentaries on Galen and Avicenna. The doctors, by depending on books of print ('Bücher der Buchstaben'), had neglected the true books of nature. They were merely purveyors of secondhand information learned from unreliable sources. They merely retailed phantasies derived from Pliny, Aristotle, Avicenna or Galen, rather than utilizing the grace of God to overtake these ancient authorities.

Whereas *De pestilitate* was a miscellaneous jumble, the Carinthian Trilogy was one of Paracelsus' most polished works, prepared with the expectation of imminent publication in 1538, but left unpublished because of interruption by his visit to Salzburg, where his premature death occurred in 1541. The most substantial part of the trilogy was an exposition of his theory of the role of tartar in the formation of disease. Significantly this long, technical treatise was introduced by three shorter items, a short historical chronicle about Carinthia, the *Defensiones septem* [*Seven defences*] and the *Labyrinthus medicorum* [*Doctor's Labyrinth*]. The latter two tracts contain some of the most sustained and effective polemics by Paracelsus against the medical establishment, and they draw upon social and religious themes prevalent in the protest tract literature. The Carinthian Trilogy therefore underlines the manner in which Paracelsus utilized his most technical presentations as a vehicle for his wider social and religious message.

The *Defensiones septem* contains a particularly passionate defence of the direct and combative style of his writings. Paracelsus boasts that his manner is rooted in the habits and customs of the simple country people among whom he has lived and journeyed. Self-consciously Paracelsus identified himself with the tradition of Karsthans. He aligned himself with the itinerant journeyman, dressed in coarse homespun cloth, fed not on figs, mead or wheaten bread, but on cheese, milk and oatcakes. Journeys among the fir-cones in the relentless search for knowledge was the only sound way to experience. The only way to understand nature was to tread its books with one's feet. This unpretentious and humble path to learning was repeatedly contrasted with the bankruptcy of the learned doctors whose culture was inimical to sound learning and effective medical practice. Academic physicians were caricatured on account of their fine dress, fondness for jewellery, and effete habits. They were presented as weaklings, inhabiting dark chimney corners, or women's chambers, and cosseting themselves with expensive luxury foods. Such manners were inimical to effectiveness as scholars or practitioners. In fact, the physicians surrounded by their books were captives of the Ship of Fools. Instead of following the example of Christ and the apostles and practising out of love for their poor neighbour, the learned practitioners practised for selfish gain. The physician was casting away his pearl and turning aside from the field in which the treasure of medicine resided. Their practice could not be fruitful unless they gave away their wealth and abandoned practising for profit. Then their needs would be taken care of, and they would flourish like the lilies of the field or birds of the air. Although Paracelsus made few overt comparisons, both from style and content of the critique of the medical profession, the reader would readily have made the connection with the anticlericalism of the protest tracts.

Readers would also have recognized the strong apocalyptic overtones of the *Defensiones septem*. Paracelsus opened his first defence by stating the conflict between the new and old theories of medicine. The old theory was discredited, not only because it was corrupted by generations of scholastics, but also because it was in principle irrelevant to different geographical circumstances and the special characteristics of the new age or latest monarchy, which was characterized by unprecedented social and economic change, greater population pressure and new diseases, all of which called for a new form of knowledge and much greater level of inventiveness than had previously existed.

God provided for the cure of diseases and other human needs in each preceding monarchy, but corrupt manners prevented exploitation of the abundance of nature. The example of Christ, which had itself hitherto been disregarded, provided renewed guarantee of reaping the full benefits of the light of nature. [. . .] But this teaching had been corrupted by false prophets and false apostles, who were in league with the Devil. Only the regenerate would be endowed with the full gifts of knowledge, which were implicit in the system of Paracelsus, and which constituted a 'new medicine appropriate to the present Monarchy'. For those guided by the precepts of humility and love for their neighbour, God would provide a cure for every disease, even diseases which the learned physicians claimed were incurable.

The eleven short chapters of the *Labyrinthus medicorum* elaborated the theory of the light of nature, which was central to the epistemology and methodology of Paracelsus. Predictably, Paracelsus included a further diatribe against the classical and Arab medical authorities and modern academic medicine as cultivated by the humanist medical establishment. The result of this vast exercise in paper and ink was to produce worthless tomes, filled with dead knowledge, worth no more than the type from which it was composed. Academic medicine was of no more value than the prattle of priests.

The epistemology outlined by Paracelsus was modelled on the empirical procedures of craftsmen. This form of knowledge was called *Experience, Experiment* or *Erfahrenheit*. The *Labyrinthus* outlined the way in which empirical methods could be pursued on an organized basis, to embrace all aspects of nature. The total system was called Magic, the descendant of the knowledge possessed by the wise men who travelled from the East to pay homage to the infant Christ. By contrast with the fictitious entities and dead knowledge of the academics, letters, words, sentences, etc. of empirical data could be constituted into living books, giving an insight into the real elements and species of nature. This system would reveal the whole course of disease and enable cures to be matched with diseases. In searching for appropriate analogies, Paracelsus concluded that the seeds of plants, their growth and development, provided a model for the understanding of disease, which should replace humoral theory. Therefore the medical practitioner should follow the wisdom of the farmer and abandon the fictions of the Galenists. The system of magic would reveal signatures which would appropriately link cures and diseases. This form of magic was possessed by the peasant rather than the physician.

The above body of knowledge based on sound precepts of theology was called the 'theology' or 'religion' of nature. While the knowledge through the light of nature was ascertained empirically, Paracelsus emphasized that acknowledgement of faith through the light of the Holy Ghost was a necessary precondition for the proper realization of the light of nature. The Doctors who lacked faith in God, the Trinity, and who failed to imitate the example of Mary and the saints, were destined to fall into vice and neglect their duty to the poor. Only those who loved God and followed the path of righteousness would be granted their share of the benefits of nature. If this duty was neglected no benefits would be forthcoming. At the Day of Judgement those who had failed to abide by the injunction of Christ to help the needy and who had cherished their treasure on earth would face their punishment. Paracelsus appealed to the academic physicians to abandon their vices and turn to the light of nature. Otherwise there would be no escape from the labyrinth in which they were entrapped.

Although the treatise on tartar, which concludes the Carinthian Trilogy, is largely technical in nature, the first two chapters recapitulate the major points of emphasis in the *Defensiones septem* and the *Labyrinthus*. Consequently, religious and social comment was intruded prominently into this technical treatise, and a similar impression is derived from most of the other medical and scientific writings of Paracelsus. As indicated above, similar themes echo throughout his writings and they are supported by the same biblical sources. It is impossible to avoid the conclusion that the religious framework and social criticism were essential and integral. Paracelsus linked his critique of the medical establishment with the anticlericalism of his time, and he self-consciously presented his own alternative system as a natural extension of the form of scriptural piety which commanded wide assent in reforming circles. By drawing on the modes of expression developed in the vernacular tracts, Paracelsus evolved a formula capable of appealing to a wide audience. The mood of social protest and apocalyptic tone cultivated by Paracelsus induced a sense of the heightened urgency of his message. His tracts therefore directed a potent blend of religious and technical argument against the medical establishment. His success as a propagandist is confirmed by the intense efforts made by the medical elite to suppress his work. Consequently, a variety of adverse circumstances prevented the immediate publication of the majority of his writings. Nevertheless his editors discovered a remarkable level of continuing demand for these works. Thereby Paracelsus succeeded posthumously in his mission to draw medicine into the centre of the Reformation stage. The relevance of the Reformation as a religious and social context to the genesis and reception of the ideas of Paracelsus must be taken into account in the evaluation of his location in the history of medicine. It is arguable that underplaying of the immediate context has resulted in greater emphasis on purely scientific factors or on more distant erudite sources of influence than is warranted by the evidence. Any realistic assessment of Paracelsus must recognize the unity of his vocation as apostle, prophet and healer.

29   Nicholas Goodrick-Clarke 'The philosophy, medicine and theology of Paracelsus'

Source: from *Paracelsus: Essential Readings*, Nicholas Goodrick-Clarke, Crucible (The Aquarian Press), Wellingborough, 1990, pp. 23–36.

Paracelsus was a pioneer of the new Renaissance world, which rediscovered man and his power in the universe. He broke with the closed hierarchial structures of medieval thought and determined to explore and describe the natural world. His enterprise was inspired by the Renaissance neo-Platonic conception that the whole of creation – the heavens, the earth, and all Nature – represented a macrocosm, and that its unity was reflected in a variety of possible microcosms, of which man was the most perfect. The analogies and correspondences between the macrocosm and the microcosm were central to his cosmology, theology, natural philosophy, and medicine. Such analogical speculation was present in Greek philosophy and throughout the Middle Ages, but Paracelsus was the first to apply this approach systematically to the study of Nature. These neo-Platonic ideas also underpinned his theory of knowledge. Paracelsus expressed a deep distrust of logical and rational thought as a scientific tool. Since man was the climax of creation, uniting within himself all the constituents of the world, he could have direct knowledge of Nature on account of a sympathy between the inner representative of a particular object in his own constitution and its external counterpart. For Paracelsus, this union with the object is the principal means of acquiring intimate and total knowledge. Moreover, this true knowledge does not concern the brain, the seat of conscious rational thinking, but rather the whole person.

Paracelsus was above all a naturalist. He set out to explore how Nature works and to discover the eternal laws by which it is governed. The work of Nature constitutes a visible reflection of the invisible work of God. Nature thus provides signs by means of which God grants a glimpse into His secret wisdom and design. Paracelsus' conception of Nature was rooted in his cosmological and theological ideas. Whereas God had created natural objects such as stars, herbs, and stones, He did not create their 'virtues' (essential activity or power). Prior to all creation these uncreated virtues had always been in God; in the course of creation they were distributed in the natural world as direct emanations of God. Just as all virtues in natural objects are divine and supernatural, so human ability and wisdom are also gifts from God. Paracelsus thus exhorts man to 'seek, knock and find' and further his knowledge of Nature as a religious duty to understand the work of God. The wonders of God, the cures, and the arcana (secret remedies) are lavished upon the natural world all around us. Nature can reveal these signs of God. The naturalist is engaged in an empirical search for the divine seals in Nature.

This empirical search was a mode of enquiry quite opposed to the medieval concern with an intellectual mastery of ancient authorities and traditional texts. Paracelsus contrasted his own notions of experience and science with that pseudo-knowledge based on logic and reasoning, an elaboration of abstract categories and models of reality bearing little relation to the actual objects, influences, and events in the external world. He rejected scholastic book-learning and its slavish dependence on the old ideas and systems of Aristotle (384–322 BC), Galen (c.129–199), and Avicenna (980–1037). In accordance with Gnostic ideas, Paracelsus conceived of all creation having two sides: a visible elemental (material) part and an invisible superelemental (astral) part. Man, the microcosm, likewise possesses a carnal elemental body and an astral body (*corpus sidereum*) which 'teaches man' and is able to communicate with the astral part of the macrocosm, the uncreated virtues or direct emanations of God in the world of Nature. He saw experience as a process of identification of the mind or astral body with the internal knowledge possessed by natural objects in attaining their specific ends. The researcher should try to 'overhear' the knowledge of the star, herb, or stone with respect to its activity or function. Science is thus already present as a virtue in the natural object, and it is the experience of the researcher which uncovers the astral sympathy between himself and the object. This identification with an object penetrates more deeply into the essence of the object than mere sensory perception. Paracelsus' science is both profound and holistic in its approach to Nature.

Magic was an essential part of Renaissance neo-Platonic philosophy, first exemplified in the influential works of Marsilio Ficino (1433–90). Magic in this context does not mean the cultivation of demons, but the capture and direction of the divine virtues in natural objects for the benefit of man. This 'natural magic' was fundamental to Paracelsus' world-view and science. Firstly, magic reveals the invisible influences between things, providing the basis of medicine, philosophy, and astronomy. Secondly, magic is an action or practice, by means of which the magus can bring heavenly forces down to earth, into himself, or on to other objects, which thus acquire the power of the transferred virtue, be it from a star, a plant, a gem, or any other natural object. The magus requires a strong mind in which the heavenly and earthly forces are balanced and combined. His power is spiritual and superior to matter and the elements. He becomes at least the equal of Nature and can achieve wonders with the aid of the virtues he has mastered. The magus can also transmute objects, transfer power, act at a distance, and predict events. Impressed by Ficino's idea of the priest-physician, Paracelsus saw the physician as a magus who knows all the virtues of herbs, minerals, and other objects. By a process of concentration the physician can capture the virtues of Nature in a miniscule remedy, for such an extract 'has many leas and meadows in its fist'.

Paracelsus' insistence on the union of researcher and object and his belief in natural magic strike the modern mind as subjective. Scientific thinking prides itself on an 'objective' attitude and demands distance and disassociation between observer and object. Since the time of Galileo (1564–1642), Descartes (1596–1650), and Newton (1642–1727), science and philosophy have typically striven for separation, distinction, and measurement in order to demonstrate the differences between objects and phenomena. By contrast, mystical and magical modes of thought seek similarities, sympathies, and 'wholes' in Nature and the cosmos. Paracelsus' notion of experience, his advocacy of homoeopathy, his doctrine of 'signatures' (whereby the form of an object symbolizes its virtue or essential action), all indicate a holistic world-view based on the traditions of Gnosticism and the Cabbala.[1] His rejection of abstract reason and logic as a distorted model of reality and his search for similarities and symbolical correspondences between the macrocosm and the microcosm led him towards a more empirical view of Nature and a sensitive apprehension of the world about us. The map is not the territory, but Paracelsus' map certainly represented a closer approximation to Nature than the constructs of medieval philosophy. Moreover, the spiritual relation between man and the cosmos was central to his science of the symbol, whereas this vision was lost in the science of the system from the seventeenth century onwards. [. . .]

The question whether Paracelsus embraced or rejected astrology cannot be answered simply. But such a question fails to comprehend Paracelsus' new approach to Nature and the essence of Renaissance neo-Platonism. Paracelsus used the term *astrum* to denote not only a celestial body (star or planet), but the 'astral', divine, and invisible virtue or activity essential to any natural object. While ancient and medieval astrology attributed a dominant and causal role to the stars in a strictly hierarchical conception of the cosmos and creation, Paracelsus ushers in a new age by bringing those powers down to earth and distributing them in divine virtues, signs, and seals throughout the natural world. In this way he shifts attention from the traditional generality of medieval cosmology towards the local, the specific, and the empirical. During the Renaissance man was now looking all around himself to discover the powers of Nature and how it works. Man and Nature consequently enter into an active relationship rather than remaining the passive objects of transcendental power, be this God or the stars above.

Paracelsus developed a theory of matter from these new philosophical ideas. Here again one can see how he moved towards an empirical concern with specifics. Medieval science, largely based on Aristotle and the translations of his works by the medieval Arab philosopher Avicenna, still accorded the four Elements – Earth, Water, Fire, and Air – a pre-eminent position in the theory of matter. The qualities of a substance or an object were deemed to reveal its elemental nature: cold and dry (Earth), cold and moist (Water), hot and dry (Fire), and hot and moist (Air). Although these four Elements still feature in Paracelsus' theory, they are no longer the last and irreducible components of matter. He thought that an immanent, specific, and soul-like force determined the nature and species of an object rather than its (visible) chemical components. For him, substances were but crude envelopes which disguised an underlying pattern of spiritual forces and it was this pattern, not the corporeal cover, which dictated the composition of matter. Paracelsus generally 'spiritualized' matter, in claiming that such spiritual forces are the true elements and principles, while the Elements and chemical substances are only the crystallized deposits of such forces. Taking the notion of Prime Matter ('Arche' or 'Ousia') from ancient Stoicism, Paracelsus regarded the visible Elements as the results of an interaction between the qualities of heat, cold, moisture, and dryness and this Prime Matter, a kind of vital matter-spirit.

According to Paracelsus, God created things in their 'prime', but not in their 'ultimate' matter. Paracelsus viewed all Nature as in process of transformation, whereby all objects are being perfected. He personalized the principle responsible for this process as Vulcan, an immanent virtue or power which works in the matrices (the traditional Elements) of Air, Earth, Fire, and Water. In this task Vulcan is assisted by two further powers or principles. Firstly, it needs to draw upon a reservoir of energy, which is necessary for the nourishment, growth, and preservation of all natural things. Paracelsus called this general reservoir the *Iliaster*, a type of primordial matter-energy which essentially is and expresses the entire potential of all nature. Secondly, since Vulcan draws upon a general resource, it requires a specific agent to impress the specific and individual attributes upon the elemental material world. This agent was known as the *Archeus*. Paracelsus described both Vulcan and the *Archeus* metaphorically as workmen, craftsmen, and alchemists perfecting prime matter into ultimate matter, whether in Nature at large or in the human body. These concepts show again how Paracelsus was not interested in identifying units of matter, but was searching for the 'intelligences' or *semina* (seeds) in matter, which as *archei* are responsible for all specificity in Nature.

Paracelsus accorded a central importance to Sulphur, Salt, and Mercury as the Three Principles of which all bodies consist. One would be mistaken if one thought that Paracelsus was referring here to the chemical substances known as sulphur, salt, and mercury. He used these terms to denote principles of constitution, representing organization (Sulphur), mass (Salt), and activity (Mercury), all varieties of the specific forms achieved by the immanent intelligences and *semina* of matter. But Paracelsus also used the terms in a chemical context: Sulphur represents the combustible, Mercury the smoky or volatile, and Salt the unchangeable component in any natural object. These principles are disclosed when the elemental cover is removed. For instance, when a piece of wood is burned one sees flame (Sulphur) and smoke (Mercury), while only ash (Salt) remains. These principles of constitution, together with the complex scheme of intelligences and *semina*, the Vulcan, the *Iliaster*, and the *Archeus*, are the dominant concepts in Paracelsus' theory of matter-energy and the process of life, while the ancient Elements are relegated to a secondary function as matrices, vehicles, or even mere covers for the active spiritual forces.

Ancient Greek medicine, deriving from Hippocrates and Galen, was based on a theory of the four chief fluids or humours of the body (blood, phlegm, yellow and black bile), which were supposed to determine the temperament of the individual. A predominance of blood over the other humours produced a ruddy complexion and a courageous, hopeful, amorous disposition; too much phlegm resulted in calmness, then sluggishness and apathy; yellow bile or choler caused anger and irascibility; black bile or melancholy produced introspection, sadness, and depression. Galen attributed disease to an upset of the humoral equilibrium, whereby there was an excess or deficit of one of the humours and the qualities of heat, cold, moisture, and dryness. Disease was a matter of 'distemper'. Medieval medicine, represented by the works of Galen and Avicenna, had built up an elaborate pharmacology of herbal remedies for numerous degrees of humoral imbalance, based on logical and rational extrapolations from a limited amount of original observation. On the one hand, this scholastic medicine produced the remote and bookish physician of the Middle Ages who expounded theory but did not actually treat patients; on the other hand, the apothecaries dealt in an endless variety of herbs and other remedies which had little or no relation to the disease and often made the patient's condition worse.

The ideas and developments of Paracelsus' theory of matter are plainly evident in his pioneering medicine. He opposed and destroyed the ancient humoral medicine and related ideas. He denied that the four humours and temperaments could explain the wide variety of diseases. He rejected the paramount importance of the constitution and its internal order in ancient pathology. Instead, Paracelsus developed a medical theory which related the macrocosm and microcosm, while building on his dynamic notions of matter and energy. There were two important consequences: firstly, Paracelsus saw disease as something which affects the body from outside rather than as an internal imbalance; secondly, this wider relationship between man and the external world led to a search for specific cures and remedies relating to particular diseases and disorders. Paracelsus also used chemical remedies, based on his speculations concerning Sulphur, Salt, and Mercury, with far more promising results than the effects of the old Galenic herbs. For this reason, Paracelsus is often hailed as the founder of modern medicine and iatrochemistry. [. . .]

[From Paracelsus' writings] one can deduce his extraordinary advances in medical thinking beyond the formulae and systems of humoralism. Paracelsus propounds a medicine which leads to the localization of disease. He distinguishes diseases according to the different organs affected, their different anatomical changes, and the different exogenous causes. Paracelsus dispenses with the tortuous humoralist theories which are necessary to explain, for example, how black bile from the spleen causes ulcers on the leg. He sees a specific disease and proposes a specific remedy. Since diseases are 'species' or 'fruits' distributed throughout mankind, there is an aetiology or science of their anatomy, causes, and treatments. By contrast, ancient pathology only recognized general 'distempers' and thus employed non-specific remedies such as sweating, bloodletting, and vomiting intended to evacuate any morbid matter. Paracelsus' medicine regards disease not as a constitutional phenomenon but as a parasitic invader; its cure demands the removal of a specific agent. Hence his therapy is not symptomatic but fundamental.

This concern with the local and specific, ideas which flowed naturally from the exploration of correspondences and analogies, led Paracelsus to the isolation of virtues in concentrated extracts and chemical remedies. This new pharmacy is based on a scientific procedure and has less to do with the trial and error of Galenic herbalism and nothing whatsoever to do with the ancient formulae of qualities, grades, and humours. Paracelsus is often called the father of homoeopathy. His chemical remedies are indeed based on the fine sympathies between the diseases and the arcana. This sympathy is opposed to the ancient principle of opposites in remedial action. Paracelsus denied that a 'cold' remedy can cure a 'hot' disease, unless this is due to the other properties of the remedies concerned. He claimed that cancer corresponded to arsenic in the macrocosm and asserted that arsenic itself would cure this arsenical condition. [. . .] A scorpions' venom can cure scorpion poisoning. Paracelsus thought that the specificity of an arcanum lies in its 'anatomy' or structure, the work of Vulcana and the *Archeus* in the particular elemental matrix. Because the anatomy of the remedy is identical with that of the disease agent, Paracelsus was a staunch advocate of the iso- or homoeopathic principle in medicine.

Paracelsus' philosophical inspiration led him to expose the weakness and unreality of elemental and humoral doctrines. Many important proto-scientific ideas and modern medical theories emerge in his work. His specific contributions to medicine are impressive and include: a humanitarian and ethical approach towards the patient, especially the mentally ill; a recognition of the healing power of Nature and the value of antiseptic principles; progressive views on syphilis and a rejection of guaiac and mercurial treatments[2] knowledge of the diuretic action of mercury and its curative powers in dropsy; the connection between goitre, minerals, and drinking water in certain places; studies of spa waters and observations of the beneficial digestive effects of certain acid waters (balneology); the description of the Miners' Disease as an occupational illness in which he shows the greater toxical risks in metals than in salts and recounts a concrete aetiology with numerous symptoms.

Notwithstanding, it is misleading to call Paracelsus the founder of any particular branch of medicine. [. . .] It is not appropriate to understand Paracelsus as a figure at the threshold of modern Western scientific thought. We should rather reflect on the perennial truths of his science of the symbol and their unexpected relevance to the profound problems of our scientific and technological era. He was the founder of an alternative science and medicine.

Alchemy plays a major part in the thought of Paracelsus. [. . .] Substances were produced in alchemy by a process comparable to generation in Nature. By imitating the natural generation of diverse substances and acting on the humours of metals, alchemy was supposed to be able to convert base metals into perfect metals. Alchemists believed that they could 'cure' and convert base metals into gold by a process of removing their impurities. These ideas seem very similar to those of Paracelsus. He too sought the volatile, the invisible and the virtues inside objects. He compared alchemy to medicine and the baseness of metals to disease.

Paracelsus also followed the medieval alchemists in his rejection of gold-making as the ultimate goal of alchemy. He mainly regarded alchemy as important for the curing of disease and the prolongation of life. Alchemy was another means of perfecting what Nature had left in an imperfect state. [. . .]

In his philosophy and medicine Paracelsus replaced the medieval, hierarchical conception of God, man, and Nature with a more reciprocal and direct relationship between God and man through His presence in man and Nature. Paracelsus regarded human spirit and talent as direct emanations of God. According to his essentially neo-Platonist notion, the spirit is a divine spark of the Godhead which inheres in man. Paracelsus regarded man as the crown of creation and believed in his free will and power to the extent that he could even act upon the stars. Since man had such tremendous potential, Paracelsus could not countenance the subjection of man within an arbitrary social or political structure. He believed that men should be free to develop their gifts to the utmost for communal benefit, rather than being harnessed to the political interests of a master or lord. His motto 'that man no other man shall own who to himself belongs alone' contains an explicit social and political philosophy based upon the notion of the divinely inspired individual.

As a Reformation figure, Paracelsus has often been compared to Luther. They share many traits, including coarse and boisterous language, the use of vernacular German rather than Latin as a popular means of communication, the wholesale rejection of academic predecessors, and theatrical acts intended to appeal to students and common folk such as the burning of books and public instruction. However, Paracelsus was a pacifist and a staunch advocate of the ordinary people. He sided with the rebellious peasants who risked persecution and death in their struggles against the feudal lords at Salzburg in 1525. His medicine was inspired by charitable motives and involved risks to his own health and life. He expressed his Christianity through acts of self-denial and practical works. He was always prepared to take the part of the poor and the downtrodden against the rich, mighty, and privileged. His conviction in the absolute value of each individual's link with God was paramount in his social and political attitude. Whilst inspired by similar motives, Luther ultimately upheld the authority of the secular princes of Germany against the revolting peasants. [. . .]

Paracelsus' social and political views were radical, and he is known to have had frequent contact with scattered Anabaptist groups in the 1520s and 1530s. He agreed with the diverse social reformers of his time in their critique of the contemporary powers of Church and State. But it would be wrong to identify him with secular revolutionary thought. His approach was one of balance. Paracelsus was opposed to dogma. He recognized private property within limits, upheld the rights of the individual, and regarded the family as the fundamental unit of society. He also preserved the medieval idea of Christian community life, so that his 'communism' was a matter of natural inspiration rather than systematic, rule-bound, and class-conscious. He interpreted property and poverty as religious and theological states of being rather than as economic privilege and misfortune. He exposed the antisocial and antihuman nature of commercial and professional vested interests. But he was also a conservative and entrusted his proposed plan of communalizing the land and the means of production to the Emperor and his administration.

Paracelsus was bold and uncompromising in his views and proposed reforms. Both the man and his works possess an epic quality, so that it is not surprising that his ideas and influence should have long survived his own lifetime. [. . .]

NOTES

1   Gnosticism was an early Christian heretical movement which invoked the notion of spiritual enlightenment through mystical and intuitive communion with God and nature. Cabbalism was the study of the Cabbala, the mystical writings of the Jews. It underwent a revival in the early sixteenth century and fostered a renewed interest in the Hebrew language which, as *the* original language of God and the Creation, some Christian Cabbalists believed held the key to the mysteries of nature and religion.
2   Guaiacum. The wood or bark of this tree from central and south America was widely held to possess curative powers, particularly in relation to syphilis, or the 'French Disease' as it was more widely known in Renaissance Europe. Paracelsus opposed its use, partly on the grounds of its exotic provenance, and preferred instead to argue in favour of compound mercurial preparations.

30   Mario Biagioli **(i) Galileo's early career (ii) Galileo and the Medicean stars**

Source: from *Galileo, Courtier: The Practice of Science in the Culture of Absolutism*, Mario Biagioli, University of Chicago Press, Chicago and London, 1993, pp. 5–8, 106–12.

If Galileo's science was not external to court culture and patronage concerns, neither was it determined by these concerns. The portrait I am proposing is not that of a 'slave of the system' – of somebody who fits himself within received roles and expectations in order to receive legitimation. Power does not censor or legitimate some body of knowledge that exists independently of it. By emphasizing the process of self-fashioning, I do not assume either an already existing 'Galileo' who deploys different tactics in different environments and yet remains always 'true to himself,' nor a Galileo who is passively shaped by the context that

envelops him. Rather, I want to emphasize how he used the resources he perceived in the surrounding environment to *construct* a new socioprofessional identity for himself, to put forward a new natural philosophy, and to develop a courtly
audience for it. As indicated by Prince Leopold de' Medici's convening the Accademia del Cimento between 1657 and 1667, Galileo had an impact on Florentine
court culture well after his death in 1642.

Obviously, any process of self-fashioning is not without tensions. If the court
made possible Galileo's legitimation of his new socioprofessional identity, it also
constrained it in ways that, at times, may have collided with Galileo's specific
desires. While in certain contexts the fit between Galileo's work and court discourse was remarkable, on other occasions we find irresolvable tensions between
patronage strategies and scientific authorship, or between Galileo's attempts to
draw the patron on his side to legitimize his scientific claims and the prince's
interest in preserving his power and image by not tying them to possibly problematic claims. [. . .]

The relationship between patronage, court culture, and Galileo's career is not
just a matter of the history or sociology of scientific professions. Copernicus and
some of his followers faced a crucial obstacle when they tried to legitimize their
work as not only a *mathematical* computational model but also a *physical* representation of the cosmos. The received hierarchy among the liberal arts was such
an obstacle. According to this hierarchy (one that was justified by scholastic views
on the differences between the disciplines and their methodologies), mathematics was subordinated to philosophy and theology. The mathematicians were
not expected (or supposed) to deal with the physical dimensions of natural phenomena, which (together with the causes of change and motion) were considered to be the philosophers' domain. Consequently, the philosophers perceived
Copernicus not just as putting forward a new planetary theory, but as 'invading'
their own disciplinary and professional domain. In general, this invasion was
unacceptable to them and, having higher disciplinary status than the mathematicians, the philosophers had resources to control such an invasion. The usual
tactic (one that worked quite well in institutions that accepted this disciplinary
hierarchy) was to delegitimize the mathematicians' claims by presenting them as
coming from a lower discipline.

The so-called Copernican revolution was two revolutions in one. The acceptance of dramatic cosmological changes required drastic modifications in the
organization of the disciplines that studied the cosmos. As we know, this process
was a very long one. The legitimation of Copernican astronomy implied a restruc-
turing of the hierarchies among the liberal arts which, in turn, involved an
increase in the mathematicians' social status. Such changes did not simply result
from the strength of the new theories but from an institutional migration as well.
Although the traditional disciplinary hierarchy was quite entrenched in the university, it was not so at court. There, one's status was determined by the prince's
favor rather than by the discipline one belonged to.

The court, then, was a social space in which mathematicians could gain higher
social status and credibility, thereby offsetting the disciplinary gap traditionally
existing between them and the philosophers. This increased socio-disciplinary

status would in turn contribute to the legitimation of the new worldview they were proposing. If we look at the so-called scientific revolution from the point of view of its sites of activity we may notice (at least on the Continent) a trajectory that leads from the university, to the court, and, eventually, to the scientific academy. To a large extent, Galileo's career exemplifies this trajectory of social and cognitive legitimation. After being a university mathematician, he became a natural philosopher at a court and then a member of what is often considered the first scientific academy – the Accademia dei Lincei. [. . .]

The almost exclusive focus on Galileo adopted in this book may create the impression that his career was radically different from that of other mathematicians. As I have indicated elsewhere, this is both true and untrue. Although his courtly career and title of philosopher was exceptional for a mathematician, there are many other ways in which Galileo fits well the mathematician's traditional social role. For instance, in terms of training, social status, and career pattern it would not have been easy to tell Galileo from other leading Italian mathematicians before 1610. Although Galileo's father, Vincenzio (a well-known musician and music theorist), had sent him to the University of Pisa to study medicine (and to help relieve the financial difficulties of his family), Galileo eventually left Pisa without a degree in 1585. Like many other mathematicians, Galileo did not study mathematics at the university. In Florence he studied mathematics under Ostilio Ricci, an applied mathematician and military engineer who instructed the Florentine court pages and lectured on perspective to the painters, sculptors, and architects of the Accademia del Disegno – the Medici-sponsored academy of fine arts. It was in this professional culture of applied mathematics at the crossroads of architecture, mechanics, fortifications, and the visual arts that Galileo spent his early years in Florence.

After 1588, Galileo taught mathematics, astronomy, mechanics, and fortification techniques at Siena, Pisa, and Padua – both inside and outside the universities in those cities. That he could teach in a university without a university degree suggests that mathematics was perceived as a technical rather than philosophical discipline, one that was learned through apprenticeship rather than formal university training. The position of the teachers of mathematics in the university was marginal. In addition to the disciplinary and epistemological gap that we have seen between mathematics and philosophy, mathematics was often considered as a mechanical art (because of its role in surveying, mechanics, and bookkeeping). This did not confer much status on its professors, who in fact made between one-sixth and one-eighth the salary of philosophers. Finally, the marginality of mathematicians in the university was reflected by the few chairs dedicated to their discipline (one at Padua and Pisa and two at Bologna) and by its subordinate role in the curriculum.

At Padua (where he taught from 1592 to 1610) Galileo dabbled successfully in mechanical inventions (he obtained a patent for a machine to lift water) and acted as a consultant to the Venetian Arsenal. Beside his activities as a university professor, Galileo supplemented his relatively low income by teaching mathematics, mechanics, and especially fortifications to private students – some of whom he boarded in his own house. In 1599, he took an artisan, Marcantonio

Mazzoleni, into his house as an instrument maker. Mazzoleni's chief task was to construct geometrical and military compasses, computation devices that Galileo would then sell mostly to his private students.

Up to this point, Galileo's career was typical of a competent and enterprising mathematician. Things changed abruptly in 1610 when, after improving the telescope (which had initially been developed in the Netherlands) and making several remarkable astronomical discoveries, Galileo left the University of Padua for the Medici court to become the *philosopher* (not just the *mathematician*) of the grand duke. It is at this point that Galileo's trajectory began to deviate from that of his fellow mathematicians. However, if the courtly skills and tactics that characterized much of his later career were exceptional for a mathematician, his desire for social and epistemological legitimation was rooted in the professional culture he shared with many leading mathematicians of his time. [. . .]

STARS IN CONTEXT

Some reasons for the Medici's interest in the moons of Jupiter are easy to grasp. As Galileo asserted in the dedication of the *Sidereus nuncius* [*The Starry Messenger*] these new planets were monuments to the Medici dynasty. Moreover, they were monuments of exceptional durability and worldwide visibility – at least for audiences equipped with good telescopes. But there were other reasons behind the Medici's enthusiasm for Galileo's discoveries, reasons fully apparent only to a Florentine audience familiar with the mythology the Medici had been articulating since Cosimo I established the dynasty in the middle of the sixteenth century. In this mythology, a correspondence was drawn between the cosmos and Cosimo, and Jupiter was regularly associated with Cosimo I, the founder of the dynasty and the first of the 'Medicean gods.' Consequently, while Galileo could have dedicated the newly discovered planets to any patron, the Medici were in the position to fully appreciate (and reward) the mythological significance of Galileo's discoveries.

Although the Medici had been the de-facto rulers of an allegedly republican Florence since the fifteenth century, the dukedom itself was of much more recent origin. In fact, Cosimo I became duke of Florence in 1537 and was made grand duke of Tuscany only in 1569. During the 1540s he had to create the political and administrative structure of the new state, along with a new political mythology that would stabilize the Medici rule and present it as a dynastic one. After becoming duke of Florence, Cosimo needed to establish a court out of almost nothing. The powerful Florentine families were to be transformed from former political leaders into a docile court aristocracy, and the new mythology that represented the ducal rule as natural and necessary was to indicate the role the powerful Florentine families had to assume within it.

Cosimo's strategy was to represent the Medici rule as Florence's manifest destiny. The city's horoscope, so commonly cast since the Middle Ages, was normalized to suggest the astrological necessity of Medici rule by linking that rule to the history and fate of the city. New Medici-oriented histories and Medici-sensitive reinterpretations of ancient myths were commissioned, while Medici-related imagery was introduced in Florentine art. Most important, Medici-controlled academies – among them the Accademia Fiorentina [Florentine Academy] and the Accademia del Disegno [Academy of Design] – were established to manage this cultural program.

Although Cosimo did not go so far as to commission a family history in the form of a Greek-style theogony [account of the birth of deities], he had classical theogonies allegorically reinterpreted to resemble the history of the house of Medici. This mythological program was best articulated in Vasari's frescoes decorating the Apartment of the Elements and the Apartment of Leo X in the Palazzo della Signoria [Lord's palace] – the first Medici court palace, later known as Palazzo Vecchio [Old palace].

The project's basic schema is clear enough. The Apartment of the Elements was a kind of Olympus divided into several rooms, each dedicated to a specific god (Hercules, Jupiter, Ops, Ceres, Saturn) or to a predivine entity such as the primordial 'elements'. Right below the Olympus of the Apartment of the Elements we find the Medici pantheon – the Apartment of Leo X. Each room of the Apartment of Leo X is dedicated to a member of the Medici family who was instrumental in establishing the dynasty.

Each room dedicated to a Medici in the Apartment of Leo X was put, as Vasari says, in a plumb-line relation with a god-dedicated room in the Apartment of the Elements directly above it. The frescoes of each room downstairs present a mythologized history of the member of the Medici family the room honors. Each history was made to mirror as closely as possible the classical theogony of the corresponding god. The Room of the Elements, the primordial entities that allowed for the formation of all things, corresponded to the Room of Leo X, the Medici pope who made the emergence of the Medici dynasty possible. As Vasari put it, 'There is nothing painted upstairs that does not correspond to something painted downstairs.' The heavenly order legitimized and naturalized the earthly one. Appropriately elegant stairs ensured communication between the two floors.

Vasari describes in detail the intricacies of the entire Medici mythology as presented in these frescoes. What we need to consider here is the specific correspondence established in them between Jupiter (the greatest of the gods) and Cosimo I (the founder of the grand duchy of Tuscany), for that mythological relation played a crucial role in Galileo's patronage tactics.

The correspondence between the room of Jupiter and that of Cosimo I is the pivot for the mythological narratives developed throughout the paintings of the two apartments. The paintings in the Room of Jupiter, which present his childhood, are in fact tied to Cosimo as well. Born of Ops and Saturn, the child Jupiter was saved from the father's cruelty (Saturn tended to eat his offspring) by his mother, who hid him in a cave in Crete. There, the infant Jupiter was reared by two nymphs. One of them, Amalthea, was represented as a goat and was allegorically associated with divine providence, while Melissa, the other nymph, was an allegory of divine knowledge. The message was that Cosimo absorbed, literally, those virtues in the cradle. In memory of Amalthea, Jupiter added the sign of Capricorn to the zodiac. The seven stars of Capricorn became emblems of the seven virtues, three theological and four moral. Quite conveniently, Capricorn happened to be Cosimo's sign, thereby confirming the destiny uniting the first grand duke and Jupiter. Thus Cosimo was endowed with divine providence and knowledge by Jupiter and received the seven virtues from Capricorn.

In the dedication of the *Sidereus nuncius* to Cosimo II, Galileo himself introduced the analogy between the Medicean Stars and Cosimo I's virtues, some moral, others 'Augustan.' He claimed that young Cosimo obtained those same virtues (which, according to Galileo, he displayed all the time) directly from Jupiter, which was just above the horizon at the moment of his birth. Those virtues were 'emanating' from the four stars which – like innate virtues – always revolved very closely around Jupiter and never abandoned him. Therefore, given the link between Jupiter and Cosimo I, Galileo was suggesting that Cosimo I passed on his (and Jupiter's) virtues to his successor through the Medicean Stars, and that Galileo himself, by revealing these stars, was somehow midwife to this astrologico-dynastic encounter. The correspondence between the Medicean Stars and the four moral virtues was accepted by the Medici's humanistic advisors: even in the thirty years following Galileo's condemnation, the four moral virtues were used as painterly allegorical representations of the four stars.

These mythologies were more than a sign of the Medici's imaginative pretentions. They constituted the 'master narrative' that informed the imagery used in public political ceremonies and festivals as well as the subject matter of court poetry, theater, painting, and opera. They offered a framework for court culture. When needed, this mythological imagery could be expanded by means of emblematic translations, as conveniently listed in sixteenth-century catalogues or dictionaries of emblems [. . .] The entire cultural framework was maintained and articulated by Medici-controlled institutions such as the Accademia Fiorentina and the Accademia del Disegno.

Court culture itself was permeated by these mythologies from the time of Cosimo I. Familiarity with them allowed the courtiers and the Florentine upper classes to engage in the game of interpreting the emblematic narratives displayed in Medici ceremonies and other political semiologies. As indicated by Baldassare Castiglione's *Book of the Courtier*, [. . .] skill in emblematics was a tool required of those who wanted to engage in courtly life. As Castiglione put it, 'Sometimes other discussions would turn on a variety of subjects, or there would be a sharp exchange of quick retorts; often 'emblems' as we nowadays call them, were devised; in which discussions a marvelous pleasure was had.' Emblematics provided the courtiers with more than an engaging parlor game; it also was a powerful tool for self-fashioning. Court society affirmed its own social identity by differentiating itself from the lower classes, which – although participating as spectators of some of those public ceremonies – could not fathom their full meaning. Emblematics was to court spectacles what etiquette was to court behavior: it differentiated social groups and reinforced social hierarchies by controlling access to meaning.

This mythologico-emblematic framework of Medici court society and culture constituted the background for Galileo's representation of his astronomical discoveries as emblems of the Medici dynasty. If he wanted to become a courtier by differentiating himself from the other practitioners of a low-status discipline like mathematics, Galileo had to use the same codes court society had adopted to differentiate itself successfully from the noncourtly masses. [. . .]

31 Peter Burke 'Witchcraft and magic in Renaissance Italy: Gianfrancesco Pico and his *Strix*'

Source: from *The Damned Art: Essays in the Literature of Witchcraft*, ed. Sydney Anglo, Routledge and Kegan Paul, London, Henley and Boston, 1977, chapter 2, pp. 32–50.

[I]

Recent research on the intellectual history of Italy in the fifteenth and sixteenth centuries has been marked by a reaction against what might be called the 'whig interpretation' of the Renaissance. The 'whig interpretation of history' was defined by Sir Herbert Butterfield, who coined the phrase, as the tendency of historians to see the past as the story of the conflict between progressives and reactionaries, in which the progressives, or whigs, always win, and in so doing bring about the modern world.

Jacob Burckhardt's famous book may reasonably be described as 'whig' in Butterfield's sense, for Burckhardt saw the Renaissance as the rise of modernity, the Italians of the time as 'the first-born among the sons of modern Europe'. Hence, when in his sixth chapter he came to discuss magic and witchcraft in Renaissance Italy, Burckhardt had a problem. The humanists, as he presents them, were enlightened progressives; magic and witchcraft, on the other hand, were old-fashioned and superstitious. Yet, as Burckhardt knows, humanists did not, for the most part, reject this 'popular superstition'; on the contrary, they took magic and witchcraft quite seriously. Burckhardt tries to resolve the contradiction by assuming that, had it not been for the French invasion and the Counter-Reformation, Italy would have overcome these 'fantastic fooleries' by her own powers.

Burckhardt's solution to his problem has not satisfied his successors, from Aby Warburg onwards. Eugenio Garin, Perkin Walker and Frances Yates have all suggested that the interest in magic shown by Ficino, Giovanni Pico, Cardano, Porta, Bruno, and other Italian Renaissance intellectuals is less odd than Burckhardt thought. Magic was an important part of their world-views. Magic was praised by ancient writers they respected such as Iamblichus, Porphyry, and above all, Hermes Trismegistus, whom they thought an ancient Egyptian writer. The image of man the magus which emerges from the hermetic writings fitted in very well with humanist ideas about the dignity of man. Dr Yates suggests that there was a rise in the status of the magician in the fifteenth and sixteenth centuries, just as there was a rise in the status of the artist. Magic did not merely survive into this period; it was revived. In any case it is impossible to draw a sharp distinction between 'reactionary' magic and 'progressive' science.

Burckhardt wrote about witchcraft and magic as if they were associated; Garin and Walker and Yates confine themselves to magic alone. However, in Italy the fifteenth and sixteenth centuries were not only the time of the revival of magic but also the time of the rise of the 'witch-craze', in the sense of the persecution of witches. Between 1460 and 1525, at least ten Italians published books denouncing witches. Witches were taken very seriously by a number of Renaissance popes, patrons of humanism and the arts; Eugenius IV, Nicholas V, Innocent VIII, Julius II, and Leo X all issued decrees against witches, of which the most notorious is Innocent's bull of 1484, [. . .] associated with the witch-hunters' manual the *Malleus Maleficarum* [the *Hammer of Witches*]. Although reliable figures about executions and other punishments seem impossible to obtain, it appears that the period around the year 1520 marks a peak of witch-hunting in northern Italy.

This coincidence in time between the rise of magic and the rise of the witch-craze in Italy suggests a number of questions. Should witches as well as magicians have a place in our picture of the Italian Renaissance? What was the relationship between humanists and witches? What was the relationship between witchcraft and magic?

A simple answer might run like this. The problem of Renaissance witches is a non-problem, the result of a linguistic confusion. 'Renaissance' is a term which commonly refers both to a movement and a period. Not everyone who lived in the period participated in the movement. On the contrary, there were at least two cultures in Renaissance Italy, that of the educated, who knew Latin and were interested in the revival of learning, and that of the rest, the 'people'. The educated believed in magic; the people believed in witchcraft. If the revival of magic and the rise of the witch-craze occurred together in Italy, that is pure coincidence, for witchcraft and magic in Italy [. . .] were quite different activities.

This answer is in fact too simple. Some educated Italians did believe in witchcraft; that is why they wrote treatises and issued decrees against it. In any case the distinction between magic and witchcraft was not a sharp one. There was a cluster of terms in Italian which might be translated 'magician': *mago*, *nigromante*, *incantatore* (feminine *incantatrice*), or *sortilego*. These terms referred to people whose use of rituals and spells gave them supernatural powers which they might use for good or evil. There was another cluster of terms which might be translated 'witch', notably *strega* or *stria* (masculine *strigone*), *lammia* and *fattucchiera*. These terms referred to people, mainly women, who did harm by supernatural means without ritual or spells and sometimes even without meaning to do so. A woman with the evil eye could harm children simply by looking at them. However, as the use of the term *strigimago* suggests, the two clusters were not distinguished carefully or consistently. Magicians were often thought to be wicked, and witches to use spells and rituals. This blurring of the distinction between magic and witchcraft had a tradition behind it. In the twelfth century, Hugh of St Victor had divided magic into five parts, of which one was *maleficium*, which he defined as evil deeds done by the help of demons. In the witch-trials of the fifteenth and sixteenth centuries, *maleficium* was one of the most common accusations.

Burckhardt's problem will not go away, however unhappy we may be with his attempts to solve it. The relationship between humanists, magicians and witches needs to be explored further.

[II]

Did humanists believe in witches? On what grounds? Did they distinguish between witchcraft and magic? For what reasons? To answer these questions it may be useful to begin by looking closely at a single text, although the enquiry obviously cannot end there, for the text may not express typical humanist attitudes, and there may not be any typical humanist attitudes to express. The text I have chosen was published in 1523 by Gianfrancesco Pico della Mirandola (1469–1533), the nephew of the still more famous Giovanni Pico. It is called *Strix*, 'the witch'. Unlike most sixteenth-century books on witchcraft, it is not voluminous and encyclopaedic; on the contrary, it is an elegant and lively little dialogue. It is not surprising that it was quickly published in Italian translation, and that it reached its fourth edition by 1556.

In this dialogue there are four speakers: Apistius, Phronimus, Dicaste and Strix herself. There are three parts or scenes. Scene I begins with the people of Mirandola running to see a witch. This gives Apistius, whose name means 'unbeliever', occasion to express his scepticism about witchcraft. His arguments are answered by Phronimus, whose name means 'prudent'. Then they go and find the witch, and Dicaste, 'the judge', who is in charge of the case, tells her that nothing will happen to her if she answers all their questions. Scene II, the next day, is an interrogation of the witch, and during this exchange Apistius begins to have doubts about his scepticism. Scene III, the same day, is a continuation of the discussion between Apistius and Phronimus, with frequent contributions from Dicaste, and it ends with the conversion of Apistius to the belief that witches really do exist.

Gianfrancesco Pico claims that 'when you listen to the witch speaking, you must believe that you are hearing an accurate account which I have in part seen with my own eyes and in part heard with my own ears, when the records of the trials were read to me.' He explains that his dialogue is a topical one; 'the evildoing of the witches in our region a few months ago' has led him to write, and he has dashed the work off in ten days.

What does the witch say? She confesses to various activities which she does not classify but which – employing the criteria of educated people of the time – it may be useful to divide into three groups.

In the first place, Strix declares that she goes to what she calls 'the game' (*ludus*) or 'the game of the Lady' (*Dominae ludus*): nocturnal festivities over which a lady presides and in which the participants eat, drink and make love. These festivities have several unnatural or supernatural features. Strix flies to the meeting-place on a linen-mallet – a local variation on the broom-stick – after drawing a circle and anointing herself with a special ointment. The food eaten at the game is not normal food; they kill and eat cattle, but after they have finished, they bring the animals back to life. Strix makes love to a being who is not quite like a normal man. He has goose-feet, a variation on the usual cloven hoof; he is a 'demon' or 'familiar spirit'.

So far the witch's activities (however odd) have sounded harmless enough, but she also confesses to *maleficium*. She causes thunder and hail by drawing a circle; she kills babies by pricking them with needles and sucking their blood; and she uses this blood in her magic ointment.

In the third place, the witch confesses to renouncing and mocking Christianity. She offers consecrated hosts to the 'Lady', who treads and pisses on them. Strix is allowed to continue going to Mass, but she is commanded to say under her breath 'you lie' when the Gospel is read, and at the elevation of the host she has to make a secret obscene gesture.

The other three characters in the dialogue react to this confession as differently as their names imply. Apistius the sceptic begins by declaring that the witch is a bird he has searched for but never found (*strix* meant 'owl' in classical Latin), and that a witch is something which 'the ancients never saw'. In any case, he continues, it is a mistake to believe what the common people say, and it is laughable to think that old women can fly through the air. Apistius's interest in antiquity marks him out as a humanist, and so does the fact that he is presented as well-read in poetry and philosophy, subjects which he thinks closely related, holding that Homer and other poets are full of 'hidden philosophy'. By the middle of the dialogue, Apistius has changed his position on witches. He now declares that doubting should be done in moderation and that he is prepared to agree with the other two, provided that he is compelled by arguments and evidence. By the end of the dialogue his conversion is complete. He changes not only his opinion about witches but his whole way of thinking, and he becomes Pisticus, 'the believer'.

The remaining two characters do not change their minds as the dialogue proceeds, but argue throughout that witches really do exist. Phronimus the pious is presented to the reader as a man who is well-read in the classics and so able to meet Apistius on his own ground. He too assumes that the Greek and Roman poets are full of 'hidden philosophy', and so it is crucial to his argument to show that the ancients do in fact refer to witches. However, where Apistius stressed the need for rational argument and for evidence, Phronimus emphasises 'the authority of our elders, confirmed by public opinion'. Dicaste's role is the less important one of supporting Phronimus. He is not shown to be well-read in secular literature, and he relies on the Bible and the Fathers of the Church rather than the ancient poets and philosophers. Thus the common position held by Phronimus and Dicaste is based on two different kinds of argument, which may be worth considering one by one.

Dicaste's points are the more conventional and so they may be summarised briefly. Anyone who denies the existence of witches ought to be excommunicated, he says, because this is to deny the truth of the Scriptures. In the Old Testament, there are references to witches in Deuteronomy, Leviticus, Isaiah and Jeremiah. In the New Testament, St Matthew relates that the devil carried Christ to Jerusalem and set him on a pinnacle of the temple, and this shows that the devil has the power to make witches fly through the air. Dicaste also refers to the lives of the saints; the temptation of St Antony the hermit, and the attack on him by all sorts of ferocious beasts, is an illustration of the devil's power to create illusions. Is this remark a clue to the popularity of paintings of the temptation of St Antony in the early sixteenth century?

The arguments of Phronimus are rather more unusual for the period, and their relevance to the humanists requires us to deal with them in rather more detail.

Phronimus points out that the Greeks knew about witches. Circe was a witch, for Book X of the *Odyssey* describes how she turned the companions of Odysseus into swine by means of her drugs. Incidentally, the choice of this example suggests a possible topical meaning for Dosso Dossi's famous painting of Circe (about 1520); one might add that Gianfrancesco Pico was of the same generation as Dossi and, like him, had close associations with the court of Ferrara. As for Medea, as described in Book III of Apollonius Rhodius's poem the *Argonautica* [the story of the Argonauts], she was a priestess of Hecate, a goddess often associated with witches. Medea helped Jason to win the Golden Fleece by giving him a magic ointment to make him invulnerable. She was also notorious for murdering her children. The parallel with witches' ointment and baby-killing is, if not close, obvious enough.

Again, when Apistius laughs at the idea that 'by drawing a circle . . . and mumbling I don't know what words', the old women are able to take off on their sticks, Phronimus replies that Apistius really ought to take Homer more seriously: 'we must believe that all the necromancy practised by Odysseus had its origin in the circle'. The reference here is to the opening of Book XI of the *Odyssey*, where Odysseus sacrifices to the dead before he descends to the underworld. 'I drew my sharp sword from my thigh and dug a pit . . . and about it, poured a drink-offering to the dead.'

As for Latin literature, two key witnesses called by Phronimus are Ovid and Apuleius. Ovid's *Metamorphoses* have a good deal to say about transformations, magical and otherwise, and in Book VI of his *Fasti* Ovid makes a reference to *striges*, who may be owls or women transformed into owls:

> They fly by night and look for children without nurses, snatch them from their cradles and defile their bodies. They are said to lacerate the entrails of infants with their beaks and they have their throats full of the blood they have drunk. They are called *striges*.

Ovid's treatment of the theme of the 'vampire', as we may call it, is close to the confession of Pico's Strix.

Another important piece of evidence comes from Apuleius, whose *Golden Ass* depends on the assumption that men and women can change their shapes as a result of rubbing themselves with ointment. This is how the hero, Lucius, came to be transformed into an ass, and his girl-friend's mistress, Pamphile, into an owl. Apistius does not make the objection that the *Golden Ass* is a work of fiction; perhaps novelists, like poets, offer hidden philosophy. Nor does he make the point that Strix has not actually confessed to changing her shape. Italian women accused of witchcraft not infrequently confessed to changing into cats, and perhaps Gianfrancesco, as he dashed off this dialogue in ten days, forgot to mention this detail. It should be added that the *Golden Ass* was a book which enjoyed considerable popularity in Italy, especially at the court of Ferrara, at about this time, another indication that we are dealing with a topical subject.

Phronimus may be well-read in the classics, but he does not approve of classical antiquity. Like some medieval writers, he believes that the ancient gods and goddesses really existed, but that they were all 'demons', by which he means 'devils'. In antiquity, the argument goes, the devil induced men to worship him 'under the veil of a false religion'. In the famous beauty contest, 'the devil deceived Paris in the form of three goddesses'. Proteus, so renowned for changes of shape, was a demon, and so was the goddess Diana, who was, he adds, not as chaste as she has been painted. It is Phronimus who identifies 'the game of the Lady' in which Strix had confessed to taking part, with 'the game of Diana', who went about at night with her nymphs. The game is at once a survival from classical antiquity and the work of the devil. It is tempting to juxtapose this account with the contemporary paintings of Diana and her nymphs by Correggio and Palma Vecchio. Were these paintings, like the ones by Bosch and Dossi, more topical than is usually thought?

It should be emphasised that Phronimus does not believe in the power of magic without the devil's aid. 'I do not believe that anything can be transformed into something else by means of ointments or of incantations; . . . incantations . . . do no harm without the evil work of the demons'. The witches are not really trans- formed into animals, but to human onlookers they seem to be so transformed. It is all an enormous diabolical illusion. The subtitle of the dialogue, 'the deceits of the devil', underlines this theme.

The emphasis on the power of 'demons' is buttressed with references to Plato and his followers, without any allusion to the possibility that the word *daimon* as they used it did not mean 'evil spirit', but simply a being inter- mediate between the gods and men. These demons, continues Phronimus, once 'had the world in their power', and could persuade 'kings, orators and philoso- phers' to worship them. However, since the Incarnation things have changed. Nowadays the demons 'can scarcely persuade evil old men and women' to worship them, and what used to be done openly and everywhere as something honourable 'is now done by a few, in secret, in remote and solitary places, as an evil and shameful thing'. Nevertheless devil-worship still goes on, as Apistius, after this prolonged battering with Christian and classical texts, is finally prepared to concede.

[III]

The beliefs of the four participants in the dialogue are presented vigorously and vividly. Did they also correspond to the positions held by Italians of the time? To answer this question will be our next concern. Only after an attempt has been made to relate the dialogue to the world around it and to see witchcraft through the eyes of contemporaries will it be safe to return to Burckhardt's more general problem of the relation of witchcraft to Renaissance humanism.

Did Dicaste, or someone with views like him, really exist? We are not told whether he is a lay or an ecclesiastical judge, but his arguments resemble those of a number of Dominican friars, 'the hounds of the Lord', some of whom were inquisitors and active in witch-trials. Obvious examples are the German friars Sprenger and Kramer, authors of the notorious *Malleus Maleficarum* (1486), a book cited by Pico. In Italy, denunciations of witches were published by a number of Dominicans, including Vincenzo Dodo (1506), the inquisitor Bernardo da Como (c. 1508), the inquisitor Silvestro de Prierio (1521), and his disciple

Bartolomeo de Spina (c. 1523). Like Dicaste, these writers took the confessions of witches seriously; like him, they believed in the physical reality of the game; like him, they cited the Bible and the lives of the saints in support of their arguments. A favourite text was 1 Kings, XXVIII, on the 'witch of Endor', a diviner who had a familiar [. . .], and was consulted by King Saul. These men tended to lump together magic and witchcraft, and the first use I know of the term *strigimagi* occurs in Prierio's book.

These clerical writers seem particularly interested in the sexual activities of witches and demons. The fear of women by the authors of the *Malleus* is apparent in their text and it is part of a medieval tradition of misogyny propagated by celibate clerics. As one might have expected from theologians, these writers were more concerned with the witches' denial of the Faith than with the harm they may have done their neighbours. It is heresy which the inquisitors were most keen to sniff out. They saw the witches in terms of a traditional stereotype of the heretic or false believer. Witches were supposed to go to 'synagogues' or 'sabbaths' like the Jews, or to insult the cross, as the Albigensians were supposed to do. Witches like heretics were believed to have their own rituals, which were seen as an upside-down version of the true faith. Witches were believed to tread on the cross instead of worshipping it and to worship the devil instead of treading on him (as the Virgin does in many images). They were believed to do homage to the devil backwards, using their left hand and kissing his anus. Witches were, quite literally, 'perverse'. These beliefs seem to illustrate an intellectual principle of 'least effort', for it is easier to conceptualise alien beliefs as the exact opposite of our own than to enter into their structure.

The theologians also believed that witches and other heretics engaged in sex orgies, killed children and drank their blood, just like Pico's Strix. In fifteenth-century Italy, the heretic Franciscans, or Fraticelli, and their followers were supposed to have killed children, burned them and drunk their ashes mixed with wine from a cask or *barilotto*. Was this a way of suggesting that heretics were not human? Or did the devout project on to their enemies their own secret wishes?

Did Apistius really exist? This question is rather more difficult to answer. One is tempted to identify him with Pietro Pomponazzi, a contemporary of Gianfrancesco Pico's whose philosophical views were at the opposite end of the spectrum. Where Gianfrancesco attacked Aristotle, Pomponazzi was proud to be an Aristotelian. Pomponazzi did not believe in miracles, in the sense of suspensions of the law of nature, and he did not believe in providence, in the sense of direct interventions by God in the course of history; Gianfrancesco believed in both. Pomponazzi argued that 'all prophecy . . . has a natural cause', while Gianfrancesco passionately believed that true prophecy came from God. Pomponazzi argued that angels and demons did not exist, and that the common people simply attributed to demons whatever they were unable to explain, whereas Gianfrancesco saw the work of demons everywhere. Pomponazzi did not have much to say about witchcraft in his books, but it is clear that he could not believe in it because there was no place for it in his world-view. His basic assumption was that everything has natural causes, because 'Nature proceeds in an orderly manner' [. . .]. Pomponazzi might well have said that a witch was a bird he had never seen. However, his arguments are not those of Apistius.

The same point may be made of three early-sixteenth-century Italians who wrote in defence of witches: Samuele da Cascini, Gianfrancesco Ponzinibio, and Andrea Alciato. They argue that most of the actions of which suspects are accused did not happen, and so they come out in favour of leniency.

The arguments for the defence, briefly summarised, are as follows. Cascini, a Franciscan friar, rests great weight on a theological argument. To be carried through the air to the game would involve a miracle, but 'no miracle can be involved in committing any sinful act'. The devil does not have the power to move people from one place to another for the purpose of *maleficium*. Consequently, continues Cascini, turning the tables on his opponents, inquisitors who believe that people are carried to the game 'in the body' are themselves heretics. It is true that the accused often confess to being carried in this way ('in body and soul' was Strix's phrase), but the accused are simple country folk who cannot distinguish dream from reality.

Ponzinibio, a lawyer by profession, takes up this second point, which concerns the credibility of testimony. He argues that the misdeeds to which the accused confess are 'imaginary not real', and that one should not be surprised if they take dream for reality 'since they are women, or if they are men, they are rustics, and people who are easily deceived'. The witches do not really insult the host or suck the blood of babies. Ponzinibio also makes a great deal of a text from canon law, the so-called Canon Episcopi, which declares that 'certain wicked women', who are 'seduced by the illusions of devils', believe that they ride at night with the goddess Diana. In other words, witches are wicked and they do yield to the temptations of Satan, but the game is no more than a figment of their imaginations.

If the witches are deceived, it is surely better to regard them as sick than as criminal. This step in the argument was taken by another lawyer, Alciato, who makes the dry comment that many of the supposed witches should have been 'purified' by hellebore (a standard purgative of the period) rather than by fire [. . .]. Some fifty years later, Montaigne's comment, after he had interviewed a supposed witch, was almost identical.

Have we discovered an original for Apistius? Not exactly. Cascini was a Franciscan friar, and his arguments mainly theological. Ponzinibio and Alciato are more like Apistius because they are laymen and because they agree with him that the testimony of simple people should not be taken very seriously. Alciato quotes Ovid and Virgil in support of his arguments, which brings him still closer to Apistius. However, Ponzinibio and Alciato were professional lawyers, and their arguments often concern technical legal points, whereas the arguments of Apistius do not.

There is another argument in defence of witches which Apistius does not use, the medical, to the effect that witches suffer from melancholy which engenders illusions and makes the sufferers confess to actions which they have not committed. This point was made with force later in the sixteenth century by Girolamo Cardano and Johann Weyer, both professional physicians, but it was already known in Italy in the 1460s. One is left with the impression that Gianfrancesco has created an Apistius who would be more vulnerable to attack than the real defenders of witches were.

What of Phronimus and Strix? Their cases are more complicated and will have to be considered in correspondingly greater detail.

[IV]

Some of the arguments of Phronimus had been put forward before. In a treatise written in the late 1460s, Ambrogio da Vignate had referred to the operations of Circe as an example of witchcraft. Nevertheless, the emphasis on the argument from classical antiquity is remarkable, even in a dialogue in which other points of view are expressed. It is always dangerous to assume that one of the characters in a dialogue represents the author; the point of choosing the dialogue form is often to suggest to the reader that no one of the views expressed is right, or at any rate not the whole truth. In this instance, however, it seems reasonable to identify the views of Phronimus with those of Gianfrancesco Pico himself. Of the four characters in the dialogue, only three engage in argument. Of these one, Apistius, changes his mind, and another, Dicaste, intervenes mainly to support the third. In any case some of the points made by Phronimus had been made by Gianfrancesco in his own name in earlier writings. To these we must now turn.

In spite of an active political life, Gianfrancesco Pico found the time to write a great deal. A collected edition of his works, published in 1573, runs to 1,378 folio pages, and still leaves out a number of important books, *Strix* among them. These books are dominated by a few recurrent themes; a suspicion of classical antiquity, an interest in the processes of illusion, and a fascination with the supernatural in all its forms.

One of his first books, dedicated in 1496, when he was twenty-seven, concerned *The Study of Divine and Human Philosophy*. Gianfrancesco argued that a Christian should be extremely cautious in reading pagan authors. 'Divine philosophy' is good in itself, but 'human philosophy', in other words secular learning, is good only if it is used for Christian purposes. Poetry is dangerous, for poets often mix obscenities into their verses. Learning is not really necessary for a Christian, for 'the apostles were simple men, for the most part fishermen', and 'God was not pleased to save His people by means of dialectic'. Gianfrancesco returned to this theme in his longest and most important work, the *Examination of the Vanity of Pagan Learning*, published in 1520, a critique of Aristotle in particular but one which calls into question the whole classical tradition.

A second major theme in Gianfrancesco's work is his concern with illusion. In his little treatise *On the Imagination*, published in 1501, he suggests that what is wrong with the imagination is essentially its close connection with the body, so that a man's 'phantasms' or fantasies can vary with the changing balance of his four humours. He adds that bad angels (not, be it noted, melancholy) can 'produce deceitful phantasms in men and women called witches'. In his *Examination*, which I have just mentioned, Gianfrancesco goes further and undermines reason and sensation as well. For example, he points out that an imbalance of the humours can distort sense-perception; to a man with jaundice, the whole world seems yellow. Gianfrancesco has obviously learned from the Hellenistic writer Sextus Empiricus whose defence of scepticism, [. . .] was to be influential later in the sixteenth century.

The third theme, the supernatural, dominates another of Gianfrancesco's major works, *On Foreknowledge*, published in 1506–7. Here he discusses a wide variety of ways of foretelling the future, such as: astrology; dream interpretation; prophecy; drawing lots; taking auguries; consulting oracles; chiromancy, geomancy, hydromancy, aeromancy, pyromancy (the 'reading' of hands, earth, water, air, and fire); and so on. He is opposed to all of these except true prophecy, which he thinks a gift direct from God; he thought Girolamo Savonarola, whom he knew personally, to be such a true prophet. Book IV of this treatise is particularly close to the arguments put forward in *Strix*. Gianfrancesco suggests that 'divining is always the result of a secret or open pact with the devil', and that the worship of the pagan gods was encouraged by 'the malice of demons'. The same examples occur here as Phronimus would cite some sixteen years later; the transformations of Proteus, Orpheus as a necromancer, Circe as a witch, and so on.

Like Phronimus, Gianfrancesco Pico pressed new methods into the service of traditional aims, and found new arguments for traditional conclusions. For example, the method of textual criticism developed by Valla and Erasmus and other humanists in order to understand the classics better was taken over by Gianfrancesco to further his argument that the classics were not worth studying. In the *Examination*, he made an analysis of the writings attributed to Aristotle, looking for forgeries, interpolations and corruptions, but this was in order to undermine Aristotle's authority rather than to understand him better. He never seems to have asked the fundamental questions about the text of the Bible which Valla and Erasmus did ask and which he was himself prepared to ask about Aristotle.

Gianfrancesco's use of scepticism was like his use of textual criticism. He was radically sceptical about the possibility of deriving reliable knowledge from sense-data, but he was not prepared even to raise the same fundamental question about knowledge derived from Revelation. He finds it curiously easy to believe that old women could fly through the air and raise storms. One might suggest that he was so credulous (relative to others in his own time) because he was so sceptical; since he lacked the Aristotelian faith in sense-data, he could not dismiss old wives' tales on the grounds of inherent implausibility. Yet it is ironic, to say the least, that the preface to *Strix* stresses what he has seen with his own eyes and heard with his own ears, as if his own senses were less fallible than those of others. The point is surely that scepticism was for him not a way of life but a tool, a weapon; its purpose was 'to destroy philosophy to make more room for religion'.

In short, throughout his life Gianfrancesco played the part of a Phronimus, meeting the humanists on their own ground in order to convert them. He might be described as a new Justin Martyr, for Justin was a second-century convert from paganism who spent the rest of his life trying to convert other educated pagans. Gianfrancesco translated a work he believed to have been written by Justin, the *Admonitorius*. Had he been born a generation later, Pico would have made an excellent Jesuit; like them he treated classical learning as the 'spoils of the Egyptians', something for Christians to pillage for their own ends.

[V]

The debate on witchcraft in early-sixteenth-century Italy suggests that the differences of opinion expressed in the dialogue corresponded to real disagreements between the educated men of the time, even if certain legal and medical points did not get a fair hearing. What of Strix herself? What did she think she was doing? Does her confession correspond to any reality? The attitudes and values of the uneducated in the sixteenth century are necessarily elusive, but if we do not attempt to recover them we risk misunderstanding the views of the educated as well.

To begin with the obvious: Gianfrancesco did not make up the stories he puts into the witch's mouth. They correspond closely to stories current in earlier treatises, notably the *Malleus* and the books by Bernardo da Como and Bartolomeo de Spina. Gianfrancesco certainly read the *Malleus* and he probably read the other two as well.

Do the confessions of Strix represent anything more than a literary tradition? Similar confessions were in fact made by a number of Italians who had been accused of witchcraft in the years just before Gianfrancesco wrote, notably at Breno (north of Brescia) in 1518, and at Sondrio (north-west of Breno) in 1523. At Breno the accused declared that they went on horseback to a certain mountain, where they found a multitude of people singing and dancing and were given 'a certain ointment' which would carry them there in future mounted on sticks. This festivity they called the *zuogo*, a dialect form of *giuoco*, 'game'. They also confessed to denying the faith; 'making a cross on the ground they trampled upon it and spat upon it'. Finally, they confessed to taking an oath to do 'all kinds of evil', and they were given 'a certain powder', which could kill people or raise tempests. The proceedings were supervised by a Lord, not a Lady, but the parallel between these confessions and Strix's account remains close.

The Sondrio trials follow the same pattern. For example, a certain Bartolomeo Scarpategio confessed to going to 'the game of the cask' (*il zogo del bariloto*), a term reminiscent of the trials of the fifteenth-century Fraticelli. There he saw 'a large fire . . . a great multitude of people who danced around it . . . a great lord who sat in a chair, dressed in red, who had horns on his head, and claws on his hands and feet, who was the devil'. There Bartolomeo 'denied God and the faith' (*renega la sancta fede e Messer Domenedio*), and promised to be faithful to the devil, touching his left hand. He also trod, spat and pissed on a wooden cross and 'made figs at it' (*ge fece le fiche*), precisely Strix's gesture at Mass. He carried the host there and insulted it. In return he was given a demon mistress.

In neither of these trials was any reference made to Diana, or indeed to any 'Lady', but this gap is filled by two trials at Modena, which is south of

Mirandola, in the 1530s. Domenica Barbarelli declared in 1532 that she went 'on the journey of Diana' [. . .] and that she profaned the cross and danced with demons by order of 'the Lady of the game'. Orsolina la Rossa, seven years later, confessed to going to the 'Sabbath' over which 'a certain woman' presided, and renouncing the Christian faith.

Thus we have no reason to doubt Gianfrancesco's word when he says that Strix's confession is an accurate account derived from the records of the trials at Mirandola. However, our problems do not end here; they only begin. If we try to use the confessions as a source for popular beliefs of the time, we find that they are not pure but contaminated. The confessions are the product of a situation in which an interrogator, usually a friar, is face to face with the accused, who more often than not has no formal education, while a clerk takes down what is being said. The historian has access to the clerk's record, often in Latin, of an interrogation in which the interrogator, who was often a stranger to the region, probably spoke literary Italian while the accused replied in dialect. The possibilities for misunderstanding are considerable. The interrogator has been through it all many times before and knows, all too well, what he is trying to find. The accused is new to the business and may be searching frantically for cues and clues as to what is wanted. The interrogator had power over the accused, including the power to torture, and the accused knew this. As Girolamo Cardano pointed out in the 1550s, confessions by witches are not to be trusted because 'these things are said under torture, when they know that a confession of this type will bring the torture to an end'. In other words, the accused will tell the interrogators what they expect to hear, and what they expect to hear is what they have read about in treatises like the *Malleus*. The treatises describe what is confessed in the trials, but then the confessions follow the model of the treatises. It is a vicious circle.

Have we any more chance of escaping from this circle than the accused and their interrogators? Yes, on two conditions. The first is that we allow for alternative hypotheses at almost every stage of the investigation. The second condition is that we put the question, 'Was X guilty of witchcraft?', on one side and ask a series of more open questions instead. What kinds of people were accused of being witches? What was the social context of these accusations? We can then put the crucial question of what (if anything) the accused thought they were doing, of what their actions meant to them.

What kinds of people were accused of witchcraft in Italy? Members of all the main groups in society might be accused of witchcraft on occasion, but not with the same frequency. Until more quantitative studies are made, we shall have to rely on impressions, and my impression is that in Italy, as elsewhere, women were accused of witchcraft more frequently than men, and also that the clergy were accused more frequently than the laity, relative to their proportion in the total population. It was not just any woman or priest who would be accused of witchcraft. Most vulnerable to the accusation were those who regularly foretold the future, discovered thieves, sold love-philtres, worked abortions, delivered babies and cured the sick by means of herbs, prayers and rituals. In Italy these people were known as *herbarie*, *girovaghi*, *guaritori*, *sortilegi*, and so on, terms which might best be translated into the sixteenth-century English 'cunning men' and 'wise women'.

Thus Guglielmo Campana, a parish priest of Modena, tried in 1517, detected thefts and prepared philtres; Benvegnuda, a woman accused at Breno in 1518, was said to have cured many people, especially from *maleficium*, and to possess 'an incantation to make a man love a woman or a woman a man'; Giuliano Verdena, a weaver of Mantua, tried in 1489, was said to fill a vessel with water and discover the images of thieves in it – an example of the 'hydromancy' attacked by Gianfrancesco Pico.

It is not difficult to see how people like this should have been identified as witches by inquisitors like Dicaste. They were sometimes accused by members of their local community, and this too should occasion no surprise. Since they were in close touch with the supernatural, the 'witch-doctors' were liable to be treated as witches themselves. As a witness in a trial in Modena put it in 1499, 'Knowing how to heal means knowing how to harm' [. . .] If misfortune struck, if a man were taken ill, if he found himself impotent on his wedding night, if his crops were destroyed by hail, then the wise women were the obvious scapegoat, though not the only one. We do not have the evidence to reconstruct the victim's point of view in depth and detail. We can only link the fragments of evidence by speculation, but we must do this (however briefly or reluctantly) in order to understand what was going on. Perhaps the victim felt guilty for some offence done to the accused; perhaps he felt envied. In any case it is not too difficult to see why private accusations of witchcraft were made, or why laymen appealed to the inquisitors. Thus in Lombardy in the mid-fifteenth century, the inhabitants of two communities, Bellano and Porlezza, petitioned the duke of Milan to call in the Inquisition against the local witches.

But what did the accused think they were doing? This is the most elusive of all the questions. 'Nothing at all' might be the answer in some cases, because the accuser had imagined everything. More complicated are the cases involving folk-healers. The accused tried to cure their clients by means of rituals and formulae, including prayers like the Our Father and the Hail Mary. Under interrogation they might claim to cure by the power of God and the saints; Benvegnuda, accused at Breno in 1518, declared that she cured people in the name of the Virgin Mary and St Julian. What is one to make of a man who practised love-magic using texts of the Psalms? It is virtually impossible to decide whether he thought he was acting like a good Christian or whether he was consciously playing with fire. He seems to have thought of the Psalms as possessing supernatural power by themselves; and this suggests the hypothesis that if the accused really did take away consecrated hosts from church, as they sometimes confessed to doing, like Strix in Pico's dialogue, this was to make use of its powers, not, as the inquisitors thought, to insult it. Where the healers must have known they were on trickier ground was where they worked *maleficium* against their clients' enemies, sticking pins into images and so on; and from the victim's point of view, even love-magic was a form of *maleficium*.

However, *maleficium* was not what the inquisitors were really looking for. What about the orgies, the flights through the air, the homage to the devil and all the rest of it? One possibility is (as Cardano suggested) that the accused simply admitted to whatever their interrogators seemed to want in order for the torture to end. This explanation seems plausible enough, yet it does not always work; one writer against witches, the layman Paolo de Grillandi, tells us that he was convinced of the reality of witchcraft after hearing confessions where torture was not applied. There are records of such trials still surviving, and they deserve to be taken seriously as evidence, all the more because the confessions sometimes surprised the interrogators; in other words did not conform to their stereotype of the witch. A series of cases which took the inquisitors by surprise occurred in the 1570s in the north-east corner of Italy, in Friuli; they have recently been the subject of a brilliant monograph. The accused called themselves 'go-gooders' (*benandanti*). They met at night four times a year. They denied being witches on the grounds that they fought the witches on these expeditions; they fought with sticks of fennel and the witches with sticks of maize; 'And if we win, that year is an abundant one, and if we lose there is famine that year'. They went on to explain that they did not go in the body but in the spirit; it was important that their body was lying face upwards while the spirit was away, so that it could re-enter.

This point supports another suggestion of Cardano's, that confessions of attendance at the 'sabbath' were merely descriptions of dreams. He raises the objection that it is odd for many different people to dream the same dream, but this point can be answered on the basis of twentieth-century research. There is evidence that culturally stereotyped dreams often occur in some societies. The Ojibwa Indians are a case in point, and so are the Nyakyusa of Tanzania among whom 'defenders' (*abamanga*) regularly fight witches in their dreams, just like the *benandanti*. People may dream in a stereotyped way if they expect to do so, and they often dream the folklore of their culture. The story of Diana and her ladies going about at night and entering people's houses was part of Italian folklore, the local equivalent of the English tales of Robin Goodfellow. It would not be too surprising if people dreamed of Diana, or if lonely old women had wish-fulfilment dreams of feasting and sexual intercourse and of doing their enemies harm.

It seems reasonable to conclude that the idea of witchcraft is a composite one, including popular elements, such as destructive magic and flight through the air, as well as learned or clerical elements, such as devil-worship.

[VI]

In the last few pages we have looked at witch-trials as a form of drama in which the fantasies of the victim, the accused, and the inquisitor all had their part. It is necessary, in conclusion, to explain why the plot of this drama changed over time, and so to return to the Burckhardtian problem with which we began. In England in Tudor and Stuart times there is evidence of increased demand at the village level for witches to be tried and condemned. No evidence of this kind has been found for Italy, at least so far. What changed was the clerical view of the witch.

The clerical stereotype of the witch as a human servant of Satan seems to have been formed in the fourteenth and fifteenth centuries. If we ask, Where did this stereotype come from? the answer is fairly simple: heretics had long been believed to engage in sex orgies, worship the devil, kill children and drink their blood. All that was new was the tendency to attribute these crimes to people accused of the equally traditional offence of *maleficium*.

But why should the stereotype of the heretic have been extended to include the witch? Why should inquisitors have become more concerned with witches in the fourteenth and fifteenth centuries? One possibility is that they were worried by the rise of heresy (the Lollards in the fourteenth century, the Hussites in the fifteenth) and so began to find heretics everywhere. In the case of Italy, we find inquisitors acutely concerned with both heresy and witch-craft in the 1520s, the decade of Pico's dialogue, the treatises of Prierio and Spina, but also of the penetration of Lutheran ideas into Italy.

Yet why should witches in particular come to be seen as dangerous? I believe that the arguments which Gianfrancesco Pico puts into the mouth of Phronimus give us a valuable clue and that, in Italy at least, the rise of the witch-hunts and the rise of the Renaissance are connected. In Florence, it has recently been noted, 'the advent of humanism coincided with a revival of sorcery persecution', in the late fourteenth and early fifteenth centuries. What could the connection between witches and the Renaissance be? That complex movement we call the Renaissance involved, among other things, the revival of interest in antiquity, including the ancient gods and goddesses. For some of the clergy, as for Phronimus, these gods were 'demons', so they believed that they were witnessing a revival of the demonic. In this context the confessions of certain women that they had attended 'the game of Diana' must have confirmed clerical suspicions.

The Renaissance also involved a revival of interest in magic among the learned, in Italy and elsewhere. Humanists were careful to distinguish 'spiritual' from 'demonic' magic, let alone from witchcraft. The clergy, as we have seen, did not make these distinctions. For them a rise of magic was a rise of witchcraft, which had to be fought; an interest in demons was an interest in devils. When one reads in *Pimander* (one of the hermetic writings taken most seriously by the humanists) that the soul leaves the sleeping body and consorts with demons in order to obtain magical powers, and when one turns to the confessions of the *benandanti* about their adventures out of the body, it is not difficult to see how the inquisitors might have thought that they were dealing with a unified movement.

Perhaps it is not so surprising to find cultivated Italians like Nicholas V, Innocent VIII, Leo X and Gianfrancesco Pico taking witches as seriously as they did. If men could gain control of supernatural forces for good purposes, why not also for evil? Given this possibility, the traditional rituals and fantasies of cunning men and wise women now appeared in a new and sinister light, as a conspiracy of the servants of Satan. Inquisitors were dispatched to bring the conspirators to justice, and the witch-craze got under way.

32 Anthony Harris **'Manifold impieties: The social setting'**

Source: from *Night's Black Agents: Witchcraft and Magic in Seventeenth-Century English Drama*, Anthony Harris, Manchester University Press, Manchester, 1980, chapter 1, pp. 1–18.

Daniel: These cunning men and women which deale with spirites and charmes seeming to doe good, and draw the people into manifold impieties, with all other which have familiarity with devils, or use conjurations, ought to bee rooted out, that others might see and feare.

[Gifford: *A Dialogue concerning Witches and Witchcraftes*]

[I]

There are almost as many theories as to the nature and origins of witchcraft as there are works – scholarly and otherwise – on the subject. In examining the witchcraft beliefs and practices of the sixteenth and early seventeenth centuries in England this confusion is compounded by the fact that there was at least as much disagreement among Elizabethan and Jacobean writers on the subject as there is today. Scholars happily drew fine distinctions between witches and wise women, magicians and necromancers, but unfortunately their definitions rarely coincided and, moreover, what relevance their academic hair-splitting had for the general populace, including both witches and bewitched, is highly doubtful.

Some authorities were prepared to distinguish between the exponents of 'black' and 'white' magic, using such terms as 'witch' and 'sorcerer' for the former and 'charmer' or 'blesser' for the latter. Others, however, condemned without exception all dealings with the occult, however innocuous they might appear, and such writers saw no reason to differentiate among the various practitioners. For example, William Perkins in his *Discourse of the Damned Art of Witchcraft* (1608) declared:

> For this must alwaies be remembred, as a conclusion, that by Witches we understand not those onely which kill and torment: but all Diviners, Charmers, Juglers, all Wizzards, commonly called wise men and wise women; yea, whosoever doe any thing (knowing what they doe) which cannot be effected by nature or art; and in the same number we reckon all good Witches, which doe no hurt but good, which doe not spoile and destroy, but save and deliver. [pp. 255–6]

Reginald Scot, writing in the milder vein of his *The Discoverie of Witchcraft* (1584) recounts an anecdote concerning an individual named Pope and concludes: 'This Pope is said of some to be a witch, of others he is accompted a conjuror; but commonlie called a wise man, which is all one with a soothsaier or witch' (Book XIII, chapter xxx).

Some of the problems of terminology are particularly relevant to a study of the portrayal of witchcraft and other occult practices in the drama of the period. For example, a point to be borne in mind when investigating the nature of the Weird Sisters in *Macbeth* is that to many of Shakespeare's contemporaries the word 'witch' could be applied equally to human and supernatural creatures. This is seen in Florio's *Queen Anna's New World of Words* (1611), where the Italian 'strega' is defined as 'a witch, a sorceresse. Also a hag or fairie'. The synonymous linking of witch and fairy is a further complication which is also relevant to *Macbeth*, for it removes the apparent incongruity of Hecate's command to the Weird Sisters to dance 'Like elves and fairies in a ring' (IV.i.42).

It is argued by some modern scholars that the terms 'witch' and 'fairy' were indeed identical in the Elizabethan era. Pennethorne Hughes, for example, declares in *Witchcraft* (1952) that the fairies were the surviving worshippers of the palaeolithic religion and that therefore 'the people who until the late Middle Ages were called fairies, by one name or another, were often those who, until the seventeenth century or so, were called witches' (p. 64). Lewis Spence in *British Fairy Origins* (1946), whilst carefully avoiding such a specific identification, lists numerous supposed attributes of fairies which were also applied to witches – the powers of shape-shifting and invisibility through the use of ointments, knowledge of herbal medicines, the maintenance of close links with agricultural and human fertility, for example (pp. 17–22). Katharine Briggs, whilst stressing that she is not convinced of the identical origins of witches and fairies, admits in her conclusion to *Pale Hecate's Team* (1962) that 'the strands of belief are almost inextricably entangled' (p. 222).

Elizabethan and Jacobean scholars, in the main, found less difficulty in distinguishing between witchcraft and sorcery. The latter was generally regarded as the art whereby the devil was summoned by charms or the drawing of magic circles, whereas witchcraft entailed the gaining of occult powers through a formal pact with the devil. Prospero can be seen as a sorcerer (or magus), using his magical arts for basically good ends, whilst Marlowe's Faustus and Alexander VI in Barnes's *The Devil's Charter* both begin their occult careers by practising sorcery but are subsequently seduced into demonic pacts and thus become witches.

Whilst the sorcerer retained control over the demons at his disposal, the witch, whether he or she realised it or not, was completely subservient to the devil. By the orthodox teaching of both the Roman Catholic and Protestant churches the witch was regarded as the victim of the devil, serving his ends but ultimately forfeiting his or her own soul. However, for most writers of the period the major interest lay in the cataloguing of the evil deeds – or 'maleficia' – real or imaginary that were ascribed to witches, with fewer expressing concern for the fates of the perpetrators of the alleged misdeeds.

This pattern is reflected in the contemporary dramas. In a few plays (*Dr Faustus* and *The Witch of Edmonton*, for example) there are sympathetic portrayals of the witch-figure but in the majority of works there is no such attempt. In such plays as *Macbeth* and Jonson's *The Masque of Queenes* the emphasis is wholly on the evil performed by the witches and of the effects on their victims with on concern shown for the inevitable destruction of the witches themselves.

A distinction can also be drawn between Renaissance and Classical witchcraft beliefs, and both forms are to be found in the dramas. *The Witch of Edmonton* is based on an actual case of 1621 and Elizabeth Sawyer engages our sympathy in part because in her we see embodied a realistic portrayal of the contemporary

English witch. The Dame and her followers in *The Masque of Queenes* and Erictho in Marston's *Sophinisba* are based on Classical models and although their powers are far greater than those of the homely Mother Sawyer, they appear much more remote figures, re-enacting an archaic tradition.

Elizabeth Sawyer is the epitome of the contemporary English witch-figure – a lonely, embittered old woman, set apart from her neighbours, the victim of their superstitions and the scapegoat for their misfortunes – and her essential mundanity contrasts both with the awesomeness of the classically-based creations and the flamboyance and spurious glamour of Hecate in Middleton's *The Witch*. The latter, with its Italian setting, reflects the current Continental attitudes to witch-craft and in many essential respects these differed considerably from the most widely held English beliefs. For example, with a few very doubtful exceptions, there seems to have been little conception in England of the coven or close-knit organisation of witches that was a major feature of most Continental cases. Records of Scottish trials, on the other hand, contain several references to such groups and in fact at this time witchcraft practices in Scotland were in many respects closer to the European than the English forms. (As might be expected, the Weird Sisters in *Macbeth* reveal some traits – including possible membership of a coven – which are closer to the Scottish models than to their English counterparts.)

Another basic difference between English and Continental attitudes is that, despite the occasional outbreaks of witch-hunting such as that carried out by Matthew Hopkins in the 1640s, there was nothing in England to compare with the sustained hysteria that resulted in the persecution, tortures and deaths of [many] so-called witches in Europe between the fourteenth and seventeenth centuries. C. H. L'Estrange Ewen, in *Witch Hunting and Witch Trials* (1929), concluded that the total number of executions for witchcraft in England between 1542 and 1736 was not more than one thousand (p. 112), a figure matched in the single year of 1524 in Como [in Northern Italy] alone.

Recent research has not added appreciably to Ewen's estimate but it must be borne in mind that the uneven survival of English court records excludes any firm conclusions based on these sources. For example, the fire of Warwick in 1694 destroyed nearly all of the existing legal records for a county which has had a widespread reputation for witchcraft practices from mediaeval times to the present day. On the other hand, the documents relating to the Essex Assizes have survived largely intact. Those concerned with the period between 1560 and 1680 have been analysed in detail in A. D. J. Macfarlane's *Witchcraft in Tudor and Stuart England: a Regional Study* (1970). Essex had what seems to have been a disproportionate number of witchcraft cases during the period, outnumbering the combined indictments in Hertfordshire, Kent, Surrey and Sussex, which were all fellow-members of the Home Circuit. Amongst the statistics Macfarlane deduces are that during the peak period of the 1580s witchcraft cases formed thirteen per cent of all criminal hearings, whilst the acquittal rate throughout the entire period was over fifty per cent. This contrasts markedly with the equivalent ratio on the Continent, which in France, for example, was sometimes as low as five per cent.

The Continental witchcraft persecutions appear in the main to have been insti-gated and maintained by the ecclesiastical authorities. This does not seem to have been the case in England, where throughout the Middle Ages there had been little pressure from Church or State to prosecute witches. Keith Thomas in *Reli-gion and the Decline of Magic* (1971) puts forward the attractive hypothesis that before the Reformation the great bulk of the English populace had been content to protect themselves from the powers of witchcraft through a combination of Church and folk magic. With the undermining of ecclesiastical authority – and in particular the assaults on the rituals of the Roman Catholic Church – the secu-rity of this immunity was removed. Thus, from the 1560s onwards, the people turned increasingly to the courts, ecclesiastical and secular, for defence against the powers of the occult. Thomas concludes that it was for this reason that there was an upsurge of witchcraft prosecutions during the latter part of the sixteenth century and he argues that the great majority of such accusations were of a 'grass-roots' character, emanating from the general populace.

Most scholars agree that the European witch-craze developed from the perse-cution of the Catharsists and Albigenses in thirteenth-century France. This had heralded the establishment of the Inquisition, and the growing insecurity of the Roman Catholic Church led to attempts to crush all forms of heresy. Many of the accusations made against witches were identical to those previously brought against the heretical sects. In a series of Papal Bulls, culminating in that of 1484, sorcery and witchcraft were gradually equated with heresy. The witch-mania was really unleashed by the publication, two years later, of *Malleus Maleficarum* [the *Hammer of Witches*], a handbook for procedure against witches written by the Dominicans Kramer and Sprenger. [. . .]

Although the weight of modern scholarship, therefore, disposes one to regard the mediaeval witch-craze as being founded on a tragic delusion, in examining the drama of the early seventeenth century one must attempt to reconstruct the prevailing views of the period. Whilst a very few scholars denounced the cruel and absurd persecutions that many innocent people suffered, the majority of the learned fully accepted the existence of witchcraft and saw in it a clear manifes-tation of the powers of anti-Christ, requiring the sternest measures to eradicate it. This is the overwhelming viewpoint of the surviving written evidence and it is a reasonable assumption that this attitude was accepted by the populace at large.

It is interesting to conjecture how far such opinions were carried over into the theatres and how the audiences responded to the portrayal of witchcraft and other supernatural activities on stage. A glimpse of one such reaction is provided by the anecdote of an incident during a performance of *Doctor Faustus* in Exeter. Faustus, in summoning Mephistophilis, appeared to invoke an actual devil which joined in the action, to the horror of audience and players alike. 'The players . . . contrarye to their custome spending the night in reading and in prayer got them out of the town the next morning.'

Beyond this apocryphal tale there is no firm evidence of the effect of the enact-ment of the occult on the plays' audiences. However, the Elizabethan and Jacobean playhouses were microcosms of their wider societies and it therefore seems likely that the majority of spectators would have seen in the theatrical portrayal of witchcraft an enactment of actuality and would have regarded it with the varying degrees of hostility that characterised the prevailing consensus of opinion on the subject. Indeed, as we shall see, inferences regarding the contemporary attitudes can reasonably be drawn from the treatment of witchcraft in the plays themselves. The playwrights were professionals, in the main, aiming to satisfy popular tastes and reflecting rather than leading current opinion. With few exceptions, the dramatic treatment of witchcraft, on the evidence of the surviving plays, follows a definite pattern, and this may well mirror the developing attitudes to the subject throughout the sixteenth and seventeenth centuries.

[II]

These shifting viewpoints can be traced in part through an examination of the anti-witchcraft statutes of the period. There had been considerable witchcraft activity in England during the Anglo-Saxon period, if not earlier. Documentary evidence attests to the widespread practice of nearly all the forms of 'black' and 'white' magic that survived into the post-mediaeval period, including the harming and curing of people and animals through charms and spells, the raising of storms and the destruction of crops. However, although several edicts were passed, such as that under King Alfred, which was clearly based on the Law of Moses – 'Those women who are wont to receive enchanters and magicians and wizards or witches – thou shalt not suffer them to live' – it was not until 1542, in the reign of Henry VIII, that the first law against 'conjurations and witchcraftes and sorcerie and enchantments' became one of the Statutes of the Realm.

It is significant that this Act was introduced under the secular rather than the ecclesiastical jurisdiction, for this strengthens the impression that the English Church, even before the Reformation, took a far more lenient attitude towards witchcraft and magic than did its European counterpart. Even in cases where guilt was established the punishment was generally penance or the pillory. By the mid sixteenth century the Church was apparently content to leave major witchcraft trials to the secular courts, merely dealing with minor cases or helping to determine the validity of claims of demonic possession.

Henry VIII's Statute was mainly concerned with the employment of sorcery and magical arts in treasure-hunting, although the use of enchantments 'to waste, consume or destroie anie person in his bodie, members or goodes, or to provoke anie person to unlawful love' were also made felonies, punishable by death. However, the pattern of tolerance was maintained in practice for there is only one recorded instance of the full penalty being exacted under the Act before its repeal in 1547.

The next Act 'against conjurations and witchcraftes' became law under Elizabeth I in 1563. There was a change of emphasis in that, whilst the basic elements of the previous Act, including treasure-seeking, were retained, greater stress was placed on other aspects of witchcraft. The invocation and conjuration of evil spirits became felonies and the practices were divided into: bewitching to death; injuring persons or cattle; seeking treasure or lost things; *trying* to provoke unlawful love or to kill, maim or injure a person. A second Act under Elizabeth, passed in 1580/1, introduced a political element in that the use of witchcraft to determine the length of the Queen's reign or the nature of the succession became capital offences.

Nevertheless, the generally lenient treatment of witchcraft, both in the Statute Book and in the application of the laws, was still evident. Under the 1563 Act it was only the use of witchcraft to inflict death that was subject to the extreme penalty. Other offences were punishable by a combination of prison and pillory for one year, the offence becoming a capital crime only if it was repeated.

The courts' leniency in practice is seen in the sentences that followed one of the most notorious witchcraft trials of the Elizabethan period, held at St Osyth, Essex, in 1582. During the hearings the magistrate and self-appointed prosecutor-in-chief, Brian Darcy, adopted many of the procedures hitherto found only in Continental witch-trials: false promises of leniency in return for confessions and the accusations of others; the use of young children to inculpate the accused; and, worst of all, the presumption of guilt, the onus being on the prisoners to prove their innocence in an increasingly hysterical atmosphere in which the slightest suspicion or rumour was taken as undoubted proof. In all, thirteen women were convicted, whilst six were either discharged or acquitted. However, despite the manifest injustice of much of the proceedings, most of the sentences were light. Only two of those convicted were executed and they had admitted causing six deaths by witchcraft. The others were found guilty of such charges as inflicting wasting diseases and destroying cattle, crops and farm buildings and thus, under the terms of the 1563 Act, escaped the full penalty.

This would not have been the case had they been convicted under the Statute of James I, introduced in 1604 and remaining in force until 1736. Under this Act the penalties were stiffened in that more offences, including the infliction of bodily harm, became punishable by death. In addition, certain witchcraft practices were specified in greater detail. The owning of familiar spirits was made a felony, whereas hitherto this had not been a crime in itself but merely one means of establishing guilt. Much of the evidence at St Osyth had been concerned with the alleged keeping of familiars but such accusations had been made as additional proofs of guilt rather than as culpable offences in themselves.

The new Statute led to an increase in the practice of searching a suspect's body for the 'mark' or 'teat' whereby the witch supposedly suckled her familiar. At the Lancaster trial of 1612 Anne Chattox admitted allowing a spirit to have 'a place of her right side neere to her ribbes for him to sucke upon'. She was also charged that she 'at a Buriall at the new Church in Pendle, did take three scalpes [skulls] of people, which had been buried, and then cast out of a grave . . . and tooke eight teeth out of the said Scalpes'. This was contrary to another item in the 1604 Statute which declared it a felony to 'take up anie dead man, woman or child out of his, her, or their grave, or anie other place where the bodie resteth, or the skin, bone or anie other part of anie dead person, to be emploied or used in anie maner of witchcraft, sorcerie, charm, or enchantment'. [. . .]

During the first part of James's reign, until 1616, there were at least thirty-five recorded executions for witchcraft, fifteen of these following the trials at Lancaster and Northampton in 1612. However, the popular conception of James's credulous acceptance of witch-lore and superstition requires some modification. In fact, his analytical mind demanded clear proof of guilt and, as he had declared in his *Daemonologie* (1597), 'Judges ought indeede to beware whome they condemne: For it is as great a crime (as Salamon sayeth) to condemne the innocent, as to let the guiltie escape free'. On several occasions James intervened in witchcraft cases, either to stop the trial or to pardon the condemned. The most famous instance was his unmasking in Leicester in 1616 of the boy imposter, Smythe, who had already seen nine persons sent to the gallows following his false charges of demonic possession. James's intervention saved the lives of a further six accused, although one died in prison before he could be freed. James's increasing scepticism is probably reflected in the fact that from 1616 until the end of his reign in 1625 there are only five recorded executions for witchcraft in England.

Although the Statutes represent the official view, their clauses and even more their enactment give some indication of the current general attitudes. The Acts could only be enforced in response to accusations and the trial records that have survived probably give a clearer picture of the opinions of the general populace, on occasions giving a fascinating insight into the attitudes of both accusers and accused. Some of the most interesting accounts of trials are contained not in the official records but in the pamphlets that were produced to coincide with the hearings.

The majority of these publications are anonymous and the standards of writing and printing vary greatly. Some have clearly been hastily produced by enterprising printers to capitalise on the latest sensational trials, whilst others are extremely detailed accounts, where the writer was an eye-witness of the investigations or had access to the court records. In some instances the author was the presiding magistrate or otherwise officially connected with the case and was writing to justify or publicise the court proceedings. Other publications are the work of persons closely involved with a particular episode, anxious to present their case to a wider audience than that available in the courts. The extremely circumstantial account of *The Most Strange and Admirable Discoverie of the Three Witches of Warboys* (1593), involving the alleged possession of the five daughters of Robert Throckmorton, is one such work. Another is Edward Fairfax's *A Discourse of Witchcraft* (1621) in which, following the acquittal of the persons accused of bewitching his two daughters, he attempted to clear the children and himself of any suspicion of fraud or malice by writing his version of the case.

The account of the pre-trial hearings at St Osyth in 1582. [. . .] W.W., *A true and just Recorde, of the Information, Examination and Confession of all the Witches, taken at S. Oses in the Countie of Essex* (1582) was almost certainly the work of the presiding Justice of the Peace, Brian Darcy. One of the most sinister elements of this unwholesome affair was the accumulation of an apparently damning case on the flimsiest of evidence. Under Darcy's McCarthy-like interrogatory technique, a subtle blend of gentle persuasion and brutal threats, both accusers and accused saw proof of witchcraft in the most innocent of happenings. Ursula Kemp, following her own confession which was prompted by Darcy's false promise of leniency, told of a visit to her neighbour and fellow-prisoner, Elizabeth Bennett:

> She went unto Mother Bennets house for a messe of milke, the which shee had promised her: But at her comming this examinate saith shee knocked at her dore, and no bodie made her any answere, whereupon shee went to her chamber windowe and looked in therat, saying, ho, ho, mother Bennet are you at home? And casting her eyes aside shee saw a spirit lift up a clothe lying over a pot, looking much lik a Ferret. And it beeing asked of this examinate why the spirite did looke upon her, shee said it was hungrie.

The witness has clearly accepted without question the examiner's unspoken contention that the innocuous ferret must in fact have been a familiar spirit. [. . .]

As has been seen, confessions of witchcraft were sometimes extracted under the pressure of skilful cross-examination, but on other occasions cruder means were employed. Doctor Fian, the ostensible leader of the North Berwick witches, accused of conspiring against the life of King James, suffered hideous torture at James's personal command. Certain clauses of the 1604 anti-witchcraft Act reflected James's view that witches could be detected by 'the finding of their marke, and the trying the insensiblenes therof and their fleeting [floating] on the water'. Some horrifying outbreaks of licensed cruelty ensued, where pre-trial confessions of witchcraft were extracted through the exertion of physical torture. In 1613 Mary Sutton from Milton, near Bedford, was suspected of being the cause of various mysterious fatal maladies that had afflicted both cattle and humans in the vicinity. She was seized on the orders of one Master Enger and taken to a dammed-up mill-pool.

> When being throwne in the first time she sunke some two foote into the water with a fall, but rose againe and floated upon the water like a planke. Then he commanded her to be taken out, and had women readie that searched her and found under her left thigh a kind of Teat which after the Bastard sone confest her Spirits in severale shapes as Cats, Moales, etc. used to sucke her.
>
> Then was she the second time bound crosse her thumbes and toes, according to the former direction, and then she sunke not at all, but sitting upon the water, turned round about like a wheele, or as that which commonly we call a whirlepoole. Notwithstanding Master Engers men standing on each side of the damme with a roape tossing her up and downe to make her sinke, but could not.

Although the unfortunate woman at first 'as boldlie as if she had been inocent asked them if they could doe anie more to her', it is hardly surprising that finally her spirit failed her and she not only admitted all the accusations but also inculpated her mother, confessions that led to both their executions. The indirect influence of James is also evident in the investigations into the alleged activities of the five 'Witches of Northamptonshire' who were executed in 1612. The swimming test on this occasion was ordered by the Justice of the Peace and the author of the pamphlet describing the case justifies this by a lengthy quotation from James's *Daemonologie*.

Such outbreaks of organised cruelty and officially sanctioned witch-hunting on a fairly large scale are fortunately exceptional. Nevertheless, on the limited evidence available, there does seem to have been an upsurge of witchcraft persecutions during the early part of James's reign. The scholarly writings of this period also reflect the monarch's published views, giving an overall impression of intolerance which compares unfavourably with the humane attitudes expressed in some of the learned works on witchcraft printed during the Elizabethan era. [. . .]

Reginald Scot's *The Discoverie of Witchcraft*, published in 1584, was in many ways the most significant of all the Elizabethan writings on the subject. He makes several direct references to the St Osyth hearings and does not disguise his feelings about them, and about Darcy's conduct in particular. The work is imbued with a profound anger at the folly and superstition of many of the activities associated with the persecution of witches and expresses deep concern for the victims of such attacks [. . .] and he declares thus his purposes in writing the book:

> And bicause it may appeare unto the world what trecherous and faithless dealing, what extreame and intollerable tyranie, what grosse and fond absurdities, what unnaturall and uncivil discourtesie, what cancred and spiteful malice, what outragious and barbarous crueltie, what lewd and false packing, what cunning and craftie intercepting, what bald and peevish interpretations, what abominable and devilish inventions, and what flat and plain knaverie is practised against these old women; I will set downe the whole order of the inquisition, to the everlasting, inexcusable, and apparent shame of all witchmongers.
>
> [Book I, Chapter ix]

Although Scot does not deny the existence of occult powers, his sturdy common sense convinced him that the great majority of so-called witches were, at worst, victims of their own maliciousness or folly. After listing the incredible crimes with which they were frequently charged – from 'incestuous adulterie with spirits' to the cannibalistic devouring of their own children – he roundly declares: 'If more ridiculous or abhominable crimes could have been invented, these poore women (whose cheefe fault is that they are scolds) should have been charged with them' (book II, chapter x). He concludes that: 'If it were true that witches confesse, or that all writers write, or that witchmongers report, or that fooles beleeve, we should never have butter in the chearne, nor cow in the close, nor corne in the field, nor faire weather abroad, nor health within doores' (book III, chapter xiv)

The work seems to have had considerable impact on Scot's contemporaries, although not always in the way in which the author intended. Ironically, the book is such a treasure-house of magic lore (with charms, spells and conjuring rituals set out, complete with diagrams) and contains such a host of authentic witchcraft tales and racy anecdotes that its main influence seems to have been to act as a source-book for other writers – including Shakespeare, Jonson and Middleton – most of whom culled the witchlore and ignored the accompanying ironic comments and refutations.

James I, on his accession to the English throne in 1603, ordered all copies of Scot's work to be destroyed. He had written his *Daemonologie*, published in Edinburgh in 1597 and reprinted by an enterprising London publisher in 1604, partly as a response to Scot's book [. . .] The work draws heavily on Biblical and Classical sources, in contrast to Scot's blend of ancient and contemporary lore. It was also very much influenced by current Continental writings, reflecting the Scottish affinities with European beliefs. [. . .]

James urged caution in condemning those accused of witchcraft and he also argued against the punishment of children involved in occult activities, 'for they are not that capable of reason as to practise such things' (book III). Nevertheless, he urged strong measures against the convicted:

> The prince or magistrate for further tryals cause, may continue the punishing of them such a certaine space as he thinkes convenient; But in the end to spare the life, and not to strike when God bids strike, and so severely punish in so odious a fault and treason against God, it is not only unlawful but comparable to the sin of witchcraft itselfe.
>
>   [Book III]

James's stern injunctions are seen in practice in the pamphlet account of the North Berwick conspiracy, *Newes From Scotland* (1591). The King took a leading part in the examination of several of the accused and also seems to have instigated the tortures inflicted on Fian following his abortive escape from captivity and subsequent denial of his previous confession:

> Whereupon the kinges majestie perceiving his stubbourne wilfulnesse, conceived and imagined that in the time of his absence hee had entered into new conference and league with the devill his master, and that hee had beene agayne newly marked, for the which hee was narrowly searched, but it could not in any wise bee founde, yet for more tryall of him to make him confesse, hee was commanded to have a most straunge torment, which was done in this manner following.
>
> His nailes upon all his fingers were riven and pulled off with an instrument called in Scottish a Turkas, which in England wee call a payre of pincers, and under everie nayle there was thrust in two needels over even up to the heads: At all which torments notwithstanding the Doctor never shronke anie whit, neither would he then confesse it the sooner for all the tortures inflicted upon him.
>
> Then was hee with all convenient speed, by commandement, convaied againe to the torment of the bootes, wherein hee continued a long time, and did abide so many blowes in them, that his legges were crushte and beaten together as small as might bee, and the bones and flesh so brused that the bloud and marrowe spouted forth in great abundance, whereby they were made unserviceable for ever.

Whatever doubts might later have grown within James's own mind, it is hardly surprising, in view of such well publicised evidence of his attitude towards those accused of witchcraft, that the predominant tone of the ostensibly learned and rational works on the subject should be uniformly hostile after his succession to the English throne. Typical of such writings is Perkins's *A Discourse of the Damned Art of Witchcraft*, which was written in 1602 at the end of Elizabeth's reign but, significantly, not published until 1608. Perkins approved, in certain circumstances, of the use of torture, including 'the rack or some other violent meanes to urge confession . . . *when the partie is obstinate*'. As was noted previously, he (like James) drew no distinction between the practitioners of 'black' or 'white' magic, and (again like James) he declared that they should all be subject to the same penalty. [. . .]

33 Anthony Harris '**Instrument of mischief Tragi-Comedy in The Witch of Edmonton**'

Source: from *Night's Black Agents: Witchcraft and Magic in Seventeenth-Century English Drama*, Anthony Harris, Manchester University Press, Manchester, 1980, chapter 7, pp. 90–3, 95–7, 99–107.

Old Carter: The witch, that instrument of mischief!

[*The Witch of Edmonton*, V.iii.21]

[I]

As was noted in Text 32 there were only five recorded executions for witchcraft in the last nine years of James I's reign, compared with thirty-five during the first thirteen years. The magistrates seem to have taken their cue from James's own increasing reluctance to accept many of the claims and accusations of occult powers. However, this more humane – or sceptical – attitude would clearly have taken much longer to filter through to the general populace. One of the five executions was that of Elizabeth Sawyer, who was hanged for witchcraft at Tyburn on 19 April 1621. *The Witch of Edmonton* recounts this real-life case in dramatised form and it reflects the slowly developing attitude to witchcraft in that it is the first play to contain a full-scale portrayal of a witch where the protagonist is treated with any measure of sympathy or understanding.

Although the play was not printed until 1658, the first recorded production was at Court on 29 December 1621 when it was presented by the Prince's Men. It had almost certainly been performed earlier in that year at the company's Cock-Pit Theatre, as is suggested by the lines 'Villains are strip't naked, the witch must be beaten out of her Cock-pit' (V.i.47–8). The title page of the 1658 quarto describes the work as 'A known true Story. Composed into a Tragi-Comedy' and it was clearly written to capitalise on the excitement generated by the recent witchcraft trial. The affair seems to have been something of a nine-days' wonder, for in addition to the play it was also the subject of popular ballads, now lost, which, according to Henry Goodcole, 'were sung at the time of our returning from the witches execution'. Goodcole was the chaplain of Newgate Gaol, where Elizabeth had been imprisoned, and he wrote an account of the case justifying her execution, if any such defence were needed. His work was entitled: *The Wonderfull discoverie of Elizabeth Sawyer a Witch, late of Edmonton, her conviction and condemnation and death. Together with the relation of the Divels accesse to her and their conference together*. This pamphlet was entered in the Stationers' Register on 27 April 1621, just eight days after the execution. In view of the speed with which the account was produced, it is remarkably free from the printing errors evident in many of the pamphlets of the period, especially those that have clearly been produced to coincide with currently sensational cases. At one point Agnes Ratcliffe, one of the witch's alleged victims, is referred to as Elizabeth, but generally the document is a clear and painstakingly accurate, if biassed, account of Elizabeth Sawyer's trial and subsequent confession.

The Witch of Edmonton follows the pamphlet account very closely, and also seems to make use of material from the ballads, which Goodcole refers to but dismisses as inaccurate. In dramatising the events, elements are introduced into the play which are not present in the historical account. There are two major plots apart from the Elizabeth Sawyer episodes, but the three themes are quite skilfully blended and the other sections reinforce and complement the witchcraft sequences. [. . .]

The quarto states that the work was composed 'by divers well-esteemed Poets; William Rowley, Thomas Dekker, John Ford etc.' Modern scholars ignore the 'etcetera' and are generally agreed in assigning the Mother Sawyer scenes to Dekker, the Cuddy Banks episodes to Rowley, and in giving overall responsibility for the Frank Thorney/Winnifride/Susan plot to Ford (with help from Dekker). Such arbitrary divisions are, of course, a gross over-simplification. From what we know of Jacobean collaborative techniques, such clear-cut divisions are most unlikely, particularly where the plots overlap within single scenes, but on grounds of style and character treatment, the witchcraft scenes are generally felt to bear most clearly the stamp of Dekker. [. . .]

[T]he main theme of *The Witch of Edmonton* is concerned with the life and death of Frank Thorney. This plot is a typical Jacobean domestic tragedy, telling how Frank secretly marries Winnifride, a serving-maid who is pregnant. Whether Frank is responsible for this or whether the father is in fact Winnifride's master, Sir Arthur Clarington, is not made clear but, once married, Winnifride rebuffs all advances from her aged former lover. Frank, through a combination of greed and weakness, is persuaded by his father into a bigamous union with a minor heiress, Susan Carter. The affair is resolved when Frank murders Susan and feigns an attack on his own life. His treachery is unmasked by Susan's sister, Katharine, and he goes to his death, seeking and gaining forgiveness from his wife and from Susan's father.

The dramatists use several obvious devices to link this plot with the Elizabeth Sawyer sections. Old Carter declares that Frank has been bewitched by her into murdering Susan, and Thorney's progress to the scaffold in V.iii is divided into two parts, with Elizabeth Sawyer's execution journey interposed. In both cases the prisoners make final speeches of repentance, although the witch does not receive the ready forgiveness that Frank is accorded.

A major element in the historical case was the dog which reputedly acted as Mother Sawyer's familiar spirit. In the play, the dog also appears to Frank and seems to encourage his murderous designs. It is also present when his treachery is discovered in IV.ii and in fact seems to play a part in his unmasking. This parallels its relationship with Mother Sawyer, which begins in apparent accord and ends with the spirit's desertion of the old woman. The black dog is also featured in the third plot, for it appears to Cuddy Banks, 'the Clown', who is organising a May Day morris dance at the homes of Sir Arthur and Old Carter – which, in itself, is a further linking element. However, Cuddy treats the dog as a pet rather than an evil spirit and does not fall prey to it in the same manner as do its other two victims. [. . .]

Cuddy Banks is tricked by the devil–dog into pursuing a spirit in the form of Katharine and he receives a ducking for his pains. More tragically, Mother Sawyer is also the victim of the dog's deception, for the creature, having enticed her into the devilish pact, finally forsakes her and, gloating over her downfall, leaves her to her fate: 'Out, witch! Thy trial is at hand. / Our prey being had, the devil does laughing stand' (V.i.73–4).

In contrast, Cuddy Banks, despite his apparent simplicity, is too shrewd to become similarly ensnared. His comical insistence on treating the spirit as a dog rather than a devil seems to ensure his immunity from its wiles. He rejects the dog's offer of a pact with the words: 'No, I'll see thee hang'd; thou shalt be damned first. / I know thy qualities too well. I'll give no suck to such whelps' (V.i.178–9). [. . .]

[T]here is the genuine affection, amounting to love, which Elizabeth develops for her dog-spirit. This devotion arises out of her intense loneliness, for she is reviled and abused on all sides. It is particularly pathetic that her clearest expression of these feelings comes shortly before the dog's treachery is revealed:

> Kiss me, my Tommy,
> And rub away some wrinkles on my brow
> By making my old ribs to shrug for joy
> Of thy fine tricks.
>
> [IV.i.157–60]

[. . .]

The various portrayals of corruption and repentance are aspects of the principal theme of the play, which is a consideration of individual moral responsibility. This is seen most clearly in the increasing corruption of Mother Sawyer and Frank Thorney, who both try to excuse their crimes. The witch blames the unkindness of her neighbours, declaring that she has become a witch only after enduring their unjust slanders and physical cruelty. Her first words are:

> And why on me? why should the envious world
> Throw all their scandalous malice upon me? . . .
>   Some call me witch,
> And being ignorant of myself, they go
> About to teach me how to be one.
>
> [II.i.1–10]

Frank blames destiny for his misdeeds [. . .]

> On every side I am distracted,
> Am waded deeper into mischief
> Than virtue can avoid. But on I must,
> Fate leads me, I will follow.
>
> [I.ii.190–3]

The devil–dog plays a crucial part in the ultimate crimes that each commits. It persuades Mother Sawyer to make her satanic pact and, at her behest, it brings about the death of her enemy, Anne Ratcliff; it also appears to help Frank make up his mind to murder Susan. However, it is extremely significant that the dog materialises only after the two characters have already begun to contemplate such acts. [. . .]

As long as Elizabeth Sawyer and Thorney remain innocent of sinful thoughts the dog cannot influence them. Thus the moral responsibility for their actions remains their own. This is highlighted by the fact that the simple but essentially good-hearted Cuddy Banks remains uncorrupted by the dog's temptations. Having failed to seduce Cuddy, the dog openly explains its function and methods to him, showing clearly how the devil is ready to take advantage of any inherent weakness in its prospective victims:

> I'll thus much tell thee: thou never art so distant
> From an evil spirit, but that thy oaths,
> Curses, and blasphemies pull him to thine elbow.
> Thou never tell'st a lie, but that a devil
> Is within hearing it. Thy evil purposes
> Are ever haunted, but when they come to act,
> As thy tongue slandering, bearing false witness,
> Thy hand stabbing, stealing, cozening, cheating,
> He's then within thee. Thou play'st; he bets upon thy part.
> Although thou lose, yet he will gain by thee.
>
> [V.i.128–37]

[. . .] Nevertheless, the dog–devil is not wholly successful in theatrical terms. In dramatising a well-known contemporary case in which the dog-spirit was an essential element, the playwrights were more or less obliged to portray the devil in this form but it presents practical problems, and in performance it would be difficult to create and sustain the essentially sinister qualities that a malevolent devil should possess. The humorous episodes with Cuddy Banks would be easier to handle but these might conflict with rather than complement the horrific effects necessary in other sections. [. . .]

[II]

The dramatists adhere very closely to Goodcole's narrative throughout the witch-craft sections of the play. In both the dramatic and the prose accounts the devil–dog first appears to Mother Sawyer whilst she is uttering blasphemous imprecations. The dog's first words to her, as recorded in her confession. were:

'Oh! Have I now found you cursing, swearing and blaspheming? Now you are mine.' These appear in the drama as: 'Ho! Have I found thee cursing? Now thou art / Mine own' (II.i.118–19). Mother Sawyer admitted to Goodcole that she was at first frightened by the apparition but 'hee did bid me not to feare him at all, for hee would do me no hurt at all, but would do for mee whatsoever I should require of him'. In the play the dog calms Elizabeth's fears with the words: 'Come, do not fear; I love thee much too well / To hurt or fright thee' (II.i.122–3). As in Goodcole's version, it then proceeds to tempt its victim with promises of revenge over her enemies.

The blasphemous prayer that the dog teaches Mother Sawyer is identical in each work ('Sanctibicetur nomen tuum' [Blessed be thy Name]), but the playwrights create a rhyming couplet by preceding the phrase with the line: 'If thou to death or shame pursue 'em' (II.i.173). The circumstances in which the prayer is taught are different in the two versions. Whereas in the play the witch learns the words during her first encounter with the dog, as part of its preliminary instructions to her, in the prose version the prayer is imparted on a later occasion, after the devil has caught Mother Sawyer praying to Christ. She declares: 'He charged me then to pray no more to Jesus Christ but to him the Divell.' The playwrights have ignored here the chance to introduce dramatic tension, [. . .] arising from the victim's desperate but unavailing attempts to turn back from the diabolic path.

On other occasions, however, the dramatists have developed points from the prose account to give an added dimension to the drama. For example, in Goodcole's version Elizabeth admits that she has 'handled' the dog: 'Yes, I did stroake him on the backe, and then he would becke unto me and wagge his tayle as being therewith contented.' This hint of mutual affection is built up into the pathetic picture of the friendless old woman of the play, developing the genuine love for her treacherous dog-spirit which was noted previously.

The dog's ultimate betrayal is present in both versions. In Goodcole's account, Elizabeth asserts that she has not seen the spirit for three weeks and that it has not visited her in prison. As her confessor notes, the dog has deserted her for, 'being descried in his waies and workes, immediately he fled, leaving her to shift and answere for herselfe'. In the play the desertion is quite fully developed throughout V.i. Mother Sawyer, beginning to fear that the dog has left her, summons it with her prayer. The dog appears but its colour has changed from black to white. This transformation signals the creature's new attitude to her and it proceeds to taunt her openly with her impending death: 'My whiteness puts thee in mind of thy winding sheet . . . When the devil comes to thee as a lamb, have at thy throat' (V.i.34–8).

The colour change has been adapted from the witch's declaration to Goodcole that the spirit came to her 'always in the shape of a dogge and of two collars [colours], sometimes of blacke and sometimes of white'. She also stated that the dog was usually black but 'when I was praying hee would come unto me in the white colour'. From these bare details the playwrights have created the theatrically effective symbol of the dog's dramatic change of colour, which heralds its victim's final downfall. The dog is in fact one of the most common forms for familiar spirits as they were described in contemporary witch confessions and in such accounts the colours black and white often recur. [. . .]

Elizabeth Sawyer's confession of guilt, made two days before her execution and fully recorded in the pamphlet, is also given an added dimension in the drama, which subtly reinforces the impression of the dog-spirit's power over its victim. Just before her arrest, Mother Sawyer vows that she will never confess and the dog retorts that 'ere the executioner catch thee / Full in 's claws, thou'lt confess all' (V.i.71–2). When she is accused of bewitching Frank Thorney into killing Susan (a palpably absurd charge of which she is clearly innocent) she replies as if under a fatally hypnotic spell, incriminating herself in her attempted denial:

> is every devil mine?
> Would I had one now whom I might command
> To tear you all in pieces: Tom would have done't
> Before he left me.
>
> [V.iii.28–31]

A further variation between the prose and dramatic works is that Goodcole's pamphlet describes the single trial at which Mother Sawyer was indicted and condemned for causing the death of Agnes Ratcliffe. In the play she faces two separate hearings – in IV.i and V.ii. The first is not an official trial but is closer to such pre-trial hearings as that recorded in the St Osyth pamphlet, where an attempt was made to determine whether there was sufficient evidence for the accused to be sent for trial. The scene is most effective in dramatic terms. It begins with a group of incensed townsmen, led by Old Banks, who display the frightening blend of credulity, fear and malice of a lynch mob. They see Mother Sawyer as the scapegoat for all the sins and misfortunes of the neighbourhood: 'Our cattle fall, our wives fall, our daughters fall, and maid-servants fall; and we ourselves shall not be able to stand if this beast be suffered to graze amongst us' (IV.i.12–14).

To 'prove' her guilt they use the device of thatch-burning. This involves the taking of a handful of thatch from her roof and burning it. If Mother Sawyer is a witch, she will immediately come to the spot. This was a common method of testing for witchcraft, and Goodcole states that 'an old ridiculouse custome was used, which was to plucke the Thatch of her house, and to burne it, and it being so burnt, the author of such mischiefe should presently come'. In the play, Mother Sawyer does of course enter, although the text does not make it clear whether her arrival is fortuitous or has indeed been supernaturally induced. She is surrounded, amidst cries of 'Beat her, kick her, set fire on her.' Fortunately, Sir Arthur Clarington arrives, conveniently accompanied by a Justice who shares Goodcole's scepticism, and he roundly condemns the townsmen for their folly in taking the law into their own hands.

Old Banks then accuses the old woman of being responsible for his own perverted behaviour. He confesses that:

So, sir, ever since, having a dun cow tied up in my backside, let me go thither or but cast mine eye at her, and if I should be hang'd, I cannot choose, though it be ten times in an hour, but run to the cow and, taking up her tail, kiss – saving your worship's reverence – my cow behind, that the whole town of Edmonton has been ready to bepiss themselves with laughing me to scorn.

[52–8]

There is a possible vestige here of the anal kiss, whereby witches were popularly supposed to salute the devil, whether in human or animal form. No mention of this charge is to be found in Goodcole. [. . .] The playwright (almost certainly Dekker, in view of the social comment involved) takes the opportunity to put into the old woman's mouth charges of hypocrisy and moral laxity against the higher classes which, she claims, are as near to witchcraft and devilish behaviour as anything of which she has been accused. She demands:

> What are your painted things in princes' courts,
> Upon whose eyelids lust sits, blowing fires
> To burn men's souls in sensual, hot desires,
> Upon whose naked paps a lecher's thought
> Acts sin in fouler shapes than can be wrought?

[105–9]

She ironically declares:

> The man of law
> Whose honeyed hopes the credulous client draws –
> As bees to tinkling basins – to swarm to him
> From his own hive, to work the wax in his –
> He is no witch, not he!

[130–4]

This outburst is over-sophisticated in its expression, coming from such a simple and uneducated person, but is otherwise highly effective. A further, ironic dimension is added to this scene when Mother Sawyer cries:

> Dare any swear I ever temped maiden
> With golden hooks flung at her chastity,
> To come and lose her honour, and being lost
> To pay not a denier for 't?

[140–3]

Her words have particular significance for Sir Arthur and her apparent insight into his seduction of Winnifride convinces him of her guilt. However, the Justice rightly concludes that there is no evidence to sustain the charges and he contents himself with advising Mother Sawyer to 'mend thy life, get home and pray' (l. 149). The sympathy that has been evoked for the old woman during the early part of this scene is considerable, but it is largely dissipated when we see that, far from repenting and taking the Justice's advice, she immediately renews her relationship with her dog-spirit and turns her malicious attentions to:

> That jade, that foul-tongu'd whore, Nan Ratcliffe,
> Who for a little soap lick'd by my sow,
> Struck and almost had lam'd it; did not I charge thee
> To pinch that quean to th' heart?
>
> [IV.i.170–3]

This formed the basis of the main charge brought against her at the trial, where it was alleged that she 'did witch unto death Agnes Ratcleife . . . because that Elizabeth [*sic*] Ratcleife did strike a Sowe of hers in her Sight for licking up a little Soape where shee had laide it'. In the play, at the witch's instigation, the dog turns the woman mad and, in an insanity scene typical of the period, Anne Ratcliffe confronts her enemy:

> *Ratcliffe*: Are you not Mother Sawyer?
> *Sawyer*: No, I am a lawyer.
> *Ratcliffe*: Art thou? I prithee let me scratch thy face, for thy pen has
> flay'd off a great many men's skins.
>
> [IV.i.180–3]

The face-scratching reference is not present in Goodcole but, like the thatch-burning, this was a crude method of dealing with suspected witchcraft. It was commonly believed that scratching a witch (usually 'above the breath') and so drawing blood would temporarily break an evil spell. [. . .] Anne Ratcliffe fails to scratch Elizabeth Sawyer, breaks free from her husband and others who attempt to restrain her, and beats out her [own] brains. This incident, according to Goodcole, was untrue but was featured in the current ballads inspired by the case. The madness element was developed by the dramatists from the account in the indictment, given by her husband, of Agnes Ratcliffe's fatal illness following her supposed bewitchment: 'That evening Agnes Ratcliffe fell very sicke, and was extraordinarily vexed, and in a most strange manner in her sicknesse was tormented . . . she lay foaming at the mouth and was extraordinarily distempered.'

Amongst the evidence of Elizabeth Sawyer's guilt produced at the actual trial was the testimony of three women who had physically examined the accused and had found that she 'had a private and strange marke on her body'. This of course was held to be the teat with which she suckled with blood her dog familiar. This feature is also included in the play when Mother Sawyer turns to her dog after the stress of her first unofficial trial:

> *Sawyer*: Comfort me: thou shalt have the teat anon.
> *Dog*: Bow wow: I'll have it now.
> *Sawyer*:   I am dri'd up
>   With cursing and with madness; and have yet
>   No blood to moisten these sweet lips of thine.
>
> [IV.i.151–4]

Additional evidence based on her physical appearance spoke of her habitually downcast countenance (which was hardly surprising in view of the abuse to which she was constantly subjected) and crooked, deformed body. In popular belief such an aspect could betoken a witch and the Elizabeth Sawyer of the play is portrayed in a similar manner. Goodcole states that she was partially blind in one eye, the result of an accidental injury involving 'a sticke which one of my children had in the hand'. However, the playwrights make only passing reference to this disability when one of Cuddy Banks's fellow morris-dancers says of her, 'Bless us, Cuddy, and let her curse t'other eye out' (II.i.85).

In the first speech Mother Sawyer describes herself as 'poor, deform'd, and ignorant, / And like a bow buckl'd and bent together' (II.i.3–4). [. . .]

In their treatments of Mother Sawyer's appearance, the essential difference between Goodcole and the playwrights is that whereas in the former's account the old woman's repellent aspect is merely additional proof of her guilt, in the drama it is made the cause of her first venture into witchcraft. Whatever her subsequent crimes, the first evil was inflicted on her. Because of her ugliness she has been made an outcast, the subject of malicious gossip and 'a common sink / For all the filth and rubbish of men's tongues / To fall and run into' (II.i.6–8).

Because her neighbours treat her as a witch, Elizabeth Sawyer responds by becoming one. The psychological insight displayed by the dramatists here is very much in accord with Reginald Scot's explanation of one of the principal causes of apparent witchcraft. In *The Discoverie of Witchcraft* he writes:

> One sort of such as are said to bee witches, are women which be commonly old, lame, bleare-eied, pale, fowle, and full of wrinkles . . . They are leane and deformed, shewing melancholie in their faces, to the horror of all that see them . . . These miserable wretches are so odious unto all their neighbours, and so feared, as few dare offend them, or denie them anie thing they aske: whereby they take upon them; yea, and sometimes thinke, that they can doo such things as are beyond the abilitie of humane nature . . . The witch, exspecting hir neighbours mischances, and seeing things sometimes come to passe according to her wishes, cursses and incantations . . . confesseth that she (as a goddes) hath brought such things to passe.
>
> [Book I. Chapter iii]

In Goodcole's account, Elizabeth Sawyer's motives for engaging in witchcraft are given as springing simply from her 'malice and envy'. He limits himself to a straightforward, unemotional description of the woman's downfall, taking the opportunity to point out the moral dangers of her unchristian behaviour but not committing himself to an opinion of the actual witchcraft powers, either as they are ascribed to Elizabeth Sawyer in particular or in a wider sense.

In the play there is no question of Mother Sawyer's guilt and the dog is without doubt a diabolical spirit through which she works her evil, but the whole tenor of the dramatists' treatment of the theme is akin to the humanity and rationalism expressed by Scot. Witchcraft is portrayed as a reality and is condemned and the witch is held up as an example of the dangers of meddling with the occult. Nevertheless, the playwrights show great compassion for the simple creature who, initially through the malice of others and at first committing no greater wrong than foolishness, becomes enmeshed in the devil's toils. It is an indication of King

James's changing attitude to witchcraft that the play should have been given a court performance when its portrayal of the witch figure is so much in accord with the compassionate views of Scot, whom James had previously so bitterly condemned. [. . .]

Mother Sawyer [. . .] provides us with a thoroughly convincing picture of the witch as she must have been most frequently in reality – old, solitary, and embittered but an essentially pathetic figure, brutally persecuted by her neighbours through a blend of prejudice and ill-founded suspicion. She is the helpless scapegoat for her fellow townspeople's barely suppressed feelings of guilt at their own superstitions and irrational fears. She is too wary and embittered to recognise genuine kindness when it is shown to her by Cuddy Banks but the sympathy evoked for her, particularly in the early stages of the play, leads one to hope that her final plea for divine forgiveness does not go unheard.

34 Frances E. Dolan **Witchcraft and the threat of the familiar**

Source: from *Dangerous Familiars: Representations of Domestic Crime in England 1550–1700*, Cornell University Press, Ithaca and London, 1994, pp. 218–20.

[. . .] *The Witch of Edmonton*, [. . .] vividly depicts the relation of witchcraft belief to social conflict and explores why this particular character chooses witchcraft in response to her social situation. Mother Sawyer complains that her neighbors treat her maliciously because she is poor, old, powerless, and ugly. She argues that her neighbors' accusations and suspicions make her a witch.

> Some call me witch,
> And, being ignorant of myself, they go
> About to teach me how to be one . . .
>
> . . .
>
> This they enforce upon me, and in part
> Make me to credit it.
>
> (2.1.8–10, 14–15)

If she is to be considered infamous, she wants power, specifically the power to get revenge and redress grievances: 'Tis all one/To be a witch as to be counted one' (2.1.118–19). Mother Sawyer articulates her experience of enforcement in the context of the play's other enforcements: Win must marry Frank because she is pregnant by her master; Old Thorney must convince Frank to marry to save their estate; Frank submits to the 'enforced' and bigamous marriage to avoid paternal disapproval and to insure his inheritance. The play also emphasizes Elizabeth Sawyer's isolation and vulnerability by silently erasing the husband that she mentions in Henry Goodcole's pamphlet about the case.

Creating a voice for Mother Sawyer, the play allows her to describe a process of subject-formation that involves both enforcement and agency, the two central concerns of witchcraft plays: Powerlessness, poverty, and the imputation of witch-craft are forced on her, yet she also chooses to seize whatever power she can through the outlaw status by which she is constituted. Scholars often quote this passage because, in it, the witch, generally constructed as either villain or victim, positions herself as both. To the end, Mother Sawyer refuses to accept all the blame; she questions the decorums of acceptable and unacceptable power in her culture, which promote many metamorphoses and enchantments more destructive than hers: 'A witch? Who is not?' (4.1.103).

Although the play grants Mother Sawyer a platform from which to speak and the power to redress her grievances, it ultimately eliminates her from the play's community. Nor does it grant her the prestige of tragic heroism. Even Mother Sawyer, the most complexly, vividly characterized of the stage's witches, is not a female Dr. Faustus, dominating the main plot and commanding the audience's attention. Instead, the play that bears her name confines her to the subplot; she appears in four of the play's thirteen scenes while Frank Thorney appears in seven. If Frank Thorney – a spineless, yet murderous, bigamist – has a rival as the play's protagonist, it is not Mother Sawyer, but her familiar, Dog. Dog, like Frank, appears in seven scenes. More important, Dog connects the play's multiple plots. In the main plot, he inspires Frank Thorney to kill one of his two wives; helps him to carry out the scheme; and then rejoices, 'shrugging as it were for joy,' when Frank is discovered. In the subplot in which we meet Dog, he acts as Mother Sawyer's familiar, rescuing her from lonely bitterness, acting as her ally and protector, and enabling her to avenge her grievances. When she longs to *be* a witch since she is *called* one but does not know where to begin, Dog instructs her. In the end, however, he abandons her to apprehension and execution. In the comic subplot, Dog befriends young Cuddy Banks, plays pranks, and dances in the morris. Of the three characters with whom Dog associates, only Cuddy Banks survives.

As the only character who figures in each of the three plots, Dog links three conventional, apparently distinct story lines: that of domestic violence, here enforced marriage, bigamy, and a man's murder of his wife; that of witchcraft, here an old, impoverished woman's search for revenge against her more privileged, uncharitable, suspicious neighbors; and, finally, the plot of festive inversion, here a young man's playful disregard for his father's values, which manifests itself in pranks, games, and love charms with no permanent or destructive consequences. This last plot contrasts both the main plot, in which young people obey their parents with tragic consequences, and the other subplot, in which the witch's disorderliness and reliance on a familiar to secure her desires end in murder and her own death. Dog demonstrates that witchcraft is simultaneously about domestic *and* communal relations when he intervenes in Mother Sawyer's vexed relations with her neighbors and in Frank's marriage, when he visits Frank's bedside or suckles Mother Sawyer, and when he ventures into the local community to dance in the morris or bedevil villagers. Acting as Mother Sawyer's demonic lover/infant as well as her avenger, Cuddy's loyal pet, and a prankster, Dog passes easily between the supernatural and the social, the consoling and the destructive. Although Dog stands out as an unlikely dramatic character, he is, in fact, only an especially vivid manifestation of the early modern preoccupation with 'familiar' threats and threatening 'familiars.' The interplay of the three plots, through Dog's agency, demonstrates that what links stories of murderous conflict between spouses, popular festivity, and witchcraft is the disruptive agency of the dangerous familiar. [. . .]

Index